The Boys of '61

The Boys of '61

The Personal Experiences of an
American Journalist Throughout
the American Civil War

Charles Carleton Coffin

LEONAUR

The Boys of '61: the Personal Experiences of an American Journalist Throughout the American Civil War
by Charles Carleton Coffin

Published by Leonaur Ltd

Material original to this edition and this editorial selection copyright © 2011 Leonaur Ltd

ISBN: 978-0-85706-513-1 (hardcover)
ISBN: 978-0-85706-514-8 (softcover)

http://www.leonaur.com

Publisher's Notes

The views expressed in this book are not necessarily those of the publisher.

Contents

Prefatory Note	7
Beginning of the Conflict	9
Around Washington	15
Bull Run	24
The Fall of 1861	38
Affairs in the West	54
Central Kentucky	66
The Opening of the Campaign in Tennessee	82
Pittsburg Landing, Fort Pillow and Memphis	97
Invasion of Maryland	114
Invasion of Kentucky	128
From Harper's Ferry to Fredericksburg	143
Battle of Fredericksburg	149
The Winter at Falmouth	178
Chancellorsville	184
Cavalry Operations	216
The Atlantic Coast	227
The Ironclads in Action	251
The Invasion of Pennsylvania	260
The Battle of Gettysburg	271
From the Rapidan to Cold Harbor	307
To Petersburg	350
Siege Operations	375
Third Invasion of Maryland	383
Sherman's Army	391
Christianity and Barbarism	403
Scenes in Savannah	414

Sherman in South Carolina	435
South Carolina Before the War	442
Sumter	452
Charleston	460
The Last Campaign	481
Richmond	494
The Confederate Loan	518
Surrender of Lee	538
Conclusion	551

Prefatory Note

This volume, though historic, is not a history of the Rebellion, but a record of personal observations and experiences during the war, with an occasional look at affairs in general to give clearness to the narrative.

The time has not arrived for the writing of an impartial history of the conflict between Slavery and Freedom in the United States. Reports of military operations are incomplete; documents in the archives at Washington are inaccessible; much material remains to be gathered before the patient historian can sift the wheat from the chaff. More than this, the war of ideas is not yet ended. Defeated Rebels in some parts of the South are bent on exterminating the African race. Few of those lately in rebellion plead guilty of having committed a crime; taking up arms against the government they consider to have been a blunder only. We are, therefore, too near the great events to render proper judgment upon questions in which our principles and sympathies have been enlisted.

The chapter concerning the Confederate Cotton Loan may seem to be out of place in a volume of which so large a portion is given to narrative, but I trust that it will be acceptable to the general reader, inasmuch as it reveals the efforts of the Rebels to array all Europe against the United States in the late struggle. The correspondence in my possession was picked up in the streets of Richmond, and will be of value to the future historian. The chapter in question is but an outline of the operations of the Confederates abroad.

In looking over the sheets as they came from the press, several errors relative to the organization and formation of troops in battle have been detected, which, however, will appear in but a few copies. Undoubtedly there are others, and the writer will esteem it a favour to be put right wherever he is in the wrong. Few official reports of regimental and brigade officers have been published, while the reports of division and corps commanders are only general in their statements. The true history of battles cannot be given till the history of regiments is written.

My stand-point as an observer is that of one whose instincts from early childhood have been on the side of Freedom. I have ever believed that Civil Liberty is the birthright of all men, and from the firing upon Sumter to the close of the contest had full faith that the people, under God, would subdue the Rebellion, and give freedom to the slave.

The four years have been worth a century of ordinary life; for in the mighty contest Right has triumphed over Wrong, and the human race, with a clearer perception of Truth and Justice as the sure foundation of government, is moving on to a higher civilization.

C. C. C.

The first subscription

INTRODUCTORY
Beginning of the Conflict

JUNE, 1861

After four years of war our country rests in peace. The Great Rebellion has been subdued, and the power and authority of the United States government are recognized in all the States. It has been a conflict of ideas and principles. Millions of men have been in arms. Great battles have been fought. There have been deeds of sublimest heroism and exhibitions of Christian patriotism which shall stir the hearts of those who are to live in the coming ages. Men who at the beginning of the struggle were scarcely known beyond their village homes are numbered now among

> .... *the immortal names*
> *That were not born to die!*

while the names of others who once occupied places of honour and trust, who forswore their allegiance to their country and gave themselves to do wickedly, shall be held forever in abhorrence.

It has been my privilege to accompany the armies of the Union through this mighty struggle. I was an eye-witness of the first battle at Bull Run, of Fort Donelson, Pittsburg Landing, Corinth, Island No. 10, Fort Pillow, Memphis, Antietam, Fredericksburg, Gettysburg, Fort Sumter, Wilderness, Spottsylvania, North Anna, Hanover Court-House, Cold Harbor, Petersburg, Weldon Railroad, and Five Forks. I was in Savannah soon after its occupation by Sherman on his great march to the sea, and watched his movement "northward with the sun." I walked the streets of Charleston in the hour of her deepest humiliation, and rode into Richmond on the day that the stars of the Union were thrown in triumph to the breeze above the Confederate Capitol.

It seems a dream, and yet when I turn to the numerous notebooks lying before me, and read the pencillings made on the march, the battle-field, in the hospital, and by the flickering camp-fires, it is no longer a fancy or a picture of the imagination, but a reality. The scenes return. I behold once more the moving columns,—their waving banners,—the sunlight gleaming from gun-barrel and bayonet,—the musket's flash and cannon's flame. I hear the drum-beat and the wild hurrah! Grant, Sherman, Sheridan, Meade, Burnside, Howard, Hancock, and Logan are leading them; while Sedgwick, Wadsworth, McPherson, Mansfield, Richardson, Rice, Baker, Wallace, Shaw, Lowell, Winthrop, Putnam, and thousands of patriots, are laying down their lives for their country. Abraham Lincoln walks the streets of Richmond, and is hailed as the Great Deliverer,—the ally of the Messiah!

It will be my aim in this volume to reproduce some of those scenes,—to give truthful narratives of events, descriptions of battles, incidents of life in camp, in the hospital, on the march, in the hour of battle on land and sea,—writing nothing in malice, not even towards those who have fought against the Union. I shall endeavour to give the truth of history rather than the romance; facts instead of philosophy; to make real the scenes of the mighty struggle through which we have passed.

On the 11th of June, 1861, I left Boston to become an Army Correspondent. The patriotism of the North was at flood-tide. Her drum-beat was heard in every village. Men were leaving their own affairs to serve their country. The stars and stripes waved from house-top and steeple. New York was a sea of banners. Ladies wore Union rosettes in their hair, while gentlemen's neck-ties were of "red, white, and blue." That family was poor indeed who could neither by cloth or coloured tissue-paper manifest its love for the Union. The music of the streets—vocal and instrumental—was *Hail Columbia* and *Yankee Doodle*. Everywhere,—in city and town and village, in Boston, New York, and Philadelphia,—there was the same spirit manifested by old and young, of both sexes, to put down the Rebellion, cost what it might of blood and treasure.

Baltimore presented a striking contrast to the other great cities. It was dull and gloomy. The stars and stripes waved over the Eutaw House, from the American newspaper office, where the brothers Fulton maintained unswerving loyalty. A few other residents had thrown the flag to the breeze, but Secession was powerful, and darkly plotted treason. There was frequent communication with the Rebels, who

CAPITOL AT WASHINGTON

were mustering at Manassas. Business was at a standstill. The pulses of trade had stopped. Merchants waited in vain for customers through the long summer day. Females, calling themselves ladies, daintily gathered up their skirts whenever they passed an officer or soldier wearing the army blue in the streets, and manifested in other ways their utmost contempt for all who supported the Union.

General Butler, who had subdued the rampant Secessionists by his vigorous measures, had been ordered to Fortress Monroe, and General Banks had just assumed command. His head-quarters were in Fort McHenry. A regiment of raw Pennsylvanians was encamped on the hill, by the roadside leading to the fort. Officers and soldiers alike were ignorant of military tactics. Three weeks previous they were following the plough, or digging in the coal-mines, or smelting iron. It was amusing to watch their attempts at evolution. They were drilling by squads and companies. "Right face," shouted an officer to his squad. A few executed the order correctly, some faced to the left, while others faced first right, then left, and general confusion ensued.

So, too, were the officers ignorant of proper military phrases. At one time a captain, whose last command had been a pair of draft-horses on his Pennsylvania farm, on coming to a pit in the road, electrified his company by the stentorian order to "Gee round that hole."

It was a beautiful evening, and the moon was shining brightly, when I called upon General Banks. Outside the fort were the field batteries belonging to the Baltimore Artillery which had been delivered up to Governor Hicks in April. The Secessionists raved over the transaction at the time, and in their rage cursed the Governor who turned them over to the United States authorities. Soldiers were building *abattis*, and training guns—sixty-four pounders—to bear upon the city, for even then there were signs of an upheaval of the Secession elements, and General Banks deemed it best to be prepared for whatever might happen. But the Rebels on that day were moving from Harper's Ferry, having destroyed all the property of the Baltimore and Ohio Railroad Company in the vicinity.

Passing on to Washington I found it in a hubbub. Troops were pouring in, raw, undisciplined, yet of material to make the best soldiers in the world,—poets, painters, artists, artisans, mechanics, printers, men of letters, bankers, merchants, and ministers were in the ranks. There was a constant rumble of artillery in the streets,— the jarring of baggage-wagons, and the tramping of men. Soldiers were quartered in the Capitol. They spread their blankets in the corridors, and made themselves at home in the halls. Hostilities had commenced. Ellsworth had just been carried to his last resting-place. The bodies of Winthrop and Greble were then being borne to burial, wrapped in the flag of their country.

Colonel Stone, with a number of regiments, was marching out from Washington to picket the Potomac from Washington to Point of Rocks. General Patterson was on the upper Potomac, General McClellan and General Rosecrans, with Virginia and Ohio troops, were driving the Rebels from Rich Mountain, while General McDowell was preparing to move upon Manassas.

These were all new names to the public. Patterson had served in the Mexican war, but the people had forgotten it. McClellan was known only as an engineer, who had made a report concerning the proposed railroad to the Pacific, and had visited Russia during the Crimean war. General Wool was in New York, old and feeble, too far advanced in life to take the field. The people were looking up to General Scott as the Hercules of the hour. Someone had called him the "Great Captain of the Age." He was of gigantic stature, and had fought gallantly on the Canadian frontier in 1812, and with his well-appointed army had marched in triumph into the City of Mexico. The events of the last war with England, and that with Mexico, in which General Scott was always the central figure, had been rehearsed by the stump-orators of a great political party during an exciting campaign. His likeness was familiar to every American. It was to be found in parlours, saloons, beer-shops, and in all public places,—representing him as a hero in gold-embroidered coat, epaulets, *chapeau*, and nodding plume. His was the genius to direct the gathering hosts. So the people believed. He was a Virginian, but loyal. The newspapers lauded him.

"General Scott is watching the Rebels with sleepless vigilance," was the not infrequent telegraphic despatch sent from Washington.

But he was seventy-five years of age. His powers were failing. His old wound troubled him at times. He could walk only with difficulty, and it tired him to ride the few rods between his house and the War Department. He was slow and sluggish in all his thoughts and actions. Yet the people had confidence in him, and he in himself.

The newspapers were filled with absurd rumours and statements concerning the movements and intentions of the Rebels. It was said that Beauregard had sixty thousand men at Manassas. A New York paper, having a large circulation, pictured Manassas as an impregnable position; a plain commanded by heavy guns upon the surrounding hills! It is indeed a plain, but the "commanding" hills are wanting. Rumour reported that General Joseph E. Johnston, who was in the Shenandoah valley, destroying the Baltimore and Ohio Railroad, and burning the bridges across the Potomac, had thirty thousand men; but we now know that his whole force consisted of nine regiments, two battalions of infantry, three hundred cavalry, and sixteen pieces of artillery.

It was for the interest of the Rebels to magnify their numbers and resources. These exaggerations had their effect at the War Department in Washington. General Butler proposed the early occupation of Manassas, to cut off communication by rail between Richmond and upper Virginia, but his proposition was rejected by General Scott. The troops in and around Washington were only partially organized into brigades. There was not much system. Everybody was full of zeal and energy, and there was manifest impatience among the soldiers at the inactivity of the commander-in-chief.

The same was true of the Rebels. They were mustering at Manassas. Regiments and battalions were pouring through Richmond. Southern women welcomed them with sweetest smiles, presented them with fairest flowers, and urged them on to drive the "usurper" from Washington. Southern newspapers, from the commencement, had been urging the capture of the Federal capital. Said the *Richmond Examiner*, of April 23rd:

> The capture of Washington is perfectly within the power of Virginia and Maryland, if Virginia will only make the effort by her constituted authorities. Nor is there a single moment to lose. The entire population pant for the onset....
>
> From the mountain-tops and valleys to the shores of the sea, there is one wild shout of fierce resolve to capture Washington City, at all and every human hazard. That filthy cage of unclean birds must and will assuredly be purified by fire.... It is not to

be endured that this flight of abolition harpies shall come down from the black North for their roosts in the heart of the South, to defile and brutalize the land.... Our people can take it,— they *will* take it,—and Scott the arch-traitor, and Lincoln the beast, combined, cannot prevent it. The just indignation of an outraged and deeply injured people will teach the Illinois Ape to repeat his race and retrace his journey across the borders of the free negro States still more rapidly than he came; and Scott the traitor will be given the opportunity at the same time to try the difference between Scott's tactics and the Shanghae drill for quick movements.

Great cleansing and purification are needed and will be given to that festering sink of iniquity,—that wallow of Lincoln and Scott,—the desecrated city of Washington; and many indeed will be the carcasses of dogs and caitiffs that will blacken the air upon the gallows before the work is accomplished. So let it be.

General Beauregard was the most prominent of the Rebel commanders, having been brought before the public by the surrender of Fort Sumter. Next in prominence were the two Johnstons, Joseph E. and Albert Sydney, and General Bragg. Stonewall Jackson had not been heard from. Leo had just gone over to the Rebels. He had remained with General Scott,—his confidant and chief adviser,—till the 19th of April, and was made commander of the Rebel forces in Virginia on the 22nd. The Convention of Virginia, then in session at Richmond, passed the ordinance of secession on the 17th,—to be submitted to the people for ratification or rejection five weeks later. Lee had therefore committed an act of treason without the paltry justification of the plea that he was following the lead of his State.

Such was the general aspect of affairs when, in June, I received permission from the War Department to become an army correspondent.

Chapter 1

Around Washington

June, 1861

In March, 1861, there was no town in Virginia more thriving than Alexandria; in June there was no place so desolate and gloomy. I visited it on the 17th. Grass was growing in the streets. Grains of corn had sprouted on the wharves, and were throwing up luxuriant stalks. The wholesale stores were all closed; the dwelling-houses were shut. Few of the inhabitants were to be seen. The stars and stripes waved over the Marshall House, the place where Ellsworth fell. A mile out from the city, on a beautiful plain, was the camp of the Massachusetts Fifth, in which were two companies from Charlestown. When at home they were accustomed to celebrate the anniversary of the battle of Bunker Hill. Although now in the enemy's country, they could not forget the day. They sat down to an ample collation. Eloquent speeches were made, and an ode was sung, written by one of their number.

Though many miles away
From home and friends today,
We're cheerful still;
For, brothers, side by side
We stand in manly pride,
Beneath the shadow wide
Of Bunker Hill.

Boom—boom—boom was the quick report of far-distant cannon. What could it be? A reconnoitring party of Ohio troops had gone up the Loudon railroad. Had anything happened to them? There were eager inquiries. The men fall into line, prepared for any emergency. A few hours later the train returned, bringing back the mangled bodies of those who fell in the ambuscade at Vienna.

I talked with the wounded. They were moving slowly up the road,—a regiment on platform cars, pushed by the engine. Before reaching Vienna an old man stepped out from the bushes making signs and gestures for them to stop.

"Don't go. The Rebels are at Vienna."

"Only guerrillas, I reckon," said one of the officers.

General Schenck, who was in command, waved his hand to the engineer, and the train moved on. Suddenly there were quick discharges of artillery, a rattling fire of small arms, and unearthly yells from front and flank, within an hundred yards. The unsuspecting soldiers were riddled with solid shot, canister, and rifle-balls. Some tumbled headlong, never to rise again. Those who were uninjured leaped from the cars. There was great confusion.

"Lie down!" cried some of the officers.

"Fall in!" shouted others.

Each did, for the moment, what seemed best. Some of the soldiers fired at random, in the direction of the unseen enemy. Some crouched behind the cars; others gained the shelter of the woods, where a line was formed.

"Why don't you fall into line?" was the sharp command of an officer to a soldier standing beside a tree.

"I would, sir, if I could," was the reply, and the soldier exhibited his arm, torn by a cannon shot.

They gathered up the wounded, carried them to the rear in blankets, began their homeward march, while the Rebels, eleven hundred strong, up to this moment sheltered behind a woodpile, rushed out, destroyed the cars, and retreated to Fairfax.

When the news reached Alexandria, a portion of the troops there were hastily sent forward; they had a weary march. Morning brought no breakfast, noon no dinner. A Secessionist had fled from his home, leaving his flocks and herds behind. The Connecticut boys appropriated one of the cows. They had no camp utensils, and were forced to broil their steaks upon the coals. It was my first dinner in the field. Salt was lacking, but hunger gave the meat an excellent seasoning. For table and furniture we had the head of a barrel, a jack-knife, and a chop-stick cut from a hazel-bush.

Congress assembled on the 4th of July, and the members availed themselves of the opportunity to visit the troops. Vallandigham of Ohio, who by word and act had manifested his sympathy for the Rebels, visited the Second Ohio, commanded by Colonel McCook, afterwards Major-General. I witnessed the reception given him by the

SIXTH MASSACHUSETTS REGIMENT IN BALTIMORE

boys of the Buckeye State. The officers treated him courteously, but not cordially. Not so the men.

"There is that d—d traitor in camp," said one, with flashing eyes.

"He is no better than a Rebel," said another.

"He helped slaughter our boys at Vienna the other day," said a third.

"Let us hustle him out of camp," remarked a fourth.

"Don't do anything rash. Let us inform him that his presence is not desired," said one.

A committee was chosen to wait upon Vallandigham. They performed their duty respectfully. He heard them, and became red in the face.

"Do you think that I am to be intimidated by a pack of blackguards from northern Ohio?" he said. "I shall come to this camp as often as I please,—every day if I choose,—and I give you notice that I will have you taken care of. I shall report your insolence. I will see if a pass from General Scott is not to be respected."

Turning to the officers, he began to inquire the names of the soldiers. The news that Vallandigham was there had spread throughout the camp, and a crowd was gathering. The soldiers were sore over the slaughter at Vienna, and began to manifest their hatred and contempt by groans and hisses.

"If you expect to frighten me, you have mistaken your man. I am ashamed of you. I am sorry for the honour of the State that you have seen fit to insult me," he said.

"Who has the most reason to be ashamed, you of us, or we of you?" said one of the soldiers. "We are here fighting for our country, which you are trying to destroy. What is your shame worth? You fired at us the other day. You helped kill our comrades. There isn't a loyal man in the country whose cheek does not redden with shame whenever your name is mentioned," was the indignant reply.

Vallandigham walked into the officers' quarters. The soldiers soon had an effigy, labelled "Vallandigham the traitor," hanging by the neck from a tree. They riddled it with bullets, then took it down and rode it on a rail, the fifers playing the "Rogues' March." When Vallandigham left the camp, they gave him a farewell salute of groans and hisses. A few of the soldiers threw onions and old boots at him, but his person was uninjured. He did not repeat his visit. He was so cross-grained by nature, so thorough a traitor, that through the session of Congress and through the war he lost no opportunity to manifest his hatred of the soldiers.

****

July, 1861

It was past sunset on the 9th of July, when, accompanied by a friend, I left Alexandria for Washington in an open carriage. Nearing the Long Bridge, an officer on horseback, in a red-flannel blouse, dashed down upon us, saying: "I am an officer of the Garibaldi Guard; my regiment has mutinied, and the men are on their way to Washington! I want you to hurry past them, give notice to the guard at the Long Bridge, and have the draw taken up." We promised to do so if possible, and soon came upon the mutineers, who were hastening towards the bridge. They were greatly excited. They were talking loud and boisterously in German. Their guns were loaded. There were seven nations represented in the regiment. Few of them could understand English. We knew that if we could get in advance of them, the two six-pounders looking down the Long Bridge, with grape and canister rammed home, would quell the mutiny. We passed those in the rear, had almost reached the head of the column, when out sprang a dozen in front of us and levelled their guns. *Click—click—click* went the locks.

"You no goes to Vashington in ze advance!" said one.

"You falls in ze rear!" said another.

"What does this mean?" said my friend, who was an officer. "Where is your captain?" he asked.

The captain came up.

"What right have your men to stop us, sir? Who gave them authority? We have passes, sir; explain this matter."

The captain, a stout, thick-set German, was evidently completely taken aback by these questions, but, after a moment's hesitation, replied,—

"No, zur, they no stops you; it was von mistake, zur. They will do zo no more." Then approaching close to the carriage, he lowered his voice, and in a confidential tone, as if we were his best friends, asked, "Please, zur, vill you be zo kind as to tell me vat is the passvord?"

"It's not nine o'clock yet. The sentinels are not posted. You need none."

A tall, big-whiskered soldier had been listening. He could speak English quite well, and, evidently desiring to apologize for the rudeness of his comrades, approached and said, "You see we Garibaldians are having a time of it, and—"

Here the captain gave him a vigorous push, with a "Hush!" long drawn, which had a great deal of meaning in it.

"I begs your pardons for ze interruption," said the captain, extending his hand and bowing politely.

Once more we moved on, but again the excited leaders, more furious than before, thrust their bayonets in our faces, again saying, "You no goes to Vashington in ze advance." One of them took deliberate aim at my breast, his eyes glaring fiercely.

It would have been the height of madness to disregard their demonstration. They had reached the guard at the Virginia end of the bridge, who, at a loss to know what it meant, allowed them to pass unchallenged.

Guarding Long Bridge

Now that we were compelled to follow, there was time to think of contingencies. What if our horses had started? or what if in the darkness a soldier, grieving over his imaginary wrong, and reckless of life, had misunderstood us? or what if the loyal officers of the regiment remaining at Alexandria had given notice by telegraph of what had happened, and those two cannon at the Washington end of the bridge had poured their iron hail and leaden rain along the causeway? It was not pleasant to think of these possibilities, but we were in for whatever might happen; and, remembering that God's providence is always good and never evil, we followed our escort over the bridge. They halted on the avenue, while we rode with all speed to General Mansfield's quarters.

"I'll have every one of the rascals shot!" said the gray-haired veteran commanding the forces in Washington. An hour later the Garibaldians found themselves surrounded by five thousand infantry. They laid down their arms when they saw it was no use to resist, were marched back to Alexandria, and put to the hard drudgery of camp life.

****

The soldiers had an amusing story to tell of one of their number who went into the lager-beer business, the sale of beer being then allowed. A sutler put a barrel on tap, and soon had a crowd of thirsty customers. But the head of the barrel was exposed in the rear. A soldier spying it, soon had that end on tap, and was doing a thriving business, selling at five cents a glass from his end of the barrel. He had a constant run of custom. When the crowd had satisfied their thirst, one of the soldiers approached the sutler.

"What do you charge for a glass?" he asked.
"Ten cents."
"Ten cents! Why, I can get just as much as I want for five."
"Not in this camp."
"Yes, sir, in this camp."
"Where, I should like to know?"
"Right round here."

The sutler crawled out from his tent to see about it, and stood transfixed with astonishment when he beheld the operation at the other end of his barrel. He was received with a hearty laugh, while the ingenious Yankee who was drawing the lager had the impudence to ask him if he wouldn't take a drink!

Virginia was pre-eminently the land of a feudal aristocracy, which prided itself on name and blood,—an aristocracy delighting to trace its lineage back to the cavaliers of Old England, and which looked down with haughty contempt upon the man who earned his bread by the sweat of his brow. The original "gentleman" of Virginia possessed great estates, which were not acquired by thrift and industry, but received as grants through kingly favour. But a thriftless system of agriculture, pursued unvaryingly through two centuries, had greatly reduced the patrimony of many sons and daughters of the cavaliers, who looked out of broken windows and rickety dwellings upon exhausted lands, overgrown with small oaks and diminutive pines. Yet they clung with tenacity to their pride.

"The Yankees are nothing but old scrubs," said a little Virginia girl of only ten years to me.

A young lady was brought to General Tyler's head-quarters at Falls Church to answer a charge of having given information to the enemy. Her dress was worn and faded, her shoes were down at the heel and out at the toes. There was nothing left of the estate of her fathers except a mean old house and one aged negro slave. She was reduced to absolute poverty, yet was too proud to work, and was waited upon by the superannuated negro.

"You are accused, madam, of having given information to the enemy," said General Tyler.

The lady bowed haughtily.

"You live in this old house down here?"

"I would have you understand, sir, that my name is Delaney. I did not expect to be insulted!" she exclaimed, indignantly. Words cannot describe her proud bearing. It was a manifestation of her regard for blood, gentility, name, and her hatred of labour. The history of the Rebellion was in that reply.

Virginia was also the land of sirens. A captain in a Connecticut regiment, lured by the sweet voice of a young lady, went outside of the pickets to spend a pleasant hour; but suddenly the Philistines were upon him, and he was a captive. Delilah mocked him as he was led away. Walking along the picket line on the 12th of July, I found a half-dozen Connecticut boys under a fence, keeping close watch of Delilah's mansion.

"There is a girl over there," said one of them, "who enticed our captain up to the house yesterday, when he was captured. Last night she came out and sung a song, and asked a lieutenant to go in and see her piano and take tea; but he smelt a rat, and was shy. Tonight there are four of us going to creep up close to the house, and he is going in to see the piano."

The trap was set, but the Rebels did not fall into it.

The pickets brought in a negro, one of the first contrabands who came into the lines of the army of the Potomac. He was middle-aged, tall, black, and wore a checked cotton shirt and slouched hat. His boots were as sorry specimens of old leather as ever were worn by human beings. He came up timidly to head-quarters, guarded by two soldiers. He made a low bow to the General, not only with his head, but with his whole body and legs, ending the *salaam* with a scrape of his left foot, rolling his eyes and grinning from ear to ear.

"What is your name?" asked the General.

"Sam Allston, sah."

"Who do you belong to?"

"I belongs to Massa Allston, sah, from Souf Carolina."

"Where is your master?"

"He be at Fairfax; he belong to Souf Carolina regiment, sah."

"How came you here?"

"Why, ye see, General, massa told me to go out and buy some chickens, and I come right straight down here, sah."

"You didn't expect to buy them here, did you?"

"No, sah; but I thought I would like to see de Yankees."

"I reckon I shall have to send you back, Sam."

This was said not seriously, but to test Sam's sincerity.

"I don't want to go back, sah. Wouldn't go back no how if I could help it; rather go a thousand miles away up Norf than go down Souf, sah. They knock me about down there. Massa whipped me last week, for talking with de other niggers about de war. O massa, don't send me back again! I'll do anything for you, massa."

He was the picture of anguish, and stood wringing his hands while the tears rolled down his cheeks. Freedom, with all its imagined blessings, was before him; slavery, with all its certain horrors, behind him.

The General questioned him about the Rebels.

"They say they will whip you Yankees. Dere's right smart chance of 'em at Fairfax, General Bonham in command. Souf Carolina is kinder mad at you Yankees. But now dey is kinder waiting for you to come, though they be packing up their trunks, as if getting ready to move."

All of his stories corroborated previous intelligence, and his information was of value.

"Well, Sam, I won't send you back," said the General. "You may go where you please about the camp."

"De Lord God Almighty bless you, sah!" was the joyful exclamation. There was no happier man in the world than Sam Allston that night. He had found that which his soul most longed for,—Freedom!

CHAPTER 2

Bull Run

JULY, 1861

At noon, on the 17th of July, the troops under General McDowell took up their line of march toward Fairfax, without baggage, carrying three days' rations in their haversacks. One division, under General Tyler, which had been encamped at Falls Church, marched to Vienna, while the other divisions, moving from Alexandria, advanced upon Fairfax Court-House.

It was a grand pageant, the long column of bayonets and high-waving flags. Union men whose homes were at Fairfax accompanied the march. "It does my eyes good to see the troops in motion at last," said one. "I have been exiled seven weeks. I know nothing about my family, although I have been within a dozen miles of them all the time. I came from the North three years ago. The Secessionists hated me, they threatened to hang me, and I had to leave mighty sudden."

The head of General Tyler's column reached Vienna at sunset. The infantry turned into the fields, while the artillery took positions on the hills. Near the railroad was a large woodpile, behind which the South Carolinians took shelter, when they fired upon the Ohio boys on the cars. It was convenient for bivouac fires, and the men helped themselves willingly. There I received instructions from Captain Alexander, of the engineers, an old campaigner in Mexico, which, during the four years of the war, I have never forgotten.

"Always sleep on the lee side of your bivouac fire," he said. "The fire dries the ground, the heat envelopes you like a blanket; it will keep off fever and ague. Better endure the discomfort of the smoke, better look like a Cincinnati ham, than to feel an ache in every bone in the morning, which you will be likely to feel if you spread your blankets on the windward side, for then you have little benefit of the heat, but

AID SOCIETY'S STORE-ROOM

receive the full rush of the air, which chills you on one side, while you are roasting on the other." It was wise counsel, and by heeding it I have saved my bones from many an ache.

It was at this place that a very laughable incident occurred. One of the citizens of Vienna had a bee-house well stocked with hives. A soldier espied them. He seized a hive and ran. Out came the bees, buzzing about his ears. Another soldier, thinking to do better, upset his hive, and seized the comb, dripping with honey. Being also hotly besieged, he dropped it, ran his hands through his hair, slapped his face, swung his arms, and fought manfully. Other soldiers seeing what was going on, and anxious to secure a portion of the coveted sweets, came up, and over went the half-dozen hives. The air was full of enraged insects, which stung men and horses indiscriminately, and which finally put a whole regiment to flight.

The Southern newspapers at this time were "firing the Southern heart," as they phrased it, by picturing the vandalism of the North. Beauregard, on the 5th of June, at Manassas, issued a manifesto addressed "to the people of the counties of Loudon, Fairfax, and Prince William." Thus it read:

> A reckless and unprincipled tyrant has invaded your soil. Abraham Lincoln, regardless of all moral, legal, and constitutional restraints, has thrown his abolition hosts among you, who are murdering and imprisoning your citizens, confiscating and

destroying your property, and committing other acts of violence and outrage too shocking and revolting to humanity to be enumerated.

All rules of civilized warfare are abandoned, and they proclaim by their acts, if not on their banners, that their war cry is 'Beauty and Booty.' All that is dear to man,—your honour, and that of your wives and daughters,—your fortunes and your lives, are involved in this momentous conflict.

In contrast to this fulmination of falsehoods, General McDowell had issued an order on the 2nd of June, three days previous, directing officers to transmit statements on the following points:—

First. The quantity of land taken possession of for the several field-works, and the kind and value of the crops growing thereon, if any.

Second. The quantity of land used for the several encampments, and the kind and value of the growing crops, if any.

Third. The number, size, and character of the buildings appropriated to public purposes.

Fourth. The quantity and value of trees cut down.

Fifth. The kind and extent of fencing destroyed. These statements will, as far as possible, give the value of the property taken, or of the damage sustained, and the name or names of the owners.[1]

A portion of the troops bivouacked in an oat-field, where the grain was standing in shocks, and some of the artillerymen appropriated the convenient forage.

The owner was complaining bitterly of the devastations. "They have taken my grain, and I want my pay for it," he said to me.

"Are you a Union man?" I asked.

"I was for the Union till Virginia seceded, and of course had to go with her; but whether I am a Union man or not, the government is bound to respect private property," he replied.

At that moment General Tyler rode past.

"Say, General, ain't you going to pay me for my property which your soldiers destroyed?"

"There is my quartermaster; he will settle it with you."

The man received a voucher for whatever had been taken. The

1: McDowell's Order.

THE IDEAL FREEDMAN

column took up its line of march, passed through a narrow belt of woods, and reached a hill from which Fairfax Court-House was in full view. A Rebel flag was waving over the town. There were two pieces of Rebel artillery in a field, a dozen wagons in park, squads of soldiers in sight, horsemen galloping in all directions. Nearer, in a meadow was a squadron of cavalry on picket. I stood beside Captain (since General) Hawley of Connecticut, commanding the skirmishers.

"Let me take your Sharpe's rifle," said he to a soldier. He rested it on the fence, ran his eye along the barrel, and fired. The nearest Rebel horseman, half a mile distant, slipped from his horse in an instant, and fell upon the ground. It was the first shot fired by the grand army on the march towards Manassas. The other troopers put spurs to their horses and fled towards Fairfax, where a sudden commotion was visible.

"The Rebels are in force just ahead!" said an officer who had advanced a short distance into the woods.

"First and second pieces into position," said Captain Varian, commanding a New York battery. The horses leaped ahead, and in a moment the two pieces were pointing toward Fairfax. The future historian, or the traveller wandering over the battle-fields of the Rebellion, who may be curious to know where the first cannon-shots were fired, will find the locality at Flint Hill, at that time the site of a small school-house. The cannon were on either side of the building.

"Load with shell," was the order, and the cartridges went home in an instant.

Standing behind the pieces and looking directly along the road under the shadow of the overhanging trees, I could see the Rebels in a hollow beyond a farm-house. The shells went screaming towards them, and in an instant they disappeared, running into the woods, casting away blankets, haversacks, and other equipments.

The column moved on. The occupants of the house met us with joyful countenances. The good woman, formerly from New Jersey, brought out a pan of milk, at which we took a long pull.

"I can't take pay; it is pay enough to see your countenances," she said.

Turning from Fairfax road the troops moved toward Germantown, north of Fairfax,—a place of six miserable huts, over one of which the Confederate flag was flying. Bonham's brigade of South Carolinians was there. Ayer's battery galloped into position. A shell was sent among them. They were about leaving, having been ordered to retreat by Beauregard. The shell accelerated their movements. Camp equipage, barrels of flour, clothing, entrenching tools, were left behind, and we made ourselves merry over their running.

Those were the days of romance. War was a pastime, a picnic, an agreeable diversion.

A gray-haired old negro came out from his cabin, rolling his eyes and gazing at the Yankees.

"Have you seen any Rebels this morning?" we asked.

"Gosh a'mighty, massa! Dey was here as thick as bees, ges 'fore you cum; but when dat ar bumshell cum screaming among 'em, dey ran as if de Ole Harry was after 'em."

All of this, the flight of the Rebels, the negro's story, was exhilarating to the troops, who more than ever felt that the march to Richmond was going to be a nice affair.

On the morning of the 18th the head of the column entered Centreville, once a thrifty place, where travellers from the western counties found convenient rest on their journeys to Washington and Alexandria. Its vitality was gone. The houses were old and poor. Although occupying one of the most picturesque situations in the world, it was in the last stages of decay.

A German met us with a welcome. Negro women peeped at us through the chinks of the walls where the clay had fallen out. At a large two-story house, which in former days reflected the glory of the Old Dominion, sat a man far gone with consumption. He had a pitiful story to tell of his losses by the Rebels.

Here we saw the women of Centreville, so accomplished in the practice of snuff-dipping, filling their teeth and gums with snuff, and passing round the cup with one swab for the company!

Richardson's brigade turned towards Blackburn's ford. Suddenly there was a booming of artillery, followed by a sharp skirmish, which Beauregard in his Report calls the first battle of Manassas. This was in distinction from that fought on the 21st, which is generally known as the battle of Bull Run.

It was a reconnoissance on the part of General Tyler to feel the position of the enemy. It might have been conducted more adroitly, without sacrifice. Under cover of skirmishers and artillery, their positions would have been ascertained; no doubt their batteries could have been carried if suitable arrangements had been made. But the long cannonading brought down hosts of reinforcements from Manassas. And when too late, three or four regiments were ordered down to the support of the Union troops.

The First Massachusetts received the hottest of the fire. One soldier in the thickest of the fight was shot; he passed his musket to his comrade, saying, "It is all right, Bill," and immediately expired. The soldier standing next to Lieutenant-Colonel Wells, received two shots in his arm. He handed his gun to the Colonel, saying, "Here, I can't use it; take it and use it." A great many of the soldiers had their clothes shot through. One had three balls in his coat, but came out unharmed.

As it is not intended that this volume shall be a history of the war, but rather a panorama of it, we must pass briefly in review the first great battle of the war at Bull Run, and the flight to Washington.

The day was calm and peaceful. Everywhere save upon the heights of Centreville and the plains of Manassas it was a day of rest.

I'll tell you what I heard that day,—
I heard the great guns far away,
Boom after boom!

Long before sunrise the troops of the attacking column rose from their bivouac and moved away towards the west. The sun had but just risen when Benjamin's batteries were thundering at Blackburn's ford, and Tyler was pressing upon the Stone Bridge. It was past eight o'clock before the first light ripple of musketry was heard at Sudley Springs, where Burnside was turning the left flank of the Rebels. Then came the opening of the cannonade and the increasing roar as regiment after regiment fell into line, and moved southward, through the thickets of pine. Sharp and clear above the musketry rose the cheers of the combatants.

"If you whip us, you will lick ninety thousand men. We have Johnston's army with us. Johnston came yesterday, and a lot more from Richmond," said a prisoner, boastfully.

Onward pressed the Union troops, success attending their arms. The battle was going in our favour. It was a little past three o'clock, when, standing by the broken-down stone bridge which the Rebels had destroyed, I had a full view of the action going on near Mrs. Henry's house. The field beyond the Rebel line was full of stragglers.

A correspondent of the *Charleston Mercury* thus writes of the aspect of affairs in the Rebel lines at that moment:

> When I entered the field at two o'clock the fortunes of the day were dark. The regiments so badly injured, or wounded and worn, as they staggered out gave gloomy pictures of the scene. We could not be routed, perhaps, but it is doubtful whether we were destined to a victory.

LADIES WORKING FOR THE ARMY

"All seemed about to be lost," wrote the correspondent of the *Richmond Dispatch*. There was a dust-cloud in the west. I saw it rising over the distant woods, approaching nearer each moment. A few moments later the fatal mistake of Major Barry was made.[2] Griffin and Ricketts could have overwhelmed the newly arrived troops, less than three regiments, with canister. But it was not so to be. One volley from the Rebels, and the tide of affairs was reversed; and the Union army, instead of being victor, was vanquished.

A few moments before the disaster by Mrs. Henry's house, I walked past General Schenck's brigade, which was standing in the road a few rods east of the bridge. A Rebel battery beyond the run was throwing shells, one of which ploughed through the Second Ohio, mangling two soldiers, sprinkling their warm blood upon the greensward.

While drinking at a spring, there was a sudden uproar, a rattling of musketry, and one or two discharges of artillery. Soldiers streamed past, throwing away their guns and equipments. Ayer's battery dashed down the turnpike. A baggage wagon was hurled into the ditch in a twinkling. A hack from Washington, which had brought out a party of Congressmen, was splintered to kindlings. Drivers cut their horses

---

2: See *Days and Nights on the Battlefield*. Available in a Leonaur edition.

loose and fled in precipitate haste. Instinct is quick to act. There was no time to deliberate, or to obtain information. A swift pace for a half-mile placed me beyond Cub Run, where, standing on a knoll, I had a good opportunity to survey the sight, painful, yet ludicrous to behold. The soldiers, as they crossed the stream, regained their composure and fell into a walk. But the panic like a wave rolled over Centreville to Fairfax. The teamsters of the immense wagon train threw bags of coffee and corn, barrels of beef and pork, and boxes of bread, upon the ground, and fled in terror towards Alexandria. The fright was soon over. The lines at Centreville were in tolerable order when I left that place at five o'clock.

Experience is an excellent teacher, though the tuition is sometimes expensive. There has been no repetition of the scenes of that afternoon during the war. The lesson was salutary. The Rebels on several occasions had the same difficulty. At Fair Oaks, Glendale, and Malvern we now know how greatly demoralized they became. No troops are exempt from the liability of a panic. Old players are not secure from stage fright. The coolest surgeon cannot always control his nerves. The soldiers of the Union in the battle of Bull Run were not cowards. They fought resolutely. The contest was sustained from early in the morning till three in the afternoon. The troops had marched from Centreville. The heat had been intense. Their breakfast was eaten at one o'clock in the morning. They were hungry and parched with thirst, yet they pushed the Rebels back from Sudley Springs, past the turnpike to the hill by Mrs. Henry's.

There is abundant evidence that the Rebels considered the day as lost, when Kirby Smith arrived.

Says the writer in the *Richmond Dispatch*, alluded to above:

> They pressed our left flank for several hours with terrible effect, but our men flinched not till their numbers had been so diminished by the well-aimed and steady volleys that they were compelled to give way for new regiments. The Seventh and Eighth Georgia Regiments are said to have suffered heavily.
>
> Between two and three o'clock large numbers of men were leaving the field, some of them wounded, others exhausted by the long struggle, who gave us gloomy reports; but as the fire on both sides continued steadily, we felt sure that our brave Southerners had not been conquered by the overwhelming hordes of the North. It is, however, due to truth to say that the result of this hour hung trembling in the balance. We had

lost numbers of our most distinguished officers. Generals Bartow and Bee had been stricken down; Lieutenant-Colonel Johnson of the Hampton Legion had been killed; Colonel Hampton had been wounded.

Your correspondent heard General Johnson exclaim to General Cocke just at the critical moment, 'O for four regiments!' His wish was answered, for in the distance our reinforcements appeared. The tide of battle was turned in our favour by the arrival of General Kirby Smith from Winchester, with four thousand men of General Johnson's division. General Smith heard while on the Manassas Railroad cars the roar of battle. He stopped the train, and hurried his troops across the field to the point just where he was most needed. They were at first supposed to be the enemy, their arrival at that point of the field being entirely unexpected. The enemy fell back and a panic seized them.

Smith had about seventeen hundred men instead of four thousand, but he came upon the field in such a manner, that some of the Union officers supposed it was a portion of McDowell's troops. Smith was therefore permitted to take a flanking position within close musket-shot of Rickett's and Griffin's batteries unmolested. One volley, and the victory was changed to defeat. Through chance alone it seemed, but really through Providence, the Rebels won the field. The cavalry charge, of which so much was said at the time, was a feeble affair. The panic began the moment that Smith opened upon Ricketts and Griffin. The cavalry did not advance till the army was in full retreat.

It is laughable to read the accounts of the battle published in the Southern papers. The *Richmond Dispatch* has a letter written from Manassas 23rd July, which has throughout evidences of candour, and yet this writer says, "We have captured sixty-seven pieces of artillery," while we had only thirty-eight guns on the field. Most necromancers have the ability to produce hens' eggs without number from a mysterious bag, but how they could capture sixty-seven pieces of cannon, when McDowell had but thirty-eight, is indeed remarkable. The same writer asserts that we carried into action the Palmetto State and the Confederate flags.

Here is the story of a wonderful cannon-ball. Says the writer:

A whole regiment of the enemy appeared in sight, going at double-quick down the Centreville road. Major Walton immediately ordered another shot. With the aid of our glass we could see them about two miles off. There was no obstruction, and the whole front of the regiment was exposed. *One half were seen to fall,* and if General Johnston had not at that moment sent an order to cease firing, nearly the whole regiment would have been killed!

The half that did not fall ought to be grateful to Major Walton for not firing a second shot. The writer says in conclusion:

> Thus did fifteen thousand men, with eighteen pieces of artillery, drive back ingloriously a force exceeding thirty-five thousand, supported by nearly one hundred pieces of cannon. We have captured nine hundred prisoners, sixty-seven pieces of cannon, Armstrong guns and rifled cannon, hundreds of wagons, loads of provisions and ammunition.

One writer asserted that thirty-two thousand pairs of handcuffs were taken, designed for Rebel prisoners! This absurd statement was believed throughout the South. In January, 1862, while in Kentucky, I met a Southern lady who declared that it must be true, for she had seen a pair of the handcuffs!

The war on the part of the North was undertaken to uphold the Constitution and the Union, but the battle of Bull Run set men to thinking. Four days after the battle, in Washington I met one who all his lifetime had been a Democrat, standing stanchly by the South till the attack on Sumter. Said he: "I go for liberating the niggers. We are fighting on a false issue. The negro is at the bottom of the trouble. The South is fighting for the negro, and nothing else. They use him to defeat us, and we shall be compelled to use him to defeat them."

These sentiments were gaining ground. General Butler had retained the negroes who came into his camp, calling them "contraband of war." Men were beginning to discuss the propriety of not only retaining, but of seizing, the slaves of those who were in arms against the government. The Rebels were using them in the construction of fortifications. Why not place them in the category with gunpowder, horses, and cattle? The reply was, "We must respect the Union people of the South." But where were the Union people?

There were some in Western Virginia, Kentucky, Tennessee, and Missouri; but very few in Eastern Virginia. At Centreville there was one man in the seedy village who said he was for the Union: he was a German. At a farm-house just out of the village, I found an old New-Yorker, who was for the Union; but the mass of the people, men, women, and children, had fled,—their minds poisoned with tales of the brutality of Northern soldiers. The mass of the people bore toward their few neighbours, who still stood for the Union, a most implacable hatred. I recall the woebegone look which overspread the countenance of a good woman at Vienna on Sunday night, when, as she gave me a draught of milk, I made a plain, candid statement of the disaster which had befallen our army. Her husband had been a friend to the Federal army, had given up his house for officers' quarters; had suffered at the hands of the Rebels; had once been obliged to flee, leaving his wife and family of six children, all of tender age, and the prospect was gloomy. He had gone to bed, to forget in sleep, if possible, the crushing blow. It was near midnight, but the wife and mother could not sleep. She was awake to every approaching footstep, heard every sound, knowing that within a stone's throw of the dwelling there were those, in former times fast friends, who now would be among the first to hound her and her little ones from the place; and why? because they loved the Union!

What had produced this bitterness? There could be but one answer,—Slavery. It was clear that, sooner or later, the war would become one of emancipation,—freedom to the slave of every man found in arms against the government, or in any way aiding or abetting treason. How seductive, how tyrannical this same monster Slavery!

Three years before the war, a young man, born and educated among the mountains of Berkshire County, Massachusetts, graduating at Williams College, visited Washington, and called upon Mr. Dawes, member of Congress from Massachusetts, to obtain his influence in securing a position at the South as a teacher. Mr. Dawes knew the young man, son of a citizen of high standing, respected not only as a citizen, but in the highest branch of the Legislature of the State in former times, and gladly gave his influence to obtain the situation. A few days after the battle Mr. Dawes visited the Old Capitol prison to see the prisoners which had been brought in. To his surprise he found among them the young man from Berkshire, wearing the uniform of a Rebel.

"How could you find it in your heart to fight against the flag of your country, to turn your back upon your native State, and the institutions under which you have been trained?" he asked.

"I didn't want to fight against the flag, but I was compelled to."

"How compelled?"

"Why, you see, they knew I was from the North; and if I hadn't enlisted, the ladies would have presented me with a petticoat."

He expressed himself averse to taking the oath of allegiance. It was only when allusion was made to his parents—the poignant grief which would all but break his mother's heart, were she to hear of him as a soldier in the traitors' lines,—that he gave way, and his eyes filled with tears. He could turn against his country, his State, the institutions of freedom, because his heart was in the South, because he had dreaded the finger of scorn which would have cowed him with a petticoat, but he could not blot out the influence of a mother's love, a mother's patriotism. He had not lived long enough under the hot breath of the *simoom* to have all the early associations withered and crisped. The mention of "mother" made him a child again.

With him was another Massachusetts man, who had been South many years, and who was more intensely Southern than himself. Another young man, a South Carolinian, was a law student in Harvard College when his State seceded. He went home to enlist. "If it had not been for the war I should now be taking my degree," said he. He was rejoicing over the result of the battle.

Slavery is not only tyrannical, but it is corrupting to morals. The Secessionists of St. Joseph, Missouri, in their eagerness to precipitate a Kansas regiment to destruction, burned a bridge on the Hannibal and St. Joseph Railroad, a few miles east of St. Joseph. The train left the city at three o'clock in the morning, and reached the bridge before daybreak. The regiment was not on board, and instead of destroying a thousand Union soldiers, a large number of the citizens of St. Joseph,—with women and children, friends and neighbours of the Secessionists,—were plunged into the abyss!

The action of these Missouri barbarians was applauded by the Secessionists of Washington. A friend came into my room late one evening in great excitement.

"What is the matter?"

"I am sick at heart," said he, "at what I have heard. I called upon some of my female acquaintances tonight. I knew that they were Secessionists, but did not think that they were so utterly corrupt as I find them to be. They are refined, intelligent, and have moved in the first society of Washington. They boldly declared that it was justifiable to destroy that railroad train in Missouri; that it is right to poison wells, or violate oaths of allegiance, to help on the cause of the South!"

The bitterness of the women of the South during the Rebellion is a strange phenomenon, without a parallel in history. For the women of Ireland, who in the rebellion of '98 cut off the heads of English residents, and chopped up their victims by piecemeal, were from the bogs and fens,—one remove only from the beasts; but these women of the South lay claims to a superior culture. It is one thing to be devoted heart and soul to a cause, but it is quite another to advance it at the cost of civilization, Christianity, and the womanly virtues.

The assertion that all women of the South thus gave themselves over to do wickedly, would be altogether too sweeping; a large portion may be included. Mrs. Greenhow and Belle Boyd have written out some of their exploits and machinations for the overthrow of the Union. With them, a false oath or any measure of deceit, was praiseworthy, if it would but aid the Secession cause. They are fair representatives of the females of the South.

CHAPTER 3

The Fall of 1861

OCTOBER, 1861

The months of August and September passed away without any action on the part of General McClellan, who had been appointed commander of the Army of the Potomac.

The disaster at Ball's Bluff occurred on the 21st of October, just three months after the battle of Bull Run. On the afternoon of the 22nd the news was whispered in Washington. Riding at once with a fellow-correspondent, Mr. H. M. Smith of the *Chicago Tribune*, to General McClellan's head-quarters, and entering the anteroom, we found President Lincoln there. I had met him on several occasions, and he was well acquainted with my friend. He greeted us cordially, but sat down quickly, rested his head upon his hand, and seemed to be unusually agitated. His eyes were sunken, his countenance haggard, his whole demeanour that of one who was in trouble.

"Will you please step in here, Mr. President," said an orderly from an adjoining room, from whence came the click of the telegraph. He soon came out, with his hands clasped upon his breast, his head bowed, his body bent as if he were carrying a great burden. He took no notice of any one, but with downcast eyes and faltering steps passed into the street and towards the Executive mansion.

"We have met with a sad disaster. Fifteen hundred men lost, and Colonel Baker killed," said General Marcy.

It was that which had overwhelmed the President. Colonel Baker was his personal friend. They had long been intimately acquainted. In speaking of that event afterwards, Mr. Lincoln said that it smote him like a whirlwind in a desert. Few men have been appointed of God to bear such burdens as were laid upon President Lincoln. A distracted country, a people at war, all the foundations of society broken up; the cares, trials, and perplexities which came every day without cessation, disaster upon disaster, the loss of those he loved,—Ellsworth, Baker, and his own darling Willie. A visitor at the White House the day of Ellsworth's death found him in tears.

"I will make no apology, gentlemen," said he, "for my weakness; but I knew poor Ellsworth well, and held him in great regard. Just as you entered the room, Captain Fox left me, after giving me the painful details of Ellsworth's unfortunate death. The event was so unexpected, and the recital so touching, that it quite unmanned me. Poor fellow," he added, "it was undoubtedly a rash act, but it only shows the heroic spirit that animates our soldiers, from high to low, in this righteous cause of ours. Yet who can restrain grief to see them fall in such a way as this,—not by the fortunes of war, but by the hand of an assassin?"

The first time I ever saw Mr. Lincoln was the day after his nomination by the Chicago Convention. I accompanied the committee appointed to inform him of the action of the Convention to Springfield. It was sunset when we reached the plain, unpretentious two-story dwelling,—his Springfield home. Turning to the left as we entered the hall, and passing into the library, we stood in the presence of a tall man, with large features, great, earnest eyes, a countenance which, once looked upon, forever remembered. He received the committee with dignity and yet with evident constraint of manner. The address of Mr. Ashmun, chairman of the committee, was brief, and so was Mr. Lincoln's reply. Then followed a general introduction of the party.

There was a pitcher of ice-water and goblets on a stand, but there were no liquors. The next morning a citizen narrated the following incident. When the telegraph informed Mr. Lincoln's neighbours that the committee were on their way, a few of his friends called upon him to make arrangements for their reception.

"You must have some refreshments prepared," said they.

"O certainly, certainly. What shall I get?"

"You will want some brandy, whiskey, wines, &c."

"I can't do that, gentlemen. I never have kept liquors, and I can't get them now."

"Well, we will supply them."

"No, gentlemen, I can't permit you to do what I would not do myself. I will furnish good water and enough of it, but no liquors."

He adhered to his decision; and thus at the beginning of the contest gave an exhibition of that resoluteness of character, that determination of will to adhere to what he felt was right, which was of such inestimable value to the nation, in carrying the cause of the Union triumphantly through all the dark days of the Rebellion.

****

It was sunset when Mr. Smith and myself reached Poolsville, after a rapid horseback ride from Washington. The quartermasters were issuing clothing to those who had cast away their garments while swimming the river. The night was cold. There had been a heavy fall of rain, and the ground was miry. It was a sad spectacle, those half-naked, shivering soldiers, who had lost everything,—clothes, equipments, and arms. They were almost heart-broken at the disaster.

"I enlisted to fight," said one, "but I don't want to be slaughtered. O my God! shall I ever forget that sight, when the boat went down?" He covered his face with his hands, as if to shut out the horrid spectacle.

Colonel Baker was sent across the river with the Fifteenth and Twentieth Massachusetts, a portion of the Tammany Regiment of New York, and the California regiment, Colonel Baker's own, in all about fifteen hundred men. His means of communication were only an old scow and two small boats. He was left to fight unassisted four thousand Rebels. Soon after he fell, there was a sudden rush to the boats, which, being overloaded, were instantly swamped. The Rebels had it all their own way, standing upon the bank and shooting the drowning men. Colonel Baker's body had been brought off, and was lying at Poolsville. The soldiers of his own regiment were inconsolable.

Poolsville is an insignificant village, situated in one of the richest agricultural districts of Maryland, surrounded by gentle swells of land, wooded vales, verdant slopes, broad fields, with the far-off mountain ranges and sweeping Potomac,—that combination which would be the delight of a painter who loves quiet rural scenery. The soil is fertile, and needs only good culture to yield an hundred-fold. Amid such native richness stands the village,—a small collection of nondescript houses, with overhanging roofs, wide porticos, or sheds which answer for *piazzas*, mammoth chimneys, built outside the edifice, as if they were afterthoughts when the houses were constructed. The streets are narrow, and the dwellings are huddled together as if there were but one corner lot, and all were trying to get as close to it as possible, reminding one of a crowd of boys round the old-fashioned fireplace of a country school-house on a winter's morning. There is not a new house in the place. The newest one was built many years ago. You look in vain for neat white cottages, with well-kept grounds. You are astonished at the immense number of old wagons and carriages, with rickety tops, torn canvas, broken wheels, shafts, and battered bodies,— of old lumber-carts and other weather-beaten vehicles under skeleton sheds. Look where you will, you come to the conclusion that time has sucked out the juice of everything. There is no freshness, no sign of a renewal of life or of present vitality. There are a small church, and two seedy, needy taverns,—mean-looking, uninviting places, each with its crowd of idle men, canvassing the state of public affairs.

Such was the village in 1861. The streets were alive with "little images of God cut in ebony," as Mrs. Stowe calls a negro child. Many of the "images," however, by contact with the Anglo-Saxon race, through Slavery, had become almost white. There were three or four hundred inhabitants, a few wealthy, with many poor.

We found accommodations at the best private residence in the place. The owner had a number of outlying farms, and was reported to be very wealthy. He was courteous, and professed to be a Union man. He was disposing of his hay and grain to the United States government, receiving the highest prices at his own door. Yet when conversing with him, he said, "your army," "your troops," as if he were a foreigner. A funeral procession passed the house,—a company of the Massachusetts Fifteenth, bearing to the village graveyard a comrade, who had laid down his life for his country at Ball's Bluff. Said the wife of my host to a friend as they passed:

"*Their* government has got money enough, and ought to take the bodies away; we don't want them buried here; it will make the place unhealthy."

These expressions revealed one thing: that between them and the Federal Union and the Constitution there was no bond of unity. There was no nationality binding us together. Once they would not have spoken of the army of the United States as "your army." What had caused this alienation? Slavery. An ebony-hued chattel kindled my fire in the morning and blacked my boots. A yellow chattel stood behind my chair at breakfast. A stout chattel, worth twelve hundred dollars, groomed my horse. There were a dozen young chattels at play upon the *piazza*. My host was an owner of human flesh and blood. That made him at heart a Secessionist. The army had not interfered with Slavery. Slaves found their way into the camp daily, and were promptly returned to their professedly loyal masters. Yet the presence of the troops was odious to the slaveholders.

In the quiet of affairs around Washington I visited Eastern Maryland, accompanied by two members of the press. The Rebels had closed the navigation of the Potomac by erecting batteries at Cockpit Point. General Hooker's division was at Budd's Ferry, Port Tobacco, and other places down the river. It was the last day of October,—one of the loveliest of the year,—when we started upon our excursion.

No description can convey an idea of the incomparable loveliness of the scenery,—the broad river, with the slow-moving sailboats, the glassy, unruffled surface, reflecting canvas, masts, and cordage, the many-coloured hills, rich with autumnal tints, the marble piles of the city, the broad streets, the more distant Georgetown, the thousands of white tents near and far away, with all the nice shading and blending of varied hue in the mellow light. On every hilltop we lingered to enjoy the richness of nature, and to fix in memory the picture which, under the relentless hand of war, would soon be robbed of its peculiar charms.

Ten miles out and all was changed. The neat, tasteful, comfortable residences were succeeded by the most dilapidated dwellings. The fields, green with verdure, gave place to sandy barrens. To say that everybody and everything were out at the elbows and down at the heels is not sufficient. One must see the old buildings,—the crazy roofs, the unglazed windows, the hingeless doors, the rotting stoops, the reeling barns and sheds, leaning in every direction, as if all were in drunken carousal,—the broken fences, the surrounding lumber,—of carts, wagons, and used-up carriages, to obtain a correct idea of this picture, so strongly and painfully in contrast to that from the hill-tops overlooking the capital of the country.

The first stopping-place for travellers is the "White Horse." We had heard much of the White Horse, and somehow had great expectations, or rather an undefined notion that Clark Mills or some other artist had sculptured from white marble a steed balanced on his hind legs and leaping toward the moon, like that in front of the Presidential mansion; but our great expectations dwindled like Pip's, when we descended a hill and came upon a whitewashed, one-story building,—a log-house, uninviting to man or beast. A poplar in front of the domicile supported a swinging sign, on which the country artist had displayed his marvellous skill in painting a white horse standing on two legs. It was time for dinner, and the landlady spread the table for her guests. There was no gold-tinted bill of fare, with unpronounceable French phrases, no long line of sable waiters in white aprons. My memory serves me as to the fare: *pork, pone, potatoes.*

The pork was cold, pone ditto, potatoes also. Pone is unraised corn-cake baked in the ashes, and said to be good for indigestion. It is a favourite cake in the South.

A saffron-hued young man, tall and lean, with a sharp nose and thin face, sat on the steps of the White Horse.

"The *ager* got hold of me yesterday and shook me right smart," he said. "It is a bad place for the ager. The people that used to live here have all moved away. The land is run out. They have *terbakkered* it to death. We can't raise nothing, and it ain't no use to try." He pointed to a deserted farm-house standing on a hill, and said, "There's a place the owner has left to grow up to weeds. He can't get nobody to carry it on."

A stately brick mansion, standing back from the highway once the residence of a man of wealth and taste, with blinds, portico, and carriage-house, elaborate in design and finish, was in the last stages of ruin. The portico had settled away from the house. The roof was hollowed like a weak-backed horse, the chimneys were tumbling, blinds swinging by a hinge, windows smashed, outhouses tottering with age and neglect, all presenting a most repulsive appearance. How changed from former years, when the courteous, hospitable proprietor of the estate received his guests at the magnificent portico, ushered them to his spacious halls, opened the sideboard and drank to their health, while attendant slaves took the horses to the stables! It is easy to fill up the picture,—the grand dinner, the walk over the estate, the stroll by the river, the duck-shooting on the marshes, the gang of slaves in the tobacco-patch, the army of black and yellow servants in the kitchens, chambers, and parlours. When this old house was in its glory, this section of Maryland was in its prime; but how great the change!

It was sad to think of the departed days. Our reflections were of what the place had been, what it was, and what it might have been, had Maryland in the beginning of her history accepted Freedom instead of Slavery.

Taverns are not frequent in the vicinity of Pomunkey, and it was necessary that we should seek private hospitality for the night. A first attempt for accommodations brought us to a house, but the owner had no oats, hay, or corn; a second ride in from the highway, brought us to a whitewashed farm-house, with immense outside chimneys, piazza, adjoining mud-chinked negro-quarters, with chimneys of sticks and clay, and a dozen surrounding buildings,—as usual, all tumbling to pieces. Explanations as to who we were secured kind hospitality from the host, a gray-headed man, with a family consisting of his wife, three grown-up sons, and nine adult daughters.

"Such as I have is at your service, gentlemen," said our host. But he had no hay, no oats, no corn, nothing but *shucks* for our horses. Our supper consisted of fried pork, fried salt shad, pone, wheat-cakes, pea-coffee, strawberry-leaf tea, sweetened with damp brown sugar! "We don't *raise* butter in this section of the State," said our host, in apology.

The supper was relished after an afternoon ride of thirty miles. The evening being chilly, a roaring fire was kept up in the old-fashioned fireplace. The daughters put on their most attractive attire, and left nothing untried to entertain their three visitors. Could we dance? Unfortunately we could not. It was a serious disappointment. They evidently had anticipated having "a good time." One of the ladies could play a violin, and treated us to jigs, reels, and hornpipes.

"You must sing the gentlemen a song, Jane," said one.

Jane turned scarlet at the suggestion, but finally, after polite requests and a little urging, turned her back to the company, faced the corner of the room, and sang a love-song. She could sing *Dixie*, but knew nothing of the *Star-Spangled Banner* or *Hail Columbia*. The young ladies were in sympathy with the Rebellion.

"It must be expected that Southern people should sympathize with the South," said our host.

"You own some slaves?" I said.

"I have three *servants*, sir. I think," he added, "that the people of Eastern Maryland would be more favourable towards the Union if they could be assured that the war would not finally become one of emancipation. My neighbour over there had a servant who ran away into the camp of one of the New York regiments. He went after him. The Colonel told the master to take him, but the servant wouldn't leave till the Colonel drew his pistol and threatened to shoot him. But notwithstanding that, I reckon that the war will make them restless." It was spoken frankly and unreservedly.

It was pitiable to walk round his farm in the morning, to see everywhere the last stages of decay,—poor, worn-out lands, broken-down fences, weedy fields, pastures without a blade of grass, leafless orchards, old buildings,—everything a wreck; and yet to know that he was wedded to the very institution which was reducing the country to a wilderness. He was not an owner of the estate, but a rentee. He paid one hundred and fifty dollars rental for three hundred acres of land, and yet confessed that he was growing poorer year by year. Tobacco, corn, and oats were the only crops. He could get no manure. He could make no hay. He kept two cows, but made no butter. The land was being exhausted, and he did not know what he should come to. All energy and life were gone; we saw only a family struggling against fate, and yet clinging with a death-grapple to the system that was precipitating their ruin.

"Why do you not go to Illinois?"

"O, sir, I am too old to move. Besides, this is home."

We pictured the boundless resources of the West, the fertile lands, the opportunities for bettering his condition, but our words fell upon an inert mind. As a last argument, we said: "You have a large family of daughters. In Illinois there are thousands of young men wanting wives, who will make good husbands. There are few young men here, but good homes await your daughters there."

There were blushes, smiles, and sparkling eyes from the "sacred nine." My fellow-correspondent of the *Chicago Tribune* then drew a florid picture of the West,—of the need of the State for such good-looking, virtuous ladies. His eloquence was persuasive. One of the daughters wanted to know how far it was to Illinois; but when informed that it was a thousand miles, her countenance fell. Bliss so far away was unattainable.

We passed a second night with our host, who, during our absence, sent one of the servants a dozen miles to obtain some butter, so courteous an entertainer was he. Yet he was struggling with poverty. He kept three slaves to wait upon his nine grown-up unmarried daughters, who were looking out upon a dark future. There was not a single gleam of light before them. They could not work, or, at the best, their work was of trifling account. What would become of them? That was the one question ever haunting the father.

"Why do you keep your slaves? they are a bill of cost to you every year," we said.

"I know it. They are lazy, shiftless, and they will steal, notwithstanding they have enough to eat and wear; but then I reckon I couldn't get along without them very well. Sam is an excellent groom, and Joe is a good ploughman. He can do anything if he has a mind to; but he is lazy, like all the rest. I reckon that I couldn't get along without him, though."

"Your sons can groom your horses and do your ploughing."

"Yes; but then they like to fish and hunt, you know; and you can't expect them to do the work of the servants."

The secret was out. Slavery made labour dishonourable.

Conversing with another farmer about the negroes, he said: "They steal all they can lay their hands on; and since the Yankee troops have been in camp round here, they are ten times as bad as they used to be. My chickens are fast disappearing. The officers buy them, I reckon."

We thought it quite likely; for having passed several days in General Hooker's division, we could bear testimony to the excellent fare of the officers' mess,—chickens served in all the various forms known to culinary art. It was convenient for officers thus to supply themselves with poultry. Of course the slave would say that he was the lawful owner of the poultry. Why should he have any compunctions of conscience about disposing of the chickens roosting on his master's apple-trees, when his labour, his life, his happiness, his children,—all his rights were stolen from him by his master? If the sword cut in one direction, why not in another?

A few days later, in November, we visited Annapolis, a quaint old city. The streets all centre at the State-House and St. John's Church. There are antiquated houses with mossy roofs, brass knockers on the doors, which were built two hundred years ago. We were carried back to the time of the Revolution, when Annapolis was in its glory.

One would suppose, in walking past the substantial stone mansions, that the owners were living at ease, in quiet and seclusion; that they had notes, mortgages, and bonds laid by for a rainy day: but a fair outside does not always indicate health within. In many of those old mansions, grand in proportion, elaborate with cornice, there was nothing but famine. How strong is aristocratic pride! Poverty cannot subdue it. Men and women lived there sorely pressed to keep up even a threadbare appearance, who, before the war, held soul and body together by raising negroes for the Southern market, and by waiting upon the Assembly when in session. They would have deemed it degrading to hold social intercourse with a mason or a blacksmith, or with any one compelled to earn his bread by the sweat of his brow. In poverty they nursed their pride. The castes of Hindustan were hardly more distinct. It is easy to see how a community can become lifeless under such a state of society. The labouring men had gone away,—to the West, to Baltimore, or to localities where it is not a crime to work for a livelihood. In consequence, enterprise had died, property had depreciated, and the entire place had become poverty-stricken.

November, 1861

On the succeeding Sunday I was in Washington, where a superintendent of one of the Sabbath schools was spending a portion of the hour in singing. Among other songs was Rev. S. F. Smith's national hymn,—

My country, 'tis of thee,
Sweet land of liberty.

Among the persons present were three ladies, members of a family sympathizing with secession. With unmistakable signs of disgust, they at once left the house!

Not only at church, but in the army, the spirit of slavery was rampant. The Hutchinson family visited Washington. They solicited permission from the Secretary of War, Mr. Cameron, to visit the camps in Virginia and sing songs to the soldiers, to relieve the tedious monotony of camp life. Their request was granted, and their intentions cordially commended by the Secretary; and, being thus indorsed, received General McClellan's pass. Their songs have ever been of freedom. They were welcomed by the soldiers. But there were officers in the service who believed in slavery, who had been taught in Northern pulpits that it was a divinely appointed, beneficent institution of Almighty God. Information was given to General McClellan that the Hutchinsons were poisoning the minds of the troops by singing Abolition songs; and their career as free concert givers to the patriotic soldiers was suddenly ended by the following order from head-quarters:

> By direction of Major-General McClellan, the permit given to the Hutchinson family to sing in the camps, and their pass to cross the Potomac, are revoked, and they will not be allowed to sing to the troops.

Far from the noise and strife of war, on the banks of the *Merrimack*, lived the poet of Peace and of Freedom, whose songs against oppression and wrong have sunk deep into the hearts of the people. Whittier heard of the expulsion of the Hutchinsons, and as if inspired by a spirit divine, wrote the *Ein Feste Burg Ist Unser Gott*.[3]

We wait beneath the furnace-blast
The pangs of transformation;
Not painlessly doth God recast
And mould anew the nation.
Hot burns the fire
Where wrongs expire;
Nor spares the hand
That from the land
Uproots the ancient evil.

The hand-breadth cloud the sages feared
Its bloody rain is dropping;
The poison plant the fathers spared

3: *Our God is a Strong Fortress.*

All else is overtopping.
East, West, South, North.
It curses the earth;
All justice dies,
And fraud and lies
Live only in its shadow.

What gives the wheat-field blades of steel?
What points the rebel cannon?
What sets the roaring rabble's heel
On the old star-spangled pennon?
What breaks the oath
Of the men o' the South?
What whets the knife
For the Union's life?—
Hark to the answer: Slavery!

Then waste no blows on lesser foes
In strife unworthy freemen.
God lifts today the veil, and shows
The features of the demon!
O North and South,
Its victims both,
Can ye not cry,
'Let slavery die!'
And union find in freedom?

What though the cast-out spirit tear
The nation in his going?
We who have shared the guilt must share
The pang of his o'erthrowing!
Whate'er the loss,
Whate'er the cross,
Shall they complain
Of present pain
Who trust in God's hereafter?

For who that leans on His right arm
Was ever yet forsaken?
What righteous cause can suffer harm
If He its part has taken?
Though wild and loud
And dark the cloud,
Behind its folds

*His hand upholds
The calm sky of tomorrow!*

*Above the maddening cry for blood,
Above the wild war-drumming,
Let Freedom's voice be heard, with good
The evil overcoming.
Give prayer and purse
To stay the Curse
Whose wrong we share,
Whose shame we bear,
Whose end shall gladden Heaven!*

*In vain the bells of war shall ring
Of triumphs and revenges,
While still is spared the evil thing
That severs and estranges.
But blest the ear
That yet shall hear
The jubilant bell
That rings the knell
Of Slavery forever!*

*Then let the selfish lip be dumb,
And hushed the breath of sighing;
Before the joy of peace must come
The pains of purifying.
God give us grace
Each in his place
To bear his lot,
And, murmuring not,
Endure and wait and labour!*

The expulsion of the Hutchinsons, with Whittier's ringing words, stirred people's thoughts. A change was gradually taking place in men's opinions. The negroes were beginning to show themselves useful. A detachment of the Thirteenth Massachusetts, commanded by Major Gould, was stationed on the upper Potomac. A negro slave, belonging in Winchester, came into the lines. He was intelligent, cautious, shrewd, and loyal. Major Gould did not return him to his master, but asked him if he would go back and ascertain the whereabouts of Stonewall Jackson. The negro readily assented. He was supplied with packages of medicine, needles, thread, and other light articles greatly needed in the South. With these he easily passed the Rebel pickets: "Been out to get 'em for massa," was his answer when questioned by the Rebels. Thus he passed repeatedly into the Rebel lines, obtaining information which was transmitted to Washington.

He had great influence with the slaves.

"They are becoming restless," said he, "but I tells 'em that they must be quiet. I says to 'em, keep yer eyes wide open and pray for de good time comin'. I tells 'em if de Souf whip, it is all night wid yer; but if de Norf whip, it is all day wid yer."

"Do they believe it?" Major Gould asked.

"Yes, massa, all believe it. The black men am all wid yer, only some of 'em isn't berry well informed; but dey is all wid yer. Massa tinks dey isn't wid yer, but dey is."

How sublime the picture!—a slave counselling his fellow bondmen to keep quiet and wait till God should give them deliverance!

Among the many Rebel ministers who had done what they could to precipitate the rebellion was a Presbyterian minister in the vicinity of Charlestown, Virginia. It was his custom, after closing his sermon, to invite the young men to enlist in the regiments then forming. On one of these occasions he made an address in which he gave utterance to the following sentiment: "If it is necessary to defend Southern institutions and Southern rights, I will wade up to my shoulders in blood!" This was brave; but the time came when the chivalry of the parson was put to the test. When the Rebels were routed at Bolivar, he, not being mounted on so fleet a horse as those of his flock who had given heed to his counsels and joined the cavalry, found himself left behind. A bullet lodged in the body of his horse prevented escape. He then tried his own legs, but soon found himself in the hands of the soldiers, who brought him to head-quarters. He at once claimed protection of Major Gould on the most extraordinary grounds. He had read the poems of Hannah Gould, and presumed that Major Gould, hailing from Massachusetts, must be her kinsman. When confronted with the Major he promptly exclaimed, "Major, I have read the poems of Miss Hannah Gould, and admire them; presuming that she is a relative of yours, I claim your protection and consideration."

The Major replied that he had not the honour to be a relative of that gifted lady, but that he should accord him all the consideration due to those who had rebelled against the peace and dignity of the United States, and had been taken with arms in their hands. He was marched off with the others and placed under guard.

Slavery was strongly entrenched in the capital of the nation. Congress had abolished it in the District of Columbia, but it still remained.

Said a friend to me one morning, "Are you aware that the Washington jail is full of slaves?" I could not believe that slaves were then confined there for no crime; but at once procured a pass from a senator to visit the jail, and was admitted through the iron gateway of one of the vilest prisons in the world. The air was stifled, fetid, and malarious.

Ascending the stone stairway to the third story of the building, entering a dark corridor and passing along a few steps, I came to a room twelve or fifteen feet square, occupied by about twenty coloured men. They were at their dinner of boiled beef and corn-cake. There was one old man sitting on the stone floor, silent and sorrowful. He had committed no crime. Around, standing, sitting, or lying, were the others, of all shades of colour, from jet black to the Caucasian hue, the Anglo-Saxon hair and contour of features. They were from ten to fifty years of age; some were dressed decently, and others were in rags. One bright fellow of twenty had on a pair of trousers only, and tried to keep himself warm by drawing around him a tattered blanket. A little fellow ten years old was all in rags. There was no chair or bed in the room. They must stand, or sit, or lie upon the brick and granite floor. There was no mattress or bedding; each had his little bundle of rags, and that was all. They looked up inquiringly as I entered, as if to make out the object of my visit.

ELLSWORTH ZOUAVE DRILL

One bright, intelligent boy belonged to Captain Dunnington, captain of the Capitol police during Buchanan's administration, and then commanding a Rebel battery. When Dunnington went from Washington to join the Rebels he left the boy behind, and the police had arrested him under an old Maryland law, because he had no master, and kept him in jail five months.

There was an old man from Fairfax Court-House. When the army advanced to Falls Church, his master sold his wife and child, for fear they might escape. "You see, sir, that broke me all up. O, sir, it was hard to part with them, to see 'em chained up and taken off away down South to Carolina. My mind is almost gone. I don't want to die here; I sha'n't live long. When your army fell back to Washington after the battle of Bull Run, I came to Washington, and the police took me up because I was a runaway."

There was another, a free negro, imprisoned on the supposition that he was a fugitive, and kept because there was no one to pay his jail fees. Another had been a hand on a Massachusetts schooner plying on the Potomac, and had been arrested in the streets on the suspicion that he was a slave.

Another had been employed on the fortifications, and government was his debtor. There was a little boy, ten years old, clothed in rags, arrested as a runaway. Women were there, sent in by their owners for safe keeping. There were about sixty chargeable with no crime whatever, incarcerated with felons, without hope of deliverance. They were imprisoned because negroes about town, without a master, always had been dealt with in that manner. The police, when the slaves had been reclaimed, had been sure of their pay, or if they were sold, their pay came from the auctioneer. When they saw me making notes, they imagined that I was doing something for their liberation, and with eagerness they crowded round, saying, "Please put down my name, sir," "I do want to get out, sir," and similar expressions. They followed me into the passage, gazed through the grated door, and when I said "Goodbye, boys," there came a chorus of "Goodbyes" and "God bless yous."

DECEMBER, 1861

Seeking Senator Wilson's room, I informed him of what I had witnessed, and read the memoranda taken in the jail. The eyes of that true-hearted man flashed with righteous indignation. "We will see about this," said he, springing to his feet.

He visited the jail, saw the loathsome spectacle, heard the stories of the poor creatures, and the next day introduced a resolution into the Senate, which upset forever this system of tyranny, which had been protected by the national authority.

The year closed gloomily. There were more than six hundred thousand troops under arms ready to subdue the Rebellion, but General McClellan hesitated to move. But there were indications of an early advance in the West; therefore on the last days of December I left Washington to be an observer of whatever might happen in Kentucky.

Chapter 4

Affairs in the West

January, 1862

The church-bells of Louisville were ringing the new year in as with the early morning we entered that city. There was little activity in the streets. The breaking out of the war had stopped business. The city, with a better location than Cincinnati, has had a slow growth. Cassius M. Clay gave the reason, years ago.

"Why," he asked, "does Louisville write on an hundred of her stores 'To let,' while Cincinnati advertises 'Wanted'? There is but one answer,—Slavery." Many of the houses were tenantless. The people lounged in the streets. Few had anything to do. Thousands of former residents were away, many with the Southern army, more with the Union. There was division of feeling. Lines were sharply drawn. A dozen loyal Kentuckians had been killed in a skirmish on Green River; among them Captain Bacon, a prominent citizen of Frankfort. His body was at the Galt House. Loyal Kentuckians were feeling these blows. Their temper was rising; they were being educated by such adversity to make a true estimate of Secession. Everything serves a purpose in this world. Our vision is too limited to understand much of the governmental providence of Him who notices the fall of a sparrow, and alike controls the destiny of nations; but I could see in the emphatic utterances of men upon the street, that revenge might make men patriotic who otherwise might remain lukewarm in their loyalty.

A friend introduced a loyal Tennessean, who was forced to flee from *Nashville* when the State seceded. The vigilance committee informed him that he must leave or take the consequences; which meant, a suspension by the neck from the nearest tree. He was offensive because of his outspoken loyalty. He was severe in his denunciations of the government, on account of its slowness to put down the Rebellion.

"Sir," said he, "this government is not going to put down the

Rebellion, because it isn't in earnest. You of the North are white-livered. Excuse me for saying it. No; I won't ask to be excused for speaking the truth. You are afraid to touch the negro. You are afraid of Kentucky. The little province of the United States gets down on its knees to the nation of Kentucky. You are afraid that the State will go over to the Rebels, if anything is done about the negro. Now, sir, I know what slavery is; I have lived among it all my days. I know what Secession is,—it means slavery. I know what Kentucky is,—a proud old State, which has a great deal that is good about her and a great deal of sham. Kentucky politicians are no better or wiser than any other politicians. The State is living on the capital of Henry Clay. You think that the State is great because he was great. O, you Northern men are a brave set! (It was spoken with bitter sarcasm.) You handle this Rebellion as gingerly as if it were a glass doll. Go on, go on; you will get whipped. Buell will get whipped at Bowling Green, Butler will get whipped at New Orleans. You got whipped at Big Bethel, Ball's Bluff, and Manassas. Why? Because the Rebels are in earnest, and you are not. Everything is at stake with them. They employ niggers, you don't. They seize, rob, burn, destroy; they do everything to strengthen their cause and weaken you, while you pick your way as daintily as a dandy crossing a mud-puddle, afraid of offending somebody. No, sir, you are not going to put down this Rebellion till you hit it in the tenderest spot,—the negro. You must take away its main support before it will fall."

General Buell was in command of the department, with his head-quarters at the Galt House. He had a large army at Mumfordville and other points. He issued his orders by telegraph, but he had no plan of operations. There were no indications of a movement. The Rebel sympathizers kept General Johnston, in command at Bowling Green, well informed as to Buell's inaction. There was daily communication between Louisville and the Rebel camp. There was constant illicit trade in contraband goods. The policy of General McClellan was also the policy of General Buell,—to sit still.

Events were more stirring in Missouri, and I proceeded to St. Louis, where General Halleck was in command,—a thick-set, dark-featured, black-haired man, sluggish, opinionated, and self-willed, arbitrary and cautious.

Soon after his appointment to this department he issued, on the 20th of November, his Order No. 3, which roused the indignation of earnest loyal men throughout the country. Thus read the document:

It has been represented that information respecting the numbers and condition of our forces is conveyed to the enemy by means of fugitive slaves who are admitted within our lines. In order to remedy this evil, it is directed that no such persons be hereafter permitted to enter the lines of any camp, or of any forces on the march, and that any within our lines be immediately excluded therefrom.

General Schofield was in command of Northern Missouri, under General Halleck. The guerrillas had burned nearly all the railroad bridges, and it was necessary to bring them to justice. The negroes along the line gave him the desired intelligence, and six of the leaders were in this way caught, tried by court-martial, and summarily shot. Yet General Halleck adhered to his infamous order. Diligent inquiries were made of officers in regard to the loyalty of the negroes, and no instance was found of their having given information to the enemy. In all of the slaveholding States a negro's testimony was of no account against a white man under civil law; but General Schofield had, under military law, inaugurated a new order of things,—a drum-head court, a speedy sentence, a quick execution, on negro testimony. The Secessionists and Rebel sympathizers were indignant, and called loudly for his removal.

The fine army which Fremont had commanded, and from which he had been summarily dismissed because of his anti-slavery order, was at Rolla, at the terminus of the southwest branch of the Pacific Railroad. This road, sixteen miles out from St. Louis, strikes the valley of the Maramec,—not the *Merrimack*, born of the White Hills, but a sluggish stream, tinged with blue and green, widening in graceful curves, with tall-trunked elms upon its banks, and acres of low lands, which are flooded in freshets. It is a pretty river, but not to be compared in beauty to the stream which the muse of Whittier has made classic. Nearly all the residences in this section are Missourian in architectural proportions and features,—logs and clay, with the mammoth outside chimneys, cow-yard and piggery, an oven out of doors on stilts, an old wagon, half a dozen horses, hens, dogs, pigs, in front, and lean, cadaverous men and women peeping from the doorways, with arms akimbo, and pipes between the teeth. This is the prevailing feature,—this in a beautiful, fertile country, needing but the hand of industry, the energy of a free people, vitalized by the highest civilization, to make it one of the loveliest portions of the world.

At Franklin the south-western branch of the Pacific Railroad diverges from the main stem. It is a new place, brought into existence by the railroad, and consists of a lime-kiln, a steam saw-mill, and a dozen houses. Behind the town is a picturesque bluff, with the lime-kiln at its base, which might be taken for a ruined temple of some old Aztec city. Near at hand two Iowa regiments were encamped. A squad of soldiers was on the plain, and a crowd stood upon the depot platform, anxiously inquiring for the morning papers. It was a supply station, provisions being sent up both lines. Two heavy freight trains, destined for Rolla, were upon the south-western branch. To one of them passenger cars were attached, to which we were transferred.

When the branch was opened for travel in 1859, the directors run one train a day,—a mixed train of passenger and freight cars,—and during the first week their patronage in freight was immense,—it consisted of a bear and a pot of honey! On the passage the bear ate the honey, and the owner of the honey brought a bill against the company for damages.

Beyond Franklin the road crosses the Maramec, enters a forest, winds among the hills, and finally by easy grades reaches a crest of land, from which, looking to the right or the left, you can see miles away over an unbroken forest of oak. Far to the east is the elevated ridge of land which ends in the Pilot Knob, toward the Mississippi, and becomes the Ozark Mountain range toward the Arkansas line. We looked over the broad panorama to see villages, church-spires, white cottages, or the blue curling smoke indicative of a town or human residence, but the expanse was primitive and unbroken. Not a sign of life could be discovered for many miles as we slowly crept along the line. The country is undulating, with the limestone strata cropping out on the hillsides. In the railroad cuttings the rock, which at the surface is gray, takes a yellow and reddish tinge, from the admixture of ochre in the soil. In one cutting we recognized the lead-bearing rocks, which abound through the south-western section of the State.

We looked in vain to discover a school-house. A gentleman who was well acquainted with this portion of the State, said that he knew of only two school-houses,—one in Warsaw and the other in Springfield. In a ride of one hundred and thirteen miles we saw but two churches. As Aunt Ophelia found "Topsy" virgin soil, so will those who undertake to reconstruct the South find these wilds of Southwestern Missouri. And they are a fair specimen of the South.

It was evening when we reached Rolla. When we stepped from the car in the darkness, there was a feeling that the place was a mortar-bed and the inhabitants were preparing to make bricks.

Our boots became heavy, and, like a man who takes responsibility, when we once planted our feet the tendency was for them to stay there. Guided by an acquaintance who knew the way, the hotel was reached. In the distance the weird camp-fires illuminated the low-hanging clouds. From right and left there came the roll of drums and the bugle-call. A group of men sat around the stove in the bar. The landlord escorted us to the wash-room,—a spacious, high-arched apartment, as wide as the east is from the west, as long as the north is from the south, as high-posted as the zenith, where we found a pail of water, a tin basin, and a towel, for all hands; and which all hands had used. After ablution came supper in the dining-hall, with bare beams overhead. Dinah waited upon us,—coal-black, tall, stately, worth a thousand dollars before the war broke out, but somewhat less just then, and Phillis, with a mob-cap on her head, bleached a little in complexion by Anglo-Saxon or Missourian blood.

We soon discovered that nothing was to be done by the army in this direction. The same story was current here as on the Potomac and in Kentucky,—"Not ready." General Sigel had sent in his resignation, disgusted with General Halleck. General Curtis had just arrived to take command. The troops were sore over the removal of Fremont: they idolized him. Among the forty thousand men in the vicinity were those who had fought at Wilson's Creek. The lines between Rebellion and Loyalty were more sharply drawn here than in any other section of the country. Men acted openly. The army was radical in its sentiments, believing in Fremont's order for the liberation of the slaves, which the President had set aside.

There was one other point which gave better promise of active operations,—Cairo. Therefore bidding *adieu* to Rolla, we returned to St. Louis and took the cars for Cairo.

It was an all-night ride, with a mixed company of soldiers and civilians. There were many ladies on their way to visit their husbands and brothers before the opening of the campaign. One woman had three children. "Their father wants to see them once more before he goes into battle," said the mother, sadly.

At last we found a place where men seemed to be in earnest. Cairo was alive. At the levee were numerous steamboats. Soldiers were arriving. There was a constant hammering and pounding on the gunboats, which were moored along the shore.

The mud cannot be put into the picture. There was thick mud, thin mud, sticky mud, slushy mud, slimy mud, deceptive mud, impassable mud, which appeared to the sight, to say nothing of the peculiarities that are understood by the nose; for within forty feet of our window were a horse-stable and pig-yard, where slops from the houses and washes from the sinks were trodden with the manure from the stables. Bunyan's Slough of Despond, into which all the filth and slime of this world settled, was nothing beside the slough of Cairo. There were sheds, shanties, stables, pigsties, wood-piles, carts, barrels, boxes,—the debris of everything thrown over the area. Of animate things, water-carts,—two-horse teams, which were supplying the inhabitants with drinking water from the river. There were truckmen stuck in the mud. There were two pigs in irrepressible conflict; also two dogs. Twenty feet distant, soldiers in their blue coats, officers with swords, sash and belt, ladies, and citizens, were picking their way along the sticky sidewalks. This was Cairo. Delectable Cairo!

The prominent names before the country at that period, as commanders who were to lead our armies to victory, were McClellan, Buell, T. W. Sherman, then at Port Royal, Fremont, Rosecrans, Burnside, Butler, and Banks. William Tecumseh Sherman was reputed to be flighty in the head. He had commanded the Department of the Ohio, but Buell had succeeded him. He was now a brigade commander at Paducah, under General C. F. Smith. There were several brigadiers at *Cairo*. General McClernand, who had been a member of Congress, a strong partisan of Senator Douglas, was most conspicuous. General Prentiss, who was ready to make a speech on any and every occasion, was also well known. The commander of the post was an obscure man. His name was Grant. At the beginning of the war he was in the leather business at Galena. He had been educated at West Point, where he stood well as a mathematician, but had left the service, and had become a hard-working citizen. He was Colonel of the Twenty-first Illinois, and had been made a brigadier by the President. He was in charge of the expedition to Belmont, which, though successful in the beginning, had ended almost in disaster. Having credentials from the Secretary of War, I entered the head-quarters of the commanding officer, and found a man of medium stature, thick set, with blue eyes, and brown beard closely cropped, sitting at a desk. He was smoking a meerschaum. He wore a plain blue blouse, without any insignia of rank. His appearance was clerkly. General McClellan, in Washington, commanded in state, surrounded by brilliant staffs, men in fine broadcloth, gold braid, plumed hats, and wearing clanking sabres. Orderlies and couriers were usually numerous at head-quarters.

"Is General Grant in?" was the question directed to the clerk in the corner.

"Yes, sir," said the man, removing his meerschaum from his mouth, and spitting with unerring accuracy into a spittoon by his side.

"Will you be kind enough to give this letter to him."

But the clerk, instead of carrying it into an adjoining room, to present it to the commander-in-chief, opened it, ran his eye rapidly over the contents, and said, "I am happy to make your acquaintance, sir. Colonel Webster will give you a pass."

Such was my first interview with General Grant. I have seen him many times since,—in the hour of victory, at Donelson; in the shadow of the cloud, after Pittsburg Landing; during the fearful days of the Wilderness; in the last great hours of triumph, with Lee and his army paroled prisoners of war; and there has ever been the same quiet, gentlemanly deportment.

The large hall of the St. Charles Hotel was the general resort of officers, soldiers, guests, and citizens. I was conversing with a friend the same afternoon when a short, muscular, quick-walking man, in the prime of life, wearing a navy uniform, entered. His countenance would attract attention even in a crowd, it was so mild, peaceful, and pleasant. My friend introduced him as Commander Foote.

"I shall be pleased to see you at my office, which is on the wharf-boat. I usually take a little recreation after dinner," said he.

Calling upon him the next day, I found him at leisure, having despatched the business of the forenoon. There was a Bible on his table and a hymn-book, and in one corner of the office a large package of books, just received from the Sunday-School Union, directed to "Captain A. H. Foote, U. S. N."

Noticing my eyes turned in that direction, he said: "They are for the sailors; I want to do what I can for the poor fellows. They haven't any chaplain; I read the service on Sunday and visit the crews, and talk to them; but it is very little religious instruction which they receive. I don't allow any work, except what is absolutely necessary, on Sunday. I believe man and beast need rest one day in seven. I am trying to persuade the men to leave off their grog rations, with a fair chance of success."

He was at leisure, and talked freely of matters relating to the organization of the fleet. He had to contend with great difficulties. The department had rendered him but little service. He had done his best to obtain mortars; had despatched officers to Pittsburg, where they were cast, but they were all sent East for the New Orleans fleet. He regretted it exceedingly, for with good ordnance he thought it would not be a difficult matter to reach New Orleans, though, as he modestly remarked, quoting the Scriptural proverb, *"It becomes not him who*

General Grant

General Sherman

putteth on the harness to boast." He was lacking men. Recruiting officers had been sent to Chicago, Cleveland, Buffalo, and other lake ports, but they had signally failed, because the department did not pay any advance to those in the river service, while on the seaboard advances were made. He had not men enough to man his gunboats.

The department had furnished him with but few new guns. He had been obliged to take those which were at Sackett's Harbor,—old guns far inferior to those with which Commodore Du Pont knocked Tybee and Hilton Head to pieces. He had to get gun-carriages manufactured in Cincinnati, other things at St. Louis, others at Pittsburg; but notwithstanding this, had organized a fleet which would throw a tremendous weight of metal. He was not ready to move, yet would move, whether ready or not, whenever the word was given. He believed in fighting at close quarters.

He spoke freely of the faults of the gunboats. They were too low in the water and the engines of too limited capacity. They would not be able to make much headway against the stream. He considered them an experiment, and, like all experiments, they were of course defective.

He was a close student, devoted to his profession, and bore the marks of severe thought in the wrinkles which were deepening on his brow. Time had begun to silver his hair and whiskers, but he walked with a firm step. He had rare conversational powers, and imparted information as if it were a pleasure. He was thoroughly conscientious, and had a deep sense of his responsibility. He was aware that his own reputation and standing as well as the interests of the public were at stake. He was greatly beloved by his men.

Two of the gunboats—the *Essex* and *Louisville*—were lying six or eight miles below Cairo, guarding the river. The *Essex*! How often in boyhood had I thrilled at the story of her brave fight with the *Cherub* and *Phebe* in the harbour of Valparaiso! How often I wished that Captain Porter could have had a fair chance in that terrible fight,—one of the fiercest ones fought on the sea. But there was another *Essex* commanded by another Captain Porter, son of him who refused to surrender his ship till he had lost all power to defend her.

The new craft was wholly unlike the old. That was a fast sailer, trim, and taut, and graceful as a swan upon the waters; this a black box, once a St. Louis ferry-boat. The sailors who had breathed the salt air of the sea, who had swung in mid-heaven upon the swaying masts, who had rode in glee upon the storm-tost billows,

Whose home was on the deep,

regarded the new *Essex* in disgust, and rechristened her the *Mud Turtle*. But her name, and the glorious record of her deeds, will not fade from remembrance. Coming generations shall read of her exploits with pride and pleasure. We were courteously received by her commander, Captain Wm. D. Porter, a solid man, but little more than five feet high, yet broad-chested, quick and energetic in his movements. He had a long, thick, black beard, and twinkling eyes full of fire. He had the rolling gait of a sailor, and was constantly pacing the deck. He was a rapid talker, and had a great store of adventure and anecdote. We alluded to the part taken by his father in the war of 1812, and the gallant fight against great odds in Valparaiso harbour. The eyes of the son kindled instantly.

"Yes, sir; that was a plucky fight. The old gentleman never would have given in if there had been the least ray of hope; but there was none. And he was too tender-hearted to needlessly slaughter his men."

Three days previous to our visit to the *Essex*, two Rebel boats came up from Columbus to see what the Yankees were doing. In five minutes Porter had his anchor up and steam on, pushing down to meet them half-way; but they declined the courtesy, and steamed back to Columbus.

"I followed them as fast as I could," said he, as we paced the deck. "I let them have my ten-inch Dahlgren and my two rifled forty-two pounders one after another, and drove them till their batteries on the bluff above the town opened on me. Then I wrote an invitation to Montgomery, who commands their fleet, to meet me any day and I would lick him like thunder. I fastened it to a cork and set it adrift, and saw a boat go out and pick it up. Then I elevated my ten-inch and let them have a shell right into the town. I reckon it waked them up some."

He laughed and chuckled, rubbed his hands, took a fresh quid of tobacco, and began to talk again of his father's exploits on the Pacific.

The Rebels under Major-General Bishop Polk were in force at Columbus. There was also a detachment at Mayfield, east of Columbus. A sudden movement was made by General Grant in the direction of Mayfield, not with any design of an attack, but to deceive the Rebels in regard to the real intentions. The troops landed at old Fort Jefferson, six miles below Cairo, on the Kentucky side. It was a mild day in midwinter. The soldiers marched without baggage. Not one in ten had gloves or mittens; and on the second night of the reconnoissance the cold became intense, and there was great suffering.

The soldiers kindled huge fires, and by running and walking, and constant thrashing of the hands, passed the long, weary night. There were numerous herds of swine in the woods, and fresh pork was abundant. There was roasting, frying, and broiling by every bivouac fire, and a savoury fragrance of sparerib and steak.

The dwellings of the farmers in this section of Kentucky are of the Southern style of architecture,—log-houses containing two rooms, with chimneys built against the ends. Entering one to obtain a drink of water we found two tall, cadaverous young men, both of them shaking with ague. There was a large old-fashioned fireplace, with a great roaring fire, before which they were sitting with the door wide open at their backs, and the cold air rushing upon them in torrents. Probably it did not occur to either of them that it would be better to shut the door.

A Connecticut wooden clock ticked on a rude shelf, a bed stood in one corner. The walls were hung with old clothes and dried herbs,—catnip and tansy and thoroughwort. The clay had dropped out in many places, and we could look through the chinks and see the landscape without. The foundations of the chimney had settled, and the structure was leaning away from the house. There were great cracks between the brickwork and the wood.

They claimed to be good Union men, but said that all the rest of the people round them were disloyal.

"We are having a hard time," said one. "The Secessionists were going to jump us,—to take our property because we were for the Union, and now your army has come and killed nigh about seventy-five hogs for us, I reckon. It is kinder hard, stranger, to be used so."

"But, my friend, if it had not been for the Union troops wouldn't you have lost everything, if you are a Union man?"

"Yes,—perhaps so," was the long-drawn answer, given with hesitation.

"There is a right smart heap of Southerners at Columbus, I reckon," said he. "There is Sam Wickliff and Josh Turner, and almost all the boys from this yere place, and they'll fight, I reckon, stranger."

We then learned that the officers of McClernand's division, having been deprived of the enjoyments of home-life, and finding themselves among the *belles* of Western Kentucky, had made the most of the opportunity by dancing all night.

"The gals danced themselves clean out, that is the reason they ain't about," said one of the young men, apologizing for the absence of his sisters, and added, "They is rather afraid of the Lincolnites."

The utterance of the last sentence contradicted all previous assertions of loyalty and hearty love for the Union.

The troops made sad havoc among the stock, shooting pigs and sheep for fun. After scouring the country well towards Columbus, having accomplished the object of the expedition,—that of deceiving the Rebels in regard to the movement contemplated up the Tennessee,—the force returned to Cairo.

CHAPTER 5
Central Kentucky

February, 1862

The tide of success during the year 1861 was almost wholly in favour of the Rebels; but at length there came a change, in the defeat of Zollicoffer by General Thomas at Mill Springs, on the 19th of January. I hastened to the centre of the State to watch operations which had suddenly become active in that quarter.

It was on the last day of January that the zealous porter of the Spencer House, in Cincinnati, awoke me with a thundering rap at five o'clock, shouting, "Cars for Lexington." It was still dark when the omnibus whirled away from the house. There were six or eight passengers, all strangers, but conversation was at once started by a tall, stout, red-faced, broad-shouldered man, wearing a gray overcoat and a broad brimmed, slouched hat, speaking the Kentucky vernacular.

It is very easy to become acquainted with a genuine Kentuckian. He launches at once into conversation. He loves to talk, and takes it for granted that you like to listen. The gentleman who now took the lead sat in the corner of the omnibus, talking not only to his next neighbour, but to everybody present. The words poured from his lips like water from a wide-mouthed gutter during a June shower. In five minutes we had his history,—born in "Old Kentuck," knew all the folks in Old Bourbon, had been a mule-driver, supplied Old Virginia with more mules than she could shake a stick at, had got tired of "Old Kentuck," moved up into Indiana, was going down to see the folks,—all of this before we had reached the ferry; and before arriving at the Covington shore we had his opinion of the war, of political economy, the Constitution, and the negroes.

It was remarkable that, let any subject be introduced, even though it might be most remotely related to the war, the talkers would quickly reach the negro question. Just as in theological discussions the tendency is toward original sin, so upon the war,—the discussion invariably went beyond the marshalling of armies to the negro as the cause of the war.

The gentleman in gray had not learned the sounds of the letters as given by the lexicographers of the English language, but adhered to the Kentucky dialect, giving "har" for hair, "thar" for there, with peculiar terminations.

"Yer see, I us-*ed* to live in Old Kaintuck, down thar beyond Paris. Wal, I mov*ed* up beyond Indi*a*nopolis, bought a mighty nice farm. I know'd all the folks down round Paris. Thar's old Speers, who got shot down to Mill Springs,—he was a game un; a white-haired old cuss who jined the Confederates. I know'd him. I 'tended his nigger sale sev'ral years ago, when he busted. He war a good old man, blame me if he want. He war crazy that ar day of the sale, and war down on the nigger-traders. He lost thousands of dollars that ar day, cause he hated 'em and run down his niggers,—said they wan't good when they war, just ter keep 'em out of the hands of the cussed traders.

"Wal, thar's Jim,—I remember him. He's in Confed'rate army, too. I lost a bet of tew hundred dollars with him on Letcher's 'lection,— that old drunken cuss who's disgracing Old Virginia; blow me if I didn't. That was hard on me, cause on 'lection day arter I'd voted, I started with a drove of mu*els*, four hundred on 'em nigh about, for Virginia. I felt mighty sick, I tell you, 'cause I had employed a drunken cuss to buy 'em for me, and he paid more than they war wuth. Wal, I know'd I would lose, and I did,—ten hundred dollars. Cusses, yer know, allers comes in flocks. Wal, only ges think of it, that ar drunken cuss is a kurnel in the Federal army. Blow me ef I think it's right. Men that drink too much ar'n't fit to have control of soldiers.

"Wal, I am a Kentuckian. I've got lots of good friends in the Southern army, and lots in the Union army. My idee is that government ought to confiscate the property of the Rebels, and when the war is over give it back to their wives and children. It's mighty hard to take away everything from 'em,—blow me if it a'n't. The Abolitionists want to confiscate the niggers. Wal, I know all about the niggers. They are a lazy, stealing set of cusses, the hull lot of 'em. What can we do with 'em? That's what I want to know. Now my wife, she wants niggers, but I don't. If Kentucky wants 'em, let her have 'em. It's my opinion that Kentucky is better off with 'em, 'cause she has got used to 'em.

"The people are talking about starving the Confederates, but I've been through the South, and it can't be done. They can raise everything that we can, and it's my candid opinion that government is gwine to get licked."

The arrival of the omnibus at the depot put an end to the talk.

The Licking Valley, through which the railroad to Lexington runs, is very beautiful. There are broad intervals fringed with hickory and elm, wood-crowned hills, warm, sunny vales and charming landscapes. Nature has done much to make it a paradise; art very little. The farmhouses are in the Kentucky style,—*piazzas*, great chimneys outside, negro cabins,—presenting at one view and in close contrast the extremes of wealth and poverty, power and weakness, civilization and barbarism, freedom and slavery.

The city of Lexington is a place of the past. Before railroads were projected, when Henry Clay was in the prime of manhood there, it was a place of enterprise and activity. The streets were alive with men. It was the great political and social centre of Central Kentucky. The city flourished in those days, but its glory has passed away. The great commoner on whose lips thousands hung in breathless admiration, the circumstances of his time, the men of his generation, have departed never to return. Life has swept on to other centres. In the suburbs were beautiful residences. Riches were displayed in lavish expenditure, but the town itself was wearing a seedy look. There was old rubbish everywhere about the city; there were buildings with crazy blinds, cracked walls, and leaning earthward; while even a beautiful church edifice had broken panes in its windows. The troubles of the year, like care and anxiety to a strong man, ploughing deep furrows on his face, had closed many stores, and written "To Rent" on many dwellings. A sudden paralysis had fallen, business had drooped, and society had lost its life.

The Phenix was the ancient aristocratic hotel of the place. It was in appearance all of the old time,—a three-story, stone, brick, and plaster building, with small windows, and a great bar-room or office, which in former days was the resort of politicians, men of the turf, and attendants at court. A crowd of unwashed men were in the hall, spattered with mud, wearing slouched hats, unshaven and unshorn,—a motley crew; some tilted against the walls in chairs, fast asleep, some talking in low tones and filling the room with fumes of tobacco. A half-dozen were greasing their boots. The proprietor apologized for their presence, remarking that they were teamsters who had just arrived from Somerset, and were soon to go back with supplies for General Thomas's army. There were three hundred of them, rough, uncouth, dirty, but well behaved. There was no loud talking, no profanity, indecency, or rudeness, but a deportment through the day and night worthy of all commendation.

While enjoying the fire in the reception-room two ladies entered,—one middle-aged, medium stature, having an oval face, dark hair, dark hazel eyes; the other a young lady of nineteen or twenty years, sharp features, black hair, and flashing black eyes. They were boarders at the hotel, were well dressed, though not with remarkable taste, but evidently were accustomed to move in the best circle of Lexington society. A regiment was passing the hotel.

"There are some more Yankees going down to Mill Springs, I reckon," said the elder.

"O, isn't it too bad that Zollicoffer is killed? I could have cried my eyes out when I heard of it," said the youngest. "O he was so brave, and noble, and chivalrous!"

"He was a noble man," the other replied.

"O, I should so like to see a battle!" said the youngest.

"It might not be a pleasant sight, although we are often willing to forego pleasure for the sake of gratifying curiosity," we replied.

"I should want my side to whip," said the girl.

"Yes. We all expect our side to be victorious, though we are sometimes disappointed, as was the case at Bull Run."

"Then you were at Bull Run? I take it that you belong to the army?"

"I was there and saw the fight, although I was not connected with the army."

"I am glad you were defeated. It was a good lesson to you. The Northerners have had some respect for the Southerners since then. The Southerners fought against great odds."

"Indeed, I think it was the reverse."

"No indeed, sir. The Federals numbered over sixty thousand, while Beauregard had less than thirty thousand. He did not have more than twelve thousand in the fight."

"I can assure you it is a grave mistake. General McDowell had less than thirty thousand men, and not more than half were engaged."

"Well, I wonder what he was thinking of when he carried out those forty thousand handcuffs?"

"I did not suppose any one gave credence to that absurd story."

"Absurd? Indeed, sir, it is not. I have seen some of the handcuffs. There are several pairs of them in this city. They were brought directly from the field by some of our citizens who went on as soon as they heard of the fight. I have several trophies of the fight which our men picked up."

No doubt the young lady was sincere. It was universally believed

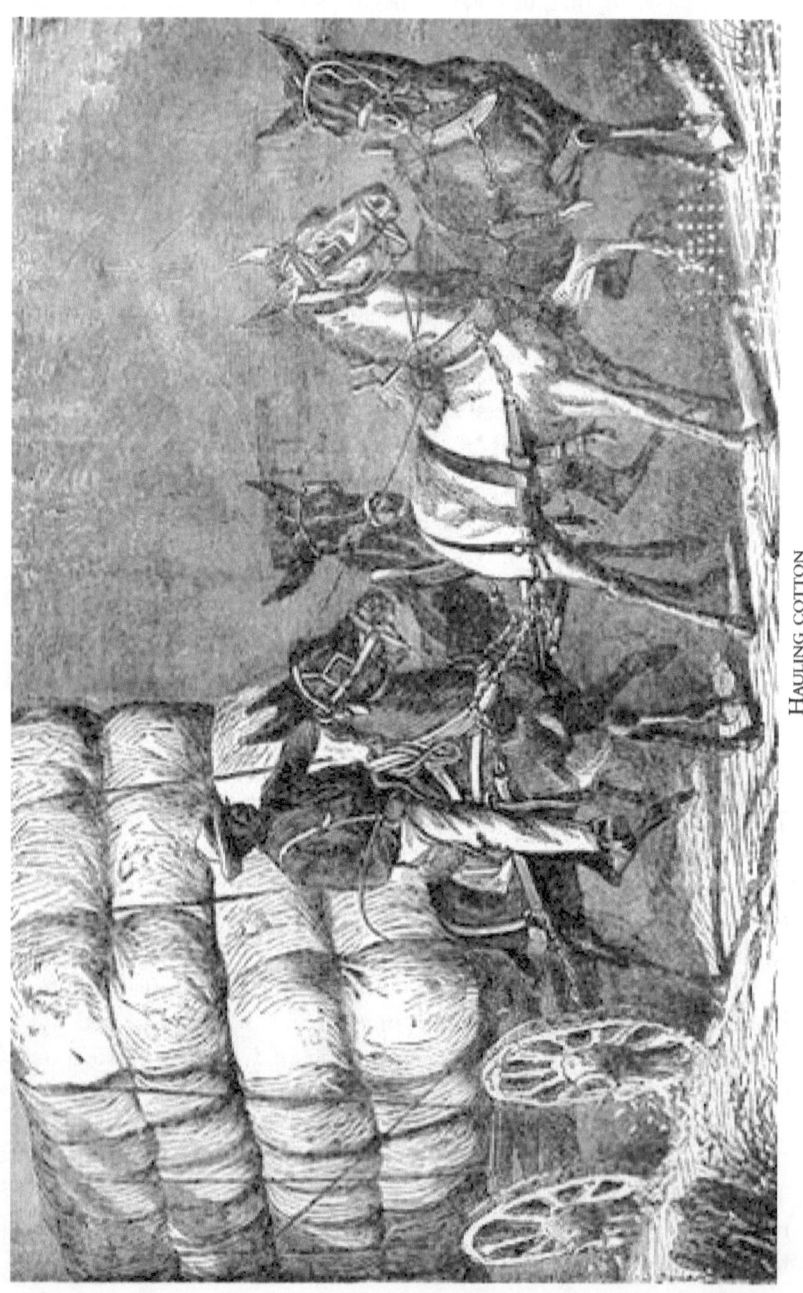

Hauling cotton

throughout the South that McDowell had thousands of pairs of handcuffs in his train, which were to be clapped upon the wrists of the Southern soldiers.

"We have some terrible uncompromising Union men in this State," said the eldest, "who would rather see every negro swept into the Gulf of Mexico, and the whole country sunk, than give up the Union. We have more Abolitionists here in this city than they have in Boston."

It was spoken bitterly. She did not mean that the Union men of the State were committed to immediate emancipation, but that they would accept emancipation rather than have the Secessionists succeed.

A gentleman came in, sat down by the fire, warmed his hands, and joined in the conversation. Said he: "I am a Southerner. I have lived all my life among slaves. I own one slave, but I hate the system. There are counties in this State where there are but few slaves, and in all such counties you will find a great many Abolitionists. It is the brutalizing influence of slavery that makes me hate it,—brutalizing to whites and blacks alike. I hate this keeping niggers to raise human stock,—to sell, just as you do horses and sheep."

In all places the theme of conversation was the war and the negroes. The ultra pro-slavery element was thoroughly secession, and the Unionists were beginning to understand that slavery was at the bottom of the rebellion. As in the dim light of the morning we already behold the approach of the full day, so they saw that these which seemed the events of an hour might broaden into that which would overthrow the entire slave system.

Anthony Trollope, an English traveller and novelist, was stopping at the hotel at the time,—a pleasant gentleman, thoroughly English in his personal appearance, with a plump face, indicative of good living and good cheer. In his work entitled *North America* he mentions the teamsters in the hall, and draws a contrast between English and American society. He says:

> While I was at supper the seventy-five teamsters were summoned into the common eating-room by a loud gong, and sat down to their meal at the public table. They were very dirty; I doubt whether I ever saw dirtier men; but they were orderly and well-behaved, and but for their extreme dirt might have passed as the ordinary occupants of a well-filled hotel in the West. Such men in the States are less clumsy with their knives and forks, less astray in an unused position, more intelligent in adapting themselves to a new life, than are Englishmen of the

same rank. It is always the same story. With us there is no level of society. Men stand on a long staircase, but the crowd congregates near the bottom, and the lower steps are very broad. In America, men stand on a common platform, but the platform is raised above the ground, though it does not approach in height the top of our staircase. If we take the average altitude in the two countries, we shall find that the American heads are the more elevated of the two. I conceived rather an affection for those dirty teamsters; they answered me civilly when I spoke to them, and sat in quietness smoking their pipes, with a dull and dirty but orderly demeanour.[4]

If Mr. Trollope, who has a very just appreciation of the character of those quiet and orderly teamsters, will but wait a century or two, perhaps he will find that democracy can build a staircase as high and complete as that reared by the aristocracy of England. We have had but two centuries for the construction of our elevated common platform, while England has had a thousand years. There the base of the staircase, where the multitude stand, is either stationary or sinking; but here the platform is always rising, and bearing the multitude to a higher plane.

A short distance north of the city of the living is the city of the dead. It is a pleasant suburb,—one which is adding week by week to its population. It is laid out in beautiful avenues, grass bordered, and shaded by grand old forest-trees. It is the resting-place of the dust of Henry Clay. The monument to his memory is not yet finished. It is a tall, round column upon a broad base, with a capital, such as the Greeks never saw or dreamed of, surmounted by a figure intended to represent the great statesman as he stood when enchaining vast audiences by his matchless oratory. Within the chamber, exposed to view through the iron-latticed door, star-embellished and bronzed, lies the sarcophagus of purest marble. It is chaste in design, ornamented with gathered rods and bonds emblematic of union, and wreathed with cypress around its sides. The pure white marble drapery is thrown partly back, exposing above the breast of the sleeper a wreath, and

Henry Clay

Upon the slab beneath the sarcophagus is this simple inscription:

I can, with unbroken confidence, appeal to the Divine Arbiter for the truth of the declaration, that I have been influenced

---

4: *North America*, by Anthony Trollope, Vol. II.

by no impure purpose, no personal motive,—have sought no personal aggrandizement, but that in all my public acts I have had a sole and single eye, and a warm devoted heart, directed and dedicated to what in my best judgment I believed to be the true interests of my country.

It is not a declaration which goes home to the heart as that simple recognition of the Christian religion which his compeer, Daniel Webster, directed should be placed above his grave in the secluded churchyard at Marshfield, but Mr. Clay was a remarkable man. Of all Americans who have lived, he could hold completest sway of popular assemblies. Hating slavery in his early life, he at last became tolerant of its existence. He cast the whole trouble of the nation upon the Abolitionists. In some things he was far-sighted; in others, obtuse. In 1843 he addressed a letter to a friend who was about to write a pamphlet against the Abolitionists, giving him an outline of the argument to be used. Thus he wrote:

> The great aim and object of your tract should be to arouse the labouring classes in the Free States against abolition. Depict the consequences to them of immediate abolition. The slaves being free, would be dispersed throughout the Union; they would enter into competition with the free labourer, with the American, the Irish, the German; reduce his wages; be confounded with him, and affect his moral and social standing. And as the ultras go for both abolition and amalgamation, show that their object is to unite in marriage the labouring white man and the labouring black man, and to reduce the white labouring man to the despised and degraded condition of the black man.
>
> I would show their opposition to colonization. Show its humane, religious, and patriotic aims, that they are to separate those whom God has separated. Why do the Abolitionists oppose colonization? To keep and amalgamate together the two races in violation of God's will, and to keep the blacks here, that they may interfere with, degrade, and debase the labouring whites. Show that the British nation is co-operating with the Abolitionists, for the purpose of dissolving the Union.[5]

This was written by a reputed statesman, who was supposed to understand the principles of political economy. The slaves being made free would enter in competition with the *free labourer*. But has not the

---

5: *North American Review*, January, 1866, p. 189.

free American labourer been forced to compete through all the years of the past with unrequited slave labour? Without inquiring into the aims and purposes of the Abolitionists,—what they intended to do, and how they were to do it,—Mr. Clay accepted the current talk of the day, and shaped his course accordingly. That letter will read strangely fifty years hence. It reads strangely now, and goes far to lower our estimate of the real greatness of one who for half a century was the idol of a great political party,—whose words were taken as the utterances of an oracle. But ideas and principles have advanced since 1843. We stand upon a higher plane, and are moving on to one still higher.

Returning to the hotel, I fell into conversation with a Presbyterian minister, who began to deplore the war.

"We should conduct it," said he, "not as savages or barbarians, but as Christians, as civilized beings, on human principles."

"In what way would you have our generals act to carry out what you conceive to be such principles?"

"Well, sir, the blockade is terribly severe on our friends in the South, who are our brothers. The innocent are suffering with the guilty. We should let them have food, and raiment, and medicines, but we should not let them have cannon, guns, and powder."

"When do you think the war would end if such a plan was adopted?"

He took a new tack, not replying to the question, but said,—

"The North began the trouble in an unchristian spirit."

"Was not the first gun fired by the Rebels upon Fort Sumter?"

"That was not the beginning of the war. It was the election of Lincoln."

"Then you would not have a majority of the people elect their officers in the constituted way?"

"Well, if Lincoln had been a wise man he would have resigned, and saved this terrible conflict."

There is a point beyond which forbearance ceases to be a virtue, and I expressed the hope that the war would be waged with shot and shell, fire and sword, naval expeditions and blockades, and every possible means, upon the men who had conspired to subvert the government. There was no reply, and he soon left the room.

Buell's right wing under General Crittenden, was at Calhoun, on Green River. Intelligence arrived that it was to be put in motion.

Leaving Lexington in the morning, and passing by cars through Frankfort,—an old town, the capital of the State, like Lexington, seedy and dilapidated,—we reached Louisville in season to take our choice of the two steamers, *Gray Eagle* and *Eugene*, to Henderson. They were both excellent boats, running in opposition, carrying passengers one hundred and eighty miles, providing for them two excellent meals and a night's lodging, all for fifty cents! People were patronizing both boats, because it was much cheaper than staying at home.

Taking the *Gray Eagle*,—a large side-wheel steamer,—we swept along with the speed of a railroad train. The water was very high and rising. The passengers were almost all from Kentucky. Some of the ladies thronging the saloon were accustomed to move in the "best society," which had not literary culture and moral worth for its standards, but broad acres, wealth in lands and distilleries. They were "raised" in Lexington or Louisville or Frankfort. They spoke of the "right smart" crowd on board, nearly "*tew*" hundred, according to their *i*dea.

But there is another class of Kentuckians as distinct from these excellent ladies as chalk from cheese. They are of that class to which David Crocket belonged in his early years,—born in a cane-brake and cradled in a trough. There were two in the saloon, seated upon an ottoman,—a brother and sister. The brother was more than six feet tall, had a sharp, thin, lank countenance, with a tuft of hair on his chin and on his upper lip. His face was of the colour of milk and molasses. He wore a Kentucky homespun suit,—coat, vest and pants of the same material, and coloured with butternut bark. He had on, although in the saloon, a broad-brimmed, slouched hat, with an ornament of blotched mud. He was evidently more at home with his hat on than to sit bareheaded,—and so consulted his own pleasure, without mistrusting that there was such a thing as politeness in the world. He had been plashing through the streets of Louisville. He had scraped off the thickest of the mud. There he sat, the right foot thrown across the left knee, with as much complacency as it is possible for a mortal to manifest. In his own estimation he was all right, although there was a gap between his pants and vest of about six inches,—a yellowish tawny streak of shirt. He sat in unconcerned silence, or stalked through the saloon with his hands in his pockets, or stretched himself at full length upon the sofa and took a comfortable snooze.

His sister,—a girl of eighteen,—had an oval face, arched eyebrows, and full cheeks, flowing, flaxen hair, and gray eyes. She wore a plain dress of gray homespun without hoops, and when standing, appeared as if she had encased herself in a meal-bag. There was no neat white collar or bit of ribbon, or cord, or tassel,—no attempt at feminine adornment. She was a "nut-brown maid,"—bronzed by exposure, with a countenance as inexpressive as a piece of putty. A dozen ladies and gentlemen who came on board at a little town twenty miles below Louisville were enjoying themselves, in a circle of their own, with the play of "Consequences." The cabin rang with their merry laughter, and we who looked on enjoyed their happiness; but there was no sign of animation in her countenance,—a block of wood could not have been more unsympathetic.

Among the ladies on board was one a resident of Owensboro', who, upon her marriage eight years before, had moved from the town of Auburn, New York, the home of Mr. Seward.

"I was an Abolitionist," she said, "before I left home, but now that I know what slavery is, I like it. The slaveholders are so independent and live so easy! They can get rich in a few years; and there is no class in the world who can enjoy so much of life as they."

It was evidently a sincere expression of her sentiments.

She was for the Union, but wanted slavery let alone. The strife in Owensboro' had been exceedingly bitter. Nearly all her old friends and neighbours were rampant Secessionists. Secession, like a sharp sword, had cut through society and left it in two parts, as irreconcilable as vice and virtue. There was uncompromising hostility ready to flame out into war at any moment in all the Kentucky towns. There was also on board a loud-talking man who walked the saloon with his hands in his pockets, looking everybody square in the face; he was intensely loyal to the Union.

"Why don't Buell move? Why don't Halleck move? It is my opinion that they are both of 'em old grannies. I want to see the Rebels licked. I have lived in Tophet for the last six months. I live in Henderson, and it has been a perfect hell ever since the Rebels fired on Fort Sumter. I have lost my property through the d—d scoundrels. I want a regiment of Union troops to go down there and clean out the devils."

It was early morning when the scream of the *Gray Eagle* roused the usual crowd of loafers from their sleep and inanition at Owensboro'. A motley mob came down to the wharf eager to hear the news. I had been informed that the place was one where whiskey distilleries abound, and the information proved to be correct. The distillery buildings were distinctly recognized by their smoking chimneys, creaking pumps, and steaming vats. The crowd on the shore had whiskey in their looks and behaviour. Among them was one enthusiastic admirer of Abraham Lincoln. He was bloated, blear-eyed, a tatterdemalion, with just enough whiskey in him to make him thick-spoken, reckless, and irresponsible in the eyes of his liquor-loving companions. While we were at a distance he swung his hat and gave a cheer for Old Abe; as we came nearer he repeated it; and as the plank was being thrown ashore he fairly danced with ecstasy, shouting, "Hurrah for Old Abe! He'll fix 'em. Hurrah for Old Abe! Hurrah for Old Abe!"

"Shet up, you drunken cuss. Hurrah for Jeff Davis!" was the response of another blear-eyed, tipsy loafer.

The steamer *Storm* was tolling its bell as the *Gray Eagle* came to the landing at Evansville, bound for Green River. Her decks were piled with bags of corn and coffee. A barge was tethered to her side, loaded with bundle hay and a half-dozen ambulances. We were just in time to reach the deck before the plank was drawn in. Then with hoarse puffs the heavily laden old craft swung into the stream and surged slowly against the swollen tide of the Ohio. Green River joins the Ohio ten miles above Evansville. It is a beautiful stream, with forest-bordered banks. At that season of the year there was nothing particularly inspiring to the muse along this stream, unless one can kindle a poetic flame in swamps, lagoons, creeks, and log-cabins standing on stilts, with water beneath, around, and often within them. On the spit of land between the Ohio and Green rivers, on posts several feet under water, was a log-cabin; a row-boat was tied to the steps, a woman and a half-dozen children stared at us from the open door. All around was forest. A gentleman on board said it was a fishing family. If so, the family, little ones and all, might ply the piscatory art from doors and windows. A more dreary, watery place cannot be imagined.

The *Storm* was not a floating palace with gilded saloons, velvet tapestry carpets, French mirrors, and a grand piano, but an old wheezy tow-boat, with great capacity below and little above. There was a room for the gentlemen, and a little box of a place for any ladies who might be under the necessity of patronizing the craft.

There were no soldiers on board, but thirty or forty passengers. We were a hard-looking set. Our clothes were muddy, our beards shaggy, our countenances far from being Caucasian in colour, with sundry other peculiarities of dress, feature, and demeanour.

There was one stout man with an enormous quantity of brown hair, and a thick yellow beard, belonging to Hopkinsville, near the Tennessee line, who had been compelled to flee for his life.

"We got up a cannon company, and I was captain. We had as neat a little six-pounder as you ever saw; but I was obliged to cut and run when the Rebels came in December; but I buried the pup and the Secessionists don't know where she is! If I ever get back there I'll make some of them cusses—my old neighbours—bite the dust. I have just heard that they have tied my brother up and almost whipped him to death. They gouged out his eyes, stamped in his face, and have taken all his property."

Here he was obliged to stop his narrative and give vent to a long string of oaths, consigning the Rebels to all the tortures and pains of the bottomless pit forever. Having disgorged his wrath, he said,—

"Now, sir, there is a grave judicial question on my mind, and I would like your opinion upon it. If you owned a darkey who should get over into Indiana, a bright, intelligent darkey, and he should take with him ten niggers from your secession neighbours, and you should happen to know it, would you send them back?"

"No, sir; I should not."

"That is my mind 'zactly. I knew you was a good Union man the moment I sot my eyes on ye." Then came an interesting explanation. He had one slave, a devoted fellow, who had become an active conductor on the underground railroad. The slave had been often to Evansville and knew the country, and had enticed away ten negroes belonging to the Secessionists in the vicinity of Hopkinsville. He had seen them all that morning, and more, had given each of them a hearty breakfast! "You see," said he, "if they belonged to Union men I would have sent 'em back; but they belonged to the—Secessionists who have driven me out, taken all my property, and do you think I'd be mean enough to send the niggers back?"

On board the *Storm* were several other men who had been driven from their homes by the Secessionists. There was one gentleman, a slaveholder from the little town of Volney, between Hopkinsville and the Cumberland River. All of his property had been taken, his negroes, if they were not sold or seized, were roaming at will. He had two brothers in the Rebel army. He was a plain, sensible, well-informed farmer. He lived close upon the Tennessee line, and was acquainted with the Southern country.

"Slavery is a doomed institution," said he; "from Kentucky, from Missouri, from Maryland and Virginia the slaves have been pouring southward. There has been a great condensation of slaves at the South where they are not wanted, and where they cannot be supported if the blockade continues. The South never has raised its own provisions. She could do it if she put forth her energies; but she never has and she will not now. The time will come, if the blockade continues, when the master will be compelled to say to the slaves, 'Get your living where you can,' and then the system, being rolled back upon itself, will be broken up. As for myself, I would like to have kept my slaves, because

I am getting along in years and I wanted them to take care of me; but as the Secessionists have taken them and driven me out, it won't make any difference to me whether the system is continued or not."

It is utterly impossible to convey to a New-Englander who has never crossed the Hudson a correct idea of a Kentucky country village, like that of Calhoun, as seen from the deck of the steamer *Storm*, in the light of a beautiful morning, so mild and spring-like that the robins, bluebirds, jays, pewits, and sparrows were filling the air with their songs, having returned from their sojourn in a Southern clime. A sentinel was plashing through the mud along the bank, guarding the ferry to the town of Rumsey, on the opposite side of the river. The bank rises abruptly into the main street of the town. First we have the McLean House, the first-class hotel of the place,—a wooden building two stories high, containing six or eight rooms. There is beyond it one brick building, then a number of smaller buildings containing a couple of rooms each, and forty rods distant a church, respectable in style and proportions. The land is undulating, and on the hillsides there are dwellings, a half-dozen of which you might call comfortable. The original forest oaks are still standing. A creek or bayou runs through the town, the receptacle of all the filth generated by ten thousand men, and thousands of mules, horses, and hogs.

Rumsey, on the opposite side of the river, is of smaller dimensions. Years ago it was a "right smart" town, but business has disappeared. The people have also gone, and now one sees a row of windowless, doorless, deserted houses, soaked in every flood of waters. Visiting the "first class" hotel of the place, we sat down in the parlour or reception-room, or whatever room it was, while the cook prepared breakfast. It was also the landlord's bed-room, occupied by himself and wife.

Calling upon the landlord for a place for toilet operations, we were invited into the kitchen which was also the dining-room and pantry and Jim's bed-room,—Jim being a tall negro, who just now is washing dishes, with a tin pan of hot water, and without any soap. Dinah is rolling biscuit, and tending the hoe-cake, which is cooking nicely on the stove. There is the flour-barrel close at hand. There is one dinner-pot, with two kettles, a pail of water, a lantern, the pepper-box, a dish of fat, a plate of butter, and a great heap of tin dishes on the table, where Dinah is moulding the biscuit, while Jim occupies the other end. The dining-table stands in the centre of the room. The plates are laid, and the whole is covered with a blue cloth, which at first sight seems to be a soldier's blanket, and which upon close inspection leaves us still in doubt whether it is a table-cloth or a bed-coverlet. There are some

BALTIMORE IN 1861

chairs, and an old desk which has lost its lid, in which are nails, a hammer, some old papers, and a deal of dust. It evidently "came down from a former generation."

We have time to notice these things while the landlord is preparing for our washing exploit, which is to be performed near Jim, with a basin on a chair.

Then we have breakfast,—beefsteak and porksteak, and buckwheat cakes, all fried in lard, sausages, potatoes, Dinah's hoe-cakes, hot flour biscuit, and a dish of hash, which will not go down at all, and coffee without milk, preferred to the water of Green River, which in its natural state is somewhat the colour of yellow snuff, and which is drank by the inhabitants of Calhoun, notwithstanding thousands of horses are stabled on its banks.

There was no movement of the troops, therefore nothing to detain us at Calhoun, and knowing that there was something of interest up the Cumberland and Tennessee rivers, we went on board the *Mattie Cook*, the downward-bound steamer. While waiting for her departure we gazed at the sights upon the shore. There was a great deal of life,—wagons, soldiers, citizens floundering through the mud to the landing, transporting goods. There were ludicrous scenes of men and teams stuck in the mortar-bed; but in the midst of life there was death. A squad of soldiers came down from camp to the hospital with a bier, and with the slow funeral dirge brought two of their comrades to the boat,—two who had just passed from the scenes of strife on earth to the eternal peace beyond. Those who bore them were by no means unaffected by the part they were called upon to perform. There were sad countenances, too, on board the boat,—two ladies, both strangers to the dead, but not indifferent to the scene. They had woman's tender sensibilities, and could not keep back the tears from their eyes, for they thought of their own sons whom they had just left, and who now stood upon the bank to say perhaps a last goodbye.

But how transitory are all the most solemn impressions of death! Ten minutes later a company of soldiers appeared for a trip down the river to Stevensport to bag, if possible, the squad of Rebels which had been prowling about the town of Stevensport. They came on board with a hurrah, and made the welkin ring with the "Red, White, and Blue." It was a pleasure to them to leave the hateful place even for a night, and be in active service.

Chapter 6

The Opening of the Campaign in Tennessee

February, 1862

At last the Rebel lines were broken. Commodore Foote had opened a gateway to the heart of the Confederacy by the capture of Fort Henry on the 6th of February. While up Green River I learned of the intended movement, and hastened to be present, but was delayed between Evansville and Paducah, and was not in season to see the engagement.

Late on the Friday evening after I saw Commodore Foote in Cairo. He had just returned from Fort Henry.

"Can you favour me with an account of the affair?" I asked.

"It will give me great pleasure to do so after I have prepared my despatches for Washington," he replied.

It was past midnight when he came to my room. He sat down, and leaned back wearily in his chair. But soon recovering his usual energy, gave the full details of the action. He had prepared his instructions to his crews several days before the battle, and upon mature thought, saw nothing to change.

To the commanders and crews he said, that it was very necessary to success that they should keep cool. He desired them to fire with deliberate aim, and not to attempt rapid firing, for four reasons, viz. that with rapid firing there was always a waste of ammunition; that their range would be wild; that the enemy would be encouraged unless the fire was effectual; that it was desirable not to heat the guns.

With these instructions he led his fleet up the narrow channel under cover of Pine Island, thus avoiding long-range shot from the rifled guns which it was known the enemy had in position to sweep the main channel. He steamed slow, to allow the troops time to gain their position.

He visited each vessel and gave personal directions. He took his own position in the pilot-house of the *Cincinnati*. The *St. Louis* was on his right hand and the *Carondelet* and *Essex* were on his left, with the *Tyler, Conestoga*, and *Lexington* in rear. There is an island a mile and a quarter below the fort. When the head of the island was reached the boats came into line and were within easy range.

"Do just as I do," was his last order to the commanders.

The Cincinnati opened, and the other vessels were quick to follow the Commodore's example.

"I had a definite purpose in view," said he, "to take the fort at all hazards. It was necessary for the success of the cause. We have had disaster upon disaster, and I intended, God helping me, to win a victory. It made me feel bad when I saw the *Essex* drop out of the line, but I knew that the fort couldn't stand it much longer. I should have opened my broadsides in a minute or two, if Tilghman had not surrendered, and that I knew would settle the question. We were not more than four hundred yards distant."

He said that when the *Essex* dropped behind the Rebels set up a tremendous cheer, and redoubled their fire; but being excited their aim was bad.

"There is nothing like keeping perfectly cool in battle," said he.

"When Tilghman came into my cabin," said the Commodore, "he asked for terms, but I informed him that his surrender must be final."

"Well, sir, if I must surrender, it gives me pleasure to surrender to so brave an officer as you," said Tilghman.

"You do perfectly right to surrender, sir; but I should not have surrendered on any condition."

"Why so? I do not understand you."

"Because I was fully determined to capture the fort or go to the bottom."

The Rebel general opened his eyes at this remark, but replied, "I thought I had you, Commodore, but you were too much for me."

"But how could you fight against the old flag?"

"Well, it did come hard at first; but if the North had only let us alone there would have been no trouble. But they would not abide by the Constitution."

"You are mistaken, sir. The North has maintained all of her Constitutional obligations. You of the South have perjured yourselves. I talked to him faithfully," said the zealous officer.

The Commodore was now nervously restless, but said: "I never slept better in my life than I did the night before going into the battle, and I never prayed more fervently than I did yesterday morning, that God would bless the undertaking, and he has signally answered my prayer. I don't deserve it, but I trust that I shall be grateful for it. But I couldn't sleep last night for thinking of those poor fellows on board the *Essex*, who were wounded and scalded. I told the surgeons to do everything possible for them. Poor fellows! I must go and see that they are well cared for."

It was one o'clock in the morning, yet exhausted as he was, he went to see that the sufferers were having every possible attention.

This was on Saturday morning; the next day he went to church as usual. The minister was not there, and after waiting awhile the audience one by one began to drop off, whereupon Commodore Foote entered the pulpit, and conducted the exercises, reading the fourteenth chapter of John's Gospel, and addressed the congregation, urging sinners to repentance, picturing the unspeakable love of Christ, and the rewards which await the righteous, and closing the services by a fervent prayer. It was as unostentatious as all his other acts, undertaken with a dutiful desire to benefit those about him, and to glorify God. That was his aim in life.

The Rebel troops which were in and around Fort Henry fled in dismay soon after the opening of the bombardment, leaving all their camp equipage. In the barracks the camp-fires were still blazing, and dinners cooking, when our troops entered. Books, letters half written, trunks, carpet-bags, knives, pistols, were left behind, and were eagerly seized by the soldiers, who rent the air with shouts of laughter, mingled with the cheers of victory.

Although not present, a letter fell into my hands written by a father in Mississippi to his sons, which gives an insight into the condition of affairs in the Confederacy at that time:

Bear Creek, Miss.
December 16, 1861
To my dear boys Sammie and Thomas:
After a long silence I will tell you some little news. I told C. D. Moore to tell you that paper was very scarce in this wooden world. I went to Vaidere to get this, and was glad to get it at 50 cents per quire.

The health of our country is pretty good. Crops are very short; corn and cotton—especially cotton—not quite half a crop, though it doesn't matter, as we can't get any money for it. For my part I know not what we are to do. I haven't a red cent.

My intention now is to plant only about eight acres in cotton; that will make enough to buy or barter my groceries. I fear, my children, we will not live to see as prosperous a time after this revolution as there was before it. I often think of the language of our Saviour: *Eloi, Eloi, lama sabacthani,*—My God, my God, why hast thou forsaken me? I verily believe all this calamity has come upon us for our wickedness. Religion is down like cotton,—not worth much; and by the actions of good brethren it might be bought for a mere trifle, though if we were to judge from its sparseness, like salt, it would be worth $40 per sack.

O my God, what will become of us? Go, if you please, to the churchyard, and you will hear nothing but secular affairs and *war, war*! Dull times everywhere. Money scarce; pork high,—10 to 12½ cents per pound; salt the same; coffee $1.50 per pound, and none to be had at that; calico 30 to 50 cents per yard; domestics 20 to 25 cents per yard; sugar 6 to 12½ cents; molasses 30 to 40 cents, and everything in the same ratio.

The capture of Fort Donelson and the troops defending it, was the first *great* achievement of the Union armies. The affair at Mill Spring, and the taking of Roanoke Island by Burnside, were important, but minor engagements when compared with the breaking in of the Rebel line of defence on the Cumberland and Tennessee. The fighting on Saturday, the last day of the series of battles, was desperate and bloody. The ground on the right in the morning, when the Rebels moved out and overwhelmed McClernand, was hotly contested. Grant's lines were so extended and necessarily thin that the Rebels were enabled to push McClernand back nearly two miles. This was done by Pillow and Bushrod Johnson, who gained McClernand's flank. Buckner, however, who was to strike McClernand's left, was slow in advancing. Had he moved as rapidly as the other divisions, McClernand would have been utterly routed. It was then that W. H. L. Wallace, of Illinois, showed his great military ability. He had been in the Mexican war, was courageous, and had that power of *presence* which made every man feel that he was under the eye of his commander. Then, too, General Logan animated his men, and held them in close contact with the Rebels till wounded.

The charge of General C. P. Smith's division on the left, in the afternoon of Saturday, was sublime. General Smith was an old soldier, who had served in Mexico. His hair was long and white, and as he rode along his lines, making arrangements for the advance, he was the most conspicuous of all men on the field. He paid no heed to the rifle and musket balls which were singing about his ears; he sat firmly on his horse. When his lines were ready, he led them, with his cap on the point of his sword.

It was sunset or nearly that hour, when his division moved to the attack of the outer works, at the southwest angle of the fort. There was a steady advance through an open field,—a rush up the hill,—a cheer,—the rout of Hanson's brigade of Rebels, the Second Kentucky, Twentieth Mississippi, and Thirtieth Tennessee,—a long, loud shout of triumph, mingled with the roar of cannon, and the rolls of musketry from the fort, pouring upon them a concentrated fire!

The scene at Donelson on Sunday morning, the day of surrender, was exceedingly exhilarating,—the marching in of the victorious divisions,—the bands playing, their flags waving, the cheers of the troops,—the gunboats firing a salute,—the immense flotilla of river steamboats gaily decorated! The *New Uncle Sam* was the boat on which General Grant had established his head-quarters. The *Uncle Sam*, at a signal from Commodore Foote, ranged ahead, came alongside one of the gunboats, and, followed by all the fleet, steamed up river past Fort Donelson, thick with Confederate soldiers,—past the entrenched camp of log-huts, past a school-house on a hill, above which waved the hospital flag,—and on to Dover, the gunboats thundering a national salute the while.

A warp was thrown ashore, the plank run out. I sprang up the bank, and mingled among the disconsolate creatures,—a care-worn, haggard, melancholy crowd which stood upon the heights above. They all told one story, claiming that they had fought well; that we outnumbered them; that there was a disagreement among their officers; that we had got General Buckner; that Floyd and Pillow had escaped; that Floyd had taken four regiments of his brigade; that there were four steamers; that they went off crowded with soldiers, the guards sunk to the water's edge.

The town of Dover is the county seat of Stewart, and a point where the farmers ship their produce. It is a straggling village on uneven ground, and contains perhaps five hundred inhabitants. There are a few buildings formerly used for stores, a doctor's office, a dilapidated church, a two-story square brick court-house, and a half-dozen decent dwellings. But the place had suffered greatly while occupied by the Secession forces. Nearly every building was a hospital. Trees had been cut down, fences burned, windows broken, and old buildings demolished for fuel.

We came upon a squad of soldiers hovering around a fire. Some were wrapped in old patched bedquilts which had covered them at home. Some had white blankets, made mostly of cotton. Others wore bright bocking, which had evidently been furnished from a merchant's stock. One had a faded piece of threadbare carpet. Their guns were stacked, their equipments thrown aside, cartridge-boxes, belts, and ammunition trampled in the mud. There were shot-guns, single and double-barrelled, old heavy rifles, flint-lock muskets of 1828, some of them altered into percussion locks, with here and there an Enfield rifle.

A few steps brought me to the main landing, where the Confederate stores were piled, and from which Floyd made his escape. The gunboats were lying off the landing, and a portion of McClernand's division was on the hills beyond, the stars and stripes and the regimental banners waving, and the bands playing. Away up on the hill Taylor's battery was firing a national salute.

There were sacks of corn, tierces of rice, sides of bacon, barrels of flour, hogsheads of sugar, sufficient for several days' rations. Then there was a dense crowd of Secessionists, evidently the rabble, or the debris of the army, belonging to all regiments. Some were sullen, some indifferent, some evidently felt a sense of relief, mingled with their apprehensions for the future. Among them were squads of our own soldiers, with smiling faces, feeling very much at home, but manifesting no disposition to add to the unhappiness of the captured.

General McClernand's division had marched down to the outskirts of the village, and was keeping guard. A private ran into the courthouse and threw the flag of the Union to the breeze from the belfry. Soldiers of our army were inspecting the shops of the place. In the basement of a store was the Confederate arsenal. There were piles of rifles, old shot-guns, many of them ticketed with the owner's name. There were many hunter's rifles, which had done good service in other days among the mountains and forests of Tennessee, but, for use in battle, of but little account.

In another building was the Commissary department. There were hogsheads of sugar, barrels of rice, boxes of abominable soap, and a few barrels of flour. Later in the day we saw soldiers luxuriating like children in the hogsheads of sugar. Many a one filled his canteen with New Orleans molasses and his pockets with damp brown sugar. Looking into a store we found a squad of soldiers taking things of no earthly use. One had a looking-glass under his arm, one a paper of files, another several brass candlesticks, one a package of bonnets.

The Mississippians and Texans were boiling over with rage against Floyd and Pillow for having deserted them.

"Floyd always was a d—d thief and sneak," said one.

Just before sunset we took a ramble through the grounds and encampments of the Rebels, who were falling into line preparatory to embarking upon the steamers. Standing on a hill beyond the village, we had at one view almost all their force. Hogarth never saw such a sight; Shakespeare, in his conceptions of Falstaff's tatterdemalions, could not have imagined the like,—not that they were deficient in intellect, or wanting in courage, for among them were noble men, brave fellows, who shed tears when they found they were prisoners of war, and who swore with round oaths that they would shoot Floyd as they would a dog, if they could get a chance, but that for grotesque appearance they were never equalled, except by the London bagmen and chiffoniers of Paris.

There were all sorts of uniforms, brown-coloured predominating, as if they were in the snuff business and had been rolled in tobacco-dust. There was sheep gray, iron gray, blue gray, dirty gray, with bed blankets, quilts, buffalo-robes, pieces of carpeting of all colours and figures, for blankets. Each had his pack on his shoulder. Judging by their garments, one would have thought that the last scrapings, the odds and ends of humanity and of dry goods, had been brought together.

The formal surrender of the fort took place in the cabin of the *New Uncle Sam* in the evening. Buckner sat on one side of the table and General Grant on the other. Buckner was attended by two of his staff. The Rebel commander was in the prime of life, although his hair had turned iron gray. He was of medium stature, having a low forehead and thin cheeks, wore a moustache and meagre whiskers. He had on a light-blue kersey overcoat and a checked neckcloth. He was smoking a cigar, and talking in a low, quiet tone. He evidently felt that he was in a humiliating position, but his deportment was such as to command respect when contrasted with the course of Floyd and Pillow. His chief of staff sat by his side.

Buckner freely gave information relative to his positions, his forces, their disposition, and his intentions. He expected to escape, and claimed that the engagements on Saturday were all in favour of the Confederates. No opprobrious words were used by any one. No discussions entered into. He asked for subsistence for his men, and said that he had only two days' provisions on hand. He had favours to ask for some of his wounded officers, all of which were readily acceded to by General Grant, who was very much at ease, smoking a cigar, and conducting the business with dignity, yet with despatch.

The prisoners were taken on board of the transports, the men on the lower deck, and the officers having the freedom of the boat. The saloons and cabins, berths and state-rooms were filled with the wounded of both armies.

"The conditions of the surrender have been most shamefully violated," said a tall, dark-haired, black-eyed Mississippi colonel, on board the *Belle* of Memphis.

"How so?" I asked.

"It was agreed that we should be treated like gentlemen, but the steward of the boat won't let us have seats at the table. He charges us a half-dollar a meal, and refuses Confederate money."

"Well, sir, you fare no worse than the rest of us. I paid for a stateroom, but the surgeon turned me out and put in a wounded man, which was all right and proper, and at which I have no complaint to make, and I shall think myself well off if I can get hard-tack."

While conversing with him, a Mississippi captain came up,—a tall, red-whiskered, tobacco-chewing, ungainly fellow, with a swaggering air. "This is d—d pretty business. They talk of reconstructing the Union, and begin by rejecting our money. I don't get anything to eat," he said.

I directed his attention to a barrel of bacon and several boxes of bread which had been opened for the prisoners, and from which they were helping themselves. He turned away in disgust, saying,—

"Officers are to be treated according to their rank,—like gentlemen,—and I'll be d—d if I don't pitch in and give somebody a licking!"

Some of the officers on board conducted themselves with perfect decorum. One young physician gave his services to our wounded.

Although Commodore Foote had been wounded in the gunboat attack upon the fort, he intended to push up the river to Nashville, and intercept General Albert Sidney Johnston, who he knew must be falling back from Bowling Green, but he was stopped by a despatch from General Halleck to General Grant. "Don't let Foote go up the river."

The gunboats could have reached Nashville in eight hours. Floyd and Pillow, who made their escape from Donelson at sunrise, reached the city before noon, while the congregations were in the churches. Had Commodore Foote followed he would have been in the city by three o'clock, holding the bridges, patrolling the rivers, and cutting off Johnston's retreat. Buell had between thirty and forty thousand men,

Johnston less than twenty. On the heel of the demoralization incident to the rout at Mill Springs, Fort Henry, and the loss at Donelson, the entire Rebel army in the West could have been destroyed, but for the dictation of General Halleck, sitting in the planter's house five hundred miles distant.

"Had I been permitted to carry out my intention we should have put an end to the rebellion in the West," said Commodore Foote.

General Halleck had endeavoured to enforce his order No. 3, excluding negroes from his lines, but before daybreak on Sunday morning at Donelson a negro entered the lines, having made his way out from Dover, past the Rebel pickets. He reported that the Rebels were fleeing. Some of the officers suggested that he was sent out to lure Grant into a trap, and proposed to tie him up and give him a whipping.

"You may hang me, shoot me, do anything to me, if it a'n't as I tell you," was his earnest reply.

One hour later came the Rebel flag of truce from Buckner, asking for the appointment of Commissioners; but the information already obtained enabled Grant to reply: "I propose to move immediately upon your works."

The negro was a slave, who entered the Union lines in search of freedom,—that which his soul most longed for. General Grant did not exclude him. Like a sensible man, he took no action in the matter, gave no directions as to what should be done with him. The slave being at liberty to decide for himself, took passage on a transport for Cairo. The steamer stopped at a landing for wood, when the slave was recognized by some of the citizens, who said that he belonged to a Union man, and demanded that he should be put off the boat. The captain of the steamer was inclined to accede to their demands; but the officers on board, knowing what service he had rendered, informed the captain that he need not be under any apprehensions of arrest by civil process, as martial law was in force. They kept the negro under their protection, and gave him his liberty, thus setting at defiance General Halleck and his pro-slavery order.

March, 1862

A great many negroes came into the lines, and were welcomed by the soldiers. Among them was a boy, black as anthracite, with large, lustrous eyes, and teeth as white as purest ivory. He was thirteen years old, born in Kentucky, but for several years had lived near

Dover. His master, he said, was a gentleman, owned twenty-four slaves. He had on a greasy shirt of snuff-coloured jean, the genuine negro cloth, such as one half the Southern army was compelled to wear. His slouched hat was tipped back upon his head, showing a countenance indicative of intelligence.

"Well, my boy, what is your name?" I asked.

"Dick, massa."

"Where do you live?"

"About fourteen miles from Dover, massa, up near de rollin' mill."

"Is your master a Secessionist?"

"He was Secesh, massa, but he be Union now."

This was correct testimony, the master appearing with great boldness at General Grant's head-quarters to let it be known he was for the Union.

"Are you a slave, Dick?"

"I was a slave, but I's free now; I's 'fiscated."

"Where were you when the fight was going on at Fort Donelson?"

"At home; but when massa found de fort was took he started us all off for de Souf, but we got away and come down to Dover, and was 'fiscated."

The master was a Secessionist till his twenty-four chattels, which he was trying to run South, became perverse and veered to the North with much fleetness. Not only were these twenty-four started South, but ten times twenty-four, from the vicinity of Dover, and an hundred times twenty-four from Clarkesville, Nashville, and all along the Cumberland. When Donelson fell, the edifice of the Secessionists became very shaky in one corner.

Columbus was occupied on the 5th of March, the Rebels retiring to Island No. 10. Visiting the post-office, I secured several bushels of Southern newspapers, which revealed a state of general gloom and despondency throughout the Confederacy. Inspired by the events of 1861,—the battles of Bull Run, Belmont, and other engagements,— the Southern muse had struck its lyre.

The battle of Belmont had kindled a poetic flame in the breast of Jo. Augustine Signaigo, in the *Memphis Appeal*. The opening stanza is as follows:

Now glory to our Southern cause, and praises be to God,
That He hath met the Southron's foe, and scourged him with his rod;
On the tented plains of Belmont, there in their might the Vandals came,
And gave unto Destruction all they found, with sword and flame;

> But they met a stout resistance from a little band that day,
> Who swore that they would conquer, or return to mother clay.

After a description of the fight, we have the following warning in the tenth stanza:

> Let the horrors of this day to the foe a warning be,
> That the Lord is with the South, that His arm is with the free;
> That her soil is pure and spotless as her clear and sunny sky,
> And he who dare pollute it on her soil shall basely die;
> For His fiat hath gone forth, e'en among the Hessian horde,
> That the South has got His blessing, for the South is of the Lord.

The *New Orleans Picayune* had an *Ode on the Meeting of the Southern Congress*, by Henry Timrod, which opened in the following lofty lines:

> Hath not the morning dawned with added light!
> And will not evening call another star
> Out of the infinite regions of the night
> To mark this day in Heaven? At last, we are
> A nation among nations; and the world
> Shall soon behold, in many a distant port,
> Another flag unfurled!

This poet gave the following contrast between the North and South:

> Look where we will, we cannot find a ground
> For any mournful song!
> Call up the clashing elements around,
> And test the right and wrong!
> On one side,—pledges broken, creeds that lie,
> Religion sunk in vague philosophy;
> Empty professions; Pharisaic leaven;
> Souls that would sell their birth-right in the sky;
> Philanthropists who pass the beggar by,
> And laws which controvert the laws of Heaven!
> And, on the other, first, a righteous cause!
> Then, honour without flaws,
> Truth, Bible reverence, charitable wealth,
> And for the poor and humble, laws which give
> Not the mean right to buy the right to live,
> But life, home and health.
> To doubt the issue were distrust in God!
> If in his providence He had decreed
> That, to the peace for which we pray,

Through the Red Sea of War must lie our way,
Doubt not, O-brothers, we shall find at need
A Moses with his rod!"

The *Vicksburg Citizen* had thirty stanzas rehearsing the events of the year 1861. Two or three selections will be sufficient to show that the muse halted a little now and then:

Last year's holidays had scarcely passed,
Before momentous events came thick and fast;
Mississippi on the 9th of January went out,
Determined to stand strong, firm and stout.

* * * * * * * *

Major Anderson would not evacuate Sumter,
When Gen. Beauregard made him surrender,—
And sent him home to his abolition master,
Upon a trot, if not a little faster.

Then Old Abe Lincoln got awful mad,
Because his luck had turned out so bad;
And he grasped his old-fashioned steel pen,
And ordered out seventy-five thousand men.

May the Almighty smile on our Southern race,
May Liberty and Independence grow apace,
May our Liberties this year be achieved,
And our distress and sorrow graciously relieved.

The bombardment of Island No. 10 commenced on the 9th of March, and continued nearly a month. General Pope moving overland, captured New Madrid, planted his guns, and had the Rebel steamboats in a trap. The naval action of March 17th was grand beyond description. The mortars were in full play. The *Cincinnati*, *Benton*, and *St. Louis* were lashed together, and anchored with their bows downstream. The *Carondelet* and *Mound City* were placed in position to give a cross-fire with the other three, while the *Pittsburg* was held in reserve.

It was past one o'clock in the afternoon of as beautiful a day as ever dawned upon the earth, when a ball of bunting went up to the top of the *Benton's* flagstaff, and fluttered out into the battle signal. Then came a flash, a belching of smoke from her bows, a roar and reverberation rolling far away,—a screaming in the air, a tossing up of earth and an explosion in the Rebel works.

The highest artistic skill cannot portray the scene of that afternoon,—the flashes and flames,—the great white clouds, mounting above the boats, and floating majestically away over the dark gray forests,—the mortars throwing up vast columns of sulphurous cloud, which widen, expand, and roll forward in fantastic folds,—the shells one after another in swift succession rising, rotating, rushing upward and onward, sailing a thousand feet high, their course tracking a light gossamer trail, which becomes a beautiful parabola, and then the terrific explosion,—a flash, a handful of cloud, a strange whirring of the ragged fragments of iron hurled upwards, outwards, and downwards, crashing through the forests!

I was favoured with a position on the *Silver Wave* steamer, lying just above the *Benton*, her wheels slowly turning to keep her in position to run down and help the gunboats if by chance they were disabled. The Rebel batteries on the mainland and on the Island, the Rebel steamers wandering up and down like rats in a cage, were in full view. With my glass I could see all that took place in and around the nearest battery. Columns of water were thrown up by the shot from the gunboats, like the first gush from the hose of a steam fire-engine, which falls in rainbow-coloured spray. There were little splashes in the stream when the fragments of shell dropped from the sky. Round shot skipped along the surface of the river, tearing through the Rebel works, filling the air with sticks, timbers, earth, and branches of trees, as if a thunderbolt had fallen. There were explosions followed by volumes of smoke rising from the ground like the mists of a summer morning. There was a hissing, crackling, and thundering explosion in front and rear and overhead. But there were plucky men in the fort, who at intervals came out from their bomb-proof, and sent back a defiant answer. There was a flash, a volume of smoke, a hissing as if a flying fiery serpent were sailing through the air, growing louder, clearer, nearer, more fearful and terrific, crashing into the *Benton*, tearing up the iron plating, cutting off beams, splintering planks, smashing the crockery in the pantry, and breaking up the Admiral's writing-desk.

Howling and screeching and whizzing,
The bomb-shells arched on high,
And then, like fiery meteors,
Dropped swiftly from the sky.

All through the sunny hours, till evening, the gunboats maintained their position. While around the bright flashes, clouds of smoke, and heavy thunderings brought to mind the gorgeous imagery of Revelation, descriptive of the last judgment.

While the bombardment was at its height, I received a package of letters, entrusted to my care. There was one postmarked from a town in Maine, directed to a sailor on the St. Louis. Jumping on board a tug, which was conveying ammunition to the gunboats, I visited the vessel to distribute the letters. A gun had burst during the action, killing and wounding several of the crew. It was a sad scene. There were the dead,—two of them killed instantly, and one of them the brave fellow from Maine. Captain Paulding opened the letter, and found it to be from one who had confided to the noble sailor her heart's affections,—who was looking forward to the time when the war would be over, and they would be happy together as husband and wife.

"Poor girl! I shall have to write her sad news," said the captain.

Day after day and night after night the siege was kept up, till it grew exceedingly monotonous. I became so accustomed to the pounding that, though the thirteen-inch mortars were not thirty rods distant from my quarters, I was not wakened by the tremendous explosions. Commodore Foote found it very difficult to fight downstream, as the water was very high, flooding all the country. Colonel Bissell, of General Pope's army, proposed the cutting of a canal through the woods, to enable the gunboats to reach New Madrid. It was an Herculean undertaking. A light-draft transport was rigged for the enterprise. Machinery was attached to the donkey-engine of the steamer by which immense cotton-wood trees were sawed off four feet under water.

There was something very enchanting in the operation,—to steam out from the main river, over corn-fields and pasture lands, into the dark forests, threading a narrow and intricate channel, across the country,—past the Rebel batteries. A transport was taken through, and a tugboat, but the channel was not deep enough for the gunboats.

Captain Stembel, commanding the *Benton*,—a brave and competent officer, Commodore Foote's right-hand man,—proposed to run the batteries by night to New Madrid, capture the Rebel steamer which Pope had caught in a trap, then turning head up stream take the Rebel batteries in reverse. The Commodore hesitated. He was cautious as well as brave. At length he accepted the plan, and sent the *Pittsburg* and *Carondelet* past the batteries at night. It was a bold undertaking, but accomplished without damage to the gunboats. The current was swift and strong, and they went with the speed of a race-horse.

Their presence at New Madrid was hailed with joy by the troops. Four steamboats had worked their way through the canal. A regiment was taken on board each boat. The Rebels had a battery on the other side of the river at Watson's Landing, which was speedily silenced by the two gunboats. The troops landed, and under General Paine drove the Rebels from their camp, who fled in confusion, throwing away their guns, knapsacks, and clothing.

General Pope sent over the balance of his troops, and with his whole force moved upon General Mackall, the Rebel commander, who surrendered his entire command, consisting of nearly seven thousand prisoners, one hundred and twenty three guns, and an immense amount of supplies.

The troops of General Paine's brigade came across a farm yard which was well stocked with poultry, and helped themselves. The farmer's wife visited the General's head-quarters to enter a complaint.

"They are stealing all my chickens, General! I sha'n't have one left," she exclaimed, excitedly.

"I am exceedingly sorry, ma'am," said the General, with great courtesy; "but we are going to put down the rebellion if it takes every chicken in the State of Tennessee!"

The woman retired, evidently regarding the Yankees as a race of vandals.

EAST TENNESSEE REFUGEES

CHAPTER 7

Pittsburg Landing, Fort Pillow and Memphis

April, 1862

The battle of Pittsburg Landing, or Shiloh as it is sometimes called, was fought on the 6th and 7th of April. It was a contest which has scarcely been surpassed for manhood, pluck, endurance, and heroism. In proportion to the numbers engaged the loss in killed and wounded was as great as that of any battle of the war. The disasters to the Rebel cause in Tennessee moved Davis to hurry reinforcements to Corinth, which was the new base of Johnston's operations. Beauregard was sent into the department. He had the reputation of being a great commander, because he commanded the Rebel batteries in the attack on Sumter, and had received the glory of winning the victory at Bull Run. Time is the test of honour. Men, like the stars, have their hours of rising and setting. He was in the zenith of his fame.

Albert Sydney Johnston was still in command, but he was induced to move from Corinth to Pittsburg Landing and attack Grant before Buell, who was slowly moving across the country from Nashville, could join him.

Buell marched with great deliberation. He even gave express orders that there should be six miles' space between the divisions of his army. The position at Pittsburg Landing was chosen by General Smith, as being a convenient base for a movement upon Corinth. It had some natural advantages for defence,—Lick Creek and a ravine above the Landing,—but nothing was done towards erecting barricades or breastworks. There are writers who maintain that the attack of the Rebels was expected; but if expected, would not prudence have dictated the slashing of trees, the erection of breastworks, and a regular disposition of the forces? On Friday and Saturday the Rebel cavalry appeared in our front, but were easily driven back towards Corinth.

Nothing was done towards strengthening the line; no orders were issued in anticipation of a battle till the pickets were attacked on Sunday morning, while the troops were cooking their coffee, and while many of the officers were in bed.

Pittsburg is the nearest point to Corinth on the river. The road winds up the bank, passes along the edge of a deep ravine, leading southwest. It forks a half-mile from the Landing, the left-hand path leading to Hamburg up the river, and the main road leading to Shiloh Church, four miles from the Landing. The accompanying sketch of the church was taken the week after the battle, with the head-quarter tents of General Sherman around it. Its architecture is exceedingly primitive. It is a fair type of the inertness of the people of that region at the time. It is about twenty-five or thirty feet square, built of logs, without pulpit or pews, with rude benches for seats. Once it was chinked with clay, but the rains have washed out the mortar, and the wind comes in through all the crevices. It is thoroughly ventilated. It would make a good corn-crib for an Illinois farmer.

A brook meanders through the forest, furnishing water for the worshipping assemblies. South of the church, and across the brook, is a clearing,—an old farm-house where Beauregard wrote his despatch to Jeff Davis on Sunday night, announcing a great victory. There are other little clearings, which have been long under cultivation. The people were too indolent to make new openings in the forest, where centuries of mould had accumulated. The country was but little further advanced than when Daniel Boone passed through the Cumberland Gap. Civilization came and made a beginning; but the blight of slavery was there. How the tillage and culture of New England or Ohio would crown those swells of land with sheaves of grain! What corn and clover fields, pastures of honeysuckle, gardens of roses! Within four miles of one of the most beautiful rivers in the world,—in a country needing only industry to make it a paradise,—the mourning dove filled the air with its plaintive notes in the depths of an almost unbroken forest, while the few people, shiftless and destitute of the comforts of civilization, knew no better than to fight against their own best interests.

The majority of the poor whites of the South are very ignorant. Few of them have ever attended school. In Tennessee, by the census of 1850, there were more than seventy thousand native-born American adults who could not read. Not one half of the prisoners captured at Donelson could read or write. While the army was lying before Corinth, I visited a Mississippi school-house,—a log building chinked with mud, covered with long split oak shingles. It had a huge fireplace, built of stones, and a chimney laid up with sticks and mud. There were openings for two windows, but frames, sash, and glass all were wanting. There was no floor but the beaten earth,—no desks. Stakes were driven into the ground, upon which slabs of oak were laid for seats. The teacher's desk was a large dry-goods box.

The State of North Carolina, with a white population of five hundred and fifty-three thousand, had eighty thousand native whites, over twenty years of age, who had never attended school. In the State of Virginia, North Carolina, South Carolina, Georgia, and Alabama, five States having a population of two million six hundred and seventy thousand, there were two hundred and sixty-two thousand native-born Americans, over twenty years of age, unable to read or write! It will be no easy matter to awaken aspirations in the minds of this class. They have been so long inert, so long taught to believe that labour is degrading, that rapid progress of Southern society cannot be expected immediately, unless emigration infuses a new vitality into the community.

Ignorance was on the increase throughout the South. Public schools were of little value where they existed, and the county was so sparsely settled in many places there were not scholars enough to form one. The school fund arising from the sale of public lands was often appropriated to other uses. In Arkansas it had been squandered by worthless officials. The planters and wealthy farmers employed teachers in their families. Before the war, thousands of young ladies from the North were thus engaged. They sat at the planter's table and associated with his daughters; but, however intelligent, refined, or agreeable they might be, they were not admitted as their equals in society. Such teaching as they received, although the teacher might be faithful, was of little account. The children, proud and haughty, daily hearing of the inferiority of the people of the North, were not always disposed to receive instruction, much less to submit to correction, at the hands of a "Yankee schoolma'am." To be chivalrous, courteous, high-minded, and generous toward woman has ever been the boast of the men of the South; but, during the months immediately preceding the outbreak of the Rebellion, insulting and abusive language was freely uttered in the presence of Northern ladies. There was rudeness not only of language, but in some instances of action. The young bloods of the aristocracy, learning to crow as they heard the old cocks, not infrequently rose in rebellion against the authority of the teacher. Especially was this the case with teachers employed in the public schools. A Yankee schoolmaster or schoolmistress was one who could be insulted

A Mississippi school-house

with impunity; and so bitter was the hatred, that, weeks before the first gun was fired at Sumter, Northern teachers were forced to leave their schools and retire from the Confederacy.

To General Sherman more than to any division commander is credit due for the victory at Pittsburg Landing. When the first volley of musketry reverberated through the forest on Sunday morning he leaped into his saddle. He was conspicuous everywhere, riding along the lines regardless of the bullets which riddled his clothes. Early in the battle he was wounded in the wrist, but wrapping a bandage round his arm, continued in the field. Three horses were shot under him. He was a conspicuous mark for the Rebel riflemen. His fearless example was inspiring to the men. And so through the long hours of the day he was able to hold his position by the church, till the giving way of Prentiss and Hurlburt, nearer the river, made it necessary to fall back. Here Grant first exhibited those qualities of character which have made him the great military commander of the age.

"We will beat them yet. They can't pass this ravine," were his words of encouragement as he selected the final line, leading to the landing.

The contest was virtually decided at five o'clock on Sunday afternoon, when Breckenridge attempted to cross the gorge near the river and was hurled back with great loss. Johnston and Beauregard made a great mistake in attacking at a point within reach of the gunboats. Had they come in on the Purdy road, between Shiloh Church and Crump's Landing, in all human probability there would have been a far different record for the historians of the future. Had they attacked northwest of the church instead of south of it, they would have taken Grant in reverse, and forced him to change the whole front of his army; they would have had no ravine to cross, would have been beyond reach of the gunboats, and would have stood a fair chance of cutting off Lewis Wallace, who was at Crump's Landing, from all connection with the main army. The defeat of the Rebels was decisive, and yet Beauregard sent the following despatch to Richmond:

Corinth
April 8th, 1862
To the Secretary of War at Richmond
We have gained a great and glorious victory. Eight to ten thousand prisoners, and thirty-six pieces of cannon. Buell reinforced Grant, and we retired to our entrenchments at Corinth, which we can hold. Loss heavy on both sides.
Beauregard

On the same day he sent a flag of truce to General Grant with the following message, also asking leave to bury the Confederate dead:

> Sir, at the close of the conflict yesterday, my forces being exhausted by the extraordinary length of the time during which they were engaged with yours on that and the preceding day, and it being apparent that you had received and were still receiving reinforcement, I felt it my duty to withdraw my troops from the immediate scene of the conflict.

From Shiloh to the close of the war, Beauregard's popularity was on the wane, and the Southern people lost confidence in him. I was at Island No. 10 when the battle was fought, but joined the army the week after.

As the army moved towards Corinth, there was abundant evidence that the defeat of the Rebels was most disastrous,—that their retreat was hasty. Blankets, knapsacks, haversacks, here and there muskets, wagons, one overturned in a slough, one with its tongue broken, tents, harnesses, oats, corn, flour, tent-poles, were confusedly scattered along the way. The carcasses of dead horses tainted the air. There were piles of earth newly heaped above those who died from their wounds. They fled in a fright on Monday night. I came unexpectedly upon a little log-hut, on a by-path leading toward Monterey. Two of McCook's cavalry rode up in advance of me. A widow woman, middle aged, with a little girl and two little boys occupied it. She kindly gave me a drink of water, and informed me that there were three Confederate wounded in the other room. I looked in upon them for a moment. Suffering had wasted them, and they had no disposition to talk of the past or the future. The good woman had been kind to them, but she had seen a great deal of sorrow. On Monday night one hundred wounded were brought to her house. Her two horses had been seized by the Rebels, her corn eaten, and no equivalent returned. She conversed unreservedly; deplored the war, and wished it over. There were seven new-made graves in her garden, and in her door-yard a heap of cinders and ashes, and charred brands,—fragments of wagons and tent-poles. On the upper Corinth road fifty wounded were lying, cared for by our surgeons.

I recall some of the scenes of the movement upon Corinth. Here is an open forest, undulating land with little or no underbrush; thousands of wagons, all plodding on, not in slow, easy motion, but by fits and starts, with cutting, slashing, shouting, swearing, a chorus of profanity resounding through the forests. A mule sticks fast; he tumbles;

his mate falls upon him. The drivers become enraged; then follows a general melee, a long halt, frantic attempts to start again, an unloading and reloading. Other trains in the rear, tired of waiting, turn to the right or left, perhaps to pass the little slough safely, only to meet with a similar mishap ten rods farther along. A battery struggles along, with twelve horses attached to a single piece of artillery. The entire forest is cut up by passing teams. Mingled with the thousands of wagons are regiments. They, too, are in confusion. Buell's and Grant's forces have become mixed. The divisions have been ordered to move, but evidently with no prearranged system. As far as the eye can see it is one grand hurly-burly,—one frantic struggle to make headway,—and this for a half-dozen miles. What a waste of horse-flesh! Here are six mules attempting to draw six boxes of bread,—weight perhaps six hundred pounds. The cavalry bring out their supplies on horses, each cavalryman bringing a bag of oats. There is cursing, swearing, pounding. The army in Flanders could not have been more profane. The brutality of the drivers is terrible. A miserable fellow, destitute of sense and humanity, strikes a mule over the head, felling the animal to the ground. Noble horses are remorselessly cut up by these fiendish beings in human form. There is no check upon their cruelty. You see dead horses everywhere. All the finer sensibilities become callous. One must see, but not feel. There would be pleasure in snatching a whip from the hands of these savages and giving them a dose of their own medicine. General Halleck advanced with extreme caution. He built four lines of breastworks, each line nearly ten miles long, so that if driven from one he could fall back to another. He sunk deep wells for water, he was preparing to be besieged instead of opening a siege.

He doubted all the reports of his scouts,—disbelieved the stories of negroes who came to him,—issued Order No. 57, that all "unauthorized persons" in his lines should be sent out, especially fugitive slaves,—threw up redoubts, dragged his heavy siege-guns through the mud from the Landing,—planted them behind sodded earthworks, erected bomb-proof magazines,—issued his final orders to his army of an hundred thousand men,—opened fire from his heavy guns,—threw forward his skirmishers, and found—a deserted town!

Joining the fleet upon the Mississippi once more on the 3rd of June, I found Commodore (now Admiral) Davis in command, Admiral Foote having been relieved at his own request. His wound was painful, and he was so debilitated that he was unable to discharge his duties. The idea was generally entertained that the Rebels had evacuated Fort Pillow. The evacuation of Corinth was the basis for expectation of such an event. Fires were seen over the point on the bluffs and beyond, toward Randolph. Of course no one could say what was burning, but from the past conduct of Rebels, it was reasonable to suppose that the evacuation had taken place, inasmuch as there was an ominous silence of Rebel batteries. But they suddenly waked up. Ascending to the pilot-house of the steamer, I could see handfuls of white cloud above and beyond the dense foliage of the forest. Then there came a dull, heavy roar,—*boom*—*boom*—*boom*,—and the nearer explosion of the shells which burst in the air above our gunboats. Not evacuated! They were there lively as ever.

This sudden and unexpected demonstration aroused Captain Maynadier, and right merrily answered the mortars till noon. Then there was a respite, while the mortar crews sat down beneath the dark green foliage of the forest, sheltered from the burning sun, and ate their rations, and rested the while.

Seven or eight miles below Craighead Point is Lanier's plantation. The proprietor being a Secessionist, burned his cotton, but for some cause he had lost faith, or pretended to lose faith, in the Confederacy, and desired to be permitted to return to his comfortable home, there to remain unmolested. He sent a note to Colonel Fitch, commanding the land forces, soliciting an interview. His request was granted, and he so ingratiated himself into Colonel Fitch's good feeling that he became again an occupant of his homestead.

Subsequently it was ascertained that he was supplying the Rebel fleet with ice, spring chickens, garden vegetables, &c. It was decided to spring a trap upon the gentlemen of the Southern navy. A small party was sent out by Colonel Fitch, which reached the locality undiscovered. After a few minutes' reconnoissance, eight men were discovered helping themselves to ice in Mr. Lanier's ice-cellar. They were surprised. One resisted, but was shot, and the rest, after a short parleying, surrendered. They were brought to the *Benton*, but were very uncommunicative and sour.

The loss of a lieutenant and seven men was not well relished at Fort Pillow. Soon after noon the guns on the bluff commenced a vigorous but random fire, as if ammunition cost nothing, and it were mere pastime to burn powder and hurl shell over the point at our fleet. It was very pleasant to see the round shot plump into the water all around our gunboats, with an occasional shell puffing into cloud overhead, and raining fragments of iron into the river,—for with such random firing, there was but little danger of being hit.

The day had been hot and sultry, but just before nightfall a huge bank of clouds rolled up in the western horizon, and burst with the fury of a tornado upon the fleet. Some of the transports dragged their anchors before the gale, but all kept up steam; they were not long in making head against the breeze. There was but little rain, but a dense cloud of dust was whirled up from the sandbars.

I was surprised to see, when the storm was at its height, two of our rams steam rapidly down to the point and turn their prows towards the Rebel batteries. They disappeared in the whirling dust-cloud, vanishing from sight like ships at sea when night comes on. They steamed swiftly down the stream and turned Craighead Point.

Their mission, at such a moment, was to take advantage of the storm,—of the enveloping dust-cloud,—to ascertain what the Rebels were doing. We could hear the sudden waking up of heavy guns,—those that had spoken to us in the past,—just as, in high party times, great orators hold forth the night before election. The rams were discovered, and at once the batteries were in a blaze. Then they quietly steamed across the bend, in face of the batteries, turned their prows up stream, and appeared in sight once more. Onward rolled the cloud, and the Rebel cannon belched and thundered, firing shot at random into the river. *Bang—bang—bang,*—two or three at a time,—roared the guns. It was amusing, laughable, to see the rams returning, and hear the uproar below.

The dust-cloud, with its fine, misty rain, rolled away. The sun shone once more, and bridged the Mississippi with a gorgeous rainbow. While admiring it, a Rebel gunboat poked her nose around the point. Then, after a little hesitancy, her entire body, to see what we were up to. She was a black craft, bearing the flag of the Confederacy. Seeing how far off we were, she steamed boldly past the point, upstream far enough to get a sight of the entire Federal fleet; turned slowly, placed her head downward, to be ready for a quick run home, if need be; then turned her paddles against the current, and surveyed us leisurely. The *Mound City* and *Cairo* being nearest, opened fire upon the craft. A signal was run up from the *Benton,* and immediately from the chimneys of the entire fleet rose heavy columns of blackest smoke, which mingled with the white puffs of steam, and rolled away into the blackness of the receding storm. The sun had gone down.

Unheeding the shot falling close at her bows, or whistling over her decks, the steamer took her own time and slowly descended the stream and disappeared beyond the jutting headland.

At sunset on the 4th of June, the Rebel batteries opened a fierce and sudden fire upon the gunboats. Then there came heavy explo-

Gunboats in Line

sions, rising columns of smoke, faint and white at first, but increasing in volume and blackness. Another,—a third, a fourth,—expanding into one broad column, all along the height occupied by the Rebel batteries. Daylight was fading away, the lurid flames filled the southern sky, and a heaving, surging bank of smoke and flame laid along the tree-tops of the intervening forest. Occasionally there were flashes and faint explosions, and sudden puffs of smoke, spreading out like flakes of cotton or fleeces of whitest wool. This was all we could see. We were ignorant of what was feeding the flames, whether steamers or bales of cotton, or barracks or tents or houses, but were sure that it was a burning of that which had cost a pile of Confederate notes. After taking possession of the works in the morning, the fleet pursued the retreating Rebels down the river.

It was dark when we came to anchor four miles above the city of Memphis on the 5th of June.

"I think that we shall have a lively time in the morning," said the Admiral. My own quarters were on board of the *J. H. Dickey*, which lay a mile upstream. I was astir before daylight on the 6th. The air was clear,—the sky without a cloud. The stars were fading in the west, and the columns of light were rising in the east. The gunboats—five of them—were in a line across the stream, with the steam escaping from their pipes. The city was in full view. People were gathering upon the banks gazing upon the fleet. A dark column of smoke rose from above the green foliage of the forest opposite the city, but whether produced by burning buildings or by the Rebel fleet, was wholly a matter of conjecture.

The tugboat *Jessie Benton*, tender to the Admiral, came up to the advance boat, which was lying by our side.

"The Admiral thinks that the Rebel fleet is below the city, and that we are to have a fight. You can go down if you want to," said the captain.

I was on board in an instant, leaving the other gentlemen of the press asleep in their state-room. The soldiers were heaving the anchors as we approached the fleet, shouting in chorus, "Yeave ho! yeave ho!" The drummer-boys were beating to quarters, the marines were mustering, officers and sailors all were busy.

The Admiral was standing on the upper deck with Captain Phelps, commanding the *Benton*, by his side. The Admiral is a tall, well-proportioned man, about fifty years old, with gray hair and blue eyes. He is a perfect gentleman,—kind, courteous, and affable, not only to his officers, but to the crews. Captain Phelps is shorter, and smaller in stature. His features are sharply cut. He stands erect, looks upon the preparations with keen eyes, giving orders with precision and promptness. The *Benton* in a few moments is ready for action, so quickly are his orders executed.

"Drop down toward the city, sir, and see if you can discover the Rebel fleet," is the word of the Admiral to our captain.

We pass through the fleet, and move slowly downstream, followed by the *Benton* and *Carondelet*, which drift with the current.

June, 1862

The sun was beginning to gild the spires of the city, and its slant rays came streaming over the waters into our faces. Men, women, and children were gathering upon the levee, on foot, on horseback, and in carriages. The crowd became more dense. Were they assembling to welcome us? Should we steam down to them, and ask them what they thought of the Rebellion? The Rebel flag was flying from the cupola of the court-house, and from a tall flagstaff on the levee. I remembered that on the 6th of May, thirteen months before, on the evening after the secession of the State, the people had torn down the stars and stripes, borne them out to the suburbs of the city, dug a grave, and buried the flag, trampling it in the mire!

Suddenly a Rebel gunboat steamed out into the stream, from the shelter of the Arkansas woods;—another,—another,—till eight had ranged themselves in two lines of battle. "Helm aport!" shouted our captain to the pilot, and we were rushing up stream again. The Admiral was not quite ready for action, and the *Benton* and *Carondelet* returned to their original position.

The appearance of the Rebel fleet,—the orderly formation of the battle line,—looked like work. The affair of the 10th of May, when the Rebel gunboats stole round Craighead Point above Fort Pillow, and sunk the *Cincinnati*, was sufficiently spirited to warrant the supposition that an engagement would be desperate. Several of the Rebel boats were fitted out at Memphis, and were manned by the old rivermen of that city, who would fight with great bravery under the eyes of their fellow-citizens, their wives and sweethearts.

"Let the sailors have breakfast," said the Admiral, who believed in fighting on a full stomach. I took mine on deck,—a cup of coffee, hard-tack, and a slice of salt junk,—for the movements in front of the city were too interesting to be lost sight of. The *Little Rebel*, the flag-ship of Commodore Montgomery, was passing from boat to boat. With my glass I could see the officers of the vessels. Montgomery was issuing his final orders.

Suddenly the Rebel fleet began to move up stream. A flag went up to the head of the *Benton's* flagstaff. It was the signal to be ready for action. Sailors dropped their plates, knives and forks, and sprang to their guns. The *Benton* was nearest the Tennessee shore, then the *Carondelet*, the *St. Louis*, *Louisville*, and *Cairo*. Our own little tug was close by the flag-ship, keeping its place in the stream by the slow working of its engine.

The Rebel fleet was composed of the *Van Dorn*, *General Price*, *General Bragg*, *Jeff Thompson*, *General Lovell*, *General Beauregard*, *Sumter*, and *Little Rebel*,—all gunboats and all rams, built expressly with a view of butting our fleet out of existence. The *Beauregard* was nearest the shore, next the *Little Rebel*, then the *General Price*, next the *General Bragg* and the *General Beauregard*, which composed the front line. Immediately in rear was the *General Lovell*, near the Memphis shore, her position being directly in front of the city wharf boat; next the *Van Dorn*, then the *Jeff Thompson* and lastly the *Sumter*.

How strange, peculiar, and indescribable are one's feelings when going into battle! There is a light-heartedness,—a quickening of all the springs of life. There is thrill in every nerve,—an exhilaration of spirit,—a tension of every fibre. You see every movement, hear every sound, and think not only of what is before you, but of home, of the loved ones there,—of the possibility that you may never behold them again. Some men review their lives, and ask themselves if they have left anything undone which ought to have been done,—if their lives have been complete.

The *Little Rebel* was opposite the *Benton*. There was a flash,—a puff of smoke from her side,—a screaming of something unseen in the air over my head,—a frightful sound. The shot fell far in our rear. Another puff from the *Beauregard*, and the shot fell near the *Benton*. A third came from the *General Price*, aimed at the *Carondelet*, passed very near her larboard ports, and almost took our own boat in the bow. My fear was all gone. I was in the fight. There was no possibility of escaping from it. Wherever the boat went I must go. I should be just as safe to keep cool as to be excited. Besides, it was a new experience,—a new sight,—a grand exhibition. Interest, curiosity, and reason mastered fear. I sat down in an arm-chair on the deck beside the pilot-house, and made rapid notes of all that I saw. I transcribe them:

5.40 a. m. Cairo opens with a stern gun,—shot strikes close under hull of *Little Rebel*. Our boats' bows up stream. Rebels advancing slowly. *Bang—bang—bang—bang* from each of the vessels. A whole broadside from *Cairo*. Another from *Louisville*. Air full of strange noises. Shells burst overhead. Pieces raining all round us. Columns of water tossed up. Both fleets enveloped in smoke. Very little wind. Splinters thrown out from *General Price*. Can see a shot-hole with my glass. Rebel fleet half-mile distant. Comes to a standstill.

6.00. Queen of the West cutting loose from shore. *Monarch* also. Great black clouds of smoke rolling up from their stacks. Steam hissing from their pipes. Commodore Ellet on the *Queen*. Stands beside the pilot-house. Sharpshooters looking from loopholes. *Queen* wheels out into stream. Passes between *Benton* and *Carondelet*. Are near enough to say good morning to Commodore Ellet and wish him success. *Monarch* following *Queen*, passing between *Cairo* and *St. Louis*.

6.25. Rebels moving down stream.

6.35. Signal from *Benton* to round to and come to close quarters. *Queen* surging ahead under full speed. Ploughs a wide furrow. Aiming for *Beauregard*. Rebel fleet all opening on her. Shot crash through her. Exciting scene. Sharpshooters at work. *Beauregard* puts her helm down. Sheers off. *Queen* rushes by. Has missed her aim. Coming round in a curve. Strikes the *General Price*. Tremendous crash. Men jumping into water. *Beauregard* falling upon *Queen of the West*. Another crash. *Monarch* close at hand. Smashes into *Beauregard*. Cracking of rifles and muskets. *Queen of the West* sinking. *Monarch* throwing out a warp. Towing her ashore. *Benton* close upon the *General Lovell*. Shot strikes *Lovell* in bow. Rips from stem to stern. Water full of timber and fragments. *Lovell* sinking. Man on deck. Left arm shattered, crying help! help! help! Commotion on shore. *Lovell* goes down with a lurch. River full of poor wretches struggling for life. Throwing up their arms. Stream sweeps them away. *Little Rebel* fleeing to Arkansas shore. The *Jeff Thompson* on fire.

7.05. Rebel fleet broken. Their guns all silent. *Beauregard* sinking. We run alongside. Rebel officers lay shattered. Sides of vessel spotted with blood. Pool of blood on deck. Crew fled. Taken off by *Little Rebel*. Help lift wounded Rebel officer on our boat. Thanked us, and said, "You are kinder than my own comrades, for one of them was mean enough to steal my watch and pick my pocket." *Little Rebel* run ashore. Crew fleeing into woods. *Cairo* gives them parting broadside. Rebels crawling up the bank dripping with water.

7.10. Boats of *Benton* and *Carondelet* picking up the wretches. Van Dorn escaping downstream.

7.25. Fight over. *Van Dorn* out of sight. Last gun fired. *Jeff Thompson* on fire in every part. Grand explosion. Whole interior of boat lifted five hundred feet high. Flames. Volumes of smoke. Bursting shells. Timbers, planks, fragments, raining all around us.

It was a complete annihilation of the Rebel fleet. Not a man was lost on our gunboats, and Commodore Ellet was the only one wounded.

The Rebel fleet began the action in good style, but maintained the line of battle a few minutes only. The appearance of the rams threw them into disorder. On the other hand, the line of battle taken by Commodore Davis was preserved to the end. Everything was as systematic and orderly as in a well-regulated household. The thought occurred, as I saw the steady onward movement of the fleet, which, after once starting to close in with the Rebels, did not for an instant slacken speed, that he was clearing the river of all Rebel obstructions with the same ease that a housewife sweeps dirt through a doorway. His orders were few. The main thing was to get to close quarters.

Embracing an early opportunity to reach the shore, I mingled freely with the crowd, to see how the thing was relished and to study the feelings of the people. Some looked exceedingly sour; some disconsolate; a few were defiant; many of the people were evidently good-natured, but deeply humiliated. A gentleman, resident of the city, informed me that he did not think the people cared anything about the Union, or had any desire to return to it, but they had an intense hatred of the tyranny to which they had been subjected, and were ready to welcome anything which would relieve them.

The *Avalanche* of that morning, hardly issued when the conflict began, said:

> There was not a little excitement about the levee last night, occasioned by an officer coming down in a skiff announcing that three of the Federal gunboats were in the 'shute' above the

Island. The signals and movements of the boats seemed to confirm the report, but we have no idea that it was true.

Yesterday was quite lively. All reports about Fort Pillow were listened to with interest, and they were not a few. By noon it was known that the fort was evacuated, and there was not a little excitement in consequence. Nearly all the stores were closed, and those that were open, with few exceptions, were rather indisposed to sell. Even a spool of cotton could not be had yesterday in stores which the day before had plenty and to spare. Besides the soldiers from Fort Pillow a fleet made us a visit which attracted much attention and formed the subject of general conversation. All seemed to regret what had been done and wished it were otherwise. So prevailing was the excitement that the common mode of salutation on Main Street was, 'When do you think the Federals will be here?' Each one made arrangements according to the tenor of the reply. Many persons were packing up to leave.

In a word, all who could began to consider anxiously the question whether to go or stay. There was much running about on the streets, and evidently more or less excitement on every countenance. Some took matters coolly, and still believe that the Federals will never go to Memphis by river. All obstructions to their progress have not been removed and probably will not be. In fact, the prospect is very good for a grand naval engagement, which shall eclipse anything ever seen before. There are many who would like the engagement to occur, who do not much relish the prospect of its occurring very near the city. They think deeper water and scope and verge enough for such an encounter may be found farther up the river. All, however, are rejoiced that Memphis will not fall till conclusions are first tried on water and at the cannon's mouth.

The "conclusions" had been tried and the people had seen their fleet unceremoniously knocked to pieces.

There were thousands of negroes on the levee, interested spectators of the scene. I asked one athletic man what he thought of it? "O massa, I tinks a good deal of it. Uncle Abe's boats mighty powerful. Dey go through our boats jus like dey was eggshells." Another one standing by at once became interested in the conversation. Said he, "Captain Jeff Thompson, he cotch it dis time! He; hi! O how de balls did whiz!" There was an unmistakable sign of pleasure on the countenances of the coloured population.

In fifteen minutes after the occupation of the city, enterprising news-boys accompanying the fleet were crying, "Here's the New York *Herald*! *Times* and *Tribune*! Chicago and St. Louis papers!"

How wonderfully had the upper Mississippi been repossessed! One by one the Rebel obstructions had been removed. How often had we been told that they were impregnable! How often that the gunboats would be destroyed! How often that never would the river be opened till the Confederacy was a recognized independent power! One short year and their labours,—the ditch-digging, the cannon-casting, boat-building, their braggadocio, had come to naught.

The part taken by Commodore Ellet was glorious. He was a brave, gallant, dashing officer, the son of a noble mother, who lived in Philadelphia. Mr. Stuart, President of the Christian Commission, relates that later in the war he called to see her, at her request, to receive a large donation. He found a lady eighty-four years of age. A grandson had been killed in battle, the body had been brought home, and was lying in the house. Said Mrs. Ellet: "I have given my two sons, Commodore Ellet and General Ellet, and four grandchildren to my country. I don't regret this gift. If I had twenty sons I would give them all, for the country must be preserved. And if I was twenty years younger, I would go and fight myself to the last!"

WITH DISPATCH

CHAPTER 8

Invasion of Maryland

AUGUST, 1862

Great events were transpiring in Virginia. The magnificent army which passed down the Potomac in March, which had thrown up the tremendous fortifications at Yorktown, which had fought at Williamsburg, Fair Oaks, Gaines's Mills, Savage Station, Glendale, and Malvern, was once more at Washington. Manassas was a bloody plain. Pope had been defeated, sacrificed by Fitz John Porter. Day after day the booming of cannon had been heard in Washington, borne by the breezes along the wooded valley of the Potomac; far away at first, then nearer at Chantilly and Fairfax Court-House. Then came the stream of fugitives, and broken, disheartened ranks back to Arlington. The streets of Washington were thick with hungry, war-worn men. Long lines of ambulances wended into the city, with wounded for the hospitals, already overcrowded. The soldiers had pitiful tales to tell of the scenes of the Peninsula, and of the gory field of Manassas,—how near they came to victory,—how Hooker and Heintzelman rolled back the lines of Stonewall Jackson,—how Fitz John Porter lingered within an hour's march of the conflict, tardily coming into line, and moving away when lightly pressed by the enemy. There were curses loud and deep breathed against Porter, Pope, and McClellan. The partisans of Porter and McClellan called Pope a braggadocio, while the soldiers who had fought with obstinacy, who had doubled up Jackson in the first day's battle, retorted that McClellan was a coward, who, through all the engagements on the Peninsula took good care to be out of the reach of hostile bullets or cannon shot. The cause of the Union was gloomy. Burnside had been hurried up from North Carolina to aid in repelling the invader. The sun shone peacefully through the August days,—summer passed into autumn,

And calm and patient Nature kept
Her ancient promise well,

Though o'er her bloom and greenness swept
The battle's breath of hell.

Adversity is a test of faith. In those darkest hours there was no faltering of hope. The heart of the nation was serene. The people believed that God would give them the victory. The soldiers believed it. Those who were passing away from earth, who with quickened sight beheld the events of the hour in the light of eternity, trusted that Providence would give the victory to their companions in arms.

Colonel Broadhead, of Michigan, lying upon the battle-field of Manassas, with the shadow of death stealing over him, wrote a most touching farewell letter to his wife, in which he expressed his convictions as to who was responsible for the defeat.

My Dear Wife:
I write to you mortally wounded, from the battle-field. We have again been defeated, and ere this reaches you your children will be fatherless. Before I die let me implore that in some way it may be stated that General—has been outwitted, and that—is a traitor. Had they done their duty as I did mine, and had led as I did, the dear old flag had waved in triumph. I wrote to you yesterday morning. Today is Sunday, and today I sink to the green couch of our final rest. I have fought well, my darling; and I was shot in the endeavour to rally our broken battalions. I could have escaped, but would not until all our hope was gone, and was shot,—about the only one of our forces left on the field. Our cause is just, and our generals,—not the enemy's,—have defeated us. In God's good time he will give us the victory.

And now, goodbye, wife and children. Bring them up—I know you will—in the fear of God and love for the Saviour. But for you and the dear ones dependent, I should die happy. I know the blow will fall with crushing weight on you. Trust in Him who gave manna in the wilderness.

Dr. North is with me. It is now after midnight, and I have spent most of the night in sending messages to you. Two bullets have gone through my chest, and directly through my lungs. I suffer little now, but at first the pain was acute. I have won the soldier's name, and am ready to meet now, as I must, the soldier's fate. I hope that from heaven I may see the glorious old flag wave again over the undivided country I have loved so well.

Farewell, wife and friends, we shall meet again.

GENERAL McCLELLAN AT WILLIAMSBURG

The military authorities were often indebted to newspaper correspondents for intelligence concerning the movements of the Rebels. One of the most indefatigable of the corps was Mr. U. H. Painter, of the *Philadelphia Inquirer*. He was at Bristow Station when Stuart made his first appearance in Pope's rear, capturing the baggage of that officer. Mr. Painter was taken prisoner, but, true to his profession, kept his eyes and ears open, listening to all that was said by Stuart and his subordinate officers. Being in citizen's dress, he managed to slip through the guard, but not till after he had obtained important information relative to the movements of the enemy. Reaching Washington, he at once sent an attaché of the paper up the Potomac to Point of Rocks, also informed the government that the Rebels were intending to invade

Maryland. No credence was given to his assertion; the government believed that Washington was the point aimed at. The Rebels made their appearance at Point of Rocks, the messenger on watch gave Mr. Painter information by telegraph that Stuart was crossing. That gentleman informed the government of the fact, and forwarded a despatch to his paper. The Washington papers in the afternoon contained semi-official denials of the despatch to the *Inquirer*. But information from the Baltimore and Ohio Railroad Company that the Rebels had possession of the road at Point of Rocks could not be disputed. Even then the government was slow to believe that the Rebels seriously intended a movement upon Maryland.

General Lee was flushed with success. He had reason to think well of himself and of his troops. He had raised the siege of Richmond, transferred the war to the vicinity of Washington, had defeated Pope on the old battle-ground of Manassas, and driven the Union forces into the defences of the capital. The troops believed that they could accomplish anything,—overcome all obstacles,—sweep away the Union army, and march to Baltimore, Philadelphia, and New York; and yet Lee had made a miscalculation of the power of endurance on the part of his troops, and the first invasion of the North failed, not only because of the courage and tenacity of the Union soldiers at Antietam, but also because the Rebel army had lost much of its aggressive power through hard marching, constant fighting, and want of food. Jackson had so worn down his troops that in the first day's fight at Manassas he was defeated by Hooker and Heintzelman, and had it not been for the timely arrival of Longstreet, would have been driven from the field. In the second day's fight he could only hold his own, while Longstreet, meeting with little opposition, was able to turn Pope's left flank, and win the victory.

Lee entered Maryland as a liberator, believing that the people would rise *en masse* to welcome him; but he was greatly mistaken.

Taking the train from Philadelphia, I went to Harrisburg, Lancaster, and York in Pennsylvania, and thence into western Maryland. Everywhere the people were arming. All the able-bodied men were drilling. All labour was at a stand-still. The fires of the foundries went out; the farmers left their uncut grain in the field. Men worth millions of dollars were in the ranks as privates. Members of Congress, professors of colleges with their classes, iron-masters with their workmen, ministers and the able-bodied men of their congregations, were hastening to the rendezvous. The State Capitol grounds were swarming with men, receiving arms and ammunition. It was a glorious exhibition of patriotism; yet I could but think that they would offer a feeble resistance in the open field to well-drilled troops. At Bunker Hill raw militia stood the fire of British veterans; but such instances of pluck are rare in history.

September, 1862

Going up the Cumberland Valley I reached Greencastle on the 14th of September, ten miles from Hagerstown. I could hear a dull and heavy booming of cannon to the south, in the direction of South Mountain; but the Rebels were at Hagerstown, and had made a dash almost up to Greencastle. The only troops in the place were a few companies watching the border, and momentarily expecting the Rebels to appear. Citizens of Maryland, some from Virginia, Union men, were there, ready to run farther North on the slightest alarm.

The little village was suddenly excited by the cry, "They are coming!" "They are coming!" It was not a body of Rebels, however, but the Union cavalry, which had cut their way out from Harper's Ferry in the night before the pusillanimous surrender of Colonel Miles. They crossed the pontoon bridge, moved up the Potomac, through wood-paths and by-ways, twice coming in contact with the Rebel pickets, and falling in with Longstreet's ammunition trains between Hagerstown and Williamsport, consisting of one hundred wagons, which were captured. Many of the teamsters were slaves, who were very glad to see the Yankees. They were contented under their capture.

"Were you not frightened when you saw the Yankees?" I asked of one.

"Not de leastest bit, massa. I was glad to see 'em. Ye see, we all wanted to get Norf. De captain of de guard, he tell me to whip up my horses and get away, but I done cut for de woods right towards de Norf."

He chuckled merrily over it, and said, "I's in de service of de Union now."

He was driving the horses with evident satisfaction at the sudden change in his fortunes.

When John Brown woke the world from its dreaming at Harper's Ferry, he had an accomplice named Cook, who escaped and concealed himself in the mountains of Pennsylvania, but who was hunted down by Fitz Hugh Miller of Chambersburg. Among the Rebel prisoners was this same Fitz Hugh, dressed in a suit of rusty gray, with a black ostrich plume in his hat, sun-burned, dusty, having a hang-dog look. He was a captain in the Rebel service. The Dutch blood of the citizens, usually as calm and steady in its flow as the rivers of their Fatherland, came up with a rush.

"Hang him! Down with the traitor! Kill him!" they shouted. They rushed to seize him, but the guards kept the populace at bay. The excitement increased. Miller appealed to the guards to protect him. He was quickly hurried into the jail, which was strongly guarded. A great change had taken place in the opinions of the people. They had been indifferent to the questions of the hour, but the Rebel raid, by which they had lost their horses, had taught them an excellent lesson. Self-interest is sometimes a stimulant to patriotism. They even began to look with complacency upon what John Brown had done.

The Rebels evacuated Hagerstown on the morning of the 16th of September, and an hour later I entered it on the first train, which was greeted by the people with shouts and hurrahs and demonstrations of joy, as if it brought emancipation from long bondage. Some of the citizens had manifested sympathy with the Rebels. Still there were groups of excited men in the streets, shouting, "We'll hang the cusses. We've spotted them, and if they ever come back we'll be the death of them, as sure as there is a God."

The battle of South Mountain had been fought, and the hostile armies were concentrating for a trial of strength along the peaceful banks of the Antietam.

I was awakened at daylight on the morning of the 17th of September by the booming of cannon. It was a dull, leaden morning. The clouds hung low upon the mountains, and swept in drifts along the hillsides. The citizens of Hagerstown were astir,—some standing on the house-tops, listening to the increasing thunder of the cannonade, some in the church-steeples, others making haste to visit the field of battle. I had no horse, but finding a stable-keeper, was soon the owner of one. The horse-dealer was quite willing to dispose of his animals. "Horse-flesh is mighty onsartin these days," said he. "The Rebels took my best ones, and if they should come here again, I reckon they would clean me out."

My first impulse was to push directly down the Sharpsburg turnpike and gain the rear of the Rebels, enter their lines as a citizen, and see the battle from their side.

"Don't do it, sir," said a citizen.

Upon reflection, it appeared to be good advice, and so turning about (for I had already gone a mile or more in that direction) I took the Boonsboro pike and rode rapidly towards the battle-field. Two or

General McClellan at the battle of Antietam

three miles out I came across a Rebel soldier,—barefoot and bareheaded, pale, sallow, worn out by hard marching, lying under an oak-tree by the roadside. His gun was by his side. He raised his head and held up his hand, as if to implore me not to harm him. He belonged to a Georgia regiment, and had dropped by the way, too feeble to keep his place in the ranks. He was taken care of by two citizens.

Striking off from the turnpike in a by-path, then across fields, through oak groves, directed by the roar of battle, descending a steep hill, and fording the Antietam, I gained the battle-field in rear of the right wing, where Hooker was in command. Passing beyond the field hospitals, I reached the hill, on Poffenberg's farm.

The fire was raging fearfully in front of Sumner; but Hooker's and Mansfield's cannon were silent, cooling their brazen lips after the morning's fever. In the hollow behind the ridge, east of Poffenberg's house, the Pennsylvania Reserve Corps—what was left of them—were lying, sad, yet not disheartened. How changed from what they were a year before, then fifteen thousand strong!

"We cannot lose many more," said one, as I talked of the morning's action. Gibbons's brigade, of Hooker's corps, had crossed the turnpike, and was holding the ground in the woods between it and the Potomac.

Ascending the ridge, I came upon Battery B, Fourth Artillery, also Cooper's and Easton's Pennsylvania batteries, the New Hampshire Ninth and Rhode Island Fifth,—thirty pieces bearing on the cornfield and the wood-crowned hill, where, alas! a thousand of as brave men as ever breathed were lying, who just before had moved to meet the enemy.

The firing was hot and heavy a few rods south.

The fight began with the pickets in the night, and was taken up by the artillery at daylight. The Rebels had concentrated a heavy force on their left, we on our right, because the lay of the land required it, the right being our strongest ground, and their left their weakest. The ridge behind Poffenberg's house was the door-post on which our fortunes hinged. Not so with them,—theirs was a double door, its hinge being in the woods bordering the turnpike south of the toll-house.

Hooker gave Meade, with the Pennsylvania Reserves, the right, Ricketts the left, and placed Doubleday in support in rear. Mansfield joined Hooker's left, but was an hour behind time. Sumner was slow to come into action. Hooker advanced, drove in the Rebel pickets, found a Rebel battery on his extreme right, which, as soon as he came within its range began to plough him with a flanking fire.

Meade obliqued to the right, poured in a few volleys, and drove the enemy across the turnpike. This was the extreme left of the enemy's line. Hooker crossed the turnpike a few rods north of Poffenberg's, marched through the fields to the ridge by the cornfield. Having obtained possession of the ridge east of Poffenberg's, he planted his batteries and opened a fierce cannonade upon the Rebels.

The ground in front of Hooker was the scene of repeated struggles. In the afternoon the Rebels made a desperate attempt to regain what they had lost. They came down through the cornfield, west of the turnpike, under cover of their batteries. Hooker, Dana, Sedgwick, Hartsuff, Richardson, and Mansfield, all general officers, had been carried from the field wounded. General Howard was in command of the right wing. I was talking with him, when an officer dashed up and said, "General, the Rebels are coming down on us."

We were in the open field, a few rods southeast of Poffenberg's barn. General Howard rode forward a few steps, looked through the leafy branches of the oaks along the turnpike. We could see the dark lines of the enemy moving through the cornfield. "Tell the batteries to give them the heaviest fire possible," he said. It was spoken as deliberately as if he had said to his servant, "Bring me a glass of water." How those thirty pieces of artillery opened! Crack! crack! crack! and then a volley by artillery! How those gray lines wavered, swayed to and fro, and melted away!

In Poffenberg's door-yard, along the turnpike, were two noble horses, both killed by the same cannon-shot, smashing the head of one and tearing the neck of the other. The dead of the Pennsylvania Reserves laid under the palings of the garden fence. The gable of the house was torn to pieces by a shell. In the field in front dead men in blue and dead men in gray were thickly strewn; and still farther out, along the narrow lane which runs southwest from the house, they were as thick as the withered leaves in autumn. How the battle-storm howled through those woods, fiercer than the blasts of November! It was a tornado which wrenched off the trunks of oaks large enough for a ship's keelson,—riving them, splintering them with the force of a thunderbolt.

If the blow which Hooker gave had been a little more powerful,—if Mansfield had been ordered in at the same instant with Hooker,—if Sumner had fallen upon the Rebel centre at the same time,—there can be but little doubt as to what would have been the result. But the battle of Antietam was fought by piecemeal. Hooker exhausted his strength before Mansfield came up; Mansfield was repulsed before Sumner came in; while Burnside, who had the most difficult task of all, was censured by McClellan for not carrying the bridge early in the morning. Yet Franklin, who arrived at noon, was only partially engaged, while Porter was ordered to stand a silent spectator through the day. The several corps of the Union army were like untrained teams of horses,—each pulled with all its strength, but no two succeeded in pulling together.

It was not far from twelve o'clock when the arrangements were completed for Sumner's movement. The artillery prepared the way for advance, by pouring in a heavy fire from all directions. The configuration of the ground admitted of this. The cornfield sloped toward the Antietam, and by careful scrutiny the Rebels could be seen lying down to avoid the shot and shells. It was a moment of anxious expectation to us who beheld the movement.

The divisions moved past the cemetery, past Roulet's house, the left of French's and the right of Richardson's, joining in the ravine. A few rods beyond the house the Rebel skirmishers opened a galling fire. Our own advanced rapidly, drove them in through the nearest cornfield. They fled to the road, and the field beyond.

The road is narrow, and by long usage and heavy rains, has become a trench, a natural rifle-pit about two and a half feet deep. The Rebels had thrown off the top rails of the fence in front, and strengthened the position by making them into *abatti*,—imitating the example set by General Stark on the north-eastern slope of Bunker Hill, in 1775.

The roadway was their first line; their second was in the corn, five or six rods farther west.

The Union troops advanced in front of the road, when up rose the first Rebel line. The fence became a line of flame and smoke. The cornfield beyond, on higher ground, was a sheet of fire. With a rush and cheer, the men in blue moved up to the fence, ploughed through and through by the batteries above, cut and gashed by the leaden hail, thrust the muzzles of their guns into the faces of the Rebels and fired.

The first Rebel line was nearly annihilated, and the dead lying beneath the tasselled corn were almost as many as the golden ears upon the stalks. Visiting the spot when the contest was over, I judged from a little counting that a thousand of the enemy's dead were in the road and the adjoining field. A shell had thrown seven into one heap,—some on their faces, some on their backs,—fallen as a handful of straws would fall when dropped upon the ground. But not they alone suffered. The bloody tide which had surged through all the morning between the ridges above, along the right, had flowed over the hill at this noontide hour. The yellow soil became crimson; the russet corn-leaves turned to

THE SUNKEN ROAD

red, as if autumn had put on in a moment her richest glory. How costly! Five thousand men,—I think I do not exaggerate,—wounded and dead, lay along that pathway and in the adjoining field![6]

To Burnside was assigned the duty of carrying the stone bridge, two miles below the turnpike, and taking the batteries which were in position south of Sharpsburg. It was a difficult task. A high-banked stream, bordered by willows; a narrow bridge; a steep hill; cleared lands, with no shelter from the batteries in front and on both his flanks, after he should have succeeded in crossing the stream.

Burnside planted his cannon on the high hills or ridges east of the river, and kept them in play a long time before any attempt was made on the bridge by infantry. The Rebel batteries replied, and there was an incessant storm of shot and shell.

The road on the eastern side winds down a ravine to the river, which is an hundred feet below the summit of the hills where his artillery was posted. It is a narrow path, with a natural embankment on the right hand, covered with oaks. There is a piece of bottom land eight or ten rods wide on the eastern side of the river. The bridge is narrow and about seventy-five feet long. After crossing the stream the road runs diagonally up the bank toward the north. On the western side are willows fringing the stream, their graceful branches bending down to the water, and covering the opposite shore. The bank is very abrupt. A small force on either side can hold the bridge against a large body of men.

The bridge was carried in the afternoon by a desperate charge. I was watching operations in the centre at the time, and saw only the smoke of the contest on the left, and heard its deafening roar. Riding down there later in the day, I witnessed the last attack. Both parties had put on new vigour at the sunset hour. The fire kindled along the line. Far upon the right was the smoke of thirty cannon, rising in a white sulphurous cloud. The woods opposite, where the Rebel batteries were, flamed like a furnace. A little nearer Sumner's artillery was thundering and hurling its bolts into the Rebels by the Dunker church. Ayers's battery was pouring a deadly fire into the cornfield, west of Roulet's, where the Rebel line was lying under cover. Above, on the highest hillock, a half-mile from Sharpsburg, a heavy Rebel battery boomed defiance. Richardson's artillery, immediately in front, was sending shells upon the hill and into Sharpsburg, where hay-

---

6: The illustration of the battle overleaf is an accurate representation drawn by Mr. Wand, who witnessed the battle. The battery in the foreground is north of the house of Mr. Roulet, near the centre of Sumner's line. French's and Richardson's divisions are seen in the middle of the picture, and the Rebels under D. H. Hill and Longstreet beyond.

Battle of Antietam

For the boys in blue

stacks, houses and barns were burning, rolling up tall pillars of cloud and flame to heaven. At our left Burnside's heavy guns worked mightily, answered by the opposing batteries. The musketry had ceased, save a few volleys rolling from beyond the willows in the valley, and a little dripping, like rain-drops after a shower. It was a continuous roll of thunder. The sun went down, reddened in the smoky haze.

After the retreat of Lee, I rode over the ground occupied by the Rebels, and surveyed the field from every point. The dead were thickly strewn. A Rebel battery had occupied the ground around the Dunker church, a small brick building on the turnpike, a mile south of Poffenberg's. At its door-step lay a major, a captain, and eleven men, all dead. A wounded horse, unable to lie down, was standing near a dismantled caisson. Almost human was the beseeching look of the dumb beast! Nearby was a soldier lying with his eyes fixed on heaven. He had died calmly. His pocket Bible was open upon his breast. Taking it up my eye fell upon the words: *"Though I walk through the valley of the shadow of death I will fear no evil, for thou art with me; thy rod and thy staff, they comfort me."* All the turmoil of life was over. He had done his duty, and had passed on to his reward.[7]

Lee recrossed the Potomac without molestation from McClellan, and the two armies went into camp, as if mutually agreed upon having a season of rest after the hardships of the campaign.

7: Want of space compels me to give only a sketch of the battle; but a full, circumstantial, and detailed account of the positions and movements of the two armies may be found in "Following the Flag," published by Messrs. Ticknor and Fields of Boston.

CHAPTER 9

Invasion of Kentucky

OCTOBER, 1862

Simultaneous with Lee's advance into Maryland was that of General Bragg into Kentucky. As there were no indications that McClellan would follow Lee into Virginia, I hastened to Kentucky to observe the events transpiring in that department. General Buell was still in command of the Union forces. He had been lying quiet through the summer, occupying Chattanooga on the east, Florence on the west, and spreading his troops over a large territory. There were detachments at Nashville, McMinnville, Murfreesboro, and Mumfordville. This force in Tennessee was piled in the form of a pyramid, Florence and Chattanooga being the base and Nashville the apex. In addition there was a force under General Morgan holding Cumberland Gap, a passage in the mountains at the extreme south-western part of Virginia, where the Old Dominion rests like the point of a ploughshare against the mountains which separate it from Kentucky. Since Daniel Boone passed through it, the Gap has been the great thoroughfare between the West and East. The distance from the Gap, where Morgan was keeping watch and ward, to Chattanooga, is about one hundred and forty miles. Through this gateway the Rebels resolved to enter Kentucky, replenish their stores, make a demonstration upon Cincinnati, capture Louisville, cut off Buell's supplies and communications, outflank him, destroy his army, transfer the war to the Ohio River, and redeem Kentucky. Buell was in repose, unconscious of General Bragg's intentions.

Bragg formed his army in three columns near Knoxville,—one to move upon the Gap, approaching it from the west, the second, under Kirby Smith, to move directly upon Lexington, Danville, and Frankfort, the third to capture the six thousand at Mumfordville, and then joining the second division at Lexington, push on in conjunction with it to Louisville. John Morgan, the commander of the Rebel cavalry, moved in advance and captured Morgan's supply trains on the 17th of August. It was the first intimation General Morgan or Buell had of the intentions of the Rebels. Morgan knew not what was going on in his rear. The Rebels prudently refrained from attacking him. The pass would fall into their hands when all their plans were ripe. Morgan held his position till the 17th of September, when, having exhausted his provisions, he spiked his guns, destroyed the fortifications, and all his tent equipage, and marched north to the Ohio River, through the mountains, reaching it without loss.

The centre column of the Rebels moved upon Frankfort, gathering up cattle, horses, goods of all kinds, cloth, clothes, boots, shoes, grain, and everything which could minister to their comfort. They visited the wealthy farmers of the bluegrass region, selected the best Kentucky stock, purchased all the new wheat, set the flour-mills a humming, keeping the millers at it day and night. Never were millers so busy, each miller tending his grinding with a Rebel bayonet at his door, the glittering of which reminded him that he had a duty to perform to the Confederacy.

At Frankfort, the capital of the State, they took possession of the state-house, inaugurated a governor, had a grand procession, with speeches, and a banquet, and a general gala-day. They invited the merchants to open their stores, made princely purchases of goods, paying liberally in the legal currency of the Confederacy. They sent off long lines of wagons toward the South laden with supplies. The Kentucky farmers were relieved of their negroes as well as of their horses. They *took* the negroes, saying to their masters, "Swear allegiance to the Confederacy and you shall be paid, but otherwise they shall be confiscated."

Thousands of slaves fled across the Ohio, for fear of being captured. Thus the war was a double reverse acting mill, grinding slavery to powder in the State. For six weeks the Rebels had it all their own way.

The third column moved upon Mumfordville, surprised the six thousand men in that place, and pushed on towards Louisville. The Rebel forces were far on their way before Buell awoke from his dreaming. He gathered in his divisions, and keeping west of Bragg, made haste to reach Louisville. If after taking Mumfordville Bragg had pushed on rapidly, he doubtless could have taken Louisville, but waiting a day, the golden opportunity was lost. He was evidently well pleased with his reception at Lexington and Frankfort. A Rebel writer thus describes the former:

> The entrance of our troops into Lexington was the occasion of the most inspiring and touching scenes. Streets, windows, and gardens were filled with ladies and little girls with streamers of red and blue ribbons and flags with stars. Beautiful women seized the hard brown hands of our rough and ragged soldiers, and with tears and smiles thanked them again and again for coming into Kentucky and freeing them from the presence and insults of the hated and insolent Yankees. For hours the enthusiasm of the people was unbounded. At every corner of the streets baskets of provisions and buckets of water were placed for the refreshment of our weary soldiers, and hundreds of our men were presented with shoes and hats and coats and tobacco by the grateful people. Private residences were turned for the time into public houses of entertainment, free to all who could be persuaded to go and eat. But if the reception of the infantry was enthusiastic, the tears, the smiles, and shouts and cheers of wild delight which greeted General John Morgan's cavalry, as they came dashing through the streets amidst clouds of dust, was without a parallel. The wildest joy ruled the hours. The bells of the city pealed forth their joyous welcome, whilst the waving of thousands of white handkerchiefs and tiny confederate flags attested the gladness and delight of every heart.[8]

There were also gay times in Frankfort. Mr. Harris was inaugurated Provisional Governor of the State by special order of General Bragg, which read as follows:

> Headquarters Army of Kentucky
> Lexington
> October 2, 1862
> Installation of the Provisional Governor at Frankfort on Saturday, October 4th, at 12 M. Major-General Smith is charged with the management of the military escort, guard, and salute.
>
> The Governor will be escorted from his quarters by a squadron of cavalry, and accompanied by the Commander of the Confederate State forces, Major-General Buckner, Brigadier-General Preston, and their respective staffs. The Commanding

---

8: Pollard's *Second Year of the War*, p. 152.

General will present the Governor to the people, and transfer in behalf of the Confederate States the civil orders of the State, and public records and property.

By order

Braxton Bragg

General Commanding

A host of generals graced the occasion,—Bragg, Kirby Smith, Buckner, Stevenson, Claiborne, Heath, Churchill, Preston Smith, and William Preston. The Capital Hotel, where the politics of the country were wont to be discussed by Henry Clay, Crittenden, and other great lights of former days, was crowded by the chivalry of the South. The landlord found his larder depleting, his liquors disappearing, but he had baskets full of Confederate notes, in exchange for food, fire, and lodging, liquors and cigars. The ladies kept open house, and invited the Rebel officers to tea on the auspicious occasion.

Meanwhile General Dumont's division of Union troops, and General Sill's division were approaching Frankfort from the north. General Bragg was dining with the accomplished Mrs. Preston, when a messenger dashed into town with the intelligence of the advance of the Union troops. Governor Harris,—six hours a Governor,—packed his carpet-bag in great haste. The brilliant throng of Rebel officers mounted their horses, the ladies took down their miniature flags, while the citizens of the place prepared to change their politics. The Rebel force in the town consisted of two regiments of infantry and one of cavalry, guarding the turnpike bridge across the Kentucky river.

The Union cavalry came thundering down the hill. It was in the evening; and without halting to ascertain who or what they were to encounter, dashed across the bridge. The Rebels gave one irresolute volley and fled precipitately from the town, which was once more and for a finality in the hands of the Union men. Four days later the battle of Perryville was fought, and then the Rebels retired from the State with their booty.

Their visit was at once a curse and a blessing,—a curse, because of the havoc, the desolation, and pillage; a blessing, because it brought Kentuckians to a sharp corner. The President had just issued his Proclamation of freedom, and Kentucky slaveholders were grumbling, and were ready to shake hands with the Rebels. They had welcomed their Southern friends, who had robbed and plundered them without stint.

There was a marked change visible in the opinions of most men. The high-handed outrages, the authorized thieving, the forcing of

Confederate notes upon the people, making it treason to refuse them in exchange for horses, cattle, clothes, and provisions, the confiscation of negroes, the grotesque appearance of the Rebel soldiers,—

Some in rags, some in tags,
But none in velvet gowns,

as reads the old nursery rhyme, dissipated the illusion in which many men had indulged. Bunyan's two pilgrims, Christian and Faithful, met a black man clothed in white garments, as they journeyed over the enchanted ground, who, with many fair speeches, would have turned them from the glittering gates of the golden city; but when the robe dropped from his limbs they saw that he was hideous, and that to follow him was to go back again to the city of Destruction. So Kentucky had seen the flatterer. The white robe had fallen; he was repulsive. Ladies who wished to welcome the Rebels as soldiers of the chivalrous South shrank with horror from the filthy crowd. The enchantment was ended. Loyalty was taking root.

Yet there were many old planters, partisans of an effete party,—once Democratic in principle,—who clung to slavery with a tenacity like that of barnacles to a worm-eaten hulk. The *Louisville Journal* condemned the Proclamation, giving utterance to the voice of the slaveholders, declaring that the Proclamation would have no binding force in that State; but the soldiers hailed it with joy. They felt that slavery was the cause of the war, and were longing to see it overthrown. Bragg having left the State, many masters began to look up their slaves, some of whom had fled to the Union lines for protection.

One wing of the army was resting at Williamstown, about twenty-five miles south of Cincinnati, in which was a division commanded by General Q. A. Gillmore; then a brigadier who, in common with many other officers, believed in what was called the "Kentucky policy." When the army began a forward movement in pursuit of Bragg, General Gillmore issued an order, known as General Order No. 5, which reads as follows:

> All contrabands, except officers' servants, will be left behind when the army moves tomorrow morning. Public transportation will in no case be furnished to officers' servants.
>
> Commanders of regiments and detachments will see this order promptly enforced.

Among the regiments of the division was the Twenty-Second Wisconsin, Colonel Utley, an officer who had no sympathy with slavery.

He had a cool head and a good deal of nerve. He had read the Proclamation of President Lincoln, and made up his mind to do what was right, recognizing the President as his Commander-in-Chief, and not the State of Kentucky. There were negroes accompanying his regiment, and he did not see fit to turn them out. Three days later he received the following note:

> October 18, 1862
> *Colonel*:
> You will at once send to my head-quarters the four contrabands, John, Abe, George, and Dick, known to belong to good and loyal citizens. They are in your regiment, or were this morning.
> Your obedient servant,
> Q. A. Gillmore
> Brigadier-General

Colonel Utley, instead of sending the men, replied:

> Permit me to say, that I recognize your authority to command me in all military matters pertaining to the military movements of the army. I do not look upon this as belonging to that department. I recognize no authority on the subject of delivering up contrabands save that of the President of the United States.
>
> You are, no doubt, conversant with that Proclamation, dated September 22, 1862, and the law of Congress on the subject. In conclusion, I will say, that I had nothing to do with their coming into camp, and shall have nothing to do with sending them out.

The note was despatched to division head-quarters. Soon after an officer called upon Colonel Utley.

"You are wanted, sir, at General Gillmore's quarters."

Colonel Utley made his appearance before General Gillmore.

"I sent you an order this evening."

"Yes, sir, and I refused to obey it."

"I intend to be obeyed, sir. I shall settle this matter at once. I shall repeat the order in the morning."

"General, to save you the trouble and folly of such a course, let me say that I shall not obey it."

The Colonel departed. Morning came, but brought no order for the delivery of the contrabands to their former owner.

As the regiment passed through Georgetown, a large number of slaves belonging to citizens of that place fled from their masters, and found shelter in the army. Some of the officers who had less nerve than Colonel Utley gave them up, or permitted the owners to come and take them. A Michigan regiment marching through the town had its lines entered by armed citizens, who forcibly took away their slaves. Colonel Utley informed the inhabitants that any attempt to take contrabands from his lines would be resisted.

"Let me say to you, gentlemen," he said to a delegation of the citizens, "that my men will march with loaded muskets, and if any attempt is made upon my regiment, I shall sweep your streets with fire, and close the history of Georgetown. If you seriously intend any such business, I advise you to remove the women and children."

The regiment marched the next morning with loaded muskets. The citizens beheld their negroes sheltered and protected by a forest of gleaming bayonets, and wisely concluded not to attempt the recovery of the uncertain property.

The day after its arrival in Nicholasville, a large, portly gentleman, lying back in an elegant carriage, rode up to the camp, and making his appearance before the Colonel, introduced himself as Judge Robertson, Chief Justice of the State of Kentucky.

"I am in pursuit of one of my boys, who I understand is in this regiment," he said.

"You mean one of your slaves, I presume?"

"Yes, sir. Here is an order from the General, which you will see directs that I may be permitted to enter the lines and get the boy," said the Judge, with great dignity.

"I do not permit any civilian to enter my lines for any such purpose," said the Colonel.

The Judge sat down, not greatly astonished, for the reputation of the Twenty-Second Wisconsin, as an abolition regiment, was well established. He began to argue the matter. He talked of the compromises of the Constitution, and proceeded to say:—

"I was in Congress, sir, when the Missouri Compromise was adopted, and voted for it; but I am opposed to slavery, and I once wrote an essay on the subject, favouring emancipation."

"Well, sir, all that may be. If you did it from principle, it was commendable; but your mission here today gives the lie to your professions. I don't permit negro-hunters to go through my regiment; but I will see if I can find the boy, and if he is willing to go I will not hinder him."

The Colonel went out and found the negro Joe, a poor, half-starved, undersized boy, nineteen years old. He told his story. He belonged to

Slaves fleeing to the army for protection

the Judge, who had let him to a brutal Irish man for $50 a year. He had been kicked and cuffed, starved and whipped, till he could stand it no longer. He went to the Judge and complained, but had been sent back only to receive a worse thrashing for daring to complain. At last he took to the woods, lived on walnuts, green corn, and apples, sleeping among the corn-shucks and wheat-stacks till the army came. There were tears in Joe's eyes as he rehearsed his sufferings.

The Colonel went back to the Judge.

"Have you found him?"

"I have found a little yellow boy, who says that he belongs to a man in Lexington. Come and see him."

"This man claims you as his property, Joe; he says that you ran away and left him," said the Colonel.

"Yes, sah, I belongs to him," said Joe, who told his story again in a plain, straightforward manner, showing a neck scarred and cut by the whip.

"You can talk with Joe, sir, if you wish," said the Colonel.

"Have not I always treated you well?" the Judge asked.

"No, massa, you hasn't," was the square, plump reply.

"How so?"

"When I came to you and told you I couldn't stand it any longer, you said, 'Go back, you dog!'"

"Did not I tell you that I would take you away?"

"Yes, massa, but you never did it."

The soldiers came round and listened. Joe saw that they were friends. The Judge stood speechless a moment.

"Joe," said the Colonel, "are you willing to go home with your master?"

"No, sah, I isn't."

"Judge Robertson, I don't think you can get that boy. If you think you can, there he is, try it. I shall have nothing to do with it," said the Colonel, casting a significant glance around to the soldiers who had gathered about them.

The Judge saw that he could not lay hands upon Joe. "I'll see whether there is any virtue in the laws of Kentucky," he said, with great emphasis.

"Perhaps, Judge, it will be as well for you to leave the camp. Some of my men are a little excitable on the subject of slavery."

"You are a set of nigger-stealers," said the Judge, losing his temper.

"Allow me to say, Judge, that it does not become you to call us nigger-stealers. You talk about nigger-stealing,—you who live on the sweat and blood of such creatures as Joe! Your dwellings, your churches, are built from the earnings of slaves, beaten out of them by brutal overseers. You hire little children out to brutes,—you clothe them in rags,—you hunt them with hounds,—you chain them down to toil and suffering! You call us thieves because we have given your Joe food and protection! Sir, I would rather be in the place of Joe than in that of his oppressor!" was the indignant outburst of the Colonel.

"Well, sir, if that is the way you men of the North feel, the Union never can be saved,—never! You must give up our property."

"Judge, allow me to tell you what sort of Unionism I have found in Kentucky. I have not seen a half-dozen who did not damn the President. You may put all the pure Unionism in Kentucky in one scale, and a ten-pound nigger baby in the other, and the Unionism will kick the beam. Allow me to say, further, that if the perpetuity or restoration of the Union depends upon my delivering to you with my own hands that little half-starved dwarf of a slave, the Union may be cast into hell with all the nations that forget God!"

"The President's Proclamation is unconstitutional. It has no bearing on Kentucky. I see that it is your deliberate intention to set at naught the laws," said the Judge, turning away, and walking to General Gillmore's head-quarters.

"You are wanted at the General's head-quarters," said an aid, soon after, to Colonel Utley.

The Colonel obeyed the summons, and found there not only Judge Robertson, but several fine old Kentucky gentlemen; also Colonel Coburn, the commander of the brigade, who agreed with General Gillmore in the policy then current. Colonel Coburn said:

"The policy of the commanding generals, as I understand it, is simply this: that persons who have lost slaves have a right to hunt for them anywhere in the State. If a slave gets inside of the lines of a regiment, the owner has a right to enter those lines, just as if no regiment was there, and take away the fugitive at his own pleasure."

"Precisely so. The Proclamation has no force in this State," said the Judge.

"I regret that I am under the necessity of differing in opinion from my commanding officers, to whom I am ready at all times to render strict *military* obedience, but (the Colonel raised his voice) *I reverse the Kentucky policy!* I hold that the regiment stands precisely as though there were no slavery in Kentucky. We came here as free men, from a free State, at the call of the President to uphold a free government.

We have nothing to do with slavery. The Twenty-Second Wisconsin, while I have the honour to command it, will never be a regiment of nigger-catchers. I will not allow civilians to enter my lines at pleasure; it is unmilitary. Were I to permit it, I should be justly amenable to a court-martial. Were I to do it, spies might enter my lines at all times and depart at pleasure."

There was silence. But Judge Robertson was loath to go away without his flesh and blood. He made one more effort. "Colonel, I did not come to your lines as a spy, but with an order from your General. Are you willing that I should go and get my boy?"

The Colonel reflected a moment.

"Yes, sir, and I will remain here. I told you before that I should have nothing to do with it."

"Do you think that the men will permit me to take him?"

"I have no orders to issue to them in the matter; they will do just as they please."

"Will you send the boy into some other regiment?"

This was too much for the Colonel. He could no longer restrain his indignation. Looking the Judge squarely in the face, he vented his anger in scathing words.

The Judge departed, and at the next session of the Court Colonel Utley was indicted for man-stealing; but he has not yet been brought to trial. The case is postponed till the day of Judgment, when a righteous verdict will be rendered.

The Judge returned to Lexington, called a public meeting, at which he made a speech, denouncing the Twenty-Second Wisconsin as an abolition regiment, and introducing resolutions declaring that the Union never could be restored if the laws of the State of Kentucky were thus set at defiance. This from the Judge, while his son was in the Rebel service, fighting against the Union.

But the matter was not yet over. A few days later, the division containing the Twenty-Second Wisconsin, commanded by General Baird, *vice* Gillmore, was ordered down the river. It went to Louisville, followed by the slave-hunters, who were determined to have their negroes.

Orders were issued to the colonels not to take any contrabands on board the boats, and most of them obeyed. Colonel Utley issued no orders.

A citizen called upon him and said,—

"Colonel, you will have trouble in going through the city unless you give up the negroes in your lines."

The regiment was then on its march to the wharf.

"They have taken all the negroes from the ranks of the other regiments, and they intend to take yours."

The Colonel turned to his men and said, quietly, "Fix bayonets."

The regiment moved on through the streets, and reached the Gault House, where the slaveholders had congregated. A half-dozen approached the regiment rather cautiously, but one bolder than the rest sprang into the ranks and seized a negro by the collar.

A dozen bayonets came down around him, some not very gently. He let go his hold and sprang back again quite as quickly as he entered the lines. There was a shaking of fists and muttered curses, but the regiment passed on to the landing, just as if nothing had happened.

General Granger, who had charge of the transportation, had issued orders that no negro should be allowed on the boats without free papers.

General Baird saw the negroes on the steamer, and approaching Colonel Utley, said,—

"Why, Colonel, how is this? Have all of these negroes free papers?"

"Perhaps not all, but those who haven't, *have declared their intentions!*" said the Colonel.

The Twenty-Second took transportation on the steamer *Commercial*. The captain of the boat was a Kentuckian, who came to Colonel Utley in great trepidation, saying: "Colonel, I can't start till those negroes are put on shore. I shall be held responsible. My boat will be seized and libelled under the laws of the State."

"I can't help that, sir; the boat is under the control and in the employ of the government. I am commander on board, and you have nothing to do but to steam up and go where you are directed. Otherwise I shall be under the necessity of arresting you."

The captain departed and began his preparations. But now came the sheriff of Jefferson County with a writ. He wanted the bodies of George, Abraham, John, and Dick, who were still with the Twenty-Second. They were the runaway property of a fellow named Hogan, who a few days before had figured in a convention held at Frankfort, in which he introduced a series of Secession resolutions.

"I have a writ for your arrest, but I am willing to waive all action on condition of your giving up the fugitives which you are harbouring contrary to the peace and dignity of the State," said the sheriff.

"I have other business to attend to just now. I am under orders from my superiors in command to proceed down the river without any delay, and must get the boat under way," said the Colonel, bowing, politely.

"But, Colonel, you are aware of the consequences of deliberately setting at defiance the laws of a sovereign State," said the sheriff.

"Are you all ready there?" said the Colonel, not to the sheriff, but to the officer of the day who had charge of affairs.

"Yes, sir."

"Then cast off."

The game of bluff had been played between the Twenty-Second Wisconsin and the State of Kentucky, and Wisconsin had won.

The sheriff jumped ashore. There were hoarse puffs from the steam-pipes, the great wheels turned in the stream, the *Commercial* swung from her moorings, and the soldiers of Wisconsin floated down the broad Ohio with the stars and stripes waving above them.

By their devotion to principle, by the firmness of their commander, they had given the cause of Freedom a mighty uplift in the old State of Kentucky.

I recall an evening in the Louisville Hotel. Officers of the army,— majors, captains, lieutenants,—were there from camp, chatting with the ladies. It was a pleasant company,—an hour of comfort and pleasure. The evening was chilly, and a coal-fire in the grate sent out its genial warmth. The cut glass of the chandeliers sparkled with ruby, purple, and amethyst in the changing light. In the anterooms there were chess-players absorbed in the intellectual game, with a knot of silent spectators.

At the dinner-table Mr. Brown was my servant. His complexion was a shade darker than mine. He served me faithfully, wearing a white cotton jacket and apron. He entered the parlour in the evening, not wearing his hotel uniform, but faultlessly dressed as a gentleman. He brought not a lady, but a double-bass viol. He was followed by two fellow-servants, one with a violin, the other with a banjo. The one with the violin was a short, thick-set, curly-headed African,—black as the King of Dahomey. The other was whiter than most of the officers in the room.

They were the hotel table-waiters and also a quadrille band. The violinist did not know B flat from F sharp. Musical notation was Greek to him; but he had rhythm, a quick, tuneful ear, and an appreciation of the beautiful in music rarely found among the many thousands who take lessons by the quarter. He did not give us *Old Tar River, Uncle Ned*, and *O Susannah*, but themes from Labitsky and Donizetti,—melodies which once heard are long remembered. His two comrades accompanied him in time and tune. For the young ladies and officers it was a delightful hour. Mr. Brown was the factotum, calling the changes with as much steadiness and precision, while handling the double-bass, as Hall or Dodworth at the grand ball to the Prince of Wales. So we were served by four thousand dollars' worth of body and soul!

The doorway leading into the hall was a portrait-gallery of dusky faces,—Dinah, Julia, Sam, and James; old aunt Rebecca, with a yellow turban on her head; young Sarah, three feet high, bare-legged, bare-armed, in a torn, greasy calico dress,—her only garment; young Toney, who had so much India-rubber in his heels that he capered irrepressibly through the hall and executed a double-shuffle. While the grand stairway, leading to the halls above was piled with dark, eager faces, reminding one of the crowded auditory looking upon Belshazzar's feast in the great picture of Allston,—fifteen, twenty, thirty thousand dollars' worth of bones, blood, and brains!

The violinist was in trouble. The screws would not stick, and in spite of his spitting in the holes, his twisting and turning, he was obliged to stop in the middle of the dance. He made strenuous efforts to keep his instrument in tune. A man in shoulder-straps, leading a fair-haired, graceful maiden, his partner in the dance, with a clenched fist and an oath informed the musician that if he didn't fix that quick he would knock his head off! It was a little glimpse of the divine, beneficent missionary institution ordained of God for the elevation of the sons of Ham!

It was not difficult to make a transition in thought to a South Carolina rice-swamp or Louisiana sugar-plantation or Arkansas cotton-field, where a master's passion was law, and where knocking off men's heads was not so rare a performance.

Among the dusky crowd gazing in upon the waltzers was a girl, sixteen or seventeen years old,—a brunette, with cherry lips, sparkling black eyes, and cheeks as fresh and fair as apricots. She was a picture of health. She gazed with evident delight, and yet there was always upon her countenance a shade of sadness. In form and feature she was almost wholly Anglo-Saxon, and more than Anglo-Saxon in beauty.

I met her in the hall during the day having charge of a young child, and had marked her beauty, ease, grace, and intelligence, and supposed that she was a boarder at the hotel,—the daughter or young wife of some officer, till seeing her the central figure of the dusky group. Then the thought came flashing, "She is a slave!"

She could have joined in the cotillon with as much grace as any of the fair dancers.

Her father, I learned, was a high-born Kentuckian, and her grandfather was from one of the first families of Virginia; but her great-great-great-grandmother was born in Africa, and that was the reason why she stood a silent spectator in the hall, instead of whirling with the gay colonel in the dance.

Chapter 10
From Harper's Ferry to Fredericksburg

November, 1862

Returning to Virginia I accompanied the army of the Potomac in the march from Berlin and Harper's Ferry to the Rappahannock. The roads were excellent, the days mild, the air clear. Beautiful beyond description the landscape, viewed from the passes of the Blue Ridge. Westward in the valley of the Shenandoah was Longstreet's corps, traced by rising clouds of dust and the smoke of innumerable camp-fires.

Eastward was the great army of the Union, winding along the numerous roads, towards the south. Many of the soldiers had their pets,—one had two yellow dogs in leading-strings. A gray-bearded old soldier carried a young puppy with its eyes not yet open, in his arms as tenderly as if it were a child. A Connecticut boy had a little kitten on his shoulders, which kept its place contentedly. Occasionally the lad caressed it, while kitty laid its face against that of the beardless boy and purred with pleasure.

The march was tediously slow. General McClellan was averse to making it at all. He had delayed from day to day, and from week to week, till ordered by the President to advance. He had no well-considered plan of operations.

The President's patience was exhausted, and at Warrenton he was deprived of the command of the army.

General Burnside, his successor, took the command reluctantly; but he was quick in deciding upon a plan. General McClellan's line of march was towards Gordonsville. Burnside decided to move upon Fredericksburg. The movement was made with great rapidity, and

Burnside only failed of seizing the place because the pontoons were not there at the time appointed. Lee came and occupied the town, threw up his earthworks, and planted his batteries. Burnside planned to have Franklin cross the Rappahannock below Port Royal, Hooker above it, while Sumner was to cross opposite the town; but a heavy storm frustrated the movement.

It was generally supposed that the army would go into winter quarters, and many of the correspondents accordingly returned to their homes. My friend and companion in the West, Mr. Richardson, left the army of the Potomac in disgust, and proceeded West again in search of adventure. His wishes were more than gratified soon after at Vicksburg, where he fell into the hands of the Rebels, who boarded him awhile at the Libby in Richmond, and afterward at the Salisbury prison in North Carolina. He ungraciously turned his back upon his Rebel friends one night, took all his baggage, and left without paying his bills.

He gained the Union lines in Tennessee after months of imprisonment, with his desires for adventure in that direction fully satisfied.

Nearly one half of the correspondents with the various armies either fell into the hands of the Rebels or were wounded. Several died of diseases contracted in the malarious swamps. As a class they were daring, courageous, venturesome, always on the alert, making hard rides, day and night, on the battle-field often where the fire was hottest,—writing their accounts seated on a stump, spreading their blankets where night overtook them, or frequently making all-night rides after a day of excitement, hardship, and exposure, that the public might have early information of what had transpired. Their statements were often contradictory. Those first received by the public were not infrequently full of errors, and sometimes were wholly false, for the reason that many papers had a correspondent a few miles in rear of the army, at the base of supplies, who caught up every wild rumour and sent it flying over the land.

Gold speculators improved every occasion to gull the public by false news. There is reason to believe that men in high official positions were in collusion with operators in bullion, to the mutual advantage of all concerned.

The press of the country, reflecting the feelings of the people, pronounced the campaign at an end. The friends of General McClellan were clamorous for his return. Congress and political advisers in Washington demanded that Burnside should move somewhere. They knew nothing of the obstacles in his path.

December, 1862

In a letter written on the 9th of December, 1862, the following view of the situation was presented by the correspondent of the *Boston Journal*:

It is a clear, cold morning. The sky is without a cloud. Standing near General Sumner's quarters, I have a wide sweep of vision. The quarters of the veteran general commanding the right grand division are in a spacious mansion, newly constructed, the property of a wealthy planter, whose estate is somewhat shorn of its beauty by the ravages of war. The fences are all gone, the forests are fast disappearing, the fine range of cedars which lined the Belleplain road are no longer to be seen. All around are the white tents of the command, the innumerable camp-fires sending up blue columns of smoke. The air is calm. You hear the rumbling of distant baggage-trains, the clatter of hundreds of axes felling the forests for fuel,—the bugle-call of the cavalrymen, and the rat-a-plan of the drummers, and mingling with all, the steady, constant flow of the falling waters of the winding stream.

Looking far off to the southeast, across the interval of the river, you see a white cloud of steam moving beneath the fringe of a forest. It is a locomotive from Richmond, dragging its train of cars with supplies for the Rebel camps. The forests and hills beyond are alive with men. Resting my glass against the side of the building to keep it steady, I can count the men grouped around the camp-fires, turning at times to keep themselves warm. Others are bringing in wood. An officer rides along. A train of wagons is winding down the hill toward the town. All along the range of hills are earthworks with sandbag embrasures, and artillery behind,—not quaker guns, I think, but field artillery, so ranged that a movement directly across the river would be marching into the jaws of death,—as hazardous and destructive as the charge of the Light Brigade at Balaklava.

I know that there is a clamour for an onward movement, a desire and expectation for an advance; but I think there are few men in the country who, after taking a look at the Rebel positions, would like to lead in a movement across the stream.

Looking into the town of Fredericksburg we see but few smokes ascending from the chimneys, but few people in the streets. It is almost wholly deserted. The women and children have gone to Richmond, or else are shivering in camp. Close upon the river-bank on either side face the pickets, within easy talking distance of each other. There has been no shooting of late. There is constant badinage. The Rebel picket asks the Yankee when he is going to Richmond. The Yankee asks the Rebel if he don't want a pair of boots. I am sorry to say that such conversation is mixed with profane words. Each party seems to think that hard words hit hard.

Last night the southern sky was red with the blaze of Rebel camp-fires. Far off to the southeast I see a hazy cloud, and columns of smoke, indicating the presence of a large army. I do not doubt that if we attempt to cross we shall meet with terrible opposition from a force nearly if not quite as large as our own.

If the President or General Halleck insist upon Burnside's making the movement, it will be made with whatever power, energy, determination, and bravery the army can exhibit. I am as anxious as anyone can be to see a great blow given to the Rebellion; but I am not at all anxious to see the attempt made against such disadvantages as are apparent to the most casual observer from this position.[9]

It was an unreasonable demand which the public made upon Burnside. He had been just one month in command of the army. His first plan had failed through the remissness of others; his second effort to move had been made abortive by the storm. He could not attempt again the movement with any hope of success, for Lee had taken precautions against an attack upon his flank. Neither the public, the politician, nor the War Department would consent to his going into winter quarters. He had no alternative other than to devise a new plan. These considerations are to be kept in remembrance in reviewing the battle of Fredericksburg.

General Burnside obtained correct information of the position held by General Lee. Jackson's corps was separated from Longstreet's by a ravine, but General Lee had constructed a road through the woods and across a ravine, by which troops could be readily marched to the right or left, as they might be needed. He was satisfied that Lee did not expect him to cross at the town, but lower down the river. He decided, therefore, to cross the Rappahannock, and make a desperate push to obtain possession of the road, which would divide Lee's army.

9: Letter to *Boston Journal*, December 9, 1862.

FREDERICKSBURG

The plan was accepted by a council of officers on the 10th of December. Preparations wore made that night for the passage of the river in three places. The artillery was drawn in position along the bank,—about one hundred and fifty pieces, some of which were thirty-pounders. Orders were issued to the troops to be ready at a moment's warning. General Woodbury, with a brigade of engineers, was ordered down to the river.

Soon after dark on the night of the 10th, the brigade, with its long train of boats on wheels, came down from the Stafford hills. Boats sufficient for the construction of two bridges halted near the railroad; enough for two more went a third of a mile downstream, opposite the lower end of the town, while the remainder went a mile and a half farther down, almost to Mr. Bernard's house. Sumner and Hooker were to use those opposite the town, and Franklin those at Bernard's. A brigade of troops was ordered to protect the engineers in their work. The gunners stood beside their guns, ready to open fire if the Rebels opposed them. The engineers took the boats from the wagons, pushed them out over the thin ice, anchored them in the stream, and commenced laying the timbers and planks. A dense fog hung over the river, which concealed their operations, and before daybreak the bridges were nearly completed. The Seventeenth and Eighteenth Mississippi regiments of Barksdale's brigade, and the Eighth Florida, of Perry's brigade, were on picket along the river, while the Thirteenth and Twenty-First Mississippi and Third Georgia were in reserve in the town.

Lee was wary. He expected an advance of the Union army. His scouts were alert. All the commanders were ordered to be vigilant. So keeping a sharp lookout, the sentinels walked the bank through the long winter night, peering into the darkness, and listening to catch the meaning of the confused hum which floated to them across the stream.

Chapter 11

Battle of Fredericksburg

December, 1862

At five o'clock on the morning of the 11th of December two signal-guns were fired on the heights of Fredericksburg. Deep and heavy their roar, rolling along the valley, echoing from hill to hill, and rousing the sleepers of both armies. We who listened upon the Falmouth hills knew that the crossing was not a surprise, but that the Rebels were ready for battle. And now as the day dawned there came a rattling of musketry along the river. The Rebel pickets opened the fire. The gunners at the batteries were quick to respond, and sent grape and canister across the stream. The Rebel pickets at the lower bridges soon retired, and the engineers completed their work. But in the town the Mississippians took shelter in the buildings, and poured a deadly fire upon the bridge-builders. Almost every soldier who attempted to carry out a plank fell. For a while the attempt was relinquished.

"The bridge must be completed," said General Burnside.

Once more the brave engineers attempted it. The fog still hung over the river. Those who stood on the northern bank could only see the flashes of the rifles on the other shore. The gunners were obliged to fire at random, but so energetic their fire the engineers were able to carry the bridge within eighty or ninety feet of the shore, and then so deadly in turn was the fire of the Rebels that it was murder to send men out with a plank.

General Burnside stood on the *piazza* of the Phillips House, a mile from the pontoons. General Sumner and General Hooker were there. Aids and couriers came and went with messages and orders.

"My bridge is completed, and I am ready to cross," was Franklin's message at half past nine.

"You must wait till the upper bridge is completed," was the reply to Franklin.

Two hours passed. A half-dozen attempts were made to complete the upper bridge without success. Brave men not belonging to the engineers came down to the bank, surveyed the scene, and then volunteering their services, seized planks and boards, ran out upon the bridge, but only to fall before the sharpshooters concealed in the cellars of the houses not ten rods distant. Captain Brainard of the Fiftieth New York, with eleven men, volunteered to finish the nearly completed work. They went out upon the run. Five fell at one volley, and the rest returned. Captain Perkins of the same regiment led another party. He fell with a ghastly wound in his neck. Half of his men are killed or wounded. These were sacrifices of life with nothing gained. It was soul-inspiring to witness such heroic devotion, but heart-sickening to stand on the bank and see them slaughtered,—their blood turning to crimson the turbid waters of the Rappahannock.

General Burnside had no desire to injure the town, but under the usages of war he had a right to bombard it; for the Rebels had concealed themselves in the houses, making use of them to slaughter his men.

"Bring all your guns to bear upon the city and batter it down," was the order issued to General Hunt, chief of artillery. Colonel Hays had eight batteries on the right; Colonel Tompkins had eleven batteries on the right centre, opposite the upper pontoons,—some of them in the yard of Mr. Lacey's house, near the river; Colonel Tyler had seven batteries a little farther down on the left centre; while Captain De Russey had seven batteries opposite the lower pontoons. There were in all thirty-five batteries, with a total of one hundred and seventy-nine guns, all bearing upon the town. The artillerymen received the orders to prepare for action with a hurrah. They had chafed all the morning, and longed for an opportunity to avenge the death of their gallant comrades.

The hour had come. They sprang to their pieces. The fire ran from the right to the left,—from the heavy twenty-four-pounders on the heights of Falmouth to the smaller pieces on the hills where Washington passed his boyhood. The air became thick with the murky clouds. The earth shook beneath the terrific explosions of the shells, which went howling over the river, crashing into the houses, battering down walls, splintering doors, ripping up floors. Sixty solid shot and shells a minute were thrown, and the bombardment was kept up till nine thousand were fired. No hot shot were used, but the explosions set fire to a block of buildings, which added terrible grandeur to the scene.

The Rebel army stood upon the heights beyond the town and

watched the operations. Lee's Rebel artillery was silent, and the Mississippians concealed in the houses were alone participants in the contest.

The fog lifted at last and revealed the town. The streets were deserted, but the houses, the church-steeples, the stores were riddled with shot; yet no impression had been made on the Mississippians.

Burnside's artillerymen could not depress their guns sufficiently to shell them out. A working party went out upon the bridge, but one after another was killed or wounded.

The time had come for a bold movement. It was plain that the Mississippians must be driven out before the bridge could be completed, and that a party must go over in boats, charge up the hill, and rout them from their hiding-places. Who would go? Who attempt the hazardous enterprise? There were brave men standing on the bank by the Lacey House, who had watched the proceedings during the long hours. They were accustomed to hard fighting: Hall's brigade, composed of the Seventh Michigan, Nineteenth and Twentieth Massachusetts, and Forty-Second New York. They had fought at Fair Oaks, Savage Station, Glendale, Malvern, and Antietam. The Twentieth had been in all these battles, and also at Ball's Bluff.

"We will go over and clean out the Rebels," was the cry of this brigade.

"You shall have the privilege of doing so," said General Burnside.

There were not boats enough for all,—not enough for one regiment even. A portion of the Seventh Michigan was selected to go first, while the other regiments stood as a supporting force.

The men run down the winding path to the water's edge, jump into the boats, and push out into the stream. It is a moment of intense anxiety. No one knows how large the force opposing them. The Rebel sharpshooters are watching the movement from their hiding-places. They have a fair view and can pick their men. The men in the boats know it, yet they move steadily onward, steering straight across the stream, without a thought of turning back, though their comrades are falling,—some headlong into the river, others dropping into the boats. The oarsmen pull with rapid strokes. When one falls another takes his place. Two thirds the distance over,—the boats ground in shoal water. The soldiers wait for no word of command, but with a common impulse, with an ardour which stops not to count the cost, they leap into the water, wade to the shore, and charge up the bank. Some fall to rise no more, but their surviving comrades rush up the slippery slope. A loud hurrah rings out from the soldiers who watch them from the Falmouth shore. Up, up they go, facing death, firing not, intent only to get at the foe and win victory with the bayonet! They smash the windows, batter down doors, driving or capturing the foe.

Loud and hearty the cheers of the regiments upon the other shore. The men of the Nineteenth and Twentieth Massachusetts would give anything to be there. All the while the cannon are roaring, hurling solid shot and shell into the doomed city.

They leaped in the rocking shallops.
Ten offered where one could go;
And the breeze was alive with laughter
Till the boatmen began to row.

Then the shore, where the Rebels harboured,
Was fringed with a gush of flame,
And buzzing, like bees, o'er the water
The swarms of their bullets came.

Not a whisper! Each man was conscious
He stood in the sight of death;
So he bowed to the awful presence,
And treasured his living breath.

And many a brave, stout fellow,
Who sprang in the boats with mirth,
Ere they made that fatal crossing,
Was a load of lifeless earth.

But yet the boats moved onward;
Through fire and lead they drove,
With the dark, still mass within them,
And the floating stars above.

Cheer after cheer we sent them,
As only armies can,—
Cheers for old Massachusetts,
Cheers for young Michigan!

They formed in line of battle;
Not a man was out of place.
Then with levelled steel they hurled them
Straight in the Rebels' face.

'O help me, help me, comrade!
For tears my eyelids drown,
As I see their starry banners
Stream up the smoking town.'[10]

10: Boker's *Crossing at Fredericksburg*.

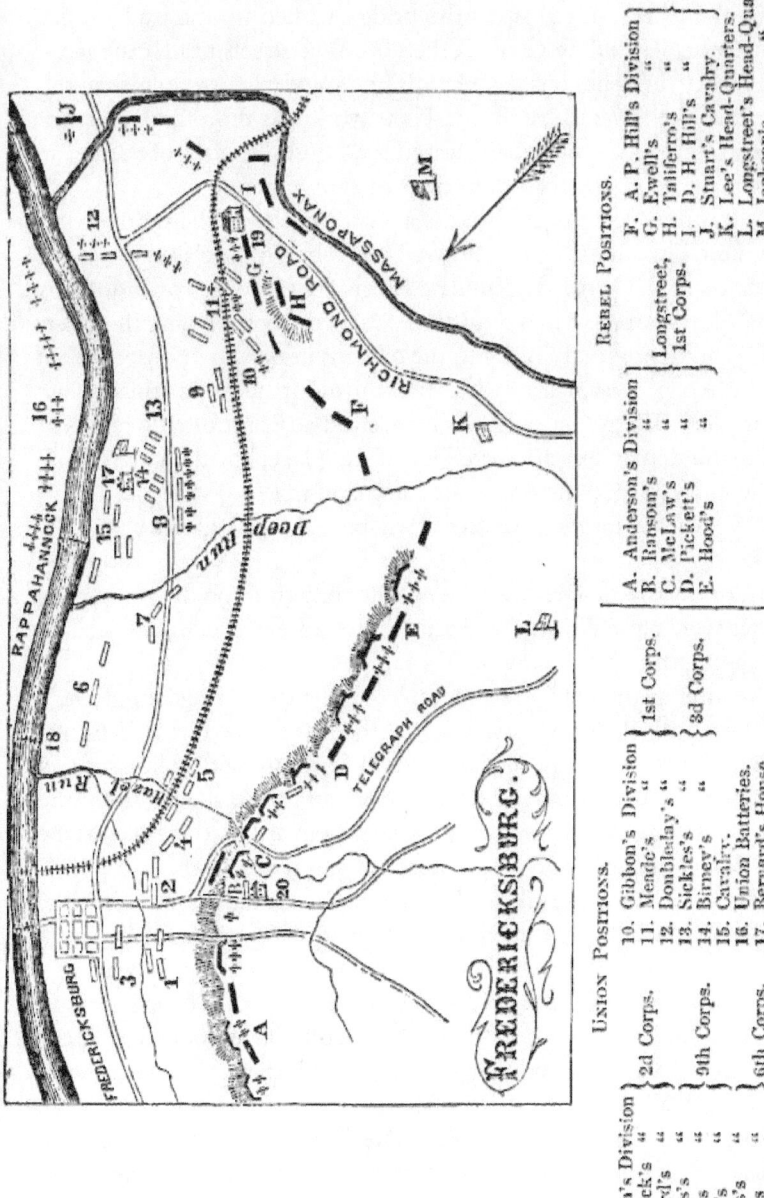

When the bridge-builders saw the soldiers charge up the hill, they too caught the enthusiasm of the moment, and finished their work. The other regiments of the brigade, before the last planks were laid, rushed down the bank, ran out upon the bridge, dashed up the bank, joined their comrades, and drove the Rebels from the streets nearest the river.

History furnishes but few records of more daring exploits than this action of the Seventh Michigan. Their work was thorough and complete. In fifteen minutes they cleared the houses in front of them, and took more prisoners than their own party numbered.

It was now half past four in the afternoon, one of the shortest days of winter. The sun was going down. The Rebels had delayed the crossing through the entire day. General Burnside was severely censured by some Northern as well as Southern papers for bombarding the town; he had no desire to do injury to the citizens in person or property, but the stubborn resistance of the Rebels made it necessary thus to use his artillery. When General Sumner arrived at Falmouth, three weeks before, he demanded the surrender of the place; but the citizens and the women begged the officer in command not to give it up.

"We would rather have the town burned than given up to the Yankees,"[11] said they.

But now the Yankees were there, marching through the streets. The houses were battered, torn, and rent. Some were in flames, and a battle was raging through the town.

As soon as the bridge was completed, the other brigades of General Howard's division moved across the river. The Rebel batteries, which till now had kept silence, opened furiously with solid shot and shell, but the troops moved steadily over, and took shelter along the river bank. The Rebels were falling back from street to street, and the men from Michigan and Massachusetts were pressing on.

I stood upon the bank of the river and watched the scene in the deepening twilight. Far up the streets there were bright flashes from the muskets of the Rebels, who fired from cellars, chamber windows, and from sheltered places. Nearer were dark masses of men in blue, who gave quick volleys as they moved steadily on, demolishing doors, crushing in windows, and searching every hiding-place. Cannon were flaming on all the hills, and the whole country was aglow with the camp fires of the two great armies. The Stafford hills were alive with men,—regiments, brigades, and divisions moving in column from their encampments to cross the river. The sky was without a cloud. The town was lighted by lurid flames. The air was full of hissings,—the sharp cut-

---

11: Richmond Examiner, December 15, 1862.

ting sounds of the leaden rain. The great twenty-pounder guns on the heights of Falmouth were roaring the while. There were shouts, hurrahs, yells, and groans from the streets. So the fight went on till the Rebels were driven wholly from the town to their entrenchments beyond.

The Seventeenth Mississippi was the most actively engaged of the Rebel regiments. Its commander, Lieutenant-Colonel Fizer, in his report, says:

> The Yankees made nine desperate attempts to finish their bridges, but were repulsed at every attempt. They used their artillery incessantly, with a heavy detachment of sharpshooters, for twelve hours, we holding our position firmly the whole time, until about half past four, p. m., when they increased their artillery and infantry, and their batteries becoming so numerous and concentrated, we could not use our rifles. Being deprived of all protection, we were compelled to fall back to Caroline Street, and from there were ordered from town. The casualties of the regiment during the engagement were one hundred and sixteen wounded, killed, and missing.[12]

When the soldiers of the Seventh Michigan leaped into the boats, a drummer-boy joined them,—Robert Henry Hendershot. He was only twelve years old, but his dark eyes flashed brightly under the excitement of the moment. His drum was upon his neck.

"Get out, you can't go," said an officer.

"I want to go," said Robert.

"No, you will get shot. Out with you."

Robert jumped into the water, but instead of going ashore, remained to push off the boat; and then, instead of letting go his hold, clung to the gunwale, and was taken across.

As the boat grounded upon the other shore, a piece of shell tore through his drum. He threw it away, seized the gun of a fallen soldier, rushed up the hill, and came upon a Rebel soldier, slightly wounded. "Surrender!" said Robert, pointing his gun at him. The Rebel gave up his gun, and Robert marched him to the rear. When he returned to the other side of the river, General Burnside saw him, and said,—

"Boy, I glory in your spunk! If you keep on in this way a few more years, you will be in my place."

His regiment, after the battle, was sent West, and Robert was in the battles of Lebanon, Murfreesboro, Chattanooga, and McMinnville, where he fought gallantly.

12: Lieutenant-Colonel Fizer's Report.

As the Rebels had used the houses for a defence, the soldiers, now that they were in possession of the town, appropriated to their own use whatever suited their fancy. Their great desire was to obtain tobacco, and the tobacco shops were first broken open. A large quantity had been thrown into the river by the Rebel authorities to prevent its falling into the hands of the Yankees; but the soldiers soon fished it up, dried it by their bivouac fires, and through the long night, while keeping watch, enjoyed their pipes at the expense of the enemy. Soldiers who did not care for tobacco helped themselves to flour, meat, potatoes, sugar, and molasses. They had a merry night cooking bacon and eggs, frying pork, making hot cakes in the kitchens. The houses were ransacked; beds, blankets, carpets, sofas, rocking-chairs, settees, and lounges were carried into the streets. Some dressed themselves in old-fashioned and antiquated clothes which they found in the chambers.

It was a carnival night. One fellow appropriated a heavy volume of Congressional documents, which he carried about several days. Another found a stuffed monkey in one of the houses, which he shouldered and bore away. One soldier had a dozen custard-cups on a string around his neck. Another, finding a nice beaver hat, threw aside his old cap and took his place again in the ranks, the sport of all his comrades, for being so nice a gentleman. It was not, however, an indiscriminate pillage of the whole town. A great many dwellings were not entered at all, and the owners, after the evacuation of the city, found their premises but little injured. In the houses nearest the river the soldiers felt that they were entitled to whatever they could lay their hands on. But those who had taken mattresses and bedding were obliged to give them up. The surgeons in charge of the hospitals seized the articles for the benefit of the wounded.

"Rev. Arthur B. Fuller is killed," said an acquaintance, as I stood upon the bank of the river. "His body is lying in the street."

He had been chaplain of the Massachusetts Sixteenth through all the Peninsula campaign, working hard day and night in the hospital, till his health had given out, and he had been honourably discharged. He had preached his last sermon on the Sunday before; but although no longer in the service, knowing that there was to be a great battle, so intense was his patriotism that he could not go away, but remained to do what he could. He took a musket, became a volunteer, and went over with the regiments.

"I must do something for my country. What shall I do?" he asked of Captain Dunn in the streets of Fredericksburg on that fatal evening.

"Now is a good time for you,—fall in on the left," said the captain, who saw that he was cool and collected, although the bullets were falling thick and fast around them. He stood in front of a grocery store, loaded his musket and fired, and then coolly loaded again. He was taking aim once more when he was shot by a sharpshooter. The Rebels advanced, and Captain Dunn was obliged to fall back. He lay where he fell till the enemy were driven from the town, when his body was recovered. The Rebels had picked his pockets. They stabbed a wounded man who was lying by his side. The soldiers of his regiment who had listened to his teachings in life came in groups to gaze with silent sorrow upon the marble brow of him who had been a faithful teacher, and who gave his life freely for his country.

At his funeral obsequies in Boston, Rev. E. O. Haven said of him:

Could he whose mangled body now lies before you, from which the deadly bullet has expelled the noble Christian's soul, rise again and speak out as he was wont to do in ringing words, they would not be apologetic, but words of exultation. Were it possible for him to be at once fallen in battle and yet alive with us, I know that he would fill our souls with his own holy enthusiasm. I know that he would make us understand and feel the magnitude of his thought and the love of his heart, when he offered to his country, in what he thought her bitterest trial, the sight of his eye and the strength of his arm, and above all the moral example of his character, won by many years' devotion to the good of his fellow-men. He offered all this to his country, and he did right. It was an overflowing love. He gave his life for liberty to all men, instead of slavery for negroes, vassalage for the great majority of the whites, and a despotism,—greatest curse of all,—for a few. He offered his life to inspire the army with noble purpose, and if need be, to inspire the nation. He knew that his life might be taken, and is not now surprised; but there comes a voice from his spirit to us saying, Waste not your sympathies in inactive sorrow, but connect the strong tide of your emotion into vigorous thought and powerful action. Weep not for me, but weep for yourselves and your children,— or see to it that they are so protected as not to need your tears.

Rev. James Freeman Clarke was his playmate in boyhood, and his friend through life, and standing by his coffin, looking for the last time upon his face, said:

Arthur Fuller was like the most of us, a lover of peace; but he saw, as we have had to see, that sometimes true peace can only come through war. In this last struggle at Fredericksburg he took a soldier's weapon, and went on with the little forlorn hope, who were leading the advance through the streets. He had not been in battle much before, but more among the sick in hospitals. Perhaps he thought it right to show the soldiers that in an hour of emergency he was ready to stand by their side. So he went with a courage and devotion which all must admire, and fell, adding his blood also to the precious blood which has been shed as an atonement for the sins of the nation. May that blood not be shed in vain. May it be accepted by God as a costly sacrifice, and may we as a people, when our necessary trials and punishments are sufficiently endured, become that righteous and happy nation God meant us to be; setting an example to mankind of a Christian republic in which there is no master and no slave, no tyrant and no victim,—not a mere rabble scrambling for gain, but brothers, co-operating in building up a grand commonwealth of true liberty, justice, and humanity. Let our friends go or stay, let us live or die,—

> *So wake we to higher aims,*
> *Of a land that has lost for a little her love of gold,*
> *And love of peace; that was full of wrongs, shames,*
> *Horrible, hateful, monstrous, not to be told,*
> *And hail once more the banner of battle unrolled!*
> *Though many an eye shall darken, and many shall weep,*
> *Yet many a darkness into light shall leap.*

To die thus, full of devotion to a noble cause, is not to die,—it is to live. It is rising into a higher life. It is passing up into the company of the true and noble, of the brave and generous,—it is going to join heroes and martyrs of all ages, who have not counted life dear when given to a good cause. Such devoted offerings by the young and brave surrendering up their lives raise us all above the fear of death. What matters it when we die, so that we live holy?—

> *They are the dead, the buried,*
> *They who do still survive,*
> *In sin and sense interred;—*
> *The dead!—they are alive!*

Foothold having been secured on the southern bank of the Rappahannock, the army began to cross. A third pontoon bridge was constructed at the lower end of the town. A thick fog hung over the river on the morning of the 12th. The air was calm, and I could distinctly hear the confused hum of preparation for the great battle. Burnside's troops were moving into position, and so were Lee's; but all the movements of both armies were concealed by the fog.

The Rebel pickets still clung to the outskirts of the town. At noon the fog disappeared, drifting up the Rappahannock. Suddenly the Rebel batteries on the hills above the town began to throw shells upon the Second Corps, which had crossed the upper bridge and was forming in the streets. Colonel Tyler, who commanded the heavy guns on the Falmouth hills, was quick to reply. The batteries in the centre opened, also those on the left. The distance from the most remote battery on the right to the farthest on the left was five miles. The Second and Ninth Corps were in the town, the front line was in the streets and the rear line along the bank of the river. Artillery trains and wagons loaded with ammunition were going over. Solid shot from the Rebel batteries tossed up the water in the river. Shells were bursting in the town.

The First and Sixth Corps, under Franklin, had crossed at the lower bridge by the house of Mr. Bernard, and were moving over the wide plain. The Bernard House, where Franklin had established his headquarters, was a fine old mansion surrounded by trees. Beyond the house there was a smooth interval, with here and there a hollow, where the troops could find shelter from the artillery-fire of the enemy.

General Stoneman was moving down from the Falmouth hills with Birney's and Sickles's divisions. Opposite Falmouth, on the Rebel left, was Longstreet's corps, with Anderson's division on Stanisbury Hill,— his pickets stationed along the canal, which winds around its base. Next to Anderson was Ransom's division, on Maryee's Hill, directly in rear of the town. Two roads run up the hill, leading west,—the Gordonsville plank-road and the Orange turnpike. Mr. Maryee's house stands between them. It is a fine brick dwelling, with a stately portico before it, with a beautiful lawn sloping towards the city, shaded by oaks and adorned with flowering shrubs. From the roof of the mansion General Longstreet can obtain a fair view of what is going on in the Union lines. He can see the troops gathering in the streets and behold the dark masses under Franklin moving out past the Bernard House.

At the base of the hill he can see some of his own soldiers, sheltered behind a stone-wall along the Old Telegraph road, which is dug like a canal into the side of the hill. It is a sheltered position, and their rifles and muskets will sweep the level field in front towards the town. His heaviest cannon and his largest howitzers are in position around Maryee's house, behind earthworks. The Washington Artillery, which was in the first battle of Manassas, and which fought through all battles of the Peninsula, at Groveton and Antietam, is there.

Ransom's division extends to Hazel Run,—a stream which comes down through a deep ravine from the west, gurgling over a rocky bed, and turning the great wheel of a grist-mill, just hid from sight as you look up the river from the town. An unfinished railroad embankment is thrown up in the run,—the Gordonsville road,—which was in construction when the war broke out. There is a hollow in the smooth field in front of the telegraph road,—a place to be kept in remembrance. There is a higher elevation beyond Maryee's house, which overlooks the town, and all the plain below, called Lee's Hill, where Lee has placed his guns of longest range.

Across the ravine is McLaw's division, behind an embankment which extends up the hill and into the woods along the Telegraph road. Beyond McLaw's is Pickett's division; then Hood's division, which forms the right of Longstreet's command, and reaches to Deep Run. Longstreet's head-quarters are in rear of Hood.

Across Deep Run are the head-quarters of Lee, who can stand by his tent and look down upon the battle-field. He can see what Couch and Wilcox are doing in the town. He is directly in front of Bernard's mansion, and can also behold all the movements of the Union troops on the plain. A. P. Hill's division of Jackson's corps is in front of him,—Hill's left resting on Deep Run, and his right reaching to Captain Hamilton's house, where the railroad crosses the old Richmond road. Hill's troops are partially concealed in the woods. Behind Hill are the divisions of Early and Taliferro,—Taliferro being on the right, near Hamilton's house. Farther in the rear, on the hill, is D. H. Hill's division, which is held in reserve. There are fourteen guns—from Pegram's, McIntosh's, Crenshaw's, Latham's, and Johnson's batteries—on the hill near Hamilton's.

Mr. Bernard has been a large slaveholder. His estate is known in the county round by the name of Mansfield. His negroes live in humble homes,—in cabins near the railroad, out towards Hamilton's. There, around the cabins, Jackson has placed twenty-one guns from Davidson's, Raines's, Caskie's, and Braxton's batteries. To the right of these, and between Bernard's and the railroad, are twelve guns,—Wooding's and Carpenter's batteries.

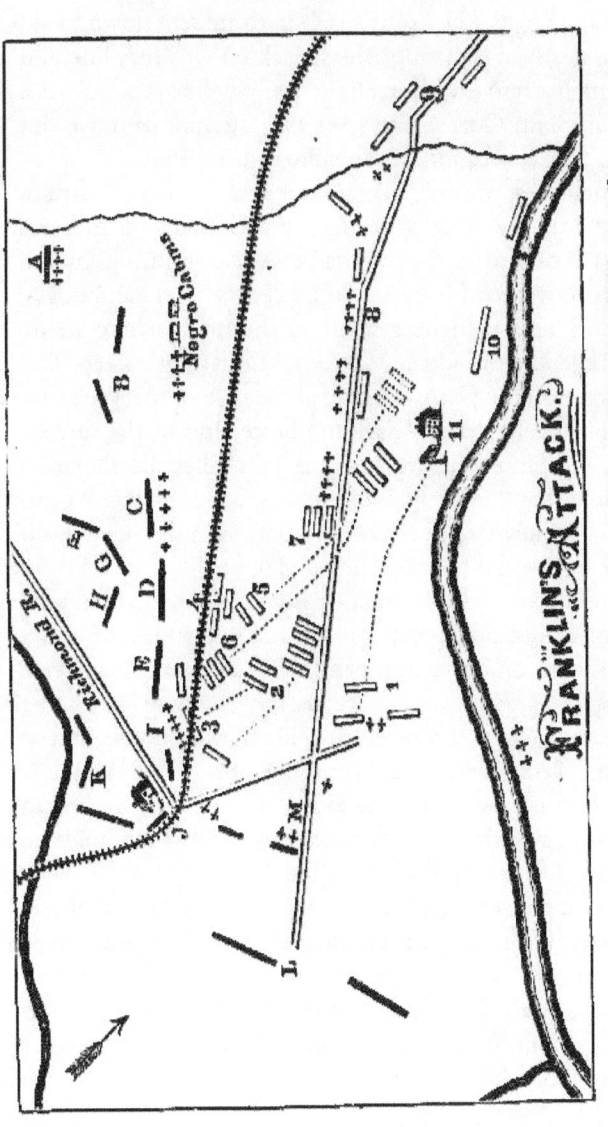

The diagram represents the position of the troops as witnessed from Franklin's Head-quarters, looking south.

UNION POSITIONS.

1. Doubleday.
2. Meade's First Position.
3. Meade's Second Position.
4. Gibbon.
5. Sickles.
6. Birney.
7. Newton.
8. Howe.
9. Brooks.
10. Burns.
11. Franklin's Head-quarters.

REBEL POSITIONS.

A. Hood.
B. Lane, Pender.
C. Thomas's Brigade.
D. Gregg's "
E. Archer's "
F., G, H. Taliferro's Division
I. Batteries.
J. Ewell's Division.
K. D. H. Hill's Division.
L. Stuart.
M. Batteries.

The road from Fredericksburg to Port Royal runs parallel to the river, about half a mile distant from the stream.

General Stuart, with two brigades of cavalry and his batteries of light artillery, hold the road. The Louisiana Guards are sent down to aid him. His line runs nearly at right angles with Jackson's infantry line, and extends from the railroad to the river. His batteries will have a cross-fire upon the First and Sixth Corps, whenever they attempt to move out from Bernard's to gain possession of the railroad at Hamilton's.

Such is the field,—a smooth plain, a mile wide and two miles long, around Bernard's, reaching up to the town. Bernard's farm is cut across by the Port Royal road, the old road to Richmond, and by the railroad. The Port Royal road is bordered by cedars, thick-set hedges, and a deep ditch. There are fences dividing the interval into fields. Deep Run is fringed with alders. Maryee's Hill is quite steep. The Rebel cannon sweep all the plain, the field at the base of Maryee's, and the town itself. The Rebel troops have the protection of the sunken road, of the rifle-pits along the crests of the hills. They are sheltered by woods, by ravines, by the hedges and fences, but Burnside has no cover for his troops. They must march out upon the plain, charge up the hillsides, and receive the fire of a sheltered foe.

To win a victory, even with a superior force, under such circumstances, there must be not only great courage and self-possession, but a well-laid plan and harmonious action of all subordinate commanders.

Burnside's plan was to make a vigorous movement with a large portion of his army to gain the railroad at Hamilton's house, and at the same time rout Longstreet from his position on Maryee's Hill. If he succeeded at Hamilton's, even if he failed at Maryee's, Lee would be compelled to evacuate the town, because Burnside would hold the railroad over which Lee received his supplies.

In the council of officers, held on the night of the 11th, General Franklin, who had about sixty thousand men, urged such a movement on the left. There was delay in issuing the orders, which gave Lee ample time to strengthen his position. The plan adopted was substantially that which Franklin had urged. These were Burnside's directions to Franklin:

> General Hardee will carry this despatch to you, and remain with you through the day. The general commanding directs that you keep your whole command in 'position' for a rapid movement down the old Richmond road; and you will send out at once a division at least, to pass below Smithfield, to seize, if

possible, the heights near Captain Hamilton's, on this side of the Massaponax, taking care to keep it well supported and its line of retreat open. He has ordered another column of a division or more to be moved from General Sumner's command, up the Plank-road to its intersection with the Telegraph road, where they will divide, with a view of seizing the heights on both those roads. Holding these heights, with the heights near Captain Hamilton's, will, he hopes, compel the enemy to evacuate the whole ridge between these points.

In a letter to General Halleck, written on the 10th, a week after the battle, General Burnside explains his plan more fully:

> The enemy had cut a road in rear of the line of heights where we made our attack, by means of which they connected the two wings of their army and avoided a long detour around through a bad country. I obtained from a coloured man information in regard to this road, which proved to be correct. I wanted to obtain possession of this road, and that was my reason for making my attack on the extreme left. I did not intend to make an attack on the right till that position was taken, which I supposed would stagger the enemy, cutting their line in two; and then I proposed to make a direct attack in front and drive them out of their works.

The day (the 12th) passed, and night came on before the army was in position to make the attack. At sunset the batteries along the lines opened fire, but the shells for the most part burst harmlessly, and the soldiers, accustomed to danger, cooked their coffee by the glimmering bivouac fires, spread their blankets on the ground, and lay down to sleep, giving no heed to the cannon's roar or the constant firing along the picket lines.

THE MORNING

The morning of the 13th dawned. A thick fog hung over the river, so dense that it was hardly possible to distinguish objects a hundred yards distant. General Sumner's head-quarters were by the house of Mr. Phillips, north of the river. General Burnside rode down from his own head-quarters, and met General Sumner and General Hooker, and other officers. He wore an anxious look, and justly, for it was the most responsible hour of his life. Up to that time all of his well-laid plans had failed. He had hoped to cross the river and surprise the Rebels, but two days had passed since the beginning of the movement, giving Lee time to strengthen his defences. Now the fog hung over the river, and he was afraid of collision between different divisions of his troops. But a password was whispered along the lines, and orders were issued to go forward.

While the troops were waiting for the advance the mails arrived. How eagerly were the letters and papers grasped by the soldiers! It was affecting to see them, as they read the words of love from home, dash the tears from their eyes. Home was dear to them just then.

The fog began to drift along the valley. It was like the drawing aside of a curtain. The entire battle-field was in view. Two signal-guns were fired in quick succession by the Rebels far down on the left in front of Franklin. There was a quick mounting of horses at Burnside's head-quarters. The officers had received their final orders, and dashed away to carry them into execution.

The main attack was to be led by Franklin. He had his own two corps, numbering forty thousand; Stoneman was moving to his support with twenty thousand, and Butterfield, with the Fifth Corps, could be called to aid him if needed.

Standing where General Tyler had planted his guns, I had a fair view of the entire battle-field. The position was below the town, near the lower bridge, on the Washington farm. Rebel officers were riding to and fro around Maryee's house. The gunners of the Washington Artillery were leaning upon their pieces, watching the movements in the town. The Second Corps had moved out from the streets past the old burying-ground, and was near the gas-works. The right of the line extended north of the Plank-road to the monument erected to the memory of Washington's mother.

General French's division of the Second Corps was on the right; General Hancock's was next in the line, with Howard's division, as reserve, in the rear. The Second Corps batteries were standing in the streets of the town, the officers vainly seeking positions where they could fire upon the Rebel batteries which looked down upon them from Maryee's Hill.

The Ninth Corps under Wilcox was joined to the Second Corps, and occupied the lower end of the town. General Sturgis's division was in front, with Whipple's, forming the second line. Burns's division was in reserve, near Deep Run. The Rebel ammunition trains were in sight far up Hazel Run, and on the distant hill there was a group of Rebel officers around Longstreet's head-quarters. Troops and teams were passing to and fro between Hood's and Pickett's divisions. Wilcox's troops were taking position, marching and countermarching, closing in solid mass under the shelter of the banks of Hazel Run. The right of the Sixth Corps, under General Smith, rested on Deep Run, Brooks's division joining Burns's west of the run, almost up to the railroad. Howe's division was next in line, where the Rebel batteries had full sweep of the broad interval. The ground is a dead level east of the run, extending from the river to the wooded hill, where Lee had established his head-quarters. Howe's troops were lying along the old Richmond road, where, beneath the cedars and sodded fences, the soldiers found shelter from the shells of the enemy. General Newton's division was on the left of Howe's, also lying under cover.

General Gibbon's division of Reynolds's corps, the First, was next in line. Meade stood next, directly in front of the railroad-crossing at Hamilton's,—the vital point, which, if seized and held, would force Lee out of his entrenchments. Meade had crossed the old Richmond road, and was facing south; Doubleday's division was on the extreme left, extending from Meade's left to the river, facing east, and standing nearly at right angles with Meade's division.

The battle was begun by General Meade, his divisions having been selected to lead the advance towards the railroad-crossing. The Bucktails, who had been in nearly all the engagements on the Peninsula, who first exhibited their valour at Drainsville, who were under Hooker at Antietam, were first engaged. They moved over the open field beyond Bernard's, and drove the enemy's skirmishers. The Rebel batteries—Latham's, Johnson's, McIntosh's, Pegram's, and Crenshaw's—opened a heavy fire. Jackson knew the importance of holding the position at Hamilton's, and had massed these batteries, which gave a concentrated fire upon the advancing force. Reynolds's batteries galloped into position and replied; and so for an hour the pounding of the batteries went on along the left.

Meade's division was composed of three brigades. The First was commanded by Colonel Sinclair, and was composed of the First Rifles (Bucktails), the First, Second, and Sixth regiments of the Pennsylvania Reserves. The Second Brigade was commanded by Colonel Magilton, and consisted of the Third, Fourth, Seventh, and Eighth regiments of the Pennsylvania Reserves, and the One Hundred and Forty-Second Pennsylvania Volunteers. The Third Brigade was commanded by General C. F. Jackson, and was composed of the Fifth, Ninth, Tenth, Eleventh, and Twelfth regiments of the Reserves. Attached to this division were four batteries of four guns each, Captain Ransom's Third United States artillery, Lieutenant Simpson's, Captain Amsden's, and Captain Cooper's of the First Pennsylvania regiment of artillery. Captain Ransom and Lieutenant Simpson had twelve-pounders, the others were three-inch rifled guns.

Sinclair's brigade was in the front line, and Magilton's three hundred paces in rear of it. Jackson's was in rear of the left of the two lines, with his men in column of regiments, about one hundred paces in rear of Magilton's line. These three brigades numbered about six thousand men.

The Attack on the Left

It was just nine o'clock when Meade moved from his position near the Bernard House.

A ravine comes down from the hills and forms the dividing line between the Bernard and Smithfield estates. As soon as Meade crossed the ravine, he turned the head of his column to the south, and moved to the Bowling Green or old Richmond road, where he was obliged to stop while the pioneers could cut away the hedges, level the sod fences, and bridge the ditches, in order that his artillery could pass. While he was doing this, Stuart's batteries opened fire. They were on Meade's left flank and enfiladed his lines, throwing shells directly up the road. Meade apprehended an immediate attack on his left flank, and swung his second brigade towards Stuart, facing east, while his first brigade was still facing south towards Hamilton's crossing. His line thus made two sides of a square. There was a little knoll on the left of the first brigade.

"That is the place for you," said Meade to Cooper and Ransom. The batteries were quickly wheeled into the position indicated. The gunners had a fair view of the Rebel batteries over the level plain. Simpson brought his battery up and placed it in front of the Third Brigade, and replied to Pegram. Such was the opening of the battle.

Meanwhile, Doubleday was pushing down by the river. When the Rebel batteries opened fire, he brought his own into position and gave a cross-fire, which was so severe that Stuart's Rockbridge battery was quickly silenced and the guns withdrawn. While this was going on, a body of Rebel sharpshooters crept up by the hedges and commenced firing; but two companies of marksmen were sent out by General Jackson's brigade, which drove them back.

An hour passed before Meade was ready to move again. Doubleday had advanced towards Stuart, but Gibbon was not yet upon Meade's right.

Stonewall Jackson, seeing that Doubleday was moving down the river, thought that it was Franklin's intention to turn his right flank. D. H. Hill's division, which was close by Hamilton's house, was sent upon the double-quick to help Stuart hold his line.[13] This weakened his centre. It was at this auspicious moment that Meade's division advanced alone to pierce the Rebel line.

It was twelve o'clock, and Franklin's force was in the following position: Doubleday on the left, well down towards Stuart, his batteries in full play; Meade thirty or forty rods beyond the Bowling Green road, in the open field; Gibbon and Newton just over the road; Howe up to it; Birney and Sickles filing out from the bridges, a mile in rear of Meade.

All of Franklin's batteries which were in position, one hundred and sixteen guns, commenced a rapid fire upon the woods beyond the railroad, to protect Meade in his advance. De Russey opened with his sixty pieces from the hills north of the Rappahannock, throwing shells over the heads of the advancing troops.

Jackson's batteries were equally active. There were twenty-one guns by the negro cabins in front of Howe, twelve in front of Newton, fourteen in front of Meade, while other single batteries under Stuart were playing on the left. More than two hundred and fifty pieces were roaring as Meade advanced.

It was a magnificent spectacle; but it was a moment of anxiety to Burnside, who could only judge of the progress of the battle by the following despatches, received from time to time.

> Headquarters
> Franklin's Grand Division
> General Burnside:
> *December 13, 7.40 a. m.* General Meade's division is to make the movement from our left; but it is just reported that the enemy's skirmishers are advancing, indicating an attack upon our position on the left.
>
> *9 o'clock a. m.* General Meade just moved out. Doubleday supports him. Meade's skirmishers engaged, however, at once with enemy's skirmishers. Battery opening, on Meade probably, from position on old Richmond road.
>
> *11 o'clock a. m.* Meade advanced half a mile, and holds on. In-

---
13: Jackson's Report.

fantry of enemy in woods in front of extreme left, also in front of Howe. No loss, so far of great importance. General Vinton badly, but not dangerously wounded.

Later.—*Reynolds has been forced to develop his whole line.*
An attack of some force of enemy's troops on our left seems probable, as far as can now be judged. *Stoneman has been directed to cross one division to support our left.* Report of cavalry pickets from the other side of the river, that enemy's troops were moving down the river on this side during the latter part of the night. Howe's pickets reported movements in their front, same direction. Still they have a strong force well posted, with batteries, there.

12 o'clock M. Birney's division is now getting into position. That done, Reynolds will order Meade to advance. Batteries over the river are to shell the enemy's position in the woods in front of Reynolds's left. He thinks the effect will be to protect Meade's advance. A column of the enemy's infantry is passing along the crest of the hills from right to left, as we look at it.

12.05 o'clock p. m. General Meade's line is advancing in the direction you prescribed this morning.

1 o'clock p. m. Enemy opened a battery on Reynolds, enfilading Meade. Reynolds has opened all his batteries on it; no report yet. Reynolds hotly engaged at this moment. Will report in a few moments again.

1.15 o'clock p. m. Heavy engagements of infantry. Enemy in force where battery is. Meade is assaulting the hill. Will report in a few minutes again.

1.25 o'clock p. m. Meade is in the woods in his front; seems to be able to hold on. Reynolds will push Gibbon in, if necessary. The battery and woods referred to must be near Hamilton's house. The infantry firing is prolonged and quite heavy. Things look well enough. Men in fine spirits.

1.40 o'clock p. m. Meade having carried a portion of the enemy's position in the woods, we have three hundred prisoners. Enemy's battery on extreme left retired. Tough work; men fight well. Gibbon has advanced to Meade's right; men fight well, driving the enemy. Meade has suffered severely. Doubleday to Meade's left,—not engaged.

2¼ o'clock p. m. Gibbon and Meade driven back from the

woods. Newton gone forward. Jackson's corps of the enemy attacks on the left. General Gibbon slightly wounded. General Bayard mortally wounded by a shell. Things do not look as well on Reynolds's front; still, we'll have new troops in soon.

2.25 o'clock p. m. Despatch received. Franklin will do his best. New troops gone in. Will report soon again.

3 o'clock p. m. Reynolds seems to be holding his own. Things look better, somewhat.

3.40 o'clock p. m. Gibbon's and Meade's divisions are badly used up, and I fear another advance on the enemy on our left cannot be made this afternoon. Doubleday's division will replace Meade's, as soon as it can be collected, and, if it be done in time, of course another attack will be made.

The enemy are in force in the woods on our left, towards Hamilton's, and are threatening the safety of that portion of our line. They seem to have detached a portion of their force to our front, where Howe and Brooks are now engaged. Brooks has some prisoners, and is down to the railroad. Just as soon as the left is safe, our forces here will be prepared for a front attack, but it may be too late this afternoon. Indeed, we are engaged in front anyhow. Notwithstanding the unpleasant items I relate, the morale generally of the troops is good.

4½ o'clock p. m. The enemy is still in force on our left and front. An attack on our batteries in front has been repulsed. A new attack has just opened on our left, but the left is safe, though it is too late to advance either to the left or front.

Such was the intelligence which reached General Burnside of the operations on the left. It was not very encouraging. He expected that Franklin, with sixty thousand men at his disposal, would sweep Jackson from his position by Hamilton's, and thus gain the rear of Lee's left flank, which would make it easy for Sumner with the right wing to break through the line in rear of the town. Instead of throwing forty thousand men upon Jackson, as he could have done, dealing a blow which might have broken the Rebel lines, Meade's division alone was sent forward. The fire of the batteries was terrific as he advanced, and so severe was the cannonade that the Rebel batteries which had been advanced from the main line were forced to retire, with two caissons blown up and several guns disabled.[14]

14: Lee's Report.

As the troops moved on they came to a hollow before reaching the railroad. They halted a moment on the edge of the depression and corrected their lines. It was a clear field to the railroad embankment, behind which they could see the gleaming of the sunlight on the bayonets of A. P. Hill's division.

Meade's three brigades were now in line, the first on the right, with the Sixth regiment of the Reserves thrown out as skirmishers; the Second in the centre, and the Third on the left.

The direction of Meade's advance brought him against Lane's and Archer's brigades. Lane's brigade was composed of five North Carolina regiments,—the Seventh, Eighteenth, Twenty-Eighth, Thirty-Third, and Thirty-Seventh. Archer's was composed of the First, Seventh, and Fourteenth Tennessee, and Nineteenth Georgia regiments, and Fifth Alabama battalion. They were on the railroad and in the woods. There was a gap between the brigades, and there Meade drove the entering wedge. It was a fierce and bloody contest along the railroad, in the woods, upon the hillside, in the ravine, on the open plain, and on the crest of the ridge. The fourteen guns on the hill poured a murderous fire into Meade's left flank. The guns by Deep Run, in front of Pender's brigade, enfiladed the line from the right, while in reserve were two full brigades,—Thomas's and Gregg's,—to fill the gap. But notwithstanding this, Meade, unsupported, charged down the slope, through the hollow, up to the railroad, and over it, routing the Fourteenth Tennessee and Nineteenth Georgia, of Archer's, and the whole of Lane's brigade. With a cheer the Pennsylvanians went up the hill, crawling through the thick underbrush, to the crest, doubling up Archer and knocking Lane completely out of the line. It was as if a Herculean destroyer had crumbled, with a sledge-hammer stroke, the key-stone of an arch, leaving the whole structure in danger of immediate and irretrievable ruin.

Archer shifted the Fifth Alabama from his right to his left, but was not able to stop the advancing Yankees. He had already sent to Gregg for help, and that officer was putting his troops in motion. He had sent to Ewell, who was by Hamilton's, and Trimble and Lawton were getting ready to move, Lane was still running, and the gap was widening between Archer and Pender.

Gibbon ought to have been following Meade, driving up the hill through the gap, but he halted at the railroad; his men were loath to move, for Pender's batteries were cutting across his flank. Howe and Newton and Brooks were by the Bowling Green road, showing no signs of advancing. Sickles and Birney were almost back to Bernard's mansion. Doubleday was holding the flank against Stuart, and Meade was struggling alone.

The latter officer thus speaks of his position at this moment:

> The first brigade to the right advanced several hundred yards over cleared ground, driving the enemy's skirmishers before them till they reached the woods in front of the railroad, which they entered, driving the enemy out of them to the railroad, where they were found strongly posted in ditches and behind temporary defences. The brigade (First) drove them from there and up the heights in their front. Owing to a heavy fire being received on their right flank, they obliqued over to that side, but continued forcing the enemy back till they had crowned the crest of the hill, crossed a main road which runs along the crest, and reached open ground on the other side, where they were assailed by a very severe fire from a larger force in their front, and at the same time the enemy opened a battery which completely enfiladed them from the right flank. After holding their ground for some time, no support arriving, they were compelled to fall back to the railroad.[15]

Gibbon, the nearest support to Meade, was nearly half a mile distant.[16] That officer was wounded while the fight was hottest, but of the part which he was performing he says:

> As soon as the enemy's guns slackened fire, I saw General Meade's troops moving forward into action, and I at once sent orders to my leading brigade to advance and engage the enemy. Shortly afterwards I ordered up another brigade to support the first. The fire was very heavy from the enemy's infantry, and I ordered up the Third Brigade and formed it in column on the right of my line, and directed them to take the position with the bayonet, having previously given that order to the leading brigade. But the general commanding that brigade told me that the noise and confusion was such that it was impossible to get the men to charge, or to get them to hear any order to charge. The Third Brigade—my last brigade—went in and took the position with the bayonet, and captured a considerable number

---

15: General Meade's Testimony, *Conduct of the War*, Part I. p. 696.
16: See map accompanying General Franklin's reply to *Report of Committee on Conduct of the War*.

of prisoners. During the fighting of the infantry I was establishing the batteries which belonged to my division in position to assist in the assault. I had just received the report of the success of this Third Brigade, when shortly after I saw a regiment of Rebel infantry come out on the left of my line between myself and General Meade. I rode up towards a battery that was on their left, and directed them to open fire upon that regiment. I was riding back towards the right of my line, when I was wounded, and left the field about half past two o'clock in the afternoon, I think.[17]

It will be seen by Franklin's despatches that Meade had broken the line before Gibbon was engaged. At 1.15 p. m. he telegraphed to Burnside, "Meade is assaulting the hill." Ten minutes later, at 1.25 p. m., "*Reynolds will push Gibbon in if necessary.*" At 1.40 p. m., "Meade has carried a portion of the enemy's position in the woods. We have three hundred prisoners. Gibbon has advanced to Meade's right."

It was in this advance to the railroad, when Gibbon came in collision with Pender's and Thomas's brigades, that Gibbon was wounded.

While this was going on in front, the Second and Third Brigades of Meade were enveloping Gregg's brigade of South Carolinians, which had been hurried up to retrieve the disaster to the line. There was a short but bloody contest. Three hundred South Carolinians fell in that struggle, including their commander, General Gregg, who was mortally wounded.

It was a critical moment with Stonewall Jackson. The whole of Ewell's division, under the command of General Early, was brought up to regain the ground. Lawton's brigade came first upon the Pennsylvanians, followed by Hayes's, Trimble's, and Field's brigades, with Early's own, commanded by Colonel Walker.

Had Newton, Howe, Brooks, Sickles, and Birney been near at hand, or had Gibbon been pushed promptly and effectively to Meade's support, the record of that bloody day would have been far different from what it is. But they were not there. They had not even been ordered to advance!

Unable to withstand the onset of the whole of Jackson's force (with the exception of a portion of Taliferro's reserves), Meade was obliged to fall back, and give up the position won by such heroic valour. As his troops went to the rear, they met Ward's brigade of Birney's division advancing. The Rebels were in full pursuit. Birney wheeled his

---

17: Testimony, *Conduct of the War*, Part I. p. 715.

batteries into position, and opened with canister, and the Rebels fled to the shelter of the woods.

The divisions of Howe and Newton and Sickles were slightly engaged later in the day, but only in repulsing a second advance of the Rebels. The attack which Meade had opened so gallantly, and which was attended with such good success, had failed. Less than ten thousand men had broken the enemy's line, and opened the way to victory. Of the sixty thousand men at Franklin's disposal not more than sixteen or eighteen thousand were engaged during the day,[18] and of those not more than eight thousand at any one time.

General Franklin, in vindicating himself from censure for not attacking with a larger force and more vigorously, falls back on the clause in Burnside's order, "to attack with one division at least, and to keep it well supported." It would have been better if Burnside had given explicit instructions. There must be some latitude allowed to subordinates, but there are very few men who, without particular instructions, can enter fully into the plans and intentions of the commander-in-chief. Franklin was constitutionally sluggish in his movements. The attack on the left required boldness, energy, and perseverance. Sumner was the man for the place. Burnside was peculiarly unfortunate in the selection of commanders to carry out the particular features of his plan; but Sumner having been first to arrive at Falmouth, and having taken position, it was not easy to make the change.

While the battle was raging on the left I rode over the plain. The cavalry under General Bayard was drawn up in rear of the grove surrounding the fine old Bernard mansion. General Bayard was sitting at the foot of a tree, waiting for orders, and watching the advancing columns of Meade and Gibbon. There was a group of officers around General Franklin. Howe's and Newton's divisions were lying down to avoid the Rebel shells, hurled from the heights beyond the railroad. All of Franklin's guns were in play. The earth shook with the deep concussion. Suddenly the Rebel batteries opened with redoubled fury. A shot went over my head, a second fell in front of my horse, and ploughed a furrow in the ground; a third exploded at my right, a fourth went singing along the line of a regiment lying prostrate on the earth. McCartney's, Williston's, Hexamer's, Amsden's, Cooper's, Ransom's, and a dozen other batteries were replying. Meade was driving up the hill. Wounded men were creeping, crawling, and hobbling towards the hospital. Some, slightly wounded, were uttering

---
18: Testimony of Meade and other officers, *Conduct of the War*.

fearful groans, while others, made of sterner stuff, though torn and mangled, bore their pains without a murmur.

A soldier, with his arms around the necks of two of his comrades, was being brought in. "O dear! O Lord! my foot is torn all to pieces!" he cried.

There was a hole in the toe of his boot where the ball had entered.

"It has gone clear through to the heel, and smashed all the bones. O dear! O dear! I shall have to have it cut off!" he cried, moaning piteously as his comrades laid him upon the ground to rest.

"Better cut off your boot before your foot swells."

"Yes,—do so."

I slipped my knife through the leather, and took the boot from his foot. The ball had passed through his stocking. There was but a drop or two of blood visible. I cut off the stocking, and the bullet was lying between his toes, having barely broken the skin.

"I reckon I sha'n't help lug you any farther," said one of the men who had borne him.

"Wal, if I had known that it wasn't any worse than that I wouldn't have had my boot cut off," said the soldier.

Returning to the Bernard mansion, I saw a commotion among the cavalry, and learned that their commander was mortally wounded. He had been struck by a solid shot while sitting by the tree; and they were bearing him to the hospital. He was a brave and gallant officer.

The Attack on the Right

But while this was transpiring on the left there was a terrible sacrifice of life at the foot of Maryee's Hill. Soon after noon French's and Hancock's divisions of the Second Corps, with Sturgis's division of the Ninth, advanced over the open field in rear of the town to attack the heights. Officers walked along the lines giving the last words. "Advance and drive them out with the bayonet!" were the orders.

The fifteen thousand in a compact body move to the edge of the plateau. The hills are aflame. All of Longstreet's guns are thundering. Shells burst in the ranks. The Rebel skirmishers, concealed in the houses and behind fences, fire a volley and fall back to the main line.

Onward move the divisions. We who behold them from the rear, although we know that death stands ready to reap an abundant harvest, feel the blood rushing with quickened flow through our veins, when we see how gallantly they move forward, firing no shot in return.

Now a sheet of flame bursts from the sunken road, and another from half-way up the slope, and yet another from the top of the hill. Hundreds fall; but still on, nearer to the hill rolls the wave. Still, still it flows on; but we can see that it is losing its power, and, though advancing, it will be broken. It begins to break. It is no longer a wave, but scattered remnants, thrown back like rifts of foam. A portion of Sturgis's division reaches the hollow in front of the hill and settles into it.

The Eleventh New Hampshire, commanded by Colonel Harriman, is in the front line. They are new troops, and this is their first battle; but they fight so gallantly that they win the admiration of their general.

"See!" said Sturgis to an old regiment which quailed before the fire. "See the Eleventh New Hampshire! a new regiment, standing like posts driven into the ground."

Hancock and French, unable to find any shelter, are driven back upon the town. The attack and repulse have not occupied fifteen minutes.

It is a sad sight, that field thickly strewn with dying and dead men. But in battle there is no time for the wringing of hands over disaster. The bloody work must go on.

Sturgis is in the hollow, so near the hill that the Rebel batteries on the crest cannot be depressed sufficiently to drive him out. He is within close musket-shot of Cobb's brigade, lying behind the stone-wall at the base of the hill. Sturgis's men lie down, load and fire deliberately, watching their opportunity to pick off the gunners on the hill. In vain are all the efforts of Longstreet to dislodge them. Solid shot, shells, canister, and shrapnel are thrown towards the hollow, but without avail. A solitary oak-tree near is torn and broken by the artillery fire, and pitted with musket-balls, and the ground is furrowed with the deadly missiles; but the men keep their position through the weary hours. The division is composed of two brigades,—Nagles's, containing the Sixth and Ninth New Hampshire, Seventh Rhode Island, Forty-Eighth Pennsylvania, and Second Maryland; and Ferrero's, containing the Twenty-First and Thirty-Fifth Massachusetts, Eleventh New Hampshire. Fifty-First Pennsylvania, and Fifty-First New York.

A second attempt is made upon the hill. Humphrey's division, composed of Tyler's and Briggs's brigade of Pennsylvanians, nearly all new troops, leads the advance, followed closely by Morrell's division of veterans. The lines move steadily over the field, under cover of the batteries which have been brought up and planted in the streets. Sturgis pours a constant stream of fire upon the sunken road.

Thus aided, they reach the base of the hill in front of Maryee's, deliver a few volleys, and then with thinned ranks retire once more to the shelter of the ridge.

The day is waning. Franklin has failed. He telegraphs that it is too late to make another attack on the left. Not so does Sumner think on the right. He is a brave old man, fearless in battle, counting human life of little value if victory can be won by its sacrifice. He walks to and fro by the Lacey House like a chained lion. Burnside will not let him cross the river. Time has ploughed deep furrows on his face. His hair is white as the driven snow. He is grim and gruff; his voice is deep, and he has rough words for those who falter in duty; but he has a tender heart. He dotes upon his son, and calls him "Sammy" familiarly. He cannot bear to have him gone long from his side, but yet is ready to send him into the thickest of the fight. He cannot see the day lost without another struggle, and orders a third attack.

Humphrey, Morrell, Getty, Sykes, and Howard, or portions of their divisions, are brought up. The troops have been under arms from early daylight. They have had no food. All day they have been exposed to the fire of the Rebel batteries, and have lost heavily. Brooks's division of the Sixth Corps moves up Deep Run to engage in the last attack. All the batteries on both sides of the river are once more brought into action. Getty moves up Hazel Run to take the Rebels in flank, who are protected by the sunken road at the base of the hill.

The Last Attack

It is sunset. The troops move out once more upon the open plain, and cross the field with a cheer. The ground beneath them is already crimson with the blood of their fallen comrades. They reach the base of the hill. Longstreet brings down all his reserves. The hillside, the plain, the crest of the ridge, the groves and thickets, the second range of hills beyond Maryee's, the hollow, the sunken road, are bright flashes. Two hundred cannon strike out fierce defiance,—forty thousand muskets and rifles flame!

The Rebels are driven from the stone-walls, and the sunken road, and the rifle-pit midway the hill. The blue wave mounts all but to the top of the crest. It threatens to overwhelm the Rebel batteries. But we who watch it behold its power decreasing. Men begin to come down the hill singly and in squads, and at length in masses. The third and last attempt has failed. The divisions return, leaving the plain and the hillside strewn with thousands of brave men who have fallen in the ineffectual struggle.

There was no fighting on Sunday, the 14th, but General Burnside was preparing to make another attack. He had eighteen of his old regiments in the Ninth Corps, who would go wherever he sent them. He thought that they would carry the heights.

"I hope," said General Sumner, "that you will desist from an attack. I do not know of any general officer who approves it, and I think it will prove disastrous to the army."

The advice was followed, and it was then decided to withdraw the army.

The wind on Tuesday night blew a gale from the southwest. Hay and straw were laid upon the bridges to deaden the sound of the artillery wheels. It began to rain before morning; and the Rebels, little dreaming of what was taking place, remained in their quarters.

Before daylight the whole army had recrossed the river, and the bridges were taken up. Great were their amazement and wonder when the Rebels looked down from the heights and saw the Union army once more on the northern bank, beyond the reach of their guns.

General Burnside lost about ten thousand men, while the loss of the Rebels was about five thousand. The defeat was disheartening to the army. But though repulsed, the soldiers felt that they were not beaten; they had failed because General Burnside's plans had not been heartily entered into by some of the officers. But the patriotic flame burned as brightly as ever, and they had no thought of giving up the contest.

Tattoo

CHAPTER 12

The Winter at Falmouth

DECEMBER, 1862

After the battle of Fredericksburg, both armies prepared for the winter. Two great cities of log-huts sprang up in the dense forests on both sides of the Rappahannock, peopled by more than two hundred thousand men. It was surprising to see how quickly the soldiers made themselves comfortable in huts chinked with mud and roofed with split shingles. These rude dwellings had a fireplace at one end, doors hung on leathern hinges, and bunks one above another, like berths in a steamboat.

There the men told stories, played checkers and cards, read the newspapers, wrote letters to their friends far away, and kept close watch all the while upon the Rebels.

But there were dark days and dreary nights. It tried their endurance and patriotism to stand all night upon picket, with the north-wind howling around them and the snow whirling into drifts. There were rainy days, and weeks of mud, when there was no drilling, and when there was nothing to do. Then chaplains, with books and papers under their arms, were welcomed everywhere. General Howard thus bore testimony to the labours of one who was not a chaplain, but an agent of the American Tract Society from Boston,—Rev. Mr. Alvord:

> There is a great and good man,—great because he is good and because he is practical,—who has followed the Army of the Potomac from the beginning. He takes his papers, and goes himself and circulates them as far as he is able, and, by the agency of others, gets them into nearly every regiment in the army. And you should see the soldiers cluster around him! When his wagon drives up in front of a regiment, the soldiers pour out

THE MAGIC LANTERN IN THE HOSPITAL.

with life, circle round him, and beg for books and tracts,—for anything he has. Some of them want papers to read for themselves, and others to select pieces out of them to send home. I could hardly believe it, that there was such eagerness on the part of soldiers for such reading until I saw it with my own eyes. 'Give me a paper,' 'Give me a paper,' 'Give me a tract,' 'Give me a book,' is the impatient cry. Very frequently ladies have sent tracts and books to my tent, and on the Sabbath-day I have taken them myself to distribute, and I have scarcely ever had to ask a soldier to receive one of them. Indeed, if you give to one or two, the others will feel jealous if neglected.[19]

Said a chaplain:

I am besieged by those who want something good to read. In my rounds I am followed at my elbow. 'Please, sir, can you spare me one?' They hail me from a distance: 'Are you coming down this way, chaplain?' It is a pleasant thing to pause in these travels through the parish and look back upon the white waves that rise in the wake of one's course. Sports are hushed, swearing is charmed away, all are reading,—Sabbath has come.

19: General Howard's Address at Washington.

In some regiments, where the officers co-operated with chaplains to elevate the morals of men, few oaths were heard.

One day General Howard started out with a handful of leaflets on swearing, with the intention of giving one to every man whom he heard using profane language. He went from regiment to regiment and from brigade to brigade of his division, and returned to his tent without hearing an oath.

"I have been all through my division today," he said, "visiting the hospitals, and I haven't heard a single man swear. Isn't it strange?"

One of the citizens of Falmouth came to General Howard for a guard.

"You favoured secession, I suppose," said the General.

"I stuck for the Union till Virginia went out of the Union. I had to go with her."

"You have a son in the Rebel army."

"Yes, sir; but he enlisted of his own accord."

"The soldiers steal your chickens, you say?"

"Yes, they take everything they can lay their hands upon, and I want a guard to protect my property."

"If you and all your neighbours had voted against secession, you would not need a guard. No, sir, you can't have one. When you have given as much to your country as I have I will give you one, but not till then," said the General, pointing to his empty sleeve. He lost his right arm at Fair Oaks.

It was a gloomy winter, but the Sanitary and Christian Commissions gave their powerful aid towards maintaining the health and morals and spirits of the army. The Christian Commission opened six stations, from which they dispensed supplies of books and papers and food for the sick, not regularly furnished by the medical department. Religious meetings were held nightly, conducted by the soldiers, marked by deep solemnity. Veterans who had passed through all the trials and temptations of a soldier's life gave testimony of the peace and joy they had in believing in Jesus. Others asked what they should do to obtain the same comfort. Many who had faced death unflinchingly at Williamsburg, Fair Oaks, Malvern, and Antietam, who had been ever indifferent to the claim of religion, became like little children as they listened to their comrades singing:

Rock of Ages, cleft for me,
Let me hide myself in thee.

It was not sentimentalism. A soldier who has been through a half-dozen battles is the last person in the world to indulge in sentiment. He above all men understands reality. Thus led by the sweet music and the fervent prayers of their comrades, they rejoiced in the hope that they had found forgiveness of sins through the blood of the Son of God.

At Falmouth, an old tobacco-warehouse on the bank of the river, within hail of the Rebel pickets, was cleared of rubbish, the broken ceiling and windows covered with canvas, a rude pulpit erected, where on Sabbath afternoons and every evening meetings were held, a Sabbath school was organized, also a day school. One of the soldiers established a school for the instruction of the children of the village. Often in the calm twilight of the mild winter days the Rebel picket pacing his beat upon the opposite bank stopped, and leaning upon his gun, listened to the hymns of devotion wafted on the evening air.

He could have sent a bullet whistling through the building, but there was a mutual understanding among the pickets not to fire, and so the meetings were undisturbed.

In the Forty-Fourth New York Regiment, known as the Ellsworth Avengers, were two young soldiers whose hearts were woven together with Christian zeal. They had no chaplain; but they established a

THE CHRISTIAN COMMISSION IN THE FIELD

prayer-meeting, holding it beside a stump, in a retired place. They obtained permission of the colonel to build a log chapel. They had to draw the logs a mile, but they had faith and energy, and laid out a building sixteen by thirty-two feet square. Rev. Mr. Alvord, the agent of a Tract Society, gives the following account of their labours.

> The first logs were heavy, and hardly anyone to help. Their plan at first was not very definite. They would lay down a log and then look and plan by the eye. Another log was wearily drawn and put on. The crowd came round to quiz and joke. 'Are you to have it finished before the world ends?' 'Fixing up to leave?' 'How does your saloon get on?' The more serious, in pity, tried to discourage. There was 'already an order out to move; what's the use?' 'Who wants meetings?' But these two Christian boys (S. and L.) toiled on like Noah, amidst the scoffs of the multitude. The edifice slowly rose; volunteers lent a hand. The Christian men of the regiment became interested. (There were forty or fifty in all, eighteen or twenty of whom at length aided in the work.) A sufficient height was reached, and first a roof of brush, and afterwards of patched *ponchos*, was put on, and meetings began,—or rather they *began* when it was only an open pen. In a few days Burnside's advance came, and the regiment left for the field. In their absence, plunderers stripped the cabin, and carried off a portion of its material; but on the return of our troops the same busy hands and hearts of faith were again at work. A sutler gave them the old canvas cover of his large tent, which he was about to cut up to shelter his horses with, and lo, it *precisely filled* the roof of the meeting-house,—not an inch to spare!
>
> Well, there it stands, to his glory and the credit of their perseverance. (It took about one hundred logs to build it.) You should have seen their eyes shine, as, here in my tent for tracts, they were one day giving me its history, and you should have been with us last evening. The little pulpit made of empty box boards, two chandeliers suspended from the ridge-pole of cross-sticks, wreathed with ivy, and in the socketed ends four adamant candles, each burning brilliantly. Festoons of ivy and 'dead men's fingers' (a species of woodbine called by this name), looped gracefully along the sides of the room, and in the centre from chandelier to chandelier,—their deep green, with the fine brown bark of the pine logs, and white canvas above, striped

with its rafters, sweetly contrasting. Below, a perfect pack of soldiers, in the 'Avengers" uniform, squatted low upon the pole seats, beneath which was a carpet of evergreen sprays,—all silent, uncovered, respectful; as the service opened, you could have heard a pin fall. There was nothing here to make a noise. Pew-doors, psalm-books, rustling silks, or groined arches reverberating the slightest sound of hand or footfall, there were none. Only the click of that wooden latch, and a gliding figure, like a stealthy vidette, squeezing in among the common mass, indicated the late comer. The song went up from the deep voices of men,—do you know the effect?—and before our service closed, tears rolled down from the *faces of men*. To be short, every evening of the week this house is now filled with some service, four of which are religious. When they can have no preaching, these soldiers meet for prayer.

I stole in one evening, lately, when they were at these devotions; prayer after prayer successively was offered, in earnest, humblest tones, before rising from their knees; the impenitent looking on solemnly. Officers were present and took part, and seldom have I seen such manifest tokens that God is about to appear in power. Opposition there is none. The whole regiment looks upon the house now as a matter of pride,—encourage all the meetings. It is attractive to visitors, and, when not used for religious purposes, is occupied by lyceum debates, singing clubs, &c., &c. How those two Christian boys do enjoy it! Said one of them to me, 'We have been paid for all our labour a thousand times over.'

Thus, fighting, marching, singing, praying, teaching the ignorant, trusting in God, never wavering in their faith of the ultimate triumph of right, they passed the weary winter.

Chapter 13
Chancellorsville

April, 1863

General Burnside having accepted the command of the army with reluctance, was relieved at his own request, and General Hooker was appointed his successor. He made a thorough reorganization. The system of grand divisions was abolished, and the corps organization adopted. The First Corps was commanded by General Sickles, the Fifth by General Meade, the Sixth by General Sedgwick, the Eleventh by General Howard, and the Twelfth by General Slocum. The cavalry was consolidated into a single corps, under General Stoneman. General Hooker intended to use the cavalry as it had not been used up to that time.

The vigour manifested by General Hooker in the reorganization, and the confidence of the soldiers in him as a commander, gave new hope to the army. He reduced the number of wagons in the trains, and informed the officers that they would be allowed only a limited amount of baggage. He issued orders that the troops should have rations of fresh bread, cabbages, and onions, in abundance. Merit was commended. Officers and men who had proved themselves efficient were allowed leave of absence, before the opening of the spring campaign. Regiments which had shown incapacity and loose discipline were allowed no favours. Only eleven regiments in the whole army were highly commended. Some were severely censured as wanting those qualities which make a good regiment. This administration of affairs soon produced a perceptible change in the spirits of the men.

There were frequent rains, which prevented any movement during the winter; but General Hooker was not idle. He was obtaining information, from scouts and spies, of Lee's position and the number of his troops. He kept his designs so well to himself that even his most trusted officers were not aware of them. But his plan embraced three features: a cavalry movement under Stoneman towards Richmond, from the Upper Rappahannock, to destroy Lee's communications, burning bridges and supplies; the deploy of a portion of the army down the river to attract Lee's attention; and, lastly, a sudden march of the main body up the river, to gain a position near Chancellorsville, southwest of Fredericksburg, which would compel Lee to come out and fight, or evacuate the place. If he gained the position, he could stand on the defensive and wait Lee's movements. He decided that Lee should be the attacking party.

Lee had sent two divisions of Longstreet's corps under that officer to North Carolina, and Hampton's cavalry was recruiting south of the James River. It was a favourable opportunity to strike a heavy blow.

On the 27th of April the Eleventh Corps, under Howard, and the Twelfth, under Slocum, at half past five in the morning started for Kelley's Ford by the Hartwood Church road.

The Third, under Sickles, and the Fifth, under Meade, moved at the same time, by a road nearer the river, in the same direction. The Second, under Couch, went towards United States Ford, which is only three miles from Chancellorsville. A dense fog hung over the river, concealing the movement. The Eleventh, Twelfth, and Fifth Corps marched fourteen miles during the day, and bivouacked at four o'clock in the afternoon a mile west of Hartwood Church. To Lee, who looked across the river from Fredericksburg, there was no change in the appearance of things on the Stafford hills. The camps of the Yankees were still there, dotting the landscape, teams were moving to and fro, soldiers were at drill, and the smoke of camp-fires was curling through the air.

During the evening of the 27th the pontoons belonging to the Sixth Corps were taken from the wagons, carried by the soldiers down to the river, and put into the water so noiselessly that the Rebel pickets stationed on the bank near Bernard's house had no suspicion of what was going on. The boats were manned by Russell's brigade. At a given signal they were pushed rapidly across the stream, and, before the Rebel pickets were aware of the movement, they found themselves prisoners. The First Corps went a mile farther down, to Southfield. It was daylight before the engineers of this corps could get their boats into the water. The Rebel sharpshooters who were lying in rifle-pits along the bank commenced a deadly fire. To silence them, Colonel Warner placed forty pieces of artillery on the high bank overlooking the river, under cover of which the boats crossed, and the soldiers, leaping ashore, charged up the bank and captured one hundred and fifty Rebels. The engineers in a short time had both bridges completed. General Wadsworth's division of the First Corps was the first to cross the lower bridge. General Wadsworth had become impatient, and, instead of waiting for the completion of the structure, swam his horse across the stream. General Brooks, of the Sixth Corps, was the first to cross the bridge at Bernard's.

It was now five o'clock in the morning. There was great commotion in Fredericksburg. A courier dashed into town on horseback, shouting, "The Yankees are crossing down the river."[20] The church-bells were rung. The people who had returned to the town after the battle of the 13th of December sprang from their beds. They went out and stood upon Maryee's Hill, looked across the river, and saw the country alive with troops.

All through the day the Yankee balloons were in the air at a great height, and the opposite side of the river, as far as the eye could reach, was blue with their crowded columns.[21]

The drummers beat the long-roll. "Fall in! Fall in!" was the cry, and the whole army was quickly under arms. The movement was a surprise to General Lee.

The crossing of the First and Sixth Corps was slow and deliberate. "They continued to cross," says the writer, "until two o'clock p. m., infantry, artillery, and wagons. They swarmed irregularly over the fields and bluffs, of which they had taken possession, seeming not to have fallen into ranks. About five p. m. a light rain commenced, when they pitched their tents, and seemed to make themselves at home."

In order to deceive General Lee, only Wadsworth's and Brooks's divisions were sent over in the forenoon; but portions of the other divisions, which had been concealed behind a belt of woods, were put in motion, and marched along the crest of the ridge, through an open field, in sight of the Rebels, as though on their way down the river; but, instead of crossing, were marched up through a gully around the hill to their starting-point, and were again moved over the same ground,—a circus-march, calculated to deceive the Rebels into thinking that the whole army was moving in that direction. A part of Jackson's corps had been lying at Shinker's Neck, several miles below Fredericksburg, which Lee ordered to Hamilton's crossing, occupying the same position that it held in the first battle.

It was night before the remainder of the Sixth Corps crossed the

---

20: Letter to *Richmond Examiner*.
21: *Richmond Examiner*, May 1st 1863.

stream, while the other two divisions of the First Corps still remained on the northern bank. Lee could not comprehend this new state of affairs. The night of the 28th passed, and no advance was made by the Sixth Corps. The morning of the 29th saw them in the same position, evidently in no haste to make an attack.

Meanwhile the main body of the army was making a rapid march up the river. The Eleventh Corps reached Kelley's Ford, twenty-eight miles above Falmouth, at half past four in the afternoon. The pontoons arrived at six o'clock. Four hundred men went over in the boats, and seized the Rebel rifle-pits, capturing a few prisoners, who were stationed there to guard the Ford. As soon as the bridge was completed, the troops began to cross. The Seventeenth Pennsylvania cavalry preceded the infantry, pushed out on the road leading to Culpepper, and encountered a detachment of Stuart's cavalry.

On the morning of the 29th, the Twelfth Corps, followed by the Eleventh, made a rapid march to Germanna Ford, on the Rapidan, while the Fifth Corps took the road leading to Ely's Ford. When the Twelfth Corps arrived at Germanna Ford at three o'clock in the afternoon, the Rebels were discovered building a bridge. About one hundred of them were taken prisoners. Instead of waiting for the pontoons to be laid, the Twelfth forded the stream, which was deep and swift; but the men held their cartridge-boxes over their heads, and thus kept their powder dry.

It was not till the afternoon of the 29th that Lee understood Hooker's movement. At sunset Stuart reported that a heavy column of Yankees was crossing the Germanna Ford, that there was another at Ely's, and still another at United States Ford. Lee saw that the routes, after crossing the Rapidan, converged near Chancellorsville, from whence several roads led to the rear of his position at Fredericksburg.

On the morning of the 30th, Hooker's army was in the following position: The Eleventh and Twelfth Corps at Germanna Ford, moving southeast; the Fifth Corps at Ely's Ford, moving south; the Second Corps, followed by the Third, at United States Ford, marching southwest; the First Corps passing up the river from its position below Fredericksburg, making a rapid march to join the Second Corps at United States Ford; the Sixth Corps, meanwhile, lying inactive on the plain by Bernard's house.

The movement was admirably made, each corps coming into position at the appointed place and time, showing that the plan had been well matured in the mind of the commander-in-chief.

Early on the morning of the 30th the Eleventh Corps, followed by the Twelfth, moved from Germanna Ford down the Stevensburg plank-road to the Old Wilderness Tavern, which is about a mile and a half west of Chancellorsville. The latter place, at the time of the battle, consisted of one brick house. The country around Chancellorsville is called "the Wilderness." Years ago a considerable portion of the land was cleared, but the system of cultivation carried on by the Virginians quickly exhausted the soil, and the fields were left to grow up again to bushes. A short distance beyond the old tavern is Dowdal's Tavern, near the junction of the Stevensburg plank-road, and the Orange turnpike, leading to Gordonsville. Hunting Run has its head-waters near the Stevensburg plank-road, and flows north to the Rapidan. There is an old saw-mill on the creek, which was used as a hospital by the Twelfth Corps during the battle. Near Dowdal's tavern is an old church, and on the right-hand side of the road, as we go toward Chancellorsville from Dowdal's, there is a cleared field on elevated land, which was the centre of Hooker's line at the beginning of the battle. Several roads diverge from Chancellorsville,—the Orange and Fredericksburg plank-road and the Gordonsville turnpike, both leading to Fredericksburg; also roads to United States and Ely's Fords; also one leading south across Scott's Run.

At noon of the 30th the Eleventh Corps reached its assigned position, between the Germanna road and Dowdal's tavern, forming the right flank of Hooker's line. The Third Corps, which had crossed at Ely's Ford, came down through the woods across Hunting Run, and formed on the left of the Eleventh, by the tavern. The Twelfth Corps filed past the Eleventh, along the Stevensburg road, and the Third Corps passed Chancellorsville, and moved almost to Tabernacle Church, on the Orange and Fredericksburg plank-road. The Second Corps, having crossed at United States Ford, came into position a mile or more in rear of the Eleventh and Third, while the Fifth moved up and formed a line facing southeast, reaching from Chancellorsville to Scott's Dam on the Rappahannock, a mile and a half north of Chancellorsville.

Stuart, commanding the Rebel cavalry, had skirmished with the Eleventh Corps on its march, but when the Third, which crossed at Ely's, reached Chancellorsville, Stuart found that he was cut off from direct communication with Lee, and was obliged to move to Todd's Tavern and Spottsylvania Court-House, to put himself in connection with the infantry of the Rebel army. Lee was still undecided what to do, but finally determined to leave Early's division of Jackson's corps, and Barksdale's brigade of McLaw's division, and a part of the reserve artillery under Pendleton, to hold Fredericksburg, and move with the rest of the army to Chancellorsville and fight Hooker. He had already sent Anderson's division to watch the movement. Slocum's skirmishers met Anderson's at Chancellorsville and drove them back to Tabernacle Church. Anderson, finding that Slocum was advancing, formed across the roads, and was in this position at dark on the night of the 30th.

On the morning of the 1st of May the whole Rebel army, except what was left to watch Sedgwick, was put in motion, with the intention of making a direct attack. Anderson advanced upon Slocum, who fell back under instructions to Chancellorsville, and filled the gap between the Third and Fifth. Lee followed, intending to give battle, but he found Hooker in a position of such strength that he hesitated. Lee says:

> The enemy had assumed a position of great natural strength, surrounded on all sides by a dense forest, filled with tangled undergrowth, in the midst of which breastworks of logs had been constructed, with trees felled in front so as to form an impenetrable *abatis*. His artillery swept the few narrow roads by which his position could be approached from the front, and commanded the adjacent woods. The left of his line extended from Chancellorsville towards the Rappahannock, covering the Bark-Mill Ford, where he communicated with the north bank of the river by a pontoon bridge. His right stretched westward along the Germanna road more than two miles.
>
> Darkness was approaching before the extent and strength of his lines could be ascertained, and, as the nature of the country rendered it hazardous to attack by night, our troops were halted, and formed in line of battle in front of Chancellorsville, at right angles to the plank-road.... It was evident that a direct attack upon the enemy would be attended with great difficulty and loss, in view of the strength of his position and his superiority in numbers. It was therefore resolved to endeavour to turn his right flank, and gain his rear, leaving a force in front to hold him in check, and conceal the movement. The execution of this plan was entrusted to Lieutenant-General Jackson, with his three divisions.

This movement of Lee's was very bold and hazardous. It divided his army into three parts,—one part watching the Sixth Corps at Fredericksburg, another between Chancellorsville and Fredericksburg, and the force under Jackson, accompanied by Stuart's cavalry, moving to get in the rear of Hooker. Jackson was obliged to make a long circuit by Todd's Tavern and the Furnace Road, moving first southwest toward Spottsylvania, then west toward Orange Court-House, then north toward the Rapidan, then east toward the old saw-mill on Hunting Run. Rodes's division reached the Old Wilderness Tavern about four o'clock in the afternoon. As the different divisions arrived they were formed across the Stevensburg plank-road, Rodes in front, Trimble's division under General Colston in the second, and A. P. Hill in the third line.

General Hooker, having decided to fight a defensive battle, ordered the construction of rifle-pits, and while Jackson was making this detour the position was strongly fortified against an attack from the direction of Fredericksburg. Early in the day it was reported that Lee was retreating rapidly toward Culpepper Court-House. From the cleared field occupied by Sickles the Rebel column could be seen moving southwest,—artillery, baggage-train, and infantry. It was generally believed in Hooker's army that Lee, finding the position too impregnable, was retiring. Sickles and Howard thought differently.

"Lee has divided his army, and now is the time to strike," said General Sickles to Hooker.

General Hooker hesitated. His plan was to stand wholly on the defensive. Still the column filed by.

"The enemy is on my flank," was the message from Howard. "We can hear the sound of their axes in the woods."[22]

"Now is the time to double up Lee," said Sickles, again urging an attack.[23]

"You may go out and feel the enemy, but don't go too fast, nor too far," said Hooker, at last yielding.

May, 1863

It is nearly two miles southwest from Chancellorsville to Wellford's iron furnace, which is situated on the Ny River, the north branch of the Mattapony. The road which passes the furnace, and along which Jackson was hastening, is a byroad from the plank-road east of Chancellorsville, to the Brock Road, which runs from Todd's Tavern northwest to the Old Wilderness Tavern. Archer's and Thomas's brigades of A. P. Hill's division were at the furnace when Sickles received permission to move out. They were the rear brigades of Jackson's column. Sickles lost no time in putting his divisions in motion. Berdan's sharpshooters were thrown out in advance as skirmishers, and the infantry with artillery

---

22: Howard's Report.
23: General Sickles's statement.

followed; but the artillery was compelled to halt till a bridge could be constructed across a small creek. It was about four o'clock when the head of the column reached the road over which Jackson had marched. Archer was nearly a mile west of the furnace when the sharpshooters reached the road, where they suddenly fell upon the Twenty-Third Georgia. This regiment had been detached from Colquitt's brigade of D. H. Hill's division, and was posted on the north side of the road, as a flanking party, to cover the march of the troops.

There was a sudden commotion in Archer's and Thomas's brigades. Brown's battery was wheeled into position, and, with the Twenty-Third Georgia and Fourteenth Tennessee, opened fire upon Sickles. The teamsters of the Rebel baggage-trains fled into the woods.

A courier dashed up the road to inform Archer what had happened, but before the news reached him the Twenty-Third Georgia was in the hands of Sickles. Archer faced about, and formed his lines.

Anderson all the while was skirmishing with Slocum, to attract Hooker's attention, while Jackson was getting into position, but he was now obliged to send Wright, Posey, and Mahan to the assistance of Archer and Thomas. They attacked Sickles's left flank, while Archer and Thomas attacked his right. The contest waxed warm.

"Don't go too fast," was Hooker's injunction again to Sickles.

"I want a brigade to fill the gap between myself and Howard," was Sickles's reply, and Barlow's brigade was sent. It was the best of the Eleventh Corps. Howard had placed it in reserve just where he could use it to advantage, on either flank, in front, or centre.

The Eleventh Corps was formed in the following order: General Devens's division on the right, between the Stevensburg road and the old saw-mill, facing northwest; General Schurz's division south of the plank-road, facing southwest; General Schimmelfennig's brigade of Steinwehr's division also south of the road, reaching to Dowdal's Tavern; Barlow's brigade north of the road, in rear of the centre.

There was no want of precaution on the part of General Howard. General Hooker rode along the line with Howard on Saturday forenoon. Howard says:

> At one point a regiment was not deployed and at another a gap in the woods was not filled. The corrections were made and the position strengthened. The front was covered by a good line of skirmishers. I should have stated that just at evening of the 1st the enemy made a reconnoissance on our front with a small force of artillery and infantry. General Schim-

melfennig moved out with a battalion and drove him back. During Saturday, the 2nd, the same general made frequent reconnaissances. Infantry scouts and cavalry patrols were constantly pushed out on every road. The unvarying report was, 'The enemy is crossing the plank-road and moving towards Culpepper.' At 4 p. m. I was directed to send a brigade to the support of General Sickles. I immediately took Barlow's brigade by a short route to General Sickles's right, some two and a half miles from the plank-road to the front.[24]

It was six o'clock. There was a gap from Dowdal's Tavern almost to Chancellorsville, from which Sickles had moved. Slocum had advanced beyond Chancellorsville southeast. The sending out of Sickles and Barlow, the advance of Slocum, and the position of the Second Corps, so far away to the rear, left Howard without any supports.

Jackson came through the woods upon Howard's skirmishers, who fired and fell back. The firing attracted the attention of the men along the lines, who were cooking their suppers. Occasional shots had been fired during the afternoon, and there was no alarm till the skirmishers came out of the woods upon the run, followed by the Rebels. The men seized their arms; but, before Devens could get his regiments into position, the Rebels were approaching his right flank, firing quick volleys and yelling like savages. Some of Devens's command fled, throwing away their guns and equipments. Others fought bravely. Devens, while endeavouring to rally his men, was wounded; several of his officers fell; yet he held his ground till the Rebels gained his rear and began firing into the backs of the men who stood behind the breastwork. Then the line gave way, abandoning five guns.

Howard was at his head-quarters, by Dowdal's. Schurz also was there when the attack commenced. He says:

> I sent my chief of staff to the front when firing was heard. General Schurz, who was with me, left at once to take command of his line. It was not three minutes before I followed. When I reached General Schurz's command, I saw that the enemy had enveloped my right, and that the first division (Devens's) was giving way. I first tried to change front with the deployed regiments. I next directed the artillery where to go; then formed a line, by deploying some of the reserve regiments, near the church. By this time the whole front, on the north of the plank-road, had given way. Colonel Burshbeck's brigade

---

24: Howard's Report.

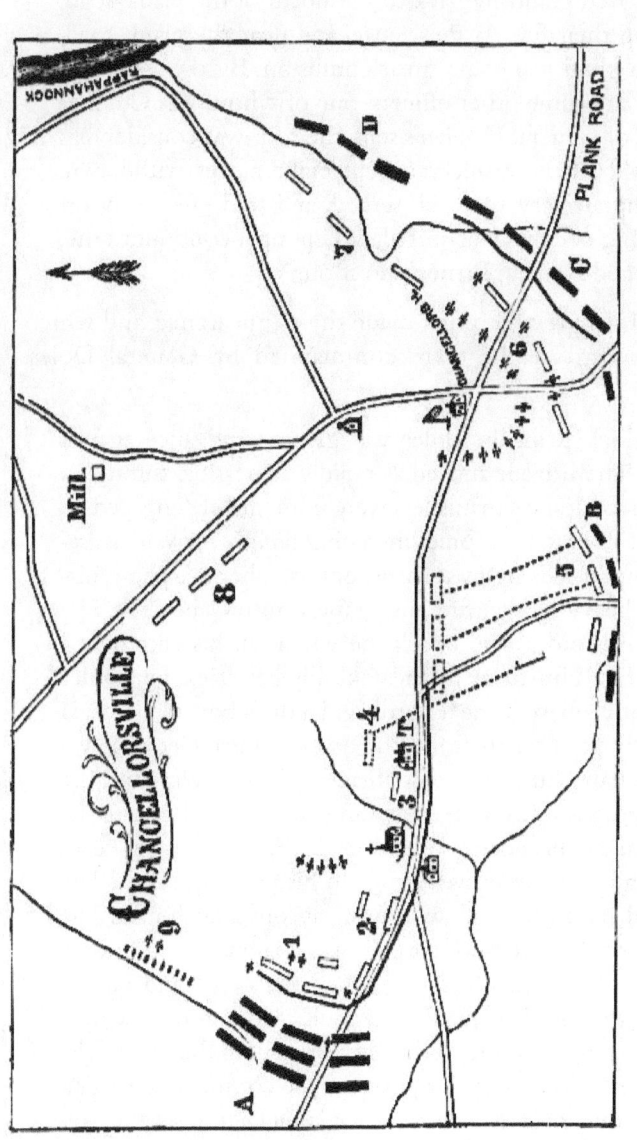

UNION POSITIONS.

1. Devens's Division.
2. Schurz's "
3. Steinwehr's Division.
4. Barlow's Brigade before moving to reinforce Sickles.
5. Sickles's (3) Corps.
6. Slocum's (12) "
7. Meade's (5) "
8. Couch's (2) "
9. Cavalry.

REBEL POSITIONS.

A. Stonewall Jackson's Corps.
   Front line Rodes's Division.
   Middle line Colston's Division.
   Third line A. P. Hill's "
B. Archer's and Wright's Brigades.
C. Anderson's Division.
D. McLaw's "
T. Tavern.

was faced about, and, lying on the other side of the rifle-pit embankment, held on with praiseworthy firmness. A part of General Schimmelfennig's and a part of Colonel Krzyzanouski's brigades moved gradually back to the north of the plank-road, and kept up their fire. At the centre, and near the plank-road, there was a blind panic and great confusion. By the assistance of my staff and some other officers, one of whom was Colonel Dickinson, of General Hooker's staff, the rout was considerably checked, and all the artillery except eight pieces withdrawn. Some of the artillery was well served, and told effectively on the advancing enemy. Captain Dilger kept up a continuous fire, till we reached General Birney's position.[25]

The Rebel troops which first made their appearance, and which enveloped Howard's right, were commanded by General Doles, who says:

> At five o'clock p. m. the order was given to advance against the enemy. The brigade moved as rapidly as possible through a very thick wood, and skirmishers were immediately engaged by those of the enemy. Our forces marching rapidly forward assisted in driving in the enemy's sharpshooters, when we were subjected to a heavy musket fire, and grape, canister, and shell. The command was ordered to attack the enemy in his entrenched position, drive him from it, and take his batteries. The order was promptly obeyed; the Fourth and Forty-Fourth Georgia assaulted his position in front; the Twenty-First Georgia was ordered to flank him so as to enfilade his entrenchments; the Twelfth Georgia was ordered forward, and to the right, to attack a force of the enemy on the right. After a resistance of about ten minutes we drove him from his position on the left, and carried his battery of two guns, caissons, and horses. The movement of the Twelfth Georgia on the right was successful. The order to forward was given, when the command moved forward at the 'double-quick' to assault the enemy who had taken up a strong position on the crest of a hill in the open field. He was soon driven from this position, the command pursuing him. He made *a stubborn resistance from behind a wattling fence*, on a hill thickly covered with pine. The whole command moved gallantly against this position, the Fourth and Forty-Fourth

---

25: Howard's Report.

Georgia in front, and the Twenty-First and Twelfth on his left flank and rear. Here we captured one gun,—a rifled piece. We pursued his retreating forces about three hundred yards over an open field, receiving a severe fire from musketry and a battery of four pieces on the crest of the hill that commanded the field below; his infantry was in large force, and well protected by rifle-pits and entrenchments. The command was ordered to take the entrenchments and the battery, *which was done after a resistance of about twenty minutes.* The enemy fled in utter confusion, leaving his battery of four pieces, his wounded, and many prisoners. The Twelfth Georgia and the larger portion of the other regiments was formed in good order, and pursued him through the pine forest, moving some five hundred yards to the front, and holding that position until after dark. Fresh troops having been placed in that position after dark, I ordered the command to retire for the purpose of replenishing ammunitions, the men being entirely out. During this engagement, which lasted from about 5½ to 9 p. m., the command captured eight pieces of artillery and many prisoners.[26]

It is manifest, that while a portion of the Eleventh Corps became panic-stricken, a large number of Howard's troops fought with great bravery. The corps numbered about thirteen thousand five hundred on the morning of May 1st.

The force under Howard at the time of the attack did not exceed eleven thousand, mainly raw German troops. Howard's total loss in killed, wounded, and prisoners was two thousand five hundred and twenty-eight. Twenty-five officers and one hundred and fifty-three men were killed, seventy-eight officers and eight hundred and forty-two wounded,—a total loss of one thousand and ninety-eight killed and wounded, which shows the severity of this brief conflict.

The Eleventh Corps has been severely censured for pusillanimous conduct in this battle; but when all of the facts are taken into consideration,—that Howard had no supports to call upon; that the Third Corps was two miles and a half from its position in the line; that Barlow's brigade had been sent away; that the attack was a surprise; that Jackson's force exceeded thirty thousand; that, notwithstanding these disadvantages, a "stubborn resistance" was offered,—praise instead of censure is due to those of the Eleventh who thus held their ground, till one fourth of their number were killed, wounded, or taken prisoners.

26: General Doles's Report, p. 63.

Almost at the beginning of the attack Devens was wounded. In the confusion and panic, there was no one to take his place till Howard arrived. Hooker was at once in his saddle.

"The enemy have attacked Howard and driven him in," was his word to Sickles.

"That can't be," said Sickles, incredulous.

"Return at once," was the order from Hooker, by a second messenger.

The heavy firing, constantly growing nearer, gave force to the instruction.

It was now quite dark. Sickles set out to return with all possible haste, but soon found that he had got to fight his way back. Jackson's left wing had swept round, till it rested upon the road, over which he had marched on his way out to the Furnace. Berry's division came first upon the enemy. A severe contest ensued, lasting till nine o'clock, when he succeeded in re-establishing his connection with Howard, who had thus far fought the battle almost alone. Lee, with Anderson's command, all the while was making a demonstration against the Twelfth and Fifth Corps east of Chancellorsville, and the Second was too far in rear to be of any service to Howard before the return of Sickles and Barlow.

Jackson gained no advantage after his first attack, but on the other hand came near experiencing a panic in his own lines. General Colston says:

> We continued to drive the enemy until darkness prevented our farther advance. The firing now ceased, owing to the difficult and tangled nature of the ground over which the troops had advanced, and the mingling of my first and second lines of battle. The formation of the troops became very much confused, and different regiments, brigades, and divisions were mixed up together.... The troops were hardly reformed and placed in position when the enemy opened, about ten o'clock, a furious fire of shot, shell, and canister, sweeping down the plank-road and the woods on each side. A number of artillery horses, some of them without drivers, and a great many infantry soldiers, belonging to other commands, rushed down the road in wild disorder; but, although many casualties occurred at this time in my division, the troops occupied their position with the utmost steadiness. It was at this time that General Nichols, of the Louisiana Brigade (Fourth), a gallant and accomplished officer, had

his leg torn off by a shell, and was carried off the field. It was also about the same time that our great, and good and ever to be lamented corps commander fell under the fire of some of the men of General Lane's brigade.[27]

Under cover of the fire of the artillery, Berry's division of the Third Corps attacked Jackson. The Rebel commander had just placed A. P. Hill's division in the front line, and was contemplating an attack upon Sickles, when Berry advanced. His biographer says:

Such was his ardour at this critical moment, and his anxiety to penetrate the movements of the enemy, doubly screened as they were by the dense forest and gathering darkness, that he rode ahead of the skirmishers, and exposed himself to a close and dangerous fire from the enemy's sharpshooters, posted in the timber. So great was the danger which he ran, that one of his staff said, 'General, don't you think this is the wrong place for you?' He replied, quickly, 'The danger is all over; the enemy is routed. Go back and tell A. P. Hill to press right on!' Soon after giving this order, General Jackson turned, and, accompanied by his staff and escort, rode back at a trot on his well-known 'Old Sorrel' toward his own men. Unhappily, in the darkness,—it was now nine or ten o'clock at night,—the little body of horsemen was mistaken for Federal cavalry charging, and the regiments on the right and left of the road fired a sudden volley into them with the most lamentable results. Captain Boswell, of Jackson's staff, was killed, and borne into our lines by his horse. Colonel Crutchfield, chief of artillery, was wounded, and two couriers killed. General Jackson received one ball in his left arm, two inches below the shoulder-joint, shattering the bone and severing the chief artery; a second passed through the same arm, between the elbow and wrist, making its exit through the palm of the hand; a third entered the palm of his right hand, about the middle, and, passing through, broke two of the bones.

He fell from his horse, and was caught by Captain Wormly, to whom he said, 'All my wounds are by my own men.'

The firing was responded to by the enemy, who made a sudden advance, *and, the Confederates falling back, their foes actually charged over Jackson's body.* He was not discovered, however, and the Federals being driven in turn, he was rescued. Ready hands placed him upon a litter, and he was borne to the rear under a

---

27: Colston's Report, p. 43.

heavy fire from the enemy. One of the litter-bearers was shot down; the General fell from the shoulders of the men, receiving a severe contusion, adding to the injury of the arm and injuring the side severely. The enemy's fire of artillery at this point was terrible. General Jackson was left for five minutes until the fire slackened, then placed in an ambulance and carried to the field hospital at Wilderness Run.[28]

Thus fell a commander endowed with qualities calculated to stir the warmest enthusiasm of the people of the South. He was brave, daring, energetic, impulsive,—the most competent of all the Rebel generals to lead a charge,—but not esteemed so able as Lee to conduct a campaign. He was deeply religious, but espoused Treason with all his heart. He was educated at the expense of the United States, and had sworn to bear faithful allegiance to his country; yet he joined the Rebels at the outset, and did what he could to inaugurate and carry to a successful issue a civil war for the overthrow of the national government and the establishing of another with slavery for its corner-stone! He prayed and fought for a system of servitude which was the sum of all villainies, and which has received the condemnation of every civilized nation of modern times.

Not according to the measure of his military prowess, nor by his sincerity of heart or religious convictions and exercises, will History judge him, but, connecting the man with the cause which he espoused, will hold him accountable for bloodshed in a war waged to sustain human slavery, under the specious doctrine of the Rights of States.

* * * * * * * *

When the assault was made on Howard, the first move on the part of Hooker was to arrange for a new line.

Captain Best, commanding the artillery of the Twelfth Corps, brought thirty-six guns into position between Chancellorsville and Dowdal's, sweeping the fields to the south and southwest, the Orangeburg plank-road, and the breastworks which Buschbeck had abandoned, and behind which the Rebels were forming for a second attack. Under cover of this fire, Birney and Whipple came back from Scott's Creek; Williams's division, which had been pushed out southeast of Chancellorsville, on the road to Fredericksburg, was drawn in.

When the Twelfth Corps got back to its place in the line, most of Howard's works were in possession of the enemy. Williams now crossed his own entrenchments, and formed in the field, facing westward.

28: *Life of Stonewall Jackson*, by Daniels, of Richmond.

Battery at Chancellorsville.

"Stand steady, old Third Brigade. Stand steady, old Second Massachusetts," was the address of the Brigadier.

So stood the line, while Best poured in his tremendous artillery fire, and while Berry pushed the Rebels back into the woods.

Jackson and A. P. Hill having been wounded, the command devolved on General Stuart, who arrived at midnight and made a reconnoissance of the lines.

East of Chancellorsville Slocum and Meade were having a severe fight with the Rebels under Lee, who says in his report:

> As soon as the sound of cannon gave notice of Jackson's attack on the enemy's right, our troops in front of Chancellorsville were ordered to press him strongly on the left, to prevent reinforcements being sent to the point assailed. They were directed not to attack in force, unless a favourable opportunity should present itself, and while continuing to cover the roads leading from their respective positions, toward Chancellorsville, to incline to the left so as to connect with Jackson's right as he closed in upon the centre. These orders were well executed, our troops advancing up to the enemy's entrenchments, while several batteries played with good effect upon his lines, until prevented by increasing darkness.[29]

Anderson's division advanced rapidly up the Fredericksburg road, charging upon Kane's brigade of Geary's division, composed of new troops, which, after a short resistance, retreated in confusion. An aid from Slocum came down to Hooker for reinforcements. "No," said Hooker, "he must hold his own. Let Geary's division, however, be thrown to the right of the road, that the artillery may be able to sweep the enemy on the left." This was done, and the heavy fire that was given by Knapp's and other batteries checked Anderson's advance. A constant demonstration was kept up by Anderson to deceive Hooker as to Lee's intentions. Thus the night passed.

The Battle of Sunday

Both armies were busy through the night, preparing for the great struggle,—Lee to attack and Hooker to defend. The wounded were sent to the rear, also the baggage trains, and the cavalry, and everything which could impede operations. Hooker's line was in the form of the letter V. The Second Corps, which had followed Berry up the

---

29: Lee's Report.

night before, occupied the right of the line, reaching nearly down to the river, joining the left flank upon Berry's division of the Third Corps, which extended to the plank-road, west of Chancellorsville. Whipple's and Birney's divisions of the Third, and Geary's division of the Twelfth, formed the point of the letter V, which enclosed Chancellorsville. The other divisions of the Twelfth Corps and the Fifth Corps forming the other side of the letter, extended from Chancellorsville to the Rappahannock. The Eleventh Corps was placed in position to support the Fifth on the extreme left of the line. During the day the First Corps under Reynolds came up the river, crossed at United States Ford, and wheeled into position on the right of the Second Corps, thus forming the extreme right of the line. The troops had been busy through the night erecting breastworks, while a large number of guns were placed in position to sweep all the roads. Stuart renewed the fight at daylight, with Hill in the front line, Colston in the second, and Rodes in the third. He advanced with the intention of breaking the line near Chancellorsville. His troops were exasperated by the loss of their leader, and were animated by revenge. They came through the woods almost in solid mass. Colston's and Rodes's men, pressing eagerly forward, and closing up the spaces between the lines. They received, without flinching, the terrible fire which flamed from Berry's and Birney's and Whipple's lines. They charged upon Sickles's outer works, and carried them.

They advanced upon the second line, but were cut up by Best's artillery. Companies and regiments melted away. Berry and Birney advance to meet them. The living waves rolled against each other like the billows of a stormy sea. The Rebels, as if maddened by the obstinacy of those who held the position, rushed up to the muzzles of the cannon. Sickles sent for reinforcements. Hooker ordered French and Hancock of the Second Corps to advance and attack Stuart in flank.

It was seven o'clock in the morning. The battle had been raging since daylight. The two divisions of the Second Corps swung out from the main line, faced southwest, and moved upon Stuart.

South of Chancellorsville there is an elevation higher than that occupied by Best's artillery. When the fog which had hung over the battle-field all the morning lifted, Stuart sent his artillery to occupy the position. Thirty pieces were planted there, which enfiladed both of Hooker's lines. A heavy artillery duel was kept up, but, notwithstanding the severity of the fire, the Union troops held the position. Stuart, instead of breaking through Sickles, found the Second Corps turning his own left flank. He says:

The enemy was pressing our left with infantry, and all the reinforcements I could obtain were sent there. Colquitt's brigade of Trimble's division, ordered first to the right, was directed to the left to support Pender. Iverson's brigade of the second line was also engaged there, and the three lines were more or less merged into one line of battle, and reported hard pressed. Urgent requests were sent for reinforcements, and notices that the troops were out of ammunition. I ordered that the ground must be held at all hazards, if necessary with the bayonet.[30]

All of the efforts of Stuart to break the line by a direct infantry attack failed. But his batteries massed on the hill were doing great damage. The shells swept down Birney's and Whipple's and Berry's ranks on the one hand, and Geary's and Williams's on the other. Hooker saw that the position could not be held without great loss of life. Preparations were accordingly made to fall back to a stronger position, where his army would be more concentrated, the lines shorter and thicker, in the form of a semicircle. Meanwhile Lee swung Anderson round and joined Stuart, making a simultaneous advance of both wings of his army, under cover of a heavy fire from all his available artillery,— pouring a storm of shells upon Chancellorsville, firing the buildings. Hooker had begun to retire before Lee advanced, withdrawing his artillery, removing his wounded, losing no prisoners.

Every attack of Anderson upon Slocum had been repulsed with great loss. A South Carolina regiment came against the Second Massachusetts. Three times the men from the Palmetto state charged upon the men of Massachusetts. Three times the flag from the Old Bay State changed hands. But, before the Rebels could carry it from the field, it was rescued, and at the close of the fight was still in the hands of the regiment. When Slocum's troops had exhausted their ammunition they emptied the cartridge-boxes of the fallen. When that was gone they held the ground by the bayonet till ordered to retire.[31]

General Lee says:

> By ten a. m. we were in full possession of the field. The troops, having become somewhat scattered, by the difficulties of the ground, and the ardour of the contest, were immediately reformed, preparatory to renewing the attack. The enemy had retired to a strong position near the Rappahannock, which he had previously fortified. His superiority of numbers, the un-

---

30: Stuart's Report.
31: *From the Potomac to the Rapidan*, by Quint.

favourable nature of the ground, which was densely wooded, and the condition of our troops, after the arduous and sanguinary conflict in which they had been engaged, rendered great caution necessary. Our preparations were just completed, when further operations were suspended by intelligence received from Fredericksburg.[32]

The new line taken by Hooker was one of great strength. No assault, with the intention of carrying it, was made by Lee. News of disaster from Fredericksburg, where Sedgwick was driving all before him, made it necessary for him to send reinforcements in that direction.

Second Battle of Fredericksburg

An important part of General Hooker's plan was Sedgwick's movement on Fredericksburg, but the battle fought there on Sunday, the 3rd of May, was wholly distinct from Chancellorsville. Early on the morning of the 2nd, Professor Lowe went up in his balloon from the Falmouth hills, and looked down upon the city.

He reported the Rebels moving towards Chancellorsville. Looking closely into the entrenchments behind Fredericksburg he discovered that the Rebels intended to hold them. The Washington Artillery was behind the breastworks by Maryee's house.

"Ten thousand of the enemy, I should judge, still there," was his report to General Butterfield, Hooker's chief of staff, who remained with Sedgwick.

During the day Reynolds withdrew and moved up the Falmouth side to United States Ford. The Rebels saw the movement, and thought that the Yankees did not dare to make a second attempt to drive them from their entrenchments.

"Now is the time for Sedgwick to attack them," was Hooker's despatch from Chancellorsville, Saturday afternoon, to General Butterfield.

As soon as night came on, Sedgwick began his preparations. The engineers were directed to take up the lower pontoons and lay a new bridge opposite the Lacy House, at the point where the Seventh Michigan and Nineteenth and Twentieth Massachusetts won for themselves great honour on the 11th of December.

"Kindle no fires; let there be no loud talking," were Sedgwick's orders to his troops on the plain by Bernard's house, below Deep

---

32: Lee's Report.

Run. The men ate their suppers of hard-tack and cold meat in silence, threw themselves upon the ground, and slept soundly in the calm moonlight. At midnight an aide rode along the lines, saying to each officer, "Get your men in readiness at once." The men sprang to their feet, folded their blankets, and were ready.

It was half past twelve Sunday morning before the forward movement began. The United States Chasseurs were in advance as skirmishers, deployed on both sides of the Bowling Green road. Shaler's brigade followed, then Wheaton's and Brown's brigades. They crossed Deep Run, where the skirmishers had a few shots with the Rebel pickets, and moved into the town.

The engineers soon had the bridge completed, and Gibbon's division of the Second Corps, which had been waiting by the Lacy House, crossed the stream.

Early stationed Barksdale, with seven companies of the Twenty-First Mississippi, between Maryee's house and the plank-road, with the Seventeenth and Thirteenth Mississippi on the hills by the Howison house, and the Eighteenth and the remainder of the Twenty-First behind the stone-wall at the base of the hill. Hayes's brigade, consisting of the Fifth, Sixth, Seventh, Eighth, and Ninth Louisianians, was on the hill near the monument, with Wilcox's brigade in its rear, guarding Banks's Ford. Early himself was by Hazel Run, with Gordon's, Hoke's, and Smith's brigades. Sedgwick's divisions were formed in the following order: Gibbon above the town in front of the monument, Newton in front of Maryee's Hill, Howe at the lower end of the town, and Brooks on the plain below.

The morning dawned. The fog prevented the Rebels from seeing the movements of Sedgwick, though Barksdale's pickets reported the town full of Yankees. From Chancellorsville came the roar of battle, the constant thunder of the cannonade. It was half past five when Shaler's brigade of Newton's division moved over the field where so many thousands fell on the 13th of December. It was a reconnoissance to ascertain the position and number of the force holding the place. The men marched on gallantly, but were forced to retire before the Mississippians and the artillery on the hill.

Sedgwick brought Hearn's, Martin's, Adams's, and Hazard's batteries, and Battery D of the Second United States regiment of artillery, into position in the town and above it, while Hexamer's, the First Maryland, and McCartney's First Massachusetts occupied the ground below Hazel Run. McCartney was on the same spot which he occupied in the first battle.

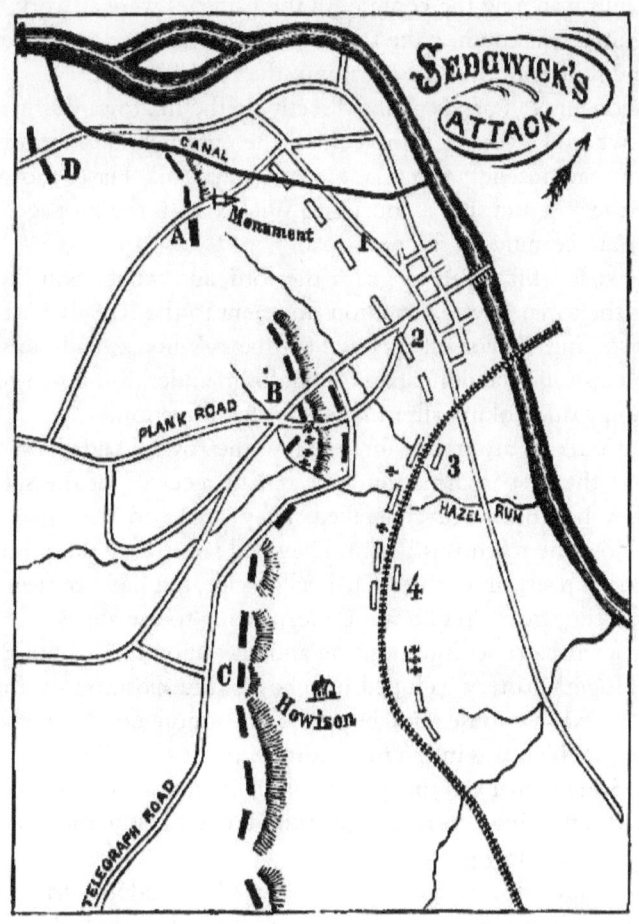

UNION POSITIONS.

1. Gibbon's Division.
2. Newton's "
3. Howe's "
4. Brooks's "

REBEL POSITIONS.

A. Hayes's Brigade.
B. Barksdale's Brigade.
C. Early's Division.
   Gordon's, Hokes's, and Smith's Brigades.
D. Wilcox's Brigade.

It was a day of peace everywhere except at Fredericksburg and Chancellorsville. The air was laden with the fragrance of flowers blooming in the gardens of the town. Thousands of spectators stood upon the Falmouth hills watching the contest. All the batteries were at work,—the heavy guns at Falmouth, at the Lacy House, and farther down, throwing shells and solid shot over the town into the Rebel lines.

Gibbon, instead of advancing directly up the hill towards the monument, where Hayes was lying behind the entrenchments, moved up the river road, intending to turn Hayes's right flank. Hayes moved his men farther up, and sent a courier to Wilcox with the message, "The Yankees are coming up the river road."[33]

Wilcox left fifty men to guard the ford, and went upon the run towards the town. It was an anxious moment to the Rebels. Barksdale and Hayes and Wilcox all met at Stanisberry's house, and consulted as to what should be done. Early their commander, was down on the Telegraph road, looking after matters in that direction.

"The Yankees are in full force below the town," said Barksdale.[34] That was the first information Wilcox had received of the startling fact. They had been out-generalled. They supposed that the movement below the town was a feint. They had seen Reynolds withdraw and march up stream towards Chancellorsville, but had not seen Gibbon cross the stream. Yet he was there, moving to the attack.

"Put your batteries into position and play upon them," said Barksdale.[35] Huger's battery galloped up, chose a fine position on the hill near Dr. Taylor's house, and began to fire upon the Massachusetts Twentieth, which was in the road, compelling it to seek shelter under the hill. So effectual was the fire that Gibbon's advance was checked.

Brooks and Howe moved against the Rebels below the town, but found them strongly posted.

Twice Newton advanced upon Maryee's Hill, and was driven back. The forenoon was waning. But though baffled, Sedgwick was not disposed to give up the attempt. He watched the contest closely, reconnoitring all the positions of the Rebels, and determined to make an attack with his whole force at once.

But while Sedgwick was making preparations, Early endeavoured to drive Brooks and Howe into the river. He advanced from the position occupied by Pender and Hood in the first battle, emerged from the woods and crossed the open field.

33: Wilcox's Report, p. 98.
34: Wilcox's Report.
35: Barksdale's Report.

It is about ten o'clock. McCartney's battery, the First Massachusetts, is on a hillock, where it has full sweep of all the plain, right and left, and in front. There are five batteries of the Rebel reserve artillery, under Pendleton, in front, which have tried in vain to drive McCartney from the spot. A solid shot kills two horses and a man; McCartney is struck by a fragment of shell; yet the battery maintains its position north of the Bowling Green road, in Bernard's field. A regiment which never before has been under fire is lying in front of the battery, sheltered by the hedges along the road,—soldiers that have enlisted for nine months. They are wanting in pluck, and as the Rebels advance, run straight up the hill towards the battery.

"Get out of the way, or I'll fire through you," shouts Lieutenant Green, who impatiently holds his artillerists in check till the fugitives are past him.

He cuts at them right and left with his sword, indignant at their cowardly conduct, anxious to have the coast clear, that he may pour a torrent of canister into the advancing foe, now close at hand.

The whole battery—six pieces—opens by a volley, sending streams of canister down the slope! But the Rebels are in earnest. Still they advance.

"Give them double-shotted canister," shouts Green to his gunners, and they ram home the charges with a will. The guns leap from the ground with the recoil!

Nearer,—across the road,—up the hill,—they come.

"Give it to them! Give it to them! Quick!" are the energetic shouts of Green, and the canister tears through the ranks. No troops can face such a destructive fire. The Rebels flee down the hill, across the road, over the field, to the shelter of the woods.

"The repulse of the enemy on the extreme left was effected almost entirely by McCartney's battery," said General Brooks.[36]

General Sedgwick determined to carry Maryee's Hill at the point of the bayonet. Some of the officers thought it an impossibility. It had been tried three times in the first battle and twice during that morning, and all attempts had failed. But Sedgwick converged his forces upon one point. He formed his columns in three lines, with the intention of moving his whole force at once,—thus preventing Early from sending any reinforcements from other parts of the lines.

The troops selected for the attack upon Maryee's Hill were the

---

36: Brooks's Report.

Sixty-First Pennsylvania and Forty-Third New York in the front line, north of the plank-road, and the First Long Island and Eighty-Second Pennsylvania in the second line, under General Shaler. South of the plank-road were the Sixth Maine and Thirty-First New York in the front line, with the Fifth Wisconsin acting as skirmishers. Next in line were the Seventh Massachusetts and Thirty-Sixth New York, Second New York and Twenty-Sixth New Jersey, of Neil's brigade. Still farther down, by Hazel Run, was the Vermont brigade.

Gibbon moved against Hayes and Wilcox, while Brooks still held the ground, and made a demonstration against Early.

It is past eleven o'clock before all the dispositions are made.

"Go upon the double-quick. Don't fire a shot. Give them the bayonet. Carry the rifle-pits, charge up the hill, and capture the guns," are the instructions.

The men throw aside everything which will hinder them, fix their bayonets, and prepare for the work. Their blood is up. They know that it is to be a desperate struggle. But it is not death that they are thinking of, but victory!

The Sixty-First Pennsylvania and Forty-Third New York move over the bridge across the canal. Their advance is the signal for all the lines. The men rise from the ground where they have been lying sheltered from the Rebel shells. The Rebel batteries above them are in a blaze. The stone-wall at the base of the hill is aflame. Barksdale sees the threatening aspect. "I am hard pressed," is his message to Wilcox. "Send me reinforcements." But Gibbon is moving on Wilcox, and the latter cannot respond.

Cool and steady the advance. The hills rain canister. The sunken road is a sheet of flame. But onward into the storm, with a cheer, heard above the roar of battle upon the distant Falmouth hills, they leap into the sunken road and capture the Rebels defending it. They climb the hill. Steep the ascent. They feel the hot breath of the cannon in their faces. Some roll to the bottom of the hill, the lamp of life extinguished forever; but their surviving comrades do not falter. They reach the crest, leap over the breastworks, and seize the guns! Maine, Massachusetts, Vermont, New York, and Wisconsin meet in the entrenchments and rend the air with victorious cheers!

Barksdale puts spurs to his horse and rides to the rear, leaving half of his brigade and eight guns in the hands of the victors.

Barksdale says:

The distance from town to the points assailed was so short,

Leading a Charge

the attack so suddenly made, and the difficulty of removing troops from one part of the line to another was so great, that it was utterly impossible for either General Wilcox or General Hayes to reach the scene of action in time to afford any assistance whatever.[37]

There was consternation in the Rebel lines. Early fled down the Telegraph road. Hayes also ran. Wilcox, who was not aware of the disaster, remained in position on Taylor's Hill, wondering what had happened. Had Sedgwick known his position, the whole of Wilcox's brigade might have been captured; but it required time to reform the lines, and Wilcox made his escape.

Long and loud and joyous were the shouts of the victors. The stronghold had been wrested from the Rebels at last.

It was Sunday noon. Hooker had just fallen back from Chancellorsville, and the Rebels were rejoicing over their success, when a messenger reached Lee with the tidings of disaster. Fredericksburg was lost, after all. It must be recovered, or the victory at Chancellorsville would be only a disastrous defeat.

Sedgwick telegraphed his success to Hooker.

"Move and attack Lee in rear," was Hooker's order.

Lee sent McLaws to hold Sedgwick in check. The time had come when Hooker should have assumed the offensive. The First Corps had arrived, but had taken no part in the battle. The Third Corps, Meade's, was in good condition; so was the Second, Hancock's, although it had fought during the forenoon. Barlow's brigade of the Eleventh was fresh; the Twelfth had fought bravely, had lost heavily, but was not demoralized. The Third Corps had suffered most of all, yet it could be relied upon for another contest. The withdrawal of McLaws left Lee's line thin towards Fredericksburg, the place to break through, and open communication with Sedgwick. The hour had come when he ought not to stand longer on the defensive, but gathering his forces in mass overwhelm Lee by a sudden and mighty onset. It was an auspicious moment,—a golden opportunity, such as does not often come to military commanders. But having formed his plan of fighting a defensive battle, he did not depart from it, and lost the victory which lay within his grasp.

Sedgwick having carried the heights of Fredericksburg, instead of following Early down the Telegraph road, made preparations to move towards Chancellorsville, and join Hooker.

Wilcox, meanwhile, brought two of Huger's rifle-guns into posi-

---

37: Barksdale's Report.

tion near Dr. Taylor's house, and opened fire. He also threw out his skirmishers, made a display of his force, and looked round to see what could be done to escape from his perilous position. Sedgwick brought up a battery, and moved forward his lines. Wilcox fled, and succeeded, by rapid marching under the shelter of a pine thicket, in gaining the plank-road, near Salem Church, where he was joined by General McLaws, and where also Barksdale rallied his troops.

The church is a brick building, without any steeple, standing on the south side of the road, about four miles out from Fredericksburg, and about a mile and a half south of the Rappahannock at Banks's Ford. There was an oak grove near the church, and in front of it an open field, but west of it there were thick woods, which effectually concealed the Rebels. It was about five o'clock in the afternoon when Sedgwick advanced up the plank-road, with Brooks's division in the road, Newton north of it, and Howe on the south side. Sedgwick's skirmishers sent back word that the Rebels were in strong force in the woods. At the same moment the Rebel batteries opened fire. One of their first shells killed a mounted orderly and his horse, and wounded Captain Reed, of General Brooks's staff.

Sedgwick brought up his artillery and commenced a fire upon the church, and the woods beyond it. Wilcox had formed his line across the plank-road. His sharpshooters were in the church. He had four pieces of artillery in the road and on each side of it. He also threw a company of sharpshooters into a school-house near the church. Kershaw's and Wofford's brigades were on the right of the road; Semmes's and Mahone's on the other side. Sedgwick's batteries were in position near the toll-gate, and so accurate and destructive was the fire of his guns that the Rebel batteries by the church were driven from their position. Russell's and Bartlett's brigades moved forward to rout the enemy from the woods, Sedgwick supposing there was but a small force to oppose him. The advance was over ground slightly ascending, through an open field, towards the woods, where the Rebel skirmishers were lying. It is a narrow belt of woods. Behind it were the church and school-house, and beyond the church the woods where the main body of the Rebels were lying. They drove the skirmishers from the belt of woods, halted a moment to reform their lines, gave three cheers, charged through the grove, routing the Rebels there concealed. They surrounded the school-house, captured the entire company of the Ninth Alabama stationed in it, put to flight a regiment lying behind the house.[38] But the re-

---

38: General Wilcox's Report.

mainder of the Ninth Alabama, with other regiments, came to the rescue, succeeded in recapturing a portion of their comrades, and forced Russell and Bartlett to retire.

It was now nearly six o'clock in the afternoon, and till night set in there was heavy fighting along the whole line. Wilcox and Semmes several times advanced upon Sedgwick, but were repulsed. So far as numbers were concerned the contest was about equal. But the Rebels were on commanding ground, and protected by the woods, while Sedgwick was in the open field. In this contest Wilcox lost four hundred and ninety-five men. He had six officers killed and twenty-three wounded. Semmes lost six hundred and eighty-three killed and wounded, Wafford five hundred and sixty-two. The whole loss of the Rebels in the fight at Salem Church was nearly two thousand. Sedgwick, instead of advancing again, waited for the Rebels to attack him, but they did not choose to come out from their strong position in the woods, and try it a second time in the field. Thus the day closed.

Sedgwick's success endangered Lee, and, unless Fredericksburg were regained, the battle was lost to the Rebels. Lee says:

> The enemy had so strengthened his position near Chancellorsville that it was deemed inexpedient to assail it with less than our whole force, which could not be concentrated until we were relieved from the danger that menaced our rear. It was accordingly resolved still further to reinforce the troops in front of General Sedgwick, in order, if possible, to drive him across the Rappahannock. Accordingly, on the 4th, General Anderson was directed to proceed with his remaining brigades to join General McLaws, the three divisions of Jackson's corps holding our position at Chancellorsville. Anderson reached Salem Church about noon, and was directed to gain the left flank of the enemy and form a junction with Early.[39]

Half of the Rebel army was arrayed against Sedgwick, who held his ground through the 4th till night. Early, during the day, retraced his steps up the Telegraph road, and, finding that Sedgwick had moved out to Salem Church, and that the fortifications were unoccupied, took possession, and thus cut Sedgwick's communications with Falmouth. When Anderson arrived he had no alternative but to retreat by Banks's Ford, where he crossed the river without loss during the night. Hooker also recrossed, took up his bridges, and the army returned again to its camp.

In reviewing this battle, it is apparent that Hooker's movement to

---
39: Lee's Report, p. 12.

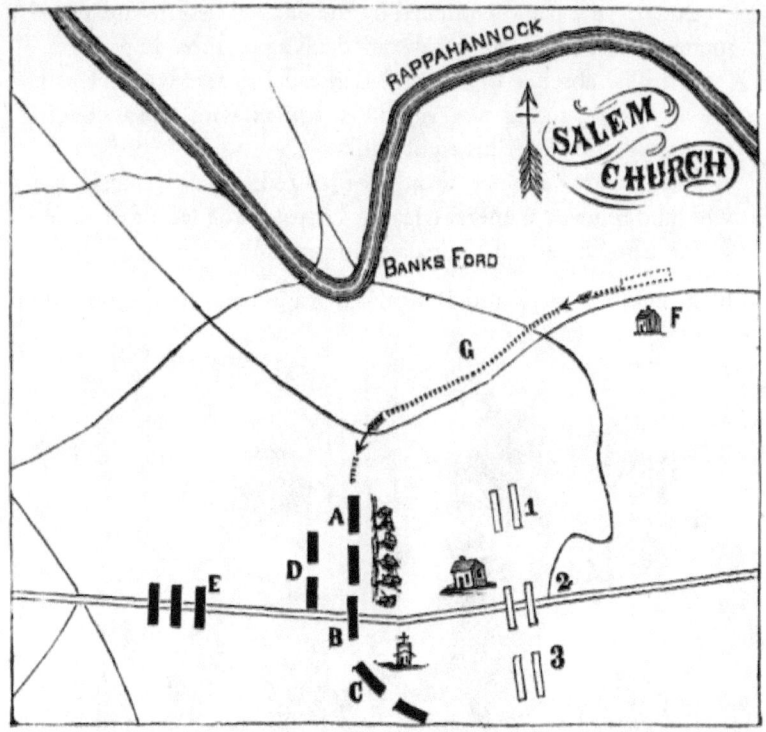

Chancellorsville was a surprise to Lee. It was excellently planned and efficiently executed,—each corps reaching its assigned position at the time appointed by the Commander-in-chief. It is plain that Hooker's departure from his original intention—to await an attack from Lee— was the cause of the disaster at the beginning of the engagement. Sickles's corps and Barlow's brigade being absent, the balance of the Eleventh Corps had no supports; and yet by Bushbeck's brigade and Dilger's battery, with such assistance as was given by a few brave men of the other brigades, Jackson's right was not only held in check, but thrown into confusion. Howard's statement of the case presents the matter in its true light.

Thus reads his report:

> Now, as to the cause of this disaster to my corps.
> 1st. Though constantly threatened, and apprised of the moving of the enemy, yet the woods were so dense that he was able to mass a large force, whose exact whereabouts neither patrols, reconnaissancers, nor scouts ascertained. He succeeded in forming a column to and outflanking my right.

2nd. By the panic produced by the enemy's reverse fire, regiments and artillery were thrown suddenly upon those in position.

3rd. The absence of General Barlow's brigade, which I had previously located in reserve and *en echelon*, with Colonel Von Gilsa's, so as to cover his right flank.

My corps was very soon reorganized, near Chancellorsville, and relieved General Meade's corps on the left of the line, where it remained till Thursday morning.[40]

Had Sickles's corps and Barlow's brigade been in the line, there

"Keep out of the draft."

40: Howard's Report, p. 9.

would have been not only no disaster, but Jackson would have been defeated at the outset; for, upon the return of those troops from Scott's Run, he was driven with great loss.

Jackson was driven by Sickles when the Third Corps returned to the line; and had Sickles and Barlow been in their proper positions when the attack was made, they could have repulsed him with greater ease.

Though Jackson's attack was successful, it is not therefore conclusively evident that Lee's plan was wise. His army was divided into three parts,—Early at Fredericksburg, Lee east of Chancellorsville, and Jackson northwest of it. Being thoroughly acquainted with the country, he was able to take his position unobserved.

There were several opportunities during the battle when Hooker could have broken Lee's lines. The battle virtually was lost to Lee on Sunday noon. Hooker had fallen back from Chancellorsville, but Sedgwick had taken Fredericksburg. Had Hooker, when he ordered Sedgwick to attack Lee in the rear, on Sunday afternoon, himself advanced, Lee would have been forced to abandon the contest; but, having resolved at the outset to stand on the defensive, the Union commander adhered to the idea, and thus Lee was able to retrieve the disaster at Fredericksburg,—far more serious than that which had happened to the Eleventh Corps.

Could we but comprehend the ways of God, we might perhaps discover that the failure of the Union army at Chancellorsville was not owing to the prowess of the Rebels, the valour of Stonewall Jackson, nor the strategy of Lee, but to another cause. When the army came into position at Chancellorsville, the commanding general is reported to have said that the Almighty could not prevent him from winning a victory. God is not mocked with impunity. There is one anthem resounding through all the ages,—*Te Deum Laudamus!*

Chapter 14
Cavalry Operations

May, 1863

The Yankees can't ride horses; they were made to go on foot and dig in the dirt; but the men of the South are true-born cavaliers, accustomed from their childhood to the sports of the field.

So said a Richmond newspaper at the beginning of the war; but Zagoni's charge at Springfield, Pleasanton's at Barber's Cross-Roads, and Dahlgren's at Fredericksburg showed that the men of the North could ride to some purpose. Up to this time the cavalry of the Army of the Potomac had taken little part in the great battles which had been fought. It had been divided by McClellan into squadrons, and attached to brigades of infantry; but Burnside, before his resignation, had begun a reorganization of the cavalry. Hooker completed the work by forming a cavalry corps, consisting of three divisions, commanded by Major-General Stoneman. The division commanders were Generals Pleasanton, Gregg, and Averill. In the month of March, Stoneman, wishing to ascertain the position of the Rebel cavalry, sent Averill's division across the Rappahannock, at Kelley's Ford. The Rebels guarding the crossing were nearly all captured. Averill pushed out towards Culpepper, but met Stuart, and after a sharp engagement retired across the river.

March and April were muddy; but Stoneman's squadrons were busy foraging the country north of the Rappahannock, while his scouts were finding their way through Stuart's lines, reaching James River, entering Richmond, ascertaining where supplies for the Rebel army were accumulated, and what troops guarded the bridges in rear of Lee's army. They discovered that the main body of the Rebel cavalry was in the vicinity of Culpepper and Orange Court-House, under Fitz-Hugh and Custis Lee.

One feature of General Hooker's plan, in the movement to Chancellorsville, was the destruction of Lee's supplies and his communications with Richmond. This part was assigned to the cavalry. Averill was sent to Bealton, on the Orange and Alexandria Railroad, as if intending a movement upon Gordonsville. Stuart sent the two Lees up the river to keep watch, which left a door open at Germanna Ford.

Stoneman sent all his unserviceable horses and men to Falmouth. Men who could not endure hardship and exposure were detailed to remain and guard the camp. The cavalrymen only knew that there was to be a movement somewhere, so well kept were Hooker's intentions.

Pleasanton was ordered to accompany Hooker to Chancellorsville, Averill was directed to cross the river at Rappahannock Station, and move towards Gordonsville, while Gregg's division was selected to strike the blow which would cripple Lee.

On the 29th of April, when the Eleventh and Twelfth Corps reached Kelley's Ford, on the Rappahannock, Gregg, who was lying there, crossed in advance, and moved west towards Culpepper. Averill at the same time forded the river at Rappahannock Station, four miles above, and moved also towards Culpepper. There was a small force of Rebel cavalry in that town, but Averill charged through the streets. The Rebels made a hasty retreat towards Gordonsville, crossing the Rapidan at the railroad and burning the bridge behind them. Averill followed, and the Lees thought that Gordonsville was the point aimed at. Gregg, instead of going to Culpepper, turned south through Stevensburg; and, while the Eleventh and Twelfth Corps were crossing the Rapidan at Germanna Ford, his troops were fording the same stream eight miles higher up.

When Gregg arrived at Raccoon Ford, he found it guarded by a strong force on the opposite side, entrenched around the house of Colonel Porter, which overlooks the ford. Gregg halted his column in the field and woods, near the house of Mr. Stringfellow, on the northern bank, and made demonstrations as if to cross. He opened with his artillery, which was replied to by the Rebels. While the enemy was thus diverted, a small force was sent to Morton's Ford, two miles below, which crossed without opposition, dashed up the road, and came upon the Rebels in rear of Colonel Porter's house. They fled towards Orange Court-House. Lieutenant Gaskell, with a portion of the Fifth United States Cavalry, followed them five miles, capturing an officer and several men. The division crossed, and bivouacked on the hills around Colonel Porter's house for the night. This movement of Gregg's compelled the Lees, who intended to fight Averill at Rapidan

Station, to make a hasty retreat towards Gordonsville, for Gregg was on their flank. Averill crossed the stream, driving back the Rebels, and by his movement deceiving the enemy. He followed them nearly to Gordonsville, remained till Gregg's division was well on its way, then recrossed the stream, and rejoined Hooker.

The night of the 30th of April was cold and the ground damp, but no fires were allowed. At two o'clock in the morning the men were roused from sleep, not by the bugle-call, but by low-spoken words. They were soon ready to move, but were obliged to wait till daylight for a guide. Four hours of valuable time were lost by this delay.

The column moved along the road which runs south from Raccoon Ford to Louisa Court-House, at Greenwood. It crossed Mountain Run soon after daylight, reached the Fredericksburg plank-road, and moved on the north fork of the North Anna. A small body dashed into Orange Spring early in the morning, and captured a lieutenant of Jackson's staff, and a wagon loaded with entrenching tools. Squadrons were sent out in all directions,—on the side-roads and by-paths, through the fields and forests,—telling the people everywhere that Hooker's whole army was on the march, creating the impression among the people that Hooker was making a swift descent upon Richmond. The soldiers helped themselves to chickens, turkeys, lambs, and obtained breakfasts in the houses of the farmers, who were astonished at their sudden appearance, and their unceremonious way of sitting down to breakfast without being asked. They visited stables, seized or exchanged horses without paying any boot. Great was the excitement among the negroes, who poured out from the cabins with wild expressions of joy. Hundreds of them joined the column, without saying goodbye to their masters. The citizens were sullen, but the women gave free utterance to their feelings.

Gregg reached Louisa Court-House, twenty miles from Raccoon Ford, at two o'clock in the afternoon. The Virginia Central Railroad, from Richmond to Gordonsville, passes through the town. A large quantity of supplies was in store there, guarded by several hundred Rebel cavalry, who, when they heard that the "Yankees" were coming, sent off what they could on a train of cars, and then fled to Gordonsville. Gregg sent out a regiment in pursuit, while the main body of his command bivouacked in the field west of the Court-House. Small bodies were detailed east and west along the railroad, tearing up the track, burning the ties, and destroying all the culverts and bridges in the vicinity.

It was the first time that the people of Louisa Court-House had

A NIGHT MARCH OF CAVALRY

been visited by the Yankees. They had lived in security, never entertaining the thought that the "Yankees" could penetrate so far into the interior. They wanted high pay for all they had to sell, but were ready to make a great discount between Confederate currency and greenbacks. Gregg was now east of Gordonsville and Averill north of it. Gregg sent a portion of the First Maine Cavalry towards the place, as if intending to proceed in that direction. Three or four miles west of the Court-House the Maine men encountered a large force, which had been sent by Fitz-Hugh Lee. The officer commanding the party sent word to Gregg, and fell back slowly; but the Rebels charged upon him, killed two, and captured twenty-eight. Gregg formed his division for battle, and the Rebels retreated towards Gordonsville.

At five o'clock in the afternoon, the railroad and depot buildings having been destroyed, the column turned southeast, crossed the South Anna, passing through Yancyville, a little village on that stream, moved down the river, and reached Thompson's Cross-Roads at eleven o'clock.

Up to this time General Stoneman had not informed his officers of his intentions. He called them together at midnight and gave them their instructions.

"You are to destroy the bridges over the North Anna, and break up Lee's communications in that direction," were his instructions to Gregg.

"Colonel Davis will destroy the bridges over the South Anna, south of the Fredericksburg Railroad."

"Colonel Wyndham, with details of regiments from his brigade, will reach the James River at Columbia, and destroy the bridge there and break up the canal."

"Colonel Kilpatrick, with the Harris Light Cavalry, will move to the Chickahominy, and burn the bridges across that stream."

Stoneman himself, with the main force, was to remain there, and cover the movement. When the object each commander had in view was accomplished, they were allowed the widest latitude for other operations.

At half past two o'clock Sunday morning, May 3rd, the various columns are in motion. It is a bright moonlight night. Gregg moves northeast, Davis east, Kilpatrick southeast, and Wyndham south.

At this moment, Lee at Chancellorsville is arranging for his second attack on Hooker; Sedgwick preparing to storm the heights of Fredericksburg; Stonewall Jackson is mortally wounded, and lying in a house at Guinea's Station. Averill is hastening to withdraw from the vicinity of Orange Court-House, when he should be moving on towards Gordonsville. Couriers are flying through the country, along the roads leading to Richmond, with the astounding intelligence that "the Yankees are coming!"

General Gregg has the First Maine and Tenth New York, with two pieces of artillery. He moves rapidly up the Central Railroad. There are no troops to oppose him. He burns the station at Beaver Dam, and Anderson's bridge across the North Anna, about three miles north of the station. He sends out detachments along the railroad, burning all the bridges in the vicinity. Another detachment moves to the South Anna, along the Richmond and Gordonsville turnpike, and destroys the bridge called the Ground-Squirrel bridge, over that stream. Having accomplished the object of the expedition, without any loss, Gregg returns and rejoins Stoneman at Thompson's Cross-Roads the 5th of May having made a forced march of seventy miles, and doing great damage.

Kilpatrick and Davis are near together in their movements, going east and southeast. Kilpatrick makes his first halt thirteen miles from Richmond. There are bodies of Rebel troops around him,—a large force at Hanover Junction, other troops in the vicinity of Ashland, and others moving out from the city to intercept him. His only safety is in a rapid, audacious movement. At daylight on Monday morning, May 4th, after a short rest for his men and horses, he is again in motion, directly toward Richmond. He strikes the Fredericksburg railroad at Hungary Station, five miles from the city, burns the depot, tears up the track, pushes directly down the Brooke pike, till he can see the spires of the city, only two miles distant.

There is great excitement in the city,—riding to and fro of officers and couriers, mustering of militia, turning out of clerks from the departments, shouldering of muskets and hasty buckling on of cartridge-boxes, forming lines and hastening out to the entrenchments. Frightened farmers ride in from all directions with the intelligence that the country is swarming with Yankees. A company of artillery and a considerable force of infantry, with cavalry pickets and scouts, which are moving out on the Brooke pike, are seized with a panic and rush back to the city. The bells are rung. The confusion and consternation increase. Men hide their valuables. Women and children cross the river to Manchester. The Union prisoners, who have been suffering the horrors of Libby Prison for many months, looking through their iron-grated windows, behold the commotion. They can hear the booming of Kilpatrick's guns. Their hearts bound with indescribable joy. They are thrilled with the thought that deliverance is at hand.

Kilpatrick captures Lieutenant Brown, an aide-de-camp of General Winder, and an escort accompanying him, within the fortifications. He paroles him, dating the parole at the city of Richmond.

"You are a mighty daring sort of fellows, but you'll certainly be captured before sundown," said the aide.

"That may all be, but we intend to do a mighty deal of mischief first," replied Kilpatrick.[41]

He leaves a portion of the troops with his artillery, which engages the Rebel batteries, while, guided by a negro, with a small detachment he moves through the fields to the railroad, burns Meadow bridge, running a train of cars into the stream. With one regiment of cavalry he reaches the Rebel fortifications, captures Rebels inside them, plants his batteries, and throws shells almost into the city of Richmond, in face of their own batteries, destroys communication with Lee, burning bridges, tearing up railroad tracks, pulling down telegraph wire, running a train of cars into the river, with rebel troops all around him.

Having accomplished this he moves northeast, for he can see Rebel columns moving up the Brooke pike and Mechanicsville road, to cut off his retreat. He dismisses all hope of returning to Stoneman. It is a critical moment. He must move in some direction at once. He consults his map.

"To horse, men! We are all right! We are safe yet."[42]

With a faithful negro to guide him, he moves through woods and fields, along by-paths and cross roads, going east and northeast, to Hanover Town, on the Pamunkey. His horses are jaded, but he makes a hard ride, reaches the place in safety, crosses the stream, sets fire to the bridge, halts his men upon the northern bank. The Rebels, in hot pursuit, come down to the other bank, mortified and chagrined and enraged at his escape. The Yankees throw up their caps, and greet them with a hearty cheer. Scouts come in and report a train of thirty wagons loaded with corn for the Rebel army nearby. Kilpatrick captures them, feeds his horses with what corn he needs, destroys the rest, moves five miles up the river, bivouacs for the night, remains till one o'clock in the morning of the 5th, then moving rapidly north to Aylett's, near Mattapony River, surprises three hundred Rebel cavalry, capturing two officers, thirty-three men, burning fifty-six wagons and a building containing twenty thousand barrels of corn and wheat, quantities of clothing and commissary stores, safely crossing the Mattapony in season to escape the advance of the Rebel cavalry

---

41: *Kilpatrick and Our Cavalry.*
42: *Kilpatrick and our Cavalry.*

in pursuit. Pushing on, later in the evening, he destroys a third wagon train, burns buildings containing a large amount of corn, near Tappahannock, then turning southeast, making a forced march of twenty miles, reaches King and Queen Court-House, where he finds a body of cavalry drawn up to dispute his passage. He prepares to charge, but suddenly discovers that it is a portion of the Twelfth Illinois of Colonel Davis's command. The meeting is a joyful one. The two commands move on together, marching southeast, reaching Gloucester Point at ten o'clock on the morning of the 7th, where they find rest and safety under the guns of the Union fortifications, making a march of nearly two hundred miles in less than five days, with a loss of only one officer and thirty-seven men, having captured and paroled upward of three hundred of the enemy.[43]

"Who will convey news to Hooker of our success?" was the question put by Kilpatrick when at Aylett's, after routing the Rebels there.

"I am ready to go," was the quick response of Lieutenant Estes of the First Maine, who was acting as aide to Kilpatrick. Ten men were detailed to accompany him. They struck across the country north, and reached the Rappahannock at Tappahannock Court-House, dashing into that place, and capturing a lieutenant and fifteen men! whom they paroled. The river was swollen, and they could not cross. The whole country was alarmed. The militia were assembling. There were three hundred on the north side of the river. The officer in command sent over a flag of truce demanding the Lieutenant to surrender; but Lieutenant Estes had no intention of giving up just then. Finding that he could not go north, he turned south. In his flight he came upon a Rebel major, two captains, and three privates, who were captured and paroled. But the militia were close upon the brave Lieutenant, who found himself and party caught in a trap between the river and the Great Dragon Swamp. Seeing that they could not escape on horseback, they abandoned their horses and took to the swamp. The militia surrounded it, and set bloodhounds on the track of the fugitives, who were finally captured, and sent off towards Richmond, under a strong guard; but before they reached the Mattapony, Kilpatrick set them at liberty and took the Rebel guard along with him to Gloucester, accompanied by thousands of negroes, on foot, in carts, wagons, and old family carriages, drawn by mules, oxen, and sometimes by cows,—packed full, and loaded down on top, by the dark-hued but light-hearted creatures, who had heard of the proclamation of President Lincoln, and were ready to accept freedom at the hands of the Yankees. After resting a few

---

43: Kilpatrick's Report.

days, Kilpatrick crossed the river on transports, marched up the tongue of land between the Rappahannock and Potomac, and joined Hooker at Falmouth, having made a complete circuit of the Rebel army.

When Colonel Wyndham left Thompson's Cross-Roads on the morning of the 3rd, he moved rapidly southwest towards the James, striking it at Columbia. The distance was about twenty miles. There were many small creeks to cross, but Wyndham reached Columbia at eight o'clock. The people had just finished breakfast when a man, riding furiously, his hair wet with foam, came dashing down the street, shouting "The Yankees are coming! the Yankees are coming!"

The people laughed; some thought him crazy. The Yankees coming? Impossible! But a column of men in blue, with gleaming sabres, dashed down the road into the village. There were no Rebel soldiers in the vicinity to oppose Wyndham. Some of the citizens fled in consternation across the James, giving the alarm. But the people over the river would not believe their stories.

"I'll go and see for myself," said an old farmer, who mounted his horse and took one of his best servants with him. He went on till he was in sight of the Yankees, then stopped and looked at them in amazement. Suddenly his servant dashed away straight towards the Yankees.

"Stop! come back!" he shouted, but the negro galloped boldly into Wyndham's lines, bringing an excellent horse, while his late master turned the other way, more amazed than ever.

Some of the soldiers told the inhabitants that they belonged to Stuart's command; and the word spread that they were not Yankees after all. A young fellow, the son of a rich farmer, rode boldly into the lines to see Stuart's cavalry.

"Has Lee licked the Yankees?" he asked.

"I reckon," said a cavalryman.

"Good!" said the boy.

"See here, my friend, my horse has gi'n out. I am on important business; I should like to exchange horses with you. General Stuart will make it all right with you when he comes this way," said the soldier, who, without further ceremony, put his saddle upon the noble-blooded animal, while the young man looked on in amazement.

Many of the Rebel cavalrymen were dressed in blue clothing, which had been stripped from prisoners, and that was the reason why the inhabitants were at a loss to know whether they were Yankees or Rebels.

Colonel Wyndham burned the bridge across the James, destroyed several canal-boats loaded with supplies, burned a warehouse filled with corn and medical stores, dug sluices in the banks of the canal, and attempted to destroy the locks, but did not succeed. He remained till four o'clock in the afternoon, then pushed down the river five miles, moved north, then northwest, and reached Stoneman at ten o'clock in the evening, accompanied by hundreds of negroes. When the alarm was given on a plantation that the Yankees were coming, the farmers made all haste to secrete their horses.

"Here! Jim, Sam, Cuffee, take the horses into the woods. Quick!" There was a grand commotion in all the stables, the negroes mounting the horses and riding into the thick bushes; but as soon as they were out of their masters' sight, they made for the Yankees by the shortest route! They were ready to do anything for their deliverers. They kept close watch while the soldiers rested; visited plantations, bringing in chickens, turkeys, calves, and lambs, and cooked delicious suppers for the whole command. They kept Stoneman informed of what was going on. He learned that in two hours after Wyndham left Columbia, a large body of cavalry entered the place in pursuit, but Wyndham moved so rapidly they could not overtake him.

A portion of Buford's brigade, the First Regulars, dashed along the Virginia Central Railroad, and tore up the track. A company went to the North Anna, drove off a guard of infantry from a bridge, captured five prisoners, burned the bridge, and returned to Stoneman without losing a man. The Fifth Regulars went down the James to Cartersville twelve miles below Columbia, to destroy a bridge. They met a portion of Lee's brigade. There was skirmishing; but while one portion of the Regulars was holding the Rebels in check, another party reached the bridge, set it on fire, and then the whole force returned to Stoneman.

The Rebels all the while were hovering round Stoneman on the southwest, but did not dare to attack him. They did not know what to make of the conflicting stories. "The Yankees are at Frederickshall, at Ashland, at Columbia, at Thompson's Cross-Roads, at Louisa, at Richmond," were the reports. The country swarmed with Yankees; every farmer had his story of woe, of stolen horses and runaway negroes; the farmers' wives and daughters mourned over lost chickens, of meat-houses broken open, jars of jelly and preserves carried away. Few of the Virginia farmers had ever seen a regiment of cavalry, and when the lines filed down the narrow roads, a squadron was magnified to a regiment, and a hundred men became a thousand.

On Tuesday afternoon, all of the detachments except Kilpatrick's and a portion of Davis's having returned, Stoneman commenced his homeward march, and recrossed the Rapidan at Raccoon Ford, in safety, though he was obliged to swim his horses through the swollen stream.

There was no enemy to molest him, none to hang upon his rear. He recrossed the Rappahannock at Kelley's Ford, and rejoined Hooker at Falmouth, having successfully accomplished what he had undertaken.

The Rebels were mortified, chagrined, and exasperated. The success which they had achieved in compelling Hooker to retire from Chancellorsville was in a measure counterbalanced by Stoneman's operations, especially by Kilpatrick's audacious exploits.

This cavalry movement was the first great raid of the war. It was not only a success, but it toughened the soldiers and prepared them for the hardships and battles which followed on the Upper Rappahannock, at Aldie, Middleburg, and Gettysburg. It gave confidence. The men felt that they were no longer the laughing-stock of the army. They had other employment now than guarding teams or keeping watch on the picket line. There was pleasurable excitement in riding through the enemy's country, making dashes into villages, charging upon the enemy, riding through the dense forests, and finding good living at every farm-house. There were plenty of volunteers for any enterprise.

A few days later Stuart attempted a counter raid in rear of the army, but was driven across the Rappahannock with ease. Then came the severe struggle at Brandy Station. Lee had started on his Gettysburg campaign, and Stuart was kept on the flank to conceal the movement, but Kilpatrick and Gregg unmasked it. Then as Stuart swung along the base of the Blue Ridge, while Lee went down the Shenandoah with the infantry, the contest was renewed in a running fight from Aldie to Snicker's Gap. In all of these engagements the superiority of the Union cavalry was fully established. The Union soldiers had learned to ride horses; and from Stoneman's raid to the capture of Jeff Davis they rode to some purpose.

CHAPTER 15

The Atlantic Coast

MARCH, 1863

The encounter between the *Merrimack* and the *Monitor* had set the world agog on the matter of armoured vessels. A fleet of ironclads had been prepared, with the special object in view of recapturing Fort Sumter. It was an event looked forward to with intense interest, not only in the North, but throughout the civilized world. Having a desire to witness that attack, I proceeded South, leaving New York on the 7th of February, 1863, on board the steamer *Augusta Dinsmore*, belonging to Adams's Express. Captain Crowell, her commander, was a sharp-eyed Connecticut Yankee, who kept the lead constantly going as we ran down the coast, and who was as well acquainted with all the soundings as the skipper of *Nantucket* immortalized by Mr. Fields, who detected the soil of Marm Hackett's garden by smell and taste, although *Nantucket* had sunk.

The harbour of Port Royal was crowded with shipping. General Foster's force from North Carolina had just arrived, to participate in a land movement. General Hunter was in command of the department, and there arose at once a question of jurisdiction, which paralyzed the operations of the army. The officers and soldiers at Port Royal, weary with doing nothing, had fitted up a theatre. The building was used for church services on Sunday. Attending the morning service the day after our arrival, I found an audience of about one hundred persons, among them General Hunter and staff. The clergyman, an Episcopalian, in a rusty black gown, stood upon the stage. A soldier played a melodeon and conducted the singing. In the afternoon there was a business meeting in the African Baptist church, which I also attended. Rev. Abraham Murchison, a tall copper-hued negro, was pastor, and presided over the deliberations. He had been a slave in Savannah, but made his way to our lines, was a storekeeper or huckster on weekdays, and preached on Sunday. The church was a plain wooden building, erected by order of General Mitchell for an African church. There were two rows of benches, a plain pine pulpit, a ventilated ceiling, from which three or four glass lamps were suspended,—all being very much like the rude churches to be found in the thinly-settled prairies of Illinois. The congregation were singing when we entered,—

Sweet fields beyond the swelling flood
Stand dressed in living green,
So to the Jews fair Canaan stood,
While Jordan rolled between.

The leader was a round-headed, compact, energetic negro, twenty-five years of age, whose zeal was bounded only by the capacity of his lungs. It was the well-known tune "Jordan," sung by millions in times past and present. The women occupied one side of the house, the men sitting opposite. It was a dusky view, looking down the aisle from my seat at the right of the pulpit. They were countenances not types of beauty, not attractive intellectually. But there was perfect decorum and solemnity. All heads were bowed when the preacher addressed the Throne of Grace. It was a prayer full of supplications and thanksgiving, expressed in fitting words.

The church had a case of discipline. Their sexton had been remiss in lighting the lamps, and was arraigned for trial. The pastor called the sexton to the front, and thus indicted him:

"John, my son, you are arraigned for not doing as you have agreed, and covenanted to do. We pay you one hundred and twenty dollars a year for lighting these yere beautiful lamps which the church have so generously provided, and, sir, you have been remiss in your duty. On Thursday night, when we were assembled for holy prayer, we were in darkness. You did wrong. You broke your obligations. You must be punished. What say you? Brethren, we will hear what he has to say."

"I lighted the lamps, sah, but they went out; de oil was bad, I reckon," said the sexton.

The pastor called upon one of the deacons to take the chair. He was of middle age, black as anthracite coal, bald-headed, and was dressed in pants and coat made of old sailcloth. By his side sat his colleague, wearing a United States soldiers' blue overcoat. The preacher, taking his stand in the aisle, laid aside his clerical authority, and became one of the brethren. "Brother cheerman, our brother am presump*tus*. He say he light de lamps and dey go out. How does he know dey go out?

He ought to stay and see dey don't go out. He am presumptus and should be punished. I move, sir, dat our brother be set aside from commin to de Lord's table till he make satisfaction."

A brother seconded the motion, and the question was put by the deacon. Two or three voted affirmatively, but nearly all negatively. The question was not understood. The preacher explained: "You is discomposed in your minds. You do not understand de question. Can any of you tell me how you voted?"

The question was put a second time, and the offending member was unanimously debarred the privileges of the church.

After the discipline a candidate for admission was presented, a stout young man, named Jonas.

"Well, my son, where are you from?" said the pastor.

"From Charleston, sir."

"Was you a member of the church there, my son?"

"Yes, sir, I was a member of the church."

"Does anyone here know anything about Jonas?"

A half-dozen responded "Yes," all agreeing that his deportment was correct.

"Did you bring your 'stificate with you?"

"No, sir; I came away in a hurry, and hadn't any time to get one."

"Yes, my son; we understand that you were obliged to leave in a hurry or not at all. But what made you become a Christian?"

"Because I felt I was a sinner."

"Did you pray, my son?"

"Yes, sir; and I feel that through the mercy of Jesus Christ my sins are pardoned."

It was a simple narrative, and expressed with evident consciousness of the solemnity of the declaration. It was plain that in spiritual things these people were further advanced than in business matters. The evidence was satisfactory, and the member received by an extension of right hand of fellowship on the part of the pastor. In the evening Rev. Mr. Murchison preached from the text, "*And they shall call upon the rocks and mountains to fall upon them,*" &c.

It was a crude, disjointed discourse, having very little logic, a great many large words, some of them ludicrously misapplied, yet contained striking thoughts, and appropriate similes. This was a congregation standing on the lowest step of civilization. Minister and people were but a twelvemonth out of bondage. All behind them was barbarism. Before them was a future, unrevealed, but infinitely better than what their past had been. Their meeting was orderly, and

I have seen grave legislative bodies in quite as much of a muddle over a simple question as that congregation of black men emerging from their long night of darkness.

On the following Sunday I was present at a service on Ladies' Island. The owner of the plantation where the meeting was held erected his house in full view of Beaufort, and near the bank of the stream where the tide ebbs and flows upon the sandy beach. It was a mean mansion, standing on posts, to give free circulation to the air underneath. In hot summer days the shade beneath the house was the resort of all the poultry of the premises. Thousands of hard-working New England mechanics live in better houses, yet from Beaufort the place made an imposing show, surrounded by orange and magnolia trees. The sandy acres of the plantation stretched towards St. Helena. A short distance from the planter's house were the weather-beaten cabins of the negroes, mere hovels, without window-panes, with mud chimneys,—the homes of generations who had gone from the darkness and hopelessness of a wearying life to the rest and quiet of the grave.

On that morning when Admiral Dupont shelled the Rebels out of the forts at Hilton Head and Bay Point, the owner of these acres made a hasty exit from his house. He sent his overseer to the cabins to hurry up the negroes, but to his surprise not a negro was to be found. The coloured people had heard the thundering down the bay. They knew its meaning. It set their hearts beating as they never had throbbed before. It was the sweetest music they ever had heard. A horseman came riding furiously up to the house, with terror in his countenance. The master hastened out to know how the battle was going.

"The Yankees have taken the forts!" said the messenger. The master became pale.

"You had better get your negroes together, and be ready for a move," said the messenger.

Sharp ears had heard all this,—the ears of Sam, a coloured man, who, seeing the herald arrive in hot haste, had the curiosity to hear what he had to say, then bounded like a deer to the cabins, running from door to door, whispering to the inmates, "To the woods! to the woods! De Yankees hab taken de forts,—massa is going to de mainland, and is going to take us wid him."

The cabins were deserted in an instant; and five minutes later, when the overseer came round to gather his drove of human cattle, he found empty hovels. The planter and his overseer were obliged to do their own hasty packing up.

The plantation was in the hands of a warm-hearted Christian gentleman from Massachusetts, Mr. Norton. The people of the estate gathered for worship in the large parlour of the house.

The room was eighteen or twenty feet square, and had a wide-mouthed fireplace, in which a cheerful fire of pitch knots was blazing. There was a settee, a mahogany sideboard, where the former owner was accustomed to quaff his wines and liquors. Seats and chairs were brought in. The big dinner-bell was rung, and the people, thirty or forty in number, came in, men, women, and children. Some of the women brought their infants. Uncle Jim, the patriarch of the plantation, was too feeble to attend. The superintendent, Mr. Norton, comforted his heart by reading to him a chapter in the Bible and offering prayers in the miserable cabin, where the old man was lying on a pile of rags. Uncle Jim was a sincere Christian. The word of God was sweet to him. His heart overflowed with thanks and praise, for the display of God's great goodness to him and his people.

A hymn was lined off by Mr. Norton, after the fashion of our fathers. William, a stout, middle-aged man, struck into St. Martin's, and the congregation joined, not reading the music exactly as good old Tansur composed it, for there were crooks, turns, slurs, and appoggiaturas, not to be found in any printed copy. It was sung harshly, nasally, and dragged out in long, slow notes.

A pure-blooded negro, Sancho, offered prayer. He had seen great hardship in life and had suffered more than his namesake, the squire, who was once unceremoniously tossed in a blanket. His prayer was the free utterance of a warm heart. It was a familiar talk with Jesus, his best friend. He improved the opportunity to mingle an exhortation with his supplication. He thus addressed the unconverted:—

"O, my poor, impenitent fellow-sinner, what you think you are doing? Where you think you are going? Death will ride up soon in a big black carriage and take you wid him down to de regions of deep darkness. Why don't you repent now, and den he will carry you up into de light of paradise!"

Looking forward to the hour of the Christian's release from the bondage of this life, he said, in conclusion, "And now, good Lord, when we have done chaw all de hard bones and swallowed all de bitter pills, we trust de good Lord will take us to himself."

After an address from the superintendent, Sancho rose.

"My belobed friends," said he, "I neber 'spected to see such a day as dis yere. For twenty years, I hired my time of old massa, I was 'bleeged to pay him twelve dollars a month in advance, and if

I didn't hab de money ready, he wollopped me. But I's a free man now. De good Lord hab done it all. I can't read. It is de great desire ob my heart to learn to read, so dat I can read de Bible all my own self; but I's too old to learn. But I rejoice dat my chillen can hab de opportunity to study de precious word. De Lord is doin great tings for us in dese yere days. Ole massa, was a purty good massa, and I prays de Lord to make him lay down his weapons ob rebellion and become a good Union man and a disciple ob de Lord Jesus, for Jesus tells us dat we must lub our enemies."

After the exercises of the religious meeting were concluded, the chairs were set aside, and they began a "praise meeting," or singing meeting. Most of their music is plaintive. The piece frequently commences with a recitative by one voice, and at the end of the first line the chorus joins. The words are often improvised to suit the occasion.

A favourite song is *Roll, Jordan, Roll,* in which the progression of the melody is very descriptive of the rolling of waves upon the beach.

Roll Jordan

There are many variations of the melody, but that here given is as I heard it sung by the negroes of Bythewood.

The verses vary only in recitation. If Mr. Jones is present he will hear, *"Mr. Jones is sitting on the tree of life."* There is no pause, and before the last roll is ended the one giving the recitative places another personage on the tree, and thus Jordan rolls along.

As the song goes on the enthusiasm rises. They sing louder and stronger. The recitative is given with increased vigour, and the chorus swells with increasing volume. They beat time, at first, with their hands, then their feet. They rise from their seats. William begins to shuffle his feet. Anna, a short, thick-set woman, wearing a chequered dress, and an apron, which once was a window-curtain, claps her hands, makes a short, quick jerk of her body, stamps her feet on the unaccented part of the measure, keeping exact syncopation. Catherine and Sancho catch the inspiration. They go round in a circle, shuffling, jerking, shouting louder and louder, while those outside of the circle respond with increasing vigour, all stamping, clapping their hands, and rolling out the chorus. William seems to be in a trance, his eyes are fixed, yet he goes on with a double-shuffle, till the perspiration stands in beads upon his face. Every joint seems hung on wires. Feet, legs, arms, head, body, and hands swing and jump like a child's dancing Dandy Jim. Sancho enters into it with all his heart, soul, mind, and might, clapping his hands, rolling his eyes, looking upward in ecstasy and outward upon the crowd, as if he were their spiritual father and guardian.

Thus it went on till nature was exhausted. When the meeting broke up, they all came round in procession, shaking hands with the superintendent and the strangers present, and singing a parting song— *There's a meeting here tonight!*

The superintendent informed me that the children who attended school could not be coaxed to take part in those praise meetings. They had learned to sing Sunday-school songs, and evidently looked upon the plantation songs of their fathers and mothers as belonging to their bondage and not worthy to be sung now that they were free.

A short distance from Hilton Head is the town of Mitchelville, laid out by the lamented astronomer, General Mitchell, who fell a victim to the yellow-fever in the summer of 1862. The town is on a broad sandy plain, bordered by groves and thickets of live-oak, palmetto, and the coast pine.

At that time there were about seventy houses,—or cabins rather,— of the rudest description, built of logs, chinked with clay brought up from the beach, roofs of long split shingles, board floors, windows with shutters,—plain board blinds, without sash or glass. Each house had a quarter of an acre of land attached. There was no paint or lime, not even whitewash, about them. It was just such a place as might be expected in a new country, where there were no saw-mills or brick-kilns,—a step in advance of a hole in the ground or a bark *wigwam*. It was the beginning of the experiment of civilization on the part of a semi-barbarous people just released from abject bondage, and far from being free men.

I looked into the first cabin, and seeing an old man sitting before the fire, greeted him with "How do you do, Uncle?" the sobriquet of all middle-aged negro men.

"'Pears how I'm rather poorly,—I's got de chills, boss."

He was a slave in Florida, made his escape from his master's plantation fifty miles inland, reached Fernandina, and entered the lines of the Union army. He was dressed in pants made of old sailcloth, and the tattered cast-off blouse of a Union soldier. The room was twelve feet square. I could see through the chinking in a hundred places. At the coping of the roof, where it should have joined the wall, there was a wide opening all around, which allowed all the warmth to escape. The furniture consisted of three tables, four chairs, a mahogany wash-stand, all of which once stood in the mansion of some island planter. There was a Dutch-oven on the hearth, the sight of which made my mouth water for the delicious tea-cakes of childhood. There were pots, kettles, baskets, and bags, and a pile of rags, old blankets which the soldiers had thrown aside. It required but a few words to thaw out Uncle Jacob, who at once commenced fumbling in his pockets, producing, after a studious search, a brown paper, carefully folded, enclosing the name of a gentleman in New York who had taken home Uncle Jacob's nephew. He wanted me to read it to him,—the name, the street, the number,—that he might learn it by heart.

"He is learning to write, boss, and I shall have a letter from him by and by," said the old man, in glee. He handed me three letters, all from men who once were slaves, not written by them individually, but by amanuenses. One was a sailor on the gunboat Ottawa, off Charleston; one was in New York city, and the third in Ohio.

"Please, boss, I should like to hab you read 'em," he said.

It was a pleasure to gratify the kind-hearted man, who listened with satisfaction beaming from every line of his countenance.

Uncle Jacob had been five months in the employ of the United States, unloading vessels at Hilton Head, and had received only his rations and a little clothing.

"Well, Uncle Jacob, which would you rather be, a freeman or a slave?" I asked.

"O, Lor' bless you, boss, I wouldn't like to be a slave again."

"Do you think you can take care of yourself?"

"Jes let gubberment pay me, boss, and see if I can't."

It was spoken with great earnestness.

In the next cabin I found Peter, who had taken the name of Brown, that of his former master. Slavery gave its victims but one name. General Mitchell said that they were entitled to another name, and he ordered that they should take that of their former masters; hence there are Peter Beauregards, James Trenholms, Susan Rhetts, Julia Barnwells, on the plantations of the Sea Islands.

"Mr. Brown, did you ever hear about the Abolitionists?" I asked.

"Yes, sir, tank you, I's he'd of 'em."

"What did you hear about them?"

"O, dey is a werry bad sort of people, sir. Old massa said dat if dey could get a chance dey would take all our pickaninnies and smash der brains out agin de trees!"

"Did you ever see an Abolitionist?"

"No, sir, tank you, nebber saw one."

"Well, Mr. Brown, I am one."

Mr. Brown started involuntarily. He looked me all over from head to feet, giving a keen search. "'Pears how I shouldn't tink you could hab de heart to do it, sir."

"Do I look as though I should like to kill your little ones?"

"No, sir, I don't tink you would."

I told him who the Abolitionists were, and what they wished to do,—that they were friends of the slaves, and always had been. He grasped my hand, and said, "God bless you, sir." And then burst into hearty laughter.

Having been informed that it would be impossible to obtain a fowl of the negroes at that season of the year, I made the attempt; but though I offered treble the value, not one would part with a hen. They were looking forward to broods of chickens which would bring them in "heaps" of money in the fall of the year. The negro race understands the value of money quite as well as we who boast of Anglo-Saxon blood.

Entering the head-quarters of the commanding officer one day, I saw a thin, spare coloured woman sitting before the fire. She nodded and smiled, ran her eyes over me, as if to take in every feature or peculiarity of my person and dress, then gazed into the fire and seemed absorbed in her own thoughts. A friend said, "That is our Sojourner Truth."

She had brought off several companies of negroes from the mainland, and had given a great deal of information concerning the movements of the Rebels. She had penetrated swamps, endured hardships, eluded Rebel pickets, visiting the plantations at midnight, and conversing with the slaves.

"I can travel all through the South, I reckon," she said.

"Are you not afraid that the Rebels will catch you?"

"Well, honey, I reckon they couldn't keep me," she said, with a smile.

She had exhibited such remarkable shrewdness and finesse in her exploits, and had rendered such valuable services to the department, that she was held in high esteem.

At that time, Mrs. Frances D. Gage, favourably known as a writer for the press, was residing on Paris Island. Seated one evening by the bright fire blazing on her hearth, I listened to her narrative of Sojourner Truth, who had been a slave, who had penetrated the far South in search of her lost children, who had run off many slaves to Canada, and who went round the country, impelled by the conviction that she had been called of God to testify against the sins of the people; hence her name, "Sojourner Truth."

The narration revealed traits of character, not infrequently seen in the negro race, and it will not be out of place in this chapter, which is intended to give the position of a race at its lowest plane of life. This wonderful woman lives in modern art. She is the original Libyan Sibyl, a statue by Mr. Story, which was more impressive than all others in the gallery of the World's Exhibition in London in 1862. Sojourner once called upon Mrs. Stowe, who has given us this account of the interview:[44]

> On her head she wore a bright Madras handkerchief, arranged as a turban, after the manner of her race. She seemed perfectly self-possessed and at her ease,—in fact, there was almost an unconscious superiority, not unmixed with a solemn twinkle of humour, in the odd, composed manner in which she looked down on me. Her whole air had at times a gloomy sort of drollery which impressed one strangely.
>
> "So, this is *you*," she said.
>
> "Yes," I answered.
>
> "Well, honey, de Lord bless ye! I jes' thought I'd like to come an' have a look at ye. You's heerd o' me, I reckon?" she added.
>
> "Yes, I think I have. You go about lecturing, do you not?"
>
> "Yes, honey, that's what I do. The Lord has made me a sign unto this nation, an' I go round a-testifyin', an' showin' on 'em their sins agin my people."

44: *Atlantic Monthly*, April, 1863.

So saying, she took a seat, and, stooping over and crossing her arms on her knees, she looked down on the floor, and appeared to fall into a sort of revery. Her great gloomy eyes and her dark face seemed to work with some undercurrent of feeling; she sighed deeply, and occasionally broke out,—

"O Lord! O Lord! Oh, the tears, an' the groans, an' the moans! O Lord!"

By this time I thought her manner so original that it might be worthwhile to call down my friends; and she seemed perfectly well pleased with the idea. An audience was what she wanted,—it mattered not whether high or low, learned or ignorant. She had things to say, and was ready to say them at all times, and to anyone.

I called down Dr. Beecher, Professor Allen, and two or three other clergymen, who, together with my husband and family, made a roomful. No princess could have received a drawing-room with more composed dignity than Sojourner her audience. She stood among them calm and erect as one of her own native palm-trees waving alone in the desert. I presented one after another to her, and at last said,—

"Sojourner, this is Dr. Beecher. He is a very celebrated preacher."

"*Is* he?" she said, offering her hand in a condescending manner, and looking down on his white head. "Ye dear lamb, I'm glad to see ye! De Lord bless ye! I loves preachers. I'm a kind o' preacher myself."

"You are?" said Dr. Beecher. "Do you preach from the Bible?"

"No, honey, can't preach from de Bible,—can't read a letter."

"Why, Sojourner, what do you preach from, then?"

Her answer was given with a solemn power of voice, peculiar to herself, that hushed everyone in the room.

"When I preaches, I has jest one text to preach from, an' I always preaches from this one. *My* text is, *when I found Jesus.*"

"Well, you couldn't have a better one," said one of the ministers.

She paid no attention to him, but stood and seemed swelling with her own thoughts, and then began this narration:

"Well, now, I'll jest have to go back, an' tell ye all about it. Ye see, we was all brought over from Africa, father an' mother an' I, an' a lot more of us; an' we was sold up an' down, an' hither an' yon; an' I can 'member, when I was a little thing, not bigger than this 'ere," pointing to her grandson, "how my ole mammy would sit out o' doors in the evenin', an' look up at the stars an' groan. She'd groan an' groan, an' says I to her,—

"'Mammy, what makes you groan so?'

"An' she'd say,—

"'Matter enough, chile! I'm groanin' to think o' my poor children: they don't know where I be, an' I don't know where they be: they looks up at the stars, an' I looks up at the stars, but I can't tell where they be.

"'Now,' she said, 'chile, when you're grown up, you may be

sold way from your mother an' all your ole friends, an' have great troubles come on ye; an' when you has these troubles come on ye, ye jes' go to God, an' He'll help ye.'

"An' says I to her,—

"'Who is God, anyhow, mammy?'

"An' says she,—

"'Why, chile, you jes' look up *dar*! It's Him that made all *dem*!'

"Well, I didn't mind much 'bout God in them days. I grew up pretty lively an' strong, an' could row a boat, or ride a horse, or work round, an' do 'most anything.

"At last I got sold away to a real hard massa an' missis. Oh, I tell you, they *was* hard! 'Peared like I couldn't please 'em nohow. An' then I thought o' what my old mammy told me about God; an' I thought I'd got into trouble, sure enough, an' I wanted to find God, an' I heerd some one tell a story about a man that met God on a threshin'-floor, an' I thought, 'Well an' good, I'll have a threshin'-floor, too.' So I went down in the lot, an' I threshed down a place real hard, an' I used to go down there every day, an' pray an' cry with all my might, a-prayin' to the Lord to make my massa an' missis better, but it didn't seem to do no good; an' so says I, one day,—

"'O God, I been a-askin' ye, an' askin' ye, an askin' ye, for all this long time, to make my massa an' missis better, an' you don't do it, an' what *can* be the reason? Why, maybe you *can't*. Well, I shouldn't wonder ef you couldn't. Well, now, I tell you, I'll make a bargain with you. Ef you'll help me git away from my massa an' missis, I'll agree to be good; but ef you don't help me, I really don't think I can be. Now,' says I, 'I want to git away; but the trouble's jest here: ef I try to git away in the night, I can't see; an' ef I try to git away in the daytime, they'll see me, an' be after me.'

"Then the Lord said to me, 'Get up two or three hours afore daylight, an' start off.'

"An' says I, 'Thank'ee, Lord! that's a good thought.'

"So up I got, about three o'clock in the mornin', an' I started an' travelled pretty fast, till, when the sun rose, I was clear away from our place an' our folks, an' out o' sight. An' then I begun to think I didn't know nothin' where to go. So I kneeled down, an' says I,—

"'Well, Lord, you've started me out, an' now please to show me where to go.'

"Then the Lord made a house appear to me, an' He said to me that I was to walk on till I saw that house, an' then go in an' ask the people to take me. An' I travelled all day, an' didn't come to the house till late at night; but when I saw it, sure enough, I went in, an' I told the folks the Lord sent me; an' they was Quakers, an' real kind they was to me. They jes' took me in, an' did for me as kind as ef I'd been one of 'em; an' after they'd giv me supper, they took me into a room where there was a great, tall, white bed; an' they told me to sleep there. Well, honey, I was kind o' skeered when they left me alone with that great white bed; 'cause I never had been in a bed in my life. It never came into my mind they could mean me to sleep in it An' so I jes' camped down under it, on the floor, an' then I slep' pretty well. In the mornin', when they came in, they asked me ef I hadn't been asleep; an' I said, 'Yes I never slep' better.' An' they said, 'Why, you haven't been in the bed!' An' says I, 'Laws, you didn't think o' sech a thing as my sleepin' in dat 'ar' *bed*, did you? I never heerd o' sech a thing in my life.'

"Well, ye see, honey, I stayed an' lived with 'em. An' now jes' look here: instead o' keepin' my promise an' bein' good, as I told the Lord I would, jest as soon as everything got a-goin' easy, *I forgot all about God.*

"Pretty well don't need no help; an' I gin' up prayin'. I lived there two or three years, an' then the slaves in New York were all set free, an' ole massa came to our house to make a visit, an' he asked me ef I didn't want to go back an' see the folks on the ole place. An' I told him I did. So he said, ef I'd jes' git into the wagon with him, he'd carry me over. Well, jest as I was goin' out to git into the wagon, *I met God!* an' says I, 'O God, I didn't know as you was so great!' An' I turned right round an' come into the house, an' set down in my room; for 't was God all around me. I could feel it burnin', burnin', burnin' all around me, an' goin' through me; an' I saw I was so wicked, it seemed as ef it would burn me up. An' I said, 'O somebody, somebody, stand between God an' me! for it burns me!' Then, honey, when I said so, I felt as it were somethin' like an *amberill* umbrella that came between me an' the light, an' I felt it was *somebody,*— somebody that stood between me an' God; an' it felt cool, like a shade; an' says I, 'Who's this that stands between me an' God? Is it old Cato?' He was a pious old preacher; but then I seemed to see Cato in the light, an' he was all polluted an' vile, like me;

an' I said, 'Is it old Sally?' an' then I saw her, an' she seemed jes' so. An' then says I, '*Who* is this?' An' then, honey, for a while it was like the sun shinin' in a pail o' water, when it moves up an' down; for I begun to feel 't was somebody that loved me; an' I tried to know him. An' I said, 'I know you! I know you! I know you!'—an' then I said, 'I don't know you! I don't know you! I don't know you!' An' when I said, 'I know you, I know you,' the light came; an' when I said, 'I don't know you, I don't know you,' it went, jes' like the sun in a pail o' water. An' finally somethin' spoke out in me an' said, '*This is Jesus!*' An' I spoke out with all my might, an' says I, '*This is Jesus!* Glory be to God!' An' then the whole world grew bright, an' the trees they waved an' waved in glory, an' every little bit o' stone on the ground shone like glass; an' I shouted an' said, 'Praise, praise, praise to the Lord!' An' I begun to feel sech a love in my soul as I never felt before,—love to all creatures. An' then, all of a sudden, it stopped, an' I said, 'Dar's de white folks, that have abused you an' beat you an' abused your people,—think o' them!' But then there came another rush of love through my soul, an' I cried out loud, 'Lord, Lord, I can love *even de white folks!*'

"Honey, I jes' walked round an' round in a dream. Jesus loved me! I knowed it,—I felt it. Jesus was my Jesus. Jesus would love me always. I didn't dare tell nobody; 'twas a great secret. Everything had been got away from me that I ever had; an' I thought that ef I let white folks know about this, maybe they'd get *Him* away,—so I said, 'I'll keep this close. I won't let anyone know.'"

"But, Sojourner, had you never been told about Jesus Christ?"

"No, honey. I hadn't heerd no preachin',—been to no meetin'. Nobody hadn't told me. I'd kind o' heerd of Jesus, but thought he was like Gineral Lafayette, or some o' them. But one night there was a Methodist meetin' somewhere in our parts, an' I went; an' they got up an' begun for to tell der 'speriences; an' de fust one begun to speak. I started, 'cause he told about Jesus. 'Why,' says I to myself, 'dat man's found him too!' An' another got up an' spoke, an' I said, 'He's found him, too!' An' finally I said, 'Why, they all know him!' I was so happy! An' then they sung this hymn": (Here Sojourner sang, in a strange, cracked voice, but evidently with all her soul and might, mispronouncing the English, but seeming to derive as much elevation and comfort from bad English as from good):

> 'There is a holy city,
> 'A world of light above,
> 'Above the stairs and regions,[45]
> 'Built by the God of love.'"

* * * * * * * *

"Well, den ye see, after a while I thought I'd go back an' see de folks on de ole place. Well, you know, de law had passed dat de culled folks was all free; an' my old missis, she had a daughter married about dis time who went to live in Alabama,—an' what did she do but give her my son, a boy about de age of dis yer, for her to take down to Alabama? When I got back to de ole place, they told me about it, an' I went right up to see ole missis, an' says I,—

"'Missis, have you been an' sent my son away down to Alabama?'

"'Yes, I have,' says she; 'he's gone to live with your young missis.'

"'O Missis,' says I, 'how could you do it?'

"'Poh!' says she, 'what a fuss you make about a little nigger. Got more of 'em now than you know what to do with.'

"I tell you, I stretched up. I felt as tall as the world!

"'Missis, says I, *I'll have my son back agin!*'

"She laughed.

"'*You* will, you nigger? How you goin' to do it? You ha'n't got no money.'

"'No, Missis,—but *God* has,—an' you'll see He'll help me!'—an' I turned round an' went out.

"O, but I *was* angry to have her speak to me so haughty an' so scornful, as ef my chile wasn't worth anything. I said to God, 'O Lord, render unto her double! It was a dreadful prayer, an' I didn't know how true it would come.

"Well, I didn't rightly know which way to turn; but I went to the Lord, an' I said to Him, 'O Lord, ef I was as rich as you be, an' you was as poor as I be, I'd help you,—you *know* I would; and, oh, do help me!' An' I felt sure then that He would.

"Well, I talked with people, an' they said I must git the case before a grand jury. So I went into the town when they was holdin' a court, to see ef I could find any grand jury. An' I stood round the court-house, an' when they was a-comin'

45: Starry regions.

out, I walked right up to the grandest-lookin' one I could see, an' says I to him,—

"'Sir, be you a grand jury?'

"An' then he wanted to know why I asked, an' I told him all about it; an' he asked me all sorts of questions, an' finally he says to me,—

"'I think, ef you pay me ten dollars, that I'd agree to get your son for you.' An' says he, pointin' to a house over the way, 'You go 'long an' tell your story to the folks in that house, an' I guess they'll give you the money.'

"Well, I went, an' I told them, an' they gave me twenty dollars; an' then I thought to myself, 'Ef ten dollars will git him, twenty dollars will git him *sartin*.' So I carried it to the man all out, an' said,—

"'Take it all,—only be sure an' git him.'

"Well, finally they got the boy brought back; an' then they tried to frighten him, an' to make him say that I wasn't his mammy, an' that he didn't know me; but they couldn't make it out. They gave him to me, an' I took him an' carried him home; an' when I came to take off his clothes, there was his poor little back all covered with scars an' hard lumps, where they flogged him.

"Well, you see, honey, I told you how I prayed the Lord to render unto her double. Well, it came true; for I was up at ole missis' house not long after, an' I heerd 'em readin' a letter to her how her daughter's husband had murdered her,—how he'd thrown her down an' stamped the life out of her, when he was in liquor; an' my ole missis, she giv a screech, an' fell flat on the floor. Then says I, 'O Lord, I didn't mean all that! You took me up too quick.'

"Well, I went in an' tended that poor critter all night. She was out of her mind,—a-cryin', an' callin' for her daughter; an' I held her poor ole head on my arm, an' watched for her as ef she'd been my babby. An' I watched by her, an' took care on her all through her sickness after that, an' she died in my arms, poor thing!"

In the spring of 1851, a Woman's Rights Convention was held in Akron, Ohio. The newspapers had ridiculed such conventions, and they were looked upon as legitimate subjects for ridicule. They had been vilified and caricatured, but there was a desire through that section of the country to hear what the women would have to say for themselves, and the church in which the meeting was held was consequently crowded. Sojourner Truth was there. Mrs. Gage was president of the meeting. She said:

> The leaders of the movement, tremblingly alive to every appearance of evil that might spring up in their midst, were many of them almost thrown into panics on the first day of the meeting, by seeing a tall, gaunt black woman, in a gray dress and uncouth sun-bonnet, march deliberately into the church and up the aisle with an air of a queen, and take her seat on the pulpit steps. A buzz of disapprobation was heard all over the house, and such words as these fell upon listening ears: 'An Abolition affair! Woman's Rights and Niggers!' 'We told you so!' 'Go it, old darkey!' "The second day the work waxed warm. Methodist, Baptist, Episcopal, and Presbyterian, and Universalist ministers came in to hear and discuss the resolutions brought forth. One claimed superior rights and privileges for man because of superior intellect; another, because of the manhood of Christ. If God had desired the equality of woman, he would have given some token of his will through the birth, life, and death of the Saviour. Another gave a theological view of the sin of our first mother. There were few women in those days who dared to speak in meeting'; and the august teachers of the people, with long-winded bombast, were seeming to get the better of us, while the boys in the galleries and sneerers among the pews were enjoying hugely the discomfiture, as they supposed, of the strong-minded. Some of the tender-skinned friends were growing indignant and on the point of losing dignity, and the atmosphere of the Convention betokened a storm.
>
> Slowly from her seat in the corner rose Sojourner Truth, who till now had hardly lifted her head.
>
> 'Don't let her speak!' gasped a half-dozen in my ear. She moved slowly and solemnly to the front, laid her old bonnet at her feet, and turned her great piercing eyes upon me. There was a hissing sound of disapprobation above and below. I rose and announced 'Sojourner Truth,' and begged the audience to keep silence a few moments. The tumult subsided at once, and every eye was fixed on this almost Amazon form, which stood nearly six feet high, head erect, and eye piercing the upper air like one in a dream. At her first word there was a

profound hush. She spoke in deep tones, which, though not loud, reached every ear in the house, and away through the throng at the doors and windows.

'Well, chillen, whar dar's so much racket dar must be som'ing out o' kilter. I tink dat 'twixt de niggas of de Souf and de women of de Norf, all a talking about de rights, de white men will be in a fix pretty soon.

'But what's all dis here talking 'bout? Dat man ober dar say dat woman needs to be helped into carriages, and lifted ober ditches, and to hab de best place eberywhar. Nobody eber helps me into carriages, or ober ditches or ober mud-puddles, or gives me any best place.' Raising herself to her full height, and her voice to a pitch like rolling thunder, she asked, 'And arn't I a woman? Look at me. Look at my arm,' and she laid bare her right arm to her shoulder, showing its tremendous muscular power. 'I have ploughed, and planted, and gathered into barns, and no man could head me; and arn't I a woman? I have borne thirteen chillen, and seen most of 'em sold off into slavery, and when I cried out with a mother's grief, none but Jesus heard; and arn't I a woman? Den dey talks about dis ting in de head. What dis dey call it?' 'Intellect,' whispered someone near her. 'Dat's it, honey. What's dat got to do wid woman's rights or niggers' rights? If my cup won't hold but a pint, and yours holds a quart, wouldn't you be mean not to let me have my little half measure full?'

She pointed her significant finger and sent a keen glance at the minister who had made the argument. The cheering was long and loud.

'Den dat little man in black, dar, he say woman can't have as much right as man, 'cause Christ wasn't a woman. *Whar did your Christ come from?*'

'Rolling thunder could not have stilled that crowd as did those deep and wonderful tones, as she stood there with outstretched arm and eye of fire. Raising her voice she repeated, 'Whar did your Christ come from? From God and a woman. Man had nothing to do with him.'

'O what a rebuke she gave the little man! Turning again to another objector, she took up the defence of Mother Eve. It was pointed, and witty, and solemn, and eliciting at almost every sentence deafening applause; and she ended by asserting that 'if de fust woman God ever made was strong enough to turn the world upside down, all herself alone, all dese togeder,' and she glanced her eye over us, 'ought to be able to turn it back again and git it right side up again; and now dey is asking to, the men better let 'em. Bleeged to you for hearin' me, and now old Sojourner ha'n't got notin' more to say.'

Amid roars of applause she turned to her corner, leaving more than one of us with streaming eyes and hearts beating with gratitude. She had taken us up in her great strong arms and carried us over the slough of difficulty, turning the whole tide in our favour. I have never in my life seen anything like the magical influence that subdued the mobbish spirit of the day and turned the jibes and sneers of an excited crowd into notes of respect and admiration. Hundreds rushed up to shake hands with the glorious old mother and bid her God speed.

The enlistment of negro troops began at Port Royal in the fall of 1862, and by midwinter the First South Carolina, commanded by Colonel Higginson, had its ranks nearly full. There was strong prejudice in the army against employing negroes. The New Jersey troops in the department of the South were bitterly hostile. Colonel Stevenson, of Massachusetts, a gallant officer, having imprudently given utterance to his feelings upon the subject, was arrested by General Hunter, which caused a great deal of excitement in the army, and which attracted the attention of the country to the whole subject.

The day after the arrest of Colonel Stevenson, a scene occurred in the cabin of the steamer *Wyoming*, plying between Beaufort and Hilton Head, which is given as a historical note. The party consisted of several ladies, one or two chaplains, fifteen or twenty officers, four newspaper correspondents, and several civilians.

A young captain in the Tenth New Jersey opened the conversation.

"I wish," said he, "that every negro was compelled to take off his hat to a white man. I consider him an inferior being."

"You differ from General Washington, who took off his hat and saluted a negro," said one of the correspondents.

"General Washington could afford to do it," said the captain, a little staggered.

"Are we to understand that in this age a captain cannot afford to equal a negro in politeness?" was the provoking question of the correspondent.

"Do you want to be buried with a nigger, and have your bones touch his in the grave?"

"As to that I have no feeling whatever. I do not suppose that it will make much difference to the bones of either party."

"Well, when I die I want twenty niggers packed all around me," shouted the captain, excitedly, turning to the crowd to see the effect of his sarcasm.

"I presume, sir, you can be accommodated if you can get the consent of the twenty negroes."

The captain saw that he was losing his argument by losing his temper, and in calmer tones said: "I want to see the negro kept in his proper place. I am perfectly willing he should use the shovel, but it is an outrage upon the white man,—an insult to have him carry a musket."

"I would just as soon see a negro shot as to get shot myself. I am perfectly willing that all the negroes should help put down the Rebellion," said the correspondent.

"I am not willing to have them act as soldiers. Put them in the ditches, where they belong. They are an inferior race."

A second correspondent broke in. "Who are you, sir?" said he; "you who condemn the government? You forget that you as a soldier have nothing to say about the orders of the President or the laws of Congress. You say that the negro is an inferior being; what do you say of Frederick Douglass, who has raised himself from slavery to a high position? Your straps were placed on your shoulders, not because you had done anything to merit them, but because you had friends to intercede for you,—using their political influence,—or because you had money, and could purchase your commission. You hate the negro, and you want to keep him in slavery, and you allow your prejudice to carry you to the verge of disloyalty to the government which pays you for unworthily wearing your shoulder-straps."

The captain and the entire company listened in silence while another correspondent took up the question.

"Gentleman, you denounce the negro; you say that he is an inferior being. You forget that we white men claim to stand on the highest plane of civilization,—that we are of a race which for a thousand years has been in the front rank,—that the negro has been bruised, crushed, trodden down,—denied all knowledge, all right, everything; that we have compelled him to labour for us, and we have eaten the fruit of his labours. Can we expect him to be our equal in acquisition of knowledge? Where is your sense of fair play? Are you afraid that the negro will push you from your position? Are you afraid that if you allow him to aid in putting down the Rebellion, that he too will become a free man, and have aspirations like your own, and in time express toward you the same *chivalric* sentiments which you express toward him? How much do you love your country if you thus make conditions of loyalty?"

The captain made no reply. The whole company was silent. There were smiles from the ladies. The captain went out upon the deck, evidently regretting that the conversation had fallen upon so exciting a topic.

The First South Carolina Regiment of loyal blacks was in camp on Smith's plantation, four miles out from Beaufort. We rode over a sandy plain, through old cotton-fields, pine-barrens, and jungles, past a dozen negro-huts, where the long tresses of moss waved mournfully in the breeze. The men had gathered a boat-load of oysters, and were having a feast,—old and young, gray-headed men, and curly-haired children, were huddled round the pans, steaming and smoking over the pitch-knot fires.

Smith's plantation is historic ground,—the place where the Huguenots built a fort long before the Mayflower cast anchor in Cape Cod harbour. The plantation was well known to the coloured people before the war as a place to be dreaded,—a place for hard work, unmerciful whippings, with very little to eat. The house and the negro quarters were in a delightful grove of live-oaks, whose evergreen leaves, wide-spreading branches, thick foliage, and gnarled trunks, gave cooling shade. In front of the house, leading down to the fort, is a magnolia walk. Behind the house, in a circular basin,—a depression often found on sandy plains,—was the garden, surrounded by a thick-set, fantastic palmetto hedge. The great oak between the house and the garden, was the whipping-post. One of the branches was smooth, as if a swing had been slung there, and the bark had been worn by the rope swaying to the merry chattering and light-hearted laughter of children. Not that, however. There the offender of plantation law,—of a master's caprice,—had paid the penalty of disobedience; there men, women, and children, suspended by the thumbs, stripped of their clothing, received the lash. Their moans, groans, cries, and prayers fell unheeding on overseer, master, and mistress,—but heard and heeded they were in heaven, and kept in remembrance. And the hour of retribution had come, the time of deliverance was near.

What a choice spot for the punishment of the criminal! close to the house,—where the master, the mistress, their sons and daughters, the infant at the nurse's breast, could see the blood fly.

The plantation jail was in the loft of the granary, beneath a pitch-pine roof, which, under the heat of a midsummer sun, was like an oven. There was one little window in the gable for the admission of air. There were iron rings and bolts in the beams and rafters, where the slaves were chained.

The owner of the plantation was not unmindful of the religious wants of his fellow-Christians. West of the house was the plantation chapel, a whitewashed building of rough boards, twenty feet by thirty, with a rude belfry, where hung the plantation bell, which on week-days was rung at daybreak. Charmingly its music floated over the blue waters of Beaufort Bay, mingling with the morning winds, swaying the magnolia branches, calling the hands—men, women, and children—to their unrequited tasks in the cotton-field. On Sunday it called them, with silvery lips and melting sounds, to come and worship: not to study God's Word, not to bow down with him who—by the "divine missionary institution," as the Southern doctors of divinity called it, was their master, ordained of God—could separate husband and wife, or toss in a baby to boot, in a bargain; not to bow down with him, for he worshipped in Beaufort, in the ancient church;—he was a chivalric son of South Carolina, riding up in his coach, and leaving his four hundred fellow-disciples to grope their way to heaven, directed by a pious bondman, as best they might.

If one wish for a flood of reflections, he will be overwhelmed on such a spot.

The First South Carolina was at drill beneath the oak, drilling as skirmishers, advancing, retiring, rallying, deploying, loading and firing, with precision. They had already been under fire in an expedition up one of the Georgia rivers.

I had breakfasted with the captain of the steamer *Darlington*, which was used as a transport on the occasion, who showed me the numerous bullet-marks on the steamer.

"How did the negroes stand fire?" I asked.

"They fought splendidly, sir."

It was no longer an experiment whether they would make good soldiers. They had demonstrated it by their courage and patriotism. The antipathy which at the beginning was rampant quickly toned down. The deportment of the coloured soldiers under insult, their bravery in battle, compelled respect from all who had doubted their heroism or fidelity.

In the attack upon Jacksonville, which occurred on the 12th of March, an old patriarch—too old to do any fighting—harangued the troops, and told them that everyone who should be killed in a cause so holy would be pretty sure of stepping directly into heaven; but that if they hung back and showed that they were cowards, there wasn't much hope of eternal life for such! He was greatly venerated by the soldiers, for he had been a preacher.

Chapter 16

The Ironclads in Action

April, 1863

After vexatious delays, the ironclad fleet was ready for action. It was deemed desirable to test their armour, before attacking Sumter, by making a reconnoissance of Fort McAllister, on the Ogeechee.

It was late on the afternoon of March 1st, when the steamer *George Washington* left Hilton Head for a trip to Ossabow Sound. The *Passaic*, *Montauk*, *Nahant*, and *Patapsco*, ironclads of the *Monitor* pattern, were already there. The *Washington* took the "inside" route up Wilmington River and through the Rumley marshes. The gunboat *Marblehead* was guarding the entrance to the river. It was past sunset, and the tide was ebbing.

"You had better lie here till morning; there are indications that we shall hear from those fellows up there," said the commander of the *Marblehead*. Looking westward into the golden light of the departing day, we could see the spires of Savannah, also nearer the Rebel gunboats moving up and down the river.

The anchor dropped, the chain rattled through the hawsehole, the lights were extinguished, the guns put in trim; the lookout took his position; the sentinels passed to and fro, peering into the darkness; a buoy was attached to the cable, that it might be slipped in an instant; all ears listened to catch the sound of muffled oars or plashing paddle-wheels, but there was no sound save the piping of the curlew in the marshes and the surging of the tide along the reedy shores. At three o'clock in the morning we were away from our anchorage, steaming up Wilmington River. The moonlight lay in a golden flood along the waters, revealing the distant outline of the Rebel earthworks. How charming the trip! exhilarating, and sufficiently exciting, under the expectation of falling in with a hostile gunboat, to bring every nerve into action. It was sunrise when the *Washington* emerged from the marshes and came to anchor among the ironclads. The *Montauk* had just completed a glorious work,— the destruction of the *Nashville*. We had heard the roar of her guns, and the quick, ineffectual firing from Fort McAllister.

The *Nashville*, which began her piratical depredations by burning the ship *Harvey Birch*, ran into Savannah, where she had been cooped up several months. She had been waiting many weeks for an opportunity to run out to sea again. On Saturday morning, the last day of February, a dense fog hung over the marshes, the islands, and inlets of Ossabow. The *Montauk* lay at the junction of the Great and Little Ogeechee Rivers, when the fog lifted and the *Nashville* was discovered aground above the fort.

The eyes of Captain Worden sparkled as he gave the command to prepare for action. He had not forgotten his encounter with the *Merrimack*. The *Montauk* moved up stream, came within range of the fort, which opened from all its guns, but to which Captain Worden gave no heed. Taking a position about three quarters of a mile from the *Nashville* and half a mile from the fort, he opened with both guns upon the grounded steamer, to which the *Nashville* replied with her hundred-pounder. The third shell from the *Montauk* exploded inside the steamer, setting her cotton on fire. The flames spread with great rapidity. Her crew fled to the marshes, the magazine soon exploded, and the career of the *Nashville* was ended.

At high tide on the morning of the 3rd of March the *Passaic*, *Patapsco*, and *Nahant* moved up the Ogeechee, and opened fire on the fort, to test the working of their machinery. The fire was furious from the fort, but slow and deliberate from the ironclads. Several mortar-schooners threw shells in the direction of the fort. The monitors were obliged to retire with the tide. They were struck repeatedly, but the balls fell harmlessly against the iron plating. It was evident that at the distance of three fourths of a mile, or a half-mile even, the ironclads could withstand the heaviest guns, while on the other hand the fire of the monitors must necessarily be very slow. The attack was made, not with the expectation of reducing the fort, but to test the monitors before the grand attack upon Fort Sumter.

The first attack on Sumter occurred on the 7th of April. The fort stood out in bold relief, the bright noon-sun shining full upon its southern face, fronting the shallow water towards Morris Island, leaving in shadow its eastern wall toward Moultrie. The air was clear, and we who were on shipboard just beyond the reach of the Rebel guns, looking inland with our glasses, could see the city, the spires, the roofs of the houses thronged with people. A three-masted ship lay at the wharves, the Rebel rams were fired up, sail-boats were scudding across the harbour, running down toward Sumter, looking seaward, then hastening back again like little children, expectant and restless on great occasions, eager for something to be done.

The attacking fleet was in the main ship-channel,—eight little black specks but little larger than the buoys which tossed beside them, and one black, oblong block, the *New Ironsides*, the flag-ship of the fleet. It was difficult to comprehend that beneath the surface of the sea there were men as secure from the waves as bugs in a bottle. It was as strange and romantic as the stories which charmed the Arabian chieftains in the days of Haroun Al Raschid.

The ironclads were about one third of a mile apart, in the following order:

Weehawken,	*Patapsco,*	*Nantucket,*
Passaic,	*Ironsides,*	*Nahant,*
Montauk,	*Catskill,*	*Keokuk.*

The *Keokuk* was built by a gentleman who had full faith in her invulnerability. She was to be tested under fire from the Rebel batteries before accepted by the government. She had sloping sides, two turrets, and was built for a ram. The opinions generally entertained were that she would prove a failure.

General Hunter courteously assigned the steamer *Nantucket* to the gentlemen connected with the press, giving them complete control of the steamer, to go where they pleased, knowing that there was an intense desire not only in the North, but throughout the world, to know the result of the first contest between ironclads and fortifications. The *Nantucket* was a small side-wheel steamer of light draft, and we were able to run in and out over the bar at will. Just before the signal was given for the advance we ran alongside the flag-ship. The crew were hard at work hoisting shot and shells from the hold to the deck. The upper deck was bedded with sand-bags, the pilot-house wrapped with cable. All the light hamper was taken down and stowed away. The iron plating was slushed with grease. Rebel soldiers were marching across Morris Island, within easy range. A shell would have sent them in haste behind the sand-hills; but heavier work was at hand, and they were harmless just then.

It was past one o'clock when the signal for sailing was displayed from the flag-ship, and the *Weehawken*, with a raft at her prow, intended to remove torpedoes, answered the signal, raised her anchor, and went steadily in with the tide, followed by the others, which maintained their respective positions, distant from each other about one third or a half-mile. In this battle of ironclads there are no clouds of canvas, no beautiful models of marine architecture, none of the stateliness and majesty which have marked hundreds of great naval engagements. There are no human beings in sight,—no propelling power is visible. There are simply eight black specks and one oblong block gliding along the water, like so many bugs.

But Sumter has discovered them, and discharges in quick succession nine signal guns, to announce to all Rebeldom that the attack is to be made. Morris Island is mysteriously silent as the *Weehawken* advances, although she is within range. Past Fort Wagner, straight on toward Moultrie the *Weehawken* moves. The silence is prolonged. It is almost painful,—the calm before the storm, the hushed stillness before the burst of the tornado!

There comes a single puff of smoke from Moultrie,—one deep reverberation. The silence is broken,—the long months of waiting are over. The shot flies across the water, skipping from wave to wave, tossing up fountains, hopping over the deck of the *Weehawken*, and rolling along the surface with a diminishing ricochet, sinking at last close upon the Morris Island beach. Fort Wagner continues the story, sending a shot at the *Weehawken*, which also trips lightly over the deck, and tosses up a water-spout far toward Moultrie. The *Weehawken*, unmindful of this play, opens its ports, and sends a fifteen-inch solid shot toward Sumter, which, like those that have been hurled toward her, takes a half-dozen steps, making for a moment its footprints on the water, and crashes against the southwest face of the fort, followed a moment later by its eleven-inch companion. The vessel is for a moment enveloped in the smoke of its guns. Bravely done! There comes an answer. Moultrie, with the tremendous batteries on either side by the hotel and east of it, and toward the inner harbour, bursts in an instant into sheets of flame and clouds of sulphurous smoke. There is one long roll of thunder, peal on peal; deep, heavy reverberations and sharp concussions, rattling the windows of our steamers, and striking us at the heart like hammer strokes.

The ocean boils! Columns of spray are tossed high in air, as if a hundred submarine fountains were let instantly on, or a school of whales were trying which could spout highest. There is a screaming in the air, a buzzing and humming never before so loud.

At five minutes before three Moultrie began the fire. Ten minutes have passed. The thunder has rolled incessantly from Sullivan's Island. Thus far Sumter has been silent, but now it is enveloped with a cloud. A moment it is hid from view—first a line of light along its parapet, and thick folds of smoke unrolling like fleeces of wool. Other flashes burst from the casemates, and the clouds creep down the wall to the water, then slowly float away to mingle with that rising from the furnaces in the sand along the shore of Sullivan's Island. Then comes a calm,—a momentary cessation. The Rebel gunners wait for the breeze to clear away the cloud, that they may obtain a view of the monitor, to see if it have not been punched into a sieve, and if it be not already disappearing beneath the waves. But the *Weehawken* is there, moving straight on up the channel, turning now toward Moultrie. To her it has been only a handful of peas or pebbles. Some have rattled against her turret, some upon her deck, some against her sides. Instead of going to the bottom, she revolves her turret, and fire two shots at Moultrie, moving on the while to gain the south eastern wall of Sumter.

Again the forts and batteries begin, joined now by Cummings Point and long ranges from Fort Johnson. All around the *Weehawken* the shot flash, plunge, hop, skip, falling like the rain-drops of a summer shower. Unharmed, undaunted, she moves straight on, feeling her way, moving slowly, with grappling-irons dragging from the raft in front to catch up torpedoes. It is for the *Weehawken* to clear the channel, and make smooth sailing for the remainder of the fleet.

To get the position of the *Weehawken* at this moment, draw a line from Cummings Point to Moultrie, and stick a pin on the line a little nearer to Moultrie than to Morris Island. It is about one half a mile from Moultrie, about one third of a mile from Sumter.

There she is,—the target of probably two hundred and fifty or three hundred guns, of the heaviest calibre, at close range, rifled cannon throwing forged bolts and steel-pointed shot, turned and polished to a hair in the lathes of English workshops,—advancing still, undergoing her first ordeal, a trial unparalleled in history!

For fifteen minutes she meets the ordeal alone, but the channel found to be clear, the *Passaic*, the *Montauk*, and *Patapsco* follow, closing up the line, each coming in range and delivering their fire upon Sumter. At twenty minutes past three the four monitors composing the right wing of the fleet are all engaged, each pressing on to reach the north-eastern face of the fort, where the wall is weakest, each receiving as they arrive at particular points a terrible fire, seemingly from all points of the compass,—points selected by trial and practice indicated by buoys. They pass the destructive latitudes unharmed. Seventy guns a minute are counted, followed by moments of calm and scattering shots, but only to break out again in a prolonged roar of thunder. They press on, making nearer and nearer to Sumter, narrowing the distance to one thousand yards, eight hundred, six, five, four hundred yards, and send their fifteen-inch shot crashing against the fort, with deliberate, effective fire.

At first the fort and the batteries and Moultrie seem to redouble their efforts in increasing the fire, but after an hour there is a perceptible diminution of the discharges from the fort. After each shot from the ironclads, clouds of dust can be discerned rising above the fort and mingling with the smoke. Steadying my glass in the lulls of the strife, watching where the southwest breeze whiffs away the smoke, I can see increasing pock-marks and discolorations upon the walls, as if there had been a sudden breaking out of *cutaneous* disease.

The flag-ship, drawing seventeen feet of water, was obliged to move cautiously, feeling her way up the channel. Just as she came within range of Moultrie her keel touched bottom on the east side of the channel; fearing that she would run aground the anchor was let go. Finding the vessel was clear, the Admiral again moved on, signalling the left wing to press forward to the aid of the four already engaged. The *Ironsides* kept the main channel, which brought her within about one thousand yards of Moultrie and Sumter. She fired four guns at Moultrie, and received in return a heavy fire. Again she touched bottom, and then turned her bow across the channel toward Sumter, firing two guns at Cummings Point. After this weak and ineffectual effort, the tide rapidly ebbing the while, she again got clear, but gave up the attempt to advance. The *Catskill, Nantucket, Nahant,* and *Keokuk* pressed up with all possible speed to aid the four which were receiving a tremendous hammering.

See them sweep past the convergent points and radial lines! See the bubbling of the water,—the straight columns thrown up in the sunlight,—the flashes, the furrows along the waves, as if a plough driven with lightning speed were turning up the water! They are all close up to Sumter, within four or five hundred yards. Behind them are Moultrie and Fort Ripley, and Fort Beauregard, flashing, smoking, bellowing; in front is Sumter, and in the background are Fort Wagner and Cummings Point. Across the shallow waters is Fort Johnson; still farther off to the right is Castle Pinckney, too far away to do damage. From all sides the balls fall around the fleet. Calmly and deliberately the fire is returned,—with a deliberation which must have commanded the admiration of the enemy.

The *Keokuk* presented a fair mark with her sloping sides and double turrets. Her commander, Captain Rhind, although not having entire confidence in her invulnerability, was determined to come to close quarters. She was not to be outdone by the ironclads who had led the advance. Swifter than they, drawing less water, she made haste to get up with the *Weehawken*. The guns which had been trained upon the others were brought to bear upon her. Where she sailed the fire was fiercest. Her plating was but pine wood to the steel projectiles, flying with almost the swiftness of a minnie bullet. Shot which glanced harmlessly from the others penetrated her angled sides. Her after turret was pierced in a twinkling, and a two-hundred pound projectile dropped inside. A heavy shot crashed into the surgeon's dispensary, and mixed emetics, cathartics, pills and powders not according to prescriptions. The enemy noticed the effect of his shot and increased his fire. Captain Rhind was not easily daunted. He opened his forward turret and gave three shots in return for the three or four hundred rained around him. The sea with every passing wave swept through the shot-holes, and he was forced to retire or go to the bottom with all on board.

The tide was ebbing fast, and the signal for retiring was displayed by the flag-ship. It was raised, seemingly, at an inopportune moment, for the fire of the fort had sensibly diminished, while that from the ironclads was steady and true. It was past five o'clock, almost sunset, when the fleet came back. Never had there been such a hammering of iron and smashing of masonry as during two and a half hours of that afternoon. The gunboat *Bibb*, the *Ben Deford*, and the *Nantasket* had taken position in the North Channel at a respectful distance off Sullivan's Island. A mile or two east of Moultrie is Beach Inlet, where a powerful battery had been erected. While intently gazing on the contest, the correspondents and all hands on the other steamers were startled by hearing the whiff and whiz of a rifle projectile, which came diagonally across the *Nantasket*, across the bow of the *Ben Deford*, falling into the sea about one hundred yards ahead. There was a laughable cuddling down and scampering for the coal-bunkers, the engine-room, and between decks. There was an immediate hauling in of cables and motion of paddle-wheels. A second shot in admirable line fell short. We being at anchor and within range, the Rebel gunner had made nice calculations. He had already fired a half-dozen shots, which had fallen far ahead unnoticed. Cummings Point also tried to reach us with shells, but failed. One of the correspondents claimed that the press completely silenced a battery—by getting out of the way!

Steaming into the retiring fleet we ran alongside the *Keokuk*. A glance at her sides showed how terrible the fire had been. Her smokestack, turrets, sides,—all were scarred, gashed, pierced through and through. An inspection revealed ninety-four short-marks. There were none below the water-line, but each wave swept through the holes on the sides. Her pumps were going and she was kept free. Only three of her officers and crew were wounded, although she had been so badly perforated.

"All right, nobody hurt, ready for them again," was the hearty response of Captain George Rodgers, of the *Catskill*, as I stepped upon the slushed deck of that vessel and grasped the hand of her wide-awake commander. The *Catskill* had received about thirty shots. One two-hundred-pounder, thrown evidently from a barbette gun, had fallen with tremendous force upon the deck, bending, but not breaking or penetrating the iron. On the sides, on the turret, and on the pilot-house were indentations like saucers, but there was no sign of serious damage.

The *Nahant* came down to her anchorage with a gashed smokestack. Going on board, we found that eleven of her officers and crew had received contusions from the flying of bolt-heads in the turret. One shot had jammed the lower ridge of her turret, interfering with its revolution. She had been struck forty times, but—aside from the loss of a few bolt-heads, a diminished draft to her chimney, and the slight jam upon the turret—her armour was intact.

The other monitors had each a few bolts started. Four gun-carriages needed repairs,—injured not by the enemy's shot, but by their own recoil. One shot had ripped up the plating of the *Patapsco* and pierced the wood-work beneath. This was the only shot, out of the twenty-five hundred or three thousand supposed to have been fired from the forts which penetrated the monitors!

The *Weehawken* had received three heavy shot upon her side, the indentations close together. The plates were badly bent, but the shot had fallen as harmlessly as pebbles upon the side of a barn.

The *Ironsides* had received thirty balls, all of which had been turned by her armour.

One hundred and fifty-three shots were fired by the fleet, against twenty-five hundred or three thousand by the Rebels. The monitors were struck in the aggregate about three hundred and fifty times.

About six thousand pounds of iron were hurled at Fort Sumter during the short time the fleet was engaged, and probably five or six times that amount of metal, or thirty thousand pounds, was thrown at the fleet. The casualties on board the fleet were,—none killed; one mortally, one seriously, and thirteen slightly wounded.

Captain Ammen, commanding the *Patapsco*, was confident that the last shots which he fired passed through the wall of the fort. He and other commanders obeyed the signal for retiring with great reluctance. They saw that the fire of the fort was growing weaker,—that the wall was crumbling. It is now known that the Rebel commander, General Ripley, was on the point of evacuating the fort when the signal was made for the fleet to withdraw. The wall was badly shattered, and a few more shots would have made it a complete ruin.

The lower casemates were soon after filled with sand-bags, the guns having been removed. The walls were buttressed with palmetto logs, and the fort lost nearly all of its original features, but was made stronger than ever.

The *Keokuk* sunk in the morning on the bar. The sea was rough, and the water poured through the shot-holes with every wave, so that it was found impossible to keep her afloat.

Admiral Dupont decided not to renew the attack, which caused a good deal of murmuring among the soldiers in the fleet. The ironclads returned to Hilton Head for repairs, the expedition was abandoned, and Sumter was left to float its flag in defiance of Federal authority.

Chapter 17

The Invasion of Pennsylvania

June, 1863

The second invasion of the North was planned immediately after the battle of Chancellorsville. The movement of General Lee was upon a great circle,—down the valley of the Shenandoah, crossing the Potomac at Williamsport with his infantry and artillery, while General Stuart, with the main body of Rebel cavalry, kept east of the Blue Ridge to conceal the advance of the infantry.

General Hooker, at Fredericksburg, the first week in June, received positive information that Lee was breaking up his camp, and that some of his divisions were moving towards Culpepper. The dust-clouds which rose above the tree-tops indicated that the Rebel army was in motion. The Army of the Potomac immediately broke up its camp and moved to Catlett's Station, on the Orange and Alexandria Railroad, where intelligence was received that Stuart had massed the Rebel cavalry at Brandy Station for a raid in Pennsylvania.

General Pleasanton, commanding the cavalry, was sent with his entire force to look into the matter. He fell upon Stuart on the 9th of June, on the broad, open plains along the Rappahannock. A desperate battle ensued,—probably it was the greatest cavalry battle of the war,—in which Stuart was driven back upon the Rebel infantry, which was hurried up from Culpepper to his support. The object of the attack was accomplished,—Stuart's raid was postponed and Lee's movement unmasked. On the same day, Lee's advanced divisions reached Winchester, attacked General Milroy, captured the town, the cannon in the fortifications, and moved on to the Potomac.

Hastening to Pennsylvania, I became an observer of the great events which followed. The people of the Keystone State in 1862 rushed to arms when Lee crossed the Potomac, but in 1863 they were strangely

CAVALRY CHARGE

apathetic,—intent upon conveying their property to a place of security, instead of defending their homes. In '62 the cry was, *"Drive the enemy from our soil!"* in '63, *"Where shall we hide our goods?"*

Harrisburg was a Bedlam when I entered it on the 15th of June.

The railroad stations were crowded with an excited people,—men, women, and children,—with trunks, boxes, bundles; packages tied up in bed-blankets and quilts; mountains of baggage,—tumbling it into the cars, rushing here and there in a frantic manner; shouting, screaming, as if the Rebels were about to dash into the town and lay it in ashes. The railroad authorities were removing their cars and engines. The merchants were packing up their goods; housewives were secreting their silver; everywhere there was a hurly-burly. The excitement was increased when a train of army wagons came rumbling over the long bridge across the Susquehannah, accompanied by a squadron of cavalry. It was Milroy's train, which had been ordered to make its way into Pennsylvania.

"The Rebels will be here tomorrow or next day," said the teamsters.

At the State-House, men in their shirt-sleeves were packing papers into boxes. Every team, every horse and mule and handcart in the town were employed. There was a steady stream of teams thundering across the bridge; farmers from the Cumberland valley, with their household furniture piled upon the great wagons peculiar to the locality; bedding, tables, chairs, their wives and children perched on the top; kettles and pails dangling beneath; boys driving cattle and horses, excited, worried, fearing they knew not what. The scene was painful, yet ludicrous.

General Couch was in command at Harrisburg. He had but a few troops. He erected fortifications across the river, planted what few cannon he had, and made preparations to defend the place.

General Lee was greatly in need of horses, and his cavalrymen, under General Jenkins, ravaged the Cumberland Valley. A portion visited Chambersburg; another party, Mercersburg; another, Gettysburg, before any infantry entered the State.

Ewell's corps of Lee's army crossed the Potomac, a division at Williamsport, and another at Shepherdstown, on the 22nd of June, and came together at Hagerstown. The main body of Lee's army was at Winchester. Stuart had moved along the eastern base of the Blue Ridge, and had come in contact with a portion of Pleasanton's cavalry at Aldie and Middleburg. Hooker had swung the army up to Fairfax and Centreville, moving on an inner circle, with Washington for a pivot.

Visiting Baltimore, where General Schenck was in command, I

found the Marylanders much more alive to the exigencies of the hour than the Pennsylvanians. Instead of hurrying northward with their household furniture, they were hard at work building fortifications and barricading the streets. Hogsheads of tobacco, barrels of pork, old carts, wagons, and lumber were piled across the streets, and patriotic citizens stood, musket in hand, prepared to pick off any Rebel troops.

Coloured men were impressed to construct fortifications. They were shy at first, fearing it was a trap to get them into slavery, but when they found they were to defend the city, they gave enthusiastic demonstrations of joy. They went to their work singing *their Marseillaise, John Brown's body*, &c.

While writing in the Eutaw House, I heard the song sung by a thousand voices, accompanied by the steady tramp, tramp, tramp of the men marching down the street, cheering General Schenck as they passed his quarters.

How rapid the revolution! Twenty-six months before, Massachusetts troops had fought their way through the city, now the coloured men were singing of John Brown amid the cheers of the people!

General Hooker waited in front of Washington till he was certain of Lee's intentions, and then by a rapid march pushed on to Frederick. Lee's entire army was across the Potomac. Ewell was at York, enriching himself by reprisals, stealings, and confiscations. General Hooker asked that the troops at Harper's Ferry might be placed under his command, that he might wield the entire available force and crush Lee; this was refused, whereupon he informed the War Department that, unless this condition were complied with, he wished to be relieved of the command of the army. The matter was laid before the President and his request was granted. General Meade was placed in command; and what was denied to General Hooker was substantially granted to General Meade,—that he was to use his best judgment in holding or evacuating Harper's Ferry! General Halleck was military adviser to the President, and the question between him and Hooker was whether Halleck, sitting in his chair at Washington, or Hooker at the head of the army, should fight General Lee. The march of Hooker from Fairfax to Frederick was one of the most rapid of the war. The Eleventh Corps marched fifty-four miles in two days,—a striking contrast to the movement in September, 1862, when the army made but five miles a day.

It was a dismal day at Frederick when the news was promulgated that General Hooker was relieved of the command. Notwithstanding the result at Chancellorsville, the soldiers had a good degree of confidence in him. General Meade was unknown except to his own corps. He entered the war as brigadier in the Pennsylvania Reserves. He commanded a division at Antietam and at Fredericksburg, and the Fifth Corps at Chancellorsville.

General Meade cared but little for the pomp and parade of war. His own soldiers respected him because he was always prepared to endure hardships. They saw a tall, slim, gray-bearded man, wearing a slouch hat, a plain blue blouse, with his pantaloons tucked into his boots. He was plain of speech, and familiar in conversation. He enjoyed in a high degree, especially after the battle of Fredericksburg, the confidence of the President.

I saw him soon after he was informed that the army was under his command. There was no elation, but on the contrary he seemed weighed down with a sense of the responsibility resting on him. It was in the hotel at Frederick. He stood silent and thoughtful by himself. Few of all the noisy crowd around knew of the change that had taken place. The correspondents of the press knew it long before the corps commanders were informed of the fact. No change was made in the machinery of the army, and there was but a few hours' delay in its movement.

General Hooker bade farewell to the principal officers of the army on the afternoon of the 28th. They were drawn up in line. He shook hands with each officer, labouring in vain to stifle his emotion. The tears rolled down his cheeks. The officers were deeply affected. He said that he had hoped to lead them to victory, but the power above him had ordered otherwise. He spoke in high terms of General Meade. He believed that they would defeat the enemy under his leadership.

While writing out the events of the day in the parlour of a private house during the evening, I heard the comments of several officers upon the change which had taken place.

"Well, I think it is too bad to have him removed just now," said a captain.

"I wonder if we shall have McClellan back?" queried a lieutenant.

"Well, gentlemen, I don't know about Hooker as a commander in the field, but I do know the Army of the Potomac was never so well fed and clothed as it has been since Joe Hooker took command."

"That is so," said several.

After a short silence, another officer took up the conversation and said,—"Yes, the army was in bad condition when he took command of it, and bad off every way; but it never was in better condition than it is today, and the men begin to like him."

The army was too patriotic to express any dissatisfaction, and in a few days the event was wholly forgotten.

It was evident that a collision of the two armies must take place before many days, and their positions, and the lines of movement indicated that it must be near Gettysburg, which is the county seat of Adams, Pennsylvania, nearly forty miles a little north of east from Frederick, on the head-waters of the Monocacy. Rock Creek, which in spring-time leaps over huge granite boulders, runs south, a mile east of the town, and is the main stem of the Monocacy. Being a county seat, it is also a grand centre for that section of the State, contains three thousand inhabitants, and has a pleasant location, surrounded with scenery of quiet beauty, hills, valleys, the dark outline and verdure-clad sides of the Blue Ridge in the west, and the billowy Catoctin range on the south. Roads radiate in all directions. It was a central point, admitting of a quick concentration of forces.

The army commanded by General Meade consisted of seven corps. 1. Major-General Reynolds; 2. Major-General Hancock; 3. Major-General Sickles; 5. Major-General Sykes; 6. Major-General Sedgwick; 11. Major-General Howard; 12. Major-General Slocum.

As Ewell was at York, and as Lee was advancing in that direction, it was necessary to take a wide sweep of country in the march. All Sunday the army was passing through Frederick. It was a strange sight. The churches were open, and some of the officers and soldiers attended service,—a precious privilege to those who before entering the army were engaged in Sabbath schools. The stores also were open, and the town was cleaned of goods,—boots, shoes, needles, pins, tobacco, pipes, paper, pencils, and other trifles which add to a soldier's comfort.

Cavalry, infantry, and artillery were pouring through the town, the bands playing, and the soldiers singing their liveliest songs. The First Corps moved up the Emmettsburg road, and formed the left of the line; the Eleventh Corps marched up a parallel road a little farther east, through Griegerstown. The Third and Twelfth Corps moved on parallel roads leading to Taneytown. The Second and Fifth moved still farther east, through Liberty and Uniontown, while the Sixth, with Gregg's division of cavalry, went to Westminster, forming the right of the line.

The lines of march were like the sticks of a fan, Frederick being the point of divergence.

On this same Sunday afternoon Lee was at Chambersburg, directing Ewell, who was at York, to move to Gettysburg. A. P. Hill was moving east from Chambersburg towards the same point, while Longstreet's,

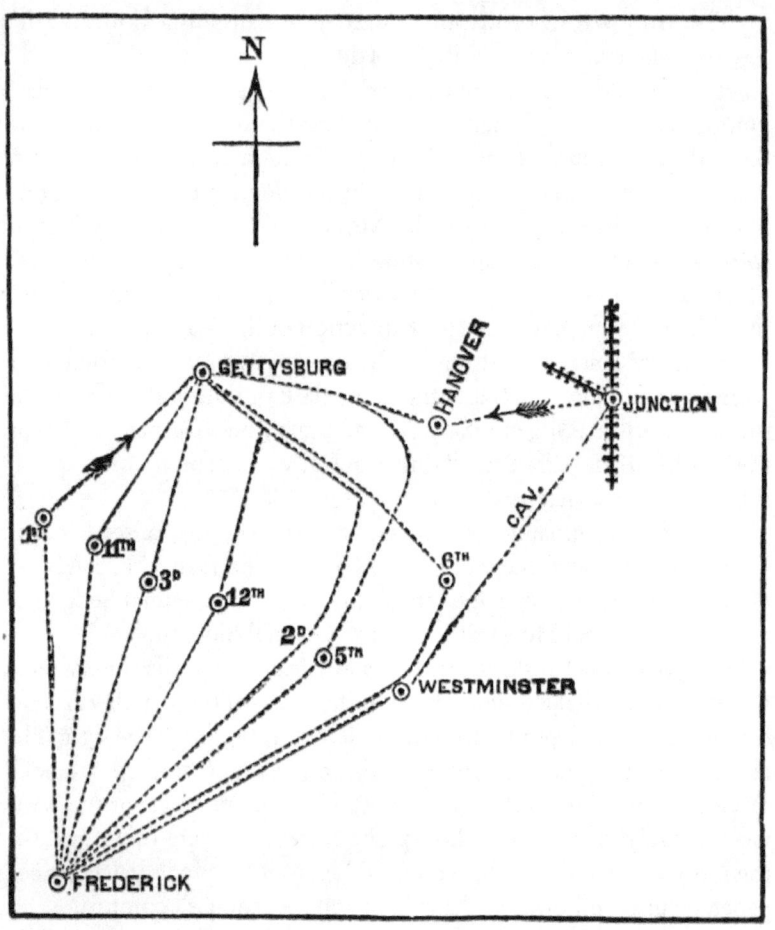

the last corps to cross the Potomac, was moving through Waynesboro' and Fairfield, marching northeast towards the same point.

It was a glorious spectacle, that movement of the army north from Frederick. I left the town accompanying the Second and Fifth Corps. Long lines of men and innumerable wagons were visible in every direction. The people of Maryland welcomed the soldiers hospitably.

When the Fifth Corps passed through the town of Liberty, a farmer rode into the village, mounted on his farm-wagon. His load was covered by white table-cloths.

"What have ye got to sell, old fellow? Bread, eh?" said a soldier, raising a corner of the cloth, and revealing loaves of sweet soft plain bread, of the finest wheat, with several bushels of ginger-cakes.

"What do you ask for a loaf?"

"I haven't any to sell," said the farmer.

"Haven't any to sell? What are ye here for?"

The farmer made no reply.

"See here, old fellow, won't ye sell me a hunk of your gingerbread?" said the soldier, producing an old wallet.

"No."

"Well, you are a mean old cuss. It would be serving you right to tip you out of your old bread-cart. Here we are marching all night and all day to protect your property, and fight the Rebs. We haven't had any breakfast, and may not have any dinner. You are a set of mean cusses round here, I reckon," said the soldier.

A crowd of soldiers had gathered, and others expressed their indignation. The old farmer stood up on his wagon-seat, took off the table-cloths, and replied:

"I didn't bring my bread here to sell. My wife and daughters set up all night to bake it for you, and you are welcome to all I've got, and wish I had ten times as much. Help your selves, boys."

"Hurrah! hurrah! hurrah!"

"Bully for you!"

"You're a brick!"

"Three cheers for the old man!"

"Three more for the old woman!"

"Three more for the girls!"

They threw up their caps, and fairly danced with joy. The bread and cakes were gone in a twinkling.

"See here, my friend, I take back all the hard words I said about you," said the soldier, shaking hands with the farmer, who sat on his wagon overcome with emotion.

On Tuesday evening, General Reynolds, who was at Emmettsburg, sent word to General Meade that the Rebels were evidently approaching Gettysburg. At the same time, the Rebel General Stuart, with his cavalry, appeared at Westminster. He had tarried east of the Blue Ridge till Lee was across the Potomac,—till Meade had started from Frederick,—then crossing the Potomac at Edwards's Ferry, he pushed directly northeast of the Monocacy, east of Meade's army, through Westminster, where he had a slight skirmish with some of the Union cavalry, moved up the pike to Littlestown and Hanover and joined Lee.

Riding to Westminster I overtook General Gregg's division of cavalry, and on Wednesday moved forward with it to Hanover Junction, which is thirty miles east of Gettysburg. There, while our horses were eating their corn at noon, I heard the distant cannonade, the opening of the great battle.

Striking directly across the country, I rejoined the Fifth Corps at Hanover. There were dead horses and dead soldiers in the streets lying where they fell. The wounded had been gathered into a school-house, and the warm-hearted women of the place were ministering to their comfort. It was evening. The bivouac fires of the Fifth Corps were gleaming in the meadows west of the town, and the worn and weary soldiers were asleep, catching a few hours of repose before moving on to the place where they were to lay down their lives for their country.

It was past eight o'clock on Thursday morning, July 2nd, before we reached the field. The Fifth Corps, turning off from the Hanover road, east of Rock Creek, passed over to the Baltimore pike, crossed Rock Creek, filed through the field on the left hand and moved towards Little Round-top, or Weed's Hill as it is now called.

Riding directly up the pike towards the cemetery, I saw the Twelfth Corps on my right, in the thick woods crowning Culp's Hill. Beyond, north of the pike, was the First Corps. Ammunition wagons were going up, and the artillerymen were filling their limber chests. Pioneers were cutting down the trees.

Reaching the top of the hill in front of the cemetery gate the battle-field was in view. To understand a battle, the movements of the opposing forces, and what they attempt to accomplish, it is necessary first to comprehend the ground, its features, the hills, hollows, woods, ravines, ledges, roads,—how they are related. A rocky hill is frequently a fortress of itself. Rail fences and stone walls are of value, and a ravine may be equivalent to ten thousand men.

Tying my horse and ascending the stairs to the top of the gateway building, I could look directly down upon the town. The houses were not forty rods distant. Northeast, three fourths of a mile, was Culp's Hill.

On the northern side of the Baltimore pike were newly mown fields, the grass springing fresh and green since the mower had swept over it. In those fields were batteries with breastworks thrown up by Howard on Wednesday night,—light affairs, not intended to resist cannon-shot, but to protect the cannoneers from sharpshooters. Howard's lines of infantry were behind stone-walls. The cannoneers were lying beside their pieces,—sleeping perhaps, but at any rate keeping close, for, occasionally, a bullet came singing past them. Looking north over the fields, a mile or two, we saw a beautiful farming country,—fields of ripened grain,—russet mingled with the green in the landscape.

Conspicuous among the buildings is the almshouse, with its brick walls, great barn, and numerous out-buildings, on the Harrisburg road. Beyond are the houses of David and John Blocher,—John Blocher's being at the junction of the Carlisle and Newville roads. Looking over the town, the buildings of Pennsylvania College are in full view, between the road leading northwest to Mummasburg, and the unfinished track of a railroad running west through a deep excavation a half-mile from the college. The Chambersburg turnpike runs parallel to the railroad. South of this is the Lutheran Theological Seminary, beautifully situated, in front of a shady grove of oaks. West and southwest we look upon wheat, clover, and corn fields, on both sides of the road leading to Emmettsburg. A half-mile west of this road is an elevated ridge of land, crowned with apple-orchards and groves of oaks. Turning to the southeast, two miles distant, is Round-top, shaped like a sugar-loaf, rocky, steep, hard to climb, on its western face, easy to be held by those who have possession, clad with oaks and pines. Nearer, a little east of the meridian, is Weed's Hill, with Plum Run at its western base, flowing through a rocky ravine. From the sides of the hill, and on its top, great boulders bulge, like plums in a pudding. It is very stony west of the hill, as if Nature in making up the mould had dumped the debris there.

Between Round-top and Weed's there is a gap, where men bent on a desperate enterprise might find a pass way. Between Weed's and the cemetery the ridge is broken down and smoothed out into fields and pastures. The road to Taneytown runs east of this low ridge, the road to Emmettsburg west of it. A small house stands on the west side of the Taneytown road, with the American flag flying in front of it. There are horses hitched to the fences, while others are nibbling the grass in the fields. Officers with stars on their shoulders are examining maps, writing, and sending off cavalrymen. It is General Meade's head-quarters. When the Rebel batteries open it will be a warm place.

Having taken a general look at the field, I rode forward towards the town, between Stewart's and Taft's batteries, in position on either side of the road. Soldiers in blue were lying behind the garden fences.

"Where are you going?" said one.

"Into the town."

"I reckon not. The Rebs hold it, and I advise you to turn about. It is rather dangerous where you are. The Rebels are right over there in that brick house."

Right over there was not thirty rods distant.

"Ping!"—and there was the sharp ring of a bullet over our heads.

General Howard was in the cemetery with his maps and plans spread upon the ground.

"We are just taking a lunch, and there is room for one more," was his kind and courteous welcome. Then removing his hat, he asked God to bless the repast. The bullets were occasionally singing over us. Soldiers were taking up the headstones and removing the monuments from their pedestals.

"I want to preserve them, besides, if a shot should strike a stone, the pieces of marble would be likely to do injury," said the General.

The flowers were blooming around us. I gathered a handful as a memento of the hour. Preparations were rapidly going on for the approaching struggle. North, west, and southwest the whole country was alive with Rebels,—long lines of men deploying in various directions, tents going up, with yellow flags above them on the distant hills, thousands of canvas-covered wagons, slowly winding along the roads, reaching as far as the eye could see towards Chambersburg, Carlisle, and Fairfield,—turning into the fields and taking positions in park. There were batteries of artillery, the cannon gleaming in the noonday sun, and hundreds of horsemen riding in hot haste on many a desperate errand.

While partaking of our refreshment, General Howard narrated the operations of the preceding day.

CHAPTER 18

The Battle of Gettysburg

JULY, 1863

On Tuesday evening, the 30th of June, General Reynolds was in camp on Marsh Run, a short distance from Emmettsburg, while General Howard, with the Eleventh Corps, was in that town. Instructions were received from General Meade assigning General Reynolds to the command of the First, Eleventh, and Third Corps. General Reynolds moved early in the morning to Gettysburg, and sent orders to General Howard to follow. General Howard received the orders at 8 o'clock in the morning. General Barlow's division of the Eleventh followed the First Corps by the most direct road while General Schurz's and General Steinwehr's divisions went by Horner's Mills, the distance being thirteen miles. General Howard, with his staff, pushed on in advance of his troops.

Buford's division of cavalry passed through Gettysburg on Tuesday and went into camp a mile and a half west of the town on the Chambersburg pike. At 9.30 a. m. on Wednesday, the Rebels of A. P. Hill's division appeared in front of him, and skirmishing commenced on the farm of Hon. Edward McPherson. General Reynolds rode into Gettysburg about 10 o'clock in advance of his troops, turned up the Chambersburg road, reconnoitred the position, rode back again, met the head of his column a mile down the Emmettsburg road, turned it directly across the fields, towards the seminary, and deployed his divisions across the Chambersburg road. General Archer's brigade of Heth's division of A. P. Hill's corps was advancing eastward, unaware of Reynolds's movement. He had passed Herr's tavern, two miles beyond the town, when he found himself face to face with General Meredith's brigade of Reynolds's command. The fight opened at once. Archer and several hundred of his men were captured. General Cutler, pushing out from the town between the half-finished railroad and the Chambersburg road, came in contact with Davis's brigade of Mississippians. The contest increased. General Reynolds, while riding along the line, was killed in the field beyond the Seminary, and the command devolved on General Doubleday.

General Howard heard the cannonade, and riding rapidly up the Emmettsburg road entered the town, sent messengers in search of General Reynolds, asking for instructions, not knowing that he had been killed.

While waiting the return of his aids, he went to the top of the college to reconnoitre the surrounding country. His aid, Major Biddle, soon came back, with the sad intelligence that General Reynolds had fallen, and that the command devolved on himself.

It was half past eleven. The Rebels were appearing in increased force. The prisoners taken said that the whole of A. P. Hill's corps was nearby.

"You will have your hands full before night. Longstreet is near, and Ewell is coming," said one, boastingly.

"After an examination of the general features of the country," said General Howard, "I came to the conclusion that the only tenable position for my limited force was on this ridge. I saw that this was the highest point. You will notice that it commands all the other eminences. My artillery can sweep the fields completely."

He pointed towards the north, where across the pike, just beyond the gateway, were Colonel Wainwright's batteries of the First Corps, and around us were Colonel Osborn's of the Eleventh. Behind us, east of the cemetery, was some of the reserve artillery.

The head of the Eleventh Corps reached Gettysburg about twelve o'clock. The first and third division passed through the town, moved out beyond the college, and joined the right of the First Corps. Howard sent three batteries and his second division, Steinwehr's, to take possession of the cemetery and the hill north of the Baltimore pike.

Thus far success had attended the Union arms. A large number of prisoners had been taken with but little loss, and the troops were holding their own against a superior force. About half past twelve cavalry scouts reported that Ewell was coming down the York road, and was not more than four miles distant. General Howard sent an aid to General Sickles, who was at Emmettsburg, requesting him to come on with all haste. Another was sent down the Baltimore pike to the Two Taverns, three miles distant, with a similar message to General Slocum. The Second Corps was there,—resting in the fields. They had heard the roar of the battle, and could see the clouds of smoke rising over the intervening hills. General Slocum was the senior officer. He received the message, but did not, for reasons best known to himself, see fit to accede to the request. He could have put the Twelfth Corps upon the ground in season to meet Ewell, but remained where he was till after the contest for the day was over.

It was a quarter before three when Ewell's lines began to deploy by John Blocher's house on the York road. The Rebel batteries were wheeled into position, and opened on Wadsworth. Weiderick's battery in the cemetery replied. Again a messenger went in haste to the delinquent officer.

"I sent again to General Slocum, stating that my right flank was attacked; that it was in danger of being turned, and asking him if he was coming up," said General Howard.

The message was delivered to Slocum, who was still at the Two Taverns, where he had been through the day. Weiderick's battery was in plain view from that position, but General Slocum did not move.

This officer on Thursday and Friday did hard service. He afterward commanded acceptably one of Sherman's wings in the march from Atlanta to the sea, but on the first day at Gettysburg his inaction, unless satisfactorily explained, will compel the impartial historian to assign him a lower place on the scroll of fame than would otherwise have been accorded him.

Sickles was too far off to render assistance. Meanwhile Ewell was pressing on towards the college. Another division of Rebels under General Pender came in from the southwest, and began to enfold the left of Howard's line.

"I want a brigade to help me!" was the word from Schurz, commanding the two divisions in front of Ewell, beyond the college.

"Send out Costa's brigade," said Howard to his chief of staff. The brigade went down through the town accompanied by a battery, and joined the line, upon the double-quick. An hour passed, of close, desperate fighting. It wanted a quarter to four. Howard confronted by four times his own force, was still holding his ground, waiting for Slocum. Another messenger rode to the Two Taverns, urging Slocum to advance.

"I must have reinforcements!" was the message from Doubleday on the left. "You must reinforce me!" was the word from Wadsworth in the centre.

"Hold out a little longer, if possible; I am expecting General Slocum every moment," was Howard's reply. Still another despatch was sent to the Two Taverns, but General Slocum had not moved. The

The Colour-Bearer

Rebel cannon were cutting Wadsworth's line. Pender was sweeping round Doubleday; Ewell was enclosing Schurz. Sickles was five miles distant, advancing as fast as he could. Slocum was where he had been from early morning, three miles distant. The tide was turning. The only alternative was a retreat. It was past four o'clock. For six hours the ground had been held against a greatly superior force.

Major Howard, the General's brother, a member of his staff, dashed down the pike in search of Slocum, with a request that he would move at once, and send one division to the right and the other to the left of Gettysburg. Slocum declined to go up to the front and take any responsibility, as he understood that General Meade did not wish to bring on a general engagement. He was willing, however, to send forward his troops as General Howard desired, and issued his orders accordingly. Under military law the question might be raised whether a senior officer had a right to throw off the responsibility which circumstances had forced upon him; also whether he could turn over his troops to a subordinate.

But before the divisions of the Twelfth Corps could get in motion, the Rebels had completely enfolded both flanks of Howard's line. The order to retreat was given. The two corps came crowding through the town. The Rebels pressed on with cheers. Most of the First Corps reached the cemetery ridge, and were rallied by Howard, Steinwehr, and Hancock. This officer had just arrived. The troops were streaming over the hill, when he reined up his steed in the cemetery. He came, under direction of General Meade, to take charge of all the troops in front. The Eleventh Corps was hard pressed, and lost between two and three thousand prisoners in the town.

The Rebels of Ewell's command pushed up the northern slope, through the hay-fields, flushed with victory; but Weiderick's battery poured canister in quick discharges into the advancing ranks, breaking the line.

The retreat was so orderly and the resistance so steady that the Rebels gave utterance to their admiration. Said General Hill:

A Yankee colour-bearer floated his standard in the field and the regiment fought around it; and when at last it was obliged to retreat, the colour-bearer retired last of all, turning round now and then to shake his fist in the face of the advancing Rebels. He was sorry when he saw him meet his doom.[46]

Three colour-bearers of the Nineteenth Indiana were shot. The

---

46: Lieutenant Freemantle.—*Blackwood's Magazine*, September, 1863.

Sergeant-Major, Asa Blanchard, ran and took the flag when the third man fell, waved it, and cried "Rally, boys!" The next moment he fell. His comrades stopped to carry him off. The Rebels were close at hand.

"Don't stop for me," he cried. "Don't let them have the flag. Tell mother I never faltered." They were his parting words to his comrades, who saved the flag.

General Hancock met General Howard and informed him of his instructions, saying, "General Meade undoubtedly supposed that I was your senior, but you outrank me."

"It is no time to talk about rank. I shall most cheerfully obey your instructions and do all in my power to co-operate with you," was Howard's reply, thus waiving the command which was his by right. They perfectly agreed in what was to be done. General Howard took charge of the troops and batteries on the right of the line, while General Hancock brought order out of confusion on the left.

The Rebels having been repulsed by the batteries, and satisfied with the work of the day, made no further attack, although they greatly outnumbered the Union force.

General Sickles arrived at seven o'clock, and General Slocum also came up, he being the senior officer, General Howard turned over the command to him, while General Hancock went back to see General Meade at Taneytown, to inform him of the state of affairs. The Third Corps filed into position on the left of the First, south of the cemetery, while the Twelfth took possession of Culp's Hill.

So closed the first day at Gettysburg.

Second Day—Thursday, July 2nd

General Meade arrived on the battle-field at three o'clock on the morning of the 2nd, and had an interview with General Howard soon after by the cemetery gate. They rode along the lines together.

"I am confident that we can hold this position," said General Howard.

"I am glad to hear you say so, for it is too late to leave it," said Meade.

The cannonade began at daybreak, the guns in the cemetery and those of the Rebels near Blocher's house keeping up a steady fire for an hour, when both parties, as if by mutual consent, became silent; but the pickets were at it all along the lines.

While I was conversing with General Howard, his brother, Major

Howard, who was keeping a sharp look upon the Rebels, came running up. "There is a splendid chance to cut them up, General; just see them!"

A column of Rebels was moving along the Chambersburg road, and stood out in bold relief.

"Let Osborn pitch in the shells from his rifled pieces," said the Major.

General Howard surveyed them a moment and replied: "We might do them some damage, but we are not quite ready to bring on a general engagement. It isn't best to hurry. We shall have enough fighting before night."

The battle had not commenced in earnest. Lee was moving his troops towards the left. The Union pickets were posted along the Emmettsburg road; some were lying down in the wheat-fields beyond it, keeping up a steady interchange of shots with the Rebels. It was a favourable time to ride over the ground where the great contest was to take place.

The first division, General Ames's, of the Eleventh Corps, was north of the Baltimore pike, the third division, Schurz's, was on both sides of it, and the second division, Steinwehr's, in the cemetery, lying behind the stone wall, which forms its western boundary. Colonel Osborn's batteries were on the crest of the ridge, in position to fire over the heads of the infantry. Robinson's division of the First Corps was posted at the left of Steinwehr's, crossing the Taneytown road. Wadsworth's and Doubleday's divisions of the First were north of the Baltimore pike, to the right of General Ames, reaching to Culp's Hill, where they joined the Twelfth Corps.

Riding down the road towards Taneytown, I came upon General Stannard's brigade of nine months' Vermont boys, lying in the open field in rear of the cemetery. Occasionally a shell came over them from the Rebel batteries, by Blocher's. It was their first experience under fire. They were in reserve, knowing nothing of what was going on the other side of the hill, yet tantalized by a flank fire from the distant batteries. A short distance farther I came to General Meade's head-quarters, in the house of Mrs. Leister. General Meade was there surrounded by his staff, consulting maps and issuing orders. General Hancock's head-quarters' flag,—the tree-foil of the Second Corps,—was waving on the ridge southwest of the house. General Slocum's,—the star-flag,—was in sight, on a conical hill a half-mile eastward. The crescent flag of the Eleventh was proudly planted on the highest elevation of the cemetery. The Maltese cross of the Fifth Corps was a half-mile south, toward Round-top.

Turning into the field and riding to the top of the ridge, I came upon Hayes's division of the Second Corps, joining Robinson's of the First; then Gibbons's and Caldwell's of the Second, reaching to a narrow roadway running west from the Taneytown road to the house of Abraham Trostle, where, a half-mile in advance of the main line, was planted the diamond flag of the Third Corps, General Sickles. Pushing directly west, through a field where the grass was ripening for the scythe, I approached the house of Mr. Codori, on the Emmettsburg road. But it was a dangerous place just then to a man on horseback, for the pickets of both armies were lying in the wheatfield west of the road. General Carr's brigade of the Third Corps was lying behind the ridge near the house of Peter Rogers. Soldiers were filling their canteens from the brook in the hollow. Further down by the house of Mr. Wentz, at the corner of the narrow road leading east from the Emmettsburg road, and in the peach-orchards on both sides of it, were troops and batteries. The Second New Hampshire, the First Maine, and the Third Michigan were there, holding the angle of the line, which here turned east from the Emmettsburg road. Thompson's battery was behind Wentz's house. General Sickles had his other batteries in position along the narrow road, the muzzles of the guns pointing southwest. Ames's New York battery was in the orchard, and the gunners were lying beneath the peach-trees, enjoying the leafy shade. Clark's New Jersey battery, Phillips's Fifth Massachusetts, and Bigelow's Ninth Massachusetts were on the left of Ames. Bigelow's was in front of Trostle's house, having complete command and the full sweep of a beautiful slope beyond the road for sixty rods.

The slope descends to a wooded ravine through which winds a brook, gurgling over a rocky bed. Beyond the brook are the stone farm-house and capacious barn of John Rose, in whose door-yard were the Union pickets, exchanging a shot now and then with the Rebels of Longstreet's corps, south of Rose's, who were lying along the Emmettsburg road.

General Barnes's division of the Third Corps was in the woods south of the narrow road, and among the rocks in front of Weed's Hill.

Sickles had advanced to the position upon his own judgment of the fitness of the movement. He believed that it was necessary to hold the ravine, down to Round-top, to prevent the enemy from passing through the gap between that eminence and Weed's Hill.

General Meade had called his corps commanders to his headquarters for consultation. Sickles did not attend, deeming it of vital importance to prepare for the advance of the enemy, and his soldiers were levelling fences and removing obstructions.

A peremptory order reached Sickles requiring his presence. He rode to the head-quarters of the army, but the conference was over, and he went back to his command followed by General Meade.

"Are you not too much extended? Can you hold your front?" asked the Commander-in-Chief.

"Yes, only I shall want more troops."

"I will send you the Fifth Corps, and you may call on Hancock for support."

"I shall need more artillery."

"Send for all you want. Call on General Hunt of the Artillery Reserve. I will direct him to send you all you want."

The pickets were keeping up a lively fire.

"I think that the Rebels will soon make their appearance," said Sickles.

A moment later and the scattering fire became a volley. General Meade took another look at the troops in position, and galloped back to his head-quarters.

General Lee, in his report, has given an outline of his intentions, he says:

> It had not been intended to fight a general battle at such a distance from our base, unless attacked by the enemy; but, finding ourselves unexpectedly confronted by the Federal army, it became a matter of difficulty to withdraw through the mountains with our large trains. At the same time the country was unfavourable for collecting supplies while in the presence of the enemy's main body, as he was enabled to restrain our foraging parties by occupying the passes of the mountains with regular and local troops. A battle thus became, in a measure, unavoidable. Encouraged by the successful issue of the engagement of the first day, and in view of the valuable results that would ensue from the defeat of the army of General Meade, it was thought advisable to renew the attack.
>
> The remainder of Ewell's and Hill's corps having arrived, and two divisions of Longstreet's, our preparations were made accordingly. During the afternoon intelligence was received of the arrival of General Stuart at Carlisle, and he was ordered to march to Gettysburg and take position on the left. A full account of these engagements cannot be given until the reports

of the several commanding officers shall have been received, and I shall only offer a general description.

The preparations for attack were not completed until the afternoon of the 2nd.

The enemy held a high and commanding ridge, along which he had massed a large amount of artillery. General Ewell occupied the left of our line, General Hill the centre, and General Longstreet the right. In front of General Longstreet the enemy held a position from which, if he could be driven, it was thought that our army could be used to advantage in assailing the more elevated ground beyond, and thus enable us to reach the crest of the ridge. That officer was directed to endeavour to carry this position, while General Ewell attacked directly the high ground on the enemy's right, which had already been partially fortified. General Hill was instructed to threaten the centre of the Federal line, in order to prevent reinforcements being sent to either wing, and to avail himself of any opportunity that might present itself to attack.

Lee had been all day perfecting his plans. He was riding along his lines at sunrise, reconnoitring Meade's position. His head-quarters were near the Theological Seminary, where, at five o'clock in the morning, Lee, Hill, Longstreet, Hood, and Heth were engaged in conversation. The conference lasted till seven o'clock, when Longstreet rode down to his corps to make arrangements for the attack. Hood had the extreme right, and McLaws stood next in line. Pickett, commanding his other division, had not arrived. It was to be held in reserve.[47]

47: The accompanying plan of the battle-field accurately represents the general positions of the troops engaged. On the right of the Union line is the Twelfth Corps; then two divisions of the First; then the Eleventh in and around the cemetery; then Robinson's division of the First; then the Second and the Fifth on the left, occupying Weed's Hill. The Third Corps is in the position it occupied at the beginning of the battle on the afternoon of the second day. It was forced back to Trostle's house. The Sixth Corps is in the position it occupied at sunset on the second day. On the third day it was in line along Weed's Hill. When Slocum went over from the right to aid in repulsing Longstreet on the second day, he passed near the two houses standing on the Taneytown road. Meade's quarters were in the house over which a flag is flying. Longstreet is in the position which he occupied at three o'clock on the afternoon of the second day, and to which he retired after failing to push Sickles beyond Trostle's. Pickett commanded a division and not a corps. But as his division took the lead in the last attack, on the third day, and as his repulse was seemingly the turning-point of the Rebellion, especial mention has been made of the part taken by the troops under his command. Hill supported him. A portion (continued on next page)

Lee chose, as his first point of attack, the position occupied by Sickles. The ground by Wentz's house is higher than the ridge, where Hancock had established his head-quarters. If he could drive Sickles from the peach-orchard by turning his left flank, and gain Weed's Hill, Meade would be compelled to retreat, and the nature of the ground was such in rear of the cemetery that a retreat might be turned into a complete rout. Meade's position was a very fair one for defence, but one from which an army could not well retire before a victorious enemy. The trains in park along Rock Creek would have been in the way. Baggage trains are exceedingly useful, but there are times when commanders do not know what to do with them. A battery in the hands of the enemy, planted on the ridge, or in the cemetery, if those places had fallen into the hands of the Rebels, would have produced confusion in Meade's rear among the teamsters, who are not always cool under fire, especially if they have refractory mules to manage. General Meade would have chosen a position fifteen or twenty miles in rear, nearer to his base of supplies, and had he been at Gettysburg on Wednesday evening, doubtless would have ordered a retreat. The question, whether to fall back or to hold the position, was seriously debated. But Howard had made the stand. He believed that the position could be held, and Lee defeated there. He did not calculate for a defeat, but for victory. Had Meade fallen back, Lee would have been wary of moving on. It was not his intention, he says, to fight a general battle so far from his base. He would have followed cautiously, if at all. Through the foresight, faith, and courage of Howard, therefore, Gettysburg has become a turning-point in history. And yet, not that alone, for the warp and woof of history are made up of innumerable threads. The Rebels, on that afternoon of Thursday, as they moved out from the woods into the fields south of the house of John Rose, had a thorough contempt for the troops in blue, standing beneath the peach-trees in Sherfy's orchard, and along the road towards Trostle's. Big Bethel, Bull Run, Richmond, Manassas, Fredericksburg, Chancellorsville,

---

of Hill's troops were with Longstreet in the attack of the second day. Ewell is in the position he occupied at dark on the second day, while two of Slocum's divisions were aiding the left of Meade's line. Lee's head-quarters were near Smucker's house. The fight on the first day began on Willoughby's Run. The Union lines on that day extended from the Middletown road along the semicircle occupied by the Rebel cannon in the diagram, to the railroad east of Blocher's. The map is reduced from an accurate survey. The best plan of this battle extant is the isometrical picture of Gettysburg, by Colonel J. B. Batchelder, who has devoted many months to the study of the field. It will ever be standard authority for the historian.

Cedar Mountain, Harper's Ferry they remembered as victories; and even Antietam and South Mountain were called drawn battles by the Rebel commander-in-chief. They had already achieved one victory on the soil of Pennsylvania. Five thousand Yankees had been captured. The troops of the Confederacy were invincible, not only while fighting at their own doors, but as invaders of the North. Such was the feeling of the soldiers. But the Rebel officers were not quite so sanguine of success as the men. An Englishman, who saw the fight from the Rebel side, says:

> At 4.30 p.m. (Wednesday) we came in sight of Gettysburg, and joined General Lee and General Hill, who were on the top of one of the ridges which form the peculiar feature of the country round Gettysburg. We could see the enemy retreating up one of the opposite ridges, pursued by the Confederates with loud yells.
>
> The position into which the enemy had been driven was evidently a strong one. General Hill now came up, and told me he had been very unwell all day, and in fact he looks very delicate. He said he had two of his divisions engaged, and had driven the enemy four miles into his present position, capturing a great many prisoners, some cannon, and some colours; he said, however, that the Yankees had fought with a determination unusual to them. He pointed out a railway cutting in which they had made a good stand; also a field, in the centre of which he had seen a man plant the regimental colours, round which the regiment had fought for some time with much obstinacy; and when at last it was obliged to retreat, the colour-bearer retired last of all, turning round every now and then to shake his fist at the advancing Rebels. General Hill said he felt quite sorry when he saw this gallant Yankee meet his doom.
>
> General Ewell had come up at 3.30 on the enemy's right and completed his discomfiture.
>
> General Reynolds, one of the best Yankee generals, was reported killed. Whilst we were talking, a message arrived from General Ewell, requesting Hill to press the enemy in front, whilst he performed the same operation on his right. The pressure was accordingly applied in a mild degree, but the enemy were too strongly posted, and it was too late in the evening for a regular attack.[48]

48: Freemantle.

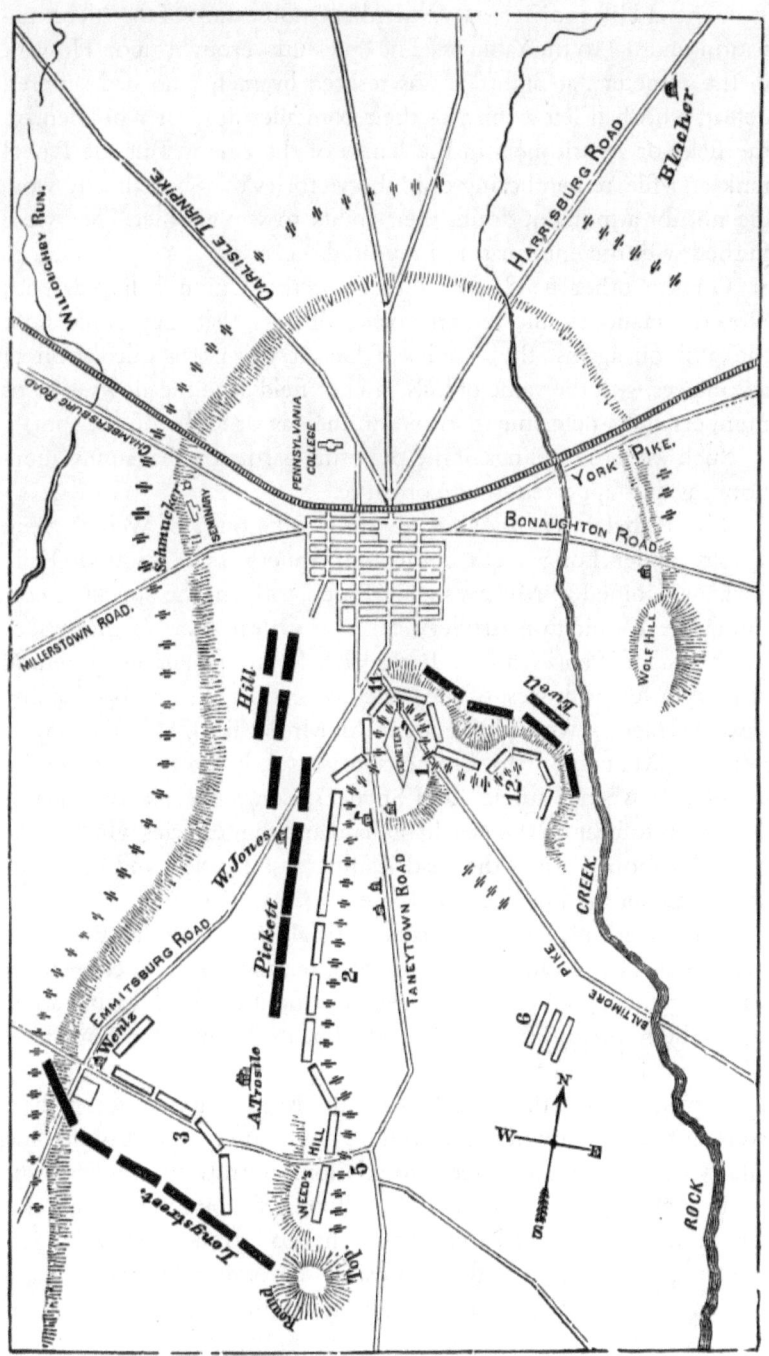

GETTYSBURG BATTLEFIELD

General Hill and General Lee had been observant of the "determination unusual to the Yankees." The "pressure" brought upon Howard in the cemetery, at nightfall, was resisted by men who had suffered defeat, who had left a third of their comrades dead or wounded on the field, or as prisoners in the hands of the enemy. But the Rebel rank-and-file, remembering only the victories they had already won, did not for a moment doubt their ability to win another. They were flushed with the enthusiasm of repeated successes.

On the other hand, the soldiers of the Union believed, with Howard, Hancock, Sickles, and other officers, that they could hold the position against the assaults of Lee. It was not a calculation of advantages,—of the value of hills, ravines, fields, and meadows,—or of numbers, but a determination to win the day or to die on the spot.

Such were the feelings of the opposing parties on that sunny afternoon, as they appeared in line of battle.

The Rebel forces moving to the attack south of Wentz's were wholly under Longstreet's command. Anderson's division of Hill's corps was joined to McLaw's and Hood's, to form the attacking column. The Washington Artillery of New Orleans was in the woods southwest of Wentz's house. Barksdale's Mississippians were behind artillery. A few rods west of the same house, on a narrow road leading towards Hagerstown, is the residence of Mr. Warfield. A third of a mile north of Wentz's, on the Emmettsburg road, is the house of Philip Snyder. Between Warfield's and Snyder's, Longstreet planted fifty or sixty guns to bear on the peach-orchard and the batteries which Sickles had stationed along the road leading past Trostle's, and upon the woods east of the house of Mr. Rose.

Longstreet's plan was to attack with all the vigour possible,—to bear down all opposition in the outset. Commanders frequently begin an engagement by feeling of the enemy's position,—advancing a few skirmishers, a regiment, or a brigade; but in this instance Longstreet advanced all but his reserve.

It was half past three. Riding rapidly to the right to see if there were signs of activity in that direction, dismounting in rear of the line, and tying my horse to a tree, I took a look northward. A mile to the north Rebel officers were in view, galloping furiously over the fields, disappearing in groves, dashing down the road to the town, and again returning. There was a battery in position beyond the railroad, and as I looked narrowly at an opening between two groves, I saw the glistening of bayonets, and a line as if a column of men were marching east toward the thick forest on Rock Creek. It was surmised that they were to attack our right upon Culp's Hill by advancing directly down Rock Creek through the woods. Prisoners captured said that Ewell had sworn a terrible oath to turn our flank, if it took his last man. To guard against such a movement, Slocum was throwing up breastworks from the crest of the hill down to Rock Creek. Two batteries were placed in position on hillocks south of the turnpike, to throw shells up the creek, should such an attempt be made. The Union Cavalry in long lines was east of the creek, and the Reserve Artillery, in parks, with horses harnessed, was in the open field south of Slocum's head-quarters.

"As near as I can make out, the Rebels have got a line of batteries in that piece of woods," said an officer who had been looking steadily across the ravine to Blocher's Hill. Laying my glass upon the breastwork, I could see the guns and the artillerymen beside their pieces, as if ready to begin the action.

Suddenly there came the roar of a gun from the south. It was Longstreet's signal. Another, another, and the fire ran from Snyder's to the Seminary, then round to Blocher's Hill.

I was at the moment near the cemetery. There came a storm of shot and shell. Marble slabs were broken, iron fences shattered, horses disembowelled. The air was full of wild, hideous noises,—the low buzz of round shot, the whizzing of elongated bolts, and the stunning explosions of shells, overhead and all around.

There was a quick response from the Union batteries. In three minutes the earth shook with the tremendous concussion of two hundred pieces of artillery.

The missiles of the Rebels came from the northeast, north, northwest, west, and southwest. The position occupied by the Vermont nine months' men was one of great exposure, as the ground in rear of the cemetery was the centre of a converging fire.

"Lie close," said General Stannard to the men. They obeyed him, but he walked to the top of the ridge and watched the coming on of the storm in the southwest.

The Fifth Corps had not moved into position, but was resting after the sixteen miles' march from Hanover.

The Rebels of Longstreet's command first in sight come out from the woods behind Warfield's house, a long line in the form of a crescent, reaching almost to Round-top. Ames's battery was the first to open upon them. Thompson, Clark, and Phillips began to thunder almost simultaneously. Bigelow, from his position, could not get a sight at them till two or three minutes later. The Third Michigan, Second New Hampshire, and Third Maine were the first regiments engaged.

The fire ran down the line towards Rose's house. The regiments in the woods along the ravine south of the house,—the Seventeenth Maine, Third Michigan, and others,—were soon in the fight. A portion of the Seventeenth Maine had been skirmishing all the morning.

Ward's brigade on the rocky ridge in front of Weed's Hill was assailed by Hood. How fearful the fight! Sickles's front line, after an obstinate struggle, was forced back. He was obliged to withdraw his batteries by Wentz's house. Bigelow retired firing by prolonge, over the rocky ground. The contest in the peach-orchard and around Rose's house was exceedingly bloody. Sickles sent his aide for reinforcements: "I want batteries and men!" said he.

"I want you to hold on where you are until I can get a line of batteries in rear of you," said Colonel McGilvery, commanding the artillery of the Third Corps, to Bigelow. "Give them canister!" he added as he rode away. Bigelow's men never had been under fire, but they held on till every charge of canister was spent, and then commenced on spherical case. Bigelow was just west of Trostle's barn. A Rebel battery hastened up and unlimbered in the field. He opened with all his guns, and they limbered up again. McGilvery's batteries were not in position, and the gallant captain and his brave men would not leave. The Rebels rushed upon the guns, and were blown from the muzzles. Others came with demoniac yells, climbing upon the limbers and shooting horses. Sergeant Dodge went down, killed instantly; also Sergeant Gilson. Lipman, Ferris, and Nutting, three of the cannoneers, were gone, twenty-two of the men wounded, and Bigelow shot through the side; also four men missing, yet they held on till McGilvery had his batteries in position!

It was a heroic resistance. Gun after gun was abandoned to the advancing Rebels. But the cannoneers were thoughtful to retain the rammers, and though the Rebels seized the pieces they could not turn them upon the slowly-retreating handful of men, who with two pieces still growled defiance. Back to Trostle's door-yard, into the garden, halting by the barn, delivering a steady fire, they held the enemy at bay till the batteries of the Fifth Corps, a little east of Trostle's, and the arrival of reinforcements of infantry, permitted their withdrawal. More than sixty horses belonging to this one battery were killed in this brief struggle at the commencement of the battle. With the seizure of each piece the Rebels cheered, and advanced with confident expectation of driving Sickles over the ridge.

But new actors came. Barnes's division of the Fifth went down through Trostle's garden and through the grove south of the house, crossed the road, and entered the woods. The Rebels were in the ravine by Rose's house. Winslow's New York battery was in a wheatfield south of Trostle's, holding them in check, while Hazlitt's battery on Weed's Hill rained a torrent of shells from its rocky fortress.

Ayer's division of Regulars, which had been lying east of Weed's Hill, moved upon the double-quick through the woods, up to the summit. The whole scene was before them: the turmoil and commotion in the woods below,—Barnes going in and the shattered regiments of the Third Corps coming out. Some batteries were in retreat and others were taking new positions. They dashed down the hillside, became a little disorganized in crossing Plum Run, but formed again and went up the ridge among the boulders, disappeared in the woods, stayed a few minutes, and then, like a shattered wreck upon the foaming sea, came drifting to the rear.

After the battle, an officer of the Seventeenth Regulars pointed out to me the line of advance.

"We went down the hill upon the run," said he. "It was like going down into hell! The Rebels were yelling like devils. Our men were falling back. It was terrible confusion: smoke, dust, the rattle of musketry, the roaring of cannon, the bursting of shells."

The Pennsylvania Reserves, under Crawford, went in. They were fighting on their own soil. Among them were soldiers whose homes were in Gettysburg.

Sickles called upon Hancock for help. Caldwell's division went down, sweeping past Trostle's into the wheat-field, dashing through Barnes's men, who were falling back. Regiments from three corps and from eight or ten brigades were fighting promiscuously. The Rebel lines were also in confusion,—advancing, retreating, gaining, and losing.

It was like the writhing of two wrestlers. Seventy thousand men were contending for the mastery on a territory scarcely a mile square! It has been called the battle of Little Round-top, but most of the fighting at this point took place between Little Round-top on Weed's Hill and the house of Mr. Rose. But there was also a contest around and upon the hill.

The advance of Hood enveloped the Union force below. The men on Hood's extreme right skirted the base of the hill, clambered over the rocks by the "Devil's Den,"—a rocky gorge,—and began to pour into the gap between Weed's and Round-top. Vincent's and Weed's brigades were holding the hill. The Twentieth Maine, Colonel Chamberlain, was on the extreme left. The Eighty-Third Pennsylvania, Forty-Fourth New York, and Sixteenth Michigan were farther north. The Twentieth Maine stood almost alone. There began to be a dropping of bullets along the line from the Rebel skirmishers creeping into the gap, and Colonel Chamberlain saw the enemy moving past his flank. He immediately extended his own left flank by forming his men in single rank. The fight was fierce. The Rebels greatly outnumbered Chamberlain, but he had the advantage of position. He was on the crest of the hill, and at every lull in the strife his men piled the loose stones into a rude breastwork. He sent for assistance, but before the arrival of reinforcements Hood's troops had gained the eastern side of the hill, and the Twentieth Maine stood in the form of the letter U, with Rebels in front, on their flank, and in rear.

It was nearly six o'clock. I was at Meade's head-quarters. The roar of battle was louder and grew nearer. Hill was threatening the centre. A cloud of dust could be seen down the Baltimore pike. Had Stuart suddenly gained our rear? There were anxious countenances around the cottage where the flag of the Commander-in-Chief was flying. Officers gazed with their field-glasses. "It is not cavalry, but infantry," said one. "There is the flag. It is the Sixth Corps."

We could see the advancing bayonets gleaming in the setting sun. Faces which a moment before were grave became cheerful. It was an inspiring sight. The troops of that corps had marched thirty-two miles during the day. They crossed Rock Creek, filed into the field, past the ammunition train, threw themselves upon the ground, tossed aside their knapsacks, and wiped the sweat from their sun-burnt cheeks.

"We want reinforcements. They are flanking us," said an officer, riding up to Meade. Word was sent to Slocum, and Williams's division of the Twelfth left their breastwork on Culp's Hill, came down upon the double-quick, leaping the stone walls between Slocum's head-quarters and the cemetery, and moved into the field west of the Taneytown road.

Stannard's brigade was attached to the First Corps, commanded by Doubleday. The Vermont boys had been lying on their faces through the long, tormenting hours. They were ready for desperate work. Doubleday dashed down to General Stannard. There is a strong contrast between these two officers. Doubleday is tall, broad-shouldered, a little stooping. He was in Sumter with Anderson when the Rebels fired the first gun at the old flag. He is cool and courageous. Stannard is short, straight, compactly built. He was a private citizen at St. Albans, Vermont, when the war began. He is a thorough citizen-soldier, as undaunted as his superior.

"You are wanted over there. Report to Hancock," said Doubleday.

The men of Vermont sprang to their feet, and went up the ridge toward the southwest upon the run. At the same time an officer rode down to the Sixth Corps. I saw the tired and weary men rise from the ground and fall into line. They also moved off upon the run toward Weed's Hill, which was all aflame. Hazlitt was firing canister from the top. Nearly all the Third, Fifth, and Second Corps batteries were at work. The sun was just setting. Sickles had been forced back from the peach-orchard, and from Rose's house, but he was still holding Trostle's. The dark lines of the Sixth Corps became lost to sight, as they moved into the woods crowning the hill. There were quicker volleys, a lighting up of the sky by sudden flashes, followed by a cheer,—not the wild yell peculiar to the Rebels, but a sharp, clear hurrah, from the men who had held the hill. Longstreet was giving up the struggle, and his men were falling back. Colonel Randall, with five companies of the Thirteenth Vermont, led the advance of General Stannard's column. Hancock had been forced to leave the guns of one of his batteries on the field near Codori's house.

The Rebel sharpshooters were lying along the Emmettsburg road, pouring in a deadly fire, under cover of which a large body of Rebels was advancing to take possession of the pieces.

"Can you retake that battery?" was Hancock's question to Randall.

"We'll do it or die, sir!"

"Then go in."

"Forward!" said Randall, turning in his saddle and waving his sword. His men gave a cheer, and broke into a run. The Colonel's horse fell, shot through the shoulder, but the Colonel dashed ahead on foot. They reached the guns, drew them to the rear. The Rebels came on with a rush. But help was at hand,—the Fourteenth Maine joined the Vermonters. Leaving the guns the soldiers faced about, charged upon the Rebels, captured eighty-three prisoners, and two Rebel cannon, and then returned! Long and loud were the cheers that greeted them.

"You must be green, or you wouldn't have gone down there," said a Pennsylvanian, who had been in a dozen battles. The blood of the Vermont boys was up, and they had not calculated the consequences of such a movement.

So closed the day on the left. But just as the contest was coming to an end around Weed's Hill, it suddenly commenced on the north side of the cemetery. Hayes's brigade of Louisiana Tigers, and Hoke's North Carolinians, belonging to Early's division of Ewell's corps, had been creeping across Spangler's farm, up the northern slope of the cemetery hill. Suddenly, with a shout they sprang upon Barlow's division, commanded by Amos. It was a short, fierce, but decisive contest. The attack was sudden, but the men of Ames's command were fully prepared. There was a struggle over the guns of two Pennsylvania batteries. The Fifth Maine battery was in an exceedingly favourable position, at an angle of the earthworks, east of the hill, and cut down the Rebels with a destructive enfilading fire. The struggle lasted scarcely five minutes,—the Rebels retreating in confusion to the town.

When Slocum went with Williams to the left there were no indications of an attack on Culp's Hill, but unexpectedly Ewell made his appearance in the woods along Rock Creek. General Green, who had been left in command, extended his line east and made a gallant fight, but not having men enough to occupy all the ground, Ewell was able to take possession of the hollow along the Creek. When Williams returned, he found his entrenchments in possession of the enemy. The men of the Twelfth threw themselves on the ground in the fields on both sides of the Baltimore pike, for rest till daybreak.

"We are doing well," was Longstreet's report to Lee at seven o'clock in the evening, from the left.[49] Ewell himself rode down through the town, to report his success on the right.

At a later hour Longstreet reported that he had carried everything before him for some time, capturing several batteries, and driving the Yankees; but when Hill's Florida brigade and some other troops gave way, he was forced to abandon a small portion of the ground he had won, together with all the captured guns except three.

It was late in the evening when I threw myself upon a pile of straw in an old farm-house, near the Baltimore pike, for a few hours' rest, expecting that with the early morning there would be a renewal of the battle.

There was the constant rumble of artillery moving into position, of ammunition and supply wagons going up to the troops. Lights were gleaming in the hollows, beneath the shade of oaks and pines, where the surgeons were at work, and where, through the dreary hours wailings and moanings rent the air; yet though within musket-shot of the enemy, and surrounded with dying and dead, I found refreshing sleep.

THIRD DAY—FRIDAY, JULY 3RD

Boom! boom! Two guns, deep and heavy, at four o'clock. It was a sultry morning. The clouds hung low upon the hills. Two more! and then more rapidly than the tick of a pendulum came the concussions. There were flashes from all the hills,—flashes in the woods

---

49: *Blackwood's Magazine,* September, 1863.

along Rock Creek. The cemetery was aflame. The door which had been opened against Slocum was to be closed, and this was the beginning of the effort.

The cannonade broke the stillness of the morning, and drowned all other sounds. Riding up the turnpike to the batteries, I had a good view of the battle-ground. General Sickles was being carried to the rear on a stretcher. He had suffered amputation. Following him was a large number of prisoners, taken in the fight upon the left. Some were haggard and care-worn,—others indifferent, or sulky, and some very jolly. "I have got into the Union after hard fighting," said one, "and I intend to stay there."

There were a few musket-shots in the woods upon the hill, from the pickets in advance. Slocum was preparing to regain what had been lost. It was seven o'clock before he was ready to move. The men moved slowly, but determinedly. The Rebels were in the rifle-pits, and opened a furious fire. A thin veil of smoke rose above the trees, and floated away before the morning breeze. Rapid the fire of musketry,— terrific the cannonade. Ewell was determined not to be driven back. He held on with dogged pertinacity. He had sworn profanely to hold the position, but in vain his effort. The rifle-pits were regained, and he was driven, inch by inch, up Rock Creek.

It took four hours to do it, however. Ewell, well knowing the importance of holding the position, brought in all of his available force. Johnson's, Rhodes's, and Early's divisions, all were engaged. To meet these General Shaler's brigade of the Sixth Corps was brought up to Culp's Hill, while Neil's brigade of the same corps was thrown in upon Early's flank east of Rock Creek, and the work was accomplished. The men fought from behind trees and rocks, with great tenacity. It was the last attempt of Lee upon Meade's right.

Gregg's and Kilpatrick's divisions of cavalry were east of Rock Creek. An orderly came dashing down the Hanover road.

"Stuart is coming round on our right!" said he. "General Pleasanton sends his compliments to General Gregg, desiring him to go out immediately and hold Stuart in check. His compliments also to General Kilpatrick, desiring him to go down beyond Round-top, and pitch in with all his might on Longstreet's left."

I was conversing with the two officers at the time.

"Good! come on, boys!" shouted Kilpatrick, rubbing his hands with pleasure. The notes of the bugle rang loud and clear above the rumble of the passing army wagons, and Kilpatrick's column swept down the hill, crossed the creek, and disappeared beyond Round-top.

A half-hour later I saw the smoke of his artillery, and heard the wild shout of his men as they dashed recklessly upon the Rebel lines. It was the charge in which General Farnsworth and a score of gallant officers gave up their lives.

General Gregg's division formed in the fields east of Wolf Hill. Stuart had already extended his line along the Bonnoughtown road. There was a brisk cannonade between the light batteries, and Stuart retired, without attempting to cut out the ammunition trains parked along the pike.

Through the forenoon it was evident that Lee was preparing for another attack. He had reconnoitred the ground with Longstreet in the morning, and decided to assault Meade's line between the cemetery and Weed's Hill with a strong force. He could form the attacking column out of sight, in the woods west of Codori's house. In advancing the troops would be sheltered till they reached the Emmettsburg road. Howard's guns in the cemetery would trouble them most by enfilading the lines. Howard must be silenced by a concentrated artillery fire. The cemetery could be seen from every part of the line occupied by the Rebels, and all the available batteries were brought into position to play upon it, and upon the position occupied by the Second Corps.

The arrangements were entrusted to Longstreet. He selected Pickett's, Pender's, Heth's, and Anderson's divisions. Pickett's were fresh troops. Heth had been wounded, and Pettigrew was in command of the division. Wilcox's and Perry's brigades of Anderson's division had the right of the first Rebel line. Pickett's division occupied the centre of the first line, followed by Pender's. Heth's division, followed by Wright's brigade of Anderson's, had the left of the line.

Wilcox and Perry's line of advance was past Klingel's house. Pickett's right swept across the Emmettsburg road by the house of Peter Rogers; his left reached to Codori's, where it joined Pettigrew's. Rhodes's division of Ewell's corps was brought down from the woods by Smucker's house, and put in position south of the town, to support Pettigrew's left. The attacking column numbered from twenty to twenty-five thousand men, but the force in support gave nearly thirty-five thousand men which Longstreet had in hand.

The movements of the Rebels, as seen from the Union lines, indicated an attack upon our extreme left. The Fifth, Third, and Sixth Corps therefore were placed well down toward Round-top.

Commencing at the Taneytown road and walking south, we have the following disposition of the troops resisting this attack. Robinson's division of the First Corps, reaching from the road along an oak grove, past a small house occupied by a coloured man. Hays's division lay behind a stone wall, and a small grove of shrub-oaks. Gibbon had no protection except a few rails gathered from the fences. There are three oak-trees which mark the spot occupied by Hall's brigade. Harrow's was just beyond it, south. In front of Harrow's, six or eight rods, were three regiments of Stannard's Vermont brigade,—the Thirteenth, Fourteenth, and Sixteenth,—lying in a shallow trench. Caldwell's division extended from Gibbon's to the narrow road leading past Trostle's house. The ridge in rear of the troops bristled with artillery. The infantry line was thin, but the artillery was compact and powerful.

Longstreet having made his disposition for the attack, and the Rebel artillery not being ready, threw himself on the ground and went to sleep.[50]

Lee reconnoitred the position from the cupola of the college, over which the Confederate hospital-flag was flying,—thus violating what has been deemed even by half-civilized races a principle of honour.

Visiting General Meade's head-quarters in the house of Mrs. Leister, in the forenoon, I saw the Commander-in-chief seated at a table with a map of Gettysburg spread out before him. General Warren, chief engineer, was by his side. General Williams, his Adjutant-General, who knew the strength of every regiment, was sitting on the bed, ready to answer any question. General Hunt, chief of artillery, was lying on the grass beneath a peach-tree in the yard. General Pleasanton, chief of the cavalry, neat and trim in dress and person, with a riding-whip tucked into his cavalry boots, was walking uneasily about. Aids were coming and going; a signal-officer in the yard was waving his flags in response to one on Round-top.

"Signal-officer on Round-top reports Rebels moving towards our left," said the officer to General Meade.

It was five minutes past one when the signal-gun for the opening of the battle was given by the Rebels on Seminary Hill. Instantly the whole line of Rebel batteries, an hundred and fifty guns, joined in the cannonade. All of the guns northeast, north, and northwest of the town concentrated their fire upon the cemetery. Those west and southwest opened on Hancock's position. Solid shot and shells poured incessantly upon the cemetery and along the ridge. The intention of Lee was soon understood,—to silence Howard's batteries because they enfiladed the attacking force ready to move over the fields toward the centre, our weakest point. If they could give to the living who held

---

50: *Blackwood's Magazine,* September, 1864.—Freemantle.

the burial-place a quiet as profound as that of the sleepers beneath the ground, then they might hope to break through the thin line of men composing the Second Corps.

But Howard was not a man to be kept quiet at such a time without especial cause. His horses were knocked to pieces, the tombstones shivered, iron railings torn, shrubs and trees cut down, here and there men killed, but his batteries were not silenced.

Mr. Wilkenson of the *New York Tribune*, who was at General Meade's head-quarters when the fire was severest, thus describes the scene:

> In the shadow cast by the tiny farm-house, sixteen by twenty, which General Meade had made his head-quarters, lay wearied staff officers and tired correspondents. There was not wanting to the peacefulness of the scene the singing of a bird, which had a nest in a peach-tree within the tiny yard of the whitewashed cottage. In the midst of its warbling a shell screamed over the house, instantly followed by another, and another, and in a moment the air was full of the most complete artillery-prelude to an infantry battle that was ever exhibited. Every size and form of shell known to British and to American gunnery shrieked, whirled, moaned, and whistled, and wrathfully fluttered over our ground. As many as six in a second, constantly two in a second, bursting and screaming over and around the head-quarters, made a very hell of fire that amazed the oldest officers. They burst in the yard,—burst next to the fence on both sides, garnished as usual with the hitched horses of aides and orderlies. The fastened animals reared and plunged with terror. Then one fell, then another,—sixteen lay dead and mangled before the fire ceased, still fastened by their halters, which gave the expression of being wickedly tied up to die painfully. These brute victims of a cruel war touched all hearts. Through the midst of the storm of screaming and exploding shells an ambulance, driven by its frenzied conductor at full speed, presented to all of us the marvellous spectacle of a horse going rapidly on three legs. A hinder one had been shot off at the hock. A shell tore up the little step at the head-quarters cottage, and ripped bags of oats as with a knife. Another soon carried off one of its two pillars. Soon a spherical case burst opposite the open door,—another ripped through the low garret. The remaining pillar went almost immediately to the howl of a fixed shot that Whitworth must have made. During this fire, the horses at twenty and thirty feet

distant were receiving their death, and soldiers in Federal blue were torn to pieces in the road, and died with the peculiar yells that blend the extorted cry of pain with horror and despair. Not an orderly, not an ambulance, not a straggler was to be seen upon the plain swept by this tempest of orchestral death, thirty minutes after it commenced. Were not one hundred and twenty pieces of artillery trying to cut from the field every battery we had in position to resist their purposed infantry attack, and to sweep away the slight defences behind which our infantry were waiting? Forty minutes,—fifty minutes,—counted watches that ran, O so languidly! Shells through the two lower rooms. A shell into the chimney, that daringly did not explode. Shells in the yard. The air thicker, and fuller, and more deafening with the howling and whirring of these infernal missiles. The Chief of Staff struck,—Seth Williams,—loved and respected through the army, separated from instant death by two inches of space vertically measured. An aide bored with a fragment of iron through the bone of the arm. And the time measured on the sluggish watches was one hour and forty minutes.

A soldier was lying on the ground a few rods distant from where I was sitting. There was a shriek, such as I hope never again to hear, and his body was whirling in the air, a mangled mass of flesh, blood, and bones!

A shell exploding in the cemetery, killed and wounded twenty-seven men in one regiment![51] and yet the troops, lying under the fences,—stimulated and encouraged by General Howard, who walked coolly along the line,—kept their places and awaited the attack.

It was half past two o'clock.

"We will let them think that they have silenced us," said General Howard to Major Osborne. The artillerists threw themselves upon the ground beside their pieces.

Suddenly there was a shout,—"Here they come!"

Every man was on the alert. The cannoneers sprang to their feet. The long lines emerged from the woods, and moved rapidly but steadily over the fields, towards the Emmettsburg road.

Howard's batteries burst into flame, throwing shells with the utmost rapidity. There are gaps in the Rebel ranks, but onward still they come. They reach the Emmettsburg road. Pickett's division appears by Klingel's house. All of Howard's guns are at work now. Pickett turns to

---

51: General Howard's Report.

the right, moving north, driven in part by the fire rolling in upon his flank from Weed's Hill, and from the Third, Fifth, and Sixth Corps batteries. Suddenly he faces east, descends the gentle slope from the road behind Codori's, crosses the meadow, comes in reach of the muskets of the Vermonters. The three regiments rise from their shallow trench. The men beneath the oak-trees leap from their low breastwork of rails. There is a ripple, a roll, a deafening roar. Yet the momentum of the Rebel column carries it on. It is becoming thinner and weaker, but they still advance.

The Second Corps is like a thin blue ribbon. Will it withstand the shock? "Give them canister! Pour it into them!" shouts Major Charles Howard, running from battery to battery. The Rebel line is almost up to the grove in front of Robinson's. It has reached the clump of shrub-oaks. It has drifted past the Vermont boys. Onward still. "Break their third line! Smash their supports!" cries General Howard, and Osborne and Wainwright send the fire of fifty guns into the column, each piece fired three times a minute! The cemetery is lost to view,—covered with sulphurous clouds, flaming and smoking and thundering like Sinai on the great day of the Lord! The front line of Rebels is melting away,—the second is advancing to take its place; but beyond the first and second is the third, which reels, breaks, and flies to the woods from whence it came, unable to withstand the storm.

Hancock is wounded, and Gibbon is in command of the Second Corps. "Hold your fire, boys; they are not near enough yet," says Gibbon, as Pickett comes on. The first volley staggers, but does not stop them. They move upon the run,—up to the breastwork of rails,—bearing Hancock's line to the top of the ridge,—so powerful their momentum.

Men fire into each other's faces, not five feet apart. There are bayonet-thrusts, sabre-strokes, pistol-shots; cool, deliberate movements on the part of some,—hot, passionate, desperate efforts with others; hand-to-hand contests; recklessness of life; tenacity of purpose; fiery determination; oaths, yells, curses, hurrahs, shoutings; men going down on their hands and knees, spinning round like tops, throwing out their arms, gulping up blood, falling; legless, armless, headless. There are ghastly heaps of dead men. Seconds are centuries; minutes, ages; but the thin line does not break!

The Rebels have swept past the Vermont regiments. "Take them in flank," says General Stannard.

The Thirteenth and Sixteenth swing out from the trench, turn a right angle to the main line, and face the north. They move forward a few steps, pour a deadly volley into the backs of Kemper's troops. With a hurrah they rush on, to drive home the bayonet. The Fifteenth, Nineteenth, Twentieth Massachusetts, and Seventh Michigan, Twentieth New York, Nineteenth Maine, One Hundred Fifty-First Pennsylvania, and other regiments catch the enthusiasm of the moment, and close upon the foe.

The Rebel column has lost its power. The lines waver. The soldiers of the front rank look round for their supports. They are gone,—fleeing over the field, broken, shattered, thrown into confusion by the remorseless fire from the cemetery and from the cannon on the ridge. The lines have disappeared like a straw in a candle's flame. The ground is thick with dead, and the wounded are like the withered leaves of autumn. Thousands of Rebels throw down their arms and give themselves up as prisoners.

How inspiring the moment! How thrilling the hour! It is the high-water mark of the Rebellion,—a turning-point of history and of human destiny!

Treason had wielded its mightiest blow. From that time the Rebellion began to wane. An account of the battle, written on the following day, and published on the 6th of July in the *Boston Journal*, contains the following passage:

> The invasion of the North was over,—the power of the Southern Confederacy broken. There at that sunset hour I could discern the future; no longer an overcast sky, but the clear, unclouded starlight,—a country redeemed, saved, baptized, consecrated anew to the coming ages.
>
> All honour to the heroic living, all glory to the gallant dead! They have not fought in vain, they have not died for naught. No man liveth to himself alone. Not for themselves, but for their children; for those who may never hear of them in their nameless graves, how they yielded life; for the future; for all that is good, pure, holy, just, true; for humanity, righteousness, peace; for Paradise on earth; for Christ and for God, they have given themselves a willing sacrifice. Blessed be their memory forevermore!

I rode along the lines, and beheld the field by the light of the gleaming stars. The dead were everywhere thickly strewn. How changed the cemetery! Three days before, its gravelled walks were smooth and clean; flowers were in bloom; birds carolled their songs amid the trees; the monuments were undefaced; the marble slabs pure and white.

"With a hurrah they rush on!"

Now there were broken wheels and splintered caissons; dead horses, shot in the neck, in the head, through the body, disembowelled by exploding shells, legs broken, flesh mangled and torn; pools of blood, scarlet stains on the headstones, green grass changed to crimson; marble slabs shivered; the ground ploughed by solid shot, holes blown out by bursting shells; dead men lying where they had fallen, wounded men creeping to the rear; cries and groans all around me! Fifty shells a minute had fallen upon that small enclosure. Not for a moment was there thought of abandoning the position. How those batteries of Osborne and Wainwright, of the Eleventh and First Corps, had lightened and thundered! There were scores of dead by the small house where the left of the Rebel line advanced, lying just as they were smitten down, as if a thunderbolt had fallen upon the once living mass!

An English officer, who saw the battle from the Rebel lines, thus says of the repulse:

> I soon began to meet many wounded men returning from the front; many of them asked in piteous tones the way to a doctor, or an ambulance. The further I got the greater became the number of the wounded. At last I came to a perfect stream of them flocking through the woods in numbers as great as the crowd in Oxford Street in the middle of the day.... They were still under a heavy fire; the shells were continually bringing down great limbs of trees, and carrying further destruction amongst their melancholy procession. I saw all this in much less time than it takes to write it, and although astonished to meet such a vast number of wounded, I had not seen enough to give me an idea of the real extent of the mischief.
>
> When I got close up to General Longstreet, I saw one of his regiments advancing through the woods in good order; so, thinking I was just in time to see the attack, I remarked to the General that 'I wouldn't have missed this for anything.' Longstreet was seated on the top of a snake-fence, in the edge of the wood, and looking perfectly calm and unperturbed. He replied, 'The devil you wouldn't! I would like to have missed it very much; we've attacked and been repulsed. Look there!'
>
> For the first time I then had a view of the open space between the two positions, and saw it covered with Confederates slowly and sulkily returning towards us in small broken parties....
>
> I remember seeing a general (Pettigrew I think it was) come up to him and report that he was unable to bring his men

up again. Longstreet turned upon him and replied with some sarcasm: 'Very well,—never mind, then, General; just let them remain where they are. The enemy is going to advance, and will spare you the trouble.' ...

Soon afterward I joined General Lee, who had in the mean while come to the front, on becoming aware of the disaster. He was engaged in rallying and in encouraging the troops, and was riding about a little in front of the woods quite alone, the whole of his staff being engaged in a similar manner further to the rear. His face, which is always placid and cheerful, did not show signs of the slightest disappointment, care, or annoyance; and he was addressing to every soldier he met a few words of encouragement, such as, 'All this will come right in the end; we will talk it over afterwards,—but in the mean time all good men must rally. We want all good men and true men just now,' &c.... He said to me, 'This has been a sad day for us, Colonel,—a sad day; but we can't expect always to gain victories.' ... I saw General Wilcox (an officer who wears a short round jacket and a battered straw hat) come up to him, and explain, almost crying, the state of his brigade. General Lee immediately shook hands with him, and said, cheerfully, 'Never mind, General. All this has been my fault,—it is I that have lost this fight, and you must help me out of it in the best way you can.'[52]

It was past eleven o'clock in the evening when I rode up from the gory field, over the ridge, where the Second Corps had stood like a wall of adamant. Meade's head-quarters were in a grove, east of the small house where he established himself at the beginning of the battle. The fire had been too hot at Mrs. Leister's. Meade was sitting on a great flat boulder, listening to the reports of his officers, brought in by couriers. It was a scene which lives in memory: a dark forest,—the evening breeze gently rustling the green leaves over our heads,—the katydids and locusts singing cheerily,—the bivouac fires glimmering on the ground, revealing the surrounding objects,—the gnarled trees, torn by cannon-shot,—the mossy stones,—the group of officers,—Williams, Warren, Howard (his right sleeve wanting an arm), Pleasanton, as trim as in the morning; Meade stooping, weary, his slouched hat laid aside, so that the breeze might fan his brow.

"Bully! bully! bully all round!" said he; and then turning to his chief of staff, Humphrey, said, "Order up rations and ammunition." To

---

52: *Blackwood's Magazine*, September, 1863.—Lieutenant-Colonel Freemantle.

General Hunt, chief of artillery, "Have your limbers filled. Lee may be up to something in the morning, and we must be ready for him."

A band came up and played "Hail to the Chief!" the "Star-spangled Banner," and "Yankee Doodle." Soul-stirring the strains. The soldiers, lying on their arms, where they had fought, heard it, and responded with a cheer. Not all: for thousands were deaf and inanimate evermore.

No accurate statement of the number engaged in this great, decisive battle of the war can ever be given. Meade's march to Gettysburg was made with great rapidity. The Provost Marshal of the army, General Patrick, committed the great error of having no rear guard to bring up the stragglers, which were left behind in thousands, and who found it much more convenient to live on the excellent fare furnished by the farmers than to face the enemy. Meade's entire force on the field numbered probably from sixty to seventy thousand. The Rebel army had made slower marches, and the soldiers could not straggle; they were in an enemy's country. Lee, therefore, had fuller ranks than Meade. His force may be estimated at ninety thousand men.

The people of the North expressed their gratitude to the heroes who had won this battle, by pouring out their contributions for the relief of the wounded. The agents of the Christian and Sanitary Commissions were quickly on the ground, and hundreds of warm-hearted men and women hastened to the spot to render aid. The morning after the battle I saw a stout Pennsylvania farmer driving his two-horse farm wagon up the Baltimore pike, loaded down with loaves of soft bread which his wife and daughters had baked.

Tender and affecting are some of the incidents of the battle-field. A delegate of the Christian Commission passing among the wounded, came to an officer from South Carolina.

"Can I do anything for you?" he asked.

"No!" was the surly reply.

He passed on, but upon his return repeated the question, and received the same answer. The day was hot, the air offensive, from putrefying wounds, and the delegate was putting cologne on the handkerchiefs of the patients.

"Colonel, let me put some of this on your handkerchief."

The wounded man burst into tears. "I have no handkerchief."

"Well, you shall have one"; and wetting his own gave it to him.

"I can't understand you Yankees," said the Colonel. "You fight us like devils, and then you treat us like angels. I am sorry I entered this war."[53]

53: Address before Alumni of Williams College, 1865. Charles Demond.

Said another Rebel,—an Irishman,—to a chaplain who took care of him, "May every hair of your head be a wax-taper to light you on your way to glory!"[54]

A chaplain passing through the hospital, came to a cot where lay a young wounded soldier who had fought for the Union.

"Poor fellow!" said the chaplain.

"Don't call me 'poor fellow!'" was the indignant reply.

"Dear fellow, then. Have you written to your mother since the battle?"

"No, sir!"

"You ought to. Here it is the tenth,—a whole week since the battle. She will be anxious to hear from you."

The lad with his left hand threw aside the sheet which covered him, and the chaplain saw that his right arm was off near the shoulder.

"That is the reason, sir, that I have not written. I have not forgotten her, sir. I have prayed for her, and I thank God for giving me so dear a mother."

Then turning aside the sheet farther, the chaplain saw that his left leg was gone. Sitting down beside the young hero the chaplain wrote as he dictated.

"Tell mother that I have given my right arm and my left leg to my country, and that I am ready to give both of my other limbs!" said he.[55]

The courage and patriotism of Spartan mothers is immortalized in story and song. "Return with your shield, or upon it," has been held up for admiration through three thousand years. The Greek fire is not extinguished; it burns today as bright and pure as ever at Salamis or Marathon.

Riding in the cars through the State of New York after the battle of Gettysburg, I fell in conversation with a middle-aged woman who had two sons in the army.

"Have they been in battle?" I asked.

"Yes, sir; one has been in fifteen battles. He was taken prisoner at Chancellorsville and was wounded at Gettysburg. The other is in the Medical Department."

"The one who was wounded at Gettysburg must have seen some hard fighting."

"Yes, sir; and I hear a good account of him from his captain. He says my son behaves well. *I told him, when he went away, that I would rather hear he was dead than that he had disgraced himself.*"

54: Ibid.
55: Rev. Mr. Auley, meeting Christian Association, Chicago.

"His time must be nearly out."

"Yes, sir, it is; but he is going to see it through, and has re-enlisted. I should like to have him at home, but I know he would be uneasy. His comrades have re-enlisted, and he is not the boy to back out. I rather want him to help give the crushing blow."

There were thousands of such mothers in the land.

Lee retreated the morning after the battle. His reasons for a retrograde movement are thus stated by himself:

> Owing to the strength of the enemy's position and the reduction of our ammunition, a renewal of the engagement could not be hazarded. and the difficulty of procuring supplies rendered it impossible to continue longer where we were. Such of the wounded as were in condition to be removed, and part of the arms collected on the field, were ordered to Williamsport. The army remained at Gettysburg during the 4th, and at night began to retire by the road to Fairfield, carrying with it about four thousand prisoners. Nearly two thousand had previously been paroled, but the enemy's numerous wounded, that had fallen into our hands after the first and second day's engagements, were left behind.[56]

Meade made no attempt to follow him with his main army, but marched directly down the Emmettsburg road, once more to Frederick, then west over South Mountain to intercept him on the Potomac. Meade had the inside of the chess-board. He was a victor. The men who had made a forced march to Gettysburg were awake to the exigency of the hour, and made a quick march back to Frederick, and over the mountains to Boonsboro'. A severe storm set in, and the roads were almost impassable, but the men toiled on through the mire, lifting the cannon-wheels from the deep ruts, when the horses were unable to drag the ordnance, singing songs as they marched foot-sore and weary, but buoyant over the great victory.

And now, as the intelligence came that Grant had taken Vicksburg, that Banks was in possession of Port Hudson, and that the Mississippi was flowing "unvexed to the sea," they forgot all their toils, hardships, and sufferings, and made the air ring with their lusty cheers. They could see the dawn of peace,—peace won by the sword. The women of Maryland hailed them as their deliverers, brought out the best stores from their pantries and gave freely, refusing compensation.

Meade left all his superfluous baggage behind, and moved in light

---

56: Lee's Report.

marching order. Lee was encumbered by his wounded, and by his trains, and when he reached Hagerstown found that Meade was descending the mountain side, and that Gregg was already in Boonsboro'.

Reinforcements were sent to Meade from Washington, with the expectation that by concentration of all available forces, Lee's army might be wholly destroyed. The elements, which had often retarded operations of the Union troops,—which had rendered Burnside's and Hooker's movements abortive in several instances, now were propitious. The Potomac was rising, and the rain was still falling. On the morning of the 13th I rode to General Meade's head-quarters. General Seth Williams, the ever-courteous Adjutant-General of the army, was in General Meade's tent. He said that Meade was taking a look at the Rebels.

"Do you think that Lee can get across the Potomac?" I asked.

"Impossible! The people resident here say that it cannot be forded at this stage of the water. He has no pontoons. We have got him in a tight place. We shall have reinforcements tomorrow, and a great battle will be fought. Lee is encumbered with his teams, and he is short of ammunition."

General Meade came in dripping with rain, from a reconnoissance. His countenance was unusually animated. He had ever been courteous to me, and while usually very reticent of all his intentions or of what was going on, as an officer should be, yet in this instance he broke over his habitual silence, and said, "We shall have a great battle tomorrow. The reinforcements are coming up, and as soon as they come we shall pitch in."

I rode along the lines with Howard in the afternoon. The Rebels were in sight. The pickets were firing at each other. There was some movement of columns.

"I fear that Lee is getting away," said Howard.

He sent an aide to Meade, with a request that he might attack.

"I can double them up," he said, meaning that, as he was on Lee's flank, he could strike an effective blow.

Kilpatrick was beyond Howard, well up towards Williamsport. "Lee is getting across the river, I think," said through a messenger.

It was nearly night. The attack was to be made early in the morning.

The morning dawned and Lee was south of the Potomac. That officer says:

> The army, after an arduous march, rendered more difficult by the rains, reached Hagerstown on the afternoon of the 6th and morning of the 7th July.

The Potomac was found to be so much swollen by the rains that had fallen almost incessantly since our entrance into Maryland, as to be unfordable. Our communications with the south side were thus interrupted, and it was difficult to procure either ammunition or subsistence, the latter difficulty being enhanced by the high waters impeding the working of the neighbouring mills. The trains with the wounded and prisoners were compelled to await at Williamsport the subsiding of the river and the construction of boats, as the pontoon bridge, left at Falling Waters, had been partially destroyed. The enemy had not yet made his appearance; but, as he was in condition to obtain large reinforcements, and our situation, for the reasons above mentioned, was becoming daily more embarrassing, it was deemed advisable to recross the river. Part of the pontoon bridge was recovered, and new boats built, so that by the 13th a good bridge was thrown over the river at Falling Waters.

The enemy in force reached our front on the 12th. A position had been previously selected to cover the Potomac from Williamsport to Falling Waters, and an attack was awaited during that and the succeeding day. This did not take place, though the two armies were in close proximity, the enemy being occupied in fortifying his own lines. Our preparations being completed, and the river, though still deep, being pronounced fordable, the army commenced to withdraw to the south side on the night of the 13th.

Ewell's corps forded the river at Williamsport, those of Longstreet and Hill crossed upon the bridge. Owing to the condition of the roads, the troops did not reach the bridge until after daylight of the 14th, and the crossing was not completed until 1 p. m., when the bridge was removed. The enemy offered no serious interruption, and the movement was attended with no loss of material except a few disabled wagons and two pieces of artillery, which the horses were unable to move through the deep mud. Before fresh horses could be sent back for them, the rear of the column had passed.[57]

Kilpatrick was astir at daybreak; he moved into Williamsport. I accompanied his column. The Rebels were on the Virginia hills, jubilant at their escape. There were wagons in the river, floating down with the current, which had been capsized in the crossing. Kilpatrick pushed

---

57: Lee's Report.

on to Falling Waters, fell upon Pettigrew's brigade, guarding the pontoons, captured two cannon and eight hundred men, in one of the most daring dashes of the war. It was poor satisfaction, however, when contrasted with what might have been done. The army was chagrined. Loud were the denunciations of Meade.

"Another campaign on the Rappahannock, boys," said one officer in my hearing.

"We shall be in our old quarters in a few days," said another.

General Meade has been severely censured for not attacking on the 13th. Lee had lost thirty thousand men. He had suffered a crushing defeat at Gettysburg. Enthusiasm had died out. His soldiers were less confident than they had been. His ammunition was nearly exhausted. He was in a critical situation.

Those were reasons why he should be attacked; but there were also reasons, which to Meade were conclusive, that the attack should not be made till the 14th: the swollen river,—the belief that Lee had no means of crossing the Potomac,—and the expected reinforcements. The delay was not from lack of spirit or over caution; but with the expectation of striking a blow which would destroy the Rebel army.

Lee went up the valley, while Meade pushed rapidly down the base of the Blue Ridge to Culpepper. But he was not in condition to take the offensive, so far from his base; and the two armies sat down upon the banks of the Rapidan, to rest after the bloody campaign.

REGIMENT AT DINNER

Chapter 19
From the Rapidan to Cold Harbor

May, 1864

There are few months in the calendar of centuries that will have a more conspicuous place in history than the month of May, 1864. It will be remembered on account of the momentous events which took place in one of the greatest military campaigns of history. We are amazed, not by its magnitude merely, for there have been larger armies, heavier trains of artillery, greater preparations, in European warfare,—but by a succession of events unparalleled for rapidity. We cannot fully comprehend the amount of endurance, the persistency, the hard marching, the harder fighting, the unwearied, cheerful energy and effort which carried the Army of the Potomac from the Rappahannock to the James in forty days, against the stubborn opposition of an army of almost equal numbers. There was not a day of rest,—scarcely an hour of quiet. Morning, noon, and midnight, the booming of cannon and the rattling of musketry echoed unceasingly through the Wilderness, around the hillocks of Spottsylvania, along the banks of the North Anna, and among the groves of Bethesda Church and Cold Harbor.

There were individual acts of valour, as heroic and soul-stirring as those of the old Cavaliers renowned in story and song, where all the energies of life were centred in one moment. There was the spirited advance of regiments, the onset of brigades, and the resistless charges of divisions,—scenes which stir the blood and fire the soul; the hardihood, the endurance, the cool, collected, reserved force, abiding the time, the calm facing of death; the swift advance, the rush, the plunge into the thickest of the fight, where hundreds of cannon, where fifty thousand muskets, filled the air with iron hail and leaden rain.

The army wintered between the Rappahannock and the Rapidan. There had been a reduction and reconstruction of its corps,—an incorporation of the First and Third with the Fifth and Sixth, with reinforcements added to the Second. The Second was commanded by Major-General Hancock, the Fifth by Major-General Warren, the Sixth by Major-General Sedgwick.

These three corps, with three divisions of cavalry commanded by General Sheridan, composed the Army of the Potomac, commanded by Major-General Meade. The Ninth Corps, commanded by Major-General Burnside, was added when the army took up its line of march.

Lee was behind Mine Run, with his head-quarters at Orange Court-House, covering the advance to Richmond from that direction.

There was concentration everywhere. General Gillmore, with what troops could be spared from the Department of the South, joined his forces to those on the Peninsula and at Suffolk under General Butler; Sigel commanded several thousand in the Shenandoah; Crook and Averell had a small army in Western Virginia; at Chattanooga, under Sherman and Thomas, was gathered a large army of Western troops; while Banks was up the Red River, moving towards Shreveport.

The *dramatis personae* were known to the public, but the part assigned to each was kept profoundly secret. There was discussion and speculation whether Burnside, from his encampment at Annapolis, would suddenly take transports and go to Wilmington, or up the Rappahannock, or the James, or the York. Would Meade move directly across the Rapidan and attack Lee in front, with every passage, every hill and ravine enfiladed by Rebel cannon? Or would he move his right flank along the Blue Ridge, crowding Lee to the seaboard? Would he not make, rather, a sudden change of base to Fredericksburg? None of the wise men, military or civil, in their speculations, indicated the line which General Grant adopted. The public accepted the disaster at Chancellorsville and the failure at Mine Run as conclusive evidence that a successful advance across the Rapidan by the middle fords was impossible, or at least improbable. So well was the secret kept, that, aside from the corps commanders, none in or out of the army, except the President and Secretary of War, had information of the line of march intended.

General Grant had a grand plan,—not merely for the Army of the Potomac, but for all of the armies in the Union service.

Banks was to take Shreveport, then sail rapidly down the Mississippi and move upon Mobile, accompanied by the naval force under Farragut. Sherman was to push Johnston from his position near Chattanooga. If Banks succeeded at Mobile, he was to move up to Montgomery and co-operate with Sherman. Such a movement would compel the Rebel General Johnston to retire from Atlanta. It would sever Alabama and Mississippi from the other States of the Confederacy.

Butler was to move up the James and seize Richmond, or cut the railroads south of the Appomattox. Sigel was to pass up the Shenandoah, while the troops in Western Virginia were to sever the railroad leading to East Tennessee.

The Army of the Potomac was to move upon Richmond,—or rather upon Lee's army. The policy of General Grant—the idea upon which he opened and conducted the campaign—must be fully comprehended before the events can be clearly understood.

That idea is thus expressed in General Grant's official report:

> From an early period in the Rebellion I had been impressed with the idea that active and continuous operations of all the troops that could be brought into the field, regardless of season and weather, were necessary to a speedy termination of the war. The resources of the enemy, and his numerical strength, were far inferior to ours; but as an offset to this, we had a vast territory, with a population hostile to the government, to garrison, and long lines of river and railroad communications to protect, to enable us to supply the operating armies.
>
> The armies in the East and West acted independently and without concert, like a balky team, no two ever pulling together, enabling the enemy to use to great advantage his interior lines of communication for transporting troops from east to west, reinforcing the army most vigorously pressed, and to furlough large numbers during seasons of inactivity on our part, to go to their homes, and do the work of producing for the support of their armies. It was a question whether our numerical strength and resources were not more than balanced by these disadvantages and the enemy's superior position.
>
> From the first, I was firm in the conviction that no peace could be had that would be stable and conducive to the happiness of the people, both North and South, until the military power of the rebellion was entirely broken.
>
> I therefore determined, first, to use the greatest number of troops practicable against the armed force of the enemy; preventing him from using the same force at different seasons against first one and then another of our armies, and the possibility of repose for refitting and producing necessary supplies

for carrying on resistance. Second, to hammer continuously against the armed force of the enemy and his resources, until, by mere attrition, if in no other way, there should be nothing left to him but an equal submission with the loyal section of our common country, to the Constitution and laws of the land.

The Army of the Potomac had no easy task to perform. Lee had the advantage of position. The Rapidan was his line. He had improved his old earthworks and thrown up new ones. His cannon covered the fords. His army was as large as when he invaded Pennsylvania. Grant must cross the Rapidan at some point. To attempt and fail would be disastrous. It was easy to say, Push on! but it was far different to meet the storm of leaden hail,—far different to see a line waver, break, and scatter to the rear, with utter loss of heart. Those were contingencies and possibilities to be taken into account.

It was no light affair to supply an army of one hundred and fifty thousand men, over a single line of railway,—to accumulate supplies in advance of the movement,—to cut loose from his base of operations, and open a new base as occasion should call. Every mile of advance increased Grant's difficulty, while every mile of retrograde movement carried Lee nearer to his base of operations.

All the speculations in regard to Burnside's destination fell to the ground when, on the 25th of April, the Ninth Corps passed through Washington, and moved into Virginia. It was a sublime spectacle. The Ninth Corps achieved almost the first successes of the war in North Carolina. It had hastened to the Potomac in time to aid in rescuing the capital when Lee made his first Northern invasion. It won glory at South Mountain, and made the narrow bridge of Antietam forever historic. It had readied Kentucky in season to aid in driving the Rebels from that State, and now, with recruited ranks,—with new regiments of as good blood as ever was poured out in the cause of right, with a new element which was to make for itself a name never again to be despised, the corps was marching through the capital of the nation, passing in review before Abraham Lincoln. The corps marched down Fourteenth Street past Willard's Hotel, where upon the balcony stood the President and General Burnside. Behold the scene! Platoons, companies, battalions, regiments, brigades, and divisions. The men are bronzed by the rays of a Southern sun, and by the March winds. The bright sunshine gleams from their bayonets; above them wave their standards, tattered by the winds, torn by cannon-ball and rifle-shot,—stained with the blood of dying heroes. They are priceless treasures, more beloved than houses, land, riches, honour, ease, comfort, wife or children. Ask them what is most dear of all earthly things, there will be but one answer,—"The flag! the dear old flag!" It is their pillar of fire by night, of cloud by day,—the symbol of everything worth living for, worth dying for!

Their banners bear the names of Bull Run, Ball's Bluff, Roanoke, Newburn, Gains's Mills, Mechanicsville, Seven Pines, Savage Station, Glendale, Malvern, Fredericksburg, Chancellorsville, Antietam, South Mountain, Knoxville, Vicksburg, Port Hudson, Gettysburg, inscribed in golden characters.

The people of Washington have turned out to see them. Senators have left their Chamber, and the House of Representatives has taken a recess to gaze upon the defenders of their country, as they pass through the city,—many of them, alas! never to return.

There is the steady tramping of the thousands,—the deep, heavy jar of the gun-carriages,—the clattering of hoofs, the clanking of sabres, the drum-beat, the bugle-call, and the music of the bands. Pavement, sidewalk, windows, and roofs are occupied by the people. A division of veterans pass, saluting the President and their commander with cheers. And now with full ranks, platoons extending from sidewalk to sidewalk, are brigades which never have been in battle, for the first time shouldering arms for their country; who till a year ago never had a country, who even now are not American citizens, who are disfranchised,—yet they are going out to fight for the flag! Their country was given them by the tall, pale, benevolent-hearted man standing upon the balcony. For the first time they behold their benefactor. They are darker hued than their veteran comrades; but they can cheer as lustily, "Hurrah! Hurrah!"

"Hurrah for Massa Linkum!"

"Three cheers for the President!"

They swing their caps, clap their hands, and shout their joy. Long, loud, and jubilant are the rejoicings of those redeemed sons of Africa. Regiment after regiment of stalwart men,—slaves once, but freemen now,—with steady step and even rank, pass down the street, moving on to the Old Dominion.

It was the first review of coloured troops by the President. He gave them freedom, he recognized them as soldiers. Their brethren in arms of the same complexion had been murdered in cold blood, after surrender, at Port Pillow and at Plymouth. And such would be their fate should they by chance become prisoners of war.

The time had come for the great movement.

On Tuesday afternoon, May 3rd, the cavalry broke camp on the Orange and Alexandria Railroad, and moved eastward,—General Gregg's division towards Ely's Ford, and General Wilson's division towards Germanna Ford, each having pontoons. At midnight the Second Corps, which had been encamped east of Culpepper, followed General Gregg. At daylight on the morning of the 4th of May, the Fifth and Sixth Corps and the reserve artillery were moving towards Germanna Ford. The supply-train—four thousand wagons—followed the Second Corps. There were but these two available roads.

The enemy was at Orange Court-House, watching, from his elevated lookout on Clark's Mountain, for the first sign of change in the Union camp. In the light of the early dawn he saw that the encampments at Culpepper were broken up, while the dust-cloud hanging over the forest toward the east was the sure indication of the movement.

General Lee put his army in instant motion to strike the advancing columns as they crossed the Rapidan. The movement of Grant was southeast, that of Lee northeast,—lines of advance which must produce collision, unless Grant was far enough forward to slip by the angle. There is reason to believe that General Grant did not intend to fight Lee at Wilderness, but that it was his design to slip past that point and swing round by Spottsylvania, and, if possible, get between Lee and Richmond. He boldly cut loose his connection with Washington, and plunged into the Wilderness, relying upon the ability of his soldiers to open a new base for supplies whenever needed.

In this first day's movement he did not uncover Washington. Burnside was still lying on the north bank of the Rappahannock. It was understood in the army that the Ninth Corps was to be a reserve to protect the capital. So, perhaps, Lee understood it. But at nightfall, on the 4th, the shelter-tents were folded, and the men of the Ninth, with six days' rations in their haversacks, were on the march along the forest-road, lighted only by the stars, joining the main army at Germanna Ford on the morning of the 5th.

The movement from the Rapidan to Cold Harbor was made in thirty days. It was a series of movements by the left flank, in part to get between Lee and his southern communications, and in part to force him to abandon strong positions.

The movements were:

From Culpepper to Wilderness.

From Wilderness to Spottsylvania.

From Spottsylvania to the North Anna.

From the North Anna to Cold Harbor.

From Cold Harbor to Petersburg.

It was thirty days of continuous marching, or fighting, building defences and bridges, opening roads, establishing new bases of supplies, through a country densely wooded, and crossing four large rivers, besides numerous smaller streams, to find always the enemy upon the other side, prepared to give desperate battle.

It was early in the morning on the 4th of May when the reveille sounded for the last time over the hills and dales of Culpepper. The last cups of coffee were drunk, the blankets folded, and then the army, which through the winter had lain in camp, moved away from the log huts, where many a jest had been spoken, many a story told,—where, through rain and mud, and heat and cold, the faithful and true-hearted men had kept watch and ward through the long, weary months,—where songs of praise and prayer to God had been raised by thousands who looked beyond the present into the future life.

So rapid was the march that the Second Corps reached Chancellorsville before night, having crossed the Rapidan at Ely's Ford. The Sixth and Fifth Corps crossed at Germanna Ford, without opposition, and before night the Army of the Potomac was upon the southern side of that stream, where it was joined by the Ninth Corps the next morning.

General Grant's quarters for the night were in an old house near the ford. Lights were to be put out at nine o'clock. There were the usual scenes of a bivouac, and one unusual to an army. The last beams of daylight were fading in the west. The drummers were beating the tattoo. Mingled with the constant rumbling of the wagons across the pontoons, and the unceasing flow of the river, was a chorus of voices,—a brigade singing a hymn of devotion. It was the grand old choral of Luther, *Old Hundred*.

Eternal are thy mercies,
Lord, Eternal truth attends thy word;
Thy praise shall sound from shore to shore,
Till suns shall rise and set no more.

Many soldiers in that army were thinking of home,—not only of loved ones, and of associations full of sweet and tender memories, but of a better abiding-place, eternal in the heavens. To thousands it was a last night on earth.

Early in the morning of the 5th Generals Meade and Grant, with their staffs, after riding five miles from Germanna Ford, halted near an old mill in the Wilderness. General Sheridan's cavalry had been pushing out south and west. Aides came back with despatches.

"They say that Lee intends to fight us here," said General Meade, as he read them.

"Very well," was the quiet reply of General Grant.

The two commanders retire a little from the crowd, and stand by the roadside in earnest conversation. Grant is of medium stature, yet has a well-developed physique, sandy whiskers and moustache, blue eyes, earnest, thoughtful, and far-seeing, a cigar in his mouth, a knife in one hand, and a stick in the other, which he is whittling to a point. He whittles slowly towards him. His thoughts are not yet crystallized. His words are few. Suddenly he commences upon the other end of the stick, and whittles energetically from him. And now he is less reticent,—talks freely. He is dressed in plain blue; and were it not for the three stars upon his shoulder, few would select him as the Lieutenant-General commanding all the armies of the Union in the field.

Meade is tall, thin, a little stooping in the shoulders, quick, comprehending the situation of affairs in an instant, energetic,—an officer of excellent executive ability.

Years ago, a turnpike was built from Fredericksburg to Orange Court-House; but in the days when there was a mania for plank roads, another corporation constructed a plank road between the same places. A branch plank road, commencing two miles west of Chancellorsville, crosses the Rapidan at Germanna Ford, running to Stevensburg, north of that stream. The turnpike runs nearly east and west, while the Stevensburg plank road runs northwest. General Grant has established his head-quarters at the crossing of the turnpike and the Stevensburg road, his flag waving from a knoll west of the road. A mile and a half out on the turnpike, on a ridge, is Parker's store, where, early in the morning, I saw long lines of Rebel infantry, the sunlight gleaming from bayonet and gun-barrel.

Before the contest begins, let us go up to the old Wilderness tavern, which stands on the Stevensburg plank road, and take a view of a portion of the battle-field. It will be a limited view, for there are few open spaces in the Wilderness.

From the tavern you look west. At your feet is a brook, flowing from the southwest, and another small stream from the northwest, joining their waters at the crossing of the turnpike and the plank road. The turnpike rises over a ridge between the two streams. On the south slope is the house of Major Lacy, owner of a house at Falmouth, used by our soldiers after the battle of Fredericksburg. It is a beautiful view,—a smooth lawn in front of the house, meadows green with the verdure of spring; beyond the meadows are hills thickly wooded,—

tall oaks, and pine and cedar thickets. On the right hand side of the turnpike the ridge is more broken, and also thickly set with small trees and bushes. A mile and a half out from the crossing of the two roads the ridge breaks down into a ravine. General Lee has possession of the western bank, Grant the eastern. It is such a mixture of woods, underbrush, thickets, ravines, hills, hollows, and knolls, that one is bewildered in passing through it, and to attempt to describe would be a complete bewilderment to writer and reader.

But General Grant has been compelled to make this ridge his right line of battle. He must protect his trains, which are still coming in on the Germanna road.

The Sixth Corps, commanded by General Sedgwick, holds the right, covering the road to Germanna Ford. The left of the Third Division reaches the turnpike, where it connects with the Fifth Corps, Warren's. Before the arrival of Burnside's force, one division of the Fifth is placed in position south of the turnpike. Now leaving a wide gap, you walk through the woods towards the southeast, and two miles from head-quarters you find the Second Corps, under Hancock, a long line of men in the thick forest, on both sides of the Orange plank road.

The forenoon of the 5th instant was devoted to taking positions. Engineers rode over the ground and examined the character of the country. A small party pushed out to Parker's store, but encountered a Rebel column advancing; but the knowledge thus obtained of the ground in that direction was of great value.

Word was sent to General Hancock, who had orders to move in direction of Spottsylvania; that Lee was taking positions. He hastened to make connection with the other corps. Had he not moved rapidly, Lee would have obtained possession of the fork of the two plank roads, the Stevensburg and the Orange road, which would have been a serious mishap. The Rebel advance was not more than a mile distant when Hancock secured it. No sooner had the pickets been thrown out, than the rattling of musketry commenced all along the line. About four in the afternoon, each commander began to feel the position of the other by advancing brigades on the right, left, and centre. An exchange of a few volleys would seemingly satisfy the parties.

It had been the practice of General Lee to begin and close a day with a grand fusillade. In this battle he adhered to his former tactics, by advancing a heavy force upon our right, and then, when the contest was at its height in that direction, attacked on the left. The rolls of musketry were very heavy and continuous for an hour. There was but little opportunity to charge bayonet. It was a close contest in a thick wood, on land which years ago was turned by the plough, but which, having by thriftless culture incident to the existence of servile labour, been worn out, now bears the smallest oaks, hazels, sassafras, and briers.

Hostilities ceased at night. Each commander learned enough of the other's operations to make dispositions for the following day. Grant had no alterations to make. Lee had forced him to accept battle there, and he must do the best he could. Longstreet arrived in the night, and was placed against Hancock, on the Rebel right, or rather on the right centre, overlapping the Second and coming against a portion of the Ninth Corps, which was assigned to the left centre. Thus these two corps and their two commanders met again in deadly conflict, having fought at the first and second Bull Run, South Mountain, Antietam, and Knoxville.

General Alexis Hays, in the front line, finding that he was outnumbered, sent word to Hancock that he must have reinforcements.

"Tell him," said Hancock to the aide, "that he shall have a fresh brigade in twenty minutes."

Twenty minutes! An age to those who see their comrades falling,—their lines growing thinner. Before the time had expired, General Hays was carried back a corpse; but though the brave man had fallen, the troops held their ground.

Night closed over the scene. Everybody knew that the contest would be renewed in the morning. Lee began the attack on the 5th, falling like a thunderbolt on the flank of Grant, but made no impression on the Union lines,—not moving them an inch from their chosen positions.

Grant resolved to take the initiative on the morning of the 6th, and orders were accordingly issued for a general attack at daybreak.

Sedgwick was to commence on the right at five o'clock, but Lee saved him the trouble. A. P. Hill forestalled the movement by advancing at half past four. The Rebel batteries by Parker's store sent a half-dozen shots into the Union lines as a signal for the beginning of the contest. Then came a slight ripple of musketry, then a roll,—long, deep, heavy,—and the crash,—indescribable, fearful to hear, terrible to think of. Fifty thousand muskets were flashing, with occasional cannon-shots, mingled with shouts, cheers, and hurrahs from the Union lines, and yells like the war-whoop of Indians,—wild, savage howls from the depths of the tangled jungle. The sun rises upon a cloudless sky. The air becomes sultry. The blood of the combatants is at fever heat. There are bayonet-charges, surgings to and fro of the opposing lines, a meeting and commingling, like waves of the ocean, sudden upspringings from the underbrush of divisions stealthily advanced. There is a continuous rattle, with intervening rolls deepening into long, heavy swells, the crescendo and the diminuendo of a terrible symphony, rising to thunder-tones, to crash and roar indescribable.

The Ninth Corps during the day was brought between the Fifth and Second. Divisions were moved to the right, to the left, and to the centre, during the two days' fight, but the positions of the corps remained unchanged, and stood as represented in the diagram.

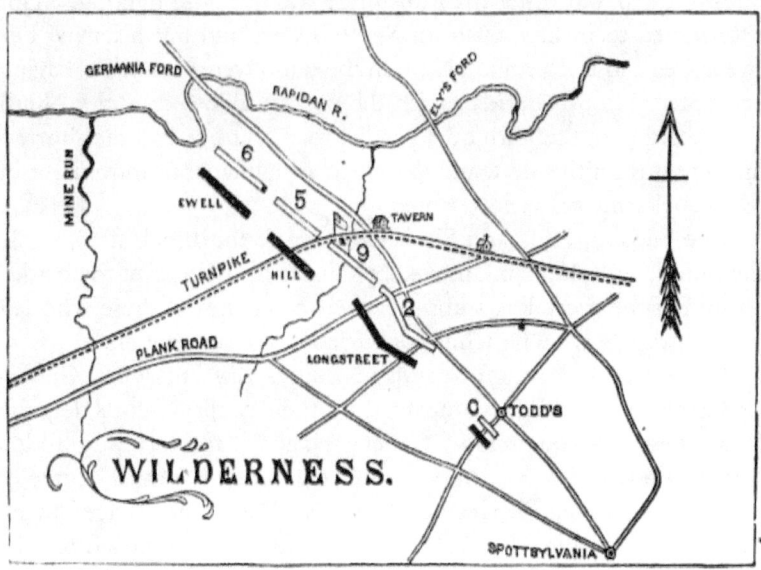

Through all those long hours of conflict there was patient endurance in front of the enemy. There were temporary successes and reverses on both sides. In only a single instance was there permanent advantage to Lee, and that he had not the power to improve. It was at the close of the contest on the 6th. The sun had gone down, and twilight was deepening into night. The wearied men of Rickett's division of the Sixth Corps, in the front line of battle on the right, had thrown themselves upon the ground. Suddenly there was a rush upon their flank. There was musketry, blinding flashes from cannon, and explosions of shells. The line which had stood firmly through the day gave way, not because it was overpowered, but because it was surprised. General Seymour and a portion of his brigade were taken prisoners. There was a partial panic, which soon subsided. The second line remained firm, the enemy was driven back, and the disaster repaired by swinging the Sixth Corps round to a new position, covered by the reserve artillery.

On the morning of the 7th the pickets reported that Lee had fallen back. Reconnoitring parties said that he was throwing up entrenchments. Grant was thoughtful through the day. He said but little. He had a cigar in his mouth from morning till night. I saw him many times during the day, deeply absorbed in thought. He rode along the centre, and examined the Rebel lines towards Parker's store. At times a shell or solid shot came from the Rebel batteries through the thick forest growth, but other than this there was but little fighting. Grant determined to make a push for Spottsylvania, and put his army between Lee and Richmond. By noon the trains were in motion, having been preceded by Sheridan with the cavalry, followed by the Ninth Corps, and then the Fifth on a parallel road. But Lee had the shortest line. He was on the alert, and there was a simultaneous movement of the Rebel army on a shorter line.

The Second, Fifth, and Sixth Corps took the Block road, while the Ninth, with the trains, moved by Chancellorsville, over the battleground of the preceding summer, where the bones of those who fell in that struggle were bleaching unburied in the summer air.

It was eleven p. m. on Saturday evening, May 7th, when Generals Grant and Meade, accompanied by their cavalry escorts, left the Wilderness head-quarters of General Hancock for a ride to Todd's Tavern, a place of two or three houses, exhibiting the usual degree of thriftlessness which characterized the Old Dominion. Twice during the ride we ran into the Rebel pickets, and were compelled to take by-paths through fields and thickets. General Grant rode at a breakneck speed. How exciting! The sudden flashing of Rebel muskets in front, the *whiz* of the minie projectile over our heads, the quick halt and right about face,—our horses stumbling over fallen timber and stumps, the clanking of sabres, the clattering of hoofs, the plunge into brambles, the tension of every nerve, the strain upon all the senses, the feeling of relief when we are once more in the road, and then the gallop along the narrow way, beneath the dark pines of the forest, till brought to a halt by the sudden challenge from our own sentinel! It is a fast life that one leads at such a time. When the reaction sets in the system is as limp as a wilted cabbage-leaf.

"Where are you going?" was the question of a cavalryman as we halted a moment.

"To Spottsylvania."

"I reckon you will have a scrimmage before you get there," said he.
"Why?"

"Well, nothing in particular, except there are forty or fifty thousand Rebs in front of you. Sheridan has had a tough time of it, and I reckon there is more work to be done."

We pushed on and reached Todd's at one o'clock on Sunday morning. The roads were full of cavalry, also the fields and woods. Sheridan had been fighting several hours, with Fitz Lee. The wounded were being brought in. Surgeons were at work. In the field, a short distance from the spot, the pickets were still firing shots. The Rebels were retiring, and Sheridan's men, having won the field, were throwing themselves upon the ground and dropping off to sleep as unconcernedly as when seeking rest in the calm repose and silence of their far-distant homes.

Fastening our horses to the front-yard fence of Todd's, making a pillow of our saddles, wrenching off the palings for a bed to keep our bones from the ground, wrapping our blankets around us, we were sound asleep in three minutes, undisturbed by the tramping of the passing troops, the jar of the artillery, the rumble of the ammunition wagons, the shouts of the soldiers, the shrieks of the wounded, and groans of the dying.

At sunrise the head-quarters of the army were removed to Piney Grove Church. No bell called the worshippers of the parish to its portal on that Sabbath morning, but other tones were vibrating the air. The Fifth Corps had come in collision with the Rebels, and while the rear-guard of the army were firing their last shots in the Wilderness, the cannonade was reopening at Spottsylvania.

The day was intensely hot. I was wearied by the events of the week,—the hard riding, the want of sleep, the series of battles,—and instead of riding out to the field, enjoyed luxurious repose beneath the apple-trees, fragrant with blossoms, and listened to the strange Sabbath symphony, the humming of bees, the songs of the birds, the roll of musketry, and the cannonade.

The second division, Robinson's, and the fourth, Cutler's (after the loss of Wadsworth, killed at the Wilderness), were engaged. Baxter's brigade of Robinson's division was thrown forward to ascertain the position of the enemy. Their advance brought on the battle. The Sixth Corps was moved to the left of Warren's on the Piney Church road, and was placed in supporting distance. In this first engagement Robinson was badly wounded in the leg.

The Second Corps having filed through the woods, after a hot and dusty march, came up behind the Fifth and Sixth. I took a ride along the lines late in the afternoon. The Fifth was moving slowly forward over undulations and through pine thickets,—a long line of men in blue, picking their way, now through dense underbrush, in a forest of moaning pines, now stepping over a sluggish stream, with briers, hazel, thorn-bushes, and alders impeding every step, and now emerging into an old field where the thriftless farmers had turned the shallow soil for spring planting.

There had been a lull in the cannonade, but it commenced again. It was as before, a spirited contest, which lasted half an hour. Warren pressed steadily on and drove the Rebels from their advanced position, forcing them to retire across the creek, but losing several hundred men before he dislodged them.

Reaching an opening in the forest, I came upon Hart's plantation, a collection of negro huts and farm buildings,—a lovely spot, where the spring wheat was already rolling in green waves in the passing breeze. Looking south over Po Creek, I could see the Catharpen road lined with horse and footmen, and could hear in the intervals of silence the rumble of wagons. A cloud of dust rose above the forest. Were the Rebels retreating, or were they receiving reinforcements? General Grant came down and looked at them. The Rebel artillerists near the court-house must have discovered us, for a half-dozen cannon-shot came ringing through the air, plunging into the newly ploughed cornfield and the clover-land, knee deep with luxuriant grass.

On Monday morning it was found that Lee's whole army was at Spottsylvania; and as our skirmishers were deployed to ascertain the position of the enemy, it was discovered that Rebels occupied all the ground in front. General Grant did not at first think Lee would make a detour of his whole force from a direct line to Richmond; he thought it must be only detachments of men which had been thrown in his way; but when he discovered what Lee's intentions were, he prepared to accept battle. Word was sent to General Burnside to take position on the extreme left. The Second Corps, which had been in rear of the Fifth, was swung to the right, while the Sixth was deflected toward the Ninth. While these dispositions were being made, the skirmishing and cannonade were never intermitted for an instant. A pontoon train was sent around to the right, to be used by Hancock. A battery was placed in position at Hart's plantation, and its rifle shot and shells interrupted the tide of travel on the Catharpen road. Riding down to the front of Hancock's corps, I found Birney, who with the Third Division held the extreme right, and had already pushed far over toward the Catharpen road.

Gibbon's division was in the centre, and Barlow's was on the left, occupying, in part, ground which the Fifth had held the night previous. It was nearly night, and the conflict was deepening. The day had been intensely hot, but, as the coolness of evening came on, both parties addressed themselves to the encounter. Barlow marched over undulating pasture-lands, through fringes of forest, into a meadow, across it, and into the dark pines beyond. Taking a favourable stand near a deserted farm-house, by the Piney Church road, I could see the dark lines move steadily on. Below me, on a hillock, were Hancock and staff directing movements. A half-dozen batteries were in position close by. One—the Third Massachusetts—was sending its shells over the heads of our men into the woods beyond the meadow. Mounting the breastworks which had been thrown up at this spot, I could see the orchard where the Rebel riflemen were lying. There was the sharp, shrill ringing of the minnie bullets whistling through the air, and at times a lurid sheet of flame from a brigade pouring in its volleys. There was the flash, the cloud of dust wherever the ragged iron tore its way, and the deafening report. I gladly availed myself of whatever protection the breastwork afforded, although a solid shot would have passed through the slight embankment as readily as a stone could be hurled through chaff. The chances were as one to several thousand of my being hit, but it is the one chance which makes a person wish he were somewhere else. The Second Corps was smartly assailed, but stood their ground and became assailants in turn,—not because they obeyed orders, but from the impulse of the men, who needed no urging. It was a remarkable feature. The men in that contest fought because they wanted to. Gibbons and Birney swung like a double-hinged door upon Longstreet's left flank and obtained possession of the ground which the Rebels occupied at the beginning of the engagement.

It became evident on Tuesday morning that General Lee had chosen Spottsylvania as a place for a trial of strength. Preparations were accordingly made for the work. General Grant's wounded impeded his movements. He decided to send them to Fredericksburg. All who could walk were started on foot. Those who could not, but who did not need ambulances, were placed in empty wagons. The long procession took its winding way, and other thousands of mangled forms were brought in to fill the empty places. It was a sad sight. It made me sick at heart, and weary of war, and how much more sick and weary when I thought of the great iniquity which had caused it.

At daybreak the cannonade recommenced, Grant's guns coming first into play. The Rebels for a while remained in silent indifference; but as continued teasing rouses a wild beast's anger, so at length they replied.

The air was calm, and the reverberation rolled far over the forest. There was constant skirmishing through the forenoon. General Grant rode along the lines, inspected the position, and issued orders for a general advance at five o'clock; but Lee took the initiative, and through the afternoon the battle raged with exceeding fierceness.

There was nothing at Spottsylvania worthy of contention,—no mountain-pass or deep-running river; but General Grant being on his way to Richmond, his adversary, like Apollyon assaulting Christian, had come out to meet him on that spot. Lee had the advantage of position and was able to concentrate his forces. It was about one o'clock when Longstreet began to press Hancock. There was a hot engagement for an hour, principally by Birney's division; but failing to move Birney, an attempt was made to pry open still wider the joint between the Second and Fifth Corps.

The relative positions of the two armies will be seen from the following diagram.

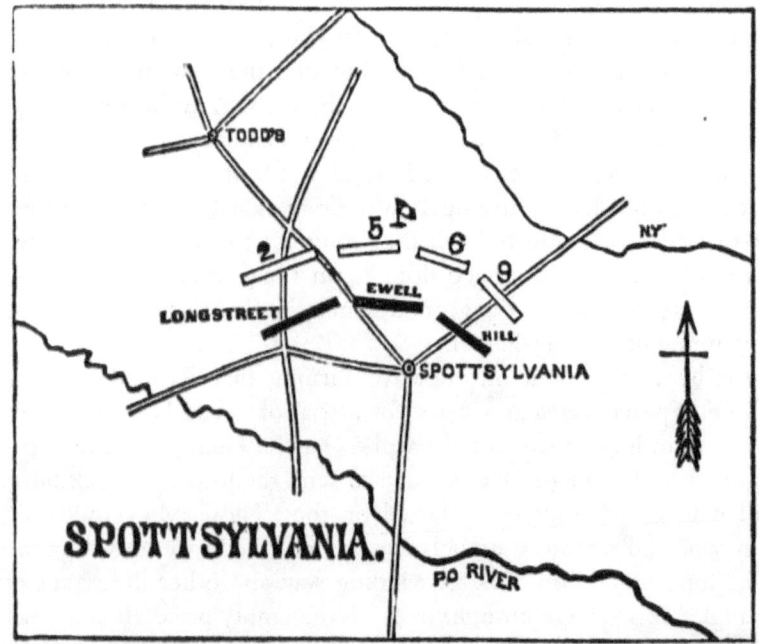

The battle was fought in the forest,—in the marshes along the Ny,—in ravines,—in pine-thickets densely shaded with the dark evergreens that shut out the rays of the noonday sun,—in open fields, where Rebel batteries had full sweep and play—with shell, and grape, and canister—from entrenched positions on the hills.

During a lull in the strife I visited the hospitals. Suddenly the battle recommenced in greater fury. The wounded began to come in at a fearful rate. The battle was drawing nearer. Shells were streaming past the hospitals. There were signs of disaster.

"Are they driving us?" was the eager inquiry of the wounded.

While the storm was at its height, a stalwart soldier who had just risen from the amputating-table, where his left arm, torn to shreds by a cannon-shot, had been severed above the elbow, leaning against the tent-pole, sang the song he often had sung in camp,—

The Union forever! Hurrah, boys! hurrah!
Down with the traitor, up with the star;
While we rally round the flag, boys, rally once again,
Shouting the battle-cry of Freedom!

His wounded comrades heard it, and joined in the chorus, raising their arms, swinging their caps, and cheering the flag they loved. It is one of memory's fadeless pictures. Is it a wonder that the recollection of that scene sometimes fills my eyes with tears?

The contest all along the line was terrific. Even now, over all the intervening time and distance, I seem to hear the unceasing rattle and roll of musketry and cannon, the cheer of the combatants, the tramping of horses, the explosion of shells, the shriek of the rifled projectile, the crash through the trees. It goes on hour after hour. The ranks are thinning. The men with stretchers bring in their bleeding burdens, and lay them gently upon the ground.

It is past seven o'clock. The shades of evening are falling. The hillside in front of the Sixth Corps is aflame. While the uproar is wildest there is a cheer, sharper and louder than the din of the conflict. It is not the savage war-cry of the enemy, but a buoyant shout. Into the storm sweeps the Vermont brigade, with bayonets firmly set, leaping over the Rebel works, and gathering hundreds of prisoners from Dale's brigade of Rebels. Ewell poured in reinforcements to strengthen his line and regain his lost work, which was stubbornly held by the Second Vermont. Far in advance of the main line lay that regiment, pouring a deadly fire upon the enemy. General Wright (in command after Sedgwick's death) sent to have the regiment withdrawn.

"We don't want to go back! Give us rations and ammunition, and we'll hold it for six months if you want us to," was the reply.

General Wright rode to General Grant. "What shall I do?" he asked.

"Pile in the men and hold it!" was the answer.

General Wright returned, but meanwhile a subordinate officer had ordered them to retire. They were loath to give up what they had won so gloriously.

General Rice, commanding a brigade in the Fifth Corps, was wounded, and borne to the rear. The surgeon laid down his knife after removing the shattered limb, and stood beside him to soothe with tender words in the last dread hour which was coming on apace. The sufferer could hear the swelling tide of battle, the deepening rolls like waves upon the ocean shore. His eyes were closing. He was approaching that ocean which has no shore. His pain was intense.

"Turn me over," said he, faintly.

"Which way?"

"Let me die with my face to the enemy!"

They were his last words. A short struggle and all was ended. A Christian patriot had finished his work on earth, and was numbered with the heroic dead.

The early dawn of Thursday, the 12th, beheld the Second Corps in motion,—not to flank the enemy, but moving, with fixed bayonets, straight on towards his entrenchments. Barlow's and Birney's divisions in columns of battalions, doubled on the centre, to give strength and firmness, led the assault. They move silently through the forest,—through the ravine in front of them, up to their own skirmish-line,—past it,—no longer marching, but running now,—dashing on with enthusiasm thrilling every nerve. They sweep away the Rebel picket-line as if it were a cobweb. On! into the entrenchments with a hurrah which startles the soldiers of both armies from their morning slumbers. Major-General Johnson and Brigadier-General Stewart, and three thousand men of Ewell's division are taken prisoners, eighteen cannon, and twenty-two standards captured.

It was the work of five minutes,—as sudden as the swoop of an eagle. Then the uproar of the day began. The second line of the enemy's works was assaulted; but, exasperated by their losses, the Rebels fought fiercely. The Ninth Corps was moved up from the left to support the Second. Longstreet, on the other hand, was brought over to help Ewell. The Fifth and Sixth became partially engaged. There were charges and counter-charges. Positions were gained and lost. From morning till night the contest raged on the right, in the centre, and on the left, swaying to and fro over the undulations and through the ravines. It was a battle of fourteen hours' duration,—in severity, in unflinching determination, in obstinacy, not exceeded by any during the war. Between forty and fifty pieces of artillery were at one time in the hands of General Hancock; but owing to the difficulties of removal, and the efforts of the enemy, he could secure only eighteen. During the day Grant advanced his lines a mile towards the court-house, and repulsed Lee in all his counter-attacks.

During the lull in the strife at Spottsylvania I spent a day in Fredericksburg, visiting the hospitals.

The city is a vast hospital; churches, public buildings, private dwellings, stores, chambers, attics, basements, all full. There are thousands upon the sidewalk. All day long the ambulances have been arriving from the field. There are but few wounded left at the front, those only whom to remove would be certain death.

A red flag has been flung out at the Sanitary Commission rooms,—a white one at the rooms of the Christian Commission. There are three hundred volunteer nurses in attendance. The Sanitary Commission

THE SANITARY COMMISSION IN THE HOSPITAL

have fourteen wagons bringing supplies from Belle Plain. The Christian Commission has less transportation facilities, but in devotion, in hard work, in patient effort, it is the compeer of its more bountifully supplied neighbour. The nurses are divided into details, some for day service, some for night work. Each State has its Relief Committee.

How patient the brave fellows are! Not a word of complaint, but thanks for the slightest favour. There was a lack of crutches. I saw an old soldier of the California regiment, who fought with the lamented Baker at Ball's Bluff, and who had been in more than twenty battles, hobbling about with the arms of a settee nailed to strips of board. His regiment was on its way home, its three years of service having expired. It was reduced to a score or two of weather-beaten, battle-scarred veterans. The disabled comrade could hardly keep back the tears as he saw them pass down the street. "Few of us left. The bones of the boys are on every battle-field where the Army of the Potomac has fought," said he.

There was the sound of the pick and spade in the churchyard, a heaving-up of new earth,—a digging of trenches, not for defence against the enemy, but for the last resting-place of departed heroes. There they lie, each wrapped in his blanket, the last bivouac! For them there is no more war,—no charges into the thick, leaden raindrops,—no more hurrahs, no more cheering for the dear old flag! They have fallen, but the victory is theirs,—theirs the roll of eternal honour. Side by side,—men from Massachusetts, from Pennsylvania, and from Wisconsin,—from all the States, resting in one common grave. Peace to them! blessings on the dear ones,—wives, mothers, children whom they have left behind.

Go into the hospitals;—armless, legless men, wounds of every description. Men on the floor, on the hard seats of church-pews, lying in one position all day, unable to move till the nurse, going the rounds, gives them aid. They must wait till their food comes. Some must be fed with a spoon, for they are as helpless as little children.

"O that we could get some straw for the brave fellows," said the Rev. Mr. Kimball, of the Christian Commission. He had wandered about town, searching for the article.

"There is none to be had. We shall have to send to Washington for it," said the surgeon in charge.

"Straw! I remember two stacks, four miles out on the Spottsylvania road. I saw them last night as I galloped in from the front."

Armed with a requisition from the Provost Marshal to seize two stacks of straw, with two wagons driven by freedmen, accompanied by four Christian Commission delegates, away we went across the battle-field of December, fording Hazel Run, gaining the heights, and reaching the straw stacks owned by Rev. Mr. Owen, a bitter Rebel.

"By whose authority do you take my property?"

"The Provost Marshal, sir."

"Are you going to pay me for it?"

"You must see the Provost Marshal, sir. If you are a loyal man, and will take the oath of allegiance, doubtless you will get your pay when we have put down the Rebellion."

"It is pretty hard. My children are just ready to starve. I have nothing for them to eat, and you come to take my property without paying for it."

"Yes, sir, war is hard. You must remember, sir, that there are thousands of wounded men,—your Rebel wounded as well as ours. If your children are on the point of starving, those men are on the point of dying. We must have the straw for them. What we don't take tonight we will get in the morning. Meanwhile, sir, if anybody attempts to take it, please say to them that it is for the hospital, and they can't have it."

Thus with wagons stuffed, we leave Rev. Mr. Owen and return to make glad the hearts of several thousand men. O how they thank us!

"Did you get it for me? God bless you, sir."

It is evening. Thousands of soldiers just arrived from Washington have passed through the town to take their places in the front. The hills around are white with innumerable tents.

A band is playing lively airs to cheer the wounded in the hospitals. I have been looking in to see the sufferers. Two or three have gone to their long home. They will need no more attention. A surgeon is at work upon a ghastly wound, taking up the arteries. An attendant is pouring cold water upon a swollen limb. In the Episcopal church a nurse is bolstering up a wounded officer in the area behind the altar. Men are lying in the pews, on the seats, on the floor, on boards on top of the pews.

Two candles in the spacious building throw their feeble rays into the dark recesses, faintly disclosing the recumbent forms. There is heavy, stifled breathing, as of constant effort to suppress cries extorted by acutest pain.

Passing into the street you see a group of women, talking about *our* wounded,—Rebel wounded, who are receiving their especial devotion. The Provost Marshal's patrol is going its rounds to preserve order.

Starting down the street, you reach the rooms of the Christian Commission. Some of the men are writing letters for the soldiers, some eating their night-rations, some dispensing supplies. Passing through the rooms, you gain the grounds in the rear,—a beautiful garden once,—not unattractive now. The air is redolent with honeysuckle and locust blossoms. The *prunifolia* is unfolding its delicate milk-white petals; roses are opening their tinted leaves.

Fifty men are gathered round a summer-house,—warm-hearted men, who have been all day in the hospitals. Their hearts have been wrung by the scenes of suffering, in the exercise of Christian charity, imitating the example of the Redeemer of men. They have dispensed food for the body and nourishment for the soul. They have given cups of cold water in the name of Jesus, and prayed with those departing to the Silent Land. The moonlight shimmers through the leaves of the locusts, as they meet at that evening hour to worship God

The little congregation breaks into singing,—

Come, thou fount of every blessing.

After the hymn, a chaplain says, "Brethren, I had service this afternoon in the First Division hospital of the Second Corps. The surgeon in charge, before prayer, asked all who desired to be prayed for to raise their hands, and nearly every man who had a hand raised it. Let us remember them in our prayers tonight."

A man in the summer-house, so far off that I cannot distinguish him, says,—

"Every man in the Second Division of the Sixth Corps hospital raised his hand for prayers tonight."

There are earnest supplications that God will bless them; that they may have patience; that Jesus will pillow their heads upon his breast, relieve their sufferings, soothe their sorrows, wipe away all their tears, heal their wounds; that he will remember the widow and the fatherless, far away, moaning for the loved and lost.

Another hymn,—

Jesus, lover of my soul,
Let me to thy bosom fly

and the delegates return to their work of mercy.

At Spottsylvania there were constant skirmishing and artillery-firing through the 13th, and a moving of the army from the north to the east of the Court-House. A rain-storm set in. The roads became heavy, and a contemplated movement—a sudden flank attack—was necessarily abandoned.

There was a severe skirmish on the 14th, incessant picket-firing on the 15th, and on the 16th another engagement all along the line,—

not fought with the fierceness of that of the 12th, but lasting through the forenoon, and resulting in the taking of a line of rifle-pits from the enemy.

On Wednesday, the 18th, there was an assault upon Lee's outer line of works. Two lines of rifle-pits were carried; but an impassable *abatis* prevented farther advance, and after a six hours' struggle the troops were withdrawn.

On the afternoon of the 19th Ewell gained the rear of Grant's right flank, and came suddenly upon Tyler's division of heavy artillery, armed as infantry, just arrived upon the field. Though surprised, they held the enemy in check, forced him back, and with aid from the Second Corps compelled him to retreat with great loss. This attack was made to cover Lee's withdrawal to the North Anna. His troops were already on the march.

Grant was swift to follow.

It is a two days' march from Spottsylvania to the North Anna. The crossings of the Mattapony were held by Rebel cavalry, which was quickly driven. Then came the gallant crossing of the Fifth Corps at Jericho Ford, the irresistible charge of Birney and Barlow of the Second Corps at Taylor's Bridge, the sweeping-in of five hundred prisoners, the severe engagements lasting three days,—all memorable events, worthy of prominence in a full history of the campaign.

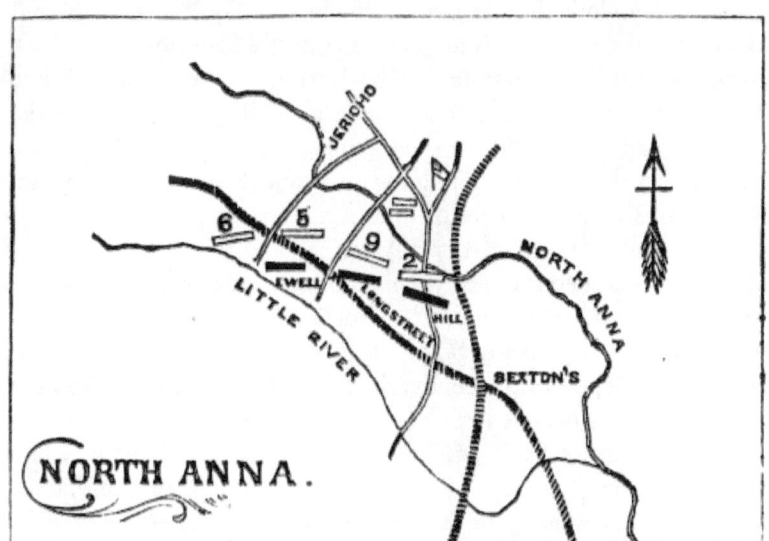

The North Anna is a rapid stream, with high banks. East of Taylor's bridge, towards Sexton's Junction, there is an extensive swamp, but westward the country is rolling. It was supposed that Lee would make a stubborn resistance at the crossings, but at Jericho Warren found only a few pickets upon the southern bank. A pontoon was laid and two divisions sent over; but moving towards the railroad a mile, they encountered Hood's and Pickett's divisions of Ewell's corps. The cannonade was heavy and the musketry sharp, mainly between Cutler's command and Ewell's, lasting till dark.

It is about two miles from Jericho crossing to the railroad, the point for which the right wing was aiming.

"I reckon that our troops didn't expect you to come this way," said Mr. Quarles, a citizen residing on the north bank, with whom I found accommodation for the night.

"I suppose you didn't expect Grant to get this side of the Wilderness?"

"We heard that he was retreating towards Fredericksburg," was the response.

He was the owner of a saw-mill. Timber was wanted for the construction of a bridge. His mill was out of repair, but there were men in the Union army accustomed to run saw-mills, and an hour was sufficient to put the machinery in order for the manufacture of lumber. It was amusing to see the soldiers lay down their guns, take up the crowbar, roll the logs into the mill, adjust the saw, hoist the gate, and sit upon the log while the saw was cutting its way. The owner of the mill looked on in disgust, as his lumber was thus freely handled.

In the first advance from Jericho bridge, the force was repulsed. The Rebels of Ewell's command came on with confidence, to drive the retreating troops into the river; but Warren had taken the precaution to place his smooth-bore guns on a hillock, south of the stream, while his rifled pieces were on the north side, in position, to give a cross-fire with the smooth-bores. When the Rebels came within reach of this concentrated fire they were almost instantly checked. It was no time to rush on, or to stand still and deliberate; they fled, uncovering the railroad, to which the Sixth advanced, tearing up the track and burning the depot. In the centre, the Ninth Corps had a severe fight, resulting in considerable loss.

It is two miles from Jericho bridge to Carmel Church, which stands in a beautiful grove of oaks. While the troops were resting beneath the trees, waiting for the order to move, a chaplain entered the church and proposed to hold religious service.

The soldiers manifested their pleasure, knelt reverently during the prayer, and listened with tearful eyes to the exhortations which followed.

It was inspiring to hear them sing:

Come, sing to me of heaven,
When I'm about to die;
Sing songs of holy ecstasy,
To waft my soul on high.

At dark on the evening of the 25th of May, I rode along the lines of the Second Corps to take a look at the Rebels. There was a steady fire of artillery. One battery of the Rebels had full sweep of the plain, and the shells were flying merrily. A thunder-storm was rising. The lightning was vivid and incessant. My head-quarters for the night were to be with a surgeon attached to the First Division of the Ninth Corps, several miles distant. The dense black clouds rising in the west made the night intensely dark, except when the lightning-flashes gleamed along the sky. It was a scene of sublime grandeur: heaven's artillery in play,—the heavy peals of thunder, mingling with the roar of the battle-field! After an hour's ride through pine thickets, over old corn-fields, half-blinded by the lightning, I reached the quarters of my friend the surgeon, whose tent was just then being packed into the wagon for a night march to a new position. The storm was close at hand, and together we fled for shelter to a neighbouring cabin. I had barely time to fasten my horse and enter the door before the storm was upon us.

The house was built of logs, chinked with mud, contained two rooms about fifteen feet square, and was occupied by a coloured family.

Others had fled for shelter to the hospitable roof. I found congregated there for the night nine surgeons, three hospital nurses, a delegate of the Christian Commission, two soldiers, two coloured women, a coloured man, three children. The coloured people had taken their only pig into the house, to save the animal from being killed by the soldiers, and had tied it to the bed-post. Their poultry—half a dozen fowls—was imprisoned under a basket. The rain fell in torrents throughout the night. Finding a place under the table for my head, with my overcoat for a pillow, and thrusting my legs under the bed which was occupied by three surgeons, I passed the night, and thought myself much more highly favoured than the forty or fifty who came to the door, but only to find a full hotel.

Instead of trying to walk over the obstacle in his path, Grant decided to go round it. Stealing a march upon Lee, he moved suddenly southeast, crossed the Pamunkey at Hanover Town, opened a new base of supplies at White House, forcing Lee to fall back on the Chickahominy.

Bayonet charge

June, 1864

On Sunday, the 29th, a great cavalry engagement took place at Hawes's shop, west of Hanover Town, in which Sheridan drove the Rebels back upon Bethesda Church. The army came into position on the 30th, its right towards Hanover Court-House. Lee was already in position, and during the day there was firing all along the line. All the corps were engaged. The Second Corps by the Shelton House, by a bayonet-charge pushed the enemy from the outer line of works which he had thrown up, while the Fifth Corps rolled back, with terrible slaughter, the mass of men which came upon its flank and front at Bethesda Church. At Cold Harbor, the Sixth, joined by the Eighteenth Army Corps, under Major-General W. F. Smith, from Bermuda Hundred, met Longstreet and Breckenridge, and troops from Beauregard. Sheridan had seized this important point,—important because of the junction of roads,—and held it against cavalry and infantry till the arrival of the Fifth and Eighteenth. The point secured, a new line of battle was formed on the 1st of June. The Ninth held the right of Bethesda Church; the Fifth was south of the church, joining the Eighteenth; the Sixth held the road from Cold Harbor to Gaines's Mills; while the Second was thrown out on the left, on the road leading to Despatch Station and the Chickahominy.

In the campaign of 1862, Cold Harbor was General McClellan's head-quarters while he was on the north bank of the Chickahominy, and Jackson, when he advanced to attack Fitz John Porter, marched down the road over which Grant moved, to that locality. It is a place of one house,—an old tavern standing at a crossing of roads, twelve miles from Richmond. The most direct route to the city runs past Gaines's Mills, where the first of the series of battles was fought before Richmond, in the seven days' contest. Jackson's head-quarters were at Cold Harbor during that engagement.

The general position of the two armies in Grant's battles at Cold Harbor is indicated by the accompanying diagram.

A huge catalpa stands in front of the old tavern, where in the peaceful days of the Old Dominion travellers rested their horses beneath the grateful shade, while they drank their toddy at the tavern bar. Two great battles were fought there by Grant, the first in the evening of the 1st of June, the second on the evening of the 3rd.

There is a line of breastworks west of the house, a few rods distant, behind which Russell's division of the Sixth Corps is lying. The road

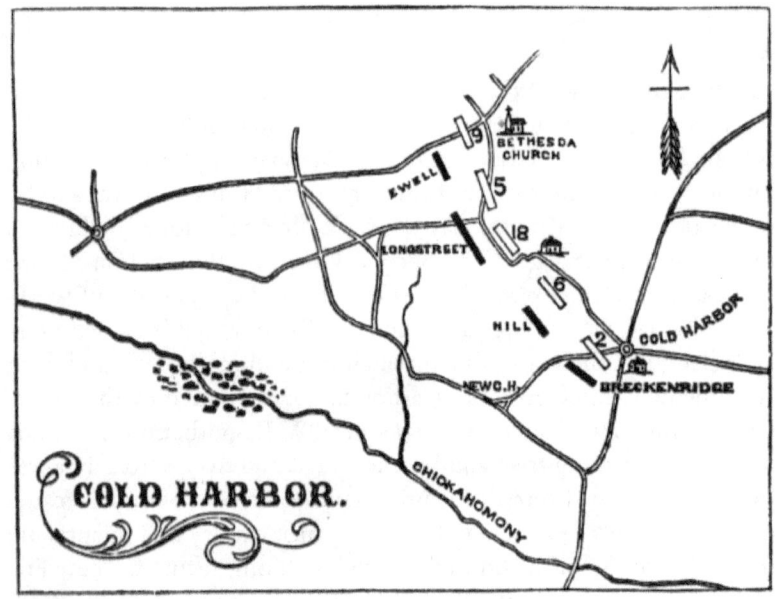

to Despatch Station runs due south; the road to New Cold Harbor southwest, the road to Bethesda Church northwest. In the battle fought on the 1st instant, Neil was east of the road leading to Despatch Station, Russell west of the house, and Ricketts northwest.

Passing toward the right one mile, we come to the house of Daniel Woody, which is in rear of the right of the line of the Eighteenth. It is the head-quarters of General Martindale, who commands the right division of the line. Next is Brooks's division in the centre, with Devens on the left, connecting with Ricketts's on the right of the Sixth.

There is a clear space west of Woody's house, a cornfield lately planted, but now trodden by the feet of Martindale's men. In front of Brooks there is a gentle swell of land, wooded with pines. On the crest of the hill there is a line of Rebel rifle-pits. In front of Devens the swell is smoothed to a plain, or rather there is a depression, as if the hillock had been scooped out of the plain. This also is wooded. The belt of timber stretches over the plain, crossing the road to Gaines's Mill, about half a mile from the tavern,—a dark strip of green twenty or thirty rods in width. Beyond the belt toward Richmond is a smooth field, half a mile in width, bounded on the farther edge, under the shadow of another belt of green, by the line of Beauregard's breastworks. The line of Rebel defence runs diagonally to the road, the distance being less between Ricketts and the work than on the left in front of Neil. This plain is swept by Rebel cannon and thousands of rifles and muskets.

It was past six o'clock—nearly seven—before the troops were in position to move upon the enemy's works. They marched through the woods, emerged upon the open field The Rebel batteries opened with redoubled fury, but the line advanced steadily. Devens found the depression in front of him almost a marsh, with trees felled, forming an *abatis*; but his men passed through, and again came into line. Burnham's brigade, of Brooks's division, containing the Tenth and Thirteenth New Hampshire, Eighth Connecticut, and One Hundred and Eighteenth New York, charged up the hill in front, and took the rifle-pits above them. Ricketts, having less distance to advance than the other divisions of the Sixth, was soonest in the fight, sweeping all before him. Before the Rebels could reload their pieces after the first volley the bayonets of the advancing columns, gleaming in the light of the setting sun, were at their throats. Half a brigade was taken prisoners, while the rest of the Rebels in front of Ricketts fled in disorder.

Russell moving along the road received an enfilading fire from artillery and musketry. The Rebels having recovered from their panic, held on with stubbornness. The broad plain over which Russell moved was fringed with fire. From dark till past ten o'clock Breckenridge tried in vain to recover what he had lost.

The loss was severe to us in killed and wounded. But it was a victory, so signal that a congratulatory order was issued by General Meade to the Sixth Corps.

Lying beneath the ever-moaning pines, with the star-lit heavens for a tent, I listened to the sounds of the battle,—steady, monotonous, like the surf on the beach. An hour's sleep, and still it was rolling in. But all things must have an end. Near midnight it died away, and there was only the chirping of the cricket, the unvarying note of the whip-poor-will, and the wind swaying the stately trees around me. Peaceful all around; but ah! beyond those forest belts were the suffering heroes, parched with thirst, fevered with the fight, bleeding for their country. How shall we thank them? How shall we reward them? What estimate shall we place upon their work? O friends, as you recall this sacrifice, let your hearts warm with devotion to your country. Do honour to the noble dead, and forget not the living,—the widow and the fatherless.

The battle of the 3rd of June was obstinate and bloody, and resulted in great loss to Grant. The artillery firing was constant through the forenoon, but Lee was too strongly entrenched to be driven.

As soon as there was a lull in the roar of battle, I improved the opportunity to visit the hospitals. There were long lines of ambulances bringing in the wounded, who were laid beneath the trees. Unconscious men were upon the tables, helpless in the hands of the surgeons,—to wake from a dreamless sleep with a limb gone, a bleeding stump of a leg or arm. Horrid the gashes where jagged iron had cut through the flesh, severing arteries and tendons in an instant. Heads, hands, legs, and arms mangled and dripping with blood,—human blood! There were moans, low murmurings, wrenched from the men against their wills. Men were babbling, in their delirium, of other scenes,—dim recollections, which were momentary realities. To be with them and not do for them,—to see suffering without power to alleviate,—gives painful tension to nerves, even though one may be familiar with scenes of carnage.

I turned from the scene all but ready to say, "Anything to stay this terrible destruction of human life." But there were other thoughts,—of retributive justice,—of sighs and groans, scourged backs, broken hearts, partings of mothers from their children,—the coffle train, and the various horrors of the accursed system of slavery, the cause of all this "wounding and hurt." I remembered that it was a contest between eternal right and infernal wrong; that He who is of infinite love and tenderness in His war against rebellion, spared not his only begotten Son;—and thus consoled and strengthened, I could wish the contest to go on till victory should crown our efforts, and a permanent peace be the inheritance of our children.

At Cold Harbor the abilities of Lee, McClellan, and Grant as commanders have been exhibited. Lee's head-quarters during the battle of Gaines's Mills were at New Cold Harbor, but during the afternoon he rode over to the old tavern and had a talk with Jackson. That battle was won by Lee after a hard struggle, not through any lack of courage on the part of the Union troops, but through McClellan's want of generalship. McClellan was ever taking counsel of his fears. He uniformly overestimated the numbers of the enemy. When Lee advanced to Munson's Hill, near Alexandria, in October, 1861, his army did not exceed sixty thousand, but McClellan estimated it at "one hundred and fifty thousand, well drilled, equipped, ably commanded, and strongly entrenched."[58] In March, 1862, when Lee evacuated Manassas, his estimate of the Rebel army was one hundred and fifteen thousand, while the actual strength was less than fifty thousand. "It seems clear that I shall have the whole force of the enemy on my hands, probably not less than one hundred thousand, and probably more," wrote McClellan to the Secretary of War upon his arrival at Yorktown.

58: McClellan's Report, p. 46.

Magruder commanded the Rebels at Yorktown. "My whole force," says he, "was less than eleven thousand."[59]

The day before the battle of Cold Harbor, McClellan's estimate of Lee's army was two hundred thousand.[60] His own force, sick and well, on the 20th, was one hundred and seventeen thousand. He had present and fit for duty on the day of battle from one hundred to one hundred and five thousand. Lee's force was two or three thousand less.

McClellan knew very little of Lee's army. He entrusted the management of the secret service to two French princes, who, however estimable they might be as individuals, had a superficial acquaintance with the English language, who knew but little of America or Americans,—whose geographical knowledge of the country in which the war was being carried on was less than that of the scholars of a New England grammar school,—who were wanting in the lawyer-like qualifications necessary to separating the true from the false in the stories of deserters, scouts, and spies. So inefficient was the secret service that McClellan had no information of Lee's movements or intentions till Jackson was at Ashland, within a few hours' march of Cold Harbor. When he saw that he was to be attacked, he moved his own head-quarters to the south side, making no effort to win the battle, thinking only of a retreat to the James.

A general who wins a battle through the blundering of an inefficient opponent cannot be called, on that account alone, a great commander. There must be genius in movements, in making use of positions and forces, so that victory is wrenched from a skilful foe, to entitle a commander to wear the bay leaves upon his brow.

McClellan's army was divided by the Chickahominy. He had about thirty thousand men on the north bank and seventy-five thousand on the south side. Lee submitted a plan to Jeff Davis, which was accepted, by which he hoped to destroy that portion of McClellan's force on the north bank. Whiting's and Ewell's divisions were put on board the cars and sent up the Virginia Central Railroad to Gordonsville, as if to join Jackson in the Shenandoah, or for a march on Washington, but Jackson was on his way towards Richmond. He commanded the united force, amounting to thirty thousand. He moved down to Ashland. A deserter informed McClellan at Cold Harbor that Jackson would attack him on the 28th.[61] Negroes came in on the next day who said that Jackson was at Hanover Court-House. McClellan's line

---

59: Magruder's Report.
60: McClellan's Report, p. 238.
61: McClellan's Report.

was twenty miles long. His extreme right was north of Richmond, at Mechanicsville; his left was southeast of the city, resting on White Oak Swamp. McClellan could have reinforced Porter, and defeated Lee, or he could have withdrawn him to the south bank, and pushed into Richmond, but he left Porter to contend with Lee's entire army, except Magruder's command of about twenty thousand men,[62] while he burned his supplies, destroyed the railroad, and made ready to march to the James. Porter held his ground till nearly night, calling for reinforcements. Had a division been sent him at the right time, Lee would have suffered a terrible defeat. Slocum, of Franklin's corps, was sent over when too late to be of essential service. Jackson extended his left south from the old tavern, and fell upon Porter's right flank, and drove the Union troops, but everywhere else Lee was repulsed with great loss. His entire loss in that battle was about nine thousand and five hundred, McClellan's about four thousand.

Lee moved out from Richmond when Jackson was at Hanover Court-House. Branch's division marched up the Brooke turnpike, A. P. Hill moved over the Mechanicsville turnpike, Longstreet and D. H. Hill by the New Bridge road. McClellan was informed of the movement. Here was his golden opportunity. By throwing nearly his entire army north of the Chickahominy, he could have met Lee outside of his entrenchments, or he could have withdrawn Porter and made a rush upon the city. Lee expected to meet the whole Union army at Cold Harbor, and in the battle supposed he was fighting McClellan's main force.

"The principal part of the enemy was on the north side," says Lee in his report. It is evident that in his plan he calculated that McClellan would not risk a battle with a divided army, and he therefore left but a small force to hold Richmond. Magruder on the other hand, saw the danger to the city. Says Magruder:

> From the time at which the enemy withdrew his forces to this side of the Chickahominy, and destroyed the bridges, to the moment of his evacuation,—that is, from Friday night until Sunday morning,—I considered the situation of our army extremely critical and perilous. The larger portion of it was on either side of the Chickahominy, the bridges had all been destroyed, and but one was rebuilt, the New Bridge, which was fully commanded by the enemy's guns at Golding's; and there were but twenty-five thousand men between his army and

---

62: Pollard, *First Year*, p. 329.

Richmond. I received repeated instructions during Saturday night from General Lee's head-quarters, enjoining upon my command the utmost vigilance, directing the men to sleep on their arms, to be prepared for whatever might occur. I passed the night without sleep, and in the superintendence of their execution. Had McClellan massed his whole force in column, and advanced it against any point of our line of battle, as was done at Austerlitz by the greatest captain of any age, though the head of his column would have suffered greatly, its momentum would have insured him success, and the occupation of our works about Richmond, and consequently the city might have been his reward. Our relief was therefore great when information reached us that the enemy had evacuated his works and was retreating.[63]

Magruder, in the above statement, unintentionally exposes the faultiness of Lee's plan, which, had McClellan improved his opportunity, would have been the loss of the Rebel capital, the rout and disorganization of Lee's army, and a historic page wholly different from that now on record.

In contrast is Grant's plan of operations. His secret-service department was managed with rare ability, by men acquainted with the English language, who were adepts in the art of sifting truth from falsehood. Grant was well informed as to Lee's numbers, the reinforcements at his disposal, and his movements. He took counsel of his courage, never of his fear. In his plan of the Wilderness campaigns, the series of movements from the Rapidan to the James, were duly considered before the orders for the advance were given. When he saw that he could not reach Richmond from the north, he decided to sweep round to the James, but not till he had made it impossible for Lee to move upon Washington, by breaking up the Virginia Central and Fredericksburg Railroad. McClellan complained that he was deprived of the control of McDowell's force at Fredericksburg, which was retained by the President to cover Washington; but the railroad from Richmond to Manassas was then in running order, with the exception of the bridge across the Rappahannock. Grant's prudence in securing Washington was as marked as his tenacity of purpose to push on towards Richmond.

The transfer of the Eighteenth Corps from Bermuda Hundred to seize Cold Harbor,—the order for which was given before the army

---

63: Magruder's Report, p. 191.

crossed the Pamunkey,—was a conception as brilliant as that of Lee's in the transfer of Jackson from the Shenandoah in '62. The march of the army to the south side of the James, which will be narrated in another chapter, was the most striking movement of the campaign, exhibiting the same quality of genius which had been exhibited at Vicksburg, and which has no parallel in the movements of any of the Rebel commanders during the war.

There was a season of rest while Grant was preparing for the march to the James. The army needed it. A month had passed, the most terrible of all the months of the war. There had been scarcely an hour of quiet from the moment when the army broke camp at Culpepper till it reached Cold Harbor. It never can be known how many were killed and wounded in that month of battle. The hospitals of Washington were crowded. Thousands of slightly wounded were granted leave of absence. Reinforcements were hurried on to fill up the wasted ranks. Lee's loss was nearly as heavy as Grant's. Richmond was overflowing with wounded; all central Virginia was a hospital. Both armies were becoming exhausted.

Lee was the attacking party at the Wilderness, but it was his last offensive movement, except as the gauge of battle was given by Grant.

The march from Spottsylvania to Cold Harbor was through a section never before visited by Union troops. At the crossing of the Ny I found quarters at a farm-house owned by a feeble, forceless, gray-bearded, black-eyed man. There was constitutionally a want of starch in his physical organization. He was free and frank, but shiftless. He owned eighty acres of land, two negroes, an old horse, and a rickety cart. His house was mean, but it was charmingly located, overlooking the broad valley of the Mattapony, and surrounded by locusts and magnolias. Nature had done a great deal towards making it a paradise, but the owner had been an indifferent steward. Lying upon the grass beneath the trees, I fell into conversation with the proprietor.

"This is Caroline County, I believe."

"Yes, sir, this is old Caroline,—a county which has sold more negroes down south than any other in Virginia."

"I was not aware of that; but I remember now a negro song which I used to hear. The burden of it was—*I wish I was back in old Caroline.*

"Quite likely, for the great business of the county has been nigger-raising, and it has been our curse. I never owned only old Peter and his wife. I wish I didn't own them, for they are old and I have got to support them; but how in the world I am to do it I don't know, for the soldiers have stripped me of everything."

"Do you mean the Union soldiers?"

"Yes, and ours (Rebels) also. First, my boys were conscripted. I kept them out as long as I could, but they were obliged to go. Then they took my horses. Then your cavalry came and took all my corn and stole my meat, ransacked the house, seized my flour, killed my pigs and chickens, and here I am, stripped of everything."

"It is pretty hard, but your leaders would have it so."

"I know it, sir, and we are getting our pay for it."

It was frankly spoken, and was the first admission I had heard from Southern lips that the South was suffering retribution for the crime of Secession. It probably did not enter his head that the selling of slaves, the breaking up of families, the sundering of heart-strings, the cries and tears and prayers of fathers and mothers, the outrages, the whippings, scourgings, branding with hot irons, were also crimes in the sight of Heaven. Broken hearts were nothing to him,—not that he was naturally worse than other men, but because slavery had blunted sensibility.

During the march the next day towards the North Anna, I halted at a farm-house. The owner had fled to Richmond in advance of the army, leaving his overseer, a stout, burly, red-faced, tobacco-chewing man. There were a score of old buildings on the premises. It had been a notable plantation, yielding luxuriant harvests of wheat, but the proprietor had turned his attention to the culture of tobacco and the breeding of negroes. He sold annually a crop of human beings for the southern market. The day before our arrival, hearing that the Yankees were coming, he hurried forty or fifty souls to Richmond. He intended to take all,—forty or fifty more,—but the negroes fled to the woods. The overseer did his best to collect them, but in vain. The proprietor raved, and stormed, and became violent in his language and behaviour, threatening terrible punishment on all the runaways, but the appearance of a body of Union cavalry put an end to maledictions. He had a gang of men and women chained together, and hurried them toward Richmond.

The runaways came out from their hiding-places when they saw the Yankees, and advanced fearlessly with open countenances. The first pleasure of the negroes was to smile from ear to ear, the second to give everybody a drink of water or a piece of hoe-cake, the third to pack up their bundles and be in readiness to join the army.

"Are you not afraid of us?"

"Afraid! Why, boss, I's been praying for yer to come; and now yer is here, thank de Lord."

"Are you not afraid that we shall sell you?"

"No, boss, I isn't. The overseer said you would sell us off to Cuba, to work in the sugar-mill, but we didn't believe him."

Among the servants was a bright mulatto girl, who was dancing, singing, and manifesting her joy in violent demonstration.

"What makes you so happy?" I asked.

"Because you Yankees have come. I can go home now."

"Is not this your home?"

"No. I come from Williamsport in Maryland."

"When did you come from there?"

"Last year. Master sold me. I spect my brother is 'long with the army. He ran away last year. Master was afraid that I should run away, and he sold me."

The negroes came from all the surrounding plantations. Old men with venerable beards, horny hands, crippled with hard work and harder usage; aged women, toothless, almost blind, steadying their steps with sticks; little negro boys, driving a team of skeleton steers,—mere bones and tendons covered with hide,—or wall-eyed horses, spavined, foundered, and lame, attached to rickety carts and wagons, piled with beds, tables, chairs, pots and kettles, hens, turkeys, ducks, women with infants in their arms, and a sable cloud of children trotting by their side.

"Where are you going?" I said to a short, thick-set, gray-bearded old man, shuffling along the road; his toes bulging from his old boots, and a tattered straw hat on his head,—his gray wool protruding from the crown.

"I do'no, boss, where I's going, but I reckon I'll go where the army goes."

"And leave your old home, your old master, and the place where you have lived all your days?"

"Yes, boss; master, he's gone. He went to Richmond. Reckon he went mighty sudden, boss, when he heard you was coming. Thought I'd like to go along with you."

His face streamed with perspiration. He had been sorely afflicted with the rheumatism, and it was with difficulty that he kept up with the column; but it was not a hard matter to read the emotions of his heart. He was marching towards freedom. Suddenly a light had shined upon him. Hope had quickened in his soul. He had a vague idea of what was before him. He had broken loose from all which he had been accustomed to call his own,—his cabin, a mud-chinked structure, with the ground for a floor, his garden patch,—to go out, in his old age, wholly un-provided-for, yet trusting in God that there would be food and raiment on the other side of Jordan.

NEGROES COMING INTO THE LINES

It was a Jordan to them. It was the Sabbath-day,—bright, clear, calm, and delightful. There was a crowd of several hundred coloured people at a deserted farm-house.

"Will it disturb you if we have a little singing? You see we feel so happy today that we would like to praise the Lord."

It was the request of a middle-aged woman.

"Not in the least. I should like to hear you."

In a few moments a crowd had assembled in one of the rooms. A stout young man, black, bright-eyed, thick-wooled, took the centre of the room. The women and girls, dressed in their best clothes, which they had put on to make their exodus from bondage in the best possible manner, stood in circles round him. The young man began to dance. He jumped up, clapped his hands, slapped his thighs, whirled round, stamped upon the floor.

"Sisters, let us bless the Lord. Sisters, join in the chorus," he said, and led off with a kind of recitative, improvised as the excitement gave him utterance. From my note-book I select a few lines:-

Recitative

We are going to the other side of Jordan.

Chorus

So glad! so glad!
Bless the Lord for freedom,
So glad! so glad!
We are going on our way,
So glad! so glad!
To the other side of Jordan,
So glad! so glad!
Sisters, won't you follow?
So glad! so glad!
Brothers, won't you follow?

And so it went on for a half-hour, without cessation, all dancing, clapping their hands, tossing their heads. It was the ecstasy of action. It was a joy not to be uttered, but demonstrated. The old house partook of their rejoicing. It rang with their jubilant shouts, and shook in all its joints.

I stood an interested spectator. One woman, well dressed, intelligent, refined in her deportment, modest in her manner, said, "It is one way in which we worship, sir. It is our first day of freedom."

The first day of freedom! Behind her were years of suffering, hardship, unrequited toil, heartaches, darkness, no hope of recompense or of light in this life, but a changeless future. Death, aforetime, was their only deliverer. For them there was hope only in the grave. But suddenly Hope had advanced from eternity into time. They need not wait for death; in life they could be free. Is it a wonder that they exhibited extravagant joy?

Apart from the dancers was a woman with light hair, hazel eyes, and fair complexion. She sat upon the broad steps of the *piazza*, and looked out upon the fields, or rather into the air, unmindful of the crowd, the dance, or the shouting. Her features were so nearly of the Anglo-Saxon type that it required a second look to assure one that there was African blood in her veins. She alone of all the crowd was sad in spirit. She evidently had no heart to join in the general jubilee.

"Where did you come from?" I asked.

"From Caroline County."

Almost everyone else would have said, "From old Caroline." There was no trace of the negro dialect, more than you hear from all classes in the South, for slavery has left its taint upon the language; it spares nothing, but is remorseless in its corrupting influences.

"You do not join in the song and dance," I said.

"No, sir."

Most of them would have said "master" or "boss."

"I should think you would want to dance on your first night of freedom, if ever."

"I don't dance, sir, in that way."

"Was your master kind to you?"

"Yes, sir; but he sold my husband and children down South."

The secret of her sadness was out.

"Where are you going? or where do you expect to go?"

"I don't know, sir, and I don't care where I go."

The conversation ran on for some minutes. She manifested no animation, and did not once raise her eyes, but kept them fixed on vacancy. Husband and children sold, gone forever,—there was nothing in life to charm her. Even the prospect of freedom, with its undefined joys and pleasures, its soul-stirring expectations, raising the hopes of those around her, moved her not. Life was a blank. She had lived in her master's family, and was intelligent. She was the daughter of her master. She was high-toned in her feelings. The dancing and shouting of those around her were distasteful. It was to her more barbaric than Christian. She felt her degradation. Freedom could not give her a birthright among the free. The daughter of her master! It was gall and wormwood; and he, her father, had sold her husband and his grandchildren!

I had read of such things. But one needs to come in contact with slavery, to feel how utterly loathsome and hateful it is. There was the broken-hearted victim, so bruised that not freedom itself, neither the ecstasy of those around her, could awaken an emotion of joy. Hour after hour the festivities went on, but there she sat upon the step, looking down the desolate years gone by, or into a dreamless, hopeless future.

It was late at night before the dancers ceased, and then they stopped, not because of a surfeit of joy, but because the time had come for silence in the camp. It was their first Sabbath of freedom, and like the great king of Israel, upon the recovery of the ark of God, they danced before the Lord with all their might.

We had a hard, dusty ride from the encampment at Mongohick to the Pamunkey. It was glorious, however, in the early morning to sweep along the winding forest-road, with the head-quarters' flag in advance. Wherever its silken folds were unfurled, there the two commanders might be found,—General Meade, commanding the Army of the Potomac, and General Grant, the commander of all the forces of the Union in the field. We passed the long line of troops, crossed the Pamunkey upon a pontoon bridge, rode a mile or two across the verdant interval, and halted beneath the oaks, magnolias, and buttonwoods of an old Virginia mansion. The edifice was reared a century ago. It was of wood, stately and substantial. How luxurious the surrounding shade; the smooth lawn, the rolled pathways bordered by box, with moss-roses, honeysuckle, and jessamines scenting the air, and the daisies dotting the greensward! The sweep of open land,—viewing it from the wide portico; the long reach of cultivated grounds; acres of wheat rolling in the breeze, like waves of the ocean; meadow-lands, smooth and fair; distant groves and woodlands,—how magnificent! It was an old estate, inherited by successive generations,—by those whose pride it had been to keep the paternal acres in the family name. But the sons had all gone. A daughter was the last heir. She gave her hand, and heart, and the old homestead,—sheep, horses, a great stock of bovines, and a hundred negroes or more,—to her husband. The family name became extinct, and the homestead of seven or eight generations passed into the hands of one bearing another name.

When McClellan was on the Peninsula, the shadow of the war-cloud swept past the place. One or two negroes ran away, but at that time they were not tolerated in camp. The campaign of 1862 left the estate unharmed. But Sheridan's cavalry, followed by the Sixth Corps, in its magnificent march from the North Anna, had suddenly and unexpectedly disturbed the security of the old plantation. There was a rattling fire from carbines, a fierce fight, men wounded and dead, broken fences, trodden fields of wheat and clover; ransacked stables, corn-bins, meat-houses, and a swift disappearing of live stock of every description.

But to go back a little. The proprietor of this estate ardently espoused Secession. His wife was as earnest as he. They hated the North. They loved the institutions and principles of the South. They sold their surplus negroes in the Richmond market. They parted husbands and wives, tore children from the arms of their mothers, and separated them forever. They lived on unrequited labour, and grew rich through the breeding of human flesh for the market.

When the war commenced, the owner of this magnificent estate enlisted in the army and was made a Colonel of cavalry. He furnished supplies and kept open house for his comrades in arms; but he fell in a cavalry engagement on the Rappahannock, in October, 1863, leaving a wife and three young children. The advance of the army, its sudden appearance on the Pamunkey, left Mrs.—— no time to remove her personal estate, or to send her negroes to Richmond for safe keeping. Fitz-Hugh Lee disputed Sheridan's advance. The fighting began on this estate. Charges by squadrons and regiments were made through the corn-fields. Horses, cattle, hogs, sheep, were seized by the cavalrymen. The garden, filled with young vegetables, was spoiled. In an hour there was complete desolation. The hundred negroes—cook, steward, chambermaid, house and field hands, old and young—all left their work and followed the army. Mrs.—— was left to do her own work. The parlours of the stately mansion were taken by the surgeons for a hospital. The change which Mrs.—— experienced was from affluence to abject poverty, from power to sudden helplessness.

Passing by one of the negro cabins on the estate, I saw a middle-aged coloured woman packing a bundle.

"Are you going to move?" I asked.

"Yes, sir; I am going to follow the army."

"What for? Where will you go?"

"I want to go to Washington, to find my husband. He ran away awhile ago, and is at work in Washington."

"Do you think it right, auntie, to leave your mistress, who has taken care of you so long?"

She had been busy with her bundle, but stopped now and stood erect before me, her hands on her hips. Her black eyes flashed.

"Taken care of me! What did she ever do for me? Haven't I been her cook for more than thirty years? Haven't I cooked every meal she ever

FORAGING

ate in that house? What has she done for me in return? She has sold my children down South, one after another. She has whipped me when I cried for them. She has treated me like a hog, sir! Yes, sir, like a hog!"

She resumed her work of preparation for leaving. That night she and her remaining children joined the thousands of coloured people who had already taken sudden leave of their masters.

Returning to the mansion to see the wounded, I met Mrs.—in the hall. She was tall, robust, dignified. She evidently did not fully realize the great change which had taken place in her affairs. The change was not complete at that moment. The coloured steward was there, hat in hand; obsequious, bowing politely, and obeying all commands. A half-hour before I had seen him in the cook's cabin, making arrangements for leaving the premises, and a half-hour later he was on his way toward freedom.

"I wish I had gone to Richmond," said the lady. "This is terrible, terrible! They have taken all my provisions, all my horses and cattle. My servants are going. What shall I do?" She sank upon the sofa, and for a moment gave way to her feelings.

"You are better off here than you would be there, with the city full of wounded, and scant supplies in the market," I remarked.

"You are right, sir. What could I do with my three little children there? Yet how I am to live here I don't know. When will this terrible war come to an end?"

But enough of this scene. I have introduced it because it is real, and because it is but one of many. There are hundreds of Southern homes where the change has been equally great. Secession is not what they who started it thought it would be. The penalties for crime always come, sooner or later. God's scales are correctly balanced. He makes all things even. For every tear wrung from the slave by injustice, for every broken heart, for the weeping and wailing of mothers for their babes sold to the far-off South, for every wrong there is retribution

Though the mills of God grind slowly,
Yet they grind exceeding small;
Though with patience he stands waiting,
With exactness grinds he all.

CHAPTER 20

To Petersburg

June, 1864

General Grant had tried to break Lee's lines at Cold Harbor, and had been repulsed with great loss. The Richmond newspapers were jubilant. "He is floundering in the swamps of Chickahominy. He has reached the graveyard of Yankee armies," said they.

The newspapers opposed to the war and in sympathy with the Rebellion, in the North, made Cold Harbor an occasion for glorifying General McClellan, their candidate for the Presidency.

"Grant is a butcher. He has sacrificed a hundred thousand lives. He acts under Lincoln's orders. Elect McClellan, and we shall have peace."

The army was dejected, but did not lose heart. It had been repulsed, had lost many brave men, but it had pushed Lee from the Wilderness to Richmond.

I conversed freely with the soldiers, and rarely found one who had not full confidence in the ability of General Grant. Round their bivouac fires the history of the Army of the Potomac was freely discussed. The old soldiers, who had fought in the first Cold Harbor battle, remembered how twenty-seven thousand men held Lee at bay on that ground through the long hours of the first of the seven days' fight in front of Richmond; how McClellan kept sixty thousand men on the south bank of the Chickahominy, inactive,—sending a brigade to their aid when too late to be of use. They recalled the scenes of those terrible demoralizing days,—how McClellan kept out of harm's way. When the battle was raging on the north bank of the Chickahominy he was south of it; when Sumner was holding Savage Station, McClellan was across White Oak Swamp; when Glendale was fought, and the Rebels under Hill routed, McClellan was at Malvern, and while Magruder was madly pushing his troops on to be slaughtered at Malvern, McClellan was on board a gunboat; how in the night the whole army was ordered away from a victorious field, from an impregnable position, while Lee was fleeing towards Richmond! Soldiers who had come later into the service remembered the failure at Fredericksburg and the retreat from Chancellorsville, and in contrast saw that Grant had pluck. It is a quality of character which soldiers admire. They could also see that there was system in his movements. They sometimes spoke of him as the Grand Flanker. "He'll flank Lee out of Richmond yet; see if he don't," said a soldier.

If Grant had failed to move Lee from his position in a direct attack, Lee also had failed to drive Grant from the junction of the roads at old Cold Harbor,—an important point, as, by opening the railroad from White House, he could easily bring up his supplies. His army was intact,—not divided, as McClellan's had been by the dark and sluggish Chickahominy.

"What will Grant do?" was a question often discussed around the mess-tables of brigadiers, colonels, and captains,—by men who were bound to obey all orders, but who nevertheless had their own ideas as to the best method of conducting the campaign. The Lieutenant-General had the whole plan of operations settled for him many times. It was amusing to see the strategic points indicated on the maps.

"He can swing in north of the city upon the high lands. The Chickahominy swamps don't extend above Mechanicsville," said one.

"But how will he get his supplies?"

"Open the Fredericksburg road. It is open now from Aquia Creek to the Rappahannock."

But Grant, instead of opening the road, determined to break it up completely, also the Virginia Central, which runs to Gordonsville, to prevent Lee from moving upon Washington. Up to this time all of his movements, while they were upon Lee's flank, had not uncovered that city; but now Washington would take care of itself.

The plan of the campaign had been well matured by General Grant before he started from Culpepper. He says:

> My idea from the start had been to beat the enemy north of Richmond if possible. Then after destroying his lines of communication north of the James River, to transfer the army to the south side, and besiege Lee in Richmond, or follow him south if he should retreat.[64]

Grant was not willing to sacrifice his men. He resolved to transfer

---

64: Grant's Official Report.

his army south of the James, and cut Lee's communications. Gregg was sent in advance, with the cavalry belonging to the Army of the Potomac, crossing the Chickahominy, and making a rapid movement by the left flank.

Lee evidently did not mistrust Grant's intention,—judging from the disposition he made of his troops, and the tardiness with which he marched to counteract the movement. The transfer of the Eighteenth Corps from Bermuda Hundred to Cold Harbor undoubtedly had its effect upon Lee's calculations. It was an indication that Grant intended to keep Washington covered.

Hunter at this time was advancing from the West. Sheridan, who had been guarding the road to White House, was withdrawn, and sent with two divisions of his cavalry up the Virginia Central road to Gordonsville, hoping to meet Hunter at Charlottesville; but Hunter had moved on Lynchburg, and the union of the forces was not effected. Sheridan's movement, however, threw dust in the eyes of Lee.

Grant knew that Petersburg was held by a handful of Rebel troops,—Wise's Legion. The citizens had been organized into a battalion, but the place could be taken by surprise. Strong earthworks had been thrown up around the city early in the war, but the troops in the city were not sufficient to man them. Grant believed that the place could be seized without difficulty; and taking a steamer at White House went to Bermuda Hundred, held a conference with Butler, who sent Gillmore with thirty-five hundred men across the Appomattox, near the Point of Rocks, to attack the city from the east. At the same time, Kautz's division of cavalry was sent, by a long detour, across the Norfolk Railroad, to enter the town from the south. Having made these arrangements, Grant returned to his army, which had been lying behind its entrenchments at Cold Harbor.

Preparations had been quietly making for a rapid march. The Second Corps had been moved down towards the Chickahominy. The Fifth was sent to Despatch Station. Gregg and Torbett, with their divisions of cavalry, were placed at Bottom's Bridge. The Rebel pickets were there on watch. Meanwhile workmen were busily engaged in opening the railroad. Lee must have known that Grant had a new movement under way, the precise nature of which it was difficult to understand.

The movement of Gillmore was a disgraceful failure. He crossed the Appomattox on the evening of the 10th of June, without molestation, marched up within sight of the city spires, discovered a formidable line of breastworks, and without making an attack, turned about and retired to Bermuda Hundred. Kautz, on the contrary, after a rapid movement, entered the city from the south, but Gillmore having retreated, could not hold it, and was obliged to retire.

Grant was justly indignant when he heard of the failure. It was a golden opportunity lost. Gillmore and Kautz could have taken and held the place till the arrival of reinforcements. Gillmore was wholly responsible for the failure. Grant once more hurried to Bermuda Hundred, to superintend in a second movement, leaving Meade to conduct the army from Cold Harbor to the James.

The grand movement from the north of Richmond, by which the whole army was placed south of that city, was begun on the 12th, in the evening. Wilson's division of cavalry was thrown across the Chickahominy, and sent to seize Long Bridge in White Oak Swamp. The Fifth Corps followed. The Rebels struck the Fifth Corps in flank, but Crawford repulsed them. The Second Corps followed the Fifth. The Sixth and Ninth crossed at Jones's Bridge, while the fifty miles of wagon trains swung far to the east and crossed the swamp fifteen miles below. Gregg covered the flank of the army with his cavalry, concealing the movement. The men had a hard time, being attacked constantly by the Rebel cavalry and infantry. It was of the utmost importance to Lee to know where Grant intended to strike, whether north of the James, by the Charles City and New Market roads, or across the James at Dutch Gap, joining his forces with Butler's, or whether his movement was directly upon Petersburg.

Lee moved on the inner circle with great caution.

The Eighteenth Corps took water transportation from White House, and arrived at Bermuda Hundred at midnight on the 14th. Grant was there. He ordered General Smith to proceed at once against Petersburg. If successful in the seizure of that place, Lee would be compelled to leave Richmond. It was in the line of his direct communication with the South. Losing that place, he would have only the Danville road, and Grant would soon deprive him of that. The Appomattox would be Grant's line of defence. Seizing it Grant could bide his time. He could become a patient watcher, and Lee would be a victim to circumstances.

Grant was quick to see the advantages to be gained. Lee was slower in arriving at a perception of the fatal consequences to himself which would result from the loss of the place; but when awakened to a sense of his danger, acted with great energy. On the other hand, Smith, who was entrusted with the execution of the enterprise, was dilatory in the execution. Birney in part is to be held responsible for the delay in the execution of the order.

"Push on and capture the place at all hazards! You shall have the whole army to reinforce you," said Grant to Smith. Grant was in such haste to have Smith move, that he did not stop to write the order. He believed that Smith could reach Petersburg before Lee could make his detour through Richmond.

A. P. Hill had already been thrown south of Richmond, and was in front of Butler. The scouts up the Appomattox reported the rumbling of heavy trains along the Richmond and Petersburg railroad. Lee was putting his troops into the cars. The dash of Kautz, and the movement of Gillmore up to the entrenchments, and his retirement without an attack, had resulted in the manning of the Petersburg batteries. A brigade had been thrown down towards City Point, five miles from Petersburg. Soon after daylight the cavalry came upon the Rebel pickets, by the City Point railroad, beyond which they found the Rebels with two cannon behind rifle-pits, in the centre of an open field on Bailey's farm.

Hinks's division of the Eighteenth Corps was composed of coloured troops, who had never been under fire. Would they fight? That was the important question. After a reconnoissance of the position by General Hinks, the troops were formed for an assault. The Rebel cannon opened. The sons of Africa did not flinch, but took their positions with deliberation. They had been slaves; they stood face to face with their former masters, or with their representatives. The flag in front of them waving in the morning breeze was the emblem of oppression; the banner above them was the flag of the free. Would an abject, servile race, kept in chains four thousand years, assert their manhood? Interesting the problem. Their brothers had given the lie to the assertion of the white man, that negroes wouldn't fight, at Wagner and Port Hudson. Would they falter?

The Rebels were on a knoll in the field, and had a clear sweep of all the approaches. The advancing troops must come out from the woods, rush up the slope, and carry it at the point of the bayonet, receiving the tempest of musketry and canister.

Hinks deployed his line. At the word of command the coloured men stepped out from the woods, and stood before the enemy. They gave a volley, and received one in return. Shells crashed through them, but, unheeding the storm, with a yell they started up the slope upon the run. They received one charge of canister, one scathing volley of musketry. Seventy of their number went down, but the living hundreds rushed on. The Rebels did not wait their coming, but fled towards Petersburg, leaving one of the pieces of artillery in the hands of their assailants, who leaped over the works, turned it in a twinkling, but were not able to fire upon the retreating foe, fleeing in consternation towards the main line of entrenchments two miles east of the city.

The coloured troops were wild with joy. They embraced the captured cannon with affectionate enthusiasm, patting it as if it were animate, and could appreciate the endearment.

"Every soldier of the coloured division was two inches taller for that achievement," said an officer describing it. These regiments were the Fifth and Twenty-Second United States coloured troops, who deserve honourable mention in history.

Brooks's division now moved up. Martindale was approaching Petersburg by the river road. By noon the whole corps was in front of the main line of works. Martindale was on the right, by the river, Brooks in the centre, Hinks on the left, with Kautz's division of cavalry sweeping down to the Jerusalem road, which enters Petersburg from the southeast.

Smith delayed unaccountably to make the attack. It was a priceless moment. A reconnoissance showed a line of strong works, in which were eighteen pieces of field artillery. The forts were well built, and connected with breastworks, but the Rebels had not soldiers enough to man them. The citizens of Petersburg had been called out to hold the town. It is evident that Smith might just as well have accomplished at one o'clock what was achieved at sunset. He was a brave officer, fearless in battle, an engineer of ability, reckless of danger, but failed to see the necessity of impetuous action. The value of time was left out of his calculations.

General Grant thus speaks of Smith's operations:

> General Smith got off as directed, and confronted the enemy's pickets near Petersburg before daylight next morning, but for some reason that I have never been able to satisfactorily understand, did not get ready to assault his main lines until near sundown. Then, with a part of his command only, he made the assault, and carried the lines northeast of Petersburg from the Appomattox River, for a distance of over two and a half miles, capturing fifteen pieces of artillery and three hundred prisoners. This was about seven p. m.[65]

The main road leading east from Petersburg ascends a hill two miles out, upon the top of which stands the house of Mr. Dunn. The house is a few rods south of the road. In front of it is a fort; another

---

65: Grant's Report.

south; a third north, and other works, with heavy embankments and deep ditches. The woods in front of the house of Mr. Dunn were cut down in 1862, when McClellan was on the Peninsula, and the trunks of the trees, blackened by fire, are lying there still, forming an *abatis*. The ground is nearly level, and the Rebel riflemen have a fair view of the entire field. It is three hundred and sixty paces from the forts to the woods, in the edge of which Hinks's division of coloured troops are lying. The guns in the forts by the house of Mr. Dunn give a direct front fire, while those by the house of Mr. Osborn on the north enfilade the line. Brooks is in position to move upon the batteries by Osborn's house, while Martindale is to advance up the railroad.

The troops were placed in line for the attack not far from one o'clock. They were exposed to the fire of the artillery. Hinks impatiently waited for orders. Two o'clock passed. The shells from the Rebel batteries were doing damage.

"Lie down!" said he to his men. They obeyed, and were somewhat sheltered.

Three o'clock! four o'clock,—five,—still no orders. Duncan's brigade was lying on both sides of the road, a short distance north of Buffum's house.

At length the word was given. Duncan threw forward a cloud of skirmishers. The Rebels opened with renewed vigour from the batteries; and the infantry, resting their muskets over the breastworks, fired at will and with great accuracy of aim. Men dropped from the advancing ranks. It was of little use to fire in return. "On! push on!" was the order. Hinks and Duncan both entered heartily into the movement. They had chafed all the afternoon at the delay; but had been admiring observers of the conduct of the troops under the fire of shells.

The skirmishers advanced quickly within close range, followed by the main line, moving more slowly over the fallen timber. The skirmishers gave a yell and pushed on, without waiting for the main body. They leaped into the ditches in front of the breastworks, and climbed on their hands and knees up the steep embankments. The Rebels above fired into their faces, and many a brave fellow rolled back dead to the bottom.

The column, perceiving the advance of their comrades, and catching the enthusiasm, broke into a run, rushing upon the forts, sweeping round the curtains, scaling the breastworks, and dashing madly at the Rebels, who fled towards Petersburg. Brooks's men at the same moment swarmed over the embankments by Osborn's, while Martindale advanced along the railroad. Fifteen pieces and three hundred men were captured, of which two thirds of the prisoners and nine cannon were taken by the coloured troops, who wheeled the guns instantly upon the enemy, and then, seizing the spades and shovels which the Rebels had left behind, reversed the fortifications and made them a stronghold.

Through the months which followed the coloured troops looked back to this exploit with pride. They never were weary of talking about it,—how they advanced, how they leaped over the entrenchments, how the Rebels went down the hill upon the run.

Smith had possession of the fortifications at 7 p. m. He ought to have moved on. There were no other works between him and Petersburg. Not a brigade from Lee had reached the city, and the disaster was calculated to demoralize the Rebel soldiers. The Second Corps had arrived. Birney, who had the advance of that corps, ought to have been on the ground by mid-afternoon, and Smith had delayed the assault on his account. He expected Birney to appear on his left, and attack by the Jerusalem plank-road; but that officer, by taking the wrong road, went several miles out of his way. Had he been in position at the time Smith expected him, the attack would have been made at 3 o'clock instead of at 7.

Smith's delay to follow up the advantage gained was an error. General Grant says:

> Between the line thus captured and Petersburg there were no other works, and there was no evidence that the enemy had reinforced Petersburg with a single brigade from any source. The night was clear,—the moon shining brightly,—and favourable to further operations. General Hancock, with two divisions of the Second Corps, had reached General Smith just after dark, and offered the service of these troops as he (Smith) might wish, waiving rank to the named commander, who, he naturally supposed, knew best the position of affairs. But instead of taking these troops and pushing on at once into Petersburg, he requested General Hancock to relieve a part of his line in the captured works, which was done before midnight.[66]

Not till the Rebel outpost on Bailey's farm fell into the hands of the coloured troops did Lee fully comprehend Grant's movement. Then there were lively movements in the Rebel ranks. All of the railroad cars in Richmond were put upon the road. Brigades were hurried through the streets, piled into the cars, and sent whirling towards Petersburg.

66: Grant's Report.

While Lee was watching the Charles City and Newmarket roads, north of the James, expecting Grant in that direction, Butler sent General Terry, with a portion of the Tenth Corps, on a reconnoissance in front of Bermuda Hundred. Terry encountered the Rebel pickets, drove them in, reached the main line, attacked vigorously, broke through, carrying all before him, and pushed on to the railroad at Port Walthall Junction, cut down the telegraph, and tore up the track.

This was an advantage not expected by Grant, who at once ordered two divisions of the Sixth Corps, under Wright, to report to Butler at Bermuda Hundred; but that officer, instead of moving rapidly, advanced leisurely, and even halted awhile.

Terry was attacked by A. P. Hill and obliged to fall back. Grant had the mortification of learning in the evening that, through the dilatory movements of the troops under Smith and Wright, his plans had failed.

In the counsels of the Almighty the time for final victory had not come. God reigns, but men act freely nevertheless. There have been numerous instances during the war where great events hung on little things. An interesting chapter might be written of the occasions where the scales were seemingly evenly balanced, and where, to the eye of faith, the breath of the Almighty turned them for the time.

At Bull Run the victory was lost to the Union arms through the mistake of Captain Barry.[67] At Pittsburg Landing, if Johnston had attacked from the northwest instead of the southwest,—if he had deflected his army a mile,—far different, in all human probability, would have been the result of that battle.

Was the arrival of the *Monitor* in Hampton Roads on that morning, after the havoc made by the Merrimac, accidental? How providential rather! How singular, if not a providence, that the wind should blow so wildly from the southwest on that night of the withdrawal of the army from Fredericksburg, wafting the rumbling of Burnside's artillery and the tramp of a hundred thousand men away from the listening ears of the enemy within close musket-shot! Events which turn the scales according to our desires we are inclined to count as special providences: but the disaster at Bull Run, the sitting down of McClellan in the mud at Yorktown; the lost opportunities for moving upon Richmond after Williamsburg and Fair Oaks; also, while the battle was raging at Gaines's Mills and at Glendale; the pusillanimous retreat from Malvern; the inaction at Antietam; Hooker's retreat from

---

67: See *My Days and Nights on the Battlefield* (available in a Leonaur edition); also testimony of Captain Ricketts and Captain Griffin, in *Report of Committee on Conduct of the War*.

Chancellorsville,—from Lee, who also was in retreat,—are inexplicable events. Meade's waiting at Boonsboro, Lee's escape, Gillmore's unexplained turning back from Petersburg, Wright's halting when everything depended on haste, Smith's delay,—all of these are mysterious providences to us, though to the Rebels they were at the time plain interpositions of God. God's system is reciprocal; everything has its use, everything is for a purpose. We read blindly, but to reason and faith there can be but one result,—the establishment of justice and righteousness between man and man and his Maker. There must be a righting of every wrong, an atonement for every crime.

> *The laws of changeless justice bind*
> *Oppressor with oppressed;*
> *And, close as sin and suffering joined,*
> *We march to fate abreast.*

It must have been evident to most observers, that as the war progressed men were brought to a recognition of God, as an overruling power in the mighty conflict. In the first uprising of the people there was pure, intense patriotism. The battle of Bull Run stung the loyal masses of the North, and filled them with a determination to redeem their tarnished honour. The failure of the Peninsular campaigns, the terrible disasters in 1862, crushed and bruised men's spirits. They began to talk of giving freedom to the slave as well as of the restoration of the Union.

"My paramount object is to save the Union, and not either to save or destroy slavery," wrote President Lincoln to Horace Greeley, August 22nd, 1862, reflecting doubtless the feelings of nearly a majority of the people. Whittier had already expressed, in the lines quoted earlier, the feelings of those who saw that slavery or the nation must die.

Two years passed, and Abraham Lincoln gave utterance to other sentiments in his second inaugural address to the people. Disaster, suffering, a view of Gettysburg battle-field, the consecration of that cemetery as the hallowed resting-place of the patriotic dead, had given him a clear insight of God's truth. Thus spoke he from the steps of the Capitol:

> The Almighty has his own purposes. Woe unto the world because of offences! for it must needs be that offences come; but woe to that man by whom the offence cometh! If we shall suppose that American slavery is one of these offences, which in the providence of God must needs come, but which, having continued through his appointed time, he now wills to remove, and that he gives to both North and South this terrible war as

the woe due to those by whom the offence came, shall we discern therein any departure from those Divine attributes which the believers in a living God always ascribe to him? Fondly do we hope, fervently do we pray, that the mighty scourge of war may speedily pass away. Yet if God wills that it continue until all the wealth piled by the bondman's two hundred and fifty years of unrequited toil shall be sunk, and until every drop of blood drawn with the lash shall be paid by another drawn by the sword, as was said three thousand years ago, so still must it be said, the judgments of the Lord are true and righteous altogether.

It was the recognition of these principles that made the people patient under the severe afflictions, the disasters, the failures. Fathers and mothers, weeping for their sons slain in battle, said to their hearts, "Be still!" for they saw that God was leading the people, through suffering, to recognize justice and righteousness as the Republic,—that thus he was saving the nation from perdition.

The heroism of the coloured soldiers, and their splendid achievements, won the respect of the army. Their patriotism was as sublime, their courage as noble, as that of their whiter-hued comrades boasting Anglo-Saxon blood, nurtured and refined by centuries of civilization.

On the morning after the battle, an officer, passing through the hospital, came upon a coloured soldier who had lost his left leg.

"Well, my boy, I see that you have lost a leg for glory," said the officer.

"No, sir; I have not lost it for glory, but for the elevation of my race!"

It was a reply worthy of historic record, to be read, through the coming centuries, by every sable son of Africa, and by every man, of whatever lineage or clime, struggling to better his condition.

The negroes manifested their humanity as well as their patriotism.

"While the battle was raging," said General Hinks, "I saw two wounded negroes helping a Rebel prisoner, who was more severely wounded, to the rear."

"Give the water to my suffering soldiers," said the wounded Philip Sidney. The incident stands upon the historic page, and has been rehearsed in story and song, as worthy of admiration. Shall not this act of two unknown coloured soldiers also have a place in history?

The time, we trust, will come when men will be rated for what they are worth,—when superiority will consist, not in brute force, but in moral qualities. The slaveholders of the South, at the beginning of the war, esteemed themselves superior to the men of the North, and immeasurably above their slaves; but in contrast,—to the shame of the

slaveholders,—stands the massacre at Fort Pillow and the humanity of the coloured soldiers in front of Petersburg.

On the night of the 16th, Burnside arrived with the Ninth Corps. Neill's division of the Sixth also arrived. Burnside attacked the Rebels, but was repulsed. The lines were reconnoitred, and it was determined to make a second assault.

About half a mile south of the house of Mr. Dunn was the residence of Mr. Shand, held by the Rebels. During the cannonade which preceded the assault, a Rebel officer entered the house and sat down to play a piano. Suddenly he found himself sitting on the floor, the stool having been knocked away by a solid shot, without injury to himself.

The house was a large two-story structure, fronting east, painted white, with great chimneys at either end, shaded by buttonwoods and gum-trees, with a peach-orchard in rear. Fifty paces from the front-door was a narrow ravine, fifteen or twenty feet deep, with a brook, fed by springs, trickling northward. West of the house, about the same distance, was another brook, the two joining about twenty rods north of the house. A Rebel brigade held this tongue of land, with four guns beneath the peach-trees. Their main line of breastworks was along the edge of the ravine east of the house. South, and on higher ground, was a *redan*,—a strong work with two guns, which enfiladed the ravine. Yet General Burnside thought that if he could get his troops into position, unperceived, he could take the tongue of land, which would break the Rebel line and compel them to evacuate the *redan*. Several attempts had been made by the Second Corps to break the line farther north, but without avail. This movement, if not successful, would be attended with great loss; nevertheless, it was determined to make the assault.

It was past midnight when General Potter led his division of the Ninth down into the ravine. The soldiers threw aside their knapsacks, haversacks, tin plates and cups, and moved stealthily. Not a word was spoken. The watches of the officers in command had been set to a second. They reached the ravine where the pickets were stationed, and moved south, keeping close under the bank. Above them, not fifteen paces distant, were the Rebel pickets, lying behind a bank of sand.

If their listening ears caught the sound of a movement in the ravine, they gave no alarm, and the troops took their positions undisturbed. The moon was full. Light clouds floated in the sky. Not a sound, save the distant rumble of wagons, or an occasional shot from the pickets, broke the silence of the night. The attacking column was composed of Griffin's and Curtin's brigades,—Griffin on the right. He had the Seventeenth Vermont and Eleventh New Hampshire in his front line, and the Ninth New Hampshire and Thirty-Second Maine in the second. Curtin had six regiments,—the Thirty-Sixth Massachusetts, and the Forty-Fifth and Forty-Eighth Pennsylvania, in his front line; the Seventh Rhode Island, Twelfth New York, and Fifty-Eighth Massachusetts in his second line.

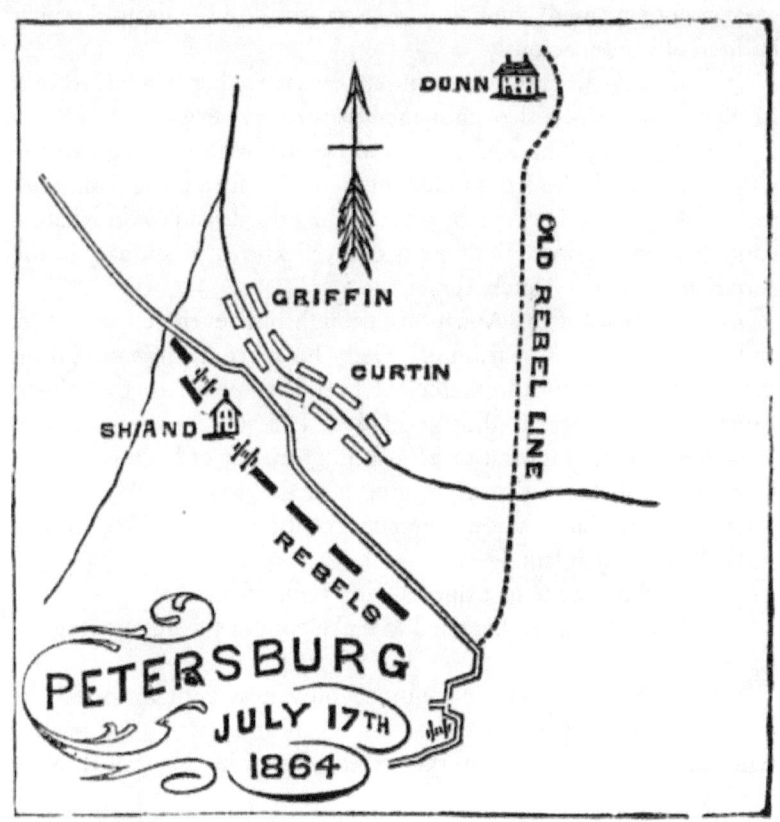

The soldiers were worn with hard marching and constant fighting, and had but just arrived from City Point, yet they took their positions without flinching. The officers gazed at the hands of their watches in the moonlight, and saw them move on to the appointed time,—fifteen minutes past three. Twenty paces,—a spring up the steep bank would carry the men to the Rebel pickets; fifty paces to the muzzles of the enemy's guns.

"All ready!" was whispered from man to man. They rose from the ground erect. Not a gun-lock clicked. The bayonet was to do the work.

"*Hurrah!*" The lines rise like waves of the sea. There are straggling shots from the Rebel pickets, four flashes of light from the

Rebel cannon by the house, two more from the *redan*, one volley from the infantry, wildly aimed, doing little damage. On,—up to the breastworks! Over them, seizing the guns! A minute has passed. Four guns, six hundred and fifty prisoners, fifteen hundred muskets, and four stands of colours are the trophies. The Rebel line is broken. The great point is gained, compelling Lee to abandon the ground which he has held so tenaciously.

In the Fifty-Seventh Massachusetts was a soldier named Edward M. Schneider. When the regiment was formed he was a student in Phillips Academy, Andover. From motives of patriotism, against the wishes of friends, he left the literature of the ancients and the history of the past, to become an actor in the present and to do what he could for future good. His father is the well-known missionary of the American Board at Aintab, Turkey.

On the march from Annapolis, though but seventeen years old, and unaccustomed to hardship, he kept his place in the ranks, from the encampment by the waters of the Chesapeake to the North Anna, where he was slightly wounded. The surgeons sent him to Port Royal for transportation to Washington, but of his own accord he returned to his regiment, joining it at Cold Harbor. While preparing for the charge upon the enemy's works, on the 17th instant, he said to the chaplain,—

"I intend to be the first one to enter their breastworks."

The brave young soldier tried to make good his words, leading the charge.

He was almost there,—not quite: almost near enough to feel the hot flash of the Rebel musketry in his face; near enough to be covered with sulphurous clouds from the cannon, when he fell, shot through the body.

He was carried to the hospital, with six hundred and fifty of his division comrades; but lay all night with his wound undressed, waiting his turn without a murmur. The chaplain looked at his wound.

"What do you think of it?"

Seeing that it was mortal, the chaplain was overcome with emotion. He remembered the last injunction of the young soldier's sister: "I commit him to your care."

The young hero interpreted the meaning of the tears,—that there was no hope.

"Do not weep," said he; "it is God's will. I wish you to write to my father, and tell him that I have tried to do my duty to my country and to God."

He disposed of his few effects, giving ten dollars to the Christian Commission, twenty dollars to the American Board, and trifles to his friends. Then, in the simplicity of his heart, said,—

"I have a good many friends, schoolmates, and companions. They will want to know where I am,—how I am getting on. You can let them know that I am gone, and that I die content. And, chaplain, the boys in the regiment,—I want you to tell them to stand by the dear old flag! And there is my brother in the navy,—write to him and tell him to stand by the flag and cling to the cross of Christ!"

The surgeon examined the wound.

"It is my duty to tell you that you will soon go home," said he.

"Yes, doctor, I am going home. I am not afraid to die. I don't know how the valley will be when I get to it, but it is all bright now."

Then, gathering up his waning strength, he repeated the verse often sung by the soldiers, who, amid all the whirl and excitement of the camp and battle-field, never forget those whom they have left behind them,—mother, sister, father, brother. Calmly, clearly, distinctly he repeated the lines,—the chorus of the song:

Soon with angels I'll be marching,
With bright laurels on my brow;
I have for my country fallen,—
Who will care for sister now?

The night wore away. Death stole on. He suffered intense pain, but not a murmur escaped his lips. Sabbath morning dawned, and with the coming of the light he passed away.

"I die content," said Wolfe, at Quebec, when told that the French were fleeing.

"Stand up for Jesus," said Dudley Tyng, in his last hours: words which have warmed and moved thousands of Christian hearts.

"Let me die with my face to the enemy," was the last request of General Rice, Christian, soldier, and patriot, at Spottsylvania; but equally worthy of remembrance are the words of Edward M. Schneider,—boy, student, youthful leader of the desperate charge at Petersburg. They are the essence of all that Wolfe and Tyng and Rice uttered in their last moments. His grave is near the roadside, marked by a rude paling. The summer breeze sweeps through the sighing pines above the heaved-up mound. Mournful, yet sweet, the music of the wind-harp;—mournful, in that one so young, so full of life and hope and promise, should go so soon; sweet, in that he did his work so nobly. Had he lived a century he could not have completed it more thoroughly or faithfully. His was a short soldier's life, extending only from the peaceful shades of Andover to the entrenchments of Petersburg; but O, how full!

Will the tree of Liberty prematurely decay, if nourished by such life-giving blood? It is costly, but the fruit is precious. For pain and anguish, waste and desolation, we have such rich recompense as this,—such examples of patriotic ardour, heroic daring, and Christian fortitude, that make men nobler, nations greater, and the world better by their contemplation.

I have stood by the honoured dust of those whose names are great in history, whose deeds and virtues are commemorated in brass and marble, who were venerated while living and mourned when dead; but never have I felt a profounder reverence for departed worth than for this young Christian soldier, uncoffined, unshrouded, wrapped only in his blanket, and sleeping serenely beneath the evergreen pines.

His last words—the messages to his comrades, to his father, and his brother—are worthy to live so long as the flag of our country shall wave or the cross of Christ endure.

"Stand up for the dear old flag and cling to the cross of Christ!" They are the emblems of all our hopes for time and eternity. Short, full, rounded, complete his life. Triumphant, glorious his death!

* * * * * * * *

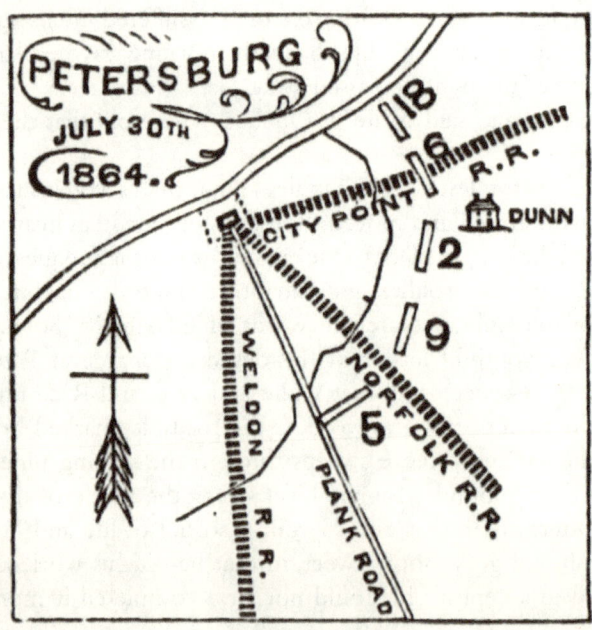

Grant determined to assault all along the line on the morning of the 18th, as nearly the entire army had arrived. Lee, however, fell back during the night to a new position nearer the city.

But the attack was made. The Eighteenth, Second, and Sixth Corps gained no advantage; but the Ninth and Fifth drove the Rebels across the Norfolk Railroad, and reached the Jerusalem plank-road. The position of the besieging army is shown by the accompanying diagram.

On the 21st of June Grant attempted to take the Weldon Railroad with the Second and Sixth Corps, but was opposed by the Rebels on Davis's farm, beyond the Jerusalem road, and a battle ensued.

The engagement was renewed the next day. There was a gap in the lines, of which A. P. Hill took advantage, and attacked Barlow's division in flank. A severe struggle followed, in which Gibbon's division lost four guns. The battle was continued on the 23rd, but no farther progress was made. The troops had been fighting, marching, or building breastworks for forty-seven days, without interruption. Daily and nightly, from the Rapidan to the Weldon road, they had been in constant action. The troops were exhausted. Grant had lost seventy thousand. The reinforcements which had reached him were inexperienced. Men when physically prostrated are indifferent to commands. Discipline becomes lax. Hundreds of efficient officers had fallen during the campaign. Brigades were commanded by majors, regiments by captains, companies by corporals. The army needed thorough reorganization. The right of the line was sufficiently near to Petersburg to commence siege operations. Entrenchments were accordingly thrown up and guns mounted, and the army enjoyed comparative rest. But it was a rest under fire, day and night, the Ninth and Eighteenth Corps especially being constantly harassed by the enemy, who were bitterly opposed to the employment of coloured troops. It was systematic hostility,—ingrained, revengeful, relentless. They would not recognize or treat them as prisoners of war. Slavery long before had proclaimed that black men had no rights which white men were bound to respect. For them was no mercy; only the fate of their compatriots at Fort Pillow awaited them, if taken in arms against their former masters, though wearing the uniform of the republic which had given them freedom and sent them to battle.

There was a tacit understanding between the soldiers of the Fifth and the enemy in front of them that there should be no picket-firing. They filled their canteens at the same spring and had friendly conversations. But not so in front of the Ninth, in which thirty were wounded or killed every twenty-four hours. Such was the unneces-

Army corps chapel near Petersburg

sary sacrifice of life to this Moloch of our generation! There were those in the army, as well as out of it, who were not willing that the coloured soldier should be recognized as a man.

"The negroes ought not to be allowed to fight," said a Massachusetts captain to me.

"Why not, sir?"

"Because the Rebels hate us for making them soldiers," was the reply; and adding, dubiously, "I don't know but that the negroes have souls; but I look upon them as a lower order of beings than ourselves."

The old prejudice remained. We were not willing to deal fairly. We asked the negro to help fight our battles, but we were willing to pay him only half a soldier's wages, as if we feared this simple act of justice might be construed as an acknowledgment of his social as well as civil equality.

Through all the weary months of fighting and exposure the wants of the soldiers were greatly relieved by the Sanitary and Christian Commissions. The warm-hearted people in the North never ceased their contributions. The machinery of both those excellent organizations was so perfect that the soldiers had quick relief.

The power of any force—moral and religious as well as mechanical—is in proportion to the directness of its application. I recall, in this connection, a hot, dry, sultry day. The sun shone from a brazen sky. The grass and shrubs were scorched, withered, and powdered with dust, which rose in clouds behind every passing wagon. Even the aspens were motionless, and there was not air enough to stir the long, lithe needles of the pines. The birds of the forest sought the deepest shade, and hushed even their twitter. It was difficult for men in robust health to breathe, and they picked out the coolest places and gave themselves up to the languor of the hour. It required an earnest effort to do anything. Yet through this blazing day men crouched in the trenches from morning till night, or lay in their shallow rifle-pits, watching the enemy,—parched, broiled, burned, not daring to raise their heads or lift their hands. To do so was to suffer death or wounds.

The hospital tents, though pitched in the woods, were like ovens, absorbing and holding the heat of the sun, whose rays the branches of the trees but partially excluded. Upon the ground lay the sick and wounded, fevered and sore, with energies exhausted, perspiration oozing from their faces, nerves quivering and trembling, pulses faint and feeble, and life ebbing away. Their beds were pine boughs. They lay as they came from the battle-field, wearing their soiled, torn, and bloody garments, and tantalized by myriads of flies.

The surgeons in charge were kind-hearted and attentive. They used all means in their power to make their patients comfortable. Was this the place where the sick were to regain their health, far from home and friends! With nothing to cheer them, hope was dying out, and despondency setting in; and memory, ever busy, was picturing the dear old home scenes, so painfully in contrast with their dismal present.

It was the Sabbath, and there were many among the suffering thousands who had been accustomed to observe the day as one of worship and rest from toil and care. In imagination they heard the pealing of church-bells, the grand and solemn music of the organ, or the hum of children's voices in the Sabbath school.

There were no clouds to shut out the sun, but the brazen dome of the sky glowed with steady heat. The Christian Commission tent had been besieged all day by soldiers, who wanted onions, pickles, lemons, oranges,—anything sour, anything to tempt the taste. A box of oranges had been brought from City Point the night before. It was suggested that they be distributed at once to the sick and wounded. "Certainly, by all means," was the unanimous voice of the Commission. I volunteered to be the distributor.

Go with me through the tents of the sufferers. Some are lying down, with eyes closed, faces pale, and cheeks sunken. The paleness underlies the bronze which the sun has burned upon them. Some are half reclining on their elbows, bolstered by knapsacks, and looking into vacancy,—thinking, perhaps, of home and kin, and wondering if they will ever see them again. Others are reading papers which delegates of the Commission have distributed. Some of the poor fellows have but one leg; others but the stump of a thigh or an arm, with the lightest possible dressing to keep down the fever. Yesterday those men, in the full tide of life, stood in the trenches confronting the enemy. Now they are shattered wrecks, having, perhaps, wife and children or parents dependent upon them; with no certainty of support for themselves even but the small bounty of government, which they have earned at such fearful sacrifice. But their future will be brightened with the proud consciousness of duty done and country saved,—the surviving soldier's chief recompense for all the toil and suffering and privation of the camp and field.

As we enter the tent they catch a sight of the golden fruit. There is a commotion. Those half asleep rub their eyes, those partially reclining sit up, those lying with their backs toward us turn over to see what is going on, those so feeble that they cannot move ask what is the matter. They gaze wistfully at our luscious burden. Their eyes gleam, but not one of them asks for an orange. They wait. Through the stern discipline of war they have learned to be patient, to endure, to remain in suspense, to stand still and be torn to pieces. They are true heroes!

"Would you like an orange, sir?"

"Thank you."

It is all he can say. He is lying upon his back. A minnie bullet has passed through his body, and he cannot be moved. He has a noble brow, a manly countenance. Tears moisten his eyes and roll down his sunken cheeks as he takes it from my hand.

"It is a gift of the Christian Commission, and I accept your thanks for those who made the contribution."

"Bully for the Christian Commission," shouts a wide-awake, jolly soldier, nearby, with an ugly wound in his left arm.

"Thank you," "God bless the Commission," "I say, Bill, aren't they bully?" are the expressions I hear behind me.

In one of the wards I came upon a soldier who had lost his leg the day before. He was lying upon his side; he was robust, healthy, strong, and brave. The hours dragged heavily. I stood before him, and yet he did not see me. He was stabbing his knife into a chip, with nervous energy, trying to forget the pain, to bridge over the lonely hours, and shut the gloom out of the future. I touched his elbow; he looked up.

"Would you like an orange?"

"By jingo! that is worth a hundred dollars!"

He grasped it as a drowning man clutches a chip.

"Where did this come from?"

"The Christian Commission had a box arrive last night."

"The Christian Commission? My wife belongs to that. She wrote to me about it last week,—that they met to make shirts for the Commission."

"Then you have a wife?"

"Yes, sir, and three children."

His voice faltered. Ah! the soldier never forgets home. He dashed away a tear, took in a long breath, and was strong again.

"Where do you hail from, soldier?"

"From old Massachusetts. I had a snug little home upon the banks of the Connecticut; but I told my wife that I didn't feel just right to stay there, when I was needed out here, and so I came, and here I am. I shall write home, and tell Mary about the Christian Commission. I have been wishing all day that I had an orange; I knew it was no use to wish. I didn't suppose there was one in camp; besides, here I am, not able to move a peg. I thank you, sir, for bringing it. I shall tell my wife all about it."

These expressions of gratitude were not indifferent utterances of courtesy, but came from full hearts. Those sun-burned sufferers recognized the religion of Jesus in the gift. The Christian religion, thus exemplified, was not a cold abstraction, but a reality, providing for the health of the body as well as the soul. It was easy to converse with those men concerning their eternal well-being. They could not oppose a Christianity that manifested such regard for their bodily comfort. Such a religion commended itself to their hearts and understandings. Thus the Commission became a great missionary enterprise. Farina, oranges, lemons, onions, pickles, comfort-bags, shirts, towels, given and distributed in the name of Jesus, though designed for the body, gave strength to the soul. To the quickened senses of a wounded soldier parched with fever, far from home and friends, an onion was a stronger argument for the religion which bestowed it than the subtle reasoning of Renan, and a pickle sharper than the keenest logic of Colenso!

Visiting Washington one day, I passed through several of the hospitals, and was present when the delegates came to the head-quarters of the Commission and narrated their experiences of the day. About fifty were present. Their work was washing and dressing wounds, aiding the sick and wounded in every way possible, distributing reading matter, writing letters for those unable to write, with religious exercises and conversation. No delegate was allowed to give jellies or wines as food, or to hold meetings in any ward, without permission of the surgeon in charge, which usually was granted. It was a rule of the Commission, and not of the Medical Department. The design was to do everything possible for the good of the men, and nothing for their hurt. One delegate said that he found fully one third of the men in his wards professing Christians. They were glad to see him, and rejoiced to obtain religious reading. A few days before he had given an old man a book entitled the *Blood of Jesus*.

"I have found Jesus, and O, he is so precious!" said the old soldier.

Another delegate said: "I found among the patients a minister who enlisted as a private. He has been in the hospital sixteen months, and has maintained his Christian character through all the trials of camp and hospital life. I found some convalescents playing cards.

"'My boys, you don't play cards on Sunday, do you?'

"'It isn't Sunday, is it? Why, hang it all, chaplain, we can't keep track of the days in the army.'

"I talked to them of home and of their mothers. The tears rolled down their cheeks. They put up their cards, and read the papers I gave them."

"I never saw men so ready to receive religious instruction," said another delegate, "or who were so easily impressed with its truths. I am satisfied that this is a golden opportunity to the Christian Church. I found a young man today who said, 'I want you, chaplain, to tell me just what I have to do to be a Christian. I will do just what you say. I want to be a Christian.' It was a sincere desire. I find that the Catholics are just as eager to have religious instruction as others."

"I found a sergeant from Massachusetts, very low, but he met me with a smile. 'It is all right, I am happy, and I die content. Tell my friends so,'" reported another.

"I have been over the river to see some detached regiments," said a chaplain. "I asked one noble-looking soldier if he loved Jesus?

"'No, I don't.'

"'Are you married?'

"'No; but I have a sister. She isn't a Christian, but she wrote to me that she wanted me to become one, and I wrote to her that I wanted her to be one; and I guess, chaplain, that everybody who believes the Bible feels just so. If they ain't good themselves, they want their friends to be.'

"I found another soldier writing a letter on a little bit of paper. I gave him a full sheet and an envelope.

"'Are you a Christian Commission man?'

"'Yes.'

"'You are a d—good set of fellows.'

"'Hold on, soldier, not quite so hard.'

"'I beg your pardon, chaplain, I didn't mean to swear, but, darn it all, I have got into the habit out here in the army, and it comes right out before I think.'

"'Won't you try to leave it off?'

"'Yes, chaplain, I will.'"

Said another delegate: "I went among the men, and they all gathered round me with great eagerness. They were a little disappointed, however, when they saw that I was a delegate of the Commission. They took me to be the paymaster.

"But I have something that is better than gold."

"'Give me some of it,' said one, who was the son of a Baptist minister, a tender-hearted Christian."

One, just returned from the army at Petersburg, said: "I came across a drummer-boy of one of the Massachusetts regiments, a member of the Sabbath school at home, who lost his Bible during the campaign, but he has written the heads of his drum all over with texts of Scripture from memory. He beats a Gospel drum."

An hour was passed with such narration interspersed with devotional exercises. Glorious their work! Sweet the music of their parting hymn:

Nearer, my God, to thee,
Nearer to thee;
E'en though it be a cross that raiseth me,
Still all my song shall be,
Nearer, my God, to thee,
Nearer to thee.

Chapter 21
Siege Operations

June, 1864

The Norfolk Railroad enters Petersburg through a ravine. In the attack upon the enemy's lines, on the 18th of June, the hollow was gained and held by Burnside's troops, their most advanced position being about four hundred feet from the Rebel line.

Lieutenant-Colonel Henry Pleasants, commanding the Forty-Eighth Pennsylvania Regiment, a practical miner, conceived the idea of excavating a tunnel under the Rebel works and exploding a mine. He submitted the plan to Burnside, who approved it. General Meade said it could not be done. Major Duane, of the Engineers, laughed at the idea. Other officers, of high rank, scouted the project. Colonel Pleasants was fully convinced of its practicability, and set his men to work.

He made application at head-quarters for a theodolite to make a triangulation of the distance, but was refused its use. He was obliged to send to Washington to obtain one. No facilities were granted him. He could neither obtain boards, lumber, or mining-picks. But his regiment, numbering four hundred men, were mostly miners, and he was confident of success. Work was accordingly commenced on the 25th of June, at noon. No wheelbarrows being provided, the men were obliged to make hand-barrows of cracker-boxes. But they were at home in the earth, and not easily discouraged by difficulties or want of proper tools to work with, and pushed forward the gallery, which was about four and a half feet high and the same in width, with great zeal. The earth brought out was covered with bushes, to conceal it from the Rebels, who by its fresh appearance might suspect where the mine was being sunk, as it was known throughout the army that mining operations had been commenced, and the Rebels had heard of it. The Richmond papers published the news, and it was heralded through the North.

At every discharge of the Rebel artillery there was danger of the caving in of the earth; but Pleasants' daring burrowers crept steadily forward, till the noise overhead, as well as previous measurements, convinced them that they were immediately under the Rebel works. The main gallery was five hundred and ten feet in length, beside which were two lateral galleries, one thirty-seven and the other thirty-eight feet in length.

A short distance from the entrance, inside of the Union fortifications, a vertical shaft was sunk, in which a fire was kept constantly burning, to produce ventilation. Eight magazines were placed in the lateral galleries, charged with four tons of powder, strongly tamped, and connected by fuses. The mine was completed on the 23rd of July.

Grant planned an assault upon the Rebel line, independently of the explosion of the mine. He sent two divisions of the Second Corps, with two divisions of Sheridan's cavalry, to the Army of the James, at Deep Bottom, where an attack was made, four guns captured, and the line extended from Deep Bottom to the New Market road. Lee attempted to recover his lost ground, but failed. Grant, in this expedition, employed an immense train of empty baggage-wagons, which, passing in sight of the Rebel pickets, made the movement an enigma to Lee. The Rebels in the fortifications had commenced a countermine, but suspended labour.

General Burnside wished that the coloured troops of his division, under General Ferrero, should lead in the assault after the mine was exploded; and the troops were drilled with that special object in view. He believed that they would make a successful charge. They were fresh, had taken but little part in the campaign, and were desirous of emulating the example of their comrades of the Eighteenth Corps. The white troops were worn with hard marching, fighting, and exposure in the trenches in front of Petersburg, where they had been on the watch day and night. The lines were so near to the Rebels that a man could not show his head above the parapet without being shot. They had acquired the habit of taking their positions by covered approaches, and had lost the resolute confidence and fearlessness manifested at the beginning of the campaigns.

General Meade objected to Burnside's plan.

> I objected not that I had any reason to believe that the coloured troops would not do their duty as well as the white troops, but that they were a new division, and had never been under fire, had never been tried, and, as this was an operation which

I knew beforehand was one requiring the very best troops, I thought it impolitic to trust to a division of whose reliability we had no evidence.[68]

The matter was referred to General Grant, who says:

General Burnside wanted to put his coloured division in front, and I believe if he had done so it would have been a success. Still I agreed with General Meade in his objections to the plan. General Meade said that if we put the coloured troops in front (we had only one division), and it should prove a failure, it would then be said, probably, that we were shoving those people ahead to get killed, because we did not care anything about them. But that could not be said if we put white troops in front.[69]

General Burnside had three divisions of white troops; as there were reasons for assigning either of the divisions to lead the assault, lots were cast, and the duty fell upon General Ledlie.

Burnside was directed by Meade to form his troops during the night, and be ready to assault at daylight on the 30th. His pioneers were to be equipped to destroy the enemy's *abatis*. Entrenching tools were provided, so that if successful in breaking the Rebel lines, the position might be quickly secured.

Portions of the Fifth and Eighteenth Corps were brought up to support the Ninth.

The field artillery was to be harnessed for immediate use. The siege artillery was to open a heavy fire. The Second Corps, at Deep Bottom, was to move to the rear of the Eighteenth, and be ready for any emergency. Sheridan, with the cavalry, was ordered to attack south and east of Petersburg. The Engineers were to have sand-bags, gabions, and fascines in readiness. The mine was to be fired at half past three, and simultaneously with the explosion the assaulting column was to rush into the gap.

"Promptitude, rapidity of execution, and cordial co-operation are essential to success," wrote General Meade, in his concluding orders.

The movements and preparations were completed before three o'clock. The moon was shining brightly, but the Rebels made no discovery of the change of position and massing of troops in rear of the Ninth Corps. The heights near the hospitals were covered by teamsters, ambulance drivers, surgeons, and civilians, waiting with intense interest for the expected upheaval.

68: Attack on Petersburg, *Report of Committee on Conduct of the War*, p. 4.
69: Ibid., p. 5.

Half past three came, and the fuse was lighted. A stream of fire ran quickly along the gallery, but no explosion followed. Had the fuse failed? Lieutenant Douty and Sergeant Reese went boldly in to ascertain, and found the fire had gone out one hundred feet from the entrance. The fuse was relighted, but it was almost five o'clock, and the anxious spectators began to speculate as to the cause of the delay. Grant and Meade were at the front. The troops thought the whole thing a failure, and began to ridicule the Pennsylvania miners.

Fleming's Rebel brigade, composed of the Seventeenth, Eighteenth, and Twenty-Second North Carolinians, was asleep over the mine. The pickets only were awake. Pegram's battery was also in the redoubt.

Finally there came a trembling of the earth, then a bursting forth of volcanic flames and rolling up of dense clouds of smoke. A mountain of rubbish rose in the air. Earth, men, planks, timbers, cannon, shot and shell, were hurled upward and outward! The sight was terribly grand. To add to the frightfulness of the eruption and the grandeur of the spectacle, one hundred guns instantly belched forth their thunders. The Rebels were surprised and panic-stricken for the moment, and ran to escape the falling earth and timbers, leaving their artillery silent. A huge gap had been made in the Rebel works, four or five hundred feet in length and twenty feet in depth.

Success depended upon the immediate occupation of the breach. Ten minutes passed before Ledlie moved, and then he only advanced to the crater. The Rebels offered no opposition. The important point to be gained and held was a ridge four hundred yards beyond. Ledlie still halted in the excavation. Wilcox and Potter soon followed him, and the three divisions became intermixed, and general confusion prevailed. An hour of precious time was lost. Ledlie made no attempt to move in or out, and Potter and Wilcox could not go forward while he blocked the way.

The enemy gradually recovered from their stupor, and began to fire from the hills, and batteries of artillery were brought up on the right and left to enfilade the crater: but not a cannon-shot was fired by the Rebels till after seven o'clock. The supporting brigades meanwhile were crowding upon those in front. The coloured troops were ordered forward. They also entered the crater, which only added to the confusion. Potter succeeded in freeing his troops from Ledlie's, and pushed on toward the crest, but being unsupported, he was obliged to retire, driven back by the canister which the enemy poured into his ranks from the new position they had taken on Cemetery Hill. The Rebel fire increased. Eight, nine, ten o'clock passed; their batteries were throwing a concentrated fire of shells and solid shot into the mingled human mass. Mahone's and Ransom's divisions of infantry were hurried to the top of the ridge, and mortars were brought into play, and the crater became a terrible scene of slaughter. Meade, seeing that further attempt to take the ridge would be not only useless, but a waste of life, permitted Burnside to withdraw his troops at discretion. Yet to retire was to run the gauntlet of almost certain death. The space between the abyss and Burnside's breastworks was swept by a cross-fire from the enemy's artillery and infantry. To remain in the crater was sure destruction; to advance was impossible; to retreat the only alternative. Permission was given the troops to retire. By degrees they fled to the rear; but it was two o'clock in the afternoon before the place was wholly evacuated.

Forty-seven officers and three hundred and seventy-two soldiers were killed, one hundred and twenty-four officers and fifteen hundred and fifty-five soldiers wounded, and nineteen hundred missing; a total loss of over four thousand men, and no substantial advantage gained.

The loss of the Rebels by the explosion was very great, as also by the heavy artillery fire.

The causes of the failure, as decided by the Committee on the Conduct of the War, were: the injudicious formation of the troops assaulting; the halting of Ledlie; lack of proper engineers; and the want of a competent head at the scene of assault.

The reasons why the attack ought to have been successful are thus stated:

1. The evident surprise of the enemy at the time of the explosion of the mine, and for some time after.

2. The comparatively small force in the enemy's works.

3. The ineffective fire of the enemy's artillery and musketry, there being scarcely any for about thirty minutes after the explosion, and our artillery being just the reverse as to time and power.

4. The fact that our troops were able to get two hundred yards beyond the crater, towards the west, but could not remain there or proceed farther for want of supports.[70]

It was a humiliating, disgraceful failure, which filled the North with mourning. The Rebels manifested their hatred of the coloured troops by shooting some of them even after they had surrendered. The *Richmond Enquirer* said that the assaulting column was led by coloured

---

70: Report of Committee.

troops, who rushed on with the cry of "No quarter," but the assertion is not true. The coloured troops were not ordered forward till late in the morning, and then advanced but a few steps beyond the crater. The *Enquirer* of August 1st doubtless gave expression to the sentiments of the Southern people respecting the treatment to be accorded to coloured soldiers. Said that paper:

> Grant's war cry of "No quarter," shouted by his negro soldiers, was returned with interest, we regret to hear not so heavily as it ought to have been, since some negroes were captured instead of being shot.... Let every salient we are called upon to defend be a Fort Pillow, and butcher every negro that Grant hurls against our brave troops, and permit them not to soil their hands with the capture of one negro.

It was the opinion of many officers who saw the advance of the coloured division, that, had they been permitted to lead the assault, the crest would have been seized and held. Such is the opinion of the Lieutenant-General already given.

The onset promised to be successful, but ended in one of the severest disasters of the war, without any compensation worthy of mention.

Sad the scene on that afternoon. The ground was thickly strewn with dying and dead. The sun blazed from a cloudless sky, and the heat was intense. The cries of the wounded were heart-rending. Officers and men on both sides stopped their ears, and turned away heart-sick at the sight. It was an exhibition of the horrible features of war which, once seen, is forever remembered.

The operation of Grant upon the enemy's lines of communication was beginning to be felt in Richmond. Wilson and Kautz on the Danville and Weldon roads, Sheridan on the Virginia Central, and Hunter in the vicinity of Lynchburg, altogether had caused an interruption of communication which advanced the prices of produce in the markets of that city.

It is amusing to read the papers published during the summer of 1864. All of Grant's movements from the Rapidan to Petersburg were retreats. Lee, in his despatches to Jeff Davis from the Wilderness, said that Grant was retreating towards Fredericksburg. It happened, however, that Lee found Grant attacking his lines at Spottsylvania on the following morning. "The enemy is falling back from Spottsylvania," said the *Examiner*, when Grant moved to the North Anna. "Grant is floundering in the swamp of the Chickahominy; he has reached McClellan's graveyard," said the Rebel press, when he was at Cold Harbor.

"Grant's attitude before Petersburg is that of a baffled, if not a ruined man," said the *Richmond Enquirer*.

"We can stand such a siege as Grant thinks he has established for twenty years to come," was the language of the *Petersburg Express*.

Another number of the *Enquirer*, June 30th, commenting upon the Richmond markets, revealed more clearly the truth.

> The extortion *now* practised upon the people in every department of necessary supply, is frightful. It is a pitiable sight to see the families of this city swarming in the markets for food, and subjected to the merciless exactions of this unrestrained avarice.

The fortunes of the Confederacy were becoming desperate. Sherman had advanced from Chattanooga, driving Johnston to Atlanta. The removal of Johnston, and the appointment of an officer in his stead who would fight the Yankees, was demanded. Jeff Davis heeded the cry, removed Johnston, and appointed Hood to succeed him. The *Enquirer* was jubilant. Said that sheet:

> There must be an end of retreating, and the risk of defeat must be encountered, or victory can never be won. The rule of Cunctator must have an end, for the rashness of Scipio can only end this war. If General Johnston has been relieved, the country will accept this action of the President as a determination henceforth to accept the risk of battle, as involving the fate and fixing the destiny of the Confederacy. To go forward and to fight is now the motto of our armies, and since Johnston would not advance, Hood has no other alternative, for his appointment has but one meaning, and that is to give battle to the foe.... Grant is hopelessly crippled at Petersburg, and Lee has but a few days ago thundered his artillery in the corporate limits of Washington City. Grant, while apparently advancing, has been really retreating, and this day is in a position from which he can advance no farther, and from which his retreat is only a question of time. Grant is exhausting the malice of disappointment and the chagrin of defeat in bombarding Petersburg; but Sherman, unless defeated by Hood, must march into Atlanta. The movements of General Lee have so weakened the army of Grant, that it is more an object of pity than of fear.[71]

Early in the campaign Grant, seeing the necessity of keeping the

---

71: *Richmond Enquirer*, July 19, 1864.

ranks of the Army of the Potomac full, had ordered the Nineteenth Corps, then on the Mississippi, to take transports for the James. His policy was concentration combined with activity. His foresight and prudence in this matter were of inestimable value, as will be seen in the ensuing chapter.

CHAPTER 22
Third Invasion of Maryland

JULY, 1864

The armies of the Union in Virginia, in the West, beyond the Mississippi, and along the Gulf were controlled by General Grant. The chess-board was continental in its dimensions, but everything upon it seemed within reach of his hand. He had two armies under his immediate direction,—the Army of the Potomac and the Army of the James. He was in constant communication with Sherman at Atlanta, and his orders reached the forces a thousand miles distant on the Mississippi! The details were left to the commanders of the various armies, but all important schemes were submitted to him for approval. But his best plans sometimes miscarried, from the neglect or inability of his subordinates to carry them into execution. Before starting from the Rapidan, General Grant ordered Hunter, who had succeeded to the command of Sigel in the Shenandoah, to proceed up the valley to Staunton and Gordonsville. When Grant was on the North Anna, he advised that officer to move on Charlottesville and Lynchburg, live on the country as he marched, and destroy the railroads, and, if possible, the James River Canal. Accomplishing that, he was to return to Gordonsville, and there join Grant. Hunter advanced. Sheridan was sent with the cavalry, while Grant was at Cold Harbor, to aid him. Sheridan broke up the Virginia Central Railroad, moved to Gordonsville, but hearing nothing of Hunter returned to the White House, and rejoined Grant at Petersburg.

Hunter moved up the valley. At the same time Generals Crook and Averill, leaving Western Virginia, met Hunter near Staunton, where they had a battle with the Rebels under General Jones, who was killed, and his force routed, with a loss of three guns and fifteen hundred prisoners.

Hunter, instead of approaching Lynchburg by Gordonsville and Charlottesville, took the road leading through Lexington and thus missed Sheridan.

He reached Lynchburg on the 16th of June, at the same time that Grant was moving from Cold Harbor to the James. Lee, seeing the danger which threatened him at the backdoor of the Rebel capital, threw reinforcements into Lynchburg, and Hunter was obliged to retreat, being far from his base, and having but a limited supply of ammunition. Having advanced upon Lynchburg from the west, instead of from the north, he was obliged to retreat in the same direction through Western Virginia, a country wellnigh barren of supplies. This left the Shenandoah open. There was no force to oppose the Rebels who were at Lynchburg. The decision of Hunter to go forward by Lexington instead of by Gordonsville disarranged Grant's plans, who did not direct him to move by Charlottesville. His letter to Halleck of the 25th of May reads: "If Hunter can possibly get to Charlottesville and Lynchburg, he should do so, living on the country. The railroads and canals should be destroyed beyond the possibility of repair for weeks. Completing this, he could find his way back to his original base, or from Gordonsville join this army." No mention was made of his advancing by Lexington; but taking that route, and being compelled to retreat by the Great Kanawha, gave Lee an opportunity to strike a blow at Washington. He was active to improve it, but Grant was quick to discover his intentions.

Ewell was sick, and Early was appointed to command the Rebel troops in the Valley. Breckenridge was sent up from Richmond. The troops took cars and moved up the Lynchburg road to Gordonsville. Early found himself at the head of twenty-five or thirty thousand men. Mosby, with his band of guerrillas, was scouring the Valley and Western Virginia. He reported a clear coast towards Washington, but that Sigel was at Martinsburg.

Early passed rapidly down the Valley, drove Sigel across the Potomac, and followed him to Hagerstown. The people of Western Maryland and Southern Pennsylvania, who had already received two unpleasant visits from the Rebels, fled in haste towards Baltimore and Harrisburg. The panic was widespread. Extravagant stories were told of the force of the enemy: Lee's whole army was advancing; he had out-generalled Grant; he had sixty thousand men across the Potomac; Washington and Baltimore were to be captured. All of which was received with exceeding coolness by the Lieutenant-General in command at City Point, who detached the Sixth Corps, ordering Ricketts's division to Baltimore and the other two divisions to Washington. The Nineteenth Corps, which had arrived at Fortress Monroe, was despatched to Washington.

The news was startling. Leaving the army at Petersburg, I hastened to City Point, to proceed to Washington. There was no commotion at General Grant's head-quarters. The chief quartermaster was looking over his reports. The clerks were at their regular work. There were numerous transports in the stream, but no indications of the embarkation of troops. General Grant was out, walking leisurely about, with his thumbs in the arm-holes of his vest, smoking his cigar so quietly and apparently unconcerned, that, had it not been for the three stars on his shoulders, a stranger would have passed him without a thought of his being the man who was playing the deepest game of war in modern times. The members of his military family were not in the least excited. Calling on Colonel Bowers, Grant's adjutant-general, I found him attending to the daily routine.

"They are having a little scare at Washington and in the North. It will do them good," said he.

"How large a force is it supposed the Rebels have in Maryland?"

"Somewhere about twenty-five thousand,—possibly thirty. Breckenridge has gone, with his command. And Early has raked and scraped all the troops possible which were outside of Richmond. Mosby is with him, and the irregular bands of the upper Potomac, and the troops which met Hunter at Lynchburg. It will not affect operations here. Lee undoubtedly expected to send Grant post-haste to Washington; but the siege will go on."

On the wall of his room was a map of the Southern States, showing by coloured lines the various gauges of all the railroads. Grant came in, looked at it, said "Good morning," and went out for another stroll about the grounds, thinking all the while.

On board our boat was a lively company, principally composed of the soldiers of the Massachusetts Sixteenth, who had served three years, and were on their way home. They were in the Peninsular campaigns. Their commander, Colonel Wyman, was killed at Glendale, where they held the ground when McCall's line was swept away. His fugitives ran through Hooker's and Sumner's lines, but the men of the Sixteenth stood firm in their places, till the drift had passed by, and moved forward to meet the exultant enemy, pouring in such a fire that the Rebel column became a mob, and fled in haste towards Richmond. They were in Grover's brigade at the second battle of Manassas. There have been few bayonet-charges pushed with such power as theirs in that battle. The Rebels were on Milroy's left flank, which was bending like a bruised reed before their advance, when Grover moved to the attack.

"We stood in these lines," said a wounded officer of the Second Louisiana, a prisoner at Warrenton, two months after that battle. "They fell upon us like a thunderbolt. They paid no attention to our volleys. We mowed them down, but they went right through our first line, then through our second, and advanced to the railroad embankment, and there we stopped them. They did it so splendidly that we couldn't help cheering them. It made me feel bad to fire on such brave fellows."

They were reduced to a squad. Their comrades were lying on nearly all the battle-fields of Virginia.

"We have had a pretty rough time of it, and I am glad we are through; but I wouldn't mind having another crack at the Johnnie's round Washington," said a soldier, lying on the deck with his knapsack for a pillow.

The whole regiment was ready to volunteer for the defence of Washington.

The cannoneers of the Twelfth New York battery were of the company. They were in Wilson's raid, had lost their guns, and felt sore. Even when their loss is owing to no fault on the part of the artillerists, they usually feel that it is humiliating. They give pet names to the dogs of war; and when a good shot has been made, affectionately pat their brazen lips.

There were members of the Sanitary and Christian Commissions, taking care of the sick and wounded; also a family of refugees from Prince George County, on the way to Maryland, to find a new home till the war was over.

Early was making the most of his opportunity. His cavalry moved at will, with no force to oppose them.

They divided into small bodies and overran the country from Frederick to Williamsport, destroying the Baltimore and Ohio Railroad, burning canal-boats, seizing horses, cattle, and supplies, from the farmers, ransacking houses as thoroughly as the soldiers of the Union had done in Virginia.

The first invasion of Maryland, in 1862, was a political as well as a military movement. It was supposed by the Rebel leaders that the State was ready to join the Confederacy, that the people were held in subjection by a military despotism. *My Maryland* was then the popular song of the South, sung in camp, on the march, and in parlours and concert-halls.

The despot's heel is on thy shore,
Maryland!
His torch is at thy temple-door,
Maryland!
Avenge the patriotic gore
That wept o'er gallant Baltimore,
And be the battle-queen of yore,
Maryland! My Maryland!

When Jackson's corps crossed the Potomac, his troops sang it with enthusiastic demonstrations, tossing up their caps. They came as liberators. Jackson's orders were strict against pillage. All property taken was to be paid for in Confederate notes,—at that time esteemed by the Rebels to be as good as greenbacks, though not very acceptable to the Marylanders. It was an invasion for conciliation. The troops respected the orders, and, aside from the loss of a few horses, the people of Maryland were well treated in that campaign. But in the second invasion, when Lee passed into Pennsylvania, no favour was shown to Maryland. Houses, stores, public and private buildings alike were sacked and burned. The soldiers foraged at will, and the one who could secure the most clothing or food was the best fellow. In this third and last invasion, officers and soldiers pillaged indiscriminately.

"Pay me twenty thousand dollars or I will burn your town," said Early to the citizens of Hagerstown, who advanced the money or its equivalent.

General Lew Wallace was in command at Baltimore. He sent what troops he could collect to the Monocacy, where he was joined by Ricketts's division of the Sixth Corps. Wallace formed his line across the railroad and awaited Early's advance. With the exception of Ricketts's division, Wallace's troops were men enlisted for one hundred days, also heavy artillerists taken from the Baltimore fortifications, invalids from the hospitals, and volunteers, numbering about nine thousand. The Rebels forded the stream and began the attack. They were held in check several hours. Wallace, after losing about twelve hundred men, was obliged to retreat.

His defeat, and the stories of the magnitude of the Rebel force, put Baltimore and Washington in great excitement. The battle at Monocacy was fought on Saturday. On Sunday morning the church-bells in Baltimore were rung, and the citizens, instead of attending worship, made haste to prepare for the enemy. Alarming reports reached that

Ruins of Chambersburg

A LAY DELEGATE IN THE HOSPITAL

city from Westminster, Reisterstown, and Cockeysville, that the Rebels were in possession of those places. Couriers dashed into Washington from Rockville, only twelve miles distant, crying that the Rebels were advancing upon the capital. On Monday morning they were near Havre-de-Grace, at Gunpowder River, where they burned the bridge, cut the telegraph, captured trains, and robbed passengers, entirely severing Baltimore and Washington from the loyal North. Only five miles from Washington, they burned the house of Governor Bradford, and pillaged Montgomery Blair's. Government employees were under arms, and troops were hastening out on the roads leading north and west, when I arrived in Washington. Loud cheers greeted Wright's two divisions of the Sixth Corps, and still louder shouts the veterans of the Nineteenth Corps, from the Mississippi, as they marched through the city. It was amusing and instructive to watch the rapid change in men's countenances. When disaster threatens, men are silent; the danger past, the tongue is loosened.

On Tuesday the Rebel sharpshooters were in front of Fort Stevens; they picked off some of the gunners, but a charge by a brigade dislodged them. They fled, leaving about one hundred dead and wounded. Forces were gathering around Early, and on Wednesday morning he hastily retreated. He recrossed the Potomac at Edwards's Ferry, and made his way, through Snicker's Gap, into the Shenandoah Valley, with an immense train of plunder, consisting of forage, grain, horses, cattle, hogs, sheep, groceries, clothing, and a forced contribution of two hundred thousand dollars from the people of Frederick, levied under threat of burning the town.

Early had no serious intention of attacking Washington, but the invasion was designed primarily to raise the siege of Petersburg, and secondarily to replenish the commissariat of the Rebel army.

Grant comprehended the movement, and instead of abandoning Petersburg, made preparations to seize the Weldon road, which, after a severe struggle, was accomplished. A few weeks later Sheridan defeated Early in the Valley, which ended the campaign of 1864 in Virginia.

Chapter 23
Sherman's Army

December, 1864

The army under General Sherman fought its way from Chattanooga to Atlanta, and then marched to the sea, capturing Fort McAllister, and opening communication with the fleet under Dupont on the 13th of December, and a few days later made its grand *entree* into Savannah. A brief review of Sherman's campaign is necessary to a clear understanding of what afterward transpired in his department.

While the Army of the Potomac was pushing through to the south side of the James, the Army of the West was moving upon Atlanta, having driven the Rebels under Johnston from Tunnel Hill, Buzzards' Roost, Resaca, Kingston, Allatoona, and Kenesaw. Johnston fought only on the defensive, and was constantly beaten, abandoning stronghold after stronghold that the Rebels had declared impregnable, and whose surrender they felt was humiliating and disgraceful.

There was a clamour throughout the South for his removal, and the appointment of a general who would take the offensive. Jeff Davis disliked Johnston on personal grounds, and appointed Hood his successor. That officer hurled his troops against Sherman's breastworks, and suffered a damaging defeat. Sherman in turn made a flank movement, and compelled Hood to evacuate Atlanta, which Sherman occupied on the 2nd of September. Jeff Davis hastened West. He conceived the idea of forcing Sherman to retreat from Atlanta to *Nashville*, by invading Tennessee. As Hood's army had been driven from Chattanooga to Dalton, losing all its strong positions, this plan is one of the most remarkable in military history. It is hardly within the sphere of sober criticism, but appropriately belongs to the comic page. "Your feet shall again press the soil of Tennessee, within thirty days," said Davis to the soldiers. "The invader shall be driven from your territory. The retreat of Sherman from Atlanta shall be like Napoleon's from Moscow."

Sherman had already contemplated a movement to Savannah, and had opened correspondence with Grant.

> Until we can repopulate Georgia it is useless to occupy it; but the utter destruction of its roads, houses, and people will cripple their military resources. By attempting to hold the roads we will lose a thousand men monthly, and will gain no result. I can make the march and make Georgia howl.... Hood may turn into Tennessee and Kentucky, but I believe he will be forced to follow me. Instead of being on the defensive, I would be on the offensive. Instead of guessing at what he means, he would have to guess at my plans. The difference in war is fully twenty-five per cent. I can make Savannah, Charleston, or the mouth of the Chattahoochee, and prefer to march through Georgia, smashing things to the sea.

Grant authorized the movement. Hood was preparing to move north.

Sherman's right wing, commanded by Howard, was composed of Osterhaus's Fifteenth Corps and the Seventeenth, under Blair; Slocum had his left wing, containing the Fourteenth Corps under Jeff. C. Davis, and the Twentieth with Williams.

The Twentieth was consolidated from the Eleventh and Twelfth Corps of the Army of the Potomac, which had fought at Fredericksburg, Chancellorsville, and Gettysburg.

Sherman sent his last despatch to Washington on the 11th of November. On the 17th, the day on which Sherman left Atlanta, Hood crossed the Tennessee River, to make the movement which was to compel Sherman to evacuate Georgia!

Sherman's southward march was a surprise to the Rebels. They affected joy, and predicted his destruction.

Said the *Augusta Constitutionalist*:

> The hand of God is in it. The blow, if we can give it as it should be given, may end the war. We urge our friends in the track of the advance to remove forage and provisions, horses, mules, and negroes, and stock, and burn the balance. Let the invader find the desolation he would leave behind him staring him in the face.... Cut trees across all roads in front of the enemy, burn

A CHARGE

the bridges, remove everything possible in time, and, before the enemy arrives, burn and destroy what cannot be removed,—leave nothing on which he can subsist; and hide the millstone and machinery of the mills.... The Russians destroyed the grand army of Napoleon, of five hundred thousand men, by destroying their country, by the fullness of fire applied to their own cities, houses, and granaries. Let Georgians imitate their unselfishness and love of country for a few weeks, and the army of Sherman will have the fate of the army of Napoleon.[72]

Said the *Savannah News*:

We have only to arouse our whole arms-bearing people,—hover on his front, his flanks, and rear,—remove from his reach or destroy everything that will subsist man or beast,—retard his progress by every means in our power,—and, when the proper time comes, fall upon him with the relentless vengeance of an insulted and outraged people, and there need be no doubt of the result.[73]

72: *Augusta Constitutionalist*, November 22, 1864.
73: *News*, November 22, 1864.

If it be true," said the *Examiner* of Richmond, "that Sherman is now attempting this prodigious design, we may safely predict that his march will lead him to the Paradise of Fools, and that his magnificent scheme will hereafter be reckoned—*With all the good deeds that never were done.*"

Almost without opposition Sherman reached the sea, and forced Hardee to evacuate Savannah. General Sherman is regarded by many people in the Southern States as the Attila of the nineteenth century, because his path from Atlanta to the Roanoke is a widespread scene of devastation. Yet he did only that which the leaders of the Rebellion and the newspapers of the South urged the people to do. They proposed to make the country a ruin in self-defence. Sherman did it to shorten the war. He says:

> We consumed the corn and fodder in the region of country for thirty miles on either side of a line from Atlanta to Savannah; also the sweet potatoes, hogs, sheep, and poultry, and carried off more than ten thousand horses and mules. I estimate the damage done to the State of Georgia as one hundred million dollars; at least twenty million dollars of which enured to our advantage, and the remainder was simple waste and destruction.[74]

This is a frank avowal. It is the official utterance of the commander who was instrumental in causing such wholesale destruction. To what end? What was gained by it? Was such destruction warranted? What will be the verdict of history? These are questions which force themselves upon every thinking mind.

General Sherman's vindication of himself is found in his correspondence with the Mayor of Atlanta and with General Hood concerning the expulsion of the non-combatants from that city.

As he could not subsist his army and the citizens also, he ordered that every person not connected with the army should leave the place. The people of that town had done what they could to overthrow the government of the United States. They had given great material aid to the Rebellion. They hated the Union as bitterly as ever, but were willing to be consumers of the food dispensed by a government which they were not willing to recognize as holding rightful authority over them. The Mayor set forth the suffering which would be entailed upon women and children, the poor and sick, by the enforcement of the order.

74: Sherman's Report.

You know the woe, the horror, and the suffering cannot be described in words," said the Mayor. "Imagination can only conceive of it, and we ask you to take these things into consideration....We solemnly petition you to reconsider this order, or modify it, and suffer this unfortunate people to remain at home and enjoy what little means they have.

The reply of General Sherman was clear and decisive.

Gentlemen:
I have your letter of the 11th, in the nature of a petition to revoke my orders removing all the inhabitants from Atlanta. I have read it carefully, and give full credit to your statements of the distress that will be occasioned by it, and yet shall not revoke my order, simply because my orders are not designed to meet the humanities of the case, but to prepare for the future struggles in which millions, yea, hundreds of millions of good people outside of Atlanta, have a deep interest. We must have peace, not only at Atlanta, but in all America. To secure this we must stop the war that now desolates our once happy and favoured country. To stop the war, we must defeat the Rebel armies that are arrayed against the laws and Constitution, which all must respect and obey. To defeat the armies, we must prepare the way to reach them in their recesses, provided with the arms and instruments which enable us to accomplish our purpose.

Now, I know the vindictive nature of our enemy, and that we may have many years of military operations from this quarter, and therefore deem it wise and prudent to prepare in time. The use of Atlanta for warlike purposes is inconsistent with its character as a home for families. There will be no manufactures, commerce, or agriculture here for the maintenance of families, and sooner or later want will compel the inhabitants to go....

War is cruelty, and you cannot refine it; and those who brought war on our country deserve all the curses and maledictions a people can pour out. I know I had no hand in making this war, and I know I will make more sacrifices today than any of you to secure peace. But you cannot have peace and a division of our country....

You might as well appeal against the thunder-storm as against these terrible hardships of war. They are inevitable, and the only way the people of Atlanta can hope once more to live in peace and quiet at home, is to stop this war, which can alone be done by admitting that it began in error and is perpetuated in pride. We don't want your negroes or your horses, or your houses or your land, or anything you have; but we do want, and will have, a just obedience to the laws of the United States. That we will have, and if it involves the destruction of your improvements, we cannot help it.

You have heretofore read public sentiment in your newspapers, that live by falsehood and excitement, and the quicker you seek for truth in other quarters the better for you. I repeat, then, that by the original compact of government, the United States had certain rights in Georgia which have never been relinquished, and never will be; that the South began the war by seizing forts, arsenals, mints, custom-houses, etc., etc., long before Mr. Lincoln was installed, and before the South had one jot or tittle of provocation. I myself have seen, in Missouri, Kentucky, Tennessee, and Mississippi, hundreds and thousands of women and children fleeing from your armies and desperadoes, hungry and with bleeding feet. In Memphis, Vicksburg, and Mississippi, we fed thousands upon thousands of the families of Rebel soldiers left on our hands, and whom we could not see starve. Now that war comes home to you, you feel very differently, you deprecate its horrors, but did not feel them when you sent car-loads of soldiers and ammunition, and moulded shells and shot to carry war into Kentucky and Tennessee, and desolate the homes of hundreds and thousands of good people, who only asked to live in peace at their old homes, and under the government of their inheritance. But these comparisons are idle. I want peace, and believe it can only be reached through Union and war; and I will ever conduct war purely with a view to perfect an early success.

But, my dear sirs, when that peace does come, you may call upon me for anything. Then will I share with you the last cracker, and watch with you to shield your home and families against danger from every quarter. Now, you must go, and take with you the old and feeble; feed and nurse them, and build for them in more quiet places proper habitations to shield them against the weather, until the mad passions of men cool down, and allow the Union and peace once more to settle on your old homes at Atlanta.

General Hood protested against the order. By a flag of truce he sent a letter, saying:

> Permit me to say, the unprecedented measure you propose transcends in studied and iniquitous cruelty all acts ever before brought to my attention in this dark history of the war. In the name of God and humanity, I protest, believing you are expelling from homes and firesides wives and children of a brave people.

To this Sherman answered on the same date:

> You style the measures proposed, 'unprecedented,' and appeal to the dark history of war for a parallel, as an act of 'studied and iniquitous cruelty.' It is not unprecedented, for General Johnston himself very wisely and properly removed the families all the way from Dalton down, and I see no reason why Atlanta should be excepted. Nor is it necessary to appeal to 'the dark history of war,' when recent and modern examples are so handy. You yourself burned dwelling-houses along your parapet; and I have seen, today, fifty houses that you have rendered uninhabitable because they stood in the way of your forts and men. You defended Atlanta on a line so close to the town that every cannon-shot and many musket-shots from our line of investment, that overshot their mark, went into the habitations of women and children. General Hardee did the same thing at Jonesboro', and General Johnston did the same last summer at Jackson, Mississippi.
>
> I have not accused you of heartless cruelty, but merely instance these cases of very recent occurrence, and could go on and enumerate hundreds of others, and challenge any fair man to judge which of us has the heart of pity for the families of 'brave people.' I say it is kindness to these families of Atlanta to remove them at once from scenes that women and children should not be exposed to; and the 'brave people' should scorn to commit their wives and children to the rude barbarians who thus, as you say, violate the rules of war as illustrated in the pages of its 'dark history.'
>
> In the name of common sense, I ask you not to 'appeal to a just God' in such a sacrilegious manner,—you who in the midst of peace and prosperity have plunged a nation into war, dark and cruel war; who dared and badgered us into battle; insulted our flag; seized our arsenals and forts that were left in

the honourable custody of a peaceful ordnance sergeant; seized and made prisoners even the very first garrisons sent to protect your people against negroes and Indians, long before any other act was committed by the, to you, 'hateful Lincoln government,' tried to force Missouri and Kentucky into rebellion, in spite of themselves; falsified the vote of Louisiana; turned loose your privateers to plunder unarmed ships; expelled Union families by the thousands, burned their houses, and declared by acts of your Congress the confiscation of all debts due Northern men for goods had and received. Talk thus to the Marines, but not to me, who have seen these things, and who will this day make as much sacrifice for the peace and honour of the South as the best-born Southerner among you. If we must be enemies, let us be men, and fight it out as we propose today, and not deal in such hypocritical appeals to God and humanity.

God will judge us in due time, and he will pronounce whether it will be humane to fight with a town full of women and the families of 'a brave people' at our back, or to remove them in time to places of safety among their own friends and people.

Notwithstanding the excesses which were committed by the foragers on Sherman's march from Atlanta to the sea, his army maintained its discipline. The soldiers while in and around Savannah were orderly and quiet. No woman was insulted; there was no debauchery, no breaking open of houses. Citizens could walk the streets and engage in business without molestation. Life and property were respected. General Sherman in his official report thus spoke of the conduct of his soldiers:

> As to the rank and file, they seem so full of confidence in themselves that I doubt if they want a compliment from me; but I must do them the justice to say that, whether called on to fight, to march, to wade streams, to make roads, clear out obstructions, build bridges, make 'corduroy,' or tear up railroads, they have done it with alacrity and a degree of cheerfulness unsurpassed. A little loose in foraging, they 'did some things they ought not to have done,' yet, on the whole, they have supplied the wants of the army with as little violence as could be expected, and as little loss as I calculated. Some of these foraging parties had encounters with the enemy which would, in ordinary times, rank as respectable battles.
>
> The behaviour of our troops in Savannah has been so manly,

so quiet, so perfect, that I take it as the best evidence of discipline and true courage. Never was a hostile city, filled with women and children, occupied by a large army with less disorder, or more system, order, and good government. The same general and generous spirit of confidence and good feeling pervades the army which it has ever afforded me especial pleasure to report on former occasions.

Although Sherman's army was composed of four corps, the Fourteenth, Fifteenth, Seventeenth, and Twentieth, he had another made up from all of these, which, though unknown in the war office, was of much service to him and of great damage to the enemy. It was known as the "Bummer" Corps. The word is not to be found in either of the American unabridged dictionaries, though it has become historic. Who made it, or how it came into use, is not known. It may have been derived from the word *bum-bailiff*, which is a corruption of bound-bailiff, a subordinate civil officer appointed to serve writs and to make executions, and bound with sureties for a faithful discharge of his trust; or from *bum-boat*, a boat used for conveying provisions, fruit, and supplies from shore to ship. From the two words we get the full meaning of the term *Bummer*.

Sherman could not start from Atlanta with sufficient supplies of bread, meat, and corn for his great march. He must live on the country. Hence he marched in four parallel columns, near enough to aid each other if attacked, yet far enough apart to mow a swath forty or fifty miles in width.

The foraging party, numbering over five thousand, always on the alert, ever in the advance, kept ahead of Kilpatrick with his cavalry.

"If I come to a town or village or plantation, and stop to obtain forage, I find that the infernal bummers have been there," said Kilpatrick.

Having authority to take provisions, the bummers were not tardy in executing their trust. They went in squads, fought the Rebel skirmishers, and defeated Wheeler's cavalry in several encounters. No matter how rich a prize there might be of poultry in a farm-yard, the appearance of a Rebel brought them into line for mutual defence.

Sometimes they came in with a dozen fresh horses loaded with chickens, turkeys, and pigs. In one instance a squad, with live fowls dangling at their saddles, was confronted by Rebel cavalry. They formed in line, fired a volley, and started upon a charge. The galloping of the horses, accompanied by the flapping of wings, the cackling of hens, gobbling of turkeys, and squealing of pigs, stampeded the horses of the enemy, and gave the bummers an easy victory.

Farm wagons were confiscated and filled with provisions,—jars of jelly, preserves, pickles, and honey, baskets of sweet potatoes and legs of bacon. They often rode grandly in family carriages, accompanied by crowds of grinning negroes, who had pointed out the places where the planters had secreted provisions, and who watched for Rebels while the bummer secured his plunder; and then, when the master was out of sight, bid goodbye forever to the old plantation, and with light hearts leaped the fences, on their way to freedom.

There were two classes of bummers,—the regular soldier of the corps, who kept his comrades well supplied with good things, and the irregular member, whose chief care was to provide for himself.

They were of great service, not only as foragers, but as flankers and scouts, keeping Sherman well informed of the whereabouts of the Rebels. Yet their lawlessness had a demoralizing tendency. Some were tender-hearted, and took only what was needed to eat, while others ransacked houses, ripped open feather-beds, smashed looking-glasses and crockery, and tumbled tables and chairs about unceremoniously, frightening women and children. But a bummer outraging a woman would have been hung by his fellows on the nearest tree, or if not by them he would have had short respite of life from the soldiers in the ranks.

While in Savannah they had no occasion to ply their vocation, as provisions were abundant. Noticing full-grown chickens picking up corn in the streets, I expressed my surprise to an officer of the Twentieth Corps.

"The fact is," he replied, "we have lived on chickens all the way from Atlanta. We have had roast chicken, fried chicken, and stewed chicken, till we are tired of it."

But when Sherman resumed his march through South Carolina, the bummers were keener than ever. The whole army was eager to begin the march. Each regiment, when it crossed the Savannah River, and set foot in South Carolina, gave a cheer. They were in the hot-bed of Secession.

"We'll make South Carolina howl!" they said.

I saw an unoccupied mansion, upon the floors of which were Brussels and tapestry carpeting, and mirrors of French plate-glass adorned the parlour. There was a library with well-filled shelves, and in the drawing-room a costly rosewood piano,—all of which in an hour were licked up by the flames.

MT. VERNON. EDWARD EVERETT. SAVANNAH.
THE CAPITOL.

Far away to the north, as far as the eye could reach, were pillars of smoke, ascending from other plantations.

"We'll purify their Secession hate by fire," said one.

The soldiers evidently felt that they were commissioned to administer justice in the premises, and commenced by firing the premises of the South Carolinians. They were avengers, and their path through that proud State was marked by fire and desolation. "South Carolina began the Rebellion, and she shall suffer for it. If it had not been for her there would have been no war. She is responsible for all the misery, woe, and bloodshed." Such was the universal sentiment.

Although Sherman's troops carried the torch in one hand and the sword in the other, and visited terrible retribution upon the Rebels, they were quick to relieve the wants of the truly loyal. A few days before reaching Savannah they came to a plantation owned by a man who through all the war had remained faithful to the Union. He had been hunted through the woods with bloodhounds by the Rebel conscript officers. Hearing the Yankees had arrived, he came out from his hiding-place, and joined the Twentieth Corps, with the intention of accompanying it to Savannah. The soldiers made up for him a purse of one hundred and thirty dollars. When it was presented he burst into tears. He could only say, so great was his emotion, "Gentlemen, I most heartily thank you. It is a kindness I never expected. I have been hunted through swamps month after month. My wife and children have been half starved, insulted, and abused, and all because we loved the old flag."

The stories which were told by those refugees, of Union men and conscripts hunted by bloodhounds, of imprisonment and murder by Rebels,—of the sufferings of the Union prisoners at Millen, Libby, Salisbury, and Andersonville,—wrought the soldiers of Sherman's army into a frenzy of wrath against South Carolina.

CHAPTER 24
Christianity and Barbarism

DECEMBER, 1864

When Sherman's army entered Savannah the people of that city were on the verge of starvation. The Rebel authorities had not accumulated sufficient supplies for a long defence. They were ignorant of the intentions of Sherman when he left Atlanta, and were unable to see through his plan till too late to put the place in condition to withstand a siege. Breastworks were hastily thrown up on the west side of the city. The eastern approaches were strongly protected by a series of forts, turrets, and batteries built by slaves at the beginning of the war, in which were heavy guns commanding the river and the roads. No one had dreamed that the Yankees would come from the west. When Sherman was fairly on his march there was consternation in all the cities along the coast. Charleston expected him. Would he not aim directly toward the cradle of Secession? The people of Mobile believed that the fleet which was gathering in the Gulf was destined to co-operate with the "ruthless invader" in an attack upon them. The inhabitants of Brunswick expected to see him there. The citizens of Savannah were equally alarmed. Proclamations and manifestoes were issued. Governor Brown called upon the Georgians to rise in their might; but their former might was weakness now. They had lost heart. They saw that their cause was failing. Their armies, successful in the beginning, had won no victory for many months. The appeals of the Governor, the manifestoes of the Rebel generals, the calls of municipal authorities, and the exhortations of Davis, awakened no enthusiasm. The planters did not hasten to the rendezvous, nor respond to the call to send provisions. The Rebel quartermasters and commissaries were active in making forced levies, and the conscription bureau was vigilant in bringing in reluctant recruits; but before preparations for defending the city were completed Sherman was thundering at the door.

When he saw the destitution, he made an appeal to the humanity of the people of the North. Boston, New York, and Philadelphia were quick to respond. In Boston thirty thousand dollars were contributed in four days, a steamer chartered, loaded, and despatched on its errand of mercy. The occasion being so unusual, I deemed it worthwhile to visit Savannah, to be an eye-witness of the reception of the timely and munificent gift.

The employment of the steamer *Greyhound* on such a mission added to the interest. She was a captured blockade-runner, built at Greenock, Scotland, in 1863, purposely to run the blockade. She made one trip into Wilmington, and was seized while attempting to escape from that port. In every timber, plank, rivet, and brace was England's hatred of the North, support of the South, and cupidity for themselves; but now she carried peace and good-will, not only to the people of Savannah, but to men of every clime and lineage, race and nation. The *Greyhound* speeding her way was a type and symbol of the American Republic, freighted with the world's best hopes, and sailing proudly forward to the future centuries.

Among the passengers on board at the time of her capture was Miss Belle Boyd, of notoriety as a spy,—bold, venturesome, and dashing, unscrupulous, bitter in her hatred of the Yankees, regardless of truth or honour, if she could but serve the Rebels. She was of great service to them in the Shenandoah. Being within the Union lines, she obtained information which on several occasions enabled Jackson to make those sudden dashes which gave him his early fame.

It was nearly dark on Saturday evening, January 14th, when the *Greyhound* discharged her pilot off Boston Light. The weather was thick, the wind southeast, but during the night it changed to the northwest and blew a gale. The cold was intense. Sunday morning found us in Holmes's Hole, covered with ice. At noon the gale abated, and we ran swiftly across the Vineyard Sound, shaping our course for Hatteras. Off Charleston we passed through the blockading fleet, which was gaily decorated in honour of the taking of Fort Fisher. The Rebel flag was floating defiantly over Sumter. On Thursday evening we dropped anchor off Port Royal, where a half-day was lost in obtaining permission from the custom-house to proceed to Savannah. The obstructions in Savannah River made it necessary to enter Warsaw Sound and go up Wilmington River. With a coloured pilot,—the only one obtainable, recommended by the Harbor-Master of Hilton Head,—the *Greyhound* put to sea once more, ran down the coast, and on Sunday morning entered the Sound. Our pilot professed to know all the crooks and turns of the river, but suddenly we found ourselves fast on a mud-bank. It was ebb-tide, and the incoming flood floated us again. Then the engines refused to work, the pumps having become foul, and the anchor was dropped just in season to save the steamer from drifting broadside upon a sandbar. It was ten miles to Thunderbolt Battery. The captain of a pilot-boat was kind enough to send Messrs. Briggs and Baldwin, of the committee of the citizens of Boston in charge of the supplies, Mr. Glidden, of the firm owning the *Greyhound*, and the writer, up to that point. We landed, and stood where the Rebels had made sad havoc of what was once a pleasant village. Some Iowa soldiers, on seediest horses and sorriest mules, were riding round on a frolic. Shiftless, long-haired, red-eyed men and women, lounging about, dressed in coarsest homespun, stared at us. A score of horses and mules were in sight, and here were collected old carts, wagons, and carriages which Sherman's boys had brought from the interior.

"We want to get a horse and wagon to take us to Savannah," said one of the party to a little old man, standing at the door of a house.

"Wal, I reckon ye can take any one of these yere," he said, pointing to the horses and mules. Such animals! Ringboned, spavined, knock-kneed, wall-eyed, sore-backed,—mere hides and bones, some of them too weak to stand, others unable to lie down on account of stiff joints.

"How far is it to Savannah?" we asked of the residents of the village.

"Three miles," said one.

"Two miles and a half, I reckon," said a second.

"Three miles and three quarters," was the estimate of a third person.

A woman, dressed in a plaid petticoat, a snuff-coloured linsey-woolsey tunic, with a tawny countenance, black hair, and flashing black eyes, smoking a pipe, said: "I'll tell yer how fur it be. Savannah be a frying-pan and Thunderbolt be the handle, and I live on the eend on it. It be four miles long, zactly."

Two coloured soldiers rode up, both on one horse, with "55" on their caps.

"What regiment do you belong to?"

"The Fifty-Fifth Massachusetts."

Their camp was a mile or so up river. A steamboat captain, who wished to communicate with the quartermaster, came upstream in his boat and kindly offered to take us to the Fifty-Fifth. It began to rain, and we landed near a fine old mansion surrounded by live-oaks, their gnarled branches draped with festoons of moss, where we thought to find accommodations for the night; but no one answered our ringing. The doors were open, the windows smashed in; marble mantels, of elaborate workmanship, marred and defaced; the walls written over with doggerel. There were bunks in the parlours, broken crockery, old boots,—debris everywhere.

The committee took possession of the premises and made themselves at home before a roaring fire, while the writer went out upon a reconnoissance, bringing back the intelligence that the camp of the Fifty-Fifth was a mile farther up the river. It was dark when we reached the hospitable shanty of Lieutenant-Colonel Fox, who, in the absence of Colonel Hartwell, was commanding the regiment, which had been there but twenty-four hours. The soldiers had no tents.

One of the committee rode into Savannah, through a drenching rain, to report to General Grover. The night came on thick and dark. The rain was pouring in torrents. Colonel Fox, with great kindness, offered to escort us to a house nearby, where we could find shelter. We splashed through the mud, holding on to each other's coat-tails, going over boots in muddy water, tumbling over logs, losing our way, being scratched by brambles, falling into ditches, bringing up against trees, halting at length against a fence,—following which we reached the house. The owner had fled, and the occupant had moved in because it was a free country and the place was inviting. He had no bed for us, but quickly kindled a fire in one of the chambers and spread some quilts upon the floor.

"I haven't much wood, but I reckon I can pick up something that will make a fire," said he. Then came the pitch-pine staves of a rice-cask; then a bedstead, a broken chair, a wooden flowerpot!

The morning dawned bright and clear. General Grover sent out horses for us, and so we reached the city after many vexatious delays and rough experiences.

The people in Savannah generally were ready to live once more in the Union. The fire of Secession had died out. There was not much sourness,—less even than I saw at Memphis when that city fell into our hands, less than was manifested in Louisville at the beginning of the war.

At a meeting of the citizens resolutions expressive of gratitude for the charity bestowed by Boston, New York, and Philadelphia were passed, also of a desire for future fellowship and amity.

A store at the corner of Bay and Barnard Streets was taken for a depot, the city canvassed, and a registry made of all who were in want. I passed a morning among the people who came for food. The air was keen. Ice had formed in the gutters, and some of the jolly young negroes, who had provided themselves with old shoes and boots from the camp-grounds of Sherman's soldiers, were enjoying the luxurious pastime of a slide on the ice. The barefooted cuddled under the sunny side of the buildings. There was a motley crowd. Hundreds of both sexes, all ages, sizes, complexions, and costumes; gray-haired old men of Anglo-Saxon blood, with bags, bottles, and baskets; coloured patriarchs, who had been in bondage many years, suddenly made freemen; well-dressed women wearing crape for their husbands and sons who had fallen while fighting against the old flag, stood patiently waiting their turn to enter the building, where through the open doors they could see barrels of flour, pork, beans, and piles of bacon, hogsheads of sugar, molasses, and vinegar. There were women with tattered dresses,—old silks and satins, years before in fashion, and laid aside as useless, but which now had become valuable through destitution.

There were women in linsey-woolsey, in negro and gunny cloth, in garments made from meal-bags, and men in Confederate gray and butternut brown; a boy with a crimson plush jacket, made from the upholstering of a sofa; men in short jackets, and little boys in long ones; the cast-off clothes of soldiers; the rags which had been picked up in the streets, and exhumed from garrets; boots and shoes down at the heel, open at the instep, and gaping at the toes; old bonnets of every description, some with white and crimson feathers, and ribbons once bright and flaunting; hats of every style worn by both sexes, palm-leaf, felt, straw, old and battered and well ventilated. One without a crown was worn by a man with red hair, suggestive of a chimney on fire, and flaming out at the top! It was the ragman's jubilee for charity.

One of the tickets issued by the city authorities, in the hand of a woman waiting her turn at the counter, read thus:

City Store
Mary Morrell
12 lbs. Flour
7 lbs Bacon
2 lbs Salt
2 qts Vinegar

Andersonville, Belle Isle, Libby Prison, Millen, and Salisbury will forever stand in suggestive contrast to this City Store in Savannah, furnished by the free-will offering of the loyal people of the North. The report of the United States Sanitary Committee reads:

> At Libby a process of slow starvation was carried on. The cornbread was of the roughest and coarsest description. Portions of the cob and husk were often found grated in with the meal. The crust was so thick and hard that the prisoners called it 'iron clad.' To render the bread eatable they grated it, and made mush of it; but the crust they could not grate. Now and then, after long intervals, often of many weeks, a little meat was given them, perhaps two or three mouthfuls. At a later period they received a pint of black peas, with some vinegar, every week; the peas were often full of worms, or maggots in a chrysalis state, which, when they made soup, floated on the surface.... But the most unaccountable and shameful act of all was yet to come. Shortly after this general diminution of rations, in the month of January, the boxes (sent by friends in the North to the prisoners), which before had been regularly delivered, and in good order, were withheld. No reason was given. Three hundred arrived every week, and were received by Colonel Ould, Commissioner of Exchange; but instead of being distributed, they were retained and piled up in warehouses nearby, in full sight of the tantalized and hungry captives."[75]

While these supplies were being distributed to the people of Savannah, thirty thousand Union prisoners in the hands of the Rebels in South-western Georgia were starving to death,—not from a scarcity of food, but in accordance with a deliberately formed plan to render them unfit for future service in the Union ranks by their inhuman treatment, should they live to be exchanged.

What a page of darkness for the future historian!

On the other hand, the Rebel prisoners in the North received invariably the same rations, in quality and quantity, given to the Union soldiers in the field, with ample clothing, fuel, and shelter. So unexceptional was their treatment, that since the war a Southern writer, desirous of removing the load of infamy resting upon the South, has advertised for statements of unkind treatment in Northern prisons![76]

Of the treatment of Union soldiers in the Southern prisons the United States Sanitary Commission says:

75: Report of the United States Sanitary Commission.
76: See the *Watchman*, New York.

The prisoners were almost invariably robbed of everything valuable in their possession; sometimes on the field, at the instant of capture, sometimes by the prison authorities, in a quasi-official way, with the promise of return when exchanged or paroled, but which promise was never fulfilled. This robbery amounted often to a stripping of the person of even necessary clothing. Blankets and overcoats were almost always taken, and sometimes other articles; in which case damaged ones were returned in their stead. This preliminary over, the captives were taken to prison.

At the trial of Wirz, the commandant of Andersonville, Dr. John C. Bates, a surgeon of the Rebel service, testified as follows:

My attention was called to a patient in my ward who was only fifteen or sixteen years of age. I took much interest in him, owing to his youth. He would ask me to bring him a potato, bread, or biscuit, which I did. I put them in my pocket. He had scurvy and gangrene. I advised him not to cook the potato, but to eat it raw. He became more and more emaciated, his sores gangrened, and for want of food, and from lice, he died. I understood that it was against orders to take anything in to the prisoners, and hence I was shy in slipping food into my pockets. Others in the ward came to their death from the same causes. When I went there, there were two thousand or two thousand five hundred sick. I judge twenty or twenty-five thousand persons were crowded together. Some had made holes and burrows in the earth. Those under the sheds were doing comparatively well. I saw but little shelter, excepting what ingenuity had devised. I found them suffering with scurvy, dropsy, diarrhoea, gangrene, pneumonia, and other diseases. When prisoners died, they were laid in wagons, head foremost, to be carried off. I don't know how they were buried. The effluvia from the hospital was very offensive. If by accident my hand was abraded, I would not go into the hospital without putting a plaster over the affected part. If persons whose systems were reduced by inanition should by chance stump a toe or scratch the hand, the next report to me was gangrene, so potent was the regular hospital gangrene. The prisoners were more thickly confined in the stockade,—like ants and bees. Dogs were kept to hunt down the prisoners who escaped. Fifty per cent of those who died might have been saved had the patients been properly cared for. The effect of the treatment of the prisoners was, morally as well as physically, injurious. There was much stealing among them. All lived each for himself. I suppose this was superinduced by their starving condition. Seeing the dying condition of some of them, I remarked to my student, 'I can't resuscitate them; the weather is chilling; it is a matter of impossibility.' I found persons lying dead sometimes among the living. Thinking they merely slept, I went to wake them up and found they had taken their everlasting sleep. This was in the hospital. I judge it was about the same in the stockade. There being no dead-house, I erected a tent for the purpose, but I soon found that a blanket or quilt had been clipped off the canvas; and as the material could not be readily supplied, the dead-house was abandoned. I don't think any more dead-houses were erected. The daily ration was less in September, October, November, and December than it was from the 1st of January to the 20th of March. The men had not over twenty ounces of food in the twenty-four hours.

The prison at Andersonville was established in January, 1864, and was used a little more than a year. It was in the form of a quadrangle, 1,295 feet long, 865 feet wide. A small stream, rising from neighbouring springs, flowed through the grounds. Within the enclosure, seventeen feet from the stockade, the dead-line was established, marked by small posts, to which a slight strip of board was nailed. Upon the inner stockade were fifty-two sentry-boxes, in which the guards stood with loaded muskets; while overlooking the enclosure were several forts, with field artillery in position, to pour grape and canister upon the perishing men at the first sign of insurrection.

Miss Clara Barton, the heroic and tender-hearted woman who, in the employ of government, visited this charnel-house to identify the graves of the victims, thus reports:

> Under the most favourable circumstances and best possible management the supply of water would have been insufficient for half the number of persons who had to use it. The existing arrangements must have aggravated the evil to the utmost extent. The sole establishments for cooking and baking were placed on the bank of the stream immediately above and between the two inner lines of the palisades. The grease and refuse from them were found adhering to the banks at the time of our visit. The guards, to the number of three thousand six hundred, were principally encamped on the upper part of the stream, and when the heavy

rains washed down the hillsides covered with thirty thousand human beings, and the outlet below failed to discharge the flood which backed and filled the valley, the water must have become so foul and loathsome that every statement I have seen of its offensiveness must fall short of the reality; and yet within rifle-shot of the prison flowed a stream, fifteen feet wide and three feet deep, of pure, delicious water. Had the prison been placed so as to include a section of 'Sweet Water Creek,' the inmates might have drank and bathed to their hearts' content.[77]

The prisoners had no shelter from the fierce sun of summer, the pelting autumn rains, or the cold of winter, except a few tattered tents. Thousands were destitute of blankets. For refuge they dug burrows in the ground. Miss Barton says:

The little caves are scooped out and arched in the form of ovens, floored, ceiled, and strengthened, so far as the owners had means, with sticks and pieces of board, and some of them are provided with fireplaces and chimneys. It would seem that there were cases, during the long rains, where the house would become the grave of its owner by falling upon him in the night.... During thirteen long months they knew neither shelter nor protection from the changeable skies above, nor the pitiless, unfeeling earth beneath....

Think of thirty thousand men penned by close stockade upon twenty-six acres of ground, from which every tree and shrub had been uprooted for fuel to cook their scanty food, huddled like cattle, without shelter or blanket, half clad and hungry, with the dewy night setting in after a day of autumn rain. The hilltop would not hold them all, the valley was filled by the swollen brook. Seventeen feet from the stockade ran the fatal dead-line, beyond which no man might step and live. What did they do? I need not ask where did they go, for on the face of the whole earth there was no place but this for them. But where did they place themselves? How did they live? Ay! how did they die?

Twelve thousand nine hundred and ninety graves are numbered on the neighbouring hillside,—the starved and murdered of thirteen months,—one thousand per month, thirty-three per day! Murdered by Jeff Davis, Robert E. Lee, James Seddon, and John C. Breckenridge! Murdered under official sanction, in accordance with pre-

---

77: Miss Barton's Report.

meditated design. Davis, Lee, Seddon, and Breckenridge may not have issued orders to starve the prisoners; but if cognizant of any inhumanity, it was in the power of Davis to stop it, and of Lee, as commander-in-chief of the army, as also of Sedden, and after him Breckenridge, secretaries of war. A word from either of these officials would have secured humane treatment.

General Lee is beloved by the Southern people for his amiability, his gentleness and generosity, as well as his unselfish devotion to the cause of Secession. But the historian will doubtless keep in mind that to be amiable is to be worthy of esteem and confidence. Those who have espoused the cause of the Union cannot discover much amiability in one who remained in the service of the government as the confidant of the commander-in-chief of the army of the United States till hostilities were commenced, and then, three days after his resignation, accepted the command of the Rebel forces in Virginia. Fort Sumter was fired upon April 12, 1861. General Lee resigned his commission in the service of the United States on the 19th, and on the 22nd took command of Rebel troops at Richmond. The State had not then seceded. The ordinance of Secession was passed by the convention on the 17th of the same month, to be submitted to popular vote for ratification on the third Tuesday of May. Without waiting for the action of the people of his State, General Lee issued his military orders and waged war against the United States.

The future historian will not overlook the fact that General Lee, if not issuing direct orders for the starvation of Union prisoners, made no remonstrance against the barbarities of Andersonville, or of the course taken to debauch the patriotism of the Union soldiers. It was promised that whoever would acknowledge allegiance to the Confederacy, or consent to make shoes or harness or clothing for the Rebels, should have the privilege of going out from the stockade, and finding comfortable quarters and plenty of food and clothing. Thus tempted, some faltered, while others died rather than be released on such terms, preferring, in their love for the flag, to be thrown like logs into the dead-cart, and tumbled into the shallow trenches on the hillside!

Among the prisoners was a lad who pined for his far-off Northern home. Often his boyish heart went out lovingly to his father and mother and fair-haired sister. How could he die in that prison! How close his eyes on all the bright years of the future! How lie down in death in that loathsome place, when, by taking the oath of allegiance to the Southern Confederacy, he could obtain freedom? His comrades were dying. Every day the dead-cart came and bore them away by scores and hundreds. What a sight their stony eyes, sunken cheeks, and swaying limbs! Around him was a crowd of living skeletons.

"Take the oath and you shall live," said the tempter. What a trial! Life was sweet. All that a man hath will he give for his life. How blessed if he could but hear once more the voice of his mother, or grasp again a father's hand! What wonder that hunger, despair, and death, and the example of some of his comrades, made him weakly hesitate?

Too feeble to walk or to stand, he crawled away from the dying and the dead, over the ground reeking with filth. He had almost reached the gate beyond which were life and liberty. A comrade, stronger and older, suspected his purpose. Through the long, weary months this brave soldier had solaced his heart by taking at times from his bosom a little flag,—the stars and stripes,—adoring it as the most sacred of all earthly things. He held it before the boy. It was the flag he loved. He had sworn to support it,—never to forsake it. He had stood beneath it in the fierce conflict, quailing not when the death-storm was thickest. Tears dimmed his eyes as he beheld it once more.

Tremblingly he grasped it with his skeleton fingers, kissed it, laid it on his heart, and cried, "God help me! I can't turn my back upon it. O comrade, I am dying; but I want you, if ever you get out of this horrible place, to tell my mother that I stood by the old flag to the last!"

And then, with the flag he loved lying on his heart, he closed his eyes, and his soul passed on to receive that reward which awaits those to whom duty is greater than life.

On Fame's eternal camping-ground
Their silent tents are spread,
And Glory guards, with solemn round,
The bivouac of the dead.

This is the contrast between Christian charity and barbaric hate,—not that all the people of the South were inhuman, or that men there are by nature more wicked than all others; but the barbarity was the legitimate outgrowth of slavery.

The armies of the South fought bravely and devotedly to establish a Confederacy with slavery for its corner-stone; but not their valour, sacrifice, and endurance, not Stonewall Jackson's religious enthusiasm or intrepidity, not Lee's military exploits, can avail to blot the horrors of Andersonville from the historic record. Their cause

Hath the primal, eldest curse upon it,
A brother's murder.

CHAPTER 25

Scenes in Savannah

DECEMBER, 1864

As I intended to spend some days in Savannah, I set out one afternoon in search of lodgings more commodious than those furnished at the Pulaski House, and I was directed to a house owned by a gentleman who, during the war, had resided in Paris,—a large brick mansion, fronting on one of the squares, elegantly finished and furnished. It had been taken care of, through the war, by two faithful negroes, Robert and his wife Aunt Nellie, both of them slaves. I rang the bell, and was ushered into the basement by their daughter Ellen, also a slave. Robert was fifty-three years of age,—a tall, stout, coal-black, slow-spoken, reflective man. Aunt Nellie was a year or two younger. Her features were of the African type; her eyes large and lustrous. Her deportment was lady-like, her language refined. She wore a gingham dress, and a white turban. Ellen, the daughter, had a fair countenance, regular features, of lighter hue than either father or mother. She appeared as much at ease as most young ladies who are accustomed to the amenities of society.

Aunt Nellie called me by name.

"I saw you yesterday at church," she said.

She placed a chair for me before the fire, which burned cheerfully on the hearth. There was a vase of amaranths on the mantel, and lithographs on the walls. A clock ticked in one corner. There were cushioned arm-chairs. The room was neat and tidy, and had an air of cheerfulness. A little boy, four or five years old, was sitting by the side of Aunt Nellie,—her grand-nephew. He looked up wonderingly at the stranger, then gazed steadily into the fire with comical gravity.

"You are from Boston, I understand," said Aunt Nellie. "I never have been to Boston, but I have been to New York several times with my master."

"Did you have any desire to stay North?"

"No, sir, I can't say that I had. This was my home; my children and friends, and my husband were all here."

"But did you not wish to be free?"

"That is a very different thing, sir. God only knows how I longed to be free; but my master was very kind. They used to tell me in New York that I could be free; but I couldn't make up my mind to leave master, and my husband. Perhaps if I had been abused as some of my people have, I should have thought differently about it."

"Well, you are free now. I suppose that you never expected to see such a day as this!"

"I can't say that I expected to see it, but I knew it would come. I have prayed for it. I didn't hardly think it would come in my time, but I knew it must come, for God is just."

"Did you not sometimes despair?"

"Never! sir; never! But O, it has been a terrible mystery, to know why the good Lord should so long afflict my people, and keep them in bondage,—to be abused, and trampled down, without any rights of their own,—with no ray of light in the future. Some of my folks said there wasn't any God, for if there was he wouldn't let white folks do as they have done for so many years; but I told them to wait,—and now they see what they have got by waiting. I told them that we were all of one blood,—white folks and black folks all come from one man and one woman, and that there was only one Jesus for all. *I knew it,—I knew it!*" She spoke as if it were an indisputable fact which had come by intuition.

Here Aunt Nellie's sister and her husband came in.

"I hope to make your better acquaintance," she said, curtseying. It is a common form of expression among the coloured people of some parts of the South. She was larger, taller, and stouter than Aunt Nellie, younger in years, less refined,—a field hand,—one who had drunk deeply of the terrible cup which slavery had held to her lips. She wore a long gray dress of coarse cloth,—a frock with sleeves, gathered round the neck with a string,—the cheapest possible contrivance for a dress, her only garment, I judged.

"These are new times to you," I said.

"It is a dream, sir,—a dream! 'Pears like I don't know where I am. When General Sherman come and said we were free, I didn't believe it, and I wouldn't believe it till the minister (Rev. Mr. French) told us that we were free. It don't seem as if I was free, sir." She looked into the fire a moment, and sat as if in a dream, but roused herself as I said,—

"Yes, you are free."

"But that don't give me back my children,—my children, that I brought forth with pains such as white women have,—that have been torn from my breast, and sold from me; and when I cried for them was tied up and had my back cut to pieces!"

She stopped talking to me, raised her eyes as if looking into heaven,—reached up her hands imploringly, and cried in agony,—

"O Lord Jesus, have mercy! How long, O Lord? Come, Jesus, and help me. 'Pears like I can't bear it, dear Lord. They is all taken from me, Lord. 'Pears like as if my heart would break. O blessed Jesus, they say that I am free, but where are my children!—my children!—my children!"

Her hands fell,—tears rolled down her cheeks. She bowed her head, and sat moaning, wailing, and sobbing.

"You wouldn't believe me," said Aunt Nellie, speaking to her. "You said that there was no use in praying for deliverance; that it was no use to trust God,—that he had forgotten us!"

She rose and approached her sister, evidently to call her mind from the terrible reality of the past. "You used to come in here and go worry, worry, worry all day and all night, and say it was no use; that you might as well die; that you would be a great deal better off if you were dead. You wouldn't believe me when I said that the Lord would give deliverance. You wouldn't believe that the Lord was good; but just see what he has done for you,—made you free. Aren't you willing to trust him now?"

The sister made no reply, but sat wiping away her tears, and sighing over the fate of her children.

"Did you not feel sometimes like rising against your masters?" I asked of the husband.

"Well, sir, I did feel hard sometimes, and I reckon that if it hadn't been for the grace which Jesus gave us we should have done so; but he had compassion on us, and helped us to bear it. We knew that he would hear us some time."

"Did you ever try to escape?"

"No, sir. I was once interested in colonization, and talked of going to Africa,—of buying myself, and go there and be free. Rev. Mr. Gurley came here and gave a lecture. He was the agent of the Colonization Society, I reckon; but just then there was so much excitement among the slaves about it, that our masters put a stop to it."

"The good people of Boston are heaping coals of fire on the heads of the slaveholders and Rebels," said Aunt Nellie.

"How so?" I asked.

"Why, as soon as General Sherman took possession of the city, you send down ship-loads of provisions to them. They have fought you with all their might, and you whip them, and then go to feeding them."

"I 'spect you intended that black and white folks should have them alike," said her sister.

"Yes, that was the intention."

"Not a mouthful have I had. I am as poor as white folks. All my life I have worked for them. I have given them houses and lands; they have rode in their fine carriages, sat in their nice parlours, taken voyages over the waters, and had money enough, which I and my people earned for them. I have had my back cut up. I have been sent to jail because I cried for my children, which were stolen from me. I have been stripped of my clothing, exposed before men. My daughters have been compelled to break God's commandment,—they couldn't help themselves,—I couldn't help them; white men have done with us just as they pleased. Now they turn me out of my poor old cabin, and say they own it. O dear Jesus, help me!"

"Come, come, sister, don't take on; but you just give thanks for what the Lord has done for you," said Aunt Nellie.

Her sister rose, stately as a queen, and said,—

"I thank you, sir, for your kind words to me tonight. I thank all the good people in the North for what they have done for me and my people. The good Lord be with you."

As she and her husband left the room, Aunt Nellie said,—

"Poor girl! she can't forget her children. She's cried for them day and night."

Never till then had I felt the full force of Whittier's burning lines:

A groan from Eutaw's haunted wood,—
A wail where Camden's martyrs fell,—
By every shrine of patriot blood,
From Moultrie's wall and Jasper's well!

By storied hill and hallowed grot,
By mossy wood and marshy glen,
Whence rang of old the rifle-shot,
And hurrying shout of Marion's men,
The groan of breaking hearts is there,—
The falling lash, the fetter's clank!
Slaves, slaves are breathing in that air
Which old De Kalb and Sumter drank!

What, ho! our countrymen in chains!
The whip on woman's shrinking flesh!
Our soil yet reddening with the stains
Caught from her scourging, warm and fresh!
What! mothers from their children riven!
What! God's own image bought and sold!
Americans to market driven,
And bartered, as the brute, for gold!

The night of the 28th of January was a fearful one in Savannah. The inhabitants experienced all the terror of a bombardment combined with the horror of a great conflagration. A fire broke out a little before midnight in a long row of wooden buildings at the west end of the city. The wind was fresh from the northwest, and the night exceedingly cold. My rooms were in the Pulaski House. I was awakened by a sudden explosion, which jarred the house, and heard the cry that the arsenal was on fire.

There was another explosion,—then a volley of shells, and large fragments came whirring through the air, striking the walls, or falling with a heavy plunge into the street.

"There are three thousand shells in the building," said a soldier running past, fleeing as if for his life.

"There are fifty tons of powder, which will go off presently," said another, in breathless haste. Fifty tons of powder! Savannah would be racked to its foundations! There would be a general crumbling of walls. Men, women, and children were running,—crying, and in fear of being crushed beneath the ruins of falling buildings.

It was the Rebel arsenal. I could not believe that the Rebels would store fifty tons of powder in the city, and waited for the general explosion. It did not come. Gradually I worked my way, under the shelter of buildings, towards the fire. The fire-engines were deserted, and the fire was having its own way, licking up the buildings, one after another, remorselessly.

It was a gorgeous sight,—the flames leaping high in air, thrown up in columns by the thirteen-inch shells, filling the air with burning timbers, cinders, and myriads of sparks. The streets were filled with fugitives. The hospitals were being cleared of sick and wounded, the houses of furniture. It was grand, but terrible. General Grover at once took measures to arrest the progress of the flames, by tearing down buildings, and bringing up several regiments, which, with the citizens and negroes, succeeded in mastering the destroying element.

In the morning there was a wilderness of chimneys, and the streets were strewn with furniture.

It was amusing to see with what good humour and nonchalance the coloured people and the soldiers regarded the conflagration.

Two negro women passed me, carrying great bundles on their heads.

"I's clean burned out," said one.

"So is I"; and they both laughed as if it was very funny.

"Let 'em burn: who cares?" said one soldier. "They have fought us, and now let 'em suffer."

"We have got to do guard duty, and it is a little more comfortable to be quartered in a house than to sleep in a shelter-tent, so let us save the place," said another; and the two went to work with a will to subdue the flames.

****

General Sherman's Special Field Order No. 15, dated January 16, 1865, permitted the freedmen to take possession of the abandoned lands. A meeting—called by General Saxton, who had been appointed Inspector—was held in the Second African Baptist Church, a large building, which was crowded to its utmost capacity by the coloured people. It was the first meeting ever held in Savannah having in view the exclusive interests of the coloured people.

The organist was playing a voluntary when I entered the church. He was a free coloured man, a native of Charleston, having a bullet-shaped head, bright, sparkling eyes, and a pleasant voice. He had lived in Savannah nine years, and was a music-teacher,—giving instruction on the violin, piano-forte, and organ, also vocal music, to persons of his own race. He was in the habit of putting in clandestinely some of the rudiments of the English language, although it was against the peace and dignity of the State. He dared to open a school, and taught in secret in the evening; but a policeman discovered that he was an incendiary, and he was compelled to hide till the matter was forgotten.

When the voluntary was completed, the choir sung Rev. Mr. Smith's *American hymn*,—

My country, 'tis of thee,
Sweet land of liberty,
Of thee I sing.

Their country! Their liberty! The words were no longer meaningless.

By request of General Saxton, they also sang Bishop Heber's *Missionary hymn*,—

From Greenland's icy mountains,
From India's coral strand,
Where Afric's sunny fountains
Roll down their golden sand,
From many an ancient river,
From many a palmy plain,
They call us to deliver
Their land from error's chain.

General Saxton addressed them.

"I have come to tell you what the President of the United States has done for you," said he.

"God bless Massa Linkum!" was the response of a thousand voices.

"You are all free."

"Glory to God! Hallelujah! Amen!" they shouted in tumultuous chorus.

He explained the cause of the war: how the Rebels fired upon the flag, how they hated freedom, and wished to perpetuate slavery, which produced the war, that, in turn, under God's providence, had made them free men. They were free, but they must labour to live. Their relations to their masters had all been changed. They could go where they pleased, do what they pleased, provided they did that which was right; but they had no claim upon their masters,—they must work for themselves. All wealth came from the soil, and by cultivating the ground they could obtain food, and thus increase their wealth. He read and explained General Sherman's order, and told them of the advancement which the freedmen had made at Beaufort. They had comfortable homes, their children were attending school, and the men and women had almost forgotten that they had been slaves. One man had accumulated ten thousand dollars in four years; another was worth five thousand. He advised them to go upon the islands and take possession of the abandoned lands. He also advised the young and able-bodied to enlist in the service of the United States. They were citizens, and they must begin to do their part as citizens. They were free, but there was still some fighting to be done to secure their liberty.

Rev. Mr. French also addressed them.

"Your freedom," said he, "is the gift of God. The President has proclaimed it, and the brave men of General Sherman's army have brought it to you."

"God bless General Sherman! Amen! That's so!" were the enthusiastic responses. They clapped their hands and gave expression to

Sherman's "bummers."

their joy in emphatic demonstrations. It was a strange sight,—a sea of turbaned heads in the body of the house, occupied by the women, wearing brightest coloured handkerchiefs, or bonnets with flaming ribbons; while above, in the galleries, were two sable clouds of faces. Every window was filled by a joyous, enthusiastic crowd.

"You are to show your late masters that you can take care of yourselves. If I were in your place I would go, if I had to live on roots and water, and take possession of the islands," said Mr. French.

"Yes, sir, dat is what we will do. We're gwine."

"Show your old masters that you can work as hard to keep out of slavery as they did to keep you in bondage. And you must have but one wife, instead of two or three, as you used to do."

There was a great sensation at this point,—an outburst of laughter echoing and re-echoing from floor to ceiling. I was utterly unable to understand how the remark was received, but the sable audience evidently looked upon it as a very funny affair. The negro race has a quick and natural appreciation of anything bordering upon the ridiculous. They boil over with uncontrollable merriment at a very small matter.

"Treat your old masters with all respect; be generous and kind to them. This is your day of rejoicing, and they are drinking their cup of sorrow. Do them good,—help them. Break off bad habits,—be good citizens, truthful and honest. Now, all of you who are ready to scratch for a living,—who are resolved to make your own way in the world,—hold up your hands."

Up went a thousand hands.

"You owe your liberty to the men of the North, to President Lincoln, to the thousands who have died,—to Jesus Christ."

Deep and solemn was the Amen,—a spontaneous outburst of gratitude, welling up from their sympathetic and affectionate natures.

A prayer was offered by Rev. Mr. Houston, of the Third African Baptist Church. It was impassioned, fervent, and earnest, in which there were thanksgiving, confession of sin, and a pleading for God's help. The President, the Union army, the Federal government, were remembered. He prayed also that God would bring the Rebels to see that they ought to lay down their arms and be at peace.

Then in conclusion they sang the hymn,—

Eternal are thy mercies, Lord,
Eternal truth attends thy word.

How gloriously the grand old choral of Luther rang! Old men sang,—tottering upon the verge of the grave, their heads white, their voices tremulous, their sight dim; women with scarred backs sang,—who had toiled unrequited in the malarious rice-swamps, who had prayed in dungeons and prisons, who had wept and moaned for their stolen babes,—for their husbands, mangled and torn by bloodhounds. But that was all of the past. The day of jubilee had dawned. They had cried day and night, "O Lord, how long!" But now they had only thanksgiving and praise.

After the meeting there was a general shaking of hands.

"Bless de Lord for dis yere day."

"May de good Lord be wid you."

"I never 'spected to see dis yere day; but de praise belongs to de good Lord; he be wid you, brudder."

Such were the congratulations. There were none of the white people of Savannah present. Before the men of the West entered the city, such a gathering, even for religious worship, would have been incendiary unless attended by white men. But it was an inauguration of a new era,—a beginning of the settlement of the question over which philanthropists, politicians, and statesmen had puzzled their philosophic brains: "What shall we do with them?"

Rev. Mr. Houston accompanied me to my room, and gave me a history of his life. He was forty-one years old, had always been a slave, and received his freedom at the hands of General Sherman. When a boy his master hired him out to the Marine Hospital. Waiting upon the sailors, he had an opportunity to hear a great deal about the world. They had books and papers. He had a desire to learn to read, and they, not having the black laws of Georgia before their eyes, taught him his letters. Then obtaining a Bible, and other books, he read with great zeal. He wanted to be a preacher, and after examination by the Baptist Association, was ordained to preach by white men. He purchased his time before the war, paying fifty dollars a month to his master, and became a provision-dealer, yet preaching on Sundays. He leased the lower story of a building fronting the market, where he sold his meat and where he lived. Above him, up two flights, was the slave-mart of Savannah. He used to go into the country, up the railroad to the centre of the State, to purchase cattle, and became well acquainted with the planters. He heard their discussions on current affairs, and thus received information upon the politics of the country. He gave an account of the state of affairs, of opinions held in the North and in the South at the time when Fremont was a candidate for the Presidency.

"We knew that he was our friend," said Mr. Houston, "and we wanted him elected. We were very much disappointed at the result of that election; but we kept hoping and praying that God would have mercy on us as a race."

"Did your people understand the points at issue between the South and the North, when the war begun?" I asked.

"Yes, sir, I think we did. When South Carolina fired on Sumter we understood that the North was fighting for the Union. The flag had been insulted, and we thought that you of the North would have spunk enough to resent the insult. Those of us who could read the papers knew that the points at issue really were between Freedom and Slavery."

"What did you think when we were defeated at Manassas? Did you not despair?"

"No, sir. I knew that the North would not give in for one defeat. Some of our people were down-hearted, but I had faith in God, sir. I felt that the war must go on till we were made free. Besides, we prayed, sir! There have been a great many prayers, sir, offered up from broken-hearted men and women,—from negro cabins, not in public,—for the success of the North. They could not offer such supplications at church; they were offered to a God who sees in secret, but who rewards openly. We are receiving all we ever asked for. Bless his holy name."

"You have seen people sold in the market, I suppose?"

"O yes, sir, thousands of them. O, sir, it seems as if I now could hear the groans and cries of mothers and fathers as they marched down those stairs out into the street in gangs,—their chains rattling and clanking on the stairs. It was hell, sir! The wailings of the damned can never be more heart-rending, as they were driven out, crying, 'O Lord! have mercy! O massa, don't! don't! O my poor children!'"

His eyes shone with a strange light. The muscles of his hands tightened. He arose and walked the room, wiped the tears from his eyes, but composing himself sat down, and said; "Iniquity was at its height when the war began, and it continued till General Sherman came. O, it was terrible! terrible! to be there in that room on the lower floor, and see the hundreds taken out,—to see them nabbed in the streets, or taken from their beds at dead of night by the sheriff, and sold at once; for since the war began white men have been obliged often to raise money suddenly, and slave property being especially insecure, we were liable to be sold at any moment. Runaway slaves were whipped unmercifully. Last summer I saw one receive five hundred lashes out on the Gulf Railroad, because he couldn't give an account of himself. The man who kept the slave-market left the city with a large number of slaves just before Sherman came, taking them South; but he is back in the city. He is a bitter old Rebel."

Mr. Houston and a party of freedmen had been to Skidaway Island to take possession of lands under General Sherman's order, and commence a colony.

They laid out a village, also farm lots of forty acres, set aside one central lot for a church, another for a school-house; then placing numbers in a hat, made the allotment. It was Plymouth Colony repeating itself. They agreed that if any others came to join them they should have equal privileges. So the *Mayflower* was blooming on the islands of the South Atlantic!

"We shall build our cabins and organize our town government for the maintenance of order," said Mr. Houston.

"I told you that I hired my time of my master," said he. "My master hired my money, and when I asked him for it he refused to pay me; and as I had no power before the law, I could not compel him, and have lost it. I have about five hundred hides, which I would like to send North. I want to purchase a portable saw-mill. We shall need lumber,—must have it to build our houses and our church."

Such was his plan,—indicating a foresight which gave promise of a prosperous future.

* * * * * * * *

Passing by a church, I saw the sexton, with brush in hand, sweeping the aisles. The edifice was a substantial, ancient structure, with a mahogany pulpit of the old style, a broad aisle, chandelier pendent from the arched roof, filigree and panel-work around the galleries. Old and aristocratic families had sat in the cushioned pews,—men of vast wealth, owning houses, lands, and slaves. A great organ loomed high up in the gallery, its gilt pipes fronting the pulpit. Marriages and funerals had been solemnized at the altar. For fifteen years, Sunday after Sunday, this sexton had faithfully discharged his duties at the church.

He was stout, thick-set, strong, with well-developed muscles and a clear eye. He was gentlemanly in his deportment, and his voice was one of the most musical I ever heard.

"Shall I take a look at the church?"

"Certainly, sir. Walk in."

His words were as if he had chanted them, so faultless the tone, inflection, and cadence. His features were well formed, but anthracite coal is not blacker than his complexion. I was interested in him at once. He leaning upon his broom, and sitting in one of the pews, had a free conversation upon the events of his life.

He was born in Norfolk, Virginia, in 1829.

"My old master died," said he, "and I fell to his son, who went off to college and got to spreeing it, lost all his property, and of course I had to be sold. I brought twelve hundred dollars,—that was in 1849,—but another man offered the man who bought me a hundred and fifty dollars bonus for his bargain, which was accepted, and I was brought to Charleston. I have always been a slave."

"But you are a free man now; just as free as I am."

"Yes, sir, so General Sherman told me. I had a talk with him; and he talked just as free with me as if I was his own brother. But I don't feel it in my heart, sir, to go away and leave my old master, now that he is poor, and calamity has come upon him."

"Has he always treated you well?"

"Yes, sir,—that is, he never scarred my back. Some masters are mighty hard, sir. I don't blame some negroes for running away from their masters now that they can, for they have been treated mighty bad, sir; but my master has had great calamity come upon him, sir. When I was brought here from Norfolk, master's son Bob, who is in Texas,—a captain in the Southern army now,—saw me, and liked me, and I liked him, and his father bought me for Bob, and Bob and I have been like brothers to each other. I have no complaint to make. But master has lost two sons in Virginia. One of them was killed in the first battle of Manassas."

"I suppose you have heard many prayers here for Jeff Davis?"

"Yes, sir, and mighty fine sermons for the Southern army, sir; and there have been solemn scenes in this church, sir. Six bodies, one Sunday, after the first battle of Manassas, were here in this broad aisle. I had the communion-table set out here, right in front of the pulpit, and there they lay,—six of 'em. I couldn't help crying when I saw 'em, for they were just like old friends to me. They used to attend the Sunday school when they were boys, and used to cut up a little wild, and it was my business to keep 'em straight. They belonged to the Oglethorpe Light Infantry, and went with Colonel Bartow. They went away gaily, and thought they were going to Richmond to have a nice time. Their mothers and sisters told them to go and fight the Yankees. They didn't expect to see them brought back dead, I reckon. It was a sad day, sir."

"Then the women were as eager as the men for the war?"

"Yes, sir,—more. They were crazy about fighting the Yankees. I know that some of the boys didn't want to fight against the flag, but the women made 'em. The men had to wear Secession badges, as something to show that they were for the South. If it hadn't been for the ladies, I reckon we wouldn't have had the war."

"What do the women think now?"

"Well, sir, some of them are as bitter as ever they were against the Yankees, but I reckon they don't care to say much; and then there are others who see it ain't no use to try to hold out any longer. There are lots of 'em who have lost their husbands and brothers and sons. I reckon there are very few of the Light Infantry left. I know 'em all, for I took care of their hall,—their armoury,—and they made me hoist the flag one day union down. That made me feel very bad, sir. I always loved the flag, and I love it now better than ever. It makes me feel bad to think that my boys fought against it (he meant the boys who attended the Sunday school). But I reckon it is the Lord's doing, sir, and that it will be a blessing to us in the end."

"Can you read and write?" I asked.

"A little, sir. I never had any one to show me, but I used to sit down here in the pews and take up the hymn-book, and spell out the words, and one day master Bob set me a copy in writing, and so I have learned a little. I can read the newspapers, sir, and have kept track of the war."

Upon the first battle of Manassas, the Peninsular campaigns, the blowing up of the Merrimac, the battles of Antietam, Gettysburg, Vicksburg, New Orleans, and Sherman's campaign, he was well informed. He had a brother who was fighting for the Union.

"He is a brave fellow, and I know he won't show the white feather," said he.

We talked upon the prospects of the coloured people now that they were free.

"I reckon, sir," said he, "that a good many of 'em will be disappointed. They don't know what freedom is. But they will find that they have got to work, or else they won't get anything to eat. They are poor, ignorant creatures; but I reckon, sir, that after a while, when things get settled, they will learn how to take care of themselves. But I think they are mighty foolish to clear out and leave their old masters, when they can have good situations, and good pay, and little to do. Then, sir, it is kind of ungrateful like, to go away and leave their old masters when the day of calamity comes. I could not do it, sir; besides, I reckon I will be better off to stay here for the present, sir."

I informed him that I was from Massachusetts.

"I know something about Massachusetts, and I reckon it is a mighty fine State, sir. I have heard you abused, and the people of Boston also.

Savannah people said hard things about you: that you were abolitionists, and wanted the negroes to have equal privileges with the white men. My father, when I was in Norfolk, undertook to get to Massachusetts, but he was hunted down in the swamps and sold South, away down to Alabama, and that is the last I have heard of him. I have always liked Massachusetts. I reckon you are a liberal people up there. I hear you have sent a ship-load of provisions to us poor people."

I gave him information upon the subject, and spoke of Mr. Everett, who made a speech at the meeting in Faneuil Hall.

"Mr. Everett! I reckon I heard him talk about General Washington once here, five or six years ago. He was a mighty fine speaker, sir. The house was crowded."

The sun was setting, and the sexton had other duties. As I left the church, he said: "Come round, sir, some afternoon, and I will take you up to the steeple, so that you can get a sight of the city, and may be you play the organ. I love to hear music, sir."

How strangely this will read fifty years hence! The words *slave,—master,—sold,—hunted down*, will make this present time seem an impossibility to those who live after us. This sexton—a slave—heard the minister preach of the loosing of the bonds of the oppressed, and of doing unto others as they would be done by, yet he found in his own experience such a Gospel a lie. His bonds were not loosened; and the boys of the Sunday school, the petted sons of Savannah, went out from their aristocratic homes to perpetuate that lie. At last through war came deliverance; and yet there was so much gentleness in the heart of this man, that in the day of calamity which came to his master, when his sons one by one were killed in their endeavours to sustain that lie; when his property disappeared like dew before the morning sun; when his pride was humiliated; when his daughters, who were expectants of immense fortunes, were compelled to do menial service,—this servant, though a free man, could not find it in his heart to leave them, and take the liberty he loved! It may have been an exceptional case; but it shows an interesting feature of Southern life. The words of this sexton of Savannah will adorn the historic page.

"I reckon, sir, that it is the Lord's doing, and that it will be a blessing to us in the end."

Society in the South, and especially in Savannah, had undergone a great change. The extremes of social life were very wide apart before the war; they were no nearer the night before Sherman marched into the city; but the morning after there was a convulsion, an upheaval, a shaking up and a settling down of all the discordant elements. The tread of that army of the West, as it moved in solid column through the streets, was like a moral earthquake, overturning aristocratic pride, privilege, and power.

Old houses, with foundations laid deep and strong in the centuries, fortified by wealth, name, and influence, went down beneath the shock. The general disruption of the former relations of master and slave, and forced submission to the Union arms, produced a common level. A reversal of the poles of the earth would hardly have produced a greater physical convulsion than this sudden and unexpected change in the social condition of the people of the city.

On the night before Sherman entered the place there were citizens who could enumerate their wealth by millions; at sunrise the next morning they were worth scarcely a dime. Their property had been in cotton, negroes, houses, land, Confederate bonds and currency, railroad and bank stocks. Government had seized their cotton; the negroes had possession of their lands; their slaves had become freemen; their houses were occupied by troops; Confederate bonds were waste paper; their railroads were destroyed; their banks insolvent. They had not only lost wealth, but they had lost their cause. And there were some who were willing to confess that they had been fighting for a system of iniquity.

One could not ask for more courteous treatment than I received during my stay in Savannah. I am indebted to many ladies and gentlemen of that city for kind invitations to pass an evening with them. There was no concealment of opinion on either side, but with the utmost good feeling full expression was given to our differing sentiments.

"We went into the war in good faith; we thought we were right; we confidently expected to establish our independence; but we are whipped, and have got to make the best of it," was the frank acknowledgment of several gentlemen.

"I hate you of the North," said a young lady. It came squarely, and the tone indicated a little irritation.

"I am very sorry for it. I can hardly think that you really hate us. You don't hate me individually?"

"O no. You come here as a gentleman. I should indeed be rude and unladylike to say that I hated you; but I mean the Yankees in general. We never can live together in peace again. For one, I hope to leave the country."

"If I were to reside here, you of course would treat me courteously so long as I was a gentleman in my deportment?"

"Certainly; but you are an individual."

"But if two individuals can live peacefully, why not ten,—or a hundred,—a thousand,—all?"

She hesitated a moment; and then, with flashing eyes and flushed countenance, which added charms to her beauty, said, "Well, it is hard—and you will not think any worse of me for saying it—to have your friends killed, your servants all taken away, your lands confiscated; and then know that you have failed,—that you have been whipped. I wish that we had the power to whip you; but we haven't, and must make the best of it. What we are to do I don't know. We have been able to have everything that money could buy, and now we haven't a dollar. I don't care anything about keeping the negroes in slavery; but there is one feeling which we Southerners have that you cannot enter into. My old mamma who nursed me is just like a mother to me; but there is one thing that I never will submit to,—that the negro is our equal. He belongs to an inferior race."

She laid down the argument in the palm of her hand with a great deal of emphasis.

"Your energy, boldness, and candour are admirable. If under defeat and disaster you sat down supinely and folded your hands, there would be little hope of your rising again; but your determination to make the best of it shows that you will adapt yourself readily to the new order of things. There never will be complete equality in society. Political and social equality are separate and distinct. Rowdies and ragamuffins have natural rights: they may have a right to vote, they may be citizens; but that does not necessarily entitle them to free entrance into our homes."

The idea was evidently new to the young lady,—and not only to her, but to all in the room. To them the abolition of slavery was the breaking down of all social distinctions. So long as the negro was compelled to enter the parlour as a servant, they could endure his presence; but freedom implied the possibility, they imagined, of his entrance as an equal, entitled to a place at their firesides and a seat at their tables. The thought was intolerable.

The poor whites of the South are far below the coloured people in ability and force of character. They are a class from which there is little to hope. Nothing rouses their ambition. Like the Indians, they are content with food for today; tomorrow will take care of itself. In the cities they swarm along the sides of buildings on sunny days, and at night crawl into their miserable cabins with little more aspiration than dogs that seek their kennels. Undoubtedly there is far less suffering among the poor of the Southern cities than among the poor of New York, where life is ever a struggle with want. The South has a milder climate, nature requires less labour for production, and the commercial centres are not overcrowded. The poor whites of the South maintain no battle with starvation, but surrender resignedly to poverty. They can exist without much labour, and are too indolent to strive to rise to a higher level of existence. The war has taken their best blood. Only shreds and dregs remain.

"What can be done for the poor whites?"

It is a momentous question for the consideration of philanthropists and statesmen.

They are very ignorant. Their dialect is a mixture of English and African, having words and phrases belonging to neither language; though the *patois* is not confined to this class, but is sometimes heard in sumptuously furnished parlours.

"I suppose that you will not be sorry when the war is over," I remarked to a lady in Savannah.

"No, sir. I reckon the Confederacy is done gone for," was the reply.

It is reported that a North Carolina colonel of cavalry was heard to address his command thus,—"'Tention, battalion. Prepare to gen orto yer critter. Git!"

The order to ride rapidly was, "Dust right smart!"

You hear young ladies say, *Paw*, for Pa, *Maw*, for Ma, and then, curiously adding another vowel sound, they say *kear* for car, *thear* for there.

The poor whites of the country are called "poor white trash," "crackers," "clay-eaters," "sand-hillers," and "swamp angels," by the educated whites. There is no homogeneity of white society. The planters, as a rule, have quite as much respect for the negroes as for the shiftless whites.

Yet these miserable wretches are exceedingly bitter against the North: it is the bitterness of ignorance,—brutal, cruel, fiendish, produced by caste, by the spirit of slavery. There is more hope, therefore, of the blacks, in the future, than of this degraded class. The coloured people believe that the people of the North are their friends. Freedom, food, schools, all were given by the Yankees; hence gratitude and confidence on the part of the freedmen; hence, on the part of the poor whites, hatred of the North and cruelty toward the negro. Idleness, not occupation, has been, and is, their normal condition. It is ingrained in their nature to despise work. Indolence is a virtue, laziness no reproach. Thus slavery arrayed society against every law of God, moral and physical.

The poor whites were in bondage as well as the blacks, and to all appearance will remain so, while the natural buoyancy of the negro makes him rise readily to new exigencies; with freedom he is at once eager to obtain knowledge and acquire landed estates.

The coloured people who had taken up lands on the islands under General Sherman's order met for consultation in the Slave Market, at the corner of St. Julian Street and Market Square. I passed up the two flights of stairs down which thousands of slaves had been dragged, chained in coffle, and entered a large hall. At the farther end was an elevated platform about eight feet square,—the auctioneer's block. The windows were grated with iron. In an anteroom at the right women had been stripped and exposed to the gaze of brutal men. A coloured man was praying when I entered, giving thanks to God for the freedom of his race, and asking for a blessing on their undertaking. After prayers they broke out into singing. Lieutenant Ketchum of General Saxton's staff, who had been placed in charge of the confiscated lands, was present, to answer their questions.

"I would like to know what title we shall have to our lands, or to the improvements we shall make?" was the plain question of a tall black man.

"You will have the faith and honour of the United States," was the reply.

Rev. Mr. French informed them that the government could not give them deeds of the land, but that General Sherman had issued the order, and without doubt President Lincoln would see it was carried out. "Can't you trust the President who gave you your freedom?" he asked.

A stout man, with a yellow complexion, rose in the centre of the house: "I have a house here in the city. I can get a good living here, and I don't want to go to the islands unless I can be assured of a title to the land; and I think that is the feeling of four fifths present."

"That's so!" "Yes, brother!" was responded. There was evidently a reluctance to becoming pioneers in such an enterprise,—to leaving the city unless the guaranty were sure.

Another man rose. "My bredren, I want to raise cotton, and I'm gwine."

It was a short but effective speech. With keen, sharp intellect, he had comprehended the great commercial question of the day. He knew that it would pay to raise cotton on lands which had been held at fabulous prices when the staple was worth but ten or fifteen cents. He was going to improve the opportunity to raise cotton, even if he did not become a holder of the estate.

"I'm gwine ye, brudder!"

"So will I!" and there was a general shaking of hands as if that were sealing a contract. Having determined to go, they joined in singing *The Freedmen's Battle-Hymn*, sung as a solo and repeated in chorus:

FREEDMEN'S BATTLE-HYMN.

I'll fight for Lib-er-ty,
I'll fight for Lib-erty,
I'll fight—I'll fight for Lib-er-ty.

Solo.
I'll fight for Liberty,
I'll fight for Liberty,
I'll fight—I'll fight for Liberty.

Chorus.
In the New Jerusalem,
In the New Jerusalem,
In the New—the New Jerusalem.

I'm not afraid to die,
I'm not afraid to die,
I'm not—I'm not afraid to die.

Chorus.
In the New, &c.

I shall meet my Saviour there,
I shall meet my Saviour there,
I shall meet—shall meet my Saviour there.

Chorus.
In the New, &c.

I shall wear a starry crown,
I shall wear a starry crown,
I shall wear—I shall wear a starry crown.

Chorus.
In the New, &c.

The coloured soldiers of Foster's army sang it at the battle of Honey Hill, while preparing to go into the fight. How gloriously it sounded now, sung by five hundred freedmen in the Savannah slave-mart, where some of the singers had been sold in days gone by! It was worth a trip from Boston to Savannah to hear it.

The next morning, in the same room, I saw a school of one hundred coloured children assembled, taught by coloured teachers, who sat on the auctioneer's platform, from which had risen voices of despair instead of accents of love, brutal cursing instead of Christian teaching. I listened to the recitations, and heard their songs of jubilee. The slave-mart transformed to a school-house! Civilization and Christianity had indeed begun their beneficent work.

FORT SUMTER

CHAPTER 26
Sherman in South Carolina

December, 1864

General Sherman received, soon after his arrival in Savannah, instructions from General Grant to hasten with his army to James River. Transports were sent down for the shipment of the troops. Grant desired to combine the two great armies, throw Sherman upon his own left flank, and sever Lee's communications with the South, and also prevent his escape. Through all the long months of summer, autumn, and winter,—from June to February,—Grant had put forth his energies to accomplish this object, but had not been able to cut the Danville road, Lee's chief line of supply or retreat. The arrival of Sherman upon the sea-coast made the plan feasible.

But that officer thought it better to march northward, driving the enemy before him, and finish up the entire Rebel forces on the Atlantic coast; besides, South Carolina deserved a retribution as severe as that which had been meted out to Georgia. He also believed that he could thus join Grant quite as soon as by the more circuitous route by water. Grant assented to the proposition, and having full confidence in the ability of his lieutenant, left him to co-operate in the manner he thought most advisable.

The Rebels expected that Sherman would move upon Charleston, but such was not his intention. He determined to make a movement which would compel its evacuation, while at the same time he could drive the forces of the Rebels in the interior of the State northward, and by destroying all the railroads in his progress, and severing Lee from the agricultural regions of the South, so cripple his resources as to paralyze the Rebel army before Richmond, and bring the war to a speedy close.

He wished to preserve his army entire, and accordingly a division of the Nineteenth Corps, which had fought under Emory in the Southwest and under Grover in the Shenandoah, having no enemy to pursue after the annihilation of Early, was sent down to garrison Savannah, Grover being made commandant of the post.

General Howard, commanding the right wing, took transports with the Seventeenth Corps, Blair's, for Beaufort, whence he pushed into the interior, striking the Charleston and Savannah Railroad at Pocotoligo, and establishing there a depot of supplies. The Fifteenth Corps, Logan's, followed, except Corse's division, which, being prevented by freshets from marching direct to Pocotoligo, moved with the left wing, commanded by Williams, joining the Twentieth Corps, and crossing the Savannah marched to Hardeeville, on the Charleston Railroad, and opened communication with Howard.

"Come with me," was the kind invitation of General Williams; "you will see high old times, I reckon. My soldiers are crazy to get into South Carolina." But believing that Sherman's movement would necessitate the evacuation of Charleston, I preferred to enter that city at the hour of her deepest humiliation.

Davis's corps, the Fourteenth, with Geary's division of the Twentieth, crossed at Sister's Ferry, fifty miles above Savannah. This detour was necessary on account of the flooding of the country by freshets. The gunboat Pontiac was sent up to cover the crossing. When Slocum reached the river at Sister's Ferry he found it three miles in width, and too deep to ford, and was obliged to wait till the 7th of February before he could cross. This movement deceived Hardee and Beauregard.

The presence of Howard at Pocotoligo looked like an advance upon Charleston, while Slocum being at Sister's Ferry indicated an attack upon Augusta. The Rebel commanders therefore undertook to hold a line a hundred miles in length. D. H. Hill was hurried to Augusta, Hardee took position at Branchville, while Beauregard remained at Charleston. This scattering of the Rebel forces made Sherman's task comparatively easy, as their combined army would hardly have been a match for Sherman in a pitched battle on a fair field. His troops had entire confidence in themselves and in their commander. Having fought their way from Chattanooga to Atlanta, having marched to the sea and taken Fort McAllister and Savannah, they believed there was no obstacle which they could not overcome in marching or fighting.

Wilmington had been captured, and Sherman proposed to receive his next supplies from the coast.

"I shall reach Goldsboro' about the 15th of March," said Sherman to his chief quartermasters, who at once made preparations to forward supplies from Morehead City in North Carolina.

Sherman held a conference with Admiral Dahlgren on the 22nd of January, and with General Foster, commanding the Department of the South. All the troops in that quarter were to be employed in a movement against Charleston. General Foster being in feeble health, Major-General Gillmore, who had charge of the department during the summer, and who had conducted the engineering operations against Wagner and Sumter, again took command.

The march of the right wing, under Howard, commenced on the 1st of February. Howard found obstructions on all the roads. The negroes from the plantations had been impressed into the Rebel service to burn bridges, fell trees, and open sluice-ways; but his Pioneer Corps was so thoroughly organized that such obstacles did not greatly impede his progress.

The Salkehatchie River runs southeast, and reaches the Atlantic midway between Charleston and Savannah. Howard moved up its southern bank, northwest, till he reached River's bridge, thirty-five miles above Pocatoligo. It was a weary march, through swamps, mud, and pine-barrens. River's bridge and Beaufort bridge were held by the Rebels, who were strongly posted. Blair, with the Seventeenth Corps, was ordered to carry the first, and Logan, with the Fifteenth, the latter. Blair detailed Mower's and Corse's divisions for the work. The troops saw before them a swamp three miles wide, overflowed, with soft mire beneath, filled with gnarled roots of gigantic trees. It was midwinter. The air was keen. They knew not the depth of the water. The forest was gloomy. Above them waved the long gray tresses of moss. There was nothing of pomp and circumstance to inspire them. It was an undertaking full of hazard. They must shiver an hour in the water, breast deep, before they could reach the enemy. But they hesitated not an instant when the order was given to move. They stepped into the water jocosely, as if upon a holiday excursion.

A Rebel brigade guarded the farther shore; flanking it, and reaching the firm land below the bridge, the troops rushed recklessly forward, and quickly drove the enemy from his strong position, losing but seventeen killed and seventy wounded.

Thus by one dash the Rebel line of the Salkehatchie was broken, and Hardee retired behind the Edisto to Branchville. The railroad from Charleston to Augusta was reached the next day, and D. H. Hill at Augusta, with one third of the Rebel force, was severed from Hardee and Beauregard. For three days Howard's men were engaged in destroying the railroad west of the Edisto,—waiting also for the left wing, which had been detained by freshets.

Kilpatrick, meanwhile, had pushed well up towards Augusta, driving Wheeler, burning and destroying property, and threatening Hill. The Rebels everywhere were in a state of consternation. They could not divine Sherman's intentions. The people of Charleston, who for four years had heard the thunder of cannon day and night down the harbour, and had come to the conclusion that it was impossible the city could ever be taken, now thought Sherman was intending to knock for admission at the back door. The people of Augusta saw that their fair town was threatened. It had been an important place to the Confederates through the war, contributing largely to help on the Rebellion by its manufacturing industry. Citizens fled from Charleston to Cheraw, Columbia, Winsboro', and other towns up the Santee and Catawba, little thinking that they were jumping from the "frying-pan into the fire."

Branchville is sixty-two miles northwest of Charleston, on the north bank of the Edisto. Hardee expected to see Sherman at that place, and made elaborate preparations to defend it, as it lay in the path to Charleston. But Sherman, instead of turning southeast, kept his eye on the north star, and moved on Orangeburg, thirteen miles north of Branchville, where also the Rebels were prepared to make a stand; but the Seventeenth Corps made one dash, and the enemy fled from a long breastwork of cotton-bales. This was on the 12th of February. Meanwhile General Hatch, with a portion of Gillmore's troops, was threatening Charleston along the coast.

A division under General Potter, accompanied by a large number of gunboats, went to Bull's Bay, north of Charleston, as if to approach the city from that quarter. The monitors were inside the bar. There were Union troops on Morris's Island, ready to move, while the batteries kept up their fire, sending shells into the city. Thus from every point except on the northern side Charleston was threatened.

It was not till Howard was well up towards Columbia that Hardee saw he had been completely flanked, and that Sherman had no intention of going to Charleston. The only force in front of Sherman was Wheeler's and Wade Hampton's cavalry, with straggling bands of infantry. Hampton's home was Columbia. He was rich, and had a palatial residence. He was an aristocrat, in principle and action. He was bitter in his hatred of the Union and the men of the North. He had fought upon nearly all the battle-fields of Virginia, and doubtless, in common with most of the people of his State, had not thought it possible the war should reach his own door. But Sherman was there, and being powerless to defend the capital of the State, he was reckless to destroy.

Columbia had been a depot of supplies through the war. In view of its occupation, Sherman gave written orders to Howard to spare all dwellings, colleges, schools, churches, and private property, but to destroy the arsenals and machinery for the manufacture of war material.

Howard threw a bridge across the river three miles above the city, and Stone's brigade of Wood's division of the Fifteenth Corps was sent across. The Mayor came out in his carriage, and made a formal surrender to Colonel Stone, who marched up the streets, where huge piles of cotton were burning. Hampton, in anticipation of the giving up of the city, had caused the cotton to be gathered, public as well as private, that it might be burned. There were thousands of bales. Negroes were employed to cut the ropes that bound them, and apply the torch. As Stone marched in the last of Hampton's troops moved out. The wind was high, and flakes of burning cotton were blown about the streets, setting fire to the buildings. The soldiers used their utmost exertions to extinguish the flames, working under the direction of their officers. The whole of Wood's division was sent in for the purpose, but very little could be done towards saving the city. The fire raged through the day and night. Hundreds of families were burned out, and reduced from opulence, or at least competency, to penury. It was a terrible scene of suffering and woe,—men, women, and children fleeing from the flames, surrounded by a hostile army, composed of men whom they had called vandals, ruffians, the slime of the North, the pests of society, and whom they had looked upon with haughty contempt, as belonging to an inferior race. Indescribable their anguish; and yet no violence was committed, no insulting language or action given by those soldiers. Sherman, Howard, Logan, Hazen, Woods,—nearly all of Sherman's officers,—did what they could to stay the flames and alleviate the distress. They experienced no pleasure in beholding the agony of the people of Columbia.

General Sherman thus vindicates himself in his official report, and charges the atrocity upon Wade Hampton:

> I disclaim on the part of my army any agency in this fire, but, on the contrary, claim that we saved what of Columbia remains unconsumed. And without hesitation I charge General Wade Hampton with having burned his own city of Columbia,—not with a malicious intent, or as the manifestation of a silly 'Ro-

man stoicism,' but from folly and want of sense, in filling it with lint, cotton, and tinder. Our officers and men on duty worked well to extinguish the flames; but others not on duty, including the officers who had long been imprisoned there, rescued by us, may have assisted in spreading the fire after it had once begun, and may have indulged in unconcealed joy to see the ruin of the capital of South Carolina.[78]

Thus Columbia, the beautiful capital of a once haughty State, became a blackened waste. The convention which passed the ordinance of Secession, when called together on the 17th of December, 1860, met in Columbia, but after organizing adjourned to Charleston, as the city was infected with small-pox. But it was the more poisonous virus of Secession which finally laid their proud city low.

The people of South Carolina are bitter in their hatred of General Sherman. They charge all the devastation committed during his march from Atlanta to Goldsboro' upon him. In their estimation he is "a fiend," and his conduct not merely "inhuman," but "devilish." Yet he only adopted the policy which the Rebel leaders urged upon their adherents, and which was vehemently advocated by the Southern press. Rebel, not loyal torches, fired Charleston, Orangeburg, and Columbia.

It is claimed that Sherman did not regard private property, but destroyed it indiscriminately with that belonging to the Confederate government. Was there any respect shown by the Rebel authorities? Cotton, resin, turpentine, stores owned by private individuals, were remorselessly given to the flames by the Rebels themselves, and their acts were applauded by the people of the South as evincing heroic self-sacrifice.

Great stress is laid upon the suffering occasioned by the pillaging and burning by Sherman's troops; but in Pennsylvania yet remain the ruins of Chambersburg as evidence of the tender mercy of the Rebels, who not only destroyed public property, but gave dwelling-houses and stores to the torch.

What act so malignant, bloody, ghastly, and fiendish as the sacking, burning, and massacre at Lawrence! What deed so damning since the barbarities of Scio or Wyoming! What woe so deep!—men, children, murdered, butchered, scalped, the bodies of the dead tossed into the flames! No relenting on the part of the Rebels, but savage, infuriate joy at the sight of the warm heart's blood of their victims! Woman's prayers and tears availed not to stay their murderous hands or move their brutal hearts.

78: Sherman's Report.

MISSISSIPPI RIVER HOSPITAL STEAMER.

The responsibility cannot be evaded by saying that Quantrel was only a guerrilla. If not holding a commission from the Rebel government, he was fighting for the Confederacy, and was ranked with Morgan and Mosby. He was an ally of Jeff Davis and General Lee. When were his acts disavowed by the Rebel government? What restraint was ever laid upon him? He passed from the scene of massacre, lighted by the flames of the burning town, safely into the Rebel lines, where instead of outlawry he found protection and favour. On what page of Confederate history shall we read the remonstrance of Lee, Davis, Stephens, Toombs, or Breckenridge? Where is the protest of the "chivalrous" gentlemen of the South? What action was taken by the Rebel Congress?

Vain the search for disavowal of or protest against the act. The historian of another generation will be able to pass right judgment upon all that has transpired during these dark years of anarchy and revolution, sorrow, tears, and anguish. The verdict of posterity will be just, and will endure through the ages.

CHAPTER 27

South Carolina Before the War

DECEMBER, 1864

To fully comprehend the fitting punishment of South Carolina we must keep in remembrance her position before the war. We must behold her as she appeared in 1860,—the leader and chief conspirator against the Republic.

She had always taken a prominent part in the political affairs of the nation. Although a State, she was hardly a republican commonwealth, and very far from being a democracy. The State was ruled by a clique, composed of wealthy men, of ancient name, who secured privileges and prerogatives for themselves at the expense of the people, who had but little voice in electing their lawgivers.

The basis of representation in the Legislature was exceedingly complex. In the House of Representatives it was a mixture of property, population, white inhabitants, taxation, and slaves. In the Senate it consisted of geographical extent, white and slave population, taxation, and property. The Senate was constituted after the "Parish system," which gave the whole control of political affairs in the State into the hands of a few wealthy men from the sea-coast.

There are two distinct classes of people in South Carolina,—the lowlanders and the uplanders. The settlers of the lowlands were emigrants from England and France, gentlemen with aristocratic ideas. The settlers of the uplands, in the western counties, were pioneers from Virginia and North Carolina,—small farmers, cultivating their own lands. During the Revolutionary war the uplanders were Whigs, the lowlanders Tories. The lowlanders had wealth, the uplanders were poor. When the Constitution was formed, organizing a State government, the lowlanders took care of their own interests. The lowlands in Colonial times were divided into parishes, and with the forming of

BATTLE OF FORT SUMTER

the Constitution each parish was to have a Senator. The uplands, not being parishes, were districts of much larger territorial area, hence political power fell into the hands of a few individuals along the coast. As white population increased in the districts, and decreased or remained stationary in the parishes, the up-country men tried to emancipate themselves from political serfdom, but there was no remedy except by an amendment to the Constitution, through a Convention called by the Legislature; and as the lowlanders had control of that body, there was no redress. The State, therefore, became an engine of political power, managed and worked by a few men from Charleston, Beaufort, St. Helena, Edisto, Colleton, and other parishes along the sea-coast.

Nature gave South Carolina sunny skies and a genial clime. The sea contributed an atmosphere which gained for Edisto and St. Helena islands the monopoly in the world's markets for cotton of finest fibre. Wealth increased with the gathering in of each new crop, and with wealth came additional power. Superiority of political privilege made the few impatient of restraint and ambitious not only to control State, but national affairs. South Carolina attempted defiance of national law in 1832, and was defeated.

The parishes governed the State solely in the interests of slavery. It gave them power, to perpetuate which they made slavery aggressive. Here is exposed the root from which Secession sprung. Free labour in the North was a plant of vigorous growth. Slavery was slow. It left worn-out lands in its track. Hard work, brutality, and sin sent its victims to an early grave. Freedom was gaining ground. Slavery must be carried into the Territories and secure a foothold in advance of free labour. So the struggle began, and through pride, passion, and malignant hatred of the North Secession was at last accomplished.

Upon the assembling of the Legislature for the choice of Presidential electors, the President of the Senate, W. D. Porter, of Charleston, said to his fellow-legislators:

> All that is dear and precious to this people,—life, fortune, name, and history,—all is committed to our keeping for weal or for woe, for honour or for shame. Let us do our part, so that those who come after us shall acknowledge that we were not unworthy of the great trusts devolved upon us, and not unequal to the great exigencies by which we were tried.... No human power can withstand or break down a united people, standing upon their own soil and defending their own firesides.[79]

They made their election. They thought it to be weal, but under God's providence it proved to be woe. A Senator said:

> We have two ways before us,—in one, whether we will or not, we must tread; for, in the event of this issue, there would be no repose. In both lie dangers, difficulties, and troubles, which no human foresight can foreshadow or perceive; but they are not equal in magnitude. One is beset with humiliation, dishonour, *emeutes*, rebellion,—with submission in the beginning to all, and at all times, and confiscation and slavery in the end. The other, it is true, has its difficulties and trials, but no disgrace. Hope, duty, and honour shine along the path. Hope beacons you to the

---

79: Proceedings of South Carolina Legislature.

end.... For himself he would unfurl the Palmetto flag, fling it to the breeze, and with the spirit of a brave man determine to live and die as became our glorious ancestors, and ring the clarion notes of defiance in the face of an insolent foe.[80]

When assembled in Hibernia Hall, in Charleston, since called Secession Hall, the delegates gave free utterance to their sentiments. Said Mr. Parker:

It is no spasmodic effort that has come suddenly upon us; it has been gradually culminating for a long period of thirty years. At last it has come to that point where one may say the matter is entirely right.

Said Lawrence M. Keitt:

I have been engaged in this movement ever since I entered political life.

Said R. Barnwell Rhett:

It is not anything produced by Mr. Lincoln's election or by the non-execution of the Fugitive Slave Law. It has been a matter which has been gathering head for thirty years.

It was the fire of 1832 flaming anew. No rights had been invaded. That Secession was inaugurated without cause must ever be the verdict of history. And history will forever hold John C. Calhoun, R. Barnwell Rhett, Right Rev. Bishop Elliott, Rev. Dr. Thornwell, and other statesmen, editors, ministers,—members of the slaveholding forum, bar, and pulpit,—responsible for all the suffering, bloodshed, and desolation which have come to the country.

Proud in spirit was South Carolina just then. The cotton crop was luxuriant. Planters were plethoric with money. The internal slave-trade established its marts of human flesh all through the South. Virginia became slave-breeding, and South Carolina slave-consuming. In former years slavery was deemed an evil, a curse; but the call for cotton, its rise in market value, with increased profit of culture and a consequent demand for labour, transformed it into a blessing, to be perpetuated for the best good of the human race.

It was found to be in perfect accordance with the teachings of the Bible. The system itself was right; the abuse of the good was only evil. Rev. Dr. Thornwell, Professor of Theology in the Presbyterian Seminary at Columbia, came boldly forward to advocate slavery as

---
80: Speech of Senator Chestnut.

a Divine institution, ordained of God for the welfare of the human race. He preached thus:

> Our slaves are our solemn trust, and while we have a right to use and direct their labours, we are bound to feed, clothe, and protect them, to give them the comforts of this life, and to introduce them to the hope of a blessed immortality. They are moral beings, and it will be found that in the culture of their moral nature we reap the largest reward from their service. *The relation itself is moral,* and in the tender affections and endearing sympathies it evokes it gives scope for the most attractive graces of human character. Strange as it may sound to those who are not familiar with the system, slavery is a school of *virtue,* and no class of men have furnished sublimer instances of heroic devotion than slaves in their loyalty and love to their masters. We have seen them rejoice at the cradle of the infant, and weep at the bier of the dead; and there are few among us who have not drawn their nourishment from their generous breasts.[81]

Such was the teaching from those who called themselves appointed of God to preach the Gospel of purity and peace. Church and State, morals and religion, everything that could give strength and respectability to their cause, were brought in to aid the work of the conspirators. So thorough were the teachings, that South Carolina became almost a unit on the question of Secession.

The people of the South charge the Union army with desecrating their church edifices. Is it a wonder that soldiers, reasoning from cause to effect, concluded that the religion which was foremost in precipitating a Rebellion which sustained such an inhuman system was not worth serious consideration? Is it a wonder that, after experiencing the horrors of Rebel prisons, they lost reverence for a religion which could uphold a government guilty of such fiendish cruelties?

Slavery was the cornerstone and foundation of the Confederacy. Never was the trade in slaves between States so thriving as during the winter of 1860. And the leaders of the Rebellion were looking forward to the time when the commerce with Africa would be reopened. Mr. Lamar of Savannah, who during the Rebellion was agent of the Confederacy in London for the purchase of army supplies, imported in the bark Wanderer a cargo of native Africans, some of whom were sold in Charleston. There was a large party in the Confederate Congress which advocated the resumption of the foreign trade, the abolition of

---

81: *Southern Presbyterian Review,* January, 1861.

Administrator's Sale, by Order of the Ordinary.

A PRIME AND ORDERLY GANG OF
68 Long Cotton Field Negroes,
Belonging to the Estate of the late Christopher J. Whaley.

WILBUR & SON
Will sell at PUBLIC AUCTION in Charleston,

At the Mart in Chalmers Street,
On Thursday, Feb. 2d, 1860,
COMMENCING AT ELEVEN O'CLOCK,

THE FOLLOWING GANG OF LONG COTTON NEGROES,
Who are said to be remarkably prime, and will be sold as per Catalogue.

NAMES.		AGES.	NAMES.		AGES.
Jimmy,	driver,	30	Carter,		36
Flora,	seamstress,	24	Taffy,		13
James,		5	Rachel,	($ 720,)	8
Charles,	($ 125,)	1	Jannett,		18
August,		52	Phebe,	($ 860,)	40
Mathias,	($ 1,220,)	18	Judy,		8
Sandy,		16	Major,		40
John,		13	Lavinia,		30
Tom,		70	Billy,	($ 550,)	10
Jack,		38	Tamor,		6
James,		6	Jimmy,		52
Leah,		5	Kate,		46
Flora,		2	Susan,		25
Andrew,		42	Thomas,	($ 380,)	6
Binah,		40	Kate,		1
Phillis,		20	Edward,	coachman,	49
Mary,		15	Amey,		22
Lymus,		10	Teneh,	washer,	30
Abram,	($ 275,)	2	Josephine,		9
Binah,		2 mos.	Sam,		11
Andrew,		29	Isaac,		5
Hagar,		25	William,		1
Dayman,		4	Amey,		27
Cuffy,		21	Louisa,	($ 750,)	8
Hagar,	($ 1,320,)	20	Joe,		3
Margaret,		85	Sam,	ruptured,	65
Lucy,	cripple,	60	Andrew,	dropsical,	61
John,		22	Daniel,		70
Ellick,	($ 1,160,)	18	Lymus,		30
Libby,		19	Lucy,	nurse,	58

TERMS.

One-third Cash; balance in one and two years, secured by bond, and mortgage of the negroes, with approved personal security. Purchasers to pay us for papers.

which in 1808 was set down as one of the grievances of the South.

It is the province of history to make a record of the bad as well as the good, shameful and humiliating though it may be. Sin and wickedness are horrible facts. To view them as such, to contemplate them in contrast with holiness and righteousness, and draw useful lessons from such contemplation, is far better than to say that they have no place in history. Posterity will wonder that a Church which called itself Christian ever gave its support and advocacy to an institution which daily brought its victims, like cattle, to the auction-block, which made no distinction of age, which was remorseless as death, and which from the cradle to the grave held its victim as with a tiger's gripe.

On the previous page is a copy of an auctioneer's handbill, which I found upon the floor of the slave-mart, with the prices paid by the buyers marked in pencil against the names of the "chattels," and now appearing in parentheses

The *Charleston Mercury* was the organ of the Secessionists from the start. It not only advocated Secession as a political principle, but filled its columns with articles holding up to ridicule and contempt the people of the North. The spirit of hate seemed to seize the whole community, in which women even exceeded their husbands. Thus wrote a Southern lady:—

> I would rather die than hold a position of inferiority and vassalage to the North, and the dominant feeling of my heart is to leave a State where men are too cowardly to protect their women and too mercenary to risk their money.[82]

"The question has thrust itself into our domestic fireside, and you find all classes,—men, women, and children,—asking what they must do to be saved," said W. F. Cullock, Collector of Charleston, in a speech at the Pulaski House, Savannah, on the opening of the Charleston and Savannah Railroad.

"Fight! Secede!" was the response from the drunken crowd.

The South Carolina Muse tuned her lyre and sang:

We'll unfurl the Lone-Star banner,
And we'll keep it waving high;
For Secession we are pledged,
For Secession we will die.

The city of Charleston was foremost for Secession. When the

82: *Charleston Mercury,* November 3, 1860.

news was received that Mr. Lincoln was elected President, a red flag, with the palmetto-tree and a lone star wrought upon it, was raised. Says the *Mercury*:

> A shout and twice three cheers greeted its appearance. The Association of 1860 assembled. The feeling was for prompt action.

The Legislature was in session at Columbia. On the 11th of the month a bill was passed calling a State convention.

> Gentlemen, hats off! Then *hip-hip-hip-hurrah!*—and *hip-hip-hip-hurrah—hurrah—hurrah—hurrah*—for the homes we love![83]

Then more soberly the editor added:

> The news of the passage of the convention resolutions by an almost unanimous vote, at Columbia, was received in this city on Saturday night with demonstrations which have, perhaps, never been equalled in the political history of the country. Our whole community seemed to breathe freer and deeper, and upon every brow sat confidence and hope. It was as though the glorious sun had suddenly dispersed cloud and mist and vapour, and sent its illuminating rays to every heart and home. Men looked each other in the face as men should do who feel that under God their destinies are in their own hands.

Thus a "daughter of South Carolina" inflamed her sisters:

> Listen, daughters of South Carolina, to the voice of a faithful sister. Should our State back out now she would be disgraced forever.... Shrink now, and we are crushed forever. Then there will be no end of the trouble you fear. Abolition emissaries will be at work all over the South, inciting the negroes in every direction. Trials must come, but let them come in the right way, and all will be well. Secede, put ourselves in a state of defence; be ready for any emergency. Should the government coerce, our sister States will come to the rescue. Let it be so. Better perish beneath the shock than to live degraded.... O women of South Carolina! Mothers, sisters, wives! do not wear the white feather now, unless, like that gallant king of old, it waves on our men to the war.[84]

Said another:

83: *Mercury*, November 12, 1860.
84: *Mercury*, November 9, 1860.

Let us women of Carolina prove that the same noble spirit which visited the mothers and maidens of '76 is alive, and glowing in the spirits of their descendants. I am myself a widowed mother, but I have said to my three sons, that if any one of them shall be craven enough to desert the State now, to temporize in her councils, or be backward if her honour calls them to the field, let him never look upon my face again.[85]

What had transpired to produce this white heat of passion? Simply that a party was coming into power opposed to the extension of slavery over free territory. True this party had also disavowed any intention of interference with slavery in the States; but restriction was loss of power,—paralysis and death at last. The grievance of South Carolina arose wholly from slavery. She claimed the right to traffic in human beings. She believed it was a natural right, authorized by the Creator of the universe, having the sanction and solemnity of the patriarchs, prophets, apostles, and Christ himself. It was a natural, moral, and scriptural right for a master to rob his brother in the Lord of his earnings during the week, commune with him on Sunday, whip him on Monday, and sell him on Tuesday. The institution being missionary in its nature, and designed to carry the Gospel to Africa, he had a right to separate husbands and wives, parents and children, break the marriage relation, and establish new alliances at will. No doubt they were sincere in their belief that the system was not only good in itself, but that it was a beneficent arrangement for the well-being of the human race. Certainly it was beneficial to the master; why should it not be to the slave? Men can be as sincerely zealous for Wrong as for Right. Eighteen hundred years ago a man zealous for the truth filled the prisons of Syria with Christians, and thought he was doing righteously in the sight of God; and human nature is the same now as then. Men and women who advocated the righteousness of slavery were scrupulous to a penny in their dealings with one another, and with coloured people who were free,—but the loss of freedom gave the right to commit robbery! Strange, also, the confusion and delusion of moral ideas. Society prided itself on its virtue. Men and women of Caucasian blood departing from morality found the door of society shut against them; but slavery being patriarchal it was not a crime, not even an offence against morality, for a planter to choose a Hagar from his slaves. Society placed no bar in his way, the Church no ban upon his action. Hagar could be taken into the master's household, appear

---

85: *Charleston Mercury*, November 17, 1860.

COOPER SHOP VOLUNTEER REFRESHMENT SALOON

in silks and satins, with Ishmael for the pet of the family, or both could be knocked off to the highest bidder in the mart, separated and sent one to the rice-swamps of Georgia and the other to the canebrakes of Louisiana, Hagar weeping and mourning for her child, and the planter, with the price of blood in his pocket, be received in any parlour in Charleston, or made Governor of the State! There were patriarchs in the convention which carried South Carolina out of the Union, who were urged on to treason by the women of the South. Ishmael would not rise in insurrection, even if his brother Isaac and father Abraham went to war.

Said another "daughter of South Carolina":

> Arming the State will keep the negroes in check. They are arrant cowards, those dear dark friends of ours. Some of you can remember how in '22 they would shrink away at the gleam of their master's sword as he armed for the nightly patrol, and the creaking of the horseman's saddles as they paraded the streets sent them hiding in every hole and corner.[86]

Isaac was eager for the fray; he burned to fight the Yankees. Hence the consummation of the treason.

86: *Charleston Mercury*, November 9, 1860.

CHAPTER 28

Sumter

FEBRUARY, 1865

Fort Sumter was evacuated by the Rebels and occupied by the Union troops on the 18th of February, 1865; but before entering upon the events of that ever-memorable morning it will give breadth and colour to the picture to glance at the scenes witnessed there at the beginning and during the Rebellion.

On the 17th of December, 1860, Governor Pickens sent a strictly confidential letter to President Buchanan.

> To spare the effusion of blood, which no human power may be able to prevent, I earnestly beg your immediate consideration of all the points I call your attention to.... I would most respectfully, and from a sincere devotion to the public peace, request that you will allow me to send a small force, not exceeding twenty-five men and an officer, to take possession of Fort Sumter immediately, in order to give a feeling of safety to the community. There are no United States troops in that fort whatever, or perhaps only four or five at present, besides some additional workmen or labourers lately employed to put the guns in order.... If Fort Sumter could be given to me as Governor, I think the public mind would be quieted, under a feeling of safety.

The State seceded on the 20th. Major Anderson with a handful of men was at Fort Moultrie. "The garrison will not be strengthened. The people will obey the call for war, and take the forts," said the *Charleston Mercury* of the 22nd.

Five days later, on the 27th, the people of Charleston looked seaward and saw Moultrie in flames, and the stars and stripes waving over Sumter. They were indignant. They considered it a breach of faith.

"Anderson has opened civil war," said the *Courier*.[87]

"His act must be repudiated by the government," said the *Mercury*.[88]

"Unless you order Anderson back, I cannot, under my convictions of patriotism and honour, continue to hold office," said the Secretary of War, John B. Floyd, of Virginia.[89]

Charleston was intensely excited.

"Assemble the Light Infantry and the Meagher Guards at the Citadel. Arm them and take possession of Castle Pinckney. Proceed immediately to Fort Moultrie; send troops to Morris Island," were the orders of Governor Pickens to Colonel Pettigrew.

"Our line of operations embraces four points: Fort Moultrie, Castle Pinckney, Fort Johnson, and Morris Island. You are indebted to the forbearance of the enemy for the liberty of transporting the reinforcements and supplies, which you ordered at midnight, and which are to be sent to your battery now in course of erection on Morris Island. A single gun from Fort Sumter would sink your transports and destroy your troops and supplies," reported General Simmons to the Governor on the 1st of January.

It was the language of war. The United States was an enemy. The guns of Moultrie were already trained on Sumter. The battery on Morris Island was for the destruction of that fort. South Carolina had begun the war in intention and in fact. The erection of the battery was war.

On the 9th of January the same battery opened fire on the *Star of the West*, steaming into the harbour, bearing the United States flag.

"You are asked to surrender the fort to the constituted authorities of South Carolina," was the demand of Governor Pickens on the 11th.

"I cannot comply with your request," was the response from Anderson.

Then came the negotiations between Charleston and Washington,— the demands upon Buchanan, the shuffling and indecision of the two-faced, unprincipled politician, who had written himself down as an "Old Public Functionary." Major Anderson was watched day and night, cut off from intercourse with the shore, deprived of fresh provisions, treated as an enemy, and compelled to see the preparations on Morris Island and on the floating battery for the reduction of the fort. Thus February and March passed away. His provisions were nearly gone. Troops were pouring into Charleston from all parts of the State and

---

87: *Courier*, December 29, 1860.
88: *Mercury*, December 29, 1860.
89: Floyd's Letter to Buchanan.

from other States. Savannah sent a company early in December. They were under the command of General Beauregard,—a small, brown, thin, wiry man, forty years old, born upon the banks of the Mississippi, in Louisiana, yet more of a Frenchman than an American.

Mr. Lincoln could not consent that Major Anderson should starve. The people of the North would not permit it. Its sentiment was for sustaining an officer who had been true to his oath, amid a general breaking down of loyalty.

Sunday dawned, the 7th of April, and Major Anderson, looking out from his prison, saw the Rebels hard at work to complete the batteries on Morris Island.

"An attempt will be made to supply Fort Sumter with provisions only," was the official notice from President Lincoln to Pickens on the 8th.

"Demand the surrender of the fort; if refused, reduce it," was the order from Montgomery.

"Surrender," was the message of Beauregard to Anderson. "I cannot; but I shall soon be starved out unless relieved," was the courteous reply.

"When will you evacuate?"

"At noon on the 15th, if I receive no supplies," wrote Anderson on the 11th.

"I shall open fire in one hour," was the last message of Beauregard, at twenty minutes past three on the morning of the 12th.

Then came the roar of the first gun, fired by old Mr. Ruffin, gray-haired, nearly fourscore. Not the young bloods of the South alone, but men and women of all ages and classes were crazy for the contest.

Shells burst in the fort, plunging through the wooden barracks and officers' quarters. Solid shot from Morris Island were hurled point-blank against the walls. All day the batteries flamed, and Sumter leisurely replied.

When darkness came on Sumter closed its port-holes and rested, but the Rebels, like spirits of evil, were at work through the night.

The second day dawned, and all the cannon were roaring again. The barracks were on fire, the smoke curling into the casemates, the hot stifling air reaching the gunners, who, wrapping themselves in wet cloths, and covering their faces, crept along the passages, rolling casks of powder into the sea. What delight on shore to see the flames mount above the walls! With what energy Moultrie, Pinckney, and Morris Island and the floating battery redoubled their fire. All but three of Anderson's cartridges were gone. The flagstaff was shot away. "The flag is down!" is the cry within the fort. Up into the storm, where the shot

DEFENCE OF FORT SUMTER

and shell are falling, walks Lieutenant Hall, planting the flag upon the parapet, where it waves till Wigfall appears at a port-hole. Then the parley,—the surrender,—and Charleston was excited as never before or since. Men and women on the house-tops, and gathered in church-steeples; business at a standstill, champagne flowing like water, costliest wines quaffed at the expense of merchants of New York; bells ringing, guns firing, ladies waving their handkerchiefs,—the city all aglow with bonfires in the evening; crowds surging through the streets, or drinking whiskey in the bar-rooms: Beauregard the Napoleon of the new era. Governor Pickens addressed the mob from the balcony of the Charleston Hotel:

> It is a glorious and exultant occasion. Fellow-citizens, I clearly saw that the day was coming when we would triumph beyond the power of man to put us down. Thank God the day has come,—thank God the war is open, and we will conquer or perish! We have defeated their twenty millions, and we have made the proud flag of the stars and stripes, that never was lowered before to any nation on this earth,—we have lowered it in humility before the glorious little State of South Carolina![90]

Intoxicated with wine and whiskey, delirious with success, insane with Secession, the jubilant crowd cheer and drink, and shout again, bidding defiance to the government, and cursing the Yankees.

Four years pass, and Sumter is repossessed by the troops of the Union. How cheering the sight to behold once more the crimson folds and fadeless stars of our country's flag waving in the sunlight over the crumbled walls!

Early in the morning we entered the harbour,—General Gillmore and staff, General Webster, chief of General Sherman's staff, with several gentlemen and ladies from Port Royal. The blockading fleet and the monitors were steaming in, their long watch through the sweltering days of summer and the stormy nights of winter at an end. They were feeling their way up the channel searching for torpedoes.

The steamer *Deer*, built on the Clyde, a few hours from Nassau, with an assorted cargo,—a low, rakish, fast-running craft, with steam escaping from her pipes,—was lying under the guns of a monitor. She had worked her way in during the night. The crestfallen captain was chewing the cud of disappointment on the quarter-deck, looking gloomily seaward the while, and doubtless wishing himself in the harbour of Nassau. Two nights before the *Syren* had passed in. The wreck of a

---

90: Speech of Governor Pickens.

third blockade-runner was lying on the sands of Sullivan's Island, near Moultrie, which months before had been run ashore by the fleet. The tide was surging through the cabin windows. Barnacles had fastened upon the hull, and long tresses of green, dank seaweed hung trailing from the iron paddle-wheels. It was a satisfaction to know that the time was at hand when Englishmen at Nassau would have to shut up shop.

We glided along the shore of Morris Island, white with tents. What heroic valour on those sands,—the assault upon Wagner, the slow, persistent excavation of the trenches, the unremitting vigilance and energy, the endurance which had forced the evacuation of Morris Island,—the turning of the guns of Wagner upon Sumter, the planting of the "Swamp-Angel" battery,—the first shell sent streaming into the city, startling the inhabitants, and awaking the unpleasant conviction that the Yankees were at their doors! So memory ran over the historic events, as we swept up the channel.

The steamer could not approach near the landing, and we were taken to the fort in small boats. We reached the interior through a low, narrow passage.

The fort bore little resemblance to its former appearance, externally or internally. None of the original face of the wall was to be seen, except on the side towards Charleston and a portion of that facing Moultrie. From the harbour and from Wagner it appeared only a tumulus,—the debris of an old ruin. All the casemates, arches, pillars, and parapets were torn up and utterly demolished. The great guns which two years before kept the monitors at bay, which flamed and thundered awhile upon Wagner, were dismounted, broken, and partially buried beneath the mountain of brick, dust, concrete, sand, and mortar. After Dupont's attack, in April, 1863, a reinforcement of palmetto-logs was made on the harbour side, and against half of the wall facing Moultrie, and the lower casemates were filled with sand-bags; but when General Gillmore obtained possession of Wagner, his fire began to crumble the parapet. The Rebels endeavoured to maintain its original height by gabions filled with sand, but this compelled a widening of the base inside by sand-bags, thousands of which were brought to the fort at night. Day after day, week after week, the pounding from Wagner was maintained so effectually that it was impossible to keep a gun in position on the side of Sumter fronting it, and the only guns remaining mounted were five or six on the side towards Moultrie, in the middle tier of casemates. Five howitzers were kept on the walls to repel an attack by small boats, the garrison keeping under cover, or seeking shelter whenever the lookout cried, "A shot!"

Cheveaux-de-frise of pointed sticks protected the fort from a scaling party. At the base outside was a barrier of interlaced wire, supported by iron posts. There was also a submerged network of wire and chains, kept in place by floating buoys.

I had the curiosity to make an inspection of the wall nearest Moultrie, to see what had been the effect of the fire of the ironclads in Dupont's attack. With my glass at that time I could see that the wall was badly honeycombed; a close inspection now proved that the fire was very damaging. There were seams in the masonry, and great gashes where the solid bolts crumbled the bricks to dust. It was evident that if the fire had been continued any considerable length of time the wall would have fallen. Its effect suggested the necessity of filling up the lower casemates.

An hour was passed in the fort, the band playing national airs, and the party inspecting the ruins and gathering relics.

Captain James of the Massachusetts Fifty-Fourth, aide to General Gillmore, was wounded in the assault on Wagner. He gazed at the ruins with a satisfaction not unmixed with melancholy, for beneath the sands of Morris Island was lying his beloved commander, Colonel Shaw.

The Rebels had refused to give up his body. "Let him lie buried beneath his niggers," was their answer to the request. And there he lies beside the brave men who followed him to death and glory, having won an immortal name no less as the commander of the first negro regiment sent to the war than by his gentle bearing as a man and bravery as a soldier. His acceptance of the command of the despised men who gladly enlisted when called to the field required at the time a devotion to principle and a decision of character, to face the gibes and sneers flung at him by negro-haters in his rear, greater than the courage to meet the enemy at the front. But he nobly led the way, and silenced every carping tongue.

For four long years the cannon of Sumter had hurled defiance at the rights of man; but the contest now was ended. Eternal principles had prevailed against every effort of Rebel hate to crush them. The strong earthworks on Sullivan's and Johnson's islands, the batteries in the harbour, Castle Pinckney and Fort Ripley, and those in the city erected by slaves, were useless forever, except as monuments of folly and wickedness. As I stood there upon the ruins of Sumter, looking down into the crater, the past like a panorama was unrolled, exhibiting the mighty events which will forever make it memorable. The silent landing of Major Anderson at the postern gate, the midnight prayer and solemn consecration of the little band to defend the flag till the last, the long weeks of preparation by the Rebels, the *Star of the West* turning her bow seaward, the 12th of April, the barracks on fire, the supplies exhausted, the hopelessness of success, the surrender, and all that had followed, were vivid memories of the moment.

How inspiring to hear the music of the band, to behold the numerous vessels of the fleet decorated from bowsprit to yardarm and topmast with flags and streamers, to recall the heroic sacrifices of those who had fought through the weary years, to know that Sumter, Moultrie, the city, and the State were redeemed from the worst system of vassalage, that our country was still a nation, renewed and regenerated by its baptism of fire and blood, that truth and right were vindicated before the world; and to look down the coming years, and know that Freedom was secured to all beneath the folds of the flag that had withstood the intrigues of cabals and the shock of battle, and that Christianity and civilization, twin agents of human progress, had received an impetus that would forever keep us in the van of nations.

Looking at that flag, involuntarily I repeated the words of the song which I heard when the shadows of night fell upon the gory field of Antietam, sung by our wounded in one of the hospitals:

Our flag is there! our flag is there!
We hail it with three loud huzzas!
Our flag is there! our flag is there!
Behold the glorious stripes and stars!
Stout hearts have fought for that bright flag,
Strong hands sustained it masthead high,
And O, to see how proud it waves,
Brings tears of joy to every eye!

CHAPTER 29

Charleston

FEBRUARY, 1865

A city of ruins,—silent, mournful, in deepest humiliation. It was early morning when we reached the wharf, piled with merchandise, not busy with commercial activity as in other days, but deserted, its timbers rotting, its planks decayed, its sheds tumbling in and reeling earthward. The slips, once crowded with steam and sailing vessels, were now vacant, except that an old sloop with a worm-eaten gunwale, tattered sails, and rigging hanging in shreds, alone remained.

A few fishermen's dories only were rocking on the waves, tethered to the wharves by rotten ropes, where the great cotton Argosies in former years had shipped or landed their cargoes.

Before the sailors had time to make fast the steamer, myself and friend[91] were up the pier. The band was playing *Hail, Columbia,* and the strains floated through the desolate city, awakening wild enthusiasm in the hearts of the coloured people, who came rushing down the grass-grown streets to welcome us.

When near the upper end of the pier we encountered an old man bending beneath the weight of seventy years,—such years as slavery alone can pile upon the soul. He bowed very low.

"Are you not afraid of us Yankees?"

"No, massa, God bless you. I have prayed many a night for you to come, and now you are here. Bless the Lord! Bless the Lord!"

He kneeled, clasped my hand, and with streaming eyes poured out his thanks to God.

Let us, before entering upon a narrative of military incidents, look at Charleston as she was at the beginning of the Rebellion, when the great cotton mart of the Atlantic coast, with lines of steamships to

---
91: James Redpath.

New York and Boston. Then her wharves not only were piled with bales of cotton and tierces of rice, or with goods from the warehouses and manufactories of New England and Great Britain, but, next to New Orleans, she was the most populous city of the South, and, in proportion to the number of inhabitants, the wealthiest. Her banks and insurance offices were as stable as those of Wall Street. She aspired to be the commercial emporium of the South. The newspapers of Charleston taught the people to believe that Secession and non-intercourse with the North would make the city the rival of New York. She first adopted the vagaries of her own son, Calhoun, on the rights of States. She proclaimed cotton king, not of America, but of the world, and in her pride believed that all nations could be brought to do her homage. She was rich and aristocratic, and looked upon the people of the North with contempt. De Bow wrote:

> The Cavaliers, Jacobites, and Huguenots who settled the South, naturally hate, contemn, and despise the Puritans, who settled the North. The former are master races; the latter a slave race, descendants of the Anglo-Saxon serfs.

Through ignorance and vanity such assertions were accepted as truths. Boys and girls of the common schools of the North could have shown that, in the contests between the Cavaliers and Puritans, the Cavaliers were defeated; that the Jacobites went down before the party which placed William of Orange on the throne.

Charleston called the people of South Carolina into council. The *Mercury*—that able but wicked advocate of Secession—threw out from its windows this motto: *One voice and millions of strong arms to uphold the honour of South Carolina!* Not the honour of the nation or of the people, but of South Carolina,—the Mephistopheles of the Confederacy, the seducer of States. With honeyed words, and well-timed flattery she detached State after State from the Union. South Carolina said, in her address to the slaveholding States:

> Whilst constituting a portion of the United States it has been *your* statesmanship which has guided it in its mighty strides to power and expansion. In the field and in the cabinet *you* have led the way to renown and grandeur.

The ministers of her churches were foremost in abetting the Rebellion. Church and State, merchant and planter, all from high to low of the white population, brought themselves to believe that their influence was world-wide, through King Cotton and his prime minister,

African Slavery. Hence the arrogance, fierce intolerance, and mad hate which had their only prototypes in the Rebellion of the Devil and his angels against Beneficent Goodness.

The siege of Charleston was commenced on the 21st of August, 1863, by the opening of the "Swamp-Angel" battery. On the 7th of September Fort Wagner was taken, and other guns were trained upon the city, compelling the evacuation of the lower half. For fourteen months it had been continued; not a furious bombardment, but a slow, steady fire from day to day. About thirteen thousand shells had been thrown into the town,—nearly a thousand a month.

They were fired at a great elevation, and were plunging shots,—striking houses on the roof and passing down from attic to basement, exploding in the chambers, cellars, or in the walls. The effect was a complete riddling of the houses. Brick walls were blown into millions of fragments, roofs were torn to pieces; rafters, beams, braces, scantlings, were splintered into jack-straws. Churches, hotels, stores, dwellings, public buildings, and stables, all were shattered. There were great holes in the ground, where cart-loads of earth had been excavated in a twinkling.

In 1860 the population of the city was 48,509,—26,969 whites, 17,655 slaves, and 3,885 free coloured. The first flight from the city was in December, 1861, when Port Royal fell into the hands of Dupont; but when it was found that the opportunity afforded at that time for an advance inland was not improved, most of those who had moved away returned. The attack of Dupont upon Sumter sent some flying again; but not till the messengers of the "Swamp Angel" dropped among them did the inhabitants think seriously of leaving. Some went to Augusta, others to Columbia, others to Cheraw. Many wealthy men bought homes in the country. The upper part of the city was crowded. Men of fortune who had lived in princely style were compelled to put up with one room. Desolation had been coming on apace. The city grew old rapidly, and had become the completest ruin on the continent. There were from ten to fifteen thousand people still remaining in it, two thirds of whom were coloured.

When Sherman flanked Orangeburg, Hardee, who commanded the Rebels in Charleston, saw that he must evacuate the place. There was no alternative; he must give up Sumter, Moultrie, and the proud old city to the Yankees. It was bitter as death! A few of the heavy guns were sent off to North Carolina, all the trains which could be run on the railroad were loaded with ammunition and commissary supplies, the guns in the forts were spiked, and the troops withdrawn.

The inhabitants had been assured that the place should be defended to the last; and in the *Courier* office we found the following sentence in type, which had been set up not twenty-four hours before the evacuation:

> There are no indications that our authorities have the first intention of abandoning Charleston, as I have ascertained from careful inquiry!

Duplicity to the end.

The Rebellion was inaugurated through deception, and had been sustained by an utter disregard of truth.

Friday and Saturday were terrible days. Carts, carriages, wagons, horses, mules, all were brought into use. The railroad trains were crowded. Men, women, and children fled, terror-stricken, broken-hearted, humbled in spirit, from their homes. How different from the 12th of April, 1861, when they stood upon the esplanade of the battery, sat upon the house-tops, clustered in the steeples, looking seaward, shouting and waving their handkerchiefs as the clouds of smoke and forked flames rolled up from Sumter!

"God don't pay at the end of every week, but he pays at last, my Lord Cardinal," said Anne of Austria.

General Hardee remained in the city till Friday night, the 17th instant, when he retired with the army, leaving a detachment of cavalry to destroy what he could not remove. Every building and shed in which cotton had been stored was fired on Saturday morning. The ironclads *Palmetto State*, *Chicora*, and *Charleston* were also given to the flames. They lay at the wharves, and had each large quantities of powder and shell on board. General Hardee knew that the explosions of the magazines would send a storm of fire upon the city. He knew it would endanger the lives of thousands; but what cared he? Governor McGrath called upon the people to destroy their houses. The newspapers pointed to Moscow as a sublime instance of heroic devotion. Human life, the wailing of infants, the feebleness of old age, weighed nothing with Hampton, Hardee, McGrath, General Lee, or Jeff Davis.

The torch was applied early on the morning of the 18th. The citizens sprang to the fire-engines and succeeded in extinguishing the flames in several places; but in other parts of the city the fire had its own way, burning till there was nothing more to devour. On the wharf of the Savannah Railroad depot were several hundred bales of cotton and several thousand bushels of rice. On Lucas Street, in a shed, were twelve hundred bales of cotton. There were numerous other sheds all filled. Nearby was the Lucas mill, containing thirty thousand bushels of rice, and Walker's warehouse, with a large amount of commissary stores, all of which were licked up by the fire so remorselessly kindled.

At the North-eastern Railroad depot there was an immense amount of cotton which was fired. The depot was full of commissary supplies and ammunition, powder in kegs, shells, and cartridges. The people rushed in to obtain the supplies. Several hundred men, women, and children were in the building when the flames reached the ammunition and the fearful explosion took place, lifting up the roof and bursting out the walls, and scattering bricks, timbers, tiles, beams, through the air; shells crashed through the panic-stricken crowd, followed by the shrieks and groans of the mangled victims lying helpless in the flames, burning to cinders in the all-devouring element. Nor was this all. At the wharves were the ironclads, burning, torn, rent, scattered over the water and land,—their shells and solid shot, iron braces, red-hot iron plates, falling in an infernal shower, firing the wharves, the buildings, and all that could burn.

There was more than this. Two magnificent Blakely guns—one at the battery, the other near the gas-works on Cooper River—were loaded to the muzzle and trains laid to burst them. The concussion shattered all the houses in the immediate vicinity.

The buildings near the North-eastern depot were swept away. All the houses embraced in the area of four squares disappeared. The new bridge leading to James Island was destroyed, the fire eating its way slowly from pier to pier through the day. The citizens did their utmost to stay the flames, but from sunrise to sunset on Saturday, all through Saturday night, Sunday, and Monday, the fire burned. How fearful this retribution for crime! Abandoned by those who had cajoled and deceived them, who had brought about their calamity, while swearing to defend them to the last, humbled, reduced from affluence to poverty, the people of Charleston were compelled to endure the indescribable agony of those days.

Colonel Bennett, commanding the Twenty-First United States Coloured Troops on Morris Island, seeing signs of evacuation on Saturday morning, the 18th, hastened up the harbour in boats with his regiment, landing at the South Atlantic wharf. His note to the Mayor was:

> In the name of the United States government I demand the surrender of the city of which you are the executive officer. Until further orders, all citizens will remain in their houses.

The mayor, meanwhile, had despatched a deputation to Morris Island with formal intelligence of the evacuation. Colonel Bennett wrote:

> My command will render every possible assistance to your well-disposed citizens in extinguishing the flames.

The Twenty-First United States Coloured Troops was made up of the old Third and Fourth South Carolina regiments, and many of them were formerly slaves in the city of Charleston. They were enlisted at a time when public sentiment was against them, in the winter of 1862-63. I was at Port Royal then, and they were employed in the quartermaster's department. They were sneered at and abused by officers and men belonging to white regiments; but Colonel Bennett continued steadfast in his determination, obtained arms after a long struggle, in which he was seconded by Colonel Littlefield, Inspector-General of coloured troops in the department. Colonel Bennett had organized four companies of the Third and Colonel Littlefield four companies of the Fourth. The two commands were united and numbered as the Twenty-First United States Coloured Troops. They went to Morris Island in 1863, took part in two or three engagements, and proved themselves good soldiers of the Union. It was their high privilege to be first in the city. The stone which the builders rejected once in the history of the world became the head stone of the corner; and in like manner the poor, despised, rejected African race, which had no rights, against whom the city of Charleston plotted iniquity and inaugurated treason, marched into the city to save it from destruction! Following the Twenty-First was a detachment of the Fifty-Fourth Massachusetts.

"Let him lie buried beneath his niggers!" Stung by the insult to the memory of their lamented commander and by the sneer at themselves, will they not now wreak their vengeance on the ill-fated city? It is their hour for retaliation. But they harbour in their hearts no malice or revenge. Conscious of their manhood, they are glad of another opportunity of showing it.

The soldiers of the Fifty-Fourth have proved their prowess on the field of battle; they have met the chivalry of South Carolina face to face, and shown their equality in courage and heroism, and on this ever-memorable day they make manifest to the world their superiority in honour and humanity.

Let the painter picture it. Let the poet rehearse it. With the old flag above them, keeping step to freedom's drum-beat, up the grass-grown streets, past the slave-marts where their families and themselves have been sold in the public shambles, laying aside their arms, working the fire-engines to extinguish the flames, and, in the spirit of the Redeemer of men, saving that which was lost.

"It was the intention of some of our officers to destroy the city," said one of the citizens; "they not only set it on fire, but they double-shotted the guns of the ironclads, and turned them upon the town, but fortunately no one was injured when they exploded."

The lower half of the city was called Gillmore's town by the inhabitants.

We visited the old office of the *Mercury*, in Broad Street. A messenger sent by the "Swamp Angel" had preceded us, entering the roof, exploding within the chimney, dumping several cart-loads of brickbats and soot into the editorial room, breaking the windows and splintering the doors. It was the room in which Secession had its incubation. The leading rebellious spirits once sat there in their arm-chairs and enthroned King Cotton. They demanded homage to his majesty from all nations. The first shell sent the *Mercury* up town to a safer locality, but when Sherman began his march into the interior, the *Mercury* fled into the country to Cheraw, right into his line of advance!

The *Courier* office in Bay Street had not escaped damage. A shell went down through the floors, ripping up the boards, jarring the plaster from the walls, and exploded in the second story, rattling all the tiles from the roof, bursting out the windows, smashing the composing-stone, opening the whole building to the winds. Another shell had dashed the sidewalk to pieces and blown a passage into the cellar, wide enough to admit a six-horse wagon. Near the *Courier* office were the Union Bank, Farmers' and Exchange Bank, and Charleston Bank, costly buildings, fitted up with marble mantels, floors of terracotta tiles, counters elaborate in carved work, and with gorgeous frescoing on the walls. There, five years ago, the merchants of the city, the planters of the country, the slave-traders, assembled on exchange, talked treason, and indulged in extravagant day-dreams of the future glory of Charleston.

The rooms were silent now, the oaken doors splintered, the frescoing washed from the walls by the rains which dripped from the shattered roof; the desks were kindling-wood, the highly-wrought cornice-work had dropped to the ground, the tiles were ploughed up, the marble mantles shivered, the beautiful plate-glass of the windows was in fragments upon the floor. The banks helped on the Rebellion,—contributed their funds to inaugurate it, and invested largely in the State securities to place the State on a war footing.

The three banks named held on January 6, 1862, six hundred and ten thousand dollars' worth of the seven per cent State stock, issued under the act of December, 1861.

The entire amount of the State loan of one million eight hundred thousand dollars issued under that act was taken by the banks of the State. Every bank with the exception of the Bank of Camden and the Commercial Bank of Columbia subscribed to the stock. The seven Charleston banks at this early stage of the war had loaned the State permanently eleven hundred and forty-two thousand dollars.[92]

At this period of the war the State had twenty-seven thousand three hundred and sixty-two troops[93] in the field, out of a white population of two hundred and ninety-one thousand, by the census of 1860,—nearly one half of the voting population, so fiercely burned the fires of Secession. But the flames had reached their whitest heat. Even at that time the people had grown weary of the war, and refused to enlist. The chief of the Military Department of the State writes:

> The activity and energy had been already abstracted, they had stricken at the sovereignty of the State; ignorance, indolence, selfishness, disaffection, and to some extent disappointed ambition, were combined and made unwittingly to aid and abet the enemy, and to become the coadjutors of Lincoln and all the hosts of abolition myrmidons.[94]

Passing from the banks to the hotels, we found a like scene of destruction. The doors of the Mills House were open. The windows had lost their glazing and were boarded up. Sixteen shots had struck the building. The rooms where Secession had been rampant in the beginning, where bottles of wine had been drunk over the fall of Sumter, echoed only to our footsteps. The Charleston Hotel, where Governor Pickens had uttered his proud, exultant, defiant words, was pierced in many places. Dining-halls, parlours, and chambers had been visited by messengers from Wagner. I gathered strawberry flowers and dandelions from the grass-green pavement in front of the hotel, trodden by the drunken multitude on that night when the flag of the Union was humbled in the dust.

No wild, tumultuous shoutings now, but silence deep, painful, sorrowful. Our own voices only echoed along the corridors and

---

92: Report of Treasurer and Finance, South Carolina, 1862.
93: Report of James Chestnut, Chief Military Department, South Carolina, January 1, 1862, p. 47.
94: Ibid., p. 24.

balconies where surged the lunatics of that hour. We passed at will along the streets, wanderers in a desolate city. Along the Battery, a beautiful promenade of the city, shaded by magnolias, and fragrant with the bloom of roses and syringas, overlooking the harbour, stood the residences of the "chivalric" men of South Carolina. From their balconies and windows the occupants had watched the first bombardment of Sumter. They had seen with joyful eyes the flames lick up the barracks, and the lowering of the flag of the Union. But now their palatial homes were wrecks, and they were fugitives. Doorless and windowless the houses. The elaborate centre pieces of stuccowork in the drawing-rooms crumbled; the bedrooms filled with bricks, the white marble steps and mahogany balusters shattered; owls and bats might build their nests in the coming spring-time undisturbed in the deserted mansions, the esplanade of the Battery, the pleasure-ground of the Charlestonians, their delight and pride, was now merely a huge embankment of earth,—a magazine of shot and shell.

The churches—where slavery had been preached as a missionary institution, where Secession had been prayed for, where *Te Deums* had been sung over the fall of Sumter and *hosannas* shouted for the great victory of Manassas—were, like the houses, wrecks. The pavements were strewn with the glass shattered from the windows of old St. Michael's, the pride and reverence of Charleston; and St. Philip's, where worshipped the rich men, where the great apostle of Secession and devotee of slavery, Calhoun, lies in his narrow cell, resembled an ancient ruin. His grave, marked by a white marble slab, was unharmed, but the bones of his fellow-sleepers had been disturbed by the shells. The yard was overrun with weeds and briers. Bombs had torn through the church. Pigeons had free access. Buzzards might roost there undisturbed.

In 1861 the heart of the city was burned out by a great fire, which swept from the Cooper River to the Ashley. How it ignited no one has told. The coloured people are fully imbued with the belief that it was sent of the Lord. No attempt had been made to rebuild the waste. All the energy of the people had been given to prosecuting the war. There had been no sound of trowel, hammer, or saw, except upon the ironclads.

The blackened area was overgrown with fire-weeds. Lean and hungry curs barked at us from the tenantless houses. Cats which once purred by pleasant firesides ran from their old haunts at our approach. The rats had deserted the wharves and moved up town with the people. The buzzards, which once picked up the garbage of the markets, had disappeared. A solitary rook cawed to us, perched on the vane of the court-house steeple. Spiders were spinning their webs in the counting-houses.

It was an indescribable scene of desolation,—of roofless houses, cannon-battered walls, crumbling ruins, upheaved pavement, and grass-grown streets; silent to all sounds of business, voiceless only to a few haggard men and women wandering amid the ruins, reflecting upon a jubilant past, a disappointed present, and a hopeless future!

Her merchants were the great men of the earth; for by their sorceries were all nations deceived. And in her was found the blood of the prophets and of the saints.

Charleston was one of the great slave-marts of the South. She was the boldest advocate for the reopening of the slave-trade. Her statesmen legislated for it; her ministers of the Gospel upheld it as the best means for Christianizing Africa and for the ultimate benefit of the whole human race. Being thus sustained, the slave-traders set up their auction-block in no out-of-the-way place. A score of men opened offices and dealt in the bodies and souls of men. Among them were T. Ryan & Son, M. M. McBride, J. E. Bowers, J. B. Oaks, J. B. Baker, Wilbur & Son, on State and Chalmers Streets. Twenty paces distant from Baker's was a building bearing the sign, "Theological Library, Protestant Episcopal Church." Standing by Baker's door, and looking up Chalmers Street to King Street, I read another sign, "Sunday-School Depository." Also, "Hibernian Hall," the building in which the ordinance of Secession was signed. In another building on the opposite corner was the Registry of Deeds. Nearby was the guard-house with its grated windows, its iron bars being an appropriate design of double-edged swords and spears. Thousands of slaves had been incarcerated there for no crime whatever, except for being out after nine o'clock, or for meeting in some secret chamber to tell God their wrongs, with no white man present. They disobeyed the law by not listening to the bell of old St. Michael's, which at half past eight in the evening, in its high and venerable tower, opened its trembling lips and shouted, "Get you home! Get you home!" Always that; always of command; always of arrogance, superiority, and caste; never of love, good-will, and fellowship. On Sunday morning it said, "Come and sit in your old-fashioned, velvet-cushioned pews, you rich ones! Go up stairs, you niggers!"

The guard-house doors were wide open. The jailer had lost his occupation. The last slave had been immured within its walls, and St. Michael's curfew was to be sweetest music thenceforth and forever. It shall ring the glad chimes of freedom,—freedom to come, to go, or to tarry by the way; freedom from sad partings of wife and husband, father and son, mother and child.

The brokers in flesh and blood took good care to be well buttressed. They set up their market in a reputable quarter, with St. Michael's and the guard-house, the Registry of Deeds and the Sunday-School Depository, the Court-House and the Theological Library around them to make their calling respectable.

But the "Swamp Angel" had splintered the pews of St. Michael's, demolished the pulpit, and made a record of its doings in the Registry building. At one stroke it opened the entire front of the Sunday-School Depository to the light of heaven. There was also a mass of evidence in the courtroom—several cart-loads of brick and plaster, introduced by General Gillmore—against the right of a State to secede.

I entered the Theological Library building through a window from which General Gillmore had removed the sash by a solid shot. A pile of old rubbish lay upon the floor,—sermons, tracts, magazines, books, papers, musty and mouldy, turning into pulp beneath the rain-drops which came down through the shattered roof.

Amid these surroundings was the Slave-Mart,—a building with a large iron gate in front, above which, in large gilt letters, was the word *Mart*.

The outer iron gate opened into a hall about sixty feet long by twenty broad, flanked on one side by a long table running the entire length of the hall, and on the other by benches. At the farther end a door, opening through a brick wall, gave entrance to a yard. The door was locked. I tried my boot-heel, but it would not yield. I called a freedman to my aid. Unitedly we took up a great stone, and gave a blow. Another, and the door of the Bastille went into splinters. Across the yard was a four-story brick building, with grated windows and iron doors,—a prison. The yard was walled by high buildings. He who entered there left all hope behind. A small room adjoining the hall was the place where women were subjected to the lascivious gaze of brutal men. There were the steps, up which thousands of men, women, and children had walked to their places on the table, to be knocked off to the highest bidder. The thought occurred to me that perhaps Governor Andrew, or Wendell Phillips, or William Lloyd Garrison would like to make a speech from those steps. I determined to secure them. While there a coloured woman came into the hall to see the two Yankees.

"I was sold there upon that table two years ago," said she.

"You never will be sold again; you are free now and forever!" I replied.

"Thank God! O the blessed Jesus, he has heard my prayer. I am so glad; only I wish I could see my husband. He was sold at the same time into the country, and has gone I don't know where."

Thus spake Dinah More.

In front of the mart was a gilt star. I climbed the post and wrenched it from its spike to secure it as a trophy. A freedman took down the gilt letters for me, and knocked off the great lock from the outer iron gate, and the smaller lock from the inner door. The key of the French Bastille hangs at Mount Vernon; and as relics of the American prison-house then being broken up, I secured these.

Entering the brokers' offices,—prisons rather,—we walked along the grated corridors, looked into the rooms where the slaves had been kept. In the cellar was the dungeon for the refractory,—bolts and staples in the floors, manacles for the hands and feet, chains to make all sure. There had evidently been a sudden evacuation of the premises. Books, letters, bills of sale, were lying on the floor.

Let us take our last look of the Divine missionary institution. Thus writes James H. Whiteside to Z. B. Oakes:

> I know of five very likely young negroes for sale. They are held at high prices, but I know the owner is compelled to sell next week, and they may be bought low enough so as to pay. Four of the negroes are young men, about twenty years old, and the other a very likely young woman about twenty-two. I have never stripped them, but they seem to be all right.

C. A. Merrill writes from Franklin:

> If I can I will come and buy some of your fancy girls and other negroes, if I can get them at a discount.

A. J. McElveen writes from Sumterville:

> I send a woman, age twenty-two. She leaves two children, and her owner will not let her have them. She will run away. I pay for her in notes, $650. She is a house woman, handy with the needle, in fact she does nothing but sew and knit, and attend to house business.

Another letter from the same:

I met a man who offered me four negroes,—one woman and three girls, all likely and fine size for the ages,—thirty-six, thirteen, twelve, and nine. The two oldest girls are the same size; all right as to teeth and person.

I cannot transfer to these pages what follows; decency forbids. Thomas Otey writes from Richmond:

> This market is fine. They are selling from twenty-five to fifty per day, and at fine prices. A yellow girl sold this morning for $1,320. No qualifications; black ones at $1,150; men at $1,400. Small ones in the ratio.

There was no longer a manifestation of lordly insolence and assumed superiority over the Yankees on the part of the whites. They spoke respectfully, but were reticent except when questioned. Once they asked questions of Yankees: "What is your occupation? What brought you to the South? What are you doing here? I believe you are a—Abolitionist, and the quicker you get out of this town the better." Such was formerly their language. So they talked to Judge Hoar, a citizen of Massachusetts. So they talked to Colonel Woodford in 1860.

In 1860, in the month of December, Lieutenant-Colonel Woodford, of the One Hundred and Twenty-Seventh New York volunteers, was in Charleston on business. He was waited on one day by a committee of citizens and informed that he had better leave the city, inasmuch as he was a Northerner, and besides was suspected of being an Abolitionist. He was put on board a steamer, and compelled to go North. He was now Provost Marshal of the Department. On the morning of the 20th he visited the office of the *Charleston Courier*. The editors had fled the city, but the business man of the establishment remained to protect it. Colonel Woodford was received very graciously. The following conversation passed between them:—

Colonel W. "Whom have I the pleasure of addressing?"

Businessman. "Mr. L—, sir."

Col. W. "Will you do me the favour to loan me a piece of paper?"

Mr. L. "Certainly, certainly, sir."

Col. W. "Shall I also trouble you for a pen and ink?"

Mr. L. "With pleasure, sir."

The ink was muddy and the pen poor, but the business man, with great alacrity, obtained another bottle and a better pen. Colonel W. commenced writing again:

Office Provost Marshal
Charleston
February 20, 1865.
Special Order, No. 1.
The *Charleston Courier* establishment is hereby taken possession of by the United States.

Mr. L. had been overlooking the writing, forgetful of courtesy in his curiosity. He could hold in no longer.

"Colonel, surely you don't mean to confiscate my property! *Why, I opposed nullification in 1830!*"

"That may be, sir, but you have done what you could to oppose the United States since 1860. If you will show me by your files that you have uttered one loyal word since January 1, 1865, I will take your case into consideration."

He could not, and the *Courier* passed into other hands.

The rich men of the city—those who had begun and sustained the Rebellion—fled when they saw that the place was to fall into the hands of the Yankees. But how bitter the humiliation! On the Sunday preceding, Rev. Dr. Porter, of the Church of the Holy Communion, preached upon the duty of fighting the Yankees to the last. "Fight! fight, my friends, till the streets run blood! Perish in the last ditch rather than permit the enemy to obtain possession of your homes!"

But on Monday morning Dr. Porter was hastening to Cheraw, to avoid being caught in Sherman's trap. The people of Charleston expected that Sherman would swing round upon Branchville, and come into the city, and therefore hastened to Columbia, Cheraw, and other northern towns of the interior, where not a few of them became acquainted with the "Bummers."

Rev. Dr. Porter owned a fine residence, which he turned over to an English lady. As there were no hotel accommodations, my friend and I were obliged to find private lodgings, and were directed to the house of the Rev. Doctor. We were courteously received by Mrs.—, a lady in middle life, still wearing the bloom of old England on her cheeks, although several years a resident of the sunny South. Rising early in the morning, for a stroll through the city before breakfast, I found the cook and chambermaid breaking out in boisterous laughter. The cook danced, clapped her hands, sat down in a chair, and reeled backward and forward in unrestrained ecstasy.

"What pleases you, Aunty?" I asked.

"O massa! I's tickled to tink dat massa Dr. Porter, who said dat no

Yankee eber would set his foot in dis yar city, had to cut for his life, and dat a Yankee slept in his bed last night! Bless de Lord for dat!"

The white women manifested their hatred to the bitter end.

"I'll set fire to my house before the Yankees shall have possession of the city!" was the exclamation of one excited lady, when it was whispered that the place was to be evacuated; but her Rebel friends saved her the trouble by applying the torch themselves.

The coloured people looked upon the Yankees as their deliverers from bondage. They spoke of their coming as the advent of the Messiah. Passing along King Street, near the citadel, with my fellow-correspondent, we met an old negress with a basket on her arm, a broad-brimmed straw hat on her head, wearing a brown dress and roundabout. She saw that we were Yankees, and made a profound courtesy.

"How do you do, Aunty?"

"O bless de Lord, I's very well, tank you," grasping my hand, and dancing for joy. "I am sixty-nine years old, but I feel as if I wan't but sixteen." She broke into a chant—

Ye's long been a-comin,
Ye's long been a-comin,
Ye's long been a-comin,
For to take de land

And now ye's a-comin,
And now ye's a-comin,
And now ye's a-comin,
For to rule de land.

And then, clapping her hands, said, "Bless de Lord! Bless de dear Jesus!"

"Then you are glad the Yankees are here?"

"O chile! I can't bress de Lord enough; but I doesn't call you Yankees."

"What do you call us?"

"I call you Jesus' aids, and I call you head man de Messiah." She burst out into a rhapsody of hallelujah and thanksgivings. "I can't bress de Lord enough; and bress you, chile: I can't love you enough for comin."

"Were you not afraid, Aunty, when the shells fell into the town?"

She straightened up, raised her eyes, and with a look of triumphant joy, exclaimed,—

"When Mr. Gillmore fired de big gun and I hear de shell a-rushin ober my head, I say, Come dear Jesus, and I feel nearer to Heaben dan I eber feel before!"

My laundress at Port Royal was Rosa, a young coloured woman, who escaped from Charleston in 1862, with her husband and four other persons, in a small boat. On that occasion Rosa dressed herself in men's clothes, and the whole party early one morning rowed past Sumter, and made for the gunboats.

"If you go to Charleston I wish you would see if my mother is there," said Rosa. "Governor Aiken's head man knows where she lives."

We went up King Street to Governor Aiken's. We found his "head man" in the yard,—a courteous black, who, as soon as he learned that we were Yankees, and had a message from Rosa to her mother, dropped all work and started with us, eager to do anything for a Yankee. A walk to John Street, an entrance through a yard to the rear of a dwelling-house, brought us to the mother, in a small room, cluttered with pots, kettles, tables, and chairs. She was sitting on a stool before the fire, cooking her scanty breakfast of corn-cake. She had a little rice meal in a bag given her by a Rebel officer. She was past sixty years of age,—a large, strong woman, with a wide, high forehead and intellectual features. She was clothed in a skirt of dingy negro cloth, a sack of old red carpeting, and poor, thin canvas shoes of her own make. Such an introduction!

"Here comes de great Messiah, wid news of Rosa!" said my introducer, with an indescribable dramatic flourish.

The mother sprang from the stool with a cry of joy. "From Rosa? From Rosa? O, thank the Lord!" She took hold of my hands, looked at me with intense earnestness and joy, and yet with a shade of doubt, as if it could not be true.

"From Rosa?"

"Yes, Aunty."

She kneeled upon the floor and looked up to heaven. She saw not us, but God and Jesus. The tears streamed from her eyes. She recounted in prayer all her long years of slavery, of suffering, of unrequited toil, and achings of the heart. "You have heard me, dear Jesus! O blessed Lamb!"

It was a conversation between herself and the Saviour. She told him the story of her life, of all its sorrows, of his goodness, kindness, and love, the tears rolling down her cheeks the while and falling in great drops upon the floor. She wanted us to stay and partake of her humble fare, pressed my hands again and again; and when we told her we must go, she asked for God's best blessing and for Jesus' love to follow us. It was a prayer from the heart. We had carried to her the news that she was free, and that her Rosa was still alive. The long looked-for jubilee morning had dawned, and we were to her God's messengers, bringing the glad tidings. It was one of the most thrilling moments I ever experienced.

This woman had been a slave, had been sold, exposed to insult, had no rights which a white man was bound to respect. So said the Chief Justice of the United States, Roger B. Taney. God ordained her, in his beneficent goodness, to be a slave. So preached Rev. Dr. Thornwell, the great South Carolina theologian; so said the Southern Presbyteries, by solemn resolutions. Remembering these things, I went out from that humble dwelling with my convictions deepened that it was God's war, and that the nation was passing through the fire in just punishment for its crimes against humanity.

The 22nd of February, Washington's birthday, was celebrated in Charleston as never before. In the afternoon a small party of gentlemen from the North sat down to a dinner. Among them were Colonel Webster, Chief of General Sherman's staff, Colonel Markland of the Post-Office Department, several officers of the army and navy, and four journalists, all guests of a patriotic gentleman from Philadelphia, Mr. Getty.

Our table was spread in the house of a caterer who formerly had provided sumptuous dinners for the Charlestonians. He was a mulatto, and well understood his art; for, notwithstanding the scarcity of provisions in the city, he was able to provide an excellent entertainment, set off with canned fruits, which had been put up in England, and had run the gauntlet of the blockade.

Sentiments were offered and speeches made, which in other days would have been called incendiary. Five years before if they had been uttered there the speakers would have made the acquaintance of Judge Lynch, and been treated to a gratuitous coat of tar and feathers, or received some such chivalric attention, if they had not dangled from a lamp-post or the nearest tree. Lloyd's Concert Band, coloured musicians, were in attendance, and *Hail Columbia*, the *Star-Spangled Banner*, and *Yankee Doodle*,—songs which had not been heard for years in that city,—were sung with enthusiasm. To stand there, with open doors and windows, and speak freely without fear of mob violence, was worth all the precious boon had cost,—to feel that our words, our actions, our thoughts even, were not subject to the misinterpretation of irresponsible inquisitors,—that we were not under Venetian espionage, but in *free* America, answerable to God alone for our thoughts, and to no man for our actions, so long as they did not infringe the rights of others.

Henceforth there shall be free speech in Charleston. A party of twenty gentlemen began the new era on the 22nd of February, and to

"John Brown" in Charleston

me it will ever be a pleasant reflection that I was one of the privileged number. While dining we heard the sound of drums and a chorus of voices. Looking down the broad avenue we saw a column of troops advancing with steady step and even ranks. It was nearly sunset, and their bayonets were gleaming in the level rays. It was General Potter's brigade, led by the Fifty-Fifth Massachusetts,—a regiment recruited from the ranks of slavery. Sharp and shrill the notes of the fife, stirring the drumbeat, deep and resonant the thousand voices singing their most soul-thrilling war-song,—*John Brown's body lies a mouldering in the grave.*

Mingling with the chorus were cheers for Governor Andrew and Abraham Lincoln!

They raised their caps, hung them upon their bayonets. Proud their bearing. They came as conquerors. Some of them had walked those streets before as slaves. Now they were freemen,—soldiers of the Union, defenders of its flag.

Around them gathered a dusky crowd of men, women, and children, dancing, shouting, mad with very joy. Mothers held up their little ones to see the men in blue, to catch a sight of the starry flag, with its crimson folds and tassels of gold.

O dark, sad millions, patiently and dumb,
Waiting for God, your hour at last has come,
And freedom's song
Breaks the long silence of your night of wrong.

Up the avenue, past the citadel, with unbroken ranks, they marched, offering no insult, uttering no epithet, manifesting no revenge, for all the wrongs of centuries heaped upon them by a people now humbled and at their mercy.

While walking down the street an hour later I inquired my way of a white woman. She was going in the same direction, and kindly volunteered to direct me.

"How do the Yankees behave?" I asked.

"O, they behave well enough, but the niggers are dreadful sassy."

"They have not insulted you, I hope."

"O no, they haven't insulted me, but they have other folks. They don't turn out when we meet them; they smoke cigars and go right up to a gentleman and ask him for a light!"

The deepest humiliation to the Charlestonians was the presence of negro soldiers. They were the provost guard of the city, with their headquarters in the citadel. Whoever desired protection papers or passes, whoever had business with the marshal or the general commanding the city, rich or poor, high-born or low-born, white or black, man or woman, must meet a coloured sentinel face to face and obtain from a coloured sergeant permission to enter the gate. They were first in the city, and it was their privilege to guard it, their duty to maintain law and order.

A Rebel officer who had given his parole, but who was indiscreet enough to curse the Yankees, was quietly marched off to the guard-house by these coloured soldiers. It was galling to his pride, and he walked with downcast eyes and subdued demeanour.

The gorgeous spectacle of the numerous war vessels in the harbour flaming with bunting from yardarm and topmast, and thundering forth a national salute in double honour of the day and the victory, deeply impressed the minds of the coloured population with the invincibility of the Yankees.

"O gosh a mighty! It is no use for de Rebs to think of standing out against de Yankees any longer. I'll go home and bring Dinah down to see de sight!" cried an old freedman as he beheld the fleet. Bright colours are the delight of the African race, and a grand display of any kind has a wonderful effect on their imagination.

Neither the white nor the coloured people comprehended the change which had taken place in their fortunes. The whites forgot that they were no longer slave-drivers. Passing down Rutledge Street one morning I saw a crowd around the door of a building. A friend who was there in advance of me said that he heard an outcry, looked in, and found a white man whipping a coloured woman. Her outcries brought a coloured sergeant of the Provost Guard and a squad of men, who quietly took the woman away, told her to go where she pleased, and informed the man that that sort of thing was "played out." Two white women were passing at the time. "O my God! To think that we should ever come to this!" was the exclamation of one. "Yes, madam, you have come to it, and will have to come to a good deal more," was the reply of my friend.

There were a few Union men in the city, who through the long struggle had been true to the old flag. They were mostly Germans. Many Union officers escaping from prison had been kindly cared for by these faithful friends, who had been subjected to such close surveillance that secretiveness had become a marked trait of character.

I saw a small flag waving from a window, and wishing to find out what sort of a Union man resided there, rang the bell. A man came to the door, of middle age, light hair, and an honest German face.

"I saw the stars and stripes thrown out from your window, and have called to shake hands with a Union man, for I am a Yankee."

CITIZENS' VOLUNTEER HOSPITAL

He grasped my proffered hand and shook it till it ached.

"Come in, sir. God bless you, sir!"

Then suddenly checking himself, he lowered his voice, looked into the adjoining rooms, peeped behind doors, to see if there were a listener near.

"We have to be careful; spies all about us," said he, not fully realizing that the soldiers of the Union had possession of the city. He showed me a large flag.

"Since the fall of Sumter," said he, "my wife and I have slept on it every night. We have had it sewed into a feather-bed."

He gazed upon it as if it were the most blessed thing in the world.

He had aided several soldiers in escaping from prison; and on one occasion had kept two officers secreted several weeks, till an opportunity offered to send them out to the blockading fleet.

During the bombardment of the city, the newspapers had published their daily bulletins,—"So many shells fired. No damage." From the proud beginning to the humiliating breaking up of the rule of Secession, the people were cheated, deluded, and deceived by false promises and lying reports. It was sad to walk amid the ruins of what had been once so fair. It seemed a city of a past age and of an extinct generation. And it was. The Charleston of former days was dead as Palmyra. Old things had passed away; a new generation will behold a wondrous change.

> *Along that dreary waste where lately rung*
> *The festal lay which smiling virgins sung,*
> *Where rapture echoed from the warbling lute,*
> *And the gay dance resounded, all was mute.*

Chapter 30

The Last Campaign

March, 1865

Hastening northward, I joined the Army of the Potomac in season to be an observer of Grant's last campaign. It was evident that the power of the Rebellion to resist was rapidly on the wane. In the West there were several small Rebel forces, but no large organized body. Hood's defeat at *Nashville* had paralyzed operations east of the Mississippi. Johnston was falling back before Sherman, without ability to check his advance.

Grant had strengthened his own army. Schofield was at Wilmington, preparing to co-operate with Sherman. Sheridan was in the Valley, at Winchester,—his cavalry in excellent condition for a move. The cavalry arm of the service had been growing in importance. Grant had fostered it, and now held it in his hand, as Jove his thunderbolts. His letter to Sheridan, written on the 20th of February, shows how thoroughly he had prepared for the finishing work:

> As soon as it is possible to travel I think you will have no difficulty about reaching Lynchburg with a cavalry force alone. From thence you could destroy the railroad and canal in every direction, so as to be of no further use to the Rebellion. Sufficient cavalry should be left behind to look after Mosby's gang. From Lynchburg, if information you might get there would justify it, you could strike south, heading the streams in Virginia to the westward of Danville, and push on and join Sherman. This additional raid, with one now about starting from East Tennessee, under Stoneman, numbering four or five thousand cavalry; one from Eastport, Mississippi, numbering ten thousand cavalry; Canby from Mobile Bay, numbering thirty-eight thou-

sand mixed troops,—these three latter pushing for Tuscaloosa, Selma, and Montgomery, and Sherman with a large army eating out the vitals of South Carolina, is all that will be wanted to leave nothing for the Rebellion to stand upon. I would advise you to overcome great obstacles to accomplish this. Charleston was evacuated on Tuesday last.

Sheridan started on the 27th of February with two divisions of cavalry, numbering about ten thousand men, reached Staunton on the 2nd of March, fell upon Early at Waynesboro', capturing sixteen hundred prisoners, eleven guns, seventeen battle-flags, and two hundred wagons; occupied Charlottesville on the 3rd, destroyed the railroad, and burned the bridge on the Rivanna River. A rain-storm delaying his trains, and obliging him to wait two days, he abandoned the attempt to reach Sherman; then dividing his force, he sent one division towards Lynchburg, which broke up the railroad, while the other went down James River, cutting the canal. He intended to cross the James at New Market, move southeast to Appomattox Court-House, strike the South Side Railroad, tear it up, and join Grant's left flank; but a freshet on the James prevented the accomplishment of his purpose. He therefore sent scouts through the Rebel lines to Grant, to inform him of the difficulties he had encountered and consequent change of plan.

"I am going to White House, and shall want supplies at that point," said he. The scouts left him on the 10th at Columbia, and reached Grant on the 12th. Sheridan made a rapid march, passing quite near Richmond on the north, and raising a midnight alarm in the Rebel capital. A citizen of Richmond writes:

> Couriers reported that the enemy were at the outer fortifications, and had burned Ben Green's house. Mr. Secretary Mallory and Postmaster-General Regan were in the saddle, and rumour says the President and the remainder of the cabinet had their horses saddled, in readiness for flight.[95]

Sheridan was not quite so near, and had no thought of attacking the city. He passed quietly down the north bank of the Pamunkey to the White House, where supplies were in waiting. He rested his horses a day or two, and then moved to Petersburg.

At daylight on the morning of the 25th of March Lee made his last offensive movement.

95: *Rebel War Clerk's Diary*, Vol. II.

Troops destroying a railroad

He conceived the idea of breaking Grant's line east of Petersburg, and destroying his supplies at City Point. The first part he successfully accomplished, but the last could not have been carried out. He massed Gordon's and Bushrod Johnson's divisions in front of the Ninth Corps, for an attack upon Fort Steadman and the batteries adjoining. The fort was held by the Fourteenth New York Heavy Artillery. It was a square redoubt, covering about one acre, and mounted nine guns, and was not more than five hundred feet from the Rebel line. The Rebels tore away their own *abatis*, and in less than a minute were inside the fort. Almost the whole garrison was captured, and the guns turned upon the batteries.

Colonel Tidball, commanding the artillery in the Ninth Corps, quickly had his men at work. General Parke, commanding the Ninth, threw Hartranft's and Wilcox's divisions in rear of Fort Steadman. They fell like a thunderbolt upon Gordon's front line, taking eighteen hundred prisoners, forcing the enemy out of the fort, and recapturing the guns.

Long and loud the *huzzas* which went up when the guns were wheeled once more upon the discomfited foe. President Lincoln saw the battle from the high ground near the house of Mr. Dunn. During the forenoon Gordon sent in a flag of truce, asking permission to bury his dead, which was granted. The Union loss was not far from eight hundred and thirty, mostly in prisoners, while Lee's exceeded three thousand. General Meade ordered a general attack. He thought that there must be a weak place in some portion of the Rebel line. The Second and Sixth Corps succeeded in taking the entrenched picket line, and holding it. Great efforts were made by Lee to regain it, but in vain. Nine hundred prisoners were captured during the afternoon.

I rode to City Point in the evening, and visited Grant's head-quarters. General Grant was well satisfied with the results of the day.

"It will tell upon the next great battle," said he. "Lee has made a desperate attempt and failed. The new recruits fought like veterans."

He had already issued his order for the grand movement which was to give the finishing blow to the Rebellion. He had been impelled to this by various causes, not the least of which was the unjust course pursued by some of the newspapers of the West, which lauded Sherman and his men, but sneered at the Army of the Potomac. The soldiers of the East had accomplished nothing, they said, and the soldiers of the West would have to finish the Rebellion. Sherman had fought his way from Chattanooga to the sea. He was driving all before him.

He would come in on Grant's left flank and rout Lee. These taunts and innuendoes were keenly felt by the men who had won the fields of Gettysburg, Antietam, Wilderness, Spottsylvania, and who had lost eighty thousand of their comrades in forty days. Grant felt it. He saw the dangerous tendency of such jealousy. He knew what the Eastern soldiers could do; that they had fought with unsurpassed bravery and heroism. To avoid sectional animosity between the East and the West, he determined to strike Lee before Sherman's arrival, and accordingly issued his order on the 24th.

But Sherman meanwhile visited Grant in person. I was sitting in the office of General Grant's Adjutant-General on the morning of the 28th of March, and saw President Lincoln, with Generals Grant, Sherman, Meade, and Sheridan, coming up the walk. Look at the men whose names are to have a conspicuous place in the annals of America. Lincoln, tall, round-shouldered, loose-jointed, large-featured, deep-eyed, with a smile upon his face. He is dressed in black, and wears a fashionable silk hat. Grant is at Lincoln's right, shorter, stouter, more compact; wears a military hat with a stiff, broad brim, has his hands in his pantaloons' pockets, and is puffing away at a cigar while listening to Sherman. Sherman, tall, with high, commanding forehead, is almost as loosely built as Lincoln; has sandy whiskers, closely cropped, and sharp, twinkling eyes, long arms and legs, shabby coat, slouch hat, his pants tucked into his boots. He is talking hurriedly, gesticulating now to Lincoln, now to Grant, his eyes wandering everywhere. Meade, also tall, with thin, sharp features, a gray beard, and spectacles, is a little stooping in his gait. Sheridan, the shortest of all, quick and energetic in all his movements, with a face bronzed by sun and wind; courteous, affable, a thorough soldier. I had not met him for many months, but he at once remembered me, and spoke of Pittsburg Landing, where I first made his acquaintance. The plan of the Lieutenant-General was then made known to his subordinates, and each departed during the day, to carry into execution the respective parts assigned them.

Grant's line was nearly forty miles long, extending from the north side of the James to Hatcher's Run. General Ord, who had succeeded Butler in command of the Army of the James, left Weitzel to maintain the position north of James River, and moved with two divisions of the Twenty-Fourth Corps under Gibbon, and one of the Twenty-Fifth under Birney, with a division of cavalry under McKenzie, to Hatcher's Run, arriving there on the morning of the 29th.

On the afternoon of the 28th Sheridan started with Crook's and

Merritt's divisions of cavalry for Dinwiddie Court-House, while Warren with the Fifth Corps crossed Hatcher's Run, and marched towards the same point.

"We have four days' rations in our haversacks, and twelve days' in our wagons," said Colonel Batchelder, Quartermaster-in-chief of the Army of the Potomac.

Lee discovered the movement, and during the evening of the 29th made a diversion against the Ninth Corps. Precisely at ten o'clock there was a signal-gun, a yell, a volley of musketry as the Rebels attacked Parke's picket-line. Then came the roar of the cannonade. The Ninth Corps was prepared. Through the afternoon there had been suspicious movements along the Rebel lines, and Parke was on the watch. It was surmised that Lee would endeavour to compel Grant to recall the Fifth and Second Corps. Parke strengthened his picket-line, and brought up his reserve artillery, to be ready in case of emergency. In three minutes nearly two hundred guns and mortars were in play. The night was dark, the wind south, and rain falling, but the battle increased in intensity. I stood upon the hill in rear of the Ninth Corps, and witnessed the display. Thirty shells were in the air at the same instant. The horizon was bright with fiery arches, crossing each other at all angles, cut horizontally by streams of fire from rifled cannon. Beneath the arches thousands of muskets were flashing. It surpassed in sublimity anything I had witnessed during the war. The slightly wounded in the hospitals of the Ninth Corps who could walk went out with me to see the fight.

"I wish I was down there with the boys," said one who the day before had received a bullet through his right hand.

After two hours of terrific cannonade the uproar ceased, Lee having found that Grant's lines were as strong as ever. The demonstration cost him several hundred soldiers. I talked with one of the wounded Rebels.

"You can't subdue us even if you take Richmond," said he; "we'll fight it out in the mountains."

"Undoubtedly you feel like fighting it out, but you may think better of it one of these days."

A delegate of the Christian Commission sat down to write a letter for him to his wife, to be sent by a flag of truce.

"Tell her," said he, "that I am kindly treated."

His voice choked and tears rolled down his cheeks. A nurse stood over him bathing his wounds to cool the fever, combing his hair, and anticipating all his wants. I recalled the words of a citizen of Savannah, who said, "I went to the stockade when your prisoners were brought down from Millen, with a basket of oranges to give to the sick and dying, but was told by the officer in command that his orders were imperative to allow no one to give anything to the prisoners."

Observe the contrast. Here were good beds, nourishing food, delicacies from the stores of the Christian and Sanitary Commissions, and kind attention. There see a crowd of wretches in rags, exposed to the winds, the rains, the broiling heat or the biting cold, eating cornmeal and water, and meat alive with maggots,—stinted till starved, held captive till hope died, till the mind wandered, and the victims became drivelling imbeciles or walking skeletons, and greeted death as a welcome release from the horrors of their prison-pen. But I have adverted to this before; still commentary is ever provoked.

Hatcher's Run, an affluent of Rowanty Creek, has a general southeast course. It is crossed by three main highways, which lead out of Petersburg towards the southwest,—the Vaughn road farthest east, Squirrel Level road next, and last the Boydtown plank-road. The Squirrel Level road forks seven miles out, one fork running to the Vaughn road and the other to the plank-road. It is nine miles from Petersburg to the toll gate on the plank-road, which is situated a few rods south of the run. The stream above this crossing of the plank-road tends west and southwest, so that if a fisherman with his rod and fly were to start at the head-waters of the creek he would travel northeast, then east, then at the bridge on the plank-road southeast, and after reaching the Vaughn road, south.

Were we to stand upon the bridge where the plank-road crosses the stream, and look northeast, we would obtain a view of the inside of the Rebel lines. The bridge was in Lee's possession, also the toll-gate on the south side, also a portion of the White Oak road, which branches from the plank road, near the toll-gate, and leads west, midway between the run and the plank-road.

The country is densely wooded, mostly with pine, with occasional clearings. Several steam saw-mills have been erected in this vicinity, which cut timber for the Petersburg market. The plank-road leads to Dinwiddie Court-House, which is fifteen miles from Petersburg. Just beyond the Court-House is Stony Creek, which has a southeast course, with a branch called Chamberlain's Bed, coming down from the north, having its rise in a swamp near the head of Hatcher's Run.

Now to understand the direction of the Rebel line of fortifications, let us in imagination start from Petersburg and walk down the plank-road. We face southwest, and walk in rear of fort after fort nine miles to Hatcher's Run, where a strong work has been erected on the north bank of the stream. We cross the bridge and find another on the south bank near the toll-house and Burgess's tavern. Here we leave the plank-road, and turning west walk along the White Oak road with Hatcher's Run north of us a mile distant. Four miles from the town we come to "Five Forks," where five roads meet, midway the head of Chamberlain's Bed and Hatcher's Run. This is an important point,—the key of Petersburg,—which, although so far away from the town, and apparently of no importance, is in reality the most vital point of all. There is no stream immediately behind or before it, but a mile south is the swamp of Chamberlain's Run; a mile north the low lands of Hatcher's Run, but here firm, hard ground. If Grant can break through this gateway he can tear up the rails of the South Side road, have unobstructed passage to the Danville road, and Richmond and Petersburg are his. It is six miles from the Forks, north, to the railroad, but that is the best place for Lee to fight, and there he establishes a strong line of works.

Grant's movement was that of fishermen stretching a seine. He kept one end of the net firmly fastened to the bank of the Appomattox, while Sheridan drew the other past Dinwiddie Court-House to Five Forks, with the intention of reaching the railroad west of Petersburg, to enclose, if possible, Lee's entire army. Such the plan,—noble in conception, grand in execution.

Sheridan had started to cut the South Side road at Burkesville, but Grant, upon deliberation, decided to strike nearer, he wrote from Gravelly Run,—three miles west of Hatcher's Run:

> I feel like ending the matter, if it is possible to do so, before going back. I do not want you to cut loose and go after the enemy's roads at present. In the morning push round the enemy if you can, and get on to his right rear.

The rain which commenced falling at midnight on the 29th continued through the 30th and the forenoon of the 31st, but Sheridan kept in motion, reached Dinwiddie at five o'clock on the 29th, where he bivouacked.

On the morning of the 30th he came in contact with the Rebels a mile beyond the Court-House, posted on the west bank of Chamberlain's Run.

W. H. F. Lee's cavalry held the right of the Rebel line, with Pickett's division of infantry on the left. During the forenoon Bushrod Johnson's division of infantry came down from Five Forks and formed on Pickett's left.

Sheridan reconnoitred the position during the forenoon, and began the attack about two p. m., but the ground was marshy, and his horses could not be used. Johnson's and Pickett's divisions, and Wise's brigade, which also had arrived, crossed the run about half past two. The fight was severe. Sheridan dismounted his men, deployed them as infantry, and contested the ground, falling back on Dinwiddie Court-House, where the battle ended at eight o'clock in the evening.

Meade ordered McKenzie's division of cavalry to hasten to the assistance of Sheridan, and at five o'clock directed Warren to push a small force down the White Oak road to communicate with that officer, and Bartlett's brigade was sent. During the night Warren's whole force moved towards Dinwiddie to attack Pickett and Johnson in the rear, and at daylight was ready for the assault; but the Rebels had decamped, and were once more in position at Five Forks.

April, 1865

On the morning of the 1st of April, Sheridan, having command of the Fifth Corps, as well as the cavalry, moved cautiously towards Five Forks. The forenoon was passed in reconnoitring the position, which was defended by the whole of Pickett's division, Wise's independent brigade of infantry, Fitz Hugh Lee's, W. H. Lee's, and Ross's divisions of cavalry, and Johnson's division of infantry.

Sheridan's order was to form the whole corps before advancing, so that all the troops should move simultaneously.

Following the Fifth Corps, we came to the Gravelly Run church, which is about one and a half miles southeast of Five Forks. A quarter of a mile northwest of the church is the house of Mr. Bass, a landmark for the future historian, for there Sheridan's line turned a right angle. Ayers's division of the Fifth marching past the church, wheeled on the north side of the house and faced west. Crawford's division passed on, and came into line north of Ayers's, while Griffin's stood in reserve on the White Oak road, in rear of Ayers's. McKenzie's cavalry, which had been some time on the ground, deflected to the right and held the ground to Hatcher's Run, which here has a course due east. McKenzie, Crawford, Ayers, and Griffin therefore faced west. Taking the other leg of the angle, we find Stagg's division of cavalry nearest the house of Mr. Bass, then Gibbs's and Fitzhugh's, Pennington's and Wells's, all facing north, and on the extreme left, Coppinger's facing northeast. Fitzhugh's division was directly south of Five Forks. This powerful body of cavalry was all under the command of Major-General Merritt.

The woods were dense, with here and there an opening.

"Keep the sun shining over your left shoulders," was Warren's order to his troops. The length of his front was about one thousand yards, and his divisions were in three lines,—numbering about twelve thousand. While the troops were forming he drew a sketch of the enemy's position for each division commander, and instructed them to explain it to each brigade commander, that there might be no mistake in the movement.

The cavalry, through the afternoon, while Warren was getting into position, kept up a skirmish fire.

Sheridan was impatient. The sun was going down and he must attack at once or retire. He could not think of doing the latter, as it would give Pickett and Johnson time to make their entrenchments exceedingly strong. He ordered Merritt to make a demonstration. That officer advanced Wells and Coppinger against Johnson's extreme right.

"I am going to strike their left flank with the Fifth Corps, and when you hear the musketry, assault all along the line," were his instructions to Merritt.

The Fifth advanced in excellent order, sweeping round Pickett's left flank, and falling on his rear. For a half-hour there was a heavy fire, but the woods being dense the loss was not very great. When the order to charge bayonet was given, the men rushed forward, leaped over the entrenchments, and captured Pickett's front line. Pickett formed a new line, which he endeavoured to hold against the Fifth. Warren ordered Crawford to take them once more in flank, and sent one of McKenzie's brigades to aid him. Ayers's and Griffin's divisions had become disorganized by the success, but reforming they advanced along the White Oak road, but were checked by Pickett's new line. Officers were urging the men forward, but there was faltering. Warren, accompanied by Captain Benvaud, rode to the front, and called upon his officers to follow his example. Quick the response. Officers of all ranks, from generals to subalterns and the colour-bearers, sprang forward. In an instant the line rallied, and with fixed bayonets leaped upon the enemy and captured the whole force opposing them. Warren's horse fell, fatally shot, and an orderly by his side was killed, within a few paces of the entrenchment. When Merritt heard the roll of musketry he ordered the attack. His cavalrymen rode fearlessly through the woods, dashed up to the entrenchments, leaped over them and carried the entire line along his front in the first grand charge. Sheridan says:

The enemy were driven from their strong line of works, completely routed; the Fifth Corps doubling up their left flank in confusion, and the cavalry of General Merritt dashing on to the White Oak road, capturing their artillery, turning it upon them, and riding into their broken ranks, so demoralized them that they made no serious stand after their line was carried, but took flight in disorder.[96]

It was now nearly dark, but Merritt and McKenzie followed the enemy, who threw away their guns and knapsacks, and sought safety in flight, or finding themselves hard pressed, surrendered.

Between five and six thousand prisoners and eighteen pieces of artillery were captured. The way was open to the South Side Railroad. Grant determined to turn the success to quick account. "Attack along the whole line," was his message to the corps commanders.

At ten o'clock Saturday evening the cannonade began. All the batteries joined, all the forts, the gunboats in the Appomattox, the batteries west of Bermuda Hundred, and the monitors by the Howlet House. There was a continual succession of flashes and an unbroken roll of thunder. The Rebels had no peace during the night.

"Send up the provost brigade," was Grant's despatch sent to City Point. The Sixty-First Massachusetts, One Hundred and Fourteenth New York, and other regiments, and Sheridan's dismounted cavalry, were out at daybreak and on the march.

"Send up the marines to guard the prisoners," was his second despatch, and the blue-jackets from the gunboats, with carbines, were sent ashore. The time had come for the mustering of every available man. The sailors took cars at City Point, and sang all the way to Hatcher's Run, as if they were having a lark.

Lee was in trouble. He sent a message to Longstreet, who was north of the James, to hurry to Petersburg. Longstreet put Ewell in command and hastened across the James, with Fields's division. Lee had three bridges, besides those in Richmond,—one at Warwick's, another at Knight's farm, and the third at Chaffin's Bluff. Longstreet, Lee's ablest general, stout, robust, with heavy black whiskers, with his staff, galloped across the middle bridge toward Petersburg, leaving his troops to follow.

The Richmond bells were ringing, not the paean of victory, as after some of their successful battles, but for the assembling of the militia to man the fortifications from which Longstreet's troops were retiring.

The beat of the alarming drum
Roused up the soldier ere the morning star,
While thronged the citizens with terror dumb,

96: Sheridan's Report.

Or whispering, with white lips,
'The foe! They come! they come!'

Let us look at Lee's lines at midnight, Saturday, April 1st. Johnson, Pickett, Wise, and W. H. F. Lee's cavalry are fleeing towards the Appomattox, beyond Hatcher's Run; A. P. Hill is holding the line east of the Run; Gordon occupies the fortifications from the Jerusalem road to the Appomattox; Longstreet is hastening down from Richmond; Ewell is north of the James, and the citizens of Richmond are jumping from their beds to shoulder muskets for service in the trenches. Lee has not yet decided to evacuate Petersburg. He will wait and see what a day may bring forth.

He had not long to wait. Parke, commanding the Ninth Corps, during the night, prepared to assault. It was precisely four o'clock when the divisions leaped from their entrenchments, and with bayonets fixed, without firing a gun, tore away the *abatis* in front of the forts, swarmed over the embankments, crawled into the embrasures, and climbed the parapet. It was the work of five minutes only, but four forts, mounting between twenty and thirty guns, were taken, with seven hundred prisoners.

Grant began early on Sunday morning to draw the farther end of the net toward Petersburg. Sheridan, with the cavalry and two divisions of the Fifth, moved upon Sutherland's Station on the South Side Railroad, eleven miles from Petersburg. Grant sent him Miles's division of the Second Corps. Wright and Ord, east of the run, at nine o'clock assaulted the works in their front, and after a severe struggle carried them, capturing all the guns and several thousand prisoners.

Humphrey, who was west of the run, now was able to leave his position and join Wright and Ord. By noon we see the net drawn close. Sheridan at Sutherland's, with the Fifth Corps, then Humphrey, Ord, and Wright; all swinging towards the city, taking fort after fort and contracting the lines.

In the morning I watched the movements on the left, but as the line advanced, hastened east in season to see the last attack on Forts Mahone and Gregg, the two Rebel strongholds south of the town. These forts were in rear of the main Rebel line, on higher ground.

The troops, in columns of brigades, moved steadily over the field, drove in the Rebel pickets, received the fire of the batteries without breaking, leaped over the breastworks with a *huzza*, which rang shrill and clear above the cannonade. Mahone was an embrasured battery of three guns; Gregg, a strong fort with sally-ports, embrasures for six guns, and surrounded by a deep ditch. Mahone was carried with a rush, the men mounting the escarpment and jumping into it, regardless of the fire poured upon them by the Rebels.

There was a long struggle for the possession of Gregg. Heth and Wilcox were there, animating the garrison. The attacking columns moved in excellent order over the field swept by the guns of the fort, and even received the canister without staggering. The fort was enveloped in smoke, showing that the defence was heroic, as well as the assault.

The lines move on. The soldiers spring into the ditch and climb the embankment. The foremost, as they reach the top, roll back upon their comrades. They are lost from sight in smoke and flame; but from the cloud there comes a hurrah, and the old flag waves in the sunlight above the stronghold which, through all the weary months, has thundered defiance.

Lee's line was broken at the centre, and Petersburg was no longer tenable.

It was inspiring to stand there, and watch the tide of victory rolling up the hill. With that Sunday's sun the hopes of the Rebels set, never to rise again. The C. S. A.,—the Confederate Slave Argosy,—freighted with blood and groans and tears, the death's-head and crossbones at her masthead, hailed as a rightful belligerent, furnished with guns, ammunition, and all needful supplies by sympathetic England and France, was a shattered, helpless wreck.

FIRE AMBULANCE

CHAPTER 31

Richmond

APRIL, 1865

There was no longer the semblance of a Confederacy. Jeff Davis and Breckenridge were fugitives, without country or home. The Rebel army was flying. Richmond was in flames. The Rebellion had gone down in a night,—in darkness as it originated, and as it ought to die.

At three o'clock, Monday morning, an explosion took place which shook Richmond to its foundations, and made even the beds in the hospital at City Point heave as if by an earthquake. It was occasioned by the blowing up of the Rebel ironclads. Semmes was again without a command, for the Rebel navy was no more. If not swept from the ocean by Union cruisers, as the *Alabama* was by the *Kearsarge*, it was crushed by the ponderous blows of Grant and his victorious legions, as the result of his successes in the field. The shock roused the army from slumber. The hosts surrounding Petersburg needed no other reveille. The soldiers were on their feet in an instant, and General Wilcox (commanding the first division of the Ninth Corps) accepted it as a signal to advance. He was lying east of the city, his right resting on the Appomattox. His men sprang forward, but found only deserted works. The last body of Rebels—the lingerers who were remaining to plunder the people of Petersburg—took to their heels, and the division entered the town without opposition.

The entire army was in motion. Engineers hurried up with pontoons, strung them across the Appomattox, and Grant began the pursuit. I entered the town soon after sunrise, and found troops pouring in from all quarters, cheering, swinging their caps, helping themselves to tobacco, rushing upon the double-quick, eager to overtake Lee.

The coloured population thronged the streets, swinging their old hats, bowing low, and shouting:

"Glory!"

"Bless de Lord!"

"I's been a praying for dis yere to happen, but didn't 'spect it quite so soon."

"It is ges like a clap of thunder," said an old negro.

"I's glad to see you. I'm been trying and wishing and praying dat de

Lord would help me get to de Yankees, and now dey has come into dis yere city," said another. The citizens of the place, also, were in the streets, amazed and confounded at what had happened. Provost General Macy, of Massachusetts, established a guard to prevent depredations and to save the army from demoralization. The Rebels, before retreating, destroyed their commissary stores and set all the tobacco warehouses on fire. I took a hurried survey of the Rebel works in front of Fort Steadman, and found them very strong. The ground was honeycombed by the shells which had been thrown from the mortars of the Ninth Corps.

General Grant was early in the town, cool, calm, and evidently well pleased with the aspect of affairs; and President Lincoln, who was at City Point, visited Petersburg during the day. He went up in a special car. The soldiers at Meade Station caught a sight of him, and cheered most heartily. He acknowledged the enthusiasm and devotion of the soldiers by bowing and thanking them for the glorious achievement of their arms. On Friday he looked care-worn, but the great victory had smoothed the deep wrinkles on his brow.

Reaching City Point at noon, I was soon in the saddle, galloping towards Richmond; crossing the Appomattox at Broadway, riding to Varina, crossing the James on the pontoons, and approaching the city by the New Market road, overtaking a division of the Twenty-Fifth Corps on the outskirts of the city. It was a hard, exhausting ride. Two miles out from the city my horse fell, and I found myself turning a summersault into the ditch; without broken bones, however, but I was obliged to moderate my speed for the remainder of the distance.

Before entering upon the narrative of my own observations, let us take a look at events transpiring in the city on Sunday. The *Sentinel* of Saturday evening said:

> We are very hopeful of the campaign which is opening, and trust that we are to reap a large advantage from the operations evidently near at hand....We have only to resolve that we never will surrender, and it will be impossible that we shall ever be taken.

"My line is broken in three places, and Richmond must be evacuated," was Lee's despatch to Jeff Davis. The messenger found him in Rev. Dr. Minnegerode's church. He read the despatch, hurried to the Executive Mansion, passed up the winding stairway to his business apartment, sat down by a small table, wrote an order for the removal of the coin in the banks to Danville, for the burning of the public documents, and for the evacuation of the city. Mrs. Davis had left the city several days previous.

Rev. Dr. Minnegerode, before closing the forenoon service, gave notice that General Ewell desired the local forces to assemble at 3 p. m. There was no evening service. Ministers and congregations were otherwise employed. Rev. Mr. Hoge, a fierce advocate for slavery as a beneficent institution, packed his carpet-bag. Rev. Mr. Duncan was moved to do likewise. Mr. Lumpkin, who for many years had kept a slave-trader's jail, had a work of necessity on this Lord's day,—the temporal salvation of fifty men, women, and children! He made up his coffle in the jail-yard, within pistol-shot of Jeff Davis's parlour window, and a stone's throw from the Monumental Church. The poor creatures were hurried to the Danville depot. This sad and weeping fifty, in handcuffs and chains, was the last slave coffle that shall tread the soil of America.

Slavery being the corner-stone of the Confederacy, it was fitting that this gang, keeping step to the music of their clanking chains, should accompany Jeff Davis, his secretaries Benjamin and Trenholm, and the Reverend Messrs. Hoge and Duncan, in their flight. The whole Rebel government was on the move, and all Richmond desired to be. No thoughts now of taking Washington, or of the flag of the Confederacy flaunting in the breeze from the dome of the national Capitol! Hundreds of officials were at the depot, waiting to get away from the doomed city. Public documents, the archives of the Confederacy, were hastily gathered up, tumbled into boxes and barrels, and taken to the trains, or carried into the streets and set on fire. Coaches, carriages, wagons, carts, wheelbarrows, everything in the shape of a vehicle, was pressed into use. There was a jumble of boxes, chests, trunks, valises, carpet-bags,—a crowd of excited men sweating as never before: women with dishevelled hair, unmindful of their wardrobes, wringing their hands, children crying in the crowd, sentinels guarding each entrance to the train, pushing back at the point of the bayonet the panic-stricken multitude, giving precedence to Davis and the high officials, and informing Mr. Lumpkin that his niggers could not be taken. O, what a loss was there! It would have been fifty thousand dollars out of somebody's pocket in 1861, and millions now of Confederate promises to pay, which the hurrying multitude and that chained slave gang were treading under foot,—trampling the bonds of the Confederate States of America in the mire, as they marched to the station; for the oozy streets were as thickly strewn with four *per cents*, six *per cents*, eight *per cents*, as forest streams with autumn leaves.

The faith of the Confederate States is pledged to provide and establish sufficient revenues for the regular payment of the interest, and for the redemp-

tion of the principal, read the bonds; but there was a sudden eclipse of faith, a collapse of confidence, a shrivelling up like a parched scroll of the entire Confederacy, which was a base counterfeit of the American Union it sought to overturn and supplant, now an exploded concern, and wound up by Grant's orders, its bonds, notes, and certificates of indebtedness worth less than the paper on which they were printed.

Soon after dark the commissaries, having loaded all the army wagons with supplies, began the destruction of what they could not carry away. In the medical purveyor's department were several hundred barrels of whiskey, which were rolled into the street and stove in by soldiers with axes. As the liquor ran down the gutter, officers and soldiers filled their flasks and canteens, while those who had no canteen threw themselves upon the ground and drank from the fiery stream. The rabble with pitchers, basins, dipped it up and drank as if it were the wine of life. The liquor soon began to show its effects. The crowd became a mob, and rushed upon the stores and government warehouses. The soldiers on guard at first kept them at bay, but as the darkness deepened the whiskey-maddened crowd became more furious. By midnight there was a grand saturnalia. The flour in the government stores was seized. Men were seen rolling hogsheads of bacon through the streets. Women filled their aprons with meal, their arms with candles. Later in the night the floating debris of the army reached the city,—the teamsters, servants, ambulance-drivers, with stragglers from the ranks, who pillaged the stores. First attacking the clothing, boot, and hat stores, then the jewellers' shops and the saloons, and lastly the dry-goods establishments. Costly panes of glass were shivered by the butts of their muskets, and the reckless crowd poured in to seize whatever for the moment pleased their fancy, to be thrown aside the next instant for something more attractive.

"As I passed the old market-house," writes a Rebel soldier, "I met a tall fellow with both arms full of sticks of candy, dropping part of his sweet burden at every step."

"Stranger," said he, "have you got a sweet tooth?"

"I told him that I did not object to candy."

"Then go up to Antoni's and get your belly full, and all for nothing."

"A citizen passed me with an armful of hats and caps. 'It is every man for himself and the Devil for us all tonight,' he said, as he rushed past me."[97]

The train which bore Jeff Davis from the city left at eight o'clock in the evening. He took his horses and coach on board for a flight across

---

97: A Rebel Courier's Experience.

the country, in case Sheridan stopped the cars. He was greatly depressed in spirits, and his countenance was haggard and care-worn. At the station there was a crowd of men who had fawned upon him,—office-holders, legislators, and public-spirited citizens who had made great sacrifices for the Rebellion,—who, now that they wished to obtain standing room upon the train, found themselves rudely thrust aside by the orders of the President. They were of no more account than the rest of the excited populace that knew Davis but to execrate him.

In the Sabbath evening twilight, the train, with the fugitive government, its stolen bullion, and its Doctors of Divinity on board, moved out from the city.

At the same hour the Governor of Virginia, William Smith, and the Legislature, embarked in a canal-boat, on the James River and Kanawha Canal, for Lynchburg. On all the roads were men, women, and children, in carriages of every description, with multitudes on horseback and on foot, flying from the Rebel capital. Men who could not get away were secretly at work, during those night-hours, burying plate and money in gardens; ladies secreted their jewels, barred and bolted their doors, and passed a sleepless night, fearful of the morrow, which would bring in the despised "Vandal horde of Yankee ruffians"; for such were the epithets they had persistently applied to the soldiers of the Union throughout the war.

But the government was not quite through with its operations in Richmond. General Ewell remained till daylight on Monday morning to clear up things,—not to burn public archives in order to destroy evidence of Confederate villainy, but to add to the crime already committed another so atrocious that the staunchest friends of the Confederacy recoiled with horror even from its contemplation.

It was past midnight when the Mayor learned that Ewell had issued orders for firing the government buildings and the tobacco warehouses. He sent a deputation of prominent citizens to remonstrate. They were referred to Major Melton, who was to apply the torch.

"It is a cowardly pretext on the part of the citizens, trumped up to save their property for the Yankees," said he.

The committee endeavoured to dissuade him from the act.

"I shall execute my orders," said he.

They went to General Ewell, who with an oath informed them that the torch would be applied at daylight. Breckenridge was there, who said that it would be a disgrace to the Confederate government to endanger the destruction of the entire city. He was Secretary of War, and could have countermanded the order. Will not history hold him accountable?

To prevent the United States from obtaining possession of a few thousand hogsheads of tobacco, a thousand houses were destroyed by fire, the heart of the city burnt out,—all of the business portion, all the banks and insurance-offices, half of the newspapers, with mills, depots, bridges, foundries, workshops, dwellings, churches,—thirty squares in all, swept clean by the devouring flames. It was the final work of the Confederate government. Inaugurated in heat and passion, carried on by hate and prejudice, its end was but in keeping with its career,—the total disregard of the rights of person and property.

In the outskirts of the city, on the Mechanicsville road, was the almshouse, filled with the lame, the blind, the halt, poor, sick, bed-ridden creatures. Ten rods distant was a magazine containing fifteen or twenty kegs of powder, which might have been rolled into the creek near at hand, and was of little value to a victorious army with full supplies of ammunition; but the order of Jeff Davis to blow up the magazines was peremptory and must be executed.

"We give you fifteen minutes to get out of the way," was the sole notice to that crowd of helpless beings lying in their cots, at three o'clock in the morning. Men and women begged for mercy; but their cries were in vain. The officer in charge of the matter was inexorable. Clothesless and shoeless, the inmates ran in terror from the spot to seek shelter in the ravines; but those who could not run while the train to fire it was being laid, rent the air with shrieks of agony. The match was applied at the time. The concussion crushed in the broad side of the house as if it had been pasteboard. Windows flew into flinders. Bricks, stones, timbers, beams, and boards were whirled through the air. Trees were twisted off like withes in the hands of a giant. The city was wrenched and rocked as by a volcanic convulsion. The dozen poor wretches whose infirmities prevented their leaving the house wore horribly mangled; and when the fugitives who had sought shelter in the fields returned to the ruins they found only the bruised and blackened remains of their fellow-inmates.

Let us take a parting glance at the Rebel army as it leaves the city.

The day is brightening in the east. The long line of baggage-wagons and the artillery has been rumbling over the bridges all night. The railroad trains have been busy in conveying the persons and property of both the government and the people; but the last has departed, and still a disappointed crowd is left at the depot. The roads leading west are filled with fugitives in all sorts of vehicles, and on horseback and on foot.

Men are rolling barrels of tar and turpentine upon the bridges. Guards stand upon the Manchester side to prevent the return of any soldier belonging to Richmond. Custis Lee's division has crossed, and Kershaw's division, mainly of South Carolinians, follows. The troops march silently; they are depressed in spirit. The rabble of Manchester have found out what fine times their friends in Richmond are having, and old women and girls are streaming across the bridges laden with plunder,—webs of cloth, blankets, overcoats, and food from the government storehouses. The war-worn soldiers, ragged and barefoot, behold it, and utter curses against the Confederate government for having deprived them of clothing and food.

General Ewell crosses the bridge, riding an iron-gray horse. He wears an old faded cloak and slouch hat. He is brutal and profane, mingling oaths with his orders. Following him is John Cabel Breckenridge, the long, black, glossy hair of other days changed to gray, his high, broad forehead wrinkled and furrowed. He is in plain black, with a *talma* thrown over his shoulders. He talks with Ewell, and gazes upon the scene. Suddenly a broad flash of light leaps up beyond the city, accompanied with a dull, heavy roar, and he sees the air filled with flying timbers of the hospital, whose inmates, almost without warning, and without cause or crime, are blown into eternity.

The last division has crossed the river. The sun is up. A match is touched to the turpentine spread along the timbers, and the bridges are in flames; also the tobacco warehouses, the flouring-mills, the arsenals, and laboratory. The Rebel troops behold the conflagration as they wind along the roads and through the green fields towards the southwest, and memory brings back the scenes of their earlier rejoicing. It is the 2nd of April, four years lacking two weeks since the drunken carousal over the passage of the ordinance of Secession.

It was a little past four o'clock when Major A. H. Stevens of the Fourth Massachusetts cavalry, and Provost Marshal of the Twenty-Fifth Army Corps, with detachments from companies E and H, started upon a reconnoissance of the enemy's entrenchments. He found them evacuated and the guns spiked. A deserter piloted the detachment safely over the torpedoes which had been planted in front of them. A mile and a half out from the city, Major Stevens met a *barouche* and five men mounted bearing a white flag. The party consisted of the Mayor, Judge Meredith of the Confederate States Court, and other gentlemen, who tendered the surrender of the city. He went into the city and was received with joy by the coloured people, who shouted their thanks to the Lord that the Yankees had come. He proceeded to the Capitol, ascended the roof, pulled down the State flag which was flying, and raised the guidons of the two companies upon the building.

RUINS OF RICHMOND

The flames were spreading, and the people, horror-struck and stupefied by the events of the night, were powerless to arrest them. On, on, from dwelling to warehouse, from store to hotel, from hotel to banks, to the newspaper offices, to churches, all along Main Street from near the Spottswood Hotel to the eastern end of the town; then back to the river, to the bridges across the James, up to the large stone fire-proof building, erected by the United States for a post-office, full of Confederate shinplasters, around this, on both sides of it, up to Capitol Square, the flames roared and leaped and crackled, consuming all the business part of the city. In the arsenal were several thousand shells, which exploded at intervals, throwing fragments of iron, burning timbers, and blazing brands and cinders over the surrounding buildings, and driving the people from their homes.

Major Stevens ordered the fire-engines into position, posted his soldiers to preserve order, and called upon the citizens to work the engines, and did what he could to stop the progress of the devouring element.

General Weitzel triumphantly entered the city at eight o'clock, the coloured soldiers singing the John Brown song. With even ranks and steady step, colours waving, drums beating, bands playing, the columns passed up the streets, flanked with fire, to the Capitol. Then stacking their guns, and laying aside their knapsacks, they sprang to the engines, or mounted the roofs and poured in buckets of water, or tore down buildings, to stop the ravages of the fire kindled by the departing Rebels,— emulating the noble example of their comrades in arms at Charleston; like them manifesting no vindictiveness of spirit, but forgetting self in their devotion to duty, forgetting wrong and insult and outrage in their desire to serve their oppressors in their hour of extremity.

The business portion was a sea of flame when I entered the city in the afternoon. I tried to pass through Main Street, but on both sides the fire was roaring and walls were tumbling. I turned into a side street, rode up to the Capitol, and then to the Spottswood Hotel. Dr. Reed's church in front was in flames. On the three sides of the hotel the fire had been raging, but was now subdued, and there was a fair prospect that it would be saved.

"Can you accommodate me with a room?"

"I reckon we can, sir, but like enough you will be burnt out before morning. You can have any room you choose. Nobody here."

I registered my name on a page which bore the names of a score of Rebel officers who had left in the morning, and took a room on the first floor, from which I could easily spring to the ground in case the hotel should be again endangered by the fire.

Throwing up the sash I looked out upon the scene. There were swaying chimneys, tottering walls, streets impassable from piles of brick, stones, and rubbish. Capitol Square was filled with furniture, beds, clothing, crockery, chairs, tables, looking-glasses. Women were weeping, children crying. Men stood speechless, haggard, woebegone, gazing at the desolation.

In Charleston the streets echoed only to the sound of my own footsteps or the snarling of hungry curs. There I walked through weeds, and trod upon flowers in the grassy streets; but in Richmond I waded through Confederate promises to pay, public documents, and broken furniture and crockery.

Granite columns, iron pillars, marble facades, broken into thousands of pieces, blocked the streets. The Bank of Richmond, Bank of the Commonwealth, Traders' Bank, Bank of Virginia, Farmers' Bank, a score of private banking-houses, the American Hotel, the Columbian Hotel, the *Enquirer* and the *Dispatch* printing-offices, the Confederate Post-Office Department, the State Court-House, the Mechanics' Institute, all the insurance offices, the Confederate War Department, the Confederate Arsenal, the Laboratory, Dr. Reed's church, several foundries and machine-shops, the Henrico County Court-House, the Danville and the Petersburg depots, the three bridges across the James, the great flouring-mills, and all the best stores of the city, were destroyed.

Soldiers from General Devens's command were on the roof of the Capitol, Governor's house, and other buildings, ready to extinguish the flames. The Capitol several times caught fire from cinders.

"If it had not been for the soldiers the whole city would have gone," said a citizen.

The coloured soldiers in Capitol Square were dividing their rations with the houseless women and children, giving them hot coffee, sweetened with sugar,—such as they had not tasted for many months. There were ludicrous scenes. One negro had three Dutch-ovens on his head, piled one above another, a stew-pan in one hand and a skillet in the other. Women had bags of flour in their arms, baskets of salt and pails of molasses, or sides of bacon. No miser ever gloated over his gold so eagerly as they over their supply of provisions. They had all but starved, but now they could eat till satisfied.

How stirring the events of that day! Lee retreating, Grant pursuing; Davis a fugitive; the Governor and Legislature of Virginia seeking safety in a canal-boat; Doctors of Divinity fleeing from the wrath they feared; the troops of the Union marching up the streets; the old flag waving over the Capitol; Rebel ironclads blowing up;

Richmond on fire; the billows rolling from square to square, unopposed in their progress by the bewildered crowd; and the Northern Vandals laying down their arms, not to the enemy in the field, but the better to battle with a foe not more relentless, but less controllable with the weapons of war. Weird the scenes of that strange, eventful night,—the glimmering flames, the clouds of smoke hanging like a funeral pall above the ruins, the crowd of homeless creatures wandering the streets.

Such resting found the soles of unblest feet!

In the morning I visited the Capitol building, which, like the Confederacy, had become exceedingly dilapidated, the windows broken, the carpets faded, the paint dingy.

General Weitzel was in the Senate Chamber issuing his orders; also General Shepley, Military Governor, and General Devens.

The door opened, and a smooth-faced man, with a keen eye, firm, quick, resolute step, entered. He wore a plain blue blouse with three stars on the collar. It was the hero who opened the way to New Orleans, and who fought the battle of the Mobile forts from the masthead of his vessel,—Admiral Farragut. He was accompanied by General Gordon of Massachusetts, commanding the Department of Norfolk. They heard the news Monday noon, and made all haste up the James, landing at Varina and taking horses to the city. It was a pleasure to take the brave Admiral's hand, and answer his eager questions as to what Grant had done. Being latest of all present from Petersburg, I could give him the desired information. "Thank God, it is about over," said he of the Rebellion.

It was a little past noon when I walked down to the river bank to view the desolation. While there I saw a boat pulled by twelve rowers coming up stream, containing President Lincoln and his little son, Admiral Porter, and three officers. Forty or fifty freedmen—sole possessors of themselves for twenty-four hours—were at work on the bank of the canal, under the direction of a lieutenant, securing some floating timber; they crowded round the President, forgetting work in their wild joy at beholding the face of the author of the great Emancipation Proclamation. As he approached I said to a coloured woman,—

"There is the man who made you free."

"What, massa?"

"That is President Lincoln."

"Dat President Linkum?"

"Yes."

Farragut at Mobile

She gazed at him a moment in amazement, joy, rapture, as if in supernal presence, then clapped her hands, jumped and shouted, "Glory! glory! glory!"

"God bless you, Sah!" said one, taking off his cap and bowing very low.

"Hurrah! hurrah! President Linkum hab come! President Linkum hab come!" rang through the street.

The lieutenant found himself without men. What cared those freedmen, fresh from the house of bondage, for floating timber or military commands? Their deliverer had come,—he who, next to the Lord Jesus, was their best friend! It was not a hurrah that they gave so much as a wild, jubilant cry of inexpressible joy.

They pressed round the President, ran ahead, and hovered upon the flanks and rear of the little company. Men, women, and children joined the constantly increasing throng. They came from all the streets, running in breathless haste, shouting and hallooing, and dancing with delight. The men threw up their hats, the women waved their bonnets and handkerchiefs, clapped their hands, and shouted, "Glory to God! glory! glory! glory!"—rendering all the praise to God, who had given them freedom, after long years of weary waiting, and had permitted them thus unexpectedly to meet their great benefactor.

"I thank you, dear Jesus, that I behold President Linkum!" was the exclamation of a woman who stood upon the threshold of her humble home, and with streaming eyes and clasped hands, gave thanks aloud to the Saviour of men.

Another, more demonstrative, was jumping and swinging her arms, crying, "Bless de Lord! Bless de Lord! Bless de Lord!" as if there could be no end of her thankfulness.

No carriage was to be had, so the President, leading his son, walked to General Weitzel's head-quarters,—Jeff Davis's mansion. Six sailors, wearing their round blue caps and short jackets and baggy pants, with navy carbines, formed the guard. Next came the President and Admiral Porter, flanked by the officers accompanying him, and the writer, then six more sailors with carbines,—twenty of us in all.

The walk was long, and the President halted a moment to rest. "May de good Lord bless you, President Linkum!" said an old negro, removing his hat and bowing, with tears of joy rolling down his cheeks. The President removed his own hat and bowed in silence: it was a bow which upset the forms, laws, customs, and ceremonies of centuries of slavery. It was a death-shock to chivalry, and a mortal wound to caste. Recognize a nigger! Disgusting. A woman in an adjoining house beheld it, and turned from the scene with unspeakable contempt. There were men in the surging mass who looked daggers from their eyes, and felt murder in their hearts, if they did not breathe it from their lips. But the hour of sacrifice had not yet come; the chosen assassin was not there; the crowning work of treason and traitors yet remained to be performed. Not the capital of the defunct slave Confederacy, but of the restored nation, was to be the scene of the last brutal act in the tragedy of horrors perpetrated in the name of Christianity. The great-hearted, noble-minded, wise-headed man, whom Providence had placed in the Executive chair to carry successfully through the bloody war of freedom against slavery to its glorious consummation, passed on to the mansion from whence the usurping President had fled.

When the soldiers saw him amid the noisy crowd they cheered lustily. It was an unexpected ovation. Such a welcome, such homage, true, heartfelt, deep, impassioned, no prince or prelate ever received.

The streets becoming impassable on account of the increasing multitude, soldiers were summoned to clear the way. How strange the event! The President of the United States—he who had been hated, despised, maligned above all other men living by the people of Richmond—was walking its streets, receiving every evidence of love and honour! How bitter the reflections of that moment to some who beheld him, who remembered, perhaps, that day in May, 1861, when Jefferson Davis entered the city,—the pageant of that hour, his speech, his promise to smite the smiter, to drench the fields of Virginia with richer blood than that shed at Buena Vista! How that part of the promise had been kept; how their sons, brothers, and friends had fallen; how all else predicted had failed; how the land had been filled with mourning; how the State had become a desolation; how their property, wealth, had disappeared! They had been invited to a gorgeous banquet; the fruit was fair to the eye, golden and beautiful, but it had turned to ashes. They had been promised a high place among the nations. Cotton was the king of kings; and England, France, and the whole civilized world would bow in humble submission to his majesty. That was the promise; but now their king was dethroned, their government overthrown, their President and his cabinet vagrants. They had been promised affluence, Richmond was to be the metropolis of the Confederacy, and Virginia the all-powerful State of the new nation. How terrible the cheat! Their thousand-dollar bonds were not worth a penny. A million dollars would not purchase a dinner. Their money was valueless, their slaves were freemen, the heart of their city

President Lincoln in Richmond

was in ashes. They had been deluded in everything. Those whom they had most trusted had most abused their confidence; and at last, in the most unfeeling and inhuman manner, had fired their dwellings, destroying property they could no longer use or levy upon, thus adding arson and robbery to the already long list of their crimes.

The people of Richmond were in despair, having no means for present subsistence, or to rebuild or commence business again. All their heroism, hardship, suffering, expenditure of treasure, and sacrifice of blood had availed them nothing. There could be no comfort in their mourning, no alleviation to their sorrow. All had been lost in an unrighteous cause, which God had not prospered, and no satisfaction could be derived from their participation in it. For try to deceive themselves as they might into a belief that the conflict was unavoidable by the encroachments of the North upon the South, they could but remember the security and peace they enjoyed in the Union, little of which they had felt or dared hope for in their Utopian scheme of slavery.

At length we reached the house from which Jeff Davis had so recently departed, where General Weitzel had established his headquarters. The President entered and sat wearily down in an arm-chair which stood in the fugitive President's reception-room. General Weitzel introduced the officers present. Judge Campbell entered. At the beginning of the war he was on the bench of the Supreme Court of the United States, afterwards espoused Secession, and was appointed assistant Secretary of War under Seddon. He was tall, and looked pale, care-worn, agitated, and bowed very low to the President, who received him with dignity, and yet cordially.

President Lincoln, accompanied by Admiral Porter, General Weitzel, and General Shepley, rode through the city, escorted by a squadron of cavalry, followed by thousands of coloured people, shouting "Glory to God!" They had seen great hardship and suffering. A few were well dressed. Some wore pants of Union blue and coats of Confederate gray. Others were in rags. The President was much affected as they crowded around the carriage to touch his hands, and pour out their thanks. "*They that walked in darkness had seen a great light.*" Their great deliverer was among them. He came not as a conqueror, not as the head of a mighty nation,—

Not with the roll of the stirring drum,
Nor the trumpet that sings of fame,

but as a plain, unpretending American citizen, a representative republican Chief Magistrate, unheralded, almost unattended, with "malice towards none, with charity for all," as he had but a few weeks previously proclaimed from the steps of the Capitol at Washington.

He visited Libby prison, breathed for a moment its fetid air, gazed upon the iron-grated windows and the reeking filth upon the slippery floors, and gave way to uncontrollable emotions.

Libby Prison! What horrors it recalls! What sighs and groans! What prayers and tears! What dying out of hope! What wasting away of body and mind! What nights of darkness settling on human souls! Its door an entrance to a living charnel-house, its iron-barred windows but the outlook of hell! It was the Inferno of the slave Confederacy. Well might have been written over its portal, *"All hope abandon, ye who enter here."*

Visiting the prison the next morning, I found it occupied by several hundred Rebels, who were peering from the grated windows, looking sadly upon the desolation around them. A large number were upon the roof, breathing the fresh air, and gazing upon the fields beyond the James, now green with the verdure of spring. Such liberty was never granted Union prisoners. Whoever approached the prison bars, or laid his hand upon them, became the victim of a Rebel bullet.

There was a crowd of women with pails and buckets at the windows, giving the prisoners provisions and talking freely with their friends, who came not only to the windows, but to the door, where the good-natured sentinel allowed conversation without restraint.

The officer in charge conducted our party through the wards. The air was saturated with vile odours, arising from the unwashed crowd,—from old rags and dirty garments, from puddles of filthy water which dripped through the floor, ran down the walls, sickening to all the senses. From this prison fifteen hundred men were hurried to the flag-of-truce boat on Sunday, that they might be exchanged before the evacuation of the city. Many thousands had lived there month after month, wasting away, starving, dying of fever, of consumption, of all diseases known to medical science,—from insanity, despair, idiocy,—having no communication with the outer world, no food from friends, no sympathy, no compassion,—tortured to death through rigor of imprisonment, by men whose hearts grew harder from day to day by the brutality they practised.

"Please give me a bit of bread, Aunty, I am starving," was the plea one day of a young soldier who saw a negro woman passing the window. He thrust his emaciated hand between the bars and clutched the bit which she cheerfully gave him; but before it had passed between his teeth he saw the brains of his benefactress spattered upon the sidewalk by the sentinel!

A. LINCOLN

Although the city was in possession of the Union forces, there were many residents who believed that Lee would retrieve the disaster.

"I was sorry," said a citizen, "to see the Stars and Stripes torn down in 1861. It is the prettiest flag in the world, but I shed tears when I saw it raised over the Capitol of Virginia on Sunday morning."

"Why so?" I asked.

"Because it was done without the consent of the State of Virginia."

"Then you still cling to the idea that a State is more than the nation."

"Yes; State rights above everything."

"Don't you think the war is almost over,—that it is useless for Lee to contend further?"

"No. He will fight another battle, and he will win. He can fight for twenty-five years in the mountains."

"Do you think that men can live in the mountains?"

"Yes; on roots and herbs, and fight you till you are weary of it, and whip you out."

A friend called upon one of the most aristocratic families of the place. He found that men and women alike were exceedingly bitter and defiant. They never would yield. They would fight through a generation, and defeat the Yankees at last.

They were proud of the Old Dominion, the mother of States and of Presidents, proud of their ancestry, of the chivalry of Virginia, and gave free expression to their hatred.

Having heard that a brigade of coloured troops had been enlisted in Richmond for the Rebel army, I made inquiries to ascertain the facts. All through the war the Rebel authorities had engaged a large number of slaves as teamsters and labourers. The immense fortifications thrown up around Richmond, Yorktown, Petersburg, Wilmington, Charleston, and Savannah were the work of slaves. The Rebels said that slavery, instead of being a weakness, was an element of strength. Slaves built the fortifications and raised the corn and wheat, which enabled the Confederacy to send all of its white fighting population to the field. But the fighting material was used up. Men were wanted. An unsparing conscription failed to fill up the ranks. Then came the agitation of the question of employing negro soldiers.

General Lee advocated the measure. "They possess," said he, "all the physical qualifications, and their habits of obedience constitute a good foundation for discipline. I think those who are employed should be freed. It would neither be just nor wise, in my opinion, to require them to serve as slaves. The best course to pursue, it seems to me, would be to call for such as are willing to come,—willing to come, with the consent of their owners. An impressment or draft would not be likely to bring out the best class, and the use of coercion would make the measure distasteful to them and to their owners."

The subject was debated in secret session in Congress, and a bill enacted authorizing their employment. A great meeting was held in the African church to "fire the Southern heart," and speeches were made. A recruiting-office was opened. The newspapers spoke of the success of the movement. Regiments were organizing.

"I fear there will soon be a great scarcity of arms when the negroes are drilled," wrote the Rebel war clerk in his diary on the 11th of March; and five days later, on the 17th, "We shall have a negro army. Letters are pouring into the department from men of military skill and character, asking authority to raise companies, battalions, and regiments of negro troops. It is the desperate remedy for the very desperate case, and may be successful. If three hundred thousand efficient soldiers can be made of this material, there is no conjecturing when the next campaign may end."

A week later the coloured troops had a parade in Capitol Square. There were so few, that the war clerk said it was "rather a ridiculous affair."

"How many coloured men enlisted?" I asked of a negro.

"'Bout fifty, I reckon, sir. Dey was mostly poor Souf Carolina darkies,—poor heathen fellers, who didn't know no better."

"Would you have fought against the Yankees?"

"No, sir. Dey might have shot me through de body wid ninety thousand balls, before I would have fired a gun at my friends."

"Then you look upon us as your friends?"

"Yes, sir. I have prayed for you to come; and do you think that I would have prayed one way and fit de other?"

"I'll tell you, massa, what I would have done," said another, taking off his hat and bowing: "I would have taken de gun, and when I cotched a chance I'd a shooted it at de Rebs and den run for de Yankees." This brought a general explosion from the crowd, and arrested the attention of some white men passing.

We were in the street west of the Capitol. I had but to raise my eyes to see the Stars and Stripes waving in the evening breeze. A few paces distant were the ruins of the Rebel War Department, from whence were issued the orders to starve our prisoners at Belle Isle, Salisbury, and Andersonville. Not far were the walls of Dr. Reed's church, where a specious Gospel had been preached, and nearby was the church of Dr. Minnegerode. The street was full of people. I was a stranger to them all, but I ventured to make this inquiry,—

"Did you ever see an Abolitionist?"

"No, massa, I reckon I neber did," was the reply.

"What kind of people do you think they are?"

"Well, massa, I specs dey is a good kind of people."

"Why do you think so?"

"'Case when I hear bad white folks swearing and cursing about 'em, I reckon dar must be something good about 'em."

"Well, my friends, I am an Abolitionist; I believe that all men have equal rights, and that I have no more right to make a slave of you than you have of me."

Every hat came off in an instant. Hands were reached out toward me, and I heard from a dozen tongues a hearty "God bless you, sir!"

White men heard me and scowled. Had I uttered those words in Richmond twenty-four hours earlier I should have had no opportunity to repeat them, but paid for my temerity with a halter or a knife; but now those men who stretched out their hands to me would have given the last drop of their blood before they would have seen a hair of my head injured, after that declaration.

The slaves were the true loyal men of the South. They did what they could to help put down the Rebellion by aiding Union prisoners to escape, by giving trustworthy information. The Stars and Stripes was their banner of hope. What a life they led! I met a young coloured man, with features more Anglo-Saxon than African, who asked,—

"Do you think, sir, that I could obtain employment in the North?"

"What can you do?"

"Well, sir, I have been an assistant in a drug store. I can put up prescriptions. I paid forty dollars a month for my time before the Confederate money became worthless, but my master thought that I was going to run away to the Yankees, and sold me awhile ago; and he was my own father, sir."

"Your own father?"

"Yes, sir! They often sell their own flesh and blood, sir!"

Among the correspondents accompanying the army was a gentleman connected with the *Philadelphia Press*, Mr. Chester, tall, stout, and muscular. God had given him a coloured skin, but beneath it lay a courageous heart. Visiting the Capitol, he entered the Senate chamber and sat down in the Speaker's chair to write a letter. A paroled Rebel officer entered the room. "Come out of there, you black cuss!" shouted the officer, clenching his fist.

Mr. Chester raised his eyes, calmly surveyed the intruder, and went on with his writing.

"Get out of there, or I'll knock your brains out!" the officer bellowed, pouring out a torrent of oaths; and rushing up the steps to execute his threat, found himself tumbling over chairs and benches, knocked down by one well-planted blow between his eyes.

Mr. Chester sat down as if nothing had happened. The Rebel sprang to his feet and called upon Captain Hutchins of General Devens's staff for a sword.

"I'll cut the fellow's heart out," said he.

"O no, I guess not. I can't let you have my sword for any such purpose. If you want to fight, I will clear a space here, and see that you have fair play, but let me tell you that you will get a tremendous thrashing," said Captain Hutchins.

The officer left the hall in disgust. "I thought I would exercise my rights as a belligerent," said Mr. Chester.

I ascended the steps of the Capitol and stood on the roof of the building to gaze upon the panorama, hardly surpassed in beauty anywhere,—a lovely combination of city, country, valley, hill, plain, field, forest, and foaming river. The events of four years came to remembrance. First, the secession of the state on the 17th of April, 1861, by the convention which sat with closed doors in the hall below, the threats of violence uttered against the Union delegates from the western counties, the wild tumult of the "People's Convention," so called, in Metropolitan Hall,—a body of Jacobins assembling to browbeat the convention in the Capitol; and when the ordinance was passed, the appearance of John Tyler, once President of the United States, with Governor Wise, among the fire-eaters, welcomed with noisy cheers; it seemed as if I could hear the voice of Tyler as he said that Virginia and the people of the South had submitted to aggression till secession was a duty, and that the Almighty would smile upon the work of that day. They were the words of a feeble old man, whose every official act was in the interest of slavery. Vehement the words of Wise, who imagined that the Yankees had seized one of his children as a hostage for himself.

"If they suppose," said he, "that hostages of my own heart's blood will stay my hand in a contest for the maintenance of sacred rights, they are mistaken. Affection for kindred, property, and life itself sink into insignificance in comparison with the overwhelming importance of public duty in such a crisis as this."

Mason, the lordly senator, and Governor Letcher, the drunken executive of the State, also addressed the crazy crowd, fired to a burning heat of madness by passion and whiskey.

On that occasion the Confederate flag was raised upon the flagstaff springing from the roof of the Capitol, although the State had not joined the Confederacy. The people were to vote on the question, and yet the Convention had enjoined that the act of secession should be kept a secret till Norfolk Navy Yard and Harper's Ferry Arsenal could be seized.[98] The newspapers of Richmond had no announcement to make the next morning that the State was no longer a member of the Union. What honourable, high-minded, "chivalrous" proceedings!

Then came the volunteers thronging the streets. Professor Jackson (Stonewall) was drilling the cadets. Three days after the passage of the ordinance of secession, troops were swarming in the yard around the Capitol, and A. H. Stephens, Vice-President of the Confederacy, and Ex-President Tyler, and the drunken Letcher were negotiating an alliance offensive and defensive between the sovereign State of Virginia and the States already confederated to establish a slaveholding republic.

Next in order was the arrival of Jeff Davis and the perambulating government of the Confederacy, to tarry a few days in Richmond before proceeding to Washington. Davis and his followers made boastful promises of what they could and would do, breathing out threatenings and slaughter against the hated Yankees. Then the hurly-burly,—the rush of volunteers, the arrival of troops, welcomed with cheers and smiles, the streets through which they passed strewn with flowers by the ladies of Richmond. The Confederate Congress and heads of departments came,—Stephens, Toombs, Cobb, Floyd, Wigfall, Memminger, Mallory,—with thousands of place-hunters, filling the city to overflowing, putting money into the pockets of the citizens,—not gold and silver, but Confederate currency, to be redeemed two years after the ratification of the treaty of peace with the United States. Beauregard, the rising star of the South, came from Charleston, to reap fresh laurels at Manassas. Richmond was solemn on that memorable Sabbath, the 21st of June, 1861, for through the forenoon the reports were that the Yankees were winning the day; but at night, when the news came from Davis that the "cowardly horde" was flying, panic-stricken, to Washington, how jubilant the crowd!

A year later there were pale faces, when the army of McClellan swept through Williamsburg. Jeff Davis packed up his furniture, and made preparations to leave the city. There was another fright when the Rebels came back discomfited from Fair Oaks.

From the roof of the Capitol anxious eyes watched the war-clouds rolling up from Mechanicsville and Cold Harbor. Those were mournful days. Long lines of ambulances, wagons, coaches, and carts, filled with

---

98: *Rebel War Clerk's Diary*, Vol. I.

wounded, filed through the streets. How fearful the slaughter to the Rebels in those memorable seven days' fighting! Deep the maledictions heaped upon the drunken Magruder for the carnage at Malvern Hill.

Beneath the roof on which I stood Stuart, Gregg, and Stonewall Jackson,—dead heroes of the Rebellion,—had reposed in state, mourned by the weeping multitude.

Before me were Libby Prison and Belle Isle. What wretchedness and suffering there! Starvation for soldiers of the Union, within sight of the fertile fields of Manchester, waving with grain and alive with flocks and herds! Nearer the Capitol was the mansion of Jeff Davis, the slave-trader's jail and the slave-market. What agony and cries of distress within the hearing of the Chief Magistrate of the Confederacy, as mothers pressed their infants to their breasts for the last time.

In front of the Capitol was the stone building erected by the United States, where for four years Jeff Davis had played the sovereign, where Benjamin, Memminger, Toombs, Mallory, Sedden, Trenholm, and Breckenridge had exercised authority, dispensing places of profit to their friends, who came in crowds to find exemption from conscription. Beyond, and on either side, was the forest of blackened chimneys, tottering walls, and smoking ruins of the fire which had swept away the accumulated wealth of years in a day. How terrible the retribution! Before the war there was quiet in the city, but there came a reign of terror, when ruffians ruled, when peaceful citizens dared not be abroad after dark. There was sorrow in every household for friends fallen in battle, and Poverty sat by many a hearthstone.

Hardest of all to bear was the charity of their enemies. Under the shadow of the Capitol the Christian and Sanitary Commissions were giving bread to the needy. Standing there upon the roof I could look down upon a throng of men, women, and children receiving food from the kind-hearted delegates, upon whose lips were no words of bitterness, but only the song of the angels,—*Peace on earth, good-will to men!*

CHAPTER 32

The Confederate Loan

April, 1865

The attitude of Great Britain towards the United States during the Rebellion will make a strange chapter in history. The first steamship returning from that country after the firing upon Fort Sumter brought the intelligence that the British government had recognized the Rebels as belligerents. Mr. Adams, the newly appointed Minister to the Court of St. James, was on his way to London, but without waiting to hear what representations he might have to make, the ministry with unseemly haste gave encouragement to the Rebels.

Palmerston, Russell, the chief dignitaries of state, and of the Church also, with the London *Times* and *Morning Post*, espoused the cause of the slaveholders, while the weavers of Lancashire, though thrown out of employment by the blockade, gave their sympathies to the North. They were ignorant of the causes which led to hostilities. The English press informed them that it was the tariff; that the people of the South had a right to secede; that the United States had no right to restrain them; that the South was fighting for liberty: but notwithstanding this, the operatives, from the beginning, ranged themselves on the side of the Union. They stood in opposition to Palmerston and the peers of the realm,—the press, the aristocracy, and the mill-owners. In this they were guided, perhaps, more by instinct than by reason.

They knew that in the North labour was free, but that the South had made slavery the corner-stone of their Confederacy. Their life was ever a battle, for Labour was the slave of Capital. They knew nothing of State rights, or the rights of belligerents, or of American tariffs, but instinct by a short road led them to the conclusion that the conflict was not merely national, but world-wide, and that the freemen of the North were fighting for the rights of men everywhere.

The London *Times* was foremost among the newspapers to prophesy the disruption of the Union. Its utterances were oracular. It claimed superior knowledge and a deeper insight of the American question than any of its contemporaries, and its opinions were accepted as truth by all Englishmen who approved the slaveholders' war. Ship-builders, cotton-brokers, and capitalists regulated their faith and works by the leading articles of that journal, and loaned their money to the South.

"The great republic is gone, and no serious attempt will be made by the North to save it," wrote Mr. W. H. Russell to the *Times* in April, 1861.

"General bankruptcy is inevitable, and agrarian and socialist riots may be expected very soon," was the despatch of that individual immediately after the battle of Bull Run.

The trades people of England believed him. The South was victor; the Confederacy was to become a nation. The agents of the South were already in England purchasing supplies, paying liberal prices. They found that Englishmen were ready to engage in any scheme of profit,—in running the blockade, building war-ships for the Confederate government, or selling arms and ammunition, in violation of the laws of the realm.

As a large number of letters written by Rebel agents and emissaries in England and France have fallen into my hands, I purpose in this chapter to give a resume of their contents, which expose the secret history of the Cotton Loan.

Soon after the beginning of hostilities the Liverpool correspondent of the *Times*, Mr. James Spence, entered heartily into the support of the cause of the South. He was engaged in commercial pursuits, but found leisure not only to keep up his correspondence with the *Times*, but to write a book entitled the *American Union*, in which he advocated the right of the South to secede, and extolled slavery as a superior condition of life for the labouring man:

> The negroes have at all times abundant food: the sufferings of fireless winters are unknown to them, medical attendance is always at command; in old age there is no fear of a workhouse; their children are never a burden or a curse; their labour, though long, is neither difficult nor unhealthy. As a rule, they have their own ground and fowls and vegetables, of which they sell a surplus. So far, then, as merely animal comforts extend, their lot is more free from suffering than those of many classes of European labourers.

Such sympathy with slavery received its reward in the appointment of Mr. Spence as financial agent of the Confederacy. Large sums of money were sent from Charleston, Savannah, and Richmond to England. Vessels found little difficulty in running the blockade during the first year of the war, and Nassau became the half-way station, and thousands of Englishmen counted up their gains from blockade-running with glee. Societies were formed in London and other principal cities, called "Confederate Aid Associations."

An address to the British public was issued, setting forth the barbarism of the North against the South, struggling for her rights.

> The women of the South have been insulted, imprisoned, flogged, violated, and outraged in a most inhuman and savage manner. Their homes and goods have been destroyed, their houses forcibly entered, the helpless and unresisting inmates murdered, the fleeing overtaken and cut down in cold blood by the savage soldiery of the North.... They are now glutting their hellish rage against the people they seek to destroy in inflicting every kind of torture, punishment, and misery that their fruitful minds can invent upon those that they would fain call fellow-citizens.... The atrocities, cruelties, crimes, and outrages committed against the South in this war are without a parallel in the history of the world....
>
> In the name of suffering Lancashire, civilization, justice, peace, liberty, humanity, Christianity, and a candid world; and by the highest considerations that can call men into action, we beg you to come forward to aid, contribute, and support a brave and valiant people that are fighting for their homes, firesides, birthright, lives, independence, sacred honour, and all that is dear to mankind.
>
> By all the sorrows, deprivations, bereavements, losses, hardships, and suffering that now engulf the Confederate people, we appeal to you to arouse, and rush to their aid with your pence, shillings, and pounds; give them your sympathy, countenance, and influence, to hurl the tyrants from their country, and obtain the greatest boon to man,—self-government. Fairest and best of earth, for the sake of violated innocence, insulted virtue, and the honour of your sex,—come in woman's majesty and omnipotence, and give strength to a cause that has for its object the highest human aims, the amelioration and exaltation of humanity.

The address was issued by Englishmen, had a wide circulation, and undoubtedly was accepted as a true representation of affairs.

Then Whittier sent his stinging words, "To Englishmen," across the Atlantic:

> *But yesterday you scarce could shake,*
> *In slave-abhorring rigor,*
> *Our Northern palms, for conscience' sake;*
> *Today you clasp the hands that ache*
> *With 'walloping the nigger'!*

> * * * * * * * *

> *And is it Christian England cheers*
> *The bruiser, not the bruised?*
> *And must she run, despite the tears*
> *And prayers of eighteen hundred years,*
> *A-muck in Slavery's crusade?*

> *O black disgrace! O shame and loss*
> *Too deep for tongue to phrase on!*
> *Tear from your flag its holy cross,*
> *And in your van of battle toss*
> *The pirate's skull-bone blazon!*

The Trent affair had inflamed the British public, and Rebel sympathizers were fierce for war, that the South might reap the advantage; but Mason and Slidell had been given up by President Lincoln, and Mr. Mason stood hat in hand at the gate of St. James. But Earl Russell could not conveniently see him just then. Lancashire had spoken. Men upon whose humble hearths no fire warmed the wintry air, in whose homes poverty was ever a guest, around whose doors the wolf of want was always prowling,—the bone and muscle of England, with whom the instinct of Liberty was stronger to persuade than distress and famine to subdue,—they, the hardy workers of England, were with the North.

At home, in the valley of the Shenandoah, Mr. Mason had been a Virginia lord. It was his nature to be proud, imperious, and haughty. He lived in the greatness of an ancient family name. He expected ready admittance at St. James; but though he rang the bell early and often, and sent in his card, Earl Russell was not "at home" to him.

He was ready to turn away in disgust, but the wants of the Confederacy compelled him to submit to whatever humiliation Earl Russell might choose to administer. He told his griefs to Mr. Benjamin, the Confederate Secretary of State, and received condolence. The Secretary wrote:

Your correspondence with Lord Russell shows with what scant courtesy you have been treated, and exhibits a marked contrast between the conduct of the English and French statesmen now in office, in their intercourse with foreign agents, eminently discreditable to the former. It is lamentable that at this late period of the nineteenth century, a nation so enlightened as Great Britain should have failed yet to discover that a principal cause of the dislike and hatred towards England, of which complaints are rife, in her Parliament and press, is the offensive arrogance of some of her public men. The contrast is striking between the polished courtesy of M. Thouvenal and the rude incivility of Lord Russell.

Your determination to submit to these annoyances in the service of your country, and to overlook personal slights, while hope remains that your continued presence in England may benefit our cause, cannot fail to command the approval of your government.[99]

Englishmen wanted to see the great republic broken to pieces, but there were repulsive features in that system of civilization which the South was attempting to establish. The Union dead were mangled at Manassas; their bones were carved into charms and amulets. Among the mountains of Tennessee old men were dragged from their beds at midnight, and hung without judge or jury, because they loved the flag of their country. In Missouri bridges were burned at night, and men, women, and children upon railroad trains were precipitated into yawning gulfs by their neighbours! This was the work of the "master race," too "refined," "chivalric," and "gentlemanly" to associate with the labouring men of the North. Were the workingmen of Old England any more worthy than they of New England to associate with the slave-masters of the South? British operatives and mechanics understood the question,—that it was a conflict between two systems of labour,—and they rejected with disdain all overtures from the South.

The intervention of England and France was necessary to insure the success of the Rebel cause, and English and European public sentiment must be brought round to the Southern side by the power of the press. Mr. Edwin De Leon therefore was made an agent of the Confederacy to subsidize the press of Europe. The wires were pulled by Mr. Benjamin, who wrote thus to Mr. De Leon:

99: Benjamin's letter to Mason, October 28, 1862.

I will take measures to forward you additional means to enable you to extend the field of your operations, and to embrace, if possible, the press of Central Europe in your campaign. Austria and Prussia, as well as the smaller Germanic powers, seem to require intelligence of the true condition of our affairs, and the nature of our struggle; and it is to be hoped that you may find means to act with efficiency in moulding public opinion in those countries.[100]

That this scheme of bribery was successful will appear further on. The British government having with precipitate haste recognized the Rebels as belligerents, English merchants were quick to follow in the track of Palmerston and Russell. Merchants, bankers, admirals of the navy, officers of the army, speculators, spendthrifts, adventurers from the slums and stews of London and Liverpool, in common with members of Parliament and peers of the realm, engaged in blockade-running, not only to enrich themselves, but to aid in establishing a government based on human slavery. The agents of the Confederacy in England found hearty welcome from all classes, especially the ship-builders.

Soon after the attack upon Sumter Mr. Mallory, Secretary of the Confederate Navy, sent Captain Bullock of Savannah to England, to engage ship-builders to fit out privateers. He found W. C. Miller & Son of Liverpool, and the Lairds of Birkenhead, ready to engage in the work of destroying American commerce. He contracted with the first for the building of the *Oreto*, or *Florida*, and with the Lairds for the *290*, or *Alabama*. He also found warm welcome from Roebuck, Gregory, and other members of Parliament, and from capitalists, who subscribed liberally in aid of the enterprise.

Funds were needed for the payment of Rebel debts in England, and the Confederate Congress passed a bill in April, 1862, authorizing the exchange of bonds for articles in kind, and Mr. Benjamin thereupon wrote to Mr. Mason, advising him of the financial arrangements which had been made:

> At your suggestion I have appointed Mr. James Spence of Liverpool financial agent, and have requested him to negotiate for the sale of five million dollars of our eight per cent bonds, if he can realize fifty per cent on them. I have already sent over two millions of bonds, and will send another million in a week or ten days. Mr. Spence is directed to confer with Messrs. Fraser,

---

100: Benjamin's letter to Mr. De Leon, December 13, 1862.

CAPTAIN WINSLOW AND THE *KEARSARGE*

ADMIRAL FARRAGUT

Trenholm & Co. who had previously been made our depositaries at Liverpool.... I have also directed Mr. Spence to endeavour to negotiate for the application of two and a half millions of coin, which I have here, for the purchase of supplies and munitions for our army. I hope that this coin will be accepted by British houses in payment at the rate of sterling in England, less freight and insurance. It seems to me that upon its transfer to British owners, they could obtain transportation for it on their vessels of war from any Confederate port, inasmuch as it would be *bona fide* British property, and in any event the holder of the transfer would have a certain security.[101]

This scheme of an alliance between British naval officers and the Rebel government was carried out, and a portion of the coin shipped in a British man-of-war, the *Vesuvius*, from Bahama, by the English consul.[102]

The bonds referred to by Mr. Benjamin were the regularly issued bonds of the Confederacy. Cotton certificates were also issued; but in addition to these means, the Rebel government deemed it advisable to bring out a loan based exclusively on cotton.

The proposition came from Mr. Slidell, who was in Paris, envoy to the Court of France, but who, instead of attending the receptions of the Emperor at the Tuileries, was endeavouring to obtain social and political recognition by giving luxurious entertainments. Napoleon was ready to recognize the Confederacy, but Palmerston and Russell hesitated, and he was not quite prepared to move alone in the matter.

He was anxious to see the great republic broken up, not that he particularly desired the establishment of the Confederacy, but for the furtherance of his own designs in Mexico. While professing to Mr. Slidell good-will, and a readiness to give substantial aid to the Rebellion, his agents, M. de Saligny, French minister in Mexico, M. Theron, French consul at Galveston, and M. Tabouelle, French vice-consul at Richmond, were intriguing to dismember Texas from the Confederacy. Mr. Benjamin wrote to Mr. Slidell:

> The Emperor of the French has determined to conquer and hold Mexico as a colony, and is desirous of interposing a weak power between his new colony and the Confederate States, in order that he may feel secure against interference with his designs on Mexico.... The evidence thus afforded of a disposition on the part of France to seize on this crisis of our fate as

---

101: Benjamin's Letter, October 24, 1862.
102: Earl Russell's letter to Mr. Adams, Diplo. Cor. 1863, Part I. p. 129.

her occasion for the promotion of selfish interests, and this too after the assurances of friendly disposition, or, at worst, impartial neutrality, which you have received from the leading public men of France, cannot but awaken solicitude.[103]

The French consuls at Galveston and Richmond were dismissed by Jeff Davis, but that did not outwardly ruffle the temper of the Emperor, nor stop the cotton loan, as will presently be seen. The Rebel congressmen looked upon Slidell's scheme with distrust, but the bill was eventually passed in secret session. The finances of the Confederacy were going to wreck. There were heavy debts in Europe, and, unless the bills were promptly paid, there would be an end of supplies. England was suffering for cotton, and the time had come for the successful negotiation of a loan, based on cotton, with great apparent advantages to the subscribers. The mill-owners of Manchester were ready to enter upon any speculation which would start their machinery; the aristocracy would subscribe out of sympathy for the slaveholders; the Liverpool shippers would take stock, as it would give employment to their blockade-runners; while the unusual risks and great chances of profit would make it attractive to the multitude with whom the Derby is the whitest day of the year.

Mr. Slidell had made the acquaintance of Baron Ermile d'Erlanger of Paris, a Jewish banker, who had a branch house in Frankfort conducted by his brother, Raphael d'Erlanger. This firm was recommended by Slidell as a suitable agency for bringing out the loan, and the contract was given them by Mr. Memminger. D'Erlanger began preparations for putting it on the market in February, 1863. He desired to issue it in England, France, Holland, and Germany at the same time, to bring to the Confederacy the financial support of Europe. The considerations were political as well as financial. He found some difficulty, however, in obtaining English agents. The Barings and Rothschilds stood aloof. He offered the London management to Messrs. John H. Gilliat & Co., but that firm declined having anything to do with it. It was offered to other bankers, but refused. He found willing agents at last in Messrs. John Henry Schroeder & Co., and the firm of Messrs. Lawrence, Son, and Pearce. In Liverpool Messrs. Frazer, Trenholm, & Co. had been acting as agents of the Confederacy, and the management was placed in their hands. Schroeder's agents in Amsterdam managed it there, while D'Erlanger's branch house in Frankfort brought it out in that city. D'Erlanger himself manipulated it in Paris.

103: Benjamin to Slidell, October 17, 1862.

D'Erlanger and Mr. Beer, of his firm, visited England, and arranged matters with Mason and Spence, and with Frazer, Trenholm, & Co., all of whom were acting as agents of the Confederacy. A special agent had been appointed by the Rebel government to take charge of the loan,—General C. J. McRae,—who was on his way from Richmond to Paris; but as the needs of the Confederacy were urgent, the loan was opened before his arrival.

The support of the press was secured,—all but two or three papers being brought, through the agency of Mr. De Leon, Mr. Mason, and Mr. Spence, to praise the Confederacy, cry down the Union, and urge recognition by France and England as the surest way to put an end to the war.

The correspondence in my possession between the parties opens on the 1st of March. Mr. Spence, sitting in his parlour in the Burlington Hotel, Old Burlington Street, London, writes to Baron d'Erlanger, who is in Paris, asking for a copy of the contract.

D'Erlanger did not place a very high estimate on the ability of Mr. Spence as a financial manager; but as he was the correspondent of the *Times*, and commercial agent of the Confederacy, thought best not to offend him. Spence, on the other hand, saw an opportunity to make money. A week later, on the 6th of March, he wrote thus to D'Erlanger:

> You said something in the last interview of £50,000 of the stock. If it had occurred to you to put down to me that quantity at the gross price of seventy-seven, I should be disposed to consider it, looking to the advantage to all concerned of having a common interest.

As the loan was issued at 90, this proposal of Mr. Spence to take it at 77,—giving him a margin of 13 per cent under the contract price,—was, in the language of bankers, "a shave" for his services as correspondent of the *Times*,—a transaction upon which more light will be thrown further on in this history.

The loan was put upon the market on the 19th of March. Fifteen per cent was to be paid at the time of subscribing. The stock was limited to three million pounds sterling ($15,000,000); but so desirous were Englishmen to take it, the applications were for £9,000,000 ($45,000,000).

On the evening of the 19th Mr. Spence wrote to D'Erlanger of its success in Liverpool:

All goes well here. The cotton trade take it up with strong interest, and it will come out for large sums. I applied very early for £20,000, and thought I should have been first, but found P—was before me, with his £100,000. You will have a lot of applications in London from the storgs,—that is, those who join to sell at the premium. Here we have no class of that kind, and our applicants, as in Manchester, being more *bona fide*, will, as a rule, take a day or two to digest its merits. The market closed here at 4¼,—quite high enough for the first day.

On the next day, the 20th, Mr. Spence writes:

We shall very much exceed a million here, I think, by noon tomorrow. The political effect will be enormous. It is the recognition of the South by the intelligence of Europe.

On the 21st, congratulations were received by D'Erlanger from Slidell, who was in London:

Allow me to congratulate you on your *magnific* success. Apart from the direct advantages of the affair, it cannot fail to give great prestige to your house.

D'Erlanger wrote to Memminger

The Emperor himself, through the medium of his Chef de Cabinet, complimented us upon the great success; a proof with what interest the operation had been received by all friends of the South.

Notwithstanding the "intelligence of Europe" had rushed to secure it, bankers of respectability—men who prized honour and integrity above pounds and pence—stood aloof, for they remembered that Mr. Jefferson Davis, President of the slaveholding Confederacy, was a repudiator. No allegation against him had been made through the press, but the *Times* came to the rescue before the attack. On the 19th, the day on which the loan was issued, Mr. Sampson, editor of the city article, said:

Those among the English people who are still suffering from Mississippi repudiation will perhaps view with wonder and regret the negotiation of a loan for a government of which Mr. Jefferson Davis, by whom that repudiation was defended in his place in Congress, is the head. But the Southern Confederacy includes Virginia, Georgia, and other honourable States, and it is by the prospect of what the Confederacy will do as a whole that people will make their calculation. The reasoning that would exclude the South from a loan on account of the conduct of Mississippi, would apply equally to the North, since the North embraces Michigan. It would also have applied to the United States loans negotiated while Mississippi was a State of the Union, and especially while Mr. Jefferson Davis was an influential member of the Federal government, and regarded with high favour by all the Northern population, by whom the remarks of the *Times* on his financial views were then declared to be nothing but the outpourings of British rancour.[104]

Turning to the *Times* of July 13th, of 1849, we find a letter written by Jeff Davis, copied from the *Washington Union*, in which the repudiator says:

The crocodile tears which have been shed over ruined creditors are on a par with the lawless denunciations which have been heaped upon that State.

To this the *Times* replied:

Taking its principles and its tone together, it is a doctrine which has never been paralleled. Let it circulate throughout Europe, that a member of the United States Senate in 1849 has openly proclaimed that at a recent period the Governor and Legislative assemblies of his own State deliberately issued fraudulent bonds for five million dollars to sustain the credit of a rickety bank, that the bonds in question having been hypothecated abroad to innocent holders, such holders have not only no claim against the community by whose Executive and Representatives this act was committed, but that they are to be taunted for appealing to the verdict of the civilized world, rather than to the judgment of the legal officers of the State by whose functionaries they have been robbed, and that the ruin of toil-worn men, of women and of children, and the crocodile tears which that ruin has occasioned, is a subject of jest on the part of those by whom it has been accomplished, and then let it be asked if any foreigner ever penned a libel on the American character equal to that against the people of Mississippi by their own Senator.[105]

104: *Times*, March 19, 1863.
105: *Times*, July 13, 1849.

Mr. Davis published a rejoinder, dated at Briarfield, Miss., August 29, 1849, addressed to the editor of the *Mississippian*:

> It is a foreigner's slander against the government, the judiciary, and the people of the Mississippi. It is an attack upon our republican government, the hypocritical cant of stock-jobbers and pensioned presses,—by the hired advocates of the *innocent* stock dealers of London change. It is a calumnious imputation.

The State of Mississippi had obtained the money in London on the solemn pledge of the faith of the State, and loaned it to the citizens; but the State had broken its pledge, repudiated the debt, and Mr. Jeff Davis eulogized the proceeding! The courts of the State decreed in 1842 that the debt was valid, and the decision was reaffirmed in 1853. Jeff Davis was then Secretary of War, and through his efforts and influence the State continued to repudiate the claims of the British bondholders. In 1863 Mississippi was indebted to Englishmen not only for the principal, $5,000,000, but for twenty-five years of unpaid interest; yet, notwithstanding this, the *Times*, eating its words of other days, came before the English people with a certificate of character for the repudiator, also publishing one from Slidell who wrote:

> I am inclined to think that the people in London confound Mr. Reuben Davis, whom I have always understood to have taken the lead on the question of repudiation, with President Jefferson Davis. I am not aware that the latter was ever identified with the question.

The *Times*, commenting upon Slidell's letter, said:

> It is satisfactory to find that the friends of the President of the Confederate States are anxious to free him from the charge of having been an advocate of the repudiation which has now been practised for exactly a quarter of a century by the State of Mississippi....
>
> Should it turn out that there has been a mistake, the announcement will be hailed with warm gratification,—not from any idle feeling of partisanship for the South, on the one hand, or the merely sordid consideration of the prospects of the bondholders on the other, but because there can be no question, whether his course be judged by Northerners or Southerners, that in his conduct of the existing war Mr. Jefferson Davis has displayed such qualities as to give the world

an interest in wishing that the dishonourable classes who are to be found in every nation should not, either now or in the future, be able to point to him as an instance of the possibility of a heartless disregard of pecuniary rights being compatible with real greatness of character. It is to be apprehended, however, that the solution will not come in the manner contemplated. Nevertheless, in another way it is not out of reach, and the best probability is that the unhappy blot upon Mr. Davis's reputation was caused by the influence of an unscrupulous community upon a then young and aspiring politician, deriving his views, perhaps, from the sophistical perversions of fraudulent lawyers, and that he has since discovered his mistake, and learnt to feel and acknowledge that if he had again to act in the matter, it would be in a very different spirit.[106]

It was necessary, for the success of the loan, to show that the South was sure of obtaining its independence, and while the editor of the city article was whitewashing Jeff Davis, the editor in chief was assuring the public that the Union was forever broken up.

Thus wrote Mr. Delaine, the editor in chief, on the 19th:

So far as it is concerned, the once United States are a mere heap of loose materials, a cauldron of molten stuff, ready to receive whatever form fortune may determine. In that vast melee are two centres, which severally strive to give law and order to the whole. At Washington a body of men, not without courage, ability, and enterprise, are labouring, not to restore the Union,—they might as well try to restore the Heptarchy,—but to reconquer what has been lost, and, let the worst come to worst, to establish a military power.

On the 27th another leader was given to American affairs. Said the editor:

As to the final issue of the war, all the world, except some politicians, soldiers, and contractors at Washington and New York, have made up their minds, ... excepting a few disappointed gentlemen of Republican tendencies, we all expect, we nearly all wish, success to the Confederate cause.

And again, on the 28th:—

There was room enough for two states on one continent, could

106: *Times*, March 23, 1863.

the Americans but have believed it. We do not affect to be surprised at the course they have taken. It was natural that a blow should be struck for the Union; but all Europe has long seen that the Union could never be restored.

That men act from motives is a fundamental truth of moral philosophy. Why the *Times* gave such earnest advocacy to the slaveholders may be inferred from what follows. Opening now the correspondence of D'Erlanger with the Rebel Secretary of the Treasury, we read, under date of June 6, 1863:

> *A great margin had to be given to interest the newspapers, pay commissions, and captivate the opinions of those who treated the loan and its support as a question of profit and loss.*

And further on, in the same letter:

> *Thanks to great pecuniary sacrifices made, and the support of all the newspapers, the subscriptions for the loan surpassed our own expectations. It reached five times the amount of the loan, and success made everybody friends.*

At a later date, J. Henry Schroeder & Co., in a note marked *private*, writes to D'Erlanger:

> For the advertisements in the *Times*, through Mr. Sampson, and later on in the *Index*, concerning the payment of the coupons, we shall do the needful.

Thus we learn, from the statement of D'Erlanger, that the *Times*, upon which John Bull pins his faith, was not only by sympathy, but through interest, the advocate of the loan and of the slave-lords' Confederacy. Its financial articles and its leaders were written to the order of D'Erlanger. By the aid of the *Times*, a Parisian Jew, taking advantage of the sympathy expressed for the South by lords, members of Parliament, bankers, businessmen, and adventurers, and of the general gullibility of the British public, was able to secure a subscription of forty-five million dollars,—or thirty million in excess of the loan! On page 532 we have seen that the Liverpool correspondent of the *Times* had been quieted by a commission of £6,500 ($30,000), not for services rendered, but to secure his interest, as explained in D'Erlanger's letter to Memminger, written on the 8th of July, 1863. The banker says:

> When our loan contract was coming back from America, this gentleman (Mr. Spence) wanted to interfere in the matter, by

all means, and claimed a partnership to the contract of one sixth, under the pretence that he was the financial agent of the Confederate government in England, and that our making the loan had put him out of business which he might otherwise have transacted for the South. We knew that Mr. Spence wrote frequently for the *Times*, that as a public writer he could do a great deal of harm if not any good. We succeeded in escaping his intrusion, and when I had made arrangements to bring out the loan in England, I followed his invitation to arrange matters with him in Liverpool, and went down there myself. I gave him £50,000 of the loan at seventy-seven, taking them back at ninety, which gave him a commission as profit of £6,500."

These extracts from D'Erlanger's correspondence will serve to show the American people that the London *Times* was in the service and pay of Jeff Davis during the Rebellion.

On the evening of the 23rd Lord Campbell called up the American question in Parliament, making a speech in favour of recognizing the Confederacy. He spoke of the remarkable success of the loan as a proof that the English public were ready to aid the South. The loan being thus bolstered up rose to four and a half *per cent* premium.

Mr. McRae having arrived in France, there was a meeting of distinguished Rebels in Paris on the 4th of June, at D'Erlanger's banking-house. Mason, Slidell, and L. J. C. Lamar, who had been purchasing supplies in London for the Confederacy,—and McRae were present. The object of the meeting was to consider the financial condition of the Confederate government in Europe. The indebtedness of the Confederacy abroad, for cannon, arms, ships, and supplies, at that time, was put down at £1,741,000 ($8,705,000). The correspondence reads:

> At the same time Ermile d'Erlanger & Co. furnished the meeting with a full statement concerning the loan. According to which, £1,850,000 ($9,250,000) of the loan is in circulation; a part of which is full paid, having been subscribed for by the creditors of the government.

The balance of £1,150,000 was in the hands of D'Erlanger for disposal. In a letter written two days later, on the 6th, by D'Erlanger to Memminger, we learn how there happened to be so large an amount of the stock on hand. Unfavourable news from America caused a feeling of uneasiness, and speculative holders began to sell at depreciated rates. D'Erlanger says:

An arrangement was thereupon entered into with Mr. Mason, and heartily approved by Mr. Slidell, which enabled us to buy for the government £1,000,000 of the stock; but so eager was the speculation, that this did not suffice, and the sum had to be extended to £1,500,000. This operation had its effect, and better tidings helped the market.

Upon this amount purchased by D'Erlanger to sustain the price of the loan, 35 *per cent* had been paid in by the subscribers. The banker writes:

> We would not have recommended the course of buying back part of the loan for the government, but for its peculiar character. The first Confederate loan was as much a political as a commercial transaction, and we have done everything that it may be regarded in both ways.... We, as well as our friends Messrs. Schroeder, are happy to have been able to lend our names and credit to the first financial operation of the South.

On the 13th of June McRae wrote to D'Erlanger a sharp letter, charging him with "unauthorized proceedings." D'Erlanger was playing a good game for himself. McRae wrote:

> These important modifications of the contract *have in every case inured to the benefit of the contractors.*

D'Erlanger replied on the same day, saying:

> The operation the repurchase of the stock was not conducted on any selfish ground, but for the political feeling attached to the loan.

It made no difference to D'Erlanger whether he bought or sold on government account, so long as he received his commissions. He objected, however, to receiving the full amount of his commission in bonds; he must have part cash. He wrote:

> We should, be under too heavy an outlay if we had to take the £150,000 commission in bonds.

This commission, therefore, up to the 15th of June, 1863, had reached the nice little sum of $750,000! D'Erlanger having disposed of the stock to good advantage, was anxious to bring out a second loan on the same terms. In a letter written to Memminger on the 8th of July we discover what those terms were.

We are ready to make a new loan contract, taking exactly the terms of the old contract, and engaging to divide with the government the profits to be realized, between the rate of 77 and the issue price.

The loan then on the market was issued at 90, which gave D'Erlanger a commission of 6½ *per cent*,—a portion of which doubtless went into the pocket of Slidell. D'Erlanger was fearful that the success of the loan would bring proposals from other banking-houses. He said:

We wish that the circumstance of our names being the first connected with a large financial transaction for the government in Europe shall tell in our favour, and that a preference shall be granted to us, which we are quite ready to merit, by making better terms to the government than any other respectable house may offer.

This proposition was indorsed by McRae, who the following week accompanied D'Erlanger to Rippaldson, where "a charming company" had gathered, and "an agreeable week was passed in the society of Madame Caroline and Miss Theresa." McRae, in a letter written on the 17th, urges a new loan, but the news from Gettysburg and Vicksburg had "lessened the appetite," and we hear no more of the proposition for a second loan.

At a later date, in December, the correspondence is in regard to the purchase of boats for the government, in which the Paris banker takes the part of Shylock:

Well then, it now appears you need my help:
Go to then; you come to me, and you say,
Shylock, we would have moneys.

McRae wanted £200,000 on government account, and applied to D'Erlanger, whose terms will be seen from the following extract from McRae's letter:

Your proposition amounts to this: That the government should pay 100 *per cent* for the use of £200,000, for probably less than six months, with no risk on the part of the lenders, as the £650,000 of bonds deposited, and the lien on the boats purchased with the sum lent, would protect them against loss in any event. My proposition was to pay 33⅓ for £200,000, for a period of probably ten or twelve months. This I considered sufficiently favourable for the lenders, as they would have been secured by the deposit of £333,333 of bonds, and a lien on the boats.

The American people, doubtless, care very little who among Rebel agents and manipulators of the loan, or who of the bondholders, made or lost money, and I pass over the details of the interesting correspondence. That D'Erlanger managed it shrewdly for his own benefit is very evident. He charged interest, commission, and exchange on all the stock passing through his hands. In the transaction £140,000, raised from the sale of bonds, was set aside as "caution money" by Mason and Slidell, who wished, for political considerations, to keep the stock at par. D'Erlanger charged commission on the repurchase of this stock, although he held it in his own name, and received interest on the same! McRae was not then in Europe, but upon arriving he refused to ratify the act of Mason and Slidell, but made a proposition to D'Erlanger that the banker should place £704,000 of unsold stock. It is not stated what commission he was to receive. The agreement was verbal, and D'Erlanger was to forfeit £140,000 if the stock was not placed at the end of six months. The months rolled away, and the stock was not placed, and D'Erlanger, instead of paying his forfeiture, held on to the £140,000 of caution money, and helped himself to the interest from government funds in his hands! McRae had no redress except to appeal to Memminger. D'Erlanger wrote a honeyed letter to the Rebel Secretary of Treasury, and offered to "compromise" by giving up one half! McRae finally accepted terms from D'Erlanger; what they were is not stated, but McRae writes a doleful letter to the banker, saying that he is afraid Memminger and Davis will censure him. D'Erlanger seems to have wound McRae round his finger at will.

Schroeder & Co. were in the "ring" with D'Erlanger, and received commission and brokerage on the entire amount of the loan, £3,000,000. D'Erlanger, Schroeder, and McRae each took £50,000 of stock in the "Franco-English Steam Navigation Company," which was to bring out cotton on government account. D'Erlanger fixed the date of issuing the bonds, and thus brought advantage to himself. Among the payments made through Mr. Mason were £55,000 to Captain Crenshaw, £26,000 to Captain North, £38,000 to Captain Maury, £31,000 to Captain Bullock and Mr. Spence. A portion of these sums went into the hands of the Lairds for the rams which they were building. Isaac Campbell & Co. received £515,000 ($2,575,000). This firm took £150,000 of the loan. Bonds to the amount of £117,000 were converted into cotton. It appears that D'Erlanger endeavoured to sweep these into his drag-net, and obtain commission and brokerage wholly unauthorized.

Since the close of the war the British holders of the loan have called upon D'Erlanger for an account of his operations, but can obtain no satisfaction. They have despatched an agent to the United States, appealing to the magnanimity of the Federal government for an adjustment and payment of their claims! Such insolent audacity has been promptly rebuked by Mr. Seward. Marvellous their stupidity and effrontery,—to ask pay for the coals on which they sought to roast us, for the rope that was to strangle the young giant of the West, whose growth they had beheld with alarm, and whose power they feared! As is evident from the correspondence in my possession, the whole scheme was well contrived and manipulated by Slidell and D'Erlanger for the benefit of themselves, and also of Campbell & Co., Schroeder & Co., Spence, the Lairds, and McRae, who, by the aid of the London *Times*, and "all the *papers*," were able to fleece the English aristocracy out of fifteen million dollars.

From mercenary motives they enlisted in the cause of slavery to destroy a friendly republican government. They had persistently asserted that a constitutional democracy like ours must ultimately fail to secure the rights and liberties of the people,—that internal war would crumble it into ruins like the ancient republics; and now they thought the fulfilment of their prophecy so near at hand it was unnecessary longer to disguise their hatred, and openly gave their "aid and comfort" to the enemy, jeering at our efforts and denouncing our measures to maintain our existence among the nations. They ventured their money on the doubtful issue and lost, and now so lugubriously bewail their folly as to make themselves ridiculous in the eyes of the world, and the laughing-stock of the American people.

PATRIOT ORPHAN HOME, FLUSHING, L. I.

CHAPTER 33

Surrender of Lee

APRIL, 1865

At three o'clock Monday morning, April 3rd, Wilcox's division of the Ninth Corps entered Petersburg just in season to see the rear guard of Lee's army disappear over the hills on the north bank of the Appomattox, having burned the bridges and destroyed all the supplies which could not be transported. Lee's army was divided,—Longstreet, Pickett, and Johnson being south of the stream, fifteen miles west of the city. Gordon, Mahone, Ewell, and Elzy, with the immense trains of supplies and batteries from Richmond, were north of the river,— all moving southwest, towards Danville, with the intention of joining Johnston in North Carolina.

"Goodbye, boys," said the women of Petersburg, some sorrowfully; others more joyful cried, "We'll drink pure coffee, with sugar in it, tomorrow. No more hard times."[107] They were weary of war.

The troops passed through the town in silence and dejection. It was a sorrowful march. The successive disasters of Sunday, the sudden breaking up, the destruction of property, the scenes of the night, soon had their effect upon the spirits of the army. Soldiers slipped from the ranks, disappeared in the woods, and threw away their muskets, sick at heart, and disgusted with war. Virginia soldiers had little inclination to abandon the Old Dominion and fight in North Carolina. They were State-rights men,—each State for itself. If Secession could cut loose from the Union, why not from the Confederacy?

Before noon the troops moving from Petersburg, and those retreating from Richmond, with all the baggage-trains and flying citizens, came together on the Chesterfield road, producing confusion and delay. Had Lee thrown his supply trains upon the Lynchburg road,

---

107: *Lee's Last Campaign*, p. 26.

and made a day's march farther west with his army, instead of taking the nearest road to Danville, he probably would have escaped; but his progress was very slow. The roads were soft, the wagons overloaded. The stalling of a single horse in the advance delayed the whole army.

The teamsters were quite as unwilling to go south as the soldiers. They were expecting every moment to hear the ringing shouts of Sheridan's men charging upon their flank or rear. There were frequent panics, which set them into a fever of excitement, and added to the confusion.

Grant determined to prevent Lee's escape if possible. The Ninth Corps was detailed to hold the town, guard the railroad, reconstruct it, and follow the other corps as a reserve. The Second, Fifth, and Sixth Corps, instead of crossing the river were sent upon the double-quick along the road which runs between the Appomattox and the South Side Railroad.

Ord, with the divisions of the Twenty-Fourth and Twenty-Fifth Corps, marched for Burkesville Junction. Sheridan, being in advance with the cavalry, reached Jettersville, on the Richmond and Danville road, forty-four miles from Richmond, on the 4th, tore up the track, entrenched his position, and waited for the infantry. Meade joined him on the morning of the 5th, while Ord, by a forced march, reached Burkesville, south of Sheridan.

Lee crossed the Appomattox at Clemenstown, moved southwest to Amelia Court-House, where he was joined by Longstreet's, Pickett's, and Johnson's troops. The Appomattox has its rise in Prince Edward county, runs northeast, approaching within fifteen miles of the James, then turns southeast, and joins the James at Petersburg.

The bridge at Clemenstown, on which Lee crossed was narrow and unsafe, and the army was much hindered. Had he not crossed at all, but marched round the bend instead, he might have slipped past Sheridan while that officer was waiting at Jettersville for Meade to join him. On the 5th Meade, finding that he was ahead of Lee, instead of marching west, turned northeast, and swept up the railroad toward Amelia, with the Fifth Corps on the right, the Second in the centre, and the Sixth on the left with the cavalry. Lee, seeing that he could not go down the railroad, instead of marching southwest, as he had done the day before, moved directly west, to give Meade the slip if possible. He abandoned wagons, caissons, and forage, and everything that impeded his march.

The Rebels had reached their Bull Run. The trains from Richmond were crossing the bridge when a panic set in. A Rebel writer says:

SURRENDER OF GENERAL LEE

While we were gazing at the wagons moving up from the bridge and entering the road leading to the Court-House, our ears caught the sound of five or six shots in succession; and, looking in the direction whence the sound came, we perceived two or three horsemen emerge from a wood about half a mile distant, and as quickly retire. We could not discern their uniform, but the supposition was, of course, that they were a part of Sheridan's cavalry. There was a slight confusion at the head of the train, and then a halt. 'The Yankees! Sheridan!' As the cry echoed from man to man, the teamsters began to turn their mules towards the river, many involving themselves with those in their rear, while others dismounted and sought the nearest wood. In five minutes the scene had been changed from quiet to the utmost disorder. The wagons were turned back with astonishing rapidity, each teamster unmercifully lashing his jaded animals, as anxious to reach the other side as an hour before he had been to get to this. The cavalry, who had been scattered over the fields cooking or eating their breakfasts, now caught the alarm, and leaving their rations grasped their bridles, mounted, and spurred their horses towards the bridge. For this point all were aiming, and the foot-sore infantry now seemed to have but a poor chance of life in the road now jammed with wagons, mules, and mounted men. The narrow defile, bounded on either side by tall rocks, was filled with horses, wagons, and men, all unable to advance a foot toward the desired point.... Upon the other side (north) the panic was even greater, the rumour prevailing that five hundred Yankees were in our front, and that a large number of our wagons had been captured and burned. Vainly plunging their sharp spurs into the steaming flanks of the poor mules, and still unable to make them trot through the mud and up the steep hills, the teamsters cut loose the traces, and remounting would gallop away, flourishing their long whips, yelling, and urging their horses to the utmost speed. Forsaking the road, they leaped the fences, thronged the fields, and sought the wood for hiding-places.... Scores of broken-down and wrecked wagons and ambulances were overturned and abandoned, their contents being strewed over the road; corn and oats, meal and flour covered the ground, while quartermaster's papers were scattered in every direction. Clothing and even medicinal stores had been in like manner thrown away.[108]

108: Rebel Courier's Experience.

When General Meade discovered Lee's new movement, he wheeled toward the left, and faced the Second and Fifth Corps northwest. The Fifth Corps moved up to Painesville, which is northwest of Amelia; but Griffin, commanding, was too late to strike Lee, whose rear-guard had passed that point. The Second Corps moved through Deatonville, which is five miles west of Jettersville, while the Sixth Corps, moving southwest, came upon the Rebels on Little Sailor's Creek, a small tributary of the Appomattox, running north. The Twenty-Fourth Corps meanwhile, marching from Burkesville up the railroad, joined the Sixth Corps at the head of the creek.

Early in the morning of the 6th General Ord directed that the Petersburg and Lynchburg Railroad bridge across the Appomattox be seized and held if possible; if not able to hold it, the troops were to destroy it. The Fifty-Fourth Pennsylvania and One Hundred and Twenty-Third Ohio were sent to do the work. They moved toward the river, but suddenly found themselves on the right flank of Lee's army, which, was in line of battle, between Sailor's Creek and the Appomattox.

Lee made a stand at this point to save his trains. He was still hoping to reach Danville. If he could fight a successful battle, his wagons would have time to slip away from Sheridan. He had already been forced ten miles out of his direct line of march, and if he failed here he must give up all expectation of reaching Danville, and strike west towards Lynchburg.

His army stood on the west bank of Sailors' Creek, facing east and southeast, behind entrenchments, with the Appomattox, which here runs northeast, behind him.

Walking along the Union lines we see that the Fifth Corps is not yet up from its long detour north toward Painesville, but the Second Corps is approaching the creek four miles above its junction with the Appomattox. One division of cavalry is on its right flank, reaching down to the river. The Sixth Corps is on the left of the Second, facing west. There is a break in the line as we go towards Ord's command, which is near Burkesville, facing northwest, with Sheridan's cavalry on both flanks.

The forenoon was passed in skirmishing on the part of the Union troops. The regiments sent to seize the bridge were not able to accomplish the task, and were driven with severe loss. But now the Second Corps came up, a foothold was gained across the creek, and Lee's left flank was forced towards the river.

It was nearly four o'clock in the afternoon before the Sixth Corps came up with the Rebels. This corps had been marching southwest;

but when the skirmishers discovered the enemy, Wright halted Seymour's division, which was in advance, faced it west, while Wheaton's division filed past Seymour's and took position on the left. The third division was in reserve. The cavalry was on the left of Wheaton. Sheridan found himself confronted by Ewell's and Kershaw's divisions, which were strongly entrenched.

Seymour and Wheaton moved from the road west, went down the steep declivity into the ravine, receiving the fire of the Rebels without flinching, crossed the creek, ascended the other bank, and dashed upon the entrenchments. At the same moment Custar's division of cavalry advanced with sabres drawn, their horses upon the run, goaded with spur and quickened by shout, till they caught the wild enthusiasm of their riders, and horses and men unitedly became as fiery Centaurs, the earth trembling beneath the tread of the thousands of hoofs, the air resounding with bugle-blasts and thrilling cheers!

The charge of this division was heroic. The Rebel artillery opened with shells, followed by canister. The infantry, protected by breastworks, were able to give a galling fire, but the squadrons swept everything before them, leaping the entrenchments, sabring all who resisted, crushing the whole of Lee's right wing by a single blow, gathering up thousands of prisoners, who stood as if paralyzed by the tremendous shock.

Entire regiments threw down their arms. Miles of wagons, caissons, ambulances, forges, arms, ammunition,—all that belonged to that portion of the line, was lost to Lee in a moment. Generals Ewell, Kershaw, Defoe, Barton, Custis Lee, Borden, and Corse were prisoners almost before they knew it.

"Further fighting is useless; it will be a waste of life," said Ewell to Custar.

"Bravely done, Custar," said Sheridan, riding up, and complimenting his lieutenant in the presence of the whole division.

It was through the co-operation of the other cavalry divisions, Crook's and Devens's and Merritt's, and of the Sixth Corps, that Custar was enabled to strike such a crushing blow. Honour is due to all. Custar had his horse killed; Lieutenant Harwell, Captain Barnhart, Lieutenant Narvall, Lieutenant Main, and Lieutenant Custar, all belonging to his staff, also had their horses shot in the splendid charge, which of itself proves that it was gallant and desperate. Officers and men alike rushed upon the enemy, rivalling each other in deeds of daring.

After receiving this paralyzing blow Lee gave up all hope of reaching Danville. He could move only in the direction of Lynchburg. Caissons, wagons, and ambulances were burned, cannon abandoned, commissary supplies left by the roadside.

It was a day of jubilee to the coloured people, who swarmed out from their cabins and appropriated the plunder.

"'Pears like as if we were spiling the Egyptians," said an old man who had gathered an immense pile of blankets and coats.

There was a skirmish at Farmville the next morning, between the cavalry and the left wing of Lee's army. The centre, and what remained of the right wing, crossed the Appomattox ten miles above Farmville,—both columns moving to Appomattox Court-House, where Lee hoped to unite his scattered forces.

Grant and Meade, with the Second and Sixth Corps, crossed at Farmville, and followed Lee along the Petersburg and Lynchburg turnpike. Ord, joined by the Fifth, starting from Burkesville, took the shortest road to Appomattox Court-House, nearly fifty miles distant, while Sheridan, with the main body of the cavalry, made a rapid movement southwest to cut off Lee's retreat. The pursuit from Sailors' Creek commenced on Friday morning, and Lee was brought to bay Saturday noon.

It was an exciting race. There were frequent interchanges of shots between the cavalry, hovering like a cloud upon Lee's flank, also captures of abandoned wagons, ambulances, caissons, pieces of artillery, and picking up of stragglers. Glimpses of the Rebel forces were sometimes had across the ravines. As a sight of the flying deer quickens the pursuit of the hound, so an occasional view of the flying enemy roused the soldiers to a wild and irrepressible enthusiasm, and their shouts and cheers rang long and loud through the surrounding woodlands.

Appomattox Court-House is at the head-waters of the Appomattox River, on the table-land between the rivulets which give rise to that stream and the James River, which makes its great southern bend at Lynchburg. The place is sometimes called Clover Hill. It is a small village,—such as are to be seen throughout the Old Dominion,—one or two good, substantial houses, surrounded by a dozen or twenty miserable cabins.

Lee succeeded in reuniting his troops, numbering not more than a division, such as once marched under his direction up the heights of Gettysburg, or moved into the fight in the Wilderness; but when reunited and ready to move upon Lynchburg, he found the cloud which had hung upon his flank and rear now enveloping him on the north, the east, the south, the west. Sheridan had swung past him, Ord and Griffin were south of him, holding the road leading to Danville, while Wright and Humphrey, east and north, were preparing to drive him over against Sheridan, who in turn would toss him down towards Ord and Griffin.

Great was the consternation in the Rebel ranks when, on Saturday morning, the Rebels discovered that Sheridan was cutting off their retreat to Lynchburg.

"Yankees at Appomattox! Sheridan!"[109] was the cry of a party of Rebel officers on a locomotive, hastening to Lynchburg in season to escape the Union cavalrymen then advancing to tear up the rails. Sheridan pounced upon the artillery, and on the afternoon of the 8th captured twenty-five pieces. Meade at the same time came upon the rear of the Rebels a mile east of the Court-House, and captured a battery. Lee's men were melting away, worn down by hard marching and fighting, and discouraged by defeat and disaster. His provisions were getting low, as the larger part of the supplies had been abandoned. His condition was critical.

It was a gloomy night. A courier brought intelligence that Sheridan had possession of Concord Station. A Rebel writer says:

> We all felt our hearts chilled by this new rumour. Concord Station was between us and Lynchburg, and we had no knowledge of any other road to that place than that which we were pursuing. Turning back, our capture was inevitable. The generals withdrew to consult, the staff officers conversed in low tones, while the soldiers, teamsters, the cause being unknown, did not hesitate to declare their impatience at the delay.[110]

Lee called his last council of war, summoning Longstreet, Pickett, Gordon, and Hill. The condition of affairs was discussed. It was a sad hour. Lee was much depressed. He did not know that the infantry under Ord and Griffin were south of him, but supposed that his way was disputed only by Sheridan. It was decided to force a passage. The attack was made; but the volleys of musketry and the vigour of the cannonade, and the long lines of men in blue, convinced him that he had little chance of escaping. The skirmishing was kept up through the day,—both parties too wearied and exhausted to fight a general battle,—yet each moment of delay made Lee's condition more hopeless.

Grant had despatched a letter to Lee on the 7th, from Farmville, asking the surrender of the army of Northern Virginia.

109: Rebel Courier's Experience.
110: Rebel Courier's Experience.

Lee replied the same day, asking for terms.

On the 8th Grant sent a second letter, insisting upon one condition only:

That the men and officers shall be disqualified for taking up arms against the United States until properly exchanged.

"I do not think the emergency has arisen to call for the surrender of this army," Lee answered; but at the same time asked for an interview at ten o'clock next morning. Sheridan had not closed all the roads to Lynchburg, but was in such a position that it was impossible for Lee to get away with his army. Breckenridge, with a large number of officers and many thousands of privates, struck northwest, through by-roads and fields, crossed James River, reached Lynchburg and passed into North Carolina.

The Second Corps was in position on Sunday morning, waiting the order to advance, when a flag of truce was displayed in front of Miles's division. Captain J. D. Cook, of General Miles's staff, was sent to receive it. He was met by Colonel Taylor, of Lee's staff, who brought a note from Lee, wishing for a suspension of hostilities to take into consideration the terms offered by General Grant on Saturday. General Meade signified by note that he had no authority to enter into an armistice, but would wait two hours before making an attack, and would communicate with General Grant.

Before the expiration of the time General Grant arrived, and a correspondence with Lee followed, which resulted in the appointment of a place of meeting for a more full consideration of the terms proposed by General Grant.

In the little village of Appomattox Court-House there is a large, square brick house, with a portico in front, the residence of Wilmer McLean. Roses were budding in the garden on that Sabbath morning, violets and daffodils were already in bloom, and the trees which shaded the dwelling were green with the verdure of spring. General Lee designated it as the place for meeting General Grant. It was a little past two o'clock in the afternoon when General Lee, accompanied by General Marshall, his chief of staff, entered the house. A few minutes later General Grant arrived, accompanied only by Colonel Parker, of his staff, chief of the Six Nations.

The meeting was in the parlour,—a square room, carpeted, furnished with a sofa and centre-table. Lee, dressed in a suit of gray, was sitting by the table when Grant entered. Time had silvered his hair and beard. He wore an elegant sword, a gift from his friends.

General Grant had left his sword behind, and appeared in the same suit he had worn in the field through the eventful days,—a plain blue frock, with double row of buttons, and shoulder-straps bearing the three silver stars, the insignia of his rank as Lieutenant-General.

The meeting was cordial. After salutations the two commanders sat down, placed their hats on the table, and conversed as freely as in other days when both were in the service of the United States. General Lee alluded to the correspondence which had passed between them.

"General, I have requested this interview, to know more fully the terms which you propose," said General Lee.

General Grant replied that he would grant a parole to officers and men, and that the officers might retain their side-arms and their personal effects. General Lee assented to the proposition, and did not ask for any modification of the terms, which were then engrossed. The paper was signed by General Lee at half past three o'clock.

After he had affixed his signature, General Lee asked for General Grant's understanding of the term "personal effects" which had been used in the instrument.

"Many of my cavalrymen own their horses," he said.

"I think that the horses must be turned over to the United States," was the reply.

"I coincide in that opinion," was Lee's rejoinder.

"But," said General Grant, "I will instruct the officers who are appointed to carry out the capitulation to allow those who own horses to take them home. They will need them to do their spring ploughing and to till their farms." "Allow me to express my thanks for such consideration and generosity on your part. It cannot fail of having a good effect," General Lee replied with emotion.

After further conversation General Lee expressed a hope that each soldier of his army might be furnished with a certificate, or some other evidence of parole, to prevent them from being forced into further service by Confederate conscripting officers.

"I will order such certificates to be issued to every man," said General Grant; and as soon as the preliminaries were settled, the head-quarters printing-press was put to work striking off blanks for that purpose.

"My army is short of rations," said Lee.

"You shall be supplied," and an order was at once issued to the commissary to furnish rations to the prisoners.

The question of terms had been discussed the evening previous around Grant's camp-fire. Grant stated that he wanted such a surrender as would break down the positions which France and England had

General Lee's Farewell

taken in recognizing the Rebels as belligerents. He did not wish for humiliating terms. He would not require a formal grounding of arms. The Rebels were Americans, and his object was to restore them to the Union and not to degrade them.

Lee returned to his army and stated the terms of capitulation, which were received with great satisfaction, especially by those who owned horses. They cheered loudly, and no doubt heartily. The terms were such as they had not expected. The newspapers of the South had persistently represented the men of the North as bloodthirsty and vindictive,—as vandals, robbers, and murderers,—capable of doing the work of fiends, and the remarkable leniency of Grant surprised them.

The terms were not altogether acceptable to Grant's army. Many of the officers remembered that General Pickett never had resigned his commission in the United States service, but that he had taken up arms against the country without any scruples of conscience. He was a deserter and a traitor, found in arms. The soldiers remembered that scores of their comrades had been shot or hung for deserting the ranks; the utmost leniency of the government was a long term of imprisonment in a penitentiary or confinement on the Dry Tortugas. Sentinels had been shot for falling asleep while on duty; yet General Pickett and his fellow-traitors were, by the terms of the parole, granted an indulgence which was equivalent to a pardon. It was General Pickett who hung the Union men of North Carolina who had enlisted in the service of the Union, but who, under the fortunes of war, had fallen into his hands. In General Pickett's estimation they had committed an unpardonable crime. He considered them as citizens of the Confederacy, and hung them upon the nearest tree. It was cold-blooded murder. But his desertion, treason, inhumanity, and murders were offset by the plea that the North could afford to be magnanimous to a conquered foe! The soldiers idolized Grant as a commander. They had no objection to his terms with the privates of Lee's army, but there was dissent from including Pickett and Ewell, and other Rebel officers who had been notoriously inhuman to Union soldiers. The Rebel soldiers were generally humane towards prisoners, especially after the first year of the war. Many instances might be cited of their kindness to the wounded on the battle-field and to prisoners in their hands. The officers in the field were also kind, but the political leaders, the women, and officers in charge of prisons were cruel and vindictive.

The hour came for Lee to part with his officers. He retained his calmness and composure, but they could not refrain from shedding tears. It was to be their last meeting. He was to lead them no more in battle.

STUDY FOR A STATUE OF LINCOLN

The occasion brought before them an acute sense that all was over,—all lost; their sacrifices, sufferings, heroism, had been in vain; their pride was humbled; instead of being victors, they were vanquished; history and the impartial verdict of mankind perhaps would hold them responsible for the blood which had been shed. It was a sad hour to that body of men in gray, wearing the stars of a perished Confederacy.

The intelligence of the capitulation was communicated to Grant's army by bulletin. As the news flew along the lines on that Sabbath morning, the cheering was prolonged and vociferous. For the first time in four years the veterans who had toiled in the mud of the Peninsula, who had been beaten back from Fredericksburg and Chancellorsville, who had stood like a wall of adamant on the banks of the Antietam, and the heights of Gettysburg, who had pressed Lee from the Wilderness to Five Forks, who had brought him to bay at last, were to have a peaceful night.

Their fighting was over, and there was to be no more charging of batteries; nor long watchings in the trenches, drenched by rains, parched by summer heat, or numbed by the frosts of winter; no more scenes of blood, of wasting away in hospitals, or murders and starvation in Rebel prisons. It was the hour of peace. In the radiant light of that Sabbath sun they could rejoice in the thought that they had once more a reunited country; that an abject people had been redeemed from slavery; that the honour of the nation had been vindicated; that the flag which traitors had trailed in the dust at the beginning of the conflict was more than ever the emblem of the world's best hopes.

CHAPTER 34

Conclusion

April, 1865

Day was breaking on the 12th of April, when General Grant, accompanied by his staff, alighted from the cars at City Point, after a tedious night ride from Burkesville. He walked slowly up the steep bank to his head-quarters, not with the air of a conqueror, but as if sleep and rest would be far more acceptable than the congratulations of a noisy crowd. Four years had passed since he left his quiet home in Illinois, a humble citizen, unknown beyond his village borders; but now his name was inseparably connected with a great moral convulsion, world-wide in its influence, enduring as time in its results. The mighty conflict of ideas had swept round the globe like a tidal wave of the ocean. Industry had been quickened in every land, and new channels of trade opened among the nations. Wherever human language was spoken, men talked of the war between Slavery and Freedom, and aspirations for good were awakened in the hearts of toiling millions in Europe, on the burning sands of Africa, and in the jungles of Hindustan, to whom life was bare existence and the future ever hopeless.

The four years of fighting were over; the Rebellion was subdued. On the first of April Lee had a large army, but suddenly he had been overwhelmed. That which seemed so formidable had disappeared like a bubble in the sunshine. Though the Rebels saw that the Confederacy was threatened as it had not been at any other period of the war, there were few, if any, who, up to the latest hour, dreamed that there could be such an overturning of affairs. That Lee had held his ground so long was a warranty that he could successfully resist all Grant's efforts to take Richmond. The Confederate Congress met daily in the capital, passed resolutions, enacted laws, and debated questions of state,

ASSASSINATION OF LINCOLN

as if the Confederacy had a place among the nations, with centuries of prosperity and glory in prospect. But their performance came to an unexpected end. The last act of the tragedy was given on the 14th,—the assassination of the President.

What drama surpasses it in interest? What period of the world's history is more replete with great events affecting the welfare of the human race? In 1861, when the curtain rose, the world beheld a nation, peaceful, happy, prosperous. Then came the spectacle,—the procession of seceding States, with bugles sounding, colours flying, the bombardment of Sumter; the uprising of the people of the North, the drum-beat heard in every village, flags floating from all the steeples, streamers and banners from all the house-tops, great battles, defeat, and victory; a ploughman and splitter of rails the liberator of the enslaved, their enlistment as soldiers of the Republic; the patriotism of the people; woman's work of love and mercy; the ghastly scenes in Southern prisons, the conflagration of cities set on fire by the Rebels, the breaking up of the Confederacy, the assassination, the capture of the Rebel chief, the return of the victorious armies, the last grand military pageant at Washington, and then the retirement of the soldiers to peaceful life! Sublime the picture!

The conflict commenced as a rebellion, but ended in revolution. Slavery has disappeared. Civil liberty is stronger than in 1861. Four millions of freedmen are candidates for citizenship, who at the beginning of the Rebellion had no rights under the flag of the Union.

Slaves rise up men; the olive waves,
With roots deep set in battle graves.

The Rebellion was an attempt to suppress Truth and Justice by tyranny. The effort might have been successful in earlier ages, but not in the nineteenth century, and never will the attempt be repeated on American soil, for the tendency of mind is towards a clearer perception of the rights of man. America uttered her protest against despotic power in 1776. "It was an experiment," said the aristocracies of Europe. The "republican bubble has burst," said Earl Russell in 1861; but the Republic lives, and the false and ignoble distinctions in the society of the Old World, which slavery attempted to establish in the New, have been reversed. America teaches this truth to the wondering nations,—that the strongest government rests, not on the few, not on property, never on injustice, but on the people, on diffused wealth and enlightened mind, on obligation to man and God.

Kings will yet lay aside their sceptres, and subjects will become sovereigns, because the people of America, by example, have shown the world that civil and religious liberty for all, as well as for the few, is of more value than human life.

How lavish the expenditure of blood! How generous the outpouring of the wine of life by the heroic dead!

Song of peace, nor battle's roar,
Ne'er shall break their slumbers more;
Death shall keep his solemn trust,
'Earth to earth, and dust to dust.'

Dead, yet living. Their patriotism, sacrifice, endurance, patience, faith, and hope can never die. Loved and lamented, but immortal. Paeans for the living, dirges for the dead. Their work is done, not for an hour, a day, a year, but for all time; not for fame or ambition, but for the poor, the degraded, the oppressed of all lands, for civilization and Christianity, for the welfare of the human race through Time and Eternity!

ALSO FROM LEONAUR
AVAILABLE IN SOFTCOVER OR HARDCOVER WITH DUST JACKET

THE LIFE OF THE REAL BRIGADIER GERARD VOLUME 1—THE YOUNG HUSSAR 1782-1807 *by Jean-Baptiste De Marbot*—A French Cavalryman Of the Napoleonic Wars at Marengo, Austerlitz, Jena, Eylau & Friedland.

THE LIFE OF THE REAL BRIGADIER GERARD VOLUME 2—IMPERIAL AIDE-DE-CAMP 1807-1811 *by Jean-Baptiste De Marbot*—A French Cavalryman of the Napoleonic Wars at Saragossa, Landshut, Eckmuhl, Ratisbon, Aspern-Essling, Wagram, Busaco & Torres Vedras.

THE LIFE OF THE REAL BRIGADIER GERARD VOLUME 3—COLONEL OF CHASSEURS 1811-1815 *by Jean-Baptiste De Marbot*—A French Cavalryman in the retreat from Moscow, Lutzen, Bautzen, Katzbach, Leipzig, Hanau & Waterloo.

THE INDIAN WAR OF 1864 *by Eugene Ware*—The Experiences of a Young Officer of the 7th Iowa Cavalry on the Western Frontier During the Civil War.

THE MARCH OF DESTINY *by Charles E. Young & V. Devinny*—Dangers of the Trail in 1865 by Charles E. Young & The Story of a Pioneer by V. Devinny, two Accounts of Early Emigrants to Colorado.

CROSSING THE PLAINS *by William Audley Maxwell*—A First Hand Narrative of the Early Pioneer Trail to California in 1857.

CHIEF OF SCOUTS *by William F. Drannan*—A Pilot to Emigrant and Government Trains, Across the Plains of the Western Frontier.

THIRTY-ONE YEARS ON THE PLAINS AND IN THE MOUNTAINS *by William F. Drannan*—William Drannan was born to be a pioneer, hunter, trapper and wagon train guide during the momentous days of the Great American West.

THE INDIAN WARS VOLUNTEER *by William Thompson*—Recollections of the Conflict Against the Snakes, Shoshone, Bannocks, Modocs and Other Native Tribes of the American North West.

THE 4TH TENNESSEE CAVALRY *by George B. Guild*—The Services of Smith's Regiment of Confederate Cavalry by One of its Officers.

COLONEL WORTHINGTON'S SHILOH *by T. Worthington*—The Tennessee Campaign, 1862, by an Officer of the Ohio Volunteers.

FOUR YEARS IN THE SADDLE *by W. L. Curry*—The History of the First Regiment Ohio Volunteer Cavalry in the American Civil War.

AVAILABLE ONLINE AT **www.leonaur.com**
AND FROM ALL GOOD BOOK STORES

ALSO FROM LEONAUR
AVAILABLE IN SOFTCOVER OR HARDCOVER WITH DUST JACKET

LIFE IN THE ARMY OF NORTHERN VIRGINIA *by Carlton McCarthy*—The Observations of a Confederate Artilleryman of Cutshaw's Battalion During the American Civil War 1861-1865.

HISTORY OF THE CAVALRY OF THE ARMY OF THE POTOMAC *by Charles D. Rhodes*—Including Pope's Army of Virginia and the Cavalry Operations in West Virginia During the American Civil War.

CAMP-FIRE AND COTTON-FIELD *by Thomas W. Knox*—A New York Herald Correspondent's View of the American Civil War.

SERGEANT STILLWELL *by Leander Stillwell*—The Experiences of a Union Army Soldier of the 61st Illinois Infantry During the American Civil War.

STONEWALL'S CANNONEER *by Edward A. Moore*—Experiences with the Rockbridge Artillery, Confederate Army of Northern Virginia, During the American Civil War.

THE SIXTH CORPS *by George Stevens*—The Army of the Potomac, Union Army, During the American Civil War.

THE RAILROAD RAIDERS *by William Pittenger*—An Ohio Volunteers Recollections of the Andrews Raid to Disrupt the Confederate Railroad in Georgia During the American Civil War.

CITIZEN SOLDIER *by John Beatty*—An Account of the American Civil War by a Union Infantry Officer of Ohio Volunteers Who Became a Brigadier General.

COX: PERSONAL RECOLLECTIONS OF THE CIVIL WAR--VOLUME 1 *by Jacob Dolson Cox*—West Virginia, Kanawha Valley, Gauley Bridge, Cotton Mountain, South Mountain, Antietam, the Morgan Raid & the East Tennessee Campaign.

COX: PERSONAL RECOLLECTIONS OF THE CIVIL WAR--VOLUME 2 *by Jacob Dolson Cox*—Siege of Knoxville, East Tennessee, Atlanta Campaign, the Nashville Campaign & the North Carolina Campaign.

KERSHAW'S BRIGADE VOLUME 1 *by D. Augustus Dickert*—Manassas, Seven Pines, Sharpsburg (Antietam), Fredricksburg, Chancellorsville, Gettysburg, Chickamauga, Chattanooga, Fort Sanders & Bean Station.

KERSHAW'S BRIGADE VOLUME 2 *by D. Augustus Dickert*—At the wilderness, Cold Harbour, Petersburg, The Shenandoah Valley and Cedar Creek..

AVAILABLE ONLINE AT **www.leonaur.com**
AND FROM ALL GOOD BOOK STORES

ALSO FROM LEONAUR
AVAILABLE IN SOFTCOVER OR HARDCOVER WITH DUST JACKET

THE RELUCTANT REBEL by *William G. Stevenson*—A young Kentuckian's experiences in the Confederate Infantry & Cavalry during the American Civil War..

BOOTS AND SADDLES by *Elizabeth B. Custer*—The experiences of General Custer's Wife on the Western Plains.

FANNIE BEERS' CIVIL WAR by *Fannie A. Beers*—A Confederate Lady's Experiences of Nursing During the Campaigns & Battles of the American Civil War.

LADY SALE'S AFGHANISTAN by *Florentia Sale*—An Indomitable Victorian Lady's Account of the Retreat from Kabul During the First Afghan War.

THE TWO WARS OF MRS DUBERLY by *Frances Isabella Duberly*—An Intrepid Victorian Lady's Experience of the Crimea and Indian Mutiny.

THE REBELLIOUS DUCHESS by *Paul F. S. Dermoncourt*—The Adventures of the Duchess of Berri and Her Attempt to Overthrow French Monarchy.

LADIES OF WATERLOO by *Charlotte A. Eaton, Magdalene de Lancey & Juana Smith*—The Experiences of Three Women During the Campaign of 1815: Waterloo Days by Charlotte A. Eaton, A Week at Waterloo by Magdalene de Lancey & Juana's Story by Juana Smith.

TWO YEARS BEFORE THE MAST by *Richard Henry Dana. Jr.*—The account of one young man's experiences serving on board a sailing brig—the Penelope—bound for California, between the years 1834-36.

A SAILOR OF KING GEORGE by *Frederick Hoffman*—From Midshipman to Captain—Recollections of War at Sea in the Napoleonic Age 1793-1815.

LORDS OF THE SEA by *A. T. Mahan*—Great Captains of the Royal Navy During the Age of Sail.

COGGESHALL'S VOYAGES: VOLUME 1 by *George Coggeshall*—The Recollections of an American Schooner Captain.

COGGESHALL'S VOYAGES: VOLUME 2 by *George Coggeshall*—The Recollections of an American Schooner Captain.

TWILIGHT OF EMPIRE by *Sir Thomas Ussher & Sir George Cockburn*—Two accounts of Napoleon's Journeys in Exile to Elba and St. Helena: Narrative of Events by Sir Thomas Ussher & Napoleon's Last Voyage: Extract of a diary by Sir George Cockburn.

AVAILABLE ONLINE AT **www.leonaur.com**
AND FROM ALL GOOD BOOK STORES

ALSO FROM LEONAUR
AVAILABLE IN SOFTCOVER OR HARDCOVER WITH DUST JACKET

ESCAPE FROM THE FRENCH by Edward Boys—A Young Royal Navy Midshipman's Adventures During the Napoleonic War.

THE VOYAGE OF H.M.S. PANDORA by Edward Edwards R. N. & George Hamilton, edited by Basil Thomson—In Pursuit of the Mutineers of the Bounty in the South Seas—1790-1791.

MEDUSA by J. B. Henry Savigny and Alexander Correard and Charlotte-Adélaïde Dard —Narrative of a Voyage to Senegal in 1816 & The Sufferings of the Picard Family After the Shipwreck of the Medusa.

THE SEA WAR OF 1812 VOLUME 1 by A. T. Mahan—A History of the Maritime Conflict.

THE SEA WAR OF 1812 VOLUME 2 by A. T. Mahan—A History of the Maritime Conflict.

WETHERELL OF H. M. S. HUSSAR by John Wetherell—The Recollections of an Ordinary Seaman of the Royal Navy During the Napoleonic Wars.

THE NAVAL BRIGADE IN NATAL by C. R. N. Burne—With the Guns of H. M. S. Terrible & H. M. S. Tartar during the Boer War 1899-1900.

THE VOYAGE OF H. M. S. BOUNTY by William Bligh—The True Story of an 18th Century Voyage of Exploration and Mutiny.

SHIPWRECK! by William Gilly—The Royal Navy's Disasters at Sea 1793-1849.

KING'S CUTTERS AND SMUGGLERS: 1700-1855 by E. Keble Chatterton—A unique period of maritime history-from the beginning of the eighteenth to the middle of the nineteenth century when British seamen risked all to smuggle valuable goods from wool to tea and spirits from and to the Continent.

CONFEDERATE BLOCKADE RUNNER by John Wilkinson—The Personal Recollections of an Officer of the Confederate Navy.

NAVAL BATTLES OF THE NAPOLEONIC WARS by W. H. Fitchett—Cape St. Vincent, the Nile, Cadiz, Copenhagen, Trafalgar & Others.

PRISONERS OF THE RED DESERT by R. S. Gwatkin-Williams—The Adventures of the Crew of the Tara During the First World War.

U-BOAT WAR 1914-1918 by James B. Connolly/Karl von Schenk—Two Contrasting Accounts from Both Sides of the Conflict at Sea During the Great War.

AVAILABLE ONLINE AT **www.leonaur.com**
AND FROM ALL GOOD BOOK STORES

www.ingramcontent.com/pod-product-compliance
Lightning Source LLC
Chambersburg PA
CBHW021823220426
43663CB00005B/114